THE
COLLECTED LETTERS
Dylan Thomas

Volume I

1931–1939

Dylan Thomas was born in Swansea on 27 October 1914. After leaving school he worked on the *South Wales Evening Post* before embarking on his literary career in London. Not only a poet, he wrote short stories, film scripts, features and radio plays, the most famous being *Under Milk Wood*. It was in New York, during his fourth US tour, that he fell ill shortly after his 39th birthday, dying there on 9 November 1953. In 1982 a memorial stone to commemorate him was unveiled in Poets' Corner in Westminster Abbey.

Also available from Orion

A Dylan Thomas Treasury
Portrait of the Artist as a Young Dog
Collected Stories
Dylan Thomas Omnibus
Selected Poems
The Love Letters of Dylan Thomas
Under Milk Wood

THE
COLLECTED LETTERS
Dylan Thomas

Volume I

1931–1939

Edited by Paul Ferris

WEIDENFELD & NICOLSON

A W&N PAPERBACK

First published in one volume in Great Britain in 1985 by J. M. Dent
Revised edition first published in Great Britain in 2000 by J. M. Dent
This two volume edition first published in Great Britain in 2017
by Weidenfeld & Nicolson
an imprint of the Orion Publishing Group Ltd
Carmelite House, 50 Victoria Embankment
London EC4Y 0DZ
An Hachette UK Company

1 3 5 7 9 10 8 6 4 2

Introduction and notes © Paul Ferris 1985, 2000

A CIP catalogue record for this book is
available from the British Library.

Volume I
ISBN (trade paperback) 978 1 4746 0799 5
Volume II
ISBN (trade paperback) 978 1 4746 0800 8

Printed in Great Britain by Clays Ltd, St Ives plc

www.orionbooks.co.uk

Contents

For Caitlin

Chronology

1914 Born 27 October, Swansea.

1925 September, enters Swansea Grammar School.

1927 14 January, newspaper *Western Mail* publishes Thomas's poem 'His Requiem', discovered (forty-four years later) to be plagiarised from a *Boy's Own Paper* of 1923.

1930 27 April, date of the first surviving poem in a poetry notebook, 'Osiris, Come to Isis'.
December, correspondence with Percy Smart begins.

1931 Summer, leaves school to be a reporter on the local newspaper, *South Wales Daily Post*.

1932 Joins Swansea Little Theatre's company of amateur players.
?December, leaves newspaper.

1933 18 May, *New English Weekly* publishes 'And death shall have no dominion'.
Summer, first visit to London.
3 September, *Sunday Referee* publishes 'That sanity be kept', which leads to correspondence with Pamela Hansford Johnson.

1934 23 February, first meeting with Pamela Hansford Johnson, in London.
13 November, moves into London lodgings.
18 December, *18 Poems*.

1936 17 July, first letter to Caitlin Macnamara.
10 September, *Twenty-five Poems*.

1937 21 April, first radio broadcast, 'Life and the Modem Poet'.
11 July, marries Caitlin Macnamara, Penzance register office.

1938 May, moves to Laugharne lives there intermittently from now on.
August, applies unsuccessfully for help to Royal Literary Fund.

1939 30 January, Llewelyn Edouard Thomas born, Hampshire.
24 August, *The Map of Love*.
20 December, *The World I Breathe* (USA).

1940 4 April, *Portrait of the Artist as a Young Dog*.
Summer, with John Davenport at Marshfield, Gloucestershire.

1941 January, applies successfully to Royal Literary Fund.
?Autumn, joins Strand Film Co in London as scriptwriter.

1943 February, *New Poems* (USA).
15 February, 'Reminiscences of Childhood', first of his nostalgic radio talks.
3 March, Aeronwy Bryn Thomas born, London.

1944 September, moves to bungalow at New Quay, Cardiganshire.

1945 Autumn, completes 'Fern Hill' at Blaen Cwm, Carmarthenshire.

1946   7 February, *Deaths and Entrances*.
        8 November, *Selected Writings* (USA).
1947   April (until August), in Italy, with family.
        15 June, 'Return Journey' (to Swansea), radio feature.
        September, moves to South Leigh, Oxfordshire.
1948   Writing feature films for Gainsborough.
1949   March, commissioned by BBC Television to adapt *Peer Gynt*.
        March, in Prague, guest of Czechoslovak Government.
        April or May, moves to the Boat House, Laugharne.
        May, accepts invitation to read at the Poetry Center, New York City.
        24 July, Colm Garan Hart Thomas born, Carmarthen.
1950   20 February, flies to New York: first US trip.
        1 June, sails for England.
1951   January, in Iran, to write film script for Anglo Iranian Oil Co.
        December, living briefly in Camden Town, London.
1952   20 January, arrives in New York, with Caitlin: second US trip.
        28 February, *In Country Sleep* (USA).
        16 May, leaves New York for England.
        10 November, *Collected Poems*.
        16 December, Jack Thomas, his father, dies.
1953   31 March, *Collected Poems* (USA).
        21 April, arrives New York: third US trip.
        14 May, first performance of *Under Milk Wood* with actors, New York.
        14 May, *The Doctor and the Devils*.
        2 June, returns to London.
        19 October, arrives New York: fourth US trip.
        5 November, collapses at Chelsea Hotel, New York City.
        9 November, dies at St Vincent's Hospital.

Introduction

Poets (one might argue) embody popular ideas of originality and rebellion against an unfeeling society. Ideally there will be hilariously bad behaviour and tragic undertones as well. From an early age Dylan Thomas sought to live by this caricature, an outlaw. Since his death in New York in 1953 the facts of his life have merged with the facts of his poetry to create a reputation that appeals to poet-lovers as much as to poetry-lovers. That explains Thomas's continuing appeal.

Perhaps it does, and perhaps it is worth looking for 'explanations' of unusual human beings. But I wonder. Biographers have combed through the ruins of Thomas's life, which is all one ever has to go on, a kind of archaeology; I certainly have. Yet revisiting these letters, fifteen years after I edited the first edition, I find a renewed satisfaction in letting his own narrative unwind.

Once past adolescence, few of Thomas's letters are about abstractions; he tends towards gossip and description. Aged twenty-five, writing on 27 November 1939 to Kenneth Patchen, an American poet, he said, 'When I read letters I nearly always whizz through the explanatory parts and the arguments and am really excited to know what the person writing has been doing with himself & with others lately, where he's been to, who he's met, what he feels like the moment he's writing, and, if I don't know him personally, what sort of person he actually is, what sort of face has he got, who he loves and doesn't, is his Sex Life a Mystery, has he got any money and if so does he want to share it, where he comes from, what sort of parents did he have, what does he do most evenings, does he know anything about the private lives of film stars, even what he had for breakfast so that I can compare . . . Or an emotional gush is very nice too.'

Thomas's poems have major pretensions; his private life very few. In everyday matters, ordinariness is what appealed to him. Domestic incidents and little disasters made up the clay he liked to work with, and his bar-talk and his letters were means of shaping it into fantasies that amused him and his circle. It was not a very elite circle, though he rubbed shoulders with literary figures, an Edith Sitwell here, a Lawrence Durrell there. People with money were always important, but they were necessary for survival, and the begging and hinting-at-poverty letters he wrote them were polished till they shone.

The friends he relaxed with were inclined to be dissident, interestingly flawed, a bit seedy. 'It's only among poor failures that I find the people I like best', he told the writer Emily Holmes Coleman in March 1937, when he was twenty-two. The following month he was writing to the poet George Barker, 'all my friends are failures, I think the glories of the world are mingy', and listing 'the people I know and like best—hack Fleet streeters, assistant assistant film-producers, professional drunks, strays and outlaws, who are always, & always will be, just about to write their autobiographies . . . In a different context—when telling the critic John Davenport about his manoeuvrings to avoid military service in 1939—he aligned himself with the shysters who were desperate for safe jobs at the Ministry of Information: 'all the half-poets, the boiled newspapermen, submen from the islands of crabs, dismissed advertisers . . .' How deplorable, in a Britain at war; how understandable.

Dylan Thomas was born in the Welsh seaport of Swansea in 1914, three months into the First World War. Both his parents were from working-class families, with close connections to rural west Wales, where siblings and cousins remained. His father, Jack Thomas, who was educated at the just-created University of Wales, developed a 'cut-glass' accent to veil his Welsh-speaking origins and ended up teaching English at Swansea Grammar School; he revered the classic authors, and provided the background of English literature against which his son grew up.

A self-centred and precocious child, spoiled by a mother who insisted that his health was delicate, Dylan entered adolescence as a serious reader and writer of poetry, whose sense of vocation was usefully complemented by his image of himself as a weakling with a cough. He saw his vocation as that of a poet and he never ceased to pursue it, when necessary at the expense of others, and certainly at the expense of himself. Dependence was or became a mould that could not be changed. 'Oh, helpless baboon!' he wrote of himself to his American publisher, James Laughlin, four years before his death amid a muddle of drink, debts and ebbing creativity in New York City at the age of thirty-nine.

The letters, of which roughly eleven hundred are collected in the two volumes of *The Collected Letters* (a hundred or so more than in the first edition), cover twenty-seven years. The first is a high-spirited piece, unpublished till now, packed with light verse, addressed to his grown-up sister Nancy c. 1926, when he would have been twelve; even then there were hints of the mockery he was always good at. By his next appearance, some four years later, his academic career has been and gone. Dylan is the dead-end schoolboy, marking time as editor of the magazine, writing to a friend, Percy Smart, who has left school already to work in a bank in London. This group of letters, also previously unpublished, is a portrait of the artist in the making: maverick, inventive, harbouring usefully unwholesome thoughts. The youthful cynicism has something darker ingrained in it. 'Even that third-former, who is running along the corridor now, has probably an inherent cancer, or a mind full of lechery. The child grows from the cradle, soaked in a morbidity and restlessness he cannot understand, does a little painful loving, fails to make money, builds his life on sand, and is struck down . . .'

Before the Smart correspondence ends, Thomas is a reporter on the local newspaper, enjoying both drunkenness and the remorse that succeeds it, his sights fixed on an artist's life with the obligatory excesses. There is often a hint with Dylan Thomas that he planned his course from the start, that he set up his biographers in advance; and it is this self-conscious approach to the business of being a poet that has done him most harm, among detractors who are looking for reasons to damage him. It is not necessarily unwise for a poet to decide that a bohemian life is the thing, and to live doggedly within the confines of the cliché, as long as there is an end-product worth having, which in this case there was. Still, Thomas did lay it on thick. Many of his poems imply the significance of the poet who is writing them, Dylan Marlais Thomas, born into provincialdom, mad with words, beating on the gates of fame, and doing it all *in public*. He has proved too flamboyant or even fraudulent for some of his successors, and there is a purist generation of academics and literary editors that turns up its nose. But he has well-armed defenders, and the popular taste for Thomas's more accessible work shows no sign of diminishing: always bearing in mind that the life may have helped.

Not long after the Smart letters, he began a friendship with Pamela Hansford Johnson, a young woman (later a successful novelist) living with her mother in south London, whose life was as circumscribed as his in suburban Swansea. The letters he wrote, over a thirteen-month period, were full of passion—for poetry more than for her—and provide a working guide to the life behind 18 *Poems* in 1934, the book that made his name. A need to reveal himself is evident; so is an air of disability. The uncertainties that made him find friends among 'poor failures' were at work already. He is undersized, unwell, unemployable. These are conditions, of course, that suit his vocation. 'A born writer', he tells Johnson (about 21 December 1933), 'is born scrofulous; his career is an accident dictated by physical or circumstantial disabilities.' In other moods he was cocky, boastful, assertive about literature, bursting with the importance of his own poetry. He was, too, endlessly descriptive of his surroundings (the shabby streets, the melancholy tramlines) and himself, the artist two hundred miles from London, hating the outer darkness of South Wales yet in an odd way relishing it as well; he would spend his life returning to it.

After the Pamela correspondence, which ended when their love affair failed to develop, the waiting was over and the game began. Thereafter the poetry, the poverty and the drinking had everyday consequences, and the fantasies of bohemian living that the early letters had toyed with were replaced by the reality.

For most of his life, Dylan presented himself as multi-faceted, unreliable, moody, an entertainer who was better at self-mockery than at boasting. He both hankered after a bourgeois way of life and despised it. 'My selfish carelessness and unpunctuality I do not try to excuse as poet's properties.

They are a bugbear & a humbug', he told Henry Treece (31 December 1938), in what he called a 'simplified confession of complicated egoism'. Money was of endless concern. During the 1930s, especially after he married Caitlin Macnamara in 1937, and the early years of the war, he was genuinely poor. Even then, as he told Kenneth Patchen (1939), he tried 'never to live below the imagined standard I had set myself . . . Sometimes, indeed, I think I am living far *above* the standard I imagine myself to have been born to deserve; but that soon grows into an unworthy thought, and the wind again, blowing from penniless places, is thick with rich cigar smoke.'

His begging letters are full of guile. Some of his admirers are still unsettled by them, preferring to concentrate on comic anecdotes about goings-on in pubs. But the sturdy beggar was the man, or an important part of him. When he cringed in a letter, it was always premeditated. 'Weasels take off their hats as I stink by', he wrote to his friend Vernon Watkins (28 May 1941), touching him for a loan that would never be repaid. If only, Dylan would say, if only I had a few pounds, I could make a fresh start. He combined the cunning of an adult with the hopeless optimism of a child. Underlying all was a harsh conviction that he was entitled to beg. '[T]he ravens—soft, white, silly ravens—will feed us', he wrote to Watkins (20 December 1938). 'Try to think of some sap, some saint', he instructed Davenport in October 1938, when a mere 'Thirty bloody pounds' (like saying a mere eight hundred pounds at the end of the century) stood between him and happiness.

A 'five-shilling fund' to which subscribers would contribute weekly was one of his schemes. 'I've got to get 12 chaps', he wrote to Davenport (July 1939), and was cross when the chaps failed to materialise. In 1941 he organised a network of correspondents to help persuade the Royal Literary Fund, which had turned him down three years earlier, to make him a grant. Word reached Thomas that Alec Waugh (who in private supported the application) had remarked, 'advise Dylan to write more stories and fewer letters'. He was furious ('When I want advice from Alec Waugh, I'll go to his brother'), but one can see what Waugh was getting at.

From 1942 Thomas had a modest wartime income writing documentary films, and after the war he became a sought-after broadcaster, wrote feature-film scripts, and went on to earn large sums reading and lecturing in America. The myth of the poet whose last years were haunted by poverty was disposed of years ago. What is true is that he and Caitlin could make money disappear as quickly as he earned it. The begging became a nightmare as well as an industry; larger and larger sums were needed, and nothing patrons did was sufficient. Drafts of a letter to Princess Caetani, an American woman who paid high prices for his poems and published them in her magazine in Italy, give a gloomy insight into his painful toying with words and phrases, as though the composition of a begging letter had become a literary end in itself.

The persona that he created for himself was the familiar one of an individual at odds with the world, whose aim in the end was merely to survive in hostile surroundings, a Charlie Chaplin-like figure who was without pride. In his letters this made for good comedy as long as his nerve held. Even at first, where he is presenting himself as the introverted poet in poor health, he is high-spirited, clever, scatological. He has a casual talent for comic verse. The 1933 letter to Johnson, quoted earlier, with the definition of a 'born writer', contained a poem 'to my Aunt, Discussing the Correct Approach to Modern Poetry'—

> '... Do not forget that "limpet" rhymes
> With "strumpet" in these troubled times,
> And commas are the worst of crimes;
> Few understand the works of Cummings,
> And few James Joyce's mental slummings,
> And few young Auden's coded chatter;
> But then it is the few that matter ...'

Twelve years later he was writing from Wales to a film producer, Donald Taylor. The war was just over; America was already the promised land that might make him solvent. The postman knocks, and

> '... I reach
> The dog-and-child-chewed mat and find?—yes, yes!—
> A bunch of letters from the far U.S.
> Ah, what epistolary pearls unseen
> Blush in these envelopes! what hippocrene!—
> "Be my pen-pal" from Truman. Or "Dear Friend,
> Shall we arrange a *personal* Lease-Lend?"
> From Betty Hutton ...
>   ... But, alas, vain hopes!
> There's nothing in those Sam-stamped envelopes
> But a request to write on "Whither Art?"
> From "Cyclorama", "Seed", "Rubato", "Fart"
> "Prognosis", "Ethic", "Crucible", and "Clef"—
> And other small reviews that pay sweet F.'

The jokes became less funny as time went on:

'At the bottom of the garden, a man, at 3/- an hour, is digging a new shitpit & will dig on, he says, until he reaches water. By that time I shall owe him this house, which is not mine' (to Davenport, 26 August 1948).

'[O]n Saturday night I fell down again and cracked some ribs, how many and how badly I won't know till I'm Xrayed tomorrow ... The pain is knifing, I cannot sit or lie, and I bellow. I wake the baby with my bullshouts. I cannot sleep. I can hardly write: this is written as I hang off a bed, yelling. Also I have gout in my toe, phlegm on my lungs, misery in my head, debts in the town, no money in my pocket, and a poem simmering on the hob' (to Margaret Taylor, 28 November 1949).

'I grow lazier and fatter and sadder and older and deafer and duller ... my children grow large and rude; I renounce my Art to make money and then make no money; I fall in love with undesirable, unloving, squat, taloned, moist unlovely women and out again like a trout' (to Ruth Witt-Diamant, 10 October 1951).

Sexual themes and statements abound. The strident sexual imagery of the earlier poems has always been evident; he liked to dwell on the biological machinery, and his taste spilt over into the letters. 'Man should be two tooled', he wrote to a friend, the Swansea journalist Charles Fisher, early in 1935, 'and a poet's middle leg is his pencil. If his phallic pencil turns into an electric drill, breaking up the tar and the concrete of language worn thin by the tricycle tyres of nature poets and the heavy six wheels of the academic sirs, so much the better . . .'

Thomas was more honest than most in making no secret of the fact that he had a dirty mind. The letters offer evidence of what he thought rather than what he did. Hints and winks suggest an improbable sexual boldness. During his first years in London he implies in one or two letters that he has a venereal infection, and clearly regards this as validating a poet's sex life. His childhood background of cramped morality in South Wales would have helped make the subject more dangerously wicked. A notebook dating from around 1936 that he left with a girlfriend, Veronica Sibthorp—two letters to her are included in these volumes—is at the National Library of Wales. It contains nonsense rhymes ('If I were Veroniker / I'd give up my moniker'), and scraps of sexual verse, the idle thoughts of a randy young man that turned later on into the controlled bawdiness of Under Milk Wood:

'I love my love with an A because she Answers
Both my hands, while both her Breasts are dancers.
I love my love with a B because she Beats
All others at Lighthousing up her teats.'

As for straightforward 'love letters', there are a couple to Emily Holmes Coleman, written before he was married; four sedate wartime letters to an actress, Ruth Wynn Owen; and many to his wife. They are not seriously erotic. A deep affection runs through the Caitlin letters, increasingly tempered by apology, guilt and a need to appease that sets one's teeth on edge. What they reveal most of all is his dependence on her, his weakness in search of her strength. This may have been true of relationships with other women, including two of the Americans he had affairs with, Elizabeth Reitell and Pearl Kazin, both of them career women with robust personalities. One tepid letter to Reitell is printed in Volume II (and at least one other exists). Also included in Volume II is part of a letter said to be to Kazin, which is at the Harry Ransom Humanities Research Center as a type-script copy. But his correspondence with mistresses is thin—although a group of letters to an American lover has come on the market in a furtive sort of way, with a condition attached that they must not be published.

As a commentator on the writing of poetry, Thomas had the reputation of being indifferent, indeed of being ready to flee from anyone who wanted to theorise out loud rather than sit down and write the stuff. This was part of his public act as the man in the loud shirt propping up the bar, but it is not borne out by the letters, which have things to say about his method. In 1933 and 1934 he was giving Pamela Hansford Johnson a running commentary as he wrote the vividly anatomical pieces that went into *18 Poems* ('Through my small, bonebound island I have learnt all I know, experienced all, and sensed all'). He was also sending lengthy critiques of her own poems, which make a useful complement to what he is saying about his own work.

Henry Treece (who was writing the first book about Thomas) and Charles Fisher were both on the receiving end of interesting technical statements from Thomas in the 1930s. The correspondence with Watkins was much concerned with the writing of particular poems. There is a letter to Hermann Peschmann (1 February 1938) where Thomas explains, not very succinctly, what a poem, 'I make this in a warring absence', is 'about' (the quotation marks are his: he didn't want to be cornered). There is a notable letter (14 August 1939) to Desmond Hawkins, who was poised to review Thomas's book *The Map of Love* for the *Spectator*, and who had written to ask him about five of the more difficult poems. Some of Thomas's exegesis is as confusing as the poems themselves, as Thomas recognised. 'I wrote it down hurriedly for you: not so much to try to elucidate things but to move them about, turn them different ways, stir them up.' But at least it throws light on the process involved, even if it is only light on the muddled frame of mind in which some of these poems of the late Thirties were written.

More nagging by editors might have helped. In an earlier letter (March 1936), Thomas responded to an inquiry from Hawkins, then literary editor of the magazine *Purpose*, who had accepted a poem, 'Find meat on bones', but was puzzled by the phrase, 'a ram rose', in a passage with sexual overtones. 'It's funny about ram', wrote Thomas. 'Once I looked up an old dictionary and found it meant red, but now I can't find it in any dictionary at all. I wanted ram in the poem to mean red *and* male *and* horny *and* driving *and* all its usual meanings. Blast it, why doesn't it mean red?' Still, 'ram rose' it remained.

Thomas worked long and hard at poems that could achieve the effects he sought. 'You must work at the talent as a sculptor works at stone', he told Pamela Hansford Johnson (15 April 1934), (employing, incidentally, the kind of phrase that Welsh-language poets use about their strict-metred verse). His poem 'Prologue' written to introduce the *Collected Poems* (1952), has a first line which rhymes with the last (the 102nd) and so on through second and last-but-one, third and last-but-two, until the rhymes meet in the middle, with lines 51 and 52. It is a scheme that few readers notice unless their attention is drawn to it: 'Why I acrosticked myself like this, don't ask me', he wrote to his editor at Dent (10 September 1952). To Desmond Hawkins (14 August 1939) he admitted that 'much of the poetry is impossibly difficult; I've asked, or rather told, words to do too much; it isn't theories that choke some of the wilder and worser lines, but sheer greed.' The crucial phrase is 'sheer greed', the obsession with words for their own sake and for the sake of their intractable nature, at which he must chip away for ever.

The only correspondent with whom he regularly discussed work in progress was Vernon Watkins, the other Swansea poet of his generation, whose comments about words and phrases were solicited and sometimes acted on. It was to Watkins that Thomas made the telling admission (perhaps it was a boast), 'You are right to write poems of all kinds; I only write poems of allsorts, and, like the liquorice sweets, they all taste the same' (1 April 1938).

Contemporary poets receive little attention from Thomas, most of it dismissive, even contemptuous: 'The English poets now are . . . a pin-legged, nibcocked, paperhearted crowd' (to Treece, mid March 1939). Thomas's judgements in the letters are inclined to be brisk, unkind and unsupported by argument. Those about whom he was rude or malicious include Edith Sitwell, George Barker, Stephen Spender ('slight, lyrical, nostalgic talent'), Louis MacNeice ('thin'), Henry Treece, C. Day Lewis ('should . . . have his balls beaten with a toffee hammer'), Geoffrey Grigson and the surrealist David Gascoyne. Major figures usually escape, although there are digs at Pound and Eliot. Auden is mocked, in part because he was homosexual. For someone who knew and liked 'queers'—see, for example, his letters to Oswell Blakeston, a literary gay of the 1930s—Thomas was quick to denigrate what he called 'bumboys', no doubt because in those days it was an easy way of damaging a reputation. In this, as in much else, he was true to the standards of Uplands, Swansea, rather than Chelsea, London.

Poets aside, Thomas also said malicious things about friends and acquaintances, and he never let the facts stand in the way of a good story or even a good sentence. It is also true that for every gibe at the shortcomings of others, there is recognition of his own. He was by nature a teller of tall stories, and the letters only hint at his talent in this department when he had a glass in his hand and a circle of admirers. It would have been excessive to correct each apparent flight of fancy with a footnote, unless he is being especially plausible: as when he tells Edith Sitwell, soon after his marriage, that he has spent ten days working on fishing-boats out of Penzance, 'and have hardly been on shore at all during the daytime'. Similarly his remark to Pamela in London that he was born in his Welsh town 'amid the smoke of the tinplate stacks' might sound convincing, although the only smoke in the Uplands came from domestic grates. The tortuous begging letters of later years, which lied and manoeuvred as he thought necessary, are another, sadder aspect of the same thing.

Most of the best letters were written before about 1948, although there are characteristic items to the very end, and the reader can find a melancholy fascination in seeing horizons darken. It is not easy to categorise Dylan Thomas's letters; and why should anyone bother? He was a complicated man, never as sure of himself as he sometimes pretended, tortured by uncertainties, dangerously reliant on others and especially on Caitlin. His happiest letters are those to his drinking pals, the 'strays and outlaws', the 'half-poets': the conversation of a man at ease with himself. Just as revealingly, the later letters to Caitlin, where he repeatedly swears his devotion, and reiterates how he misses her—during his frequent voluntary absences—have an air of desperation. The 1985 edition included a letter from Caitlin, written to Oscar Williams and Gene Derwood in America on 9 February 1953, which threw light on her dilemma, trapped in the vortex that was dragging her husband down. Unfortunately her estate is not as helpful to the editor as she was (Caitlin died in 1994), and the letter is not in this edition. The book continues to be dedicated to her.

Throughout, Thomas's sense of his own shortcomings is never far away. Aged nineteen, he wrote to Trevor Hughes of 'my islandic egoism which allows few of the day's waves to touch it'. 'Please help', he wrote to Margaret Taylor (12 April 1947); 'though I deserve nothing.' He would sacrifice anyone's interests if it helped him stay in business as a poet, but he could also tell a correspondent (W. T. Davies, July 1939) that 'I don't think it does any harm to the artist to be lonely *as* an artist . . . If he feels personally unimportant, it may be that he is.' A letter to C. Gordon Glover, a passing journalist who had interviewed him for an article (25 May 1948), is a canny assessment of 'this impermanent, oscillating, rag-bag character', a recognition of 'my still only half-squashed and forgotten bourgeois petty values; all my excruciating whimsicality; all my sloth; all my eye!' He caricatured the desire for literary reputation even while he was in the process of acquiring one. His letter to James Laughlin of 7 May 1938 is relevant: 'On, on, money to right of them, fame to the left, an income, a new suit, a special party, "Tell me Mr. Gluepot how did you start writing? do you believe in the feminine verse-ending? is Europe at the Crossroads?", lobster for tea, champagne every night, a niche in Letters, and an everlasting hole in the earth.' It was the tone of voice that made people take to him.

The present text is taken from original manuscripts or photocopies, except in a few cases where only typescripts are available, and fewer still where the editor has had to rely on the version printed in the unreliable *Selected Letters* of 1966.

As well as the new items that have surfaced since the 1985 *Collected Letters*, others have been identified but are untraceable, not least because collectors can be secretive. An asterisk before the addressee's name indicates a new letter. A number of the '1985' letters have been redated and so repositioned; for advice in this and other respects I am indebted to Professor Ralph Maud. Many footnotes have been revised and new ones added. Identifying the location of manuscripts, as shown at the end of each letter, has proved difficult in cases where those who owned letters in 1985 have disposed of them at auction or otherwise. It is impractical to pursue every item along a chain of dealers. In all cases where the location, identified in the first edition, can no longer be given with certainty, the 1985 ownership is shown, enclosed in brackets.

Concerning the style of presentation, square brackets are used in the text of letters to enclose conjectures of any kind. Where there is an editorial interpolation in addition to the conjectured or uncertain words, the editor's remarks are in italics, the remainder in ordinary type. The 1985 edition had occasional deletions, mainly for legal reasons, signified by [. . .]. Nearly all of this text has now been restored.

Obvious misspellings have been silently corrected. Many words gave Thomas trouble. Disillusion ('dissilusion'), separate ('seperate'), disappoint ('dissapoint') and propaganda ('propoganda') were among his blind spots. Also he was a careful, even laborious drafter of letters. Original versions were polished up and written out again. Especially in the case of long letters, this produced copyist's errors, 'poeple' for 'people', 'where' for 'were', 'it's' for 'its'. Wherever it seems that a misspelling was intended as a joke or to produce some verbal effect, it has been left untouched. Proper names, often misspelt over years, even in the case of friends, have been corrected, sometimes with a footnote.

Acknowledgements

Many people have taken time and trouble to help me find, date, assess and annotate letters. I mention especially Professors Walford Davies of Aberystwyth and Ralph Maud of Vancouver, the leading authorities on Dylan Thomas texts. Gwyn Jenkins and Dr Ceridwen Lloyd-Morgan at the National Library of Wales. Andrew MacAdie, who made available Dylan's first letter to Caitlin and other items in his collection; Jim Martin also let me see letters. Michael Rush, senior trustee of the Dylan Thomas copyright estate. Meic Stephens, writer and editor. David N. Thomas, who showed me the MS of his *Dylan Thomas. A Farm, Two Mansions and a Bungalow*, before Seren Books published it (2000); the information in n. 2, page 218 in Volume II, is his. Jeff Towns of Dylans Book Store, Swansea, who has an unrivalled knowledge of the market in Thomas holographs; I also adapted some of his footnotes to the letter to Loren MacIver, published by his Salubrious Press. Gwen Watkins, widow of the poet Vernon. John Whitehead of Moffat, Dumfriesshire, who wrote to me after the first edition with useful corrections.

For other assistance I am grateful to The Astrology Shop, Richard Atkinson (Casenove), Lady Avebury (daughter of Pamela Hansford Johnson), Barclays Bank (Human Resources), Michael Basinski (State University of New York at Buffalo), Dr Peter Beal (Sotheby's, London), Gilbert Bennett, Brighton Public Library, Kathleen Cann (Cambridge University Library), Chris Coover (Christie's New York), Wystan Curnow, Roy Davids, Michael Davie, Baldwyn Davies, Jane Davies (Tenby), Esmond Devas, Reg and Eileen Evans, Charles Fisher, Mark Fisher, Dr Chris Fletcher (British Library), David Gascoyne, General Dental Council, Elva Griffith (Ohio State University Libraries), Ken Hewlings (Tenby), Mary Johnson, Paul Johnson (National Library of Wales), Marilyn Jones (West Glamorgan Public Library, Swansea), Ed Knappman, Mark Le Fanu (Society of Authors), J. C. Wyn Lewis, Ray Lovell, Ann McKay (BBC), Nancy MacKechnie (Vassar University Library), Mexican Consulate, Dale Miller (Christie's East), Sarah Mindham, Leslie A. Morris and Melanie Wisner (Houghton Library, Harvard University), Timothy Murray and Rebecca Johnson Melvin (University of Delaware Library), Maurice F. Neville, Aedin O'Carroll (Location Register, University of Reading), Sonia Richmond (Phillips), Caroline Roberts (Brewers' and Licensed Retailers' Association), William Roberts (University of California at Berkeley Library),

Royal Pharmaceutical Society, Louise Ryan (Authors' Licensing & Collecting Society), Jay Satterfield and Krista L. Ovist (University of Chicago Library), Lorraine Scourfield (Boat House, Laugharne), Fiona Searle, Michael Snow, Neil Somerville (BBC Written Archives), Shayera Tangri (Wilson Library, University of North Carolina), Michael Taylor, Tenby Public Library, Aeron Thomas (Dylan's daughter), Clem Thomas (Laugharne), Dewi Thomas (Carmarthen Public Library), Kim Thomas (India Office Library), Llewelyn Thomas (Dylan's elder son), Tony Vilela (Laugharne), Tara Wenger and Cliff Farrington (Harry Ransom Humanities Research Center), Helene Whitson (San Francisco State University Library), Robert Williams, Bill Willis (Swansea), Joan Wintercorn, Sarah Wombwell (Christie's, South Kensington), Professor John Worthen, Stephen Young (*Poetry,* Chicago).

For help with research, proof-reading, indexing and general attention to the text, I am indebted as always to my wife Mary.

The following list repeats personal acknowledgements from the 1985 edition.

Graham Ackroyd, Ben Arbeid, Eric Barton, John Bayliss, Sir Theodore Brinckman (Monk Bretton Books), John Malcolm Brinnin, Victor Bonham-Carter (Society of Authors), Julian Chancellor (Society of Authors), Douglas Cleverdon, John Crichton (The Brick Row Book Shop), Roger Davenport, H. W. E. Davies, Sean Day-Lewis, Nicolette Devas (sister of Caitlin Thomas), Sheila Dickinson, Lawrence Durrell, Valerie Eliot, Charles Elliott, Frances Freeth, Jean Overton Fuller, Roland Gant, Clive Graham, Thomas B. Greenslade (Kenyon College archivist), Bernard Gutteridge, Desmond Hawkins, Ian Henderson, Nigel Henderson, Robert Hewison, Jane Aiken Hodge, Barbara Holdridge, G. Thurston Hopkins, Hubert Howard (the Camillo Caetani Foundation), Lord Howard de Walden, Dr Cyril James, Fred Janes, Glyn Jones, Professor Gwyn Jones, Mimi Josephson, P. J. Kavanagh, Ellen de Young Kay, James Laughlin, Laurie Lee, John Lehmann, Michael Levien, Mervyn Levy, Jack Lindsay, Brigit Manlier (sister of Caitlin Thomas), R. B. Marriott, Douglas Matthews, Barbara Noble, John Ormond, Ruth Wynn Owen, Ken Pearson, P. E. N., Hermann Peschmann, Gilbert Phelps, Douglas Phillips, Peter Quennell, Keidrych Rhys, Anthony Rota, Charles W. Sachs (The Scriptorium), D. S. Savage, Rupert Shephard, Philip Skelsey, Elizabeth Reitell Smith, John Sommerfield, Sir Stephen Spender, Professor Jon Stallworthy, Derek Stanford, Harald Sverdrup, Amelia Taylor, Professor Christy M. Taylor, Haydn Taylor (brother-in-law of Dylan Thomas), David Tennant, Georgia Tennant, Molly Murray Threipland, Dr Kerith Trick, Meurig Walters, E. W. White, John Wilson (bookseller).

The author and publisher thank the following corporate holders of Dylan Thomas letters for access to material; all are identified where the letters appear.

We are especially grateful to the Harry Ransom Humanities Research

Center of the University of Texas at Austin—which has the largest collection of Thomas letters—and to the State University of New York at Buffalo—whose Poetry and Rare Books Collection at the University Libraries contains the Pamela Hansford Johnson letters and the Thomas Notebooks—for their help with many inquiries.

We also formally thank the BBC Written Archives Centre; University of Birmingham Library (UK); Bodleian Library; the British Library Board; the Syndics of Cambridge University Library; the Joseph Regenstein Library, University of Chicago Library; Columbia University Libraries; University of Delaware Library; Houghton Library, Harvard University; Lilly Library, Indiana University; Chalmers Memorial Library, Kenyon College; University College of Los Angeles Library; Pierpont Morgan Library; Mount Holyoke College Library; Henry W. and Albert A. Berg Collection, New York Public Library, Astor, Lenox and Tilden Foundations; Fales Library, New York University; Ohio State University Libraries; Oxford University Press; Rosenbach Museum and Library; Royal Literary Fund; Paul Sacher Foundation, Basle; National Library of Scotland; Morris Library, Southern Illinois University at Carbondale; the Department of Special Collections, McFarlin Library, University of Tulsa; National Library of Wales; University of Washington Libraries; West Glamorgan Archive Service.

Laurence Pollinger Ltd, Viking Penguin Inc. and the Estate of Mrs Frieda Lawrence Ravagli kindly gave permission to use the three verses from 'Another Ophelia' and the two verses from 'Obsequial Ode', by D. H. Lawrence, which Thomas quoted in a letter dated 30 July 1945. The British Library and Mrs Gwen Watkins gave permission for the reproduction in facsimile of a letter from Thomas to Vernon Watkins.

Abbreviations

BBC	BBC Written Archives Centre, Caversham
Berg	Berg Collection, New York Public Library
Buffalo	University Libraries, State University of New York at Buffalo
Chicago	University of Chicago
Carbondale	Morris Library, Southern Illinois University at Carbondale
Delaware	University of Delaware
Houghton	Houghton Library, Harvard University
Indiana	Lilly Library, Indiana University
Ohio	Ohio State University Libraries
Texas	Harry Ransom Humanities Research Center, the University of Texas at Austin
Victoria	University of Victoria, Canada
Washington	University of Washington, Seattle
CP	*Dylan Thomas. Collected Poems 1934–1953*
The Poems	*Dylan Thomas: The Poems,* edited by Daniel Jones
'Notebooks'	The four surviving 'Poetry Notebooks' with Thomas's adolescent work, at Buffalo.
SL	*The Selected Letters of Dylan Thomas* (1966), edited by Constantine FitzGibbon
VW	*Dylan Thomas. Letters to Vernon Watkins* (1957), edited by Vernon Watkins.

When the whereabouts of a letter, as given in the first edition, is no longer certain, the original location is in brackets, eg *MS: (Thomas Trustees).*

The approximate value of money in Britain since Dylan Thomas's time:

Past value	*Value in year 2000*
£1.00 in 1939	£27.00
£1.00 in 1945	£23.00
£1.00 in 1950	£19.00

Majoda
New Quay
Cards
26 2 45

Dear Vernon,

I was very very glad to hear and see from you; it's been a long and complicated time since we disappointingly met, and I'm happy and relieved to think that the offence, (for my lost, preoccupied manner must really have been that) I gave when we did meet in that gabbling drunk-gray crush, the worst of the town, has, if never to be forgotten utterly, lost some disfavour. (I have just been writing at length to Llewelyn, on the occasion of a fall from a tree and a split tongue, and the effort of not talking to a boy of six has made me adopt the claptrap periods of a leader-writer, under gas.) I have found, increasingly as time goes on, or around, or backwards, or stays quite still as the brain races, the heart absorbs and expells, and the arteries harden, that the problems of physical life, of social contact, of daily posture and armour, of the choice between dissapations, of the abhorred needs enforced by a reluctance to "miss anything", that old fear of death, are as insoluble to me as those of the spirit. In few and fewer poems I can despair and, at rare moments exult with the big last, but the first force me every moment to make quick decisions and thus to plunge me into little hells and rubbishes at which I rebel with a kind of truculent acceptance. The ordinary moments of walking up 4 village streets, opening doors or letters, speaking good-days to friends or strangers, looking out of windows, making telephone calls, are so inexplicably (to me) dangerous that I am trembling all over before I get out of bed in the mornings to meet them. Waking to remember an appointment at x that coming evening is to see, before x, galleries of menacing commonplaces, chambers of errors of the day's conventions, pits of platitudes and customary gestures, all beckoning, spurning; and through, over, & out of these I must

A troubled letter from Thomas to his friend, the poet Vernon Watkins. It is printed on pages 151–2 in Volume II.

2

somehow move before the appointment, the
appointment that has now become a shining grail
in a dentist's surgery, an almost impossible
consummation of illegal pleasure to be
acheived in a room like a big gut in a
subterranean concentration-camp. And especially,
of course, in London. I wish that I could have met
Gwen "properly", and glad that she wanted to; I
was "myself" in the sense that I was no-one
else, but I was broken on a wheel of streets
and faces; equally well, I may be just as
broken in the peace — what peace? — of the
country, hysterical in my composure, hyena-ish
in my vegetabledom. I will, if I may, try to
come to stay in the pub in Stony Stratford
when next I come to London: but oh the
bony cupboards and traps and vats before that.
          I wish I could see your new poems. The
translation in Horizon I did, & remembered much
of it; it was beautiful.
     I am glad Francis is alive, well, and happy.
          I have lost Dan's address again. Will you
tell him that we are not going to Ireland for
a long time, perhaps not even this year, as
another film has risen out of some fool's mind
and must be written so that we can eat
and tremble at the approach of each quiet,
unsensational & monstrous day? The studio is
being carefully looked after. I'll write to Dan
this week & will send the letter to you.
          Love to you and Gwen from us both.
                    Ever,
                    Dylan.

I wish I could understand your letter from
Heatherslade. It was dated the 24th, which
was Saturday, but said that you were afraid
we would be unable to meet as you were
leaving on Friday. If that was not also, and
unfortunately, typical of myself, I should say
it was a piece of genuine accept-no-other
Vernon.
Don't mind this silly letter. It was lovely to
have yours.

THE COLLECTED LETTERS

Provincial Poet
1931–4

Both Thomas's parents, D. J. (David John, or Jack) and Florence Thomas, came from rural backgrounds in West Wales, and spoke Welsh. But D. J. Thomas (born in 1876) was of a pre-nationalist generation that accepted English as the dominant culture, and his ambitions looked east to England. D. J.'s youthful writing was unsuccessful, and by 1914, when his son Dylan Marlais was born, he was long established in the post he would occupy until retirement, teaching English to boys from petit-bourgeois families at Swansea Grammar School. A daughter, Nancy, was eight years older than her brother. But it was on his son that D. J. lavished the attention of a disappointed man. Books in general and poetry in particular were part of the daily scene at 5 Cwmdonkin Drive, a semi-detached house on a hill in a suburb of Swansea. Dylan Thomas began to write poetry as a child. Shortly before his eleventh birthday he went to the Grammar School, where his career was undistinguished and a trial to his father, by then the senior English master. But throughout his adolescence, he was filling notebooks with poems.

*NANCY THOMAS
[?1926]

Dylan Thomas's first known letter was written, at the age of eleven or twelve, to his sister Nancy, then nineteen or twenty, when she was staying at Blaen Cwm, a pair of stone cottages at Llangain, Carmarthenshire, owned and lived in for generations by members of his mother's family. Nancy Marles Thomas (1906–53) was on holiday with a first cousin, Doris Williams, who lived on the coast nearby at Llanstephan. The letter pokes fun at 'Grandpa' Gwynne, a maths teacher at Swansea Grammar School, and so is later than September 1925, when Thomas entered the school, not long before his eleventh birthday.

5 Cwmdonkin Drive   Uplands on Avon[1]   Swansea

Nancy—Sir!

Before I write I want this to be known:—this is not a news-letter. It is original, therefore it is a new-letter!

BOOKS! Ah! Before I go on we must stop. Books! What Fasination;[2] what charm; what undreamt-of dreams, what hours of unseppressed joy lie between the brown-gilt, (which has a guilty look) covers of Messers (pun!!) Woolworth's classics. We may not have in humble Swansea such mansons as Blaincwm, such promenades of paradise as Lammer Street,[3] such mathematical, gigantic, vast unimaginable buildings as the 'Home & Colonial Stores', but—oh—but (('but me, no buts') we have a Woolworth's.) Their latest books are—:

'Jokes'—on seeing N.M.T., by Hugh-Mur. (see it!) "Broken Windows in China". By Hoo-Flung-Dung!!

One day as I was strolling around Mumbles Cemetry[4] I came upon an old man. He looked doleful and nothing seemed to please him, not even the stately tombs. Being of a kind temprement and an inquisitive disposition I went up to the old chap clapped him on the back saying, "what ails you, old man" 'alone and palely loitering' " He said "I will tell you the cause for my woe. But first look at the scenery—:

> It was indeed a lonely spot,
> With desolation spread;

---

1 'On Avon' is a joke. 'Uplands' is the suburb where the Thomases lived.
2 In general throughout the letters, minor errors in spelling and punctuation have been silently corrected, but in this case the text is transcribed as written.
3 Lammas Street is in Carmarthen.
4 Mumbles Cemetery is in Swansea.

An eerie, solemn silence reigned,
Around the sleeping dead

No sculptured urn or marble tomb
Releived the sombre green;
A crucifix half crumbling down
Might here & there be seen.

A Dial that for centuries
Had marked the passing hour,
Broken, ruined, fallen at last
'neath Time's relentless power!

And there it lay as it had fallen,
Upon a rotting grave;
A dark damp mound beneath the wall
Where sunbeams never wave.

We sat us down upon a bench
Th' old man himself had made,
While o'er our heads a giant yew
Flung its ghastly shade.

I longed to hear the bygone tale,
And told the sad old man;
And grumbling & sighing all the while;
His plaint he thus began—:

"A bred & born philologist is what I claim to be,
But find that there are many things which greatly puzzle me.
[For in]stance take a cricket ball—you buy it—then its bought
[But i]f[1] you take & sky it right to say it's short.

[A dru]mmer is a man we know who has to do with drums,
[But] I've never met a plumber yet who had to do [with] plums.
[A che]erful man who sells you hats would be a cheerful [hatte]r,
[But i]s a serious man who sells you mats "a serious [mat]ter?"

[You] take your wife to Yarmouth, then you're a pair of [tr]ippers
[If] you slipped with her while skating would you be [a p]air of slippers?

1 The text is taken from a badly made photocopy at the British Library, and the words in square brackets have been cropped. The holograph was owned at one time by Doris, the cousin who was with Nancy when she received the letter. Doris married a Randolph Fulleylove, a dentist. The Fulleyloves showed the letter in the 1960s to a radio journalist, Colin Edwards, who meant to write a biography of Thomas (he never did), and he recorded them reading parts of the letter, which helps replace missing words in the photocopy; his tapes and a typescript are at the National Library of Wales. In 1981 the letter was sold by Sotheby's in London for £2,200 to a pseudonymous overseas buyer, 'Dr Bolus', who ignored requests to make the letter available. But a photocopy had to be deposited at the British Library before an export licence was granted, and this ultimately brought the letter into the public domain.

[If it] freezes when it's frosty, is it squosty when you [squ]eeze
[Woul]d you have to buy a biograph to write [bio]graphies?

A man is called a baker when to earn his bread he bakes,
But do we call a Quaker by that name because he quakes.
And *if* you are a dealer, of course, you have to deal,
But you *may* be a peeler though you never have to peel!

A man who brews as everybody knows is called a brewer;
But if your landlord sues you, would you say he is a suer?
A girl can change the colour of the hair upon her head,
It's strange that though you find she's died—she isn't is'nt dead!!!!!!!!

And after this original grumble the sad old man stuck his hands in his
pockets, made a gloomy contortion with his wrinkled face, & quickly
dissapeared into the shadows.

I have written nursery rhymes extra-specially for Nancy—Tommy—
Goo! Goo!

A Good Idea
When pussy turns her back to me
They say it's going to rain;
But though I turn her round about
She turns her back again.
I want it to be fine today
So I think I will creep
And sit the other side of her
When she is fast asleep.

Hide & Seek
I love to play at hide-and-seek,
But I am always found;
I don't know how it is at all,
I never make a sound.

I'm hiding in the garden now,
I've found a place that's new.
They'll never think of looking here.
Would you?

The Sea
Behold the wonders of the mighty deep,
Where crabs & lobsters learn to creep,
And little fishes learn to swim,
And clumsy sailors tumble in.

Apple-Tree Town
Three wise men lived in apple-tree-town,
So wise that each wore a gigantic frown,

But they couldn't tell whether—ahem! ahem!—
An apple seed points to the flower or the stem;
'Tis sad, but true,
That none of them knew,
Do you? Do You? Do You?

Poor, Dear Grandpa.

On Mr Gwyn of Swansea G. S. spelling boy's names wrongly. He can spell
Allbright like Allsop.[1] But he *can't spell Thomas. Poetic law won't have
it.*]
[*Interlined between* Allbright *and* Thomas *is the word* uncorrectly.]

What is the matter with grandpa Gwynn,
Whatever can the matter be,
[He's] broken his leg in trying to spell
[Dy]lan Thomas without a T.

[My][2] dear Nancy. Riddles are now all the go. [But], of course I need'ent
tell you that, when you [mov]e in the gayest Llangain society. Anyway,
here's [one] to get the craze on.—we all know [that] lions don't go to
Heaven. Missionaries do. [Wha]t is the result then when a lion swallows a
[missi]onary.

[I won]der how Rudge & Doris are progressing. Give this [?letter] to
Rudge[3]—: this is what'll happen to him—;

"*Say Good Bye when your chum is married*"

[T]his is a rhyme that might well be carried
[Pin]ned in your hat till the end of things:
[Say] good-bye when your chum is married,
[Say] good-bye when the church-bell rings.

[(] = You know what these wives are—dont you.]
Oh well, I feel *so very very tired* that I must sing this weary ditty.

"*WOWWIES*"
("Worries." N.B.—Please drop *all* the Rs.)
There's a worry in the morning because the coffee's cold,
There's the worry of the postman & the "paper" to unfold.
It's a worry getting on your boots & going to the train,
And you've got to put your hat on & take it off again.

It's a wonder how I live with such a constant strain—
I've got to put my hat on & take it off again.

---

1 'Allbright' bitter beer was brewed in Cardiff. The firm of Samuel Allsopp in Burton-on-Trent made another well-known bitter.
2 The photocopy is defective again.
3 Perhaps Randolph Fulleylove, than practising as a dentist in Llanelli.

There are worries in the noontide, & 'legion' is their name;
There's the worry of the luncheon that always tastes the same.
There's the worry of the 'baccy, that's the greatest worry save
The beastly boring worry when you know you want a shave.

That's a "really wicked wowwy," & your pardon I must crave,
If I use some tough-ish language when I mention that I shave!

There are wowwies in the evening, you've got to dress and dine;
There's the worry of the speeches that accompany the wine;
There's the wowwy of remembering what card your partner lead
AND THEN THE AWFUL WORRY OF GETTING INTO BED!!!!

Ah-a-h-a! How tired I am!
Now comes the awful 'wowwy' of finishing this letter,
One word before I end [*The word* Nancy *is deleted*] Dear—let's hope
    you're beastly better.

> Yours
> Dylan

Photocopy: British Library. MS location unknown

*PERCY SMART

Percy Eynon Smart (1912–91) was joint editor of the Swansea Grammar School magazine
with Dylan Thomas until summer 1930, when he left to work for Barclays Bank in London.
Thomas was to spend another year at school, sole editor of the magazine.

[December 1930]   Prefects' Room

Dear Percy,
    Thanks for the contribution which is joyfully accepted. I am not sure of
the Johnson quotation, so I leave it as it is.[1] After all, my edition of
Boswell has 577 pages of closely printed matter, and the life of an Editor!
(as you know) is not so much milk and honey as to allow me to spend my
valuable time in hunting up obscure (no) references.
    Life is mainly an elaborate system of give and take, but this term (I am
speaking of that Greatest of Concerns, the Magazine) it has consisted of a
little more taking than usual. Robbing myself of a moral simile, I mean we
have received more contributions this term, one or two especially good,
than in the previous year. As for Ward,[2] the less said about his literary and
business capabilities the better. He is not even willing to work. I am not
altogether sorry you refrained from writing on the joys and sorrows of early

---

1 Smart's article, 'In the centre of the world', was about London, and appeared in the
  December 1930 issue of the magazine. He quoted Samuel Johnson, 'When a man is
  tired of London, he is tired of life.'
2 A. J. Ward, a fellow-schoolboy who was 'sub-editor' of the magazine.

banking life. We all have our troubles (!), and very few of us want to increase them. Even that third-former, who is running along the corridor now, has probably an inherent cancer, or a mind full of lechery. The child grows from the cradle, soaked in a morbidity and restlessness he cannot understand, does a little painful loving, fails to make money, builds his life on sand, and is struck down before he can accomplish anything. Is it worth me lifting up my pen to write? Is anything worth anything? It is in moments like this that I emphatically reply 'no'.

Very striking and all that. I can hear you in your suburban lodgings laughing at my theatrical gestures. Every[?one] in the room look up because I am laughing at them, too. 'What's the latest story?' they ask me. I tell them.

Let me apologise for what this letter is promising to be. I remember once I wrote an essay on the Aesthetes, complaining of the young men that spend their nights in introspective orgies, and his days in committing them to paper. I have a certain sympathy with them now. Beppo, you will remember, had quite a philosophic interior under his melodramatic shell.[1] What if you could turn the Lot's wife of every divine moment that grasps you into salt? What effigies, and how much better than a water-colour of Mumbles Head[2] or a poem on Sussex lambs, even though they might both contain that personal divinity of yours.

But back to banking & the Magazine. I am glad you are enjoying your life, and, as Dad puts it, your prospects of a Dist: Career. The Mag: is going to be really good this term.

When are we going to start our argument about experiment and tradition? It's your turn to start it. Write soon.

Dylan

I will send you *two* mags. You are lucky.

MS: National Library of Wales

*PERCY SMART
[early 1931]   Grammar School

Dear Percy,

I received quite a dreadful surprise when I saw your letter this morning. Ward told me he had sent your mags. But he obviously hadn't. Well, here they are. Very good mag, even though I shouldn't say it. But modesty was never one of my strong points.

Only time for a short letter. Very busy this term with (a) two plays which I'm producing for the school, & acting in (b) the compiling of A NEW

1 Byron's poem *Beppo: a Venetian story* is an ironic account of marital misbehaviour.
2 The headland that encloses the southern extremity of Swansea Bay.

QUARTERLY MAGAZINE, CALLED 'PROSE & VERSE'. MARK THIS. IT IS IMPORTANT. 'PROSE & VERSE' IS GOING TO BE A JOLLY GOOD AND HIGHBROW AFFAIR, WELL PRINTED, WITH BRILLIANTLY COLOURED COVERS (mine), AND A WEALTH OF SPLENDID CONTRIBUTIONS. I WILL GIVE YOU SOME IDEA OF IT—TYPICAL CONTRIBUTIONS TO DATE ARE The cedars—a poem by Dan Jones,[1] detailed notes on the Persian Exhibition by Stevens,[2] a short story (v.g.) by a friend of mine Evelyn Phillips,[3] a Physcological Article by Ward (much better than usual), poems by me, short story called 'Interior' by me, essay on the Aesthetes by me. Etc. NOW I, AS EDITOR OF AN ENTIRELY NEW ARTISTIC PERIODICAL WHICH THE TOWN, SUCH AS IT IS, HAS BEEN WANTING FOR SO LONG, DEMAND SOMETHING FROM YOU. I MUST HAVE IT. AS HEAVY, ORIGINAL, OR AS ANYTHING YOU LIKE. PLEASE. IT IS NECESSARY. I AM WAITING.

Now for another point. 'Prose & Verse' is going to be run entirely by guaranteed subscriptions. We only want enough to cover the cost of printing. Can you guarantee one for yourself? Can you guarantee others to subscribe? I don't really know the price, but it won't be above 2/- [two shillings]. Try your best.

Hope you like the mag.

YOU MUST CONTRIBUTE TO 'P & V'

Not such a short letter after all.

Dylan

MS: National Library of Wales

*PERCY SMART

[?February 1931]   5 Cwmdonkin Drive Uplands Swansea

Dear Percy,

I will answer your questions in order, thanking you meanwhile for your praise of the mag—see how largely it figures in our correspondence—and your criticism of its chippiness, which, although I was fully aware of it, could not be remedied. I must confess to the pseudonym 'Simple Simon'. Modesty again. Lavender drew 'My Hat'. Francis VA wrote Blimey, and is still at large.[4]

---

1 Daniel Jenkyn Jones (1912–93), composer, became Thomas's lifelong friend. They met at the grammar school.
2 The school magazine dated April 1931 carried an unsigned article, 'Some characteristics of Persian art. The exhibition at Burlington House'.
3 Perhaps the 'E.P.' to whom Thomas's poem 'The force that through the green fuse' was dedicated in a manuscript notebook on 12 October 1933.
4 The items are from the December 1930 issue, which Smart had not previously seen. 'Simple Simon', who wrote 'Three Nursery Rhymes', was thought to be a Thomas pseudonym, but this was previously unconfirmed. Mr Lavender was the art master.

The rest of your letter was devoted to 'P & V', its opportunities etc. I will answer your questions about that. The *plans* are *not* cut and dried. Far from it. I visited my friend, thy friend, our friend, Mr Hunt, and put the project, from a printing point in view, in front of him. He dashed my hopes of having *two* coloured covers (& what colours) to the ground; he said that, owing to the number and irregular size of the colour-blocks, they would cost a small fortune. So I decided on a cover like this

```
┌─────────────────────┐
│ 1931         july   │
│                     │
│        prose        │
│        and          │
│        verse        │
│                     │
│ no 1      vol 1     │
└─────────────────────┘
```

only slightly larger and better spaced. See the absence of capitals, an old advertising dodge I have snared for better and ~~brighter~~ more artistic uses. Mr Hunt then said that the minimum number of copies it would be financially advantageous for *us* to have printed, would be 250. This was rather a blow. He was not able to tell me the cost of 250 copies then, but I will find that out quite soon. Then say it amounts to—£5, I'll price each copy so that we can get in £5 without selling all the 250. Each number we sell after that is profit, not for us, but for 'P & V', to make it Bigger, Brighter and Better—that is, my object is to get, as soon as possible, a little capital behind the enterprise. But before that's possible, or before it's even possible to print the 1st number, I *must* find out the price of printing 250 copies (two sizes larger than the School Mag, same type and paper, all matter, no illustrations, no advs:) and then get enough subscribers to guarantee the cost. Are there any flaws in this scheme? Can you suggest any improvements, additions, or anything else to ensure success, at least business success?

About your contribution, thanks for the willingness—I *do* write remarkable letters—but I leave the subject entirely to you. What 'P & V' insists on is Originality of Outlook. It is, frankly, a highbrow affair, not purposely so, but the expression of individualism (that's the keynote) which, as every contributor is intelligent above the average, can't be lowbrow. I include a copy of the Preface I have written. This should help you to write a long note, letter, or article to the Post.[1] Could I see it before you send it in?

Your remark about 'strength to strength', and 'famous men' might come true, but so might the remark of Pudovkin[2] on being introduced to the New Poets of Soviet Russia:—'You are sick youths, with nothing but chaos in your heads'. I hope not, and I don't think so.

Write as soon as you can.

Dylan

PTO

1 *South Wales Daily Post*, Swansea's principal newspaper.
2 V. I. Pudovkin, Russian film director and actor.

Preface

There seems to us no more suitable way of opening such a venturesome affair as an amateur periodical appealing only to a limited public is bound to be, than by a frank expression of what our aims and desires are. We are not, let it be understood at the first, either a private litarary group or a circle of would-be moneymakers. Our pages are open to anybody whose contributions we consider 'good enough', though obviously we cannot undertake payment. All we ask for is 'enough' subscribers for us to be able to pay the printers without loss, and unbiased criticism from those people, who, as a rule, consider it their duty to condemn whatever we of the younger generation attempt. We are not trying to write down to a public; neither are we trying to write above its head. What we feel is necessary is the expression of the individual, whether he chooses an artistic medium or not, and the most we can do in justification of this ideal is to guarantee an open magazine for you & me to put down some of our many thoughts, theories, & imaginative ideas in. This is the first number of 'Prose & Verse'. With your literary & financial assistance, let us make it the first of many.

MS: National Library of Wales

*PERCY SMART

[?7 March 1931][1] [headed paper: J. Grey Morgans,[2] M.A.   Headmaster.
The Grammar School   Swansea.]

Dear Percy,

Again I apologize at my delay in not answering your letter of the 22nd, but, knowing my customary indolence, you will be able to excuse me.

Thanks very much for the article on the Forsytes. I read it with interest. It will distinctly help towards making P and V into a succesfull (wrong spelling) and—I am hopeful—a lucrative concern. Its admirable solidity, saneness, and competence will help to balance some of the other contributions.

As I will be taking School Mag stuff into Mr Hunt early next week, I shall be able to write to you about P & V financial details.

I now approach what is rather a delicate question. I shall not be too optimistic at the reply. Can you, within the next two or three days—no more—write and send to me something for the School Mag. I'm heavy on ya, I know. Two contributions within a week is no mean task. But this is, if

---

1 '7th March' is written diagonally opposite the salutation, probably added by Smart.
2 Mr Morgans (nicknamed 'Pinky'), a lax disciplinarian who had not long been headmaster, was still having his stationery stolen by the next generation of schoolboys after Thomas; among them this editor.

not my last, my last but one term as Editor, & I *should* like you to write for the Mag as long as one of us holds that office.

Don't trouble to write telling me you will or won't. Either send the con: by Wednesday or Thursday, or don't.

I hope you will.

About your paragraph for the local paper. It is, as far as it goes, O.K. It seems to me ideal for an opening hint on the subject. Then, in a week or two, you could bring it up again with clearer details. Then—an appeal for cons: & subs. Eh? Anyway, send *this* note in as soon as you can.

You'll be interested to know that a new Debating Society has been formed in School. I am Secretary. Our first debate was 'That Modern Youth is Decadent'.[1] I moved the motion that it was, seconded by J. C. Griffiths. McQueen & N. G. Jones opposed. I lost, or my motion lost, by 14 votes to 6. That's natural, isn't it. What boy is going to say he's decadent. He is, though. I talked for a very long time, not with many facts but with a host of epigrams and condemnatory epithets. I shocked everybody. I ran down everything, especially *tender*! subjects like religion, sanctity, sport, and sex. Great Sport! You should be here for them. The next is 'Capital Punishment'.

Don't forget the School Mag.

Dylan

MS: National Library of Wales

TREVOR HUGHES

Trevor Tregaskis Hughes (1904–66), a clerk with literary ambitions, responded to an item in the local newspaper about the projected 'Prose and Verse'. He is the original of 'Raymond Price' in Thomas's later story, 'Who Do You Wish Was With Us?'

10/6/31   5 Cwmdonkin Drive   Uplands   Swansea

Dear Mr. Hughes,

Thank you very much for your short story, 'Freedom'. It is one of the few contributions I have received so far which does really suit the requirements of the type of periodical I wish to produce. Needless to say, your story is accepted without reservation. But, unless I can foster interest in the notoriously stony bosoms of the local public, neither 'Freedom', nor any of the other material at my disposal, will ever see light in the form of 'Prose & Verse'.

For it is subscribers more than contributors I need now—I am not speaking of your type of contribution which is as gratefully received as it is rarely sent—for out of the 200 subscribers at 2/- each needed to cover the cost of publication (£20) I have amassed just over twenty. More will be coming this week, but that is all I have been *absolutely guaranteed* so far.

1 The debate was reported in the April 1931 magazine.

Admittedly, I have not written to any of the people who are supposed to [be] interested in literary matters; I put the particulars and my address in the local paper, and trusted to the depth of their interest, which, I am beginning to believe, is almost legendary.

I shall wait a few days before I knock at the houses of the nouveaux riches and the Swansea bohemians, asking, in a hopeless voice, for donations; or at any rate subscriptions.

I wonder whether you could help me in a business way as much as you have helped me in a literary way. If you could gather the names of as many subscribers as possible towards 'Prose & Verse', & then give them into me, you would be doing a great deal towards furthering my project.

Hoping I shall hear from you in the near future,

I am,
Yours faithfully
D. M. Thomas

MS: Buffalo

*PERCY SMART
25th June [1931]   5 Cwmdonkin Drive   Uplands   Swansea

Dear Percy,

Your letter, with its admirable suggestion and no addresses following the names, came, as you may have observed from a close scrutiny of the Post, too late to prevent my sending in our concocted notice. But it can't be helped. I have written, (not changing the paragraph), to one or two of them but so far have had no reply. I am going to write to some more. I went up to Grey Morgans and asked if he'd like to guarantee a 2/-. Yes, he said, and what's more, he said, I'll give you a 10/- note, he said, to start the fund, he said. After a little natural reluctance at taking the money, I thanked him and got drunk. But—have no fears—I returned the money later from my own poor salary,[1] and the note now nestles closely, like a lover on a chemise, between the pages of HAR-JAN of Cassel's Encyclopedia!! all to the good. I saw Llewelyn John afterwards and he guaranteed another 10/- when I wanted it. All to the better. The snag is—go wary, the snark says, go wary the snag—that I have only 12 guaranteed subs: And out of 200, mind you, as the man said, lamenting at a football match over a passing crow's sense of humour.

You can't realize but you probably can the immense joy it gives me as an editor man—this sentence rhymes but it doesn't scan—to receive contributions from outside people, look at them with the sardonic and blasé eye symptomatic of my godless generation, and then send them back, enclosing a note written in my worst style, advising the authors to take up

---

1 Thomas is generally thought to have left school to work on the local newspaper, the *Daily Post*, after the summer term ended on 29 July 1931. He edited the July issue of the school magazine. But 'my own poor salary' suggests he was already a journalist.

pullet-breeding, & concluding with a very coarse paragraph about mid-wives in Jamaica.

A creature called Chrissie Breeze—I hope you don't know her—sent me some poems? from Neath. Her parents are probably inmates of a cerebral institution. And she should join them. One of the poems? started

> 'Twas 'neath the willow's sunny shade
> I lay to dream of love,
> The while, in every copse and glade,
> I heard the cooing of the dove.
> 'Twere bliss, I think, to sit like this,
> The pleasant sky above.

This is honestly what she wrote. Isn't it too good to be true?

Only one fellow, Trevor Hughes, sent me anything worth while. It was a short story about monks, very very good. It had a clear defined style and tons of atmosphere. Its entire absence of plot or reason didn't mar it a bit.

And now to business. Will you write something for the Post about 'P & V' & then send it here, not that I don't trust what you'll write but that I'd like to see it before publication. Say the thing isn't progressing well. Pour shame on Swansca's indifference and in the Post's lack of publicity—see where they shoved our last paragraph[1]—appeal for contributors & donors. In short, write what you think best.

And now about the School Mag: As this is my last term as editor, I naturally want to bring out an extra good number. And no number one of us (as ex co-ed:s) edits is complete without contributions from both. I'm bound to write something. So are you. Please send something as long and as Smartian as possible.

Sorry I'm so late in writing. We business men . . .

Dylan

MS: National Library of Wales

*PERCY SMART
[July 1931]   5 Cwmdonkin Drive   Uplands   Swansea

Dear Percy,

Pardon me for my exceptional delay in writing to you, exceptional even in one whose own mother cannot call him the soul of regularity. The truth is I thought I'd written, and then I knew I hadn't. Isn't memory false, or, alternatively, how false is memory. Yes, yes.

---

1 More than one reference may have appeared in the local newspaper. The *Daily Post* of 2 June 1931, using information from Thomas, had reported that the projected 'Prose and Verse' would cost two shillings, and that 'the editor, who is to be found at 5, Cwmdonkin Drive, Uplands', sought contributions whose 'only qualification must be originality of outlook and expression'. The paragraph was tucked away in the *Listener*'s daily gossip column, beside a photograph of a man-eating shark.

I may have thanked you previously for your magazine article, which, in the absence of any other title, I have called Monomania, but in case I haven't, thank you. I knew my call for a contribution would not be in vain. But how fortunate you are in your choice of casual companions. You go into a railway carriage and immediately start a 'half-intellectual' discussion about the merits of Pickwick, the paucities of Galsworthy, (that touches you on the quick, Malvolio; which does not come from any play I know) or the evils of the crossword craze. In any public place your plastic features draw out the secrets from the most reticent heart. Somebody says, 'There's weather we're having', and I say 'yes', or 'you wouldn't think this was summer would you?' and I say 'no'. Is the dissimilarity between the conversations we singly encourage owing to, as I have said, your plastic features and your honeyed voice, or my retroussé profile and my mellow tones? Ah.

I have arranged, in a consultation with the Principal of the Board of Education, that your parents *may* attend the school Prize-Day. But do not raise their spirits too high. *I* shall not be there, shall receive no prize, and hear no applause ring in my withered ears.

Prose and Verse is about as far ahead as when I wrote to you before. Your letter in the Post brought one literary contribution, of no merit at all.[1] The only thing to do is to write for an interview to some local big wap & ask him for £10 or £20 straight away. There's quite a valuable adjunct to our editorial forces in Hughes, a Swansea chap I'd never heard of until about a month ago. He's thirty years old, knows a lot of people, writes good short stories, and has a typewriter upon which he types *all* the things for Prose & V and many letters which are sent to rich people.

I am very well, thank-you.

I have two teeth missing in the front now,

And my favourite fruit is the lemon.

Write as soon as you like on any subject you like and let me congratulate you on your charming note on Bank paper.

Dylan

MS: *National Library of Wales*

*PERCY SMART

[July 1931]   5 Cwmdonkin Drive   Uplands   Swansea

Dear Percy,

Have you had my letter, asking for a return-post reply about your prizes? In the event that you haven't I shall again state the facts. You are due for the English & History prizes. The French, out of pity, goes to Jimmy Rees. The books must be worth not above 12/6 each; you may of course

---

1 Smart had sent the newspaper a further puff for 'Prose and Verse'.

amalgamate the money and have some sumptuous edition of something or other. Dad is going slowly dotty. HE WANTS YOUR REQUIREMENTS BY RETURN OF POST.

On receiving your letter, I shall write again.

Dylan

RETURN
OF
POST

MS: National Library of Wales

*PERCY SMART
[July 1931]   5 Cwmdonkin Drive   Uplands   Swansea

Dear Percy,

This term, Ward is not to blame. I put your mags: aside, left them for a day or two, and then forgot that I hadn't sent them. Blame not me, but my forgetfulness, which obviously amounts to the same thing. I've been absolutely encompassed (as Topsy says) by work lately—I've been writing a lot, enjoying myself in various ways a lot, mostly riotous, and am busily rehearsing for two plays to be produced by the Swansea Dramatic Club or Society—I don't know which. One is a cheap comedy 'Captain X', and the other is a long one-acter 'Waterloo' by Conan-Doyle, in which I play a veteran soldier of 90. Henry Irving, incidentally, made his name in that part!!!

I think you'll be pleased with the mag—I'm sorry I have only one to send you now; the other will come later when I add to my stock. I've changed the cover slightly. Don't you think it's better? There are nearly 50 pages, 49 & a bit to be exact. There is abundant variety and more photographs than ever before. I wish I was in school for another year; if I was, the mag would become really remarkable. That sounds obnoxiously immodest, but I don't mean it. It is, as Dad is never tired of telling me, experience that counts, experience, in the magazine case, with contributors & contributions.

I don't remember whether I've written to you since the paragraph in the Post appeared. If I haven't, let me thank you. It was very good. I detected the other bloke's comments. P & V is a big job. According to old Mr Davies, it would cost about £45 to bring out—that is 17/6 a page for roughly 50 pages. That, of course, is the utter maximum, & even then the old fool may be wrong. Therefore, as it's not worth printing less than 300 copies, 300 definite subscribers are required at about 3/- a head. That seems too much to ask anybody. You think it out. Add things. Correct things. Improve things. I await your reply.

How are you getting on? Rather late in the letter to ask that, but, nevertheless, how are you getting on? Send particulars, and criticize the mag.

Dylan

MS: National Library of Wales

TREVOR HUGHES
[February 1932]   5 Cwmdonkin Drive   Uplands   Swansea

Dear Trevor,
Your letter was late, but mine is later, and the trouble is I have no real excuse, except the chronic and self-condemnatory one of innate laziness, to offer you. You will, I know, brush aside my faltering cry of 'Work'. You have been one of the World's Workers long enough to realise there is always time enough to complete one's correspondence. So, humbly and with a forced smile upon my lips, I tender—what a curious word that is— apologies as sincere as they are lame. I have such little time. My right hand is injured from a colliery accident. I have no ink.

Now that the bridge of reticence is spanned (God, what style! The man's a Burke!) and the waves of consciousness met (the man's a Lawrence!) writing becomes distinctly easier. A phrase is a phrase again, an image an image now.

The purple of your dreams is untroubled—unstirred as you say. I am glad to hear that. What I shall be gladder to hear is that you are still writing. You may not know it, but you could, with practice & time, become a very considerable prose-writer. You've got something to say & a new way to say it.

My purple is turning, I think, into a dull gray. I am at the most transitional period now. Whatever talents I possess may suddenly diminish or may suddenly increase. I can, with great ease, become an ordinary fool. I may be one now. But it doesn't do to upset one's own vanity, and this letter is gradually becoming a cry from the depths.

I am playing in Noel Coward's 'Hay Fever' at the Little Theatre this season.[1] Much of my time is taken up with rehearsals. Much is taken up with concerts, deaths, meetings & dinners.[2] It's odd, but between all these I manage to become drunk at least four nights of the week. Muse or Mermaid?[3] That's the transition I spoke about. M or M? I'd prefer M any day, so that clears the air a lot.

Job[4] is a very curious man, isn't he? I agree he has no sense of humour and a dislike of alcohol, but I have heard him laugh, and he has told me, quite jocularly, that my voice, inexplicably enough, was always thicker at 3 o'clock than it was at 12.30—you see, I dine in town—(Dine? You compliment yourself, sir.)

1 Amateur players, who performed regularly in the town and district. Thomas was a member from 1932 to 1934. His sister, also a member, was in *Hay Fever*.
2 Typical events that a junior reporter had to cover.
3 A pub in the Mumbles, a village on Swansea Bay that was becoming a suburb.
4 Chief reporter of the *Post*, the 'Mr Solomon' of Thomas's story 'Old Garbo'.

When you write next, and I hope you write soon, enclose either a story you have written or the particulars of one you are writing. Otherwise, my insane annoyance will know no bounds.

I can't concentrate. My mind leaps from thought to thought like a wombat. I'll have to stop. Besides, the ink is getting low.

Don't forget to write soon.

Is your Ma any better?

How is London treating you, if at all?[1]

Mermaid?

Are you writing much?

Am I writing much?

Are we writing much?

Can you write, can I write, can we write?

Clear up this lot in your next epistle. Pardon mine, it's a Sunday morning. I've got a head like a wind-mill.

Dylan

MS: Buffalo

*PERCY SMART

[1932 ?April/May][2]   5 Cwmdonkin Drive   Uplands   S'sea

READ

THIS

FIRST

Percy [*written boldly above a deleted* Dear Trevor]

There was a time, so far away it is little higher than the grass, but ~~Yeats~~ gray not ~~Oscar~~ apple-green as grass is, high hopes had high words, and the things in the twenty-four hour dream, heartaches, irrelevancies, knowing for a moment nothing's worth knowing, the self-consciousness, the pain, & the ribs of fire across the eyes, these were not counted. So little, they could be drowned under the high hopes. Now, if a [*a word is deleted*] the high hopes have dwindled, & the words drifted away, these things have all the words I know. ~~Once in a groove call a dog~~ he Call a dog when in a groove, dog's no wish, or hope, of moving. Such weary thought, so crabbed its written, theres no truth in it you might say, there's no sense you can find, but who cares for you know I don't, and my head is burning, & my hands, their pencil silly-writing, drip damp from wrist to finger. Nerves, so the

---

1 Hughes had moved to London with his family.
2 The 'after note' of this two-part letter was written on remnants of paper with the letter-heading of the *South Wales Daily Post*. The newspaper changed its title to *South Wales Evening Post* on 14 March 1932, after it was bought by Northcliffe Newspapers. The old letter-heading would have been redundant, and the stationery was evidently cut into the small-size sheets used by reporters to feed text quickly to typesetters. In the first part of the letter, 'Queen of the May' suggests a date near 1 May.

dentist says, are all on edge. The drill is lifted & moved to the sebaceous belly of the all-flaming Christ it were over, put by, all by, the white sheets & then the white sheet, put out the light, & then it does not matter, I am so comfortable, whether the light is put out or not. Look what the stream of consciousness has done for me. I have no Joyce: I must write so mad whether I like it or not.[1] This is what comes out of the brain, though I prune the weeds. If these not weeds, these weak words, help, God help, the buds (tra la) that in the spring do sit & [?simper] high upon a plant's high lap.

For the 1000th time this morning the sub-editors' door has swung to with a noise like the falling of the walls of jericho.[2] Soon, though friend may say sooner, I shall lie upon the floor & gibber; I shall swing upon the chandeliers & yap; I shall bark like a dog, showing my discoloured teeth, crying out 'Muzzle me for the sake of Magdalena & the Eaten Heart, muzzle me, muzzle me'.

For the 1000th time this morning the telephone bell rings. Is this Mr—? [One and a half lines are deleted] No, this is Joan of Arc. Can't you hear me sizzling. Is this Mr ...? No he is away at the moment, sprinkling [?aniseed] over his grandmother, who is a staunch Tory. For the 1000th time I hear the noise of the engines, I hear the voices of men I loathe & distrust, I feel them breathe upon my cheek, I am called here, I am called there, there is an accident in Landore, there is a marriage in Killay,[3] there is a newly dug grave in garden & Mother has bought me a razor blade, a razor blade, to cut my throat so early.

For the 1000th time I say to myself 'I am dying'. Once I say to myself 'I am dead', & 1000 times again, 'To night, I shall be Queen of the May. Wake me early, preferably before the buds are in full voice.

The strain is telling on me. I lift my tumbler of neat acid. Your face, Edith, looks remarkably beautiful through its glass. I smile, but you are looking somewhere else. At the boxer perhaps, though I luv more than he does.[4] For I have written a poem about you, which, though not beautiful, is highly coloured, & liberally tinted with the conventional exotic dyes. Never to lose her, that is the high hope, Percy [Percy is heavily scrawled, replacing an illegible name, probably Trevor]. Now she is Mother, now she is Soldier, now penny paper, now Betty, [words deleted] names are), now

---

1 The 'READ THIS FIRST' part of the letter—that is, up to and including the 'Pome'—is on cheap lined paper, heavily altered and giving the impression that Thomas was drunk. Very likely he was, but the letter has an air of contrivance.

2 The preceding sentence begins the second page of the letter. Thomas's handwriting, tiny on the first page, has returned to normal size. Page 1 suggests it was written at home ('white sheets ... put out the light'). Page 2 (and page 3) were allegedly written in the Evening Post office, but that may have been part of the contrivance. 'Pome', on page 4, could have been written anywhere.

3 Landore and Killay are districts of Swansea.

4 An 'Edith' ran the teleprinter room of the Post in the 1940s, probably the same woman. 'The boxer' must be Freddie ('Half Hook') Farr, the chief reporter, who covered boxing for the paper. He appears, undisguised, in Thomas's story 'Old Garbo'.

[*words deleted*] Music, now Poems, now Maisie, now Music & Poems & [all things artistic *deleted*] Painting, now Maisie (subtle these names are) now Tumbler, now Tumbler, now Edith, now Tumbler, now Tumbler . . . and that chronologically is as far as I've got . . . but always feminine so must not lose her, P. Grip her waist. Hold her tight. Kiss her, read her, drink her.

Dylan

Pome[1]
War would be kind; this peace
Lies sveltly on the knitter's head,
Fit for old men & geese
Or rather Rodericks on their knees
Praying for woman or for cheese,
Is shabby, dull, & lie-a-bed,   EXCUSE
I would lie wounded, burst, or dead   DRAFT
Rather than breathe such peace,   OF
Be maggot-ridden by armistices   POME
Illnesseses & vilenesses

[*Continuation on printed letterhead, 'South Wales Daily Post and Cambria Daily Leader' etc.*][2]

This is an after note, almost, you might say, O my large epitome of Sane Intelligence, an aftermath. The writing is, if not beautiful, at least regular. And the thought is logical.

All about me is the sane air of the morning, the sun beaming brightly from its accustomed vantage point, and the wind, as usual, attempting to blow it off the face of the sky.

The air is chill, clean. I look at the pieces of paper I wrote on last night,[3] and think Christ! Have I written that? Is that rubbish mine? Was I drunk, or mad? Now, thank God, I am sober, sane. (What a disquieting thought it is—that last night's was my real mood, & this but a superimposed sanity, a false cleanness of mind forced upon me by the wind & the English—or rather the Welsh—morning.)[4]

Another thing strikes me. Once you said, sententiously but truly, 'How different people are inside and outside. No one would think you were a modern poet.' No, they wouldn't, would they? If you & I went—mind, I

1 Five lines and several words have been crossed out.
2 Thomas's letters were kept by Smart in no particular order. The family, who sold them after his death, have no knowledge of the chronology. But the 'after note' almost certainly belongs here.
3 The newspaper office closed after the final edition at the end of the afternoon. Either Thomas wrote pages 2 and 3 of the letter somewhere other than the reporters' room, or they were written there but not at night.
4 Thomas used a morning-after recollection of drunkenness when he wrote 'Old Garbo' (first published 1939) about a Saturday night out with Freddie Farr—'Knowing that I would never drink again, I lay in bed until midday dinner . . .'

only suggest it—into an hotel-bar, which would the barmaid think the most capable of churning out unrhymed, unrhythmical, rubbish? You, yes, you. I have a weak jaw & a loose mouth, & very wide eyes & a hat at a daft angle. I am ordinary. You, outsize in intellects, are extraordinary. Yet you have more common-sense & sanity in your big toe than I've in my whole head. Odd, very odd.

I am not going to apologize for my very egotistical letter. Letters, I maintain, between the intervals of removing a half-chewed cigar from my pocket to my mouth, should always be egotistical. A writes a letter all about A, & B about B. A receives B's letter & wants to hear about B. He does. And vice-versa.

Therefore your next letter, which I hope will

[incomplete]

MS: National Library of Wales

*PERCY SMART
[Soon after 12 December 1932]

5 Cwmdonkin Drive   Uplands   Swansea

Dear Percy,
Your letter, inside a dignified envelope, and penned, like the doctor's in the 'Giaconda Smile', with meticulous calligraphy, has come at a time when I thought that London, for once and for all, had severed the immortal Thomas–Smart connections, had transformed the senior member into a black-coated gentleman with business in the city and a number of literary & dramatic interests that were never, at any time, allowed to interfere with the successful stirrings for bread-&-butter, and the junior member— my sentence is becoming more and [more] involved—into a suburban parasite, clinging on to a hermit's uneventful life, & occasionally, when mood or calf's insanity promotes, dropping his sugared syllables of grief upon an odd piece of vellum paper.

Here, with reluctance, I start another sentence: To one so removed from the petty machinations of provincial life as yourself, whose interests now lie in the sylphs of Sadler's Wells rather than in the shaggy eunuchs of the Uplands, news of my departure from the staff of the 'Evening Post', may come in a light of the most secondary importance. But to me this departure—voluntary, may I assure my sceptical friend—may be the turning point in what has been, so far, a meteoric career, starting, that is, at a reasonable height (of both physical & mental capabilities,) and shooting, down towards (Huxley again) 'abysms of stinking mud' as quickly as it is possible.

I was offered a five-years contract with the 'Post', not so much because of my brilliance as a hack reporter—which many people, including the dyed-in-the-wool editor, (may his tribe decrease), sincerely doubted—but because I could—& many of the staff couldn't—string a grammatical sentence together in quite reasonable time. Valiantly, however, I refused the contract . . .[1] Five more years subjugated to the dictates of a puritanic chief reporter and a blousy combine would stamp out all the originality in the world & promise a life of suicides, alcohol, & church bazaars. Despite my disbelief in the worth of living, which you so securely and comfortably tilt at in your letter as though I had merely decided on pessimism because it is an easy philosophy & had not thought, thought, and thought for myself, facing, eventually, a blank wall, I have still a certain amount of faith in myself. Without it, of course, it wouldn't be worth living till tomorrow. Therefore I threw what was a comparatively safe job aside, & have now taken up the very precarious profession of free-lance journalism.

I still write for the Northcliffe press, humorous articles, specials, nature notes.[2] I have had a story accepted by, but not yet published in the Mercury. I have had printed a patriotic poem in the B.O.P.,[3] and I have a lot of stuff in hand. Whether I could live by this method I don't know. And, to date, I don't particularly care.

But, yes, in a way I do. And I can't help thinking of Lawrence's words. Lawrence handed out more straight commonsensible truths than Jesus ever did. This is Lawrence: 'It's either you fight or die, young gents. You've got no option. Don't say you can't. Start & try. Give hypocrisy the once-over, & tackle the bloody big blow-fly of money. Do it or die you've got no option'.[4]

I'm trying to do, at least, which is the best thing you can say of me.

Lulu is dead. For some reason I went to his funeral.[5] It was too fresh an afternoon, too full of pleasure, cold wind making commotion among trees, clear sky and warm sun, to bury a man. It was too fine an afternoon for him to be dead at all. But, wrapped in private miseries over the death of a haggard, hollow and diabetic old schoolmaster, the mourners carried on their business, shuffled, muttered as they moved. Rain, most certainly, should have fallen.

As a rule and of late I have tried vainly to disassociate myself from the emotions of others, focus, that is, my feelings on neutrality (if there is such a word) & remain unmoved at the griefs or laughter of others. Vainly, I

1 Thomas left the *Evening Post* in November or December 1932. The 'five-year contract' is an invention. He was sacked, or persuaded to leave.

2 This career didn't prosper. The *Evening Post* of 7 January 1933 carried an article by Thomas, 'Genius and Madness Akin in the World of Art', which referred to the painter Nina Hamnett as 'author of the banned book, *Laughing Torso*'. The book was not banned, and the newspaper had to print a fulsome apology a week later.

3 The *Boy's Own Paper* had published a poem, 'The Second Best', but years earlier, in 1927. No story appeared in the *London Mercury*.

4 Thomas was quoting and paraphrasing a Lawrence poem that begins, 'It's either you fight or you die,/young gents, you've got no option' (*Pansies*, 1929), lines 1–2 and 9–13.

5 'Lulu' was R. M. Lewis, senior French master at Swansea Grammar School, who died 8 December 1932. The funeral was on Monday 12 December at Ystalyfera, an industrial village a dozen miles from Swansea.

said. I began thinking, over the old fellow's grave, as morbidly & as selfishly as a Russian dramatist.

And when I die (I thought) will there be a procession of black-coated gentlemen, their hats at discreet angles, following *me* to the grave-yard where, prayers said and the last words of the minister hovering meaninglessly over the mourners' heads, the corpse will be lowered into its —— feet of earth. Will my mother turn on her ready tap of recollections and, cloaking misdeeds with tears, dwell tenderly upon such virtues as I may present at the gold gates—my love of dogs & little children; my belief in the devil, three-toed, three-tongued, my affections for a muse wh[ich], in its turn, has returned but little of my labour.

Will the handkerchiefs flutter, white flags in a green place, the minister wipe a tear away with a sanctimonious sleeve, the wind continue to make noise along the branches, after I have stopped and refused to be wound up again?

I doubt it, doubt it. All of which—a crazy quilt of words covering a sentiment worn thin by lady novelists and moths—must come to an end.

The trouble is, you see, that I can go on writing like that all day, turning, in that case, poor old Lulu's funeral into an occasion for precious writing, cynical, idealistic, half-baked prose; make of old Lulu's funeral an opportunity for the higher witticisms of a low mind.

There I go again. Give me pen & paper—the trick's done: a thousand conceits, couched in a hermit's language spoiling the whiteness of the page. In my ivory tower of silence sit I brooding, clad in owls' feathers, over a dubious colon, splitting an infinitive with a connoisseur's care & purpose, dipping, on occasions, into a more exotic ink-bottle & fetching out, at the end of a J. nib, little Wilde words.

That is enough. Remember me by that.

You seem to be having a gay time in spite of licking stamps for a living, and, let it be hoped, occasionally delving into the depths of bankers' dark intrigues. You haven't, I suppose, seen Peggy Ashcroft, (whom the gods desire) taking part in a play called, I believe, 'Elsa', by Schnitzler or some other German?[1] From what I gather of the plot—the play was produced in an independent theatre and is now withdrawn—you would have revelled in it. Peggy Ashcroft—close all doors!—accepts a rich man's offer of monetary gain if she unclothes herself for him. Now, keep that naughty thought to yourself, & do not let the dramatist's idea cause rash thoughts to enter your sane & diplomatic brain, & make you rush to the Sadlers' stage-doors, attempting to bribe that talented actress with a week's earnings.

In your letter you ask, though rhetorically, who, in my opinion, is the best dramatist—Shaw, Travers,[2] or Shakespeare. As a young man sd in a young man's novel:—'My two favourite authors are Blight and Mildew'. I feel I cannot improve upon that.

1 Peggy Ashcroft played the eponymous heroine in *Fräulein Elsa*, adapted from Arthur Schnitzler's novel, at the Independent Theatre Club in November 1932.
2 Ben Travers (1886–1980), popular playwright who wrote the 'Aldwych farces' of the 1920s.

Again, remember what P. G. Woodhouse sd, or rather what his character Brusilov, sd: 'Nastikov no good; Sovietski no good. I spit me of them both. Nobody no good except me. P. G. Woodhouse & Tolstoi not bad. Not bad but not good. Nobody really any good except me.' I cannot say better than that, either.[1]

As Shakespeare says, 'Exit soldier pursued by bear'. Could any words sum up a situation more brilliantly?

Dylan

I hope you like long letter!
Why not send me one like this?

MS: *National Library of Wales*

TREVOR HUGHES
[?early January 1933]   5 Cwmdonkin Drive Uplands Swansea

Dear Trevor,

In my more melancholy moods, when the brightest things can be made to appear the most drab, and when life—you probably detest such a sententious opening to a letter as much as I do—offers little more than the preferably sharp razor and the necessarily painless drug, I turn over, with a certain perverse pleasure, all my ill-fortunate experiences which amount as nearly to heartbreak as one, like myself, who has never felt the desire to fall in love, can realise.

And among those experiences I count that of losing, apparently for ever, my friendship with you. It is easier to write than to talk about it. I have a horrid fear, when talking, of plunging into a hot bath of sentimentality, but on paper the most girlish thoughts can be expressed without much fear of a sudden immersion into those wicked waters.

I realise I am writing the most utter nonsense. This is what I mean to say: When you left Swansea I thought that the end had come of a friendship, quite short, that I, at any rate, will always think of happily. We wrote letters for a time. Then they stopped for God knows what reason. Laziness on both our parts, probably. I didn't hear from you for six months. My sister stayed the night in Torrington-square & asked where you were. Nobody appeared to know. And then the day before Christmas, a much over-rated holiday, I received a letter. Thanks for it, but don't let it be in the way of a conscience-reliever. Don't lie back, a smug smile on your face,

1 Thomas was quoting from memory. In P. G. Wodehouse's *The Clicking of Cuthbert* (1922), the eminent Russian novelist, Vladimir Brusiloff, is impressing a literary gathering in suburban England: 'No novelists any good except me. Sovietski—yah! Nastikoff—bah! I spit me of zem all. No novelists anywhere any good except me. P. G. Wodehouse and Tolstoi not bad. Not good, but not bad. No novelists any good except me.'

& hands folded over a pious belly, thinking, 'Well, well, everything is alright now. I've let the cat out, done my day's accounts, and written to that little fellow in Swansea—what's his name, now? Thomas I think. No, no, Williams,' and after the strain of such concentration is over, warming your hooves before the fire, letting a contented mind dwell on the beauties of the world-to-come, where suburban gentlemen, small as agates on an alderman's thumb, hymn the Eternal Bowler.

I am writing you a long letter, and I want to hear regularly from you. Let the mind run. If you haven't any facts I won't mind—I rarely have any of my own. Spin a lot of sentences out of your guts. If nothing else, it's practice for that polished prose of yours which one day, and I don't mean maybe, is going to earn you a respectable living and the plaudits of sound literary people. You have a solidity in your writing—for once I use that word in a complimentary, not derogatory, sense—which is bound to get you somewhere one day. It's that solidity & perception of detail, sense of values, if you like, an at-the-root indestructibility of matter, which I haven't got. All I may, eventually, do is to

> Astound the salons & the cliques
> Of half-wits, publicists & freaks.

I was cut out for little else. The majority of literature is the outcome of ill men, and, though you might not know it, I am always very ill. Logically, that means I am producing, or am going to produce, literature. But I have given up believing in logic long ago. Which is a very logical thing to do. Please believe me when I do throw a little bouquet now & then. You'll have enough buckets thrown in your direction because of your literary sincerity. So treasure, like a squirrel, every complimentary bunch of flowers, for though the scent's bound to wither & the stalks drop, &, of course, he who gave the flowers be utterly forgotten, the memory—bring out your tracts! How everyone nowadays is so terribly frightened of becoming maudlin!—will last for a long time. That kind of memory, & the hope that that kind of memory fosters, are among the few things that keep a man alive. Faith, he said, smoothing his tired brow with buffalo's milk, keeps a man breathing.

> When the moon sinks behind the lawn
> With an old smell of camphor & collected roses,
> Will you & I wait for the certain sign,
> And wait for ever, one supposes,
> Watching, our hands cupped holding matches,
> Sun after moon, & then again
> The same celestial repetition.

What you want to keep out is morbidity, even though everything is despondent. Not a forced cheerfulness, nor a preoccupation with the pleasant instead of the dirty side. But there's a fountain of clearness in everyone. Bach found it, Mozart, D. H. Lawrence, W. B. Yeats & probably

Jesus Christ. Have a shot at finding it. You may succeed. I never will. And for God's sake don't take to writing poetry in my style. Try Longfellow, not me. This sounds awfully conceited. Try your own style. But then, of course, that's what you really are doing.

To answer a question of yours: I have left the Post. They offered me a five years' contract in Swansea. I refused. The sixteen months or less I was on the staff were already showing signs of a reporter's decadence. Another two years I'd have been done for. Not that I was afraid of the Mermaid's grip. I still sedulously pluck the flowers of alcohol, &, occasionally, but not as often as I wish, am pricked by the drunken thorn (an atrocious image!). No, what I feared was the slow but sure stamping out of individuality, the gradual contentment with life as it was, so much per week, so much for this, for that, so much left over for drink & cigarettes. That be no loife for such as Oi! I am attempting to earn a living now—attempting is the correct word—by free-lance journalism, & contribute, fairly regularly, humorous articles to the Post, less regularly literary articles to the *Herald*,[1] now & then funny verses to the B.O.P. (what a come-down was that, O men of Israel!) seasonable & snappy titbits for the Northcliffe Distributive Press. I had a bad poem in the Everyman,[2] & a story is accepted by Squire in the Mercury,[3]—that's where you want to plant your stuff. When the story 'The Diarists' is published, I'll send you a copy. It isn't particularly good.

I still write poems, of course. It's an incurable disease. I write prose, too, & am thinking of tackling a short novel. Thinking, I said.

The purple of your dreams is, I hope, still purple. I am glad to hear official responsibilities are not preventing you from writing fiction as they have, in the past, prevented you from writing letters.

Dylan

Remember me, quite sincerely & not as a matter of form, to your sister & mother, &, don't, on any account save the imperative dictates of the angels, fail to write soon, again, & again soon.

MS: Buffalo

TREVOR HUGHES
[8 February 1933]   5 Cwmdonkin Drive   Uplands   Swansea

Dear Trevor,
Thank you for your letter, & excuse mine, written in pencil on the world's worst paper. The only thing I hope is that it is legible.
You certainly did let the mind run, scorning even the mechanical

1 *Herald of Wales*, weekly sister-paper of the *Post*.
2 In an *Everyman* competition, 1929, two lines of a Thomas poem were commended: 'dim with arrowy air./Asleep and slender with the moon-slow hour.'
3 The poet and journalist Sir John Squire (1884–1958) founded the monthly magazine *London Mercury* and edited it until 1934.

medium of the typewriter, & penning your thoughts—they were, of course, sunk in a deeper melancholy, at least the majority of them, than mine could ever be—in immaculate calligraphy. Your letter was beautifully sincere. In my little ivory temple, immune from the winds and whips of the world, shut, if you like, Proustlike in my conservatory, I find it hard to think, in any but a cynical & theoretical manner, of the blood and withering diseases you have such firsthand knowledge of.[1] Beauty, you say, comes out of suffering. For we are born in others' pain & perish in our own. That, to those who have suffered, & in spite of it are still capable of appreciating and, sometimes, creating beauty, must appear perfectly true. I can't appreciate it, firstly because I have known little physical suffering & no actual hardships or heartbreaks, and secondly because, at the root of it all, I can't reconcile life & art. Obviously one is born before one can be an artist, but after that it doesn't matter what happens. The artistic consciousness is there or it isn't. Suffering is not going to touch it. Consciousness of beauty—& what that elusive thing is I haven't the remotest idea; woman isn't, because she dies. Nothing that dies is truly beautiful—is born with you or not at all. Suffering is not going to create that consciousness, nor happiness, nor anything else you may experience. True beauty, I shall always believe, lies in that which is undestroyable, &, logically, is therefore very little. But it is there. Not that what you have suffered does not influence you deeply & terribly. It is bound to upset & disillusion, carry you, unless you are careful, to the margins of madness. But it is not going to touch in any way at all that which really makes you an artist—knowledge of the actual world's deplorable sordidness, & of the invisible world's splendour (not heaven with God clothed like a deacon, sitting on a golden cloud, but the unseen places clouding above the brain). Suffer as much as you like, that world remains. It is only the complexion of the outer, & absurd, world that changes.

Words are so misleading. I don't urge a monastic seclusion, & preoccupation with the invisible places (you see, even my 'facile' flow of selfconscious images fails, & I am left with the word 'places', which is quite unsatisfactory). That is Roman Catholicism. (One day I may turn Catholic, but not yet.) You must *live* in the outer world, suffer in it & with it, enjoy its changes, despair at them, carry on ordinarily with moneymaking routines, fall in love, mate, & die. You *have* to do that. Where the true artist differs from his fellows is that *that* for him is not the only world. He has the inner splendour (which sounds like a piece of Lawrence or a fribble of Dean Inge).[2] The outer & inner worlds are not, I admit, entirely separate. Suffering colours the inner places, & probably adds beauty to them. So does happiness.

You may think this philosophy—only, in fact, a very slight adaptation of

1 Hughes had an invalid mother, and his brother had died of tuberculosis.
2 William Ralph Inge (1860–1954), Dean of St Paul's, known for his lugubrious writings about contemporary life.

the Roman Catholic religion—strange for me to believe in. I have always believed in it. My poems rarely contain any of it. That is why they are not satisfactory to me. Most of them are the outer poems. Three quarters of the world's literature deals with the outer world. Most modern fiction does. Some of it, of course, is purely reporting of outer incidents. Not that that need condemn it. Perhaps the greatest works of art are those that reconcile, perfectly, inner & outer.

There is nothing new in what I have been saying. But it sprang to my mind when I read your reply to my sincere advice—shun morbidity (as I haven't).

You say, or at least imply, that you couldn't, because of your terrible misfortunes. And I say that you can. Morbidity is sickness, unhealthiness. That need play no *great* part in your stories. They might be very fine stories anyway. But they will be finer without. This is not a stirring plea to be British, only to let the inner consciousness, you've got it because you *are* an artist from the little I have read of yours, develop. 'Raise up thine eyes to the hills.'

And now, when I look back over what I have written, I feel conscious that there is a terrible lot of priggery in it—intellectual & emotional priggery. It reads like a chunk of adulterated Chesterton, revised by Sir Edward Elgar. Looking over it again, I doubt its sincerity, such is the horribly argumentative, contradictory nature of my mind. Give me a sheet of paper & I can't help filling it in. The result—more often than not—is good & bad, serious & comic, sincere & insincere, lucid or nonsensical by the turns of my whirligig mentality, started from the wrong end, a mentality that ran before it walked, & perhaps will never walk, that wanted to fly before it had the right even to think of wings.

Tomorrow, the next moment, I may believe in my beastly inner & outer. I may be believing it now. It may be facile, immature humbug. Again, it may be the expression of a real belief. The prince of darkness is a gentleman.[1] But his satanic convolutions & contradictions abide by no gentlemanly conditions.

As I am writing, a telegram arrives. Mother's sister, who is in the Carmarthen Infirmary suffering from cancer of the womb, is dying. There is much lamentation in the family & Mother leaves. The old aunt will be dead by the time she arrives. This is a well-worn incident in fiction, & one that has happened time after time in real life. The odour of death stinks through a thousand books & in a thousand homes. I have rarely encountered it (apart from journalistic enquiries), & find it rather pleasant. It lends a little welcome melodrama to the drawing-room tragicomedy of my most uneventful life. After Mother's departure I am left alone in the house, feeling slightly theatrical. Telegrams, dying aunts, cancer, especially of such a private part as the womb, distraught mothers & unpremeditated train-journeys, come rarely. They must be savoured

1 Spoken by Edgar in Shakespeare's *King Lear*, Act 3, Sc. 4.

properly & relished in the right spirit. Many summer weeks I spent happily with the cancered aunt on her insanitary farm.[1] She loved me quite inordinately, gave me sweets & money, though she could little afford it, petted, patted, & spoiled me. She writes—is it, I wonder, a past tense yet— regularly. Her postscripts are endearing. She still loves—or loved—me, though I don't know why. And now she is dying, or dead, & you will pardon the theatrical writing. Allow me my moments of drama.[2]

But the foul thing is I feel utterly unmoved, apart, as I said, from the pleasant death-reek at my negroid nostrils. I haven't, really, the faintest interest in her or her womb. She is dying. She is dead. She is alive. It is all the same thing. I shall miss her bi-annual postal orders. That's all. And yet I like—liked—her. She loves—loved—me. Am I, he said, with the diarist's unctuous, egotistic preoccupation with his own blasted psychological reactions to his own trivial affairs, callous & nasty? Should I weep? Should I pity the old thing? For a moment, I feel I should. There must be something lacking in me. I don't feel worried, or hardly ever, about other people. It's self, self, all the time. I'm rarely interested in other people's emotions, except those of my pasteboard characters. I prefer (this is one of the thousand contradictory devils speaking) style to life, my own reactions to emotions rather than the emotions themselves. Is this, he pondered, a lack of soul?

There was a certain theatrical quality about your letter, too, a little of the purple dreams of the yellow nineties,[3] the red roses, the wine, & the final falling of the final curtain. And now I wish I hadn't said that. The histrionic quality was sincere. Your answer to my DO NOT BE MORBID statement was enough to shove me under the table. Go on writing future letters just as theatrically. Tons of good stuff comes out of the theatre. This again may sound facetious. I am not deriding what you spoke of. That goes too deep for the playhouse. The selfconscious can escape, momentarily, by dressing their soul-cries in ermine & astrakhan, & letting them stand before the footlights before the footlights fade out.

I am interested in what you say about your story writing—the quick, quiet, dream-come idea, the lifting of the pen, & then the faces of past miseries & horrors obliterating everything. I can realise why your output is

---

1 The farm is the Fern Hill of Thomas's poem. It is also the 'Gorsehill' of his story 'The Peaches'.
2 The aunt, Ann Jones, died late on Tuesday 7 February. Her death was the occasion of Thomas's poem 'After the funeral (In memory of Ann Jones)', the earliest draft of which is dated 'Feb 10 '33'. He began the poem the day *before* she was buried, which was on 11 February. Nor is it likely that he went to the funeral. The local newspaper (which called her 'Annie' Jones) listed Thomas's parents among the mourners, but not Dylan. By 1933, Annie and her husband Jim had given up farming and no longer lived at Fernhill.
3 *The Yellow Book* was an influential magazine of art and literature in the 1890s, a period that Thomas liked to despise.

so small. In your letter you say it will be something if we can help each other towards, I forget your exact image, the planting of seeds in the forests of literature or something like that. From my seat among the ancients may I, for one moment, shake a few stalactites off my frosty beard, & give you a little advice? I asked you, in a letter, to write from your guts. You did. And, of course, you do in your short stories. But why not, just for a few times, put a sheet of paper in front of you, & without thinking twice, write half or a quarter or all of a short story. Don't begin with a polished idea in which every incident is fixed in your mind. Just shove a girl on the seashore on a summer day & let her make her own story. Write, write, regardless of everything. Your present method of story writing—the draft after draft, the interminable going-over-again, can be compared to the method of the marksman who spends weeks & weeks polishing his rifle, weeks & [weeks] cleaning it, weeks & weeks getting the exact ammunition for it, weeks & weeks deciding on a target, weeks & weeks weighing his rifle in his hand, weeks & weeks weighing it in a different way, &, at the end of the year, having a pop at the bull's eye. Why not, for a change, fire off round after round of ammunition from any old gun you can get hold of. You'll miss hundreds of times, but you're bound to get the bull's eye a lot of times, too. You'll find the hit-or-miss, the writing with no plot, technique will help you considerably in loosening your mind & in getting rid of those old stifling memories which may, unless you are careful, get in the way of your literary progress.

I now rest my beard upon my knees again, & the crows return to their nests.

Swansea still stands where it did. No one has blown up the churches. The Watch Committee[1] still stands on its one leg & hands its glass eye round from member to member. There are the taverns & cafés. There is the hospital & the mortuary. Job—I have seen him several times since I left him—still drones around the edges of the local news like a Cornish bee. My friend Dan[2] still tears his fearsome chords from the entrails of a much-abused piano. I continue writing in the most futile manner, looking at the gas-oven, at periodic intervals, with a wistful glimmer in my eye. My sister is soon to be married.[3] She will live in London. I shall stay

---

1 The watch committee of a borough council had a minor role as a guardian of public morals, often derided. Officially it dealt with local policing and street lighting; also with films, which it could ban from cinemas.
2 Daniel Jones.
3 Nancy Thomas became engaged to Haydn Taylor, an Englishman, at Christmas 1932. He was then a commercial traveller, and was based in Swansea until September that year. Her letters to him from 5 Cwmdonkin Drive describe an unhappy family ('very quarrelsome') where there were frequent rows about drink and money. According to Nancy, her brother stole from handbags ('a £1 note was missing'), her mother used to steam open Haydn Taylor's letters, and her father frequently raged against life in general.

occasionally with her. The London Mercury has not yet printed my story. Neither have I received a cheque for it. I have just evaded a libel action through some pot-boiling article of mine for the Northcliffe Press.[1] A lone tea beckons on the table.

I have been a long time in replying to your last long letter. Please forgive me & let your next be longer.

Dylan

MS: Buffalo

GEOFFREY GRIGSON

Geoffrey Grigson (1905–85), poet, author and critic, was literary editor of the *Morning Post*. In 1933 he found time to start the influential magazine *New Verse*, which appeared every two months, and edited it until it ceased publication in 1939.

[Spring 1933]   5 Cwmdonkin Drive   Uplands   Swansea

Dear Sir,

I am sending you some poems to be considered for publication in 'New Verse', about which I read in 'John O'London's Weekly', a month or two ago. Out of a large number of poems I found it extremely difficult to choose 6 to send you. As a matter of fact, the enclosed poems were picked almost entirely at random.

If you think the poems unsuitable for publication, and if, of course, you are sufficiently interested, I could let you see some more. I probably have far better ones in some of my innumerable exercise books.[2]

A considerable period lies between the writing of some of the enclosed poems, as perhaps you will be able to see. Whether time has shown any improvement I find it hard to say, as I have developed, intellectually at least, in the smug darkness of a provincial town, and have only on rare occasions shown any of my work to any critics, generally uninterested or incompetent.

If you could see your way clear to publish any of these poems, or find in them sufficient merit to warrant the reading of some more, you would be doing me a very great favour. Grinding out poetry, whether good or bad, in such an atmosphere as surrounds me, is depressing and disheartening.

Yours sincerely,
Dylan Thomas

MS: Buffalo

---

1 The Nina Hamnett affair. See page 24, n.2.
2 Grigson returned the poems.

TREVOR HUGHES
[May 1933][1]   5 Cwmdonkin Drive   Uplands   Swansea

Dear Trevor,

Many months passed between the posting of my letter, which, as you say, you found provocative of thought, and the written result. I have a very good mind indeed to send you a shallow letter. You would probably send an answer to it by return post, for the more lengthy and profound (?) my letter, the longer do you seem to take in replying. This little reprimand over, and never, I hope, to be repeated, I can now tackle your correspondence in as serious a manner as I am able.

You ask me for criticism of your story, but I would rather, if it is the same to you, and even if it isn't, criticise the attitude of mind behind its writing & not so much the result of such an attitude.

Again I was struck by the brilliance of your letter, a subterranean brilliance, if you will, and too near the rim to be pleasant. But brilliance, nevertheless, of a high imaginative order as they say in textbooks. But how much do I prefer the passionate wordiness of your letter to the unnecessary wordiness of your story! I am not going to, even if I could, destroy your story in a couple of cheap sentences. It is a bad story, but that doesn't matter. You are, and you know it despite your self-termed apologia, capable of a much better [story] than that. It must be as unsatisfactory to you as it is to me.

This is my main contention: Why, when you can, as you show in your letter, struggle with the fundamentals of belief, & the rock-bottom ideas of artistic bewilderment, morbidity, and disillusionment, when you can write with a pen dipped in fire and vinegar, when you have something to say, however terrible it may be, and the vocabulary to say it with, do you waste time on the machinations of a Stacy Aumonier plot and on the unreal emotions of a pasteboard character whose replica one could find in a hundred novelettes of the nineties? Why go to the cafés, and French cafés at that, for your plots? You are not really interested in people. I doubt whether you are a fiction writer at all. Why go to the cafés for worn plots when the only things you are interested in are the antagonistic interplays of emotions and ideas, the rubbing together of sensibilities, brain chords and nerve chords, convolutions of style, tortuities of new expressions?

My contention boils down to the fact that the short story is not your medium. What your medium is I can do nothing but suggest. It is prose, undoubtedly, but an utterly non-commercial prose, a prose of passionate ideas, a metaphysical prose. I repeat my last letter's advice to you: Write, write, write, out of your guts, out of the sweat on your forehead and the blood in your veins.[2] Do not think about Mr Potter's guide to the salesmanship of short stories produced, apparently, on the lines of the Ford works. Do not bother your head about the length of the stuff you are

1 Probably in reply to a letter from Hughes dated 7 May (at Buffalo).
2 The advice came in the last letter but one, according to the order suggested here, which fits the best conjecture.

writing. Don't descend, that is the main point. You descended badly in the story I have at my elbow as I write. You tagged on, under some misapprehension as to the quality of the intellect of your audience, that magazine little bit about the inquest. You see that sort of ending in the Windsor and the Pall Mall periodicals, and even in the London Mercury on an off month. (Please don't think that anything I say in this letter resembles a sneer at your work. I am honestly doing my best to help you.)

You descended from the Stygian heights—a very true paradox—of your real style, which I have only seen in your letters, when you make your pseudo-French characters say, 'It is very difficult—difficile', or words to that effect. Whether the addition of the foreign word is to add atmosphere, or merely to instruct junior readers, I don't know. In either case, it's a ghastly thing to do. What you want to do is to sit down & write, regardless of plot or characters, just as you write a letter to *me*. You know Middleton Murry's[1] prose and Lawrence's non-fiction prose. Murry is not interested in plots or characters. He is interested in the symbols of the world, in the mystery and meaning of the world, in the fundamentals of the soul. And these things he writes about. These things *you* are interested in. Write about them. You have a style as individual as Murry's. Murry writes with a sober, contemplative pen, and you with an inebriate pen. But it doesn't matter a bit. Write a story (if you must write stories) about yourself searching for your soul amid the horrors of corruption and disease, about your passionate strivings after something you don't know and can't express. (This is one of the few ways [of] knowing it and expressing it.)

In one letter I remember telling you to steer clear as quickly as you could from morbidity and morbid introspection. Now I am telling you to delve deep, deep into yourself until you find your soul, and until you know yourself. These two bits of advice aren't contradictory. The true search for the soul lies so far within the last circle of introspection that it is out of it. You will, of course, have to revolve on every circle first. But until you reach that little red hot core, you are not alive. The number of dead men who walk, breathe, and talk is amazing.

(I am not taking any trouble over the phrasing of this letter. You, from your peak of sultry glory where the gods of clauses and of commas walk under the exclamatory moon, might be annoyed at my rough way with words and grammar. But the faster I write the more sincere I am in what I write.)

It is not Utopian advice that I am attempting to ladle out to you. It is terribly practical. Forget the 'annihilative reverse' of the rejection slip, and the 'intellectual catarrh'. Plunge, rather, headfirst & boldly into Charon's ferry. And who knows? Charon's ferry may turn at last into the river Jordan & purge you of ills.

You speak of a world in which the effort of thought will be unnecessary. Write of it. You speak of your 'curious surprising of beauty', and its

1 John Middleton Murry (1889–1957), writer and editor, friend of D. H. Lawrence. In 1923 he founded the monthly *Adelphi* magazine, which published work by Thomas from 1933.

metamorphosis into ugliness, your 'charred crucifix'. Write, write, write.

You are one [of] the dark-eyed company of Poe & Thompson,[1] Nerval[2] & Baudelaire, Rilke and Verlaine. Be a Thompson in prose. You complain that you haven't his genius. Of course you haven't, but you have your own red sparks of genius. And you *must* not allow the old stagnant waters to put them out. You say you have the honey. You say you have nothing but honey and greyness. You have honey and senna. Mix them together, dip your pen into them, and write.

Don't forget: To hell with all the preconceived notions of short story writing, to the world of dyspeptic editors and rejection slips, to the cardboard men & women. Into the sea of yourself like a young dog, and bring out a pearl.

Remember: you are not another Aumonier, another Manhood, another Bullett.[3] You are one of the white-faced company whose tears wash the world.

To hell with everything except the inner necessity for expression, & the medium of expression, [with] everything except the great need of forever striving after this mystery and meaning I moan about.

There is only one object: the removing of veils from your soul & scabs from your body. Reaching a self freedom is the only object. You will get nearer to it by writing as I have suggested—make your own variations— than by all the writing of clever and eminently saleable short stories. And, lastly, it doesn't matter a damn whether your stuff is printed or not. Better a bundle of pages on which you have honestly strived after something worth striving after, than a story in every magazine & an international reputation.

Come back to Wales in the Neath[4] of adversity. Leave London & come to Neath. That is particularly bad advice, I'm sure, but it is written from purely selfish motives—from a desire to see you and talk to you again, to hear you speak, to read your mad prose, & to read you my mad pomes. 3 months are all too long.

Dylan

MS: Buffalo

TREVOR HUGHES
[late July 1933]   5 Cwmdonkin Drive   Uplands   Swansea

I looked through a pile of old papers the other day, and found your last letter to me. Reading it again, I realised how very good indeed it was. I know of nothing, in any literature I have read, to compare with it. Among

1 The poet Francis Thompson (1859–1907).
2 Gérard de Nerval (1808–55), French poet; he was mentally disturbed.
3 Stacy Aumonier (1887–1928) wrote short stories, as did H. A. Manhood. Gerald Bullett (1893–1958) was a poet and novelist.
4 A small and unprepossessing town near Swansea.

the cribbed and cabinned, the bored and strangled destructivism of so much modern writing, it stands out supremely—a vast wind of pessimism (though that is not the right word) among the despondent farts of the little men. Poe has nothing on you. He had his Ravens,[1] you have a flock of monstrous carrion-pickers. Forget the Hound of Heaven[2] and bay down your own hellhounds. I am looking forward to your sequel to Burton-Hughes's Guts of Melancholia.[3] If I can but make you write always as well as you can write in the letter by my side, then I shall be doing, for once in my life, something worthwhile.

I am writing this near a two-foot statue of Echo, who cocks her marble ear at me, listening to me mouth these words aloud.

Do you want your story back? I have lost it, and one of my own in which there were four characters—a dead man and three hawks. It was very pretty.

I am writing this in an odd mood, smoking, toasting my toes. I have such a bad headache that it is hard to write connected sentences. When a new thought comes I want to put it down, slipshod, in probably a most inapt place. My pen started to write ebony.

Oh, to be a critic! 'Mr X shows promise. This week's masterpiece. Mr Y is bad.' So simple, no bother, no bleeding of writing. I think you bleed more than I do, God help you. Remember the Worm,[4] read a meaning into its symbol—a serpent's head rising out of the clean sea.

Think this selfconscious. A pal o' mine's mad, in Coney Hill, saying all the time, so his aunt says, 'Keep a straight bat, sir'. We have a new asylum.[5] It leers down the valley like a fool, or like a snail with the two turrets of its water towers two snails' horns.

How good it is to feel that I can write anything to you. Your last letter shows me that you understand, though understand what I shall never know more than I shall know the answer to the looking glass question—'Why is this me?' Remember—'Don't be morbid'. Sometimes I want to go down to the cellar to be nearer the worms. Sometimes only a worm is companion, its grey voice at your ear the only voice.

(This, too, you might laugh off. 'Juvenilia.' A shrug, a slight condescension. Boys will be old men.)

I will be in London for a fortnight, from Bank Holiday on, staying on the Thames with Nancy,[6] my sister, who married some months ago.

Write and tell me when I can come to see you, or where I can meet you

1 Edgar Allan Poe's poem 'The Raven' was first published in 1845. 'Take thy beak from out my heart, and take thy form from off my door! / Quoth the Raven, "Nevermore"'.

2 'The Hound of Heaven' is Francis Thompson's best-known poem.

3 Robert Burton wrote The Anatomy of Melancholy, first published in 1621.

4 The Worm's Head, a half-tide island off the Gower Peninsula, beyond Swansea.

5 Cefn Coed (psychiatric) hospital, on a hill a mile from Thomas's home, was opened in December 1932. 'Coney Hill' must be Colney Hatch, once a notorious lunatic asylum outside London.

6 Nancy Thomas married Haydn Taylor in May 1933. Their first home was a houseboat on the Thames at Chertsey. Thomas's visit, which took place, was almost certainly his first to London.

sometime. We might go to the ballet together.
Or we might sit and talk. Or sit.
Beachcomber would love this.[1]

Dylan

MS: Buffalo

PAMELA HANSFORD JOHNSON

Soon to find her own feet as a novelist, Pamela Hansford Johnson (1912–81) was two years older than Dylan Thomas. Their literary friendship, which became a love affair after they met in February 1934, began with a poem by Thomas, 'That sanity be kept', published in a newspaper, the *Sunday Referee*, 3 September 1933. Earlier in the year the newspaper had begun a feature, the 'Poet's Corner', edited by the eccentric Victor Neuburg (almost invariably spelt 'Neuberg' by Thomas). Johnson, who worked in a bank and lived with her mother in Clapham, submitted a poem, which appeared on 9 April, and she was drawn into Neuburg's coterie of young writers. When the *Referee* published Thomas's poem, she wrote to him.

[about 17 September 1933][2]   Blaen-Cwm[3]   Llangain nr Carmarthen

Beginning this letter in the way I do, removes the necessity of using the formal, 'madam', the stiff, 'Miss Johnson', (rather ambiguous but entirely unmeant), and the impudent, 'Pamela', (also ambiguous, also unmeant). It removes a similar obstacle in your case.

If it is 'gruesome' to reply to letters, then I am as much of a ghoul as you are. I return frequently, in the characterless scrawl God and a demure education gave me.

Incidentally, when you reply to this—and let it be long and soon—don't write to the above address. It is merely a highly poetical cottage where I sometimes spend week-ends. Reply to my nasty, provincial address.

Thank you for the poems. Mr. Neuburg has paid you a large and almost merited compliment. 'One of the few exquisite word-artists of our day', needs little praise or abuse from me. But, still, I must compliment you upon 'The Nightingale', by far the best of the three poems. Comparing that with the 'Sea Poem for G', one of the most perfect examples of bloody verse I have ever seen, and with other Referee poems, is like comparing Milton

---

1 Pseudonym of J. B. Morton, humorous columnist in the *Daily Express*.
2 Johnson's diary, 9 September: 'Had nice letter from Referee poet to whom I wrote.' 18 September: 'Charming & very, very modern, not to say rude letter from Dylan Thomas.' The present letter, the earliest that survives, is the second of these. Many presumed letters from Thomas to Johnson have disappeared. Buffalo has barely thirty, counting all the fragments, although the recipient said in her lifetime that she owned 'a hundred' of them. Her estate has no information.
3 A pair of stone cottages, near the Carmarthen-Llanstephan road, occupied by members of his mother's family. Fernhill (the farm is one word, the poem two) is a mile away.

with Stilton. I like the other two poems you sent me, but not as much, and the first stanza of 'Prothalamium', I don't like at all. Too many adjectives, too much sugar. And the fifth and sixth lines are pure cliché. 'I write from the heart', said a character in some novel I've forgotten. 'You write', was the reply, 'from the bowels as after a strong emetic.' Not that I apply that rude remark to 'Prothalamium'; I'm quoting not because of it but for the sake of it.

Of course you are not an agèd virgin. But many of the contributors to the Poet's Corner are, and woo the moon for want of a better bedfellow. I can't agree with you that the majority of the Referee poems are good. With a few exceptions they are nauseatingly bad. Yours are among the exceptions, of course. Do you remember a poem called '1914' printed a couple of weeks ago? Do you remember the 'Sea Poem'? Do you remember those few diabetic lines about an Abyssinian cat? What did you think of last week's 'Blue Gum Tree'? That is a real test of taste. Like that, you like anything. It would be hard to realise the number of people bluffed into believing 'Blue Gum Tree' to be a good poem. Its sprawling formlessness they would call, 'modern', its diction, 'harsh but effective', and some of its single lines, such as, 'The cloth of silver over a white balustrade', would send them into some sort of colourful rapture. In reality, the formlessness is the outcome of entire prosodical incompetence, the diction is not even tailor-made but ready-to-wear, and the 'colourful' lines are like cheap, vermilion splotches on a tenthrate music-hall backcloth.

In the very interesting copy you sent me of the first Poet's Corner, it is explained that when, during any week, no poetry is received, the best *verse* would be printed. That would be perfectly all right if it did happen. But the pretentious palming off of *doggerel* (not even verse) as 'arty' poetry is too much.

It was on the same grounds that I objected to 'Poet's Corner' as a title. There was a time when only poets were called poets. Now anyone with an insufficient knowledge of the English language, a Marie Corelli senti- ment,[1] and a couple of 'bright' images to sprinkle over the lines, is called a poet. He can't even leave his excretion in a private spot. They give him a public 'Corner' to leave it in. (A vulgar metaphor! I hope you don't object.)

This is in no way a biased or personal attack. It's the general principles of the thing I like to use as Aunt Sallies. Pray God I, too, am not 'arty'. A physical pacifist and a mental militarist, I can't resist having a knock—or even a blow at a dead horse—when all I put my faith in is utterly contradicted. I put my faith in poetry, and too many poets deny it.

To return to *your* poetry, (you must excuse my slight soap-box attitude): It shows a tremendous passion for words, and a real knowledge of them. Your grasp of form and your handling of metre is among the best I know to- day. And—the main thing—your thoughts are worth expressing. Have you written a great deal? When do you write? I'm interested to know all sorts of things like that, and to see some more.

1 Marie Corelli (Mary Mackay) (1855–1924), an extravagantly romantic novelist.

What I like about your poems is that they *state*, not contradict, that *they create* not destroy. Poem after poem, recording, in sickening detail, the wrinkles on the author's navel, fill the contemporary journals, poem after poem recording, none too clearly, the chaos of to-day. Out of chaos they make nothing, but, themselves part of the post-war carnage, fade away like dead soldiers. So much new verse (do you know 'New Verse'?) can be summarised into, 'Well, there's been a hell of a war; it's left us in a mess; what the hell are we going to do about it?' The answer is fairly obvious. But is it worth writing about? No, you answer in a loud voice, or at least I hope you do. You are not like that, and your 'not-ness' alone is worth all the superlatives at my command.

So you are the same age as myself.[1] You say one has enough time, when one is 21, to be modest. One has enough time ahead, too, to regret one's immodesty. The more I think of my Referee poem the less I like it. The idea of myself, sitting in the open window, in my shìrt, and imagining myself as some Jehovah of the West, is really odd. If I were some Apollo, it would be different. As a matter of fact, I am a little person with much untidy hair.

With this letter you will find two poems of mine. I am sending them to show you, or to hope to show you, that I can do much better than you think from what you have seen of mine. Incidentally, I'd better mention that the poem starting, 'No food suffices', is, though complete in itself, the woman's lament from an unfortunately unfinished play. I think this needs mention; references in the poem would otherwise cast aspersions on the nature of my sex.[2] The second poem you may not like at all; it is distinctly unfashionable.

After my violent outburst against the Referee poets, you'll probably read *my* two poems with a stern & prejudiced eye. I hope you don't, and I hope you like them. Whether you do or not, tell me.

Can I keep your poems for a little longer?

Dylan Thomas

P.S. The Woman poem is to be printed in the Adelphi. I can't resist adding that, because I like the magazine so much. The Jesus poem is probably to be printed in T. S. Eliot's Criterion, though, as a rule, the Criterion doesn't print any metaphysic verse at all. I mention the 'C' for the same reason that I mention the 'A'.[3]

P.P.S. I am staying, as you see, in Carmarthenshire & have forgotten to bring your address with me. I am trusting to luck that 13 is the right number. If it is, you will read this explanation. If it isn't, you won't. So there was no point at all in writing it. *D.T.*

MS: Buffalo

1 She was twenty-one. He was still six weeks short of his nineteenth birthday.
2 'The Woman Speaks' was the title of the poem (its first line was 'No food suffices') when it was published the following year.
3 The 'Jesus poem' was probably 'Before I knocked and flesh let enter', dated 6 September in a Notebook. It didn't appear in the *Criterion* magazine.

PAMELA HANSFORD JOHNSON
[September 1933] [two fragments]

Words! Words! I never seem to stop writing. Here is another sentence to add to the already growing confusion.

The two other poems I have included are very recent. For some reason I don't think you will like the needles & the knives.[1] I don't think I do, either, but there we are!

In time you'll have all I've ever written, if I send you such vast quantities at a time.

On reverse of same sheet
I have typed & bound on somebody else's official paper sixteen short poems for you. In the past I believe I've only sent you the longer poems. These, as all the others, are chosen haphazardly. Two, to my dim sense of criticism in regard to my own writing, are very bad. Give me a critical study, however short, upon them. And please remember that Quotation No. is not a part of the poem it faces.

MS: Buffalo

TREVOR HUGHES
[card, postmarked 11 Oct 1933]   5 Cwmdonkin Drive

Dear Trevor,

First let me apologise for not having written before this, and secondly for writing such a little note now. I have, really, the most concrete excuses, too complicated to put on a post-card. The only thing of importance is this: 'Prose and Verse', that stillborn child, is to be resurrected. Grocer Trick[2] is to do the financial and business part of it, and I, as it was arranged before, am to edit it. The high standards, formerly set, will be strictly adhered to; but there is one important, new condition: 'P & V' will print only the work of Welshmen and women—this includes those of dim Welsh ancestry and those born in Wales—who *write* in English. This condition necessarily restricts, but it is that which will make, I hope and trust, the journal an unique affair. Another highbrow periodical, especially produced from a

---

1 A Notebook poem, 'Take the needles and the knives', is dated 12 September. On 10 September, Dylan's father, D. J. Thomas, had been admitted to hospital in London, to begin treatment with radium needles for cancer of the mouth, diagnosed two weeks earlier. Dylan told people it was cancer of the throat, presumably because that sounded worse.

2 Albert Edward ('Bert') Trick (1889–1973), ran his mother's small grocery shop not far from Cwmdonkin Drive. Formerly an income-tax clerk, he was passionately concerned with both literature and left-wing politics. He was married with a small daughter. For a year or so, Thomas's intellectual life revolved around Bert Trick's parlour.

blowsy town such as this—on the furthest peaks of the literary world—is doomed to hell from the beginning. But a new highclass periodical for Welshmen? Up Cymru! I don't see why it shouldn't be a great success. Already Trick is corresponding with universities, libraries, museums, and other intellectual morgues, with spinsters, knights, and philanthropists. Do you know any Welshmen who might be interested in the project? If so, tell me when you write. And when you can, send me along all your original prose still existing. I'd like to go through it carefully and critically, picking out what is suitable for publication. You've got four or five printed pages at your disposal. I'm not going to write any more now. *Write* and tell me your views.

Dylan

MS: Buffalo

PAMELA HANSFORD JOHNSON
[15 October 1933][1]   5 Cwmdonkin Drive Uplands Swansea

Thank you. I should have been very sorry hadn't I posted the card. The mutual outpourings of a crank and a romantic (there is little doubt as to which is which) would have been lost to posterity; creeds and beliefs, that will change as the years change us, but are nevertheless sincere, would have remained unexpressed; insults and compliments, hasty judgments, wisdoms and nonsenses, would have been unsaid; and a considerably nice friendship would have been broken up almost before it began. Even now twelve heartfelt pages are titivating the senses of a Dead Letter superintendent, and three heartfelt poems are lying beneath the pillow of some postmaster's boy in the depths of Llangyfellach or Pwllddu. (I, too, know not a word of Welsh and these names are as fearsome to me as they are to you.)[2]

What have I missed in your letter? Three poems, twelve passionate pages of affirmation and denial, a thought on Shakespeare and a sob for Siegfried! Dear God, and all for three-halfpence.

There is so much to talk about in your last letter, to agree with and to argue with most violently, that I must light my cigarette, and then, with a steady hand and a more-or-less contented mind, tackle the points in order from the very beginning to the last curve on the last letter of the totally unnecessary 'Johnson'.

1 The poems by Pitt and Martineau that Thomas mentions appeared in the *Sunday Referee* on 8 October, apparently a week earlier. Johnson's diary, Monday 16 October: 'Lovely long & delightful letter from Dylan Thomas.' In those days there was a Sunday post collection, so '15 October' is a reasonable conjecture.
2 Llangyfelach (an industrial suburb of Swansea) and Pwlldu (a bay near the town) are both misspelt. Thomas was brought up in an anglicised home. Like most of his friends, he would have been able to pronounce Welsh names, but not necessarily to spell them.

1) I'm glad you're not as riddled with silliness as I am. I should have carried on for months, never writing your name, consciously avoiding such an ordinary gesture of friendliness as calling you Pamela, or Pam, or whatever I am to call you. My unusual name—for some mad reason it comes from the Mabinogion and means the 'prince of darkness'[1]—rhymes with 'Chillun', as you suggest. I don't know what Pamela rhymes with, unless the *very* cultured way of saying 'family', and therefore cannot reply with a little couplet.

2) The Vicky-Bird,[2] undoubtedly of the parrot variety, doesn't appear to like what we sent him last week. But then I always said his taste was abysmal. I sent him a very short and obscure poem with one indecent line. What did you send him to be so ignominiously placed among the spavined horses? A very short and obscure poem with *two* indecent lines? No, I hardly think so. He doesn't want to give too many prizes to the same people, on principle. He must print the work of others sometimes, and spread the vomit evenly and impartially over his pages. Miss Gertrude Pitt must show her mettle, rusty tin to me; and Mr. Martineau must patch his broken heart with a sentimental song.

3) I am in the path of Blake, but so far behind him that only the wings on his heels are in sight. I have been writing since I was a very little boy, and have always been struggling with the same things, with the idea of poetry as a thing entirely removed from such accomplishments as 'word-painting', and the setting down of delicate but usual emotions in a few, wellchosen words. There must be no compromise; there is always only the one right word: use it, despite its foul or merely ludicrous associations; I used 'double-crossed' because it was what I meant. It is part of a poet's job to take a debauched and prostituted word, like the beautiful word, 'blond', and to smooth away the lines of its dissipation, and to put it on the market again, fresh and virgin. Neuburg blabs of some unsectarian region in the clouds where poetry reaches its highest level. He ruins the truth of that by saying that the artist must, of necessity, preach socialism. There is no necessity for the artist to do anything. There is no necessity. He is a law unto himself, and his greatness or smallness rises or falls by that. He has only one limitation, and that is the widest of all: the limitation of form. Poetry finds its own form; form should never be superimposed; the structure should rise out of the words and the expression of them. I do not want to express only what other people have felt; I want to rip something away and show what they have never seen. Because of the twist in myself I

---

1 The word 'Dylan' means nothing more than 'sea', or possibly a sea-god. As a proper name it occurs briefly in the *Mabinogion*—the Welsh medieval prose romances which have echoes of older narratives—where it is bestowed on a child born to Arianrhod: 'a fine boy-child with rich yellow hair'. It was virtually unknown as a name before D. J. Thomas disinterred it for his son.

2 Victor Neuburg (1883-1940) was not entirely the figure of fun that Thomas portrayed. A bisexual who wrote poetry, he had formerly dabbled in homosexual magic with the necromancer Aleister Crowley.

will never be a very good poet: only treading the first waves, putting my hands in deeper and then taking them out again.

But even that, to me, is better than the building of perfectly ornate structures in the sand. To change the image, one is a brief adventure in the wilderness, and the other a little gallop on an ordered plot of land.

4) I apologise for No Man Believes, but I really didn't think it was obscure. I understood it so perfectly myself, but I was probably the only one who did. And even that's ungrammatical.

5) But why Wordsworth? Why quote that decay? Shelley I can stand, but old Father William was a human nannygoat with a pantheistic obsession. He hadn't a spark of mysticism in him. How could he be a metaphysicist? Metaphysics is merely the structure of logic, intellect, and supposition on a mystical basis. And mysticism is illogical, unintellectual, and dogmatic. Quote Shelley, yes. But Wordsworth was a tea-time bore, the great Frost of literature, the verbose, the humourless, the platitudinary reporter of Nature in her dullest moods. Open him at any page: and there lies the English language not, as George Moore said of Pater,[1] in a glass coffin, but in a large, sultry, and unhygienic box. Degutted and desouled. Catch him in his coy moods, walking the hills with a daffodil pressed to his lips, and his winter woollies tickling his chest. Catch him in his pompous mood, his Virginity and Victoria mood, his heavy-footed humourlessness pursuing a wanton dogma down a blind alley full of the broken bones of words. I admit the Immortality Ode is better than anything he ever did (with the exception of the pantheistic creed expressed in Tintern Abbey); among the mediocrity and rank badness it stands out like a masterpiece; but judged from a proper perspective, along the lines of Shakespeare, Dante, Goethe, Blake, John Donne, Verlaine & Yeats, it is no more than moderately good. All it says has been said before and better, and all it was incapable of saying. Try to rub away its halo of fame and the mist of veneration that has grown up around it; try to forget the drummed-in fact that he is an English mystic—: and you will see it chockful of clichés, ridiculous inversions of speech and thought, all the tricks-of-trade of the unoriginal verse-writer whose bluff has not yet been called. I put by its side the poems of Matthew Arnold, and think what a delightfully loud splash the two would make if I dropped them into the river.

Perhaps you gather that I don't like Wordsworth. I'm sorry, but he's one of the few 'accepted' whom I refuse in any way to accept at all. *This is my important point about him in summary*: He writes about mysticism but he is not a mystic; he describes what mystics have been known to feel, but he himself doesn't feel anything, not even a pain in the neck. He could well have written his Ode in the form of a treatise: 'Mysticism and its Relations to the Juvenile Mind.' Just as an experiment, read him again with my adverse opinions at the back of your mind. I changed from loving to loathing Swinburne in a day. Enough. You shall have your own back.

1 George Moore (1852–1933), Anglo-Irish novelist. Walter Pater (1839–94), philosopher and writer, known for an elegant literary style.

6) I, too, should like to meet you. This possibly can be arranged, but not before the beginning of September when I am going to see my sister near Chertsey.[1]

Don't expect too much of me (It's conceit to suppose that you would); I'm an odd little person. Don't imagine the great jawed writer brooding over his latest masterpiece in the oak study, but a thin, curly little person, smoking too [many] cigarettes, with a crocked lung, and writing his vague verses in the back room of a provincial villa.

7) David Gascoyne[2] and Reuben Mednikoff! You move in exalted company. I read the Russian Jew's (is he?) effort in the Referee, & thoroughly agree with you —as a poet he's a bloody good painter. But Gascoyne? And seventeen, too? Tut, tut, what are the boys coming to? I read a thing of his—before your letter came—in the new, New Verse,[3] and thought he was raving mad. There are more maggots in his brain than there are in mine. But if he is so young there *is* a hope that the poetry will drop away from him and that the sore it leaves will soon heal. His New Verse poem is called 'And the 7th Dream Is The Dream of Isis'. Without wishing to provide a pornographic interlude over the tea-table, I'll quote some of the actual lines:[4] This is the opening:

> 'White curtains of tortured destinies
> Encourage the waistlines of women to expand
> And the eyes of men to enlarge like pocket cameras
> Teach children to sin at the age of five
> To cut out the eyes of their sisters with nail-scissors.'

And later:

> 'The pavements of cities are covered with needles
> The reservoirs are full of human hair
> Fumes of sulphur envelop the house of ill-fame
> Out of which bloodred lilies appear
> Across the square where crowds are dying in thousands
> A man is walking a tightrope covered with moths.'

And later:

> 'She was standing at the window clothed only in a ribbon
> She was burning the eyes of snails in a candle
> She was eating the excrement of dogs and horses
> She was writing a letter to the president of france.'

---

1 A slip for 'December'. Near the end of the next letter Thomas wrote, 'You are right, of course. December it is.'

2 The poet David Gascoyne (b. 1916) published his first book of verse in 1932. During the 1930s he was close to French surrealists, and strongly influenced by them.

3 The October issue.

4 There are a number of copying errors, eg 'stairs' for 'stains' six lines from the end, and four lines are omitted.

And later still:
'The edges of leaves must be examined through microscopes
In order to see the stains made by dying flies
At the other end of the tube a woman is bathing her husband
When an angel writes the word Tobacco along the sky
The sea becomes covered with patches of dandruff
Little girls stick photographs of genitals in the windows of their homes
And virgins cover their parents' beds with tealeaves.'

And so on. All the rest is just as pretty and just as meaningless. Ugliness & eccentricity must have a purpose. So much for Mr Gascoyne. May he teach the bats in his belfry better manners. (By the way, I just thought, I hope he isn't a near & dear friend of yours. If he is, I've been very impolite.)

8) I've heard such a lot about 'Cold Comfort Farm' that I'll have to get hold of it.[1] It sounds incredible. Isn't there a Grandma Doom in it who once saw something frightful in the woodshed?

9) The Steyning incidents[2] are almost too good to be true. Mrs. Runia Tharp![3] I've been muttering the magic names all day. It's enough to Runia, and I hope you'll excuse that. Don't take any notice of what the intellectual bullies told you. Tell 'em you've got more in your little finger than they have in the whole of their fact-crammed brains.

10) But for God's sake don't defend the Sunday Referee literary whippets any more. I'm repeating myself, I know, but I regard the verses printed (with very few exceptions—you, notably) as schoolgirl posies plucked from a virgin garden, and the saccharine wallowings of near-schoolboys in the bowels of a castrated muse. Even the Bentley bodies covering the Ford engines are badly battered. I'd like to carry the image further and say that the chassis is made from a scrapheap of dis-used spare parts. Neuburg indulges in a horrid compromise: between the outlooks of the romanticist and the theorist, the mincing tread of the 'one-line and memorable passage taster and memoriser', and the galumphing of the dogmatic theorist. In fact the compromise [is] between Beer and No Beer. The result is partial inebriation—his muse is never drunk enough to be really emotional and never sober enough to be really intellectual.

11) Please don't type again; the warmest words look cold.

And now I, too, must finish, not because of any business appointment, but because I think I've written plenty. Now it is *your* turn. There are many things I want to write about, but they'll do next time. I'll expect a letter very, very soon—and as long as mine.

Dylan

---

1 *Cold Comfort Farm*, Stella Gibbons's parody of the rural novel, was published in 1932.
2 Neuburg, who lived in London, spent some of his time at Steyning, in Sussex. Johnson had been to literary get-togethers there.
3 Runia Tharp was the name adopted by Runia Sheila Macleod, a woman of means who was Neuburg's companion.

P.S. Three poems for you. Tell me if you like them or not. And why. I'll do the same if you'll send me some. The 'conversation' poem is very violent, as you will see, the 'Noise' poem very romantic, and the other in my more usual style. Take your choice, mum.

MS: Buffalo

PAMELA HANSFORD JOHNSON
[late October 1933][1]   Blaen-Cwm   Llangain   near Carmarthen

One day a very tired and bewildered young man will haunt the steps of the General Post Office, crying aloud, in broken Welsh, this one sad sentence: 'Why, in the name of God and the angelic clerks, cannot my letters be delivered to me?' He will be shooed away, but he will always return, crying his same question to a deaf Post Master and a malicious deity.

The trouble is that, for the last fortnight, I have been leading a very nomad existence, a few days in a rat-infested cottage in the heart of Wales, a few days with an eccentric friend, and a few days at home. Consequently, my letters are delivered to all three addresses, redelivered, and delivered again. Your last letter reached me on Saturday. I am replying with the greatest speed and at the greatest length.

When I came down here there were two letters of yours waiting for me— the proverbial twelve pages, and three typewritten sheets, to say nothing of the three lost poems. Now I reply to your collected correspondence.

I am staying, as you see, in a country cottage, eight miles from a town and a hundred miles from anyone to whom I can speak to on any subjects but the prospect of rain and the quickest way to snare rabbits. It is raining as I write, a thin, purposeless rain hiding the long miles of desolate fields and scattered farmhouses. I can smell the river, and hear the beastly little brook that goes gurgle-gurgle past this room. I am facing an uncomfortable fire, a row of china dogs, and a bureau bearing the photograph of myself aged seven—thick-lipped, Fauntleroy-haired, wide-eyed, and empty as the bureau itself. There are a few books on the floor beside me—an anthology of poetry from Jonson to Dryden, the prose of Donne, a Psychology of Insanity. There are a few books in the case behind me—a Bible, From Jest To Earnest, a History of Welsh Castles. Some hours ago a man came into the kitchen, opened the bag he was carrying, and dropped the riddled bodies of eight rabbits on to the floor. He said it was a good sport, showed me their torn bellies and opened heads, brought out the ferret from his pocket for me to see. The ferret might have been his own child, he fondled it so. His own eyes were as close-set as the eyes of the terrible thing he held in his hand. He called it, 'Billy fach'.

1 Dated by Thomas's references to poems which appeared in the *Sunday Referee* on 22 October. And a Notebook poem, dated 25 October, is marked 'Llangain'.

Later, when I have finished this letter, I'll walk down the lane. It will be dark then; lamps will be lit in the farmhouses, and the farmers will be sitting at their fires, looking into the blazing wood and thinking of God knows what littlenesses, or thinking of nothing at all but their own animal warmth.

But even this, grey as it is and full of the noise of sanitating water, and full of the sight of miserably wet fields, is better than the industrial small towns. I passed them in the bus coming down here, each town a festering sore on the body of a dead country, half a mile of main street with its Prudential, its Co-Op, its Star, its cinema and pub. On the pavements I saw nothing but hideously pretty young girls with cheap berets on their heads and paint smudged over their cheeks; thin youths with caps and stained fingers holding their cigarettes; women, all breast and bottom, hugging their purses to them and staring in at the shop windows; little colliers, diseased in mind and body as only the Welsh can be, standing in groups outside the Welfare Hall. I passed the rows of colliers' houses, hundreds of them, each with a pot of ferns in the window, a hundred jerry-built huts built by a charitable corporation for the men of the town to breed and eat in.

All Wales is like this. I have a friend who writes long and entirely unprintable verses beginning, 'What are you, Wales, but a tired old bitch?' and, 'Wales my country, Wales my cow.'

It's impossible for me to tell you how much I want to get out of it all, out of narrowness and dirtiness, out of the eternal ugliness of the Welsh people, and all that belongs to them, out of the pettinesses of a mother I don't care for and the giggling batch of relatives. What are you doing. I'm writing. Writing? You're always writing. What do you know? You're too young to write. (I admit that I very often look even younger than I am.) And I *will* get out. In some months I will be living in London. You shall call every day then and show me the poetry of cooking. I shall have to get out soon or there will be no need. I'm sick, and this bloody country's killing me.

All of which may sound very melodramatic. I don't want to make this letter sound like a third-rate play in which the 'artistic' hero boasts of his superiority over his fellows and moans of his highly poetical disease, or into a mere agony column. I hope you will excuse even the little bit of ranting and self pity I have indulged in.

I *did* like your illustrations, but the drawing of the oysters was far too good for the poem. I've given up tearing my hair at the products of the Neuburg Academy for the Production of Inferior Verse. I read them, put them aside, and try my hardest to forget. 'To The Hen', is the best thing I have seen in the Referee recently, but it is compensated for by the 'Cornflowers' of Miss Arlett. And now, to complete it all, the Sea Poem woman is assistant editor. Ah well. No more will my vague efforts adorn the Neuburg altar. Now even closer will I hug them to me.

But what's this about form? Are you misreading my cryptic comments?

Or have I subconsciously (that word has gone sour since Lawrence flung it at his own addled head, and the Vicky Bird roosted on it) written what I did not intend. Rhythm, certainly. It's as essential to poetry as it is to music. Rhyme, certainly, but with qualifications. I've been under the impression that I have defended form in my recent letters and spat me of the sprawling formlessness of Ezra Pound's performing Yanks and others. But, for all I know, I may have reiterated Geoffrey Grigson's vast maxim, 'Modern Art does not need logic or balance', or Herbert Read's[1] statement to the effect that modern art need have no meaning at all.

Now to your twelve pages. Twelve pages, after all, is very little if you have a lot to say. Your flattering description of yourself, aided by the drawing in your last letter, must have given you great amusement. But don't say the drawing's true. And why the desire to look like everybody else? If you were the usual gutless, unimaginative, slang-flinging flapper, your adherence to a conventional style of looks would be excusable. But you aren't. As an individual, you should *look* individual, apart from the mass member of society. For commercial, and sanitary, reasons, it is better to dress cleanly. But I do like colour. *I* don't look a bit like anybody else—I couldn't if I wanted to, and I'm damned if I *do* want to. I *like* conversational (your word) shirts. And I see no reason why I shouldn't. Man's dress is unhygienic and hideous. Silk scarlet shirts would be a vast improvement. This isn't the statement of an artistic poseur; I haven't got the tact to pose as anything. Oh to look, if nothing else, different from the striped trouser lads with their cancer-fostering stiff collars and their tight little bowlers.

I was surprised to hear that you had written only 30 poems; a bus-going life explains it. May the Kiddies' Kompleat Poetry Set be put to severe work in the future, and may I, humbly and yet critically, cast my eyes upon the virgin words.

And now I have eight poems of yours to do what I like with. And I am going to do what I like with them—criticise each in turn, not very minutely, for nothing short of fifty pages would allow it, but at least in some detail. Remember that nothing I say, Pamela, is for the sake of being smart, or to relieve any acid emotions I may have bottled up within me. I mean what I say and I mean it to help. Tell me if it is worth my while and your attention. If it is, then I will willingly, more than willingly, criticise in the same way every and any poem you have written.

Sung In A Garden At Nightfall

Delius should have written this instead of that extremely literary piece of music, Summer Night on the River. His music is a rebound, or, if you like, a second mood. First comes the idea of the creation, then the mental poem, then the composition of the music: a wrong method of approach. The nostalgia that runs through him like a vein drips 'jasmine-sweet' from your song. I'm glad that the colour of your poem book is green, the colour

1 Sir Herbert Read (1893–1968), author and critic, published several volumes of poetry, but was best known for influential studies of writers, literature and painting.

of youth when a minor heartbreak or the twiddly bit on an oboe is more effective than the sight of God or the feel of a surgical needle stuck into the tongue. And this is prejudiced, I know. But I like the Garden Song, and if in places it is more intestinal than emotional, that is all to the good. And I confess to a slight retching at the phrases, 'Woven of saffron with a weft of blue', 'veiled with violet', 'The air is jasmine-sweet'. And I confess that 'The lashes of the rose are sealed with dew' is very pretty. But the whole poem I should like to see upon the cover of a chocolate box; its flavours would mix well with the taste of coffee-centres and crème de menthe.

You have such a lot of the abilities that go towards making a *very* good poet that it seems a shame you don't take a firmer grasp on your susceptibilities to the easier emotions and images. The best advice in the world to a poetess is—Be a poet! Think of Mrs Browning and Emily Brontë. One wrote in quite a competent, female manner, the other androgynously. It's Neuburg's Heshe all over again, and Lawrence's Bull-Cow.

Laze, if you will, in a gossamer evening, confiding with your summer lover (impersonal! impersonal!); think your thoughts, and weep over the jail-like attitude of the poplars. But make more out of that experience than a pretty patchwork of derivative images and puce emotions. The garden (God wot!) must fit the mind like a glove. You yourself make it hell or heaven. Nothing is beautiful unless you think it. Make of your Woodforde-Finden garden[1] a valley Wagner might have been proud of, a little place Debussy would have lolled in, a rugby field for an infant Honneger. But don't take it as you find it. The garden was nothing. You descended on it like a bat from Chopin's belfry, and, lo, it was saccharine.

The Béguinage

This is by far the best poem that I've seen of yours. It's hard to imagine that the same mind created this and the previous song. It is beautifully simple; two of the verses are perfect. The idea, the form, & the expression, go hand-in-hand with a most satisfying delicacy. Out of more than fifty lines I can find only two that, in the slightest way, make discord. And those lines, oddly enough, are the two that begin the poem. I read them and expected Sousa orchestrated by Milhaud; I read on and got Mozart—a clumsy way of expressing my delight at fortyeight lines and my dislike of two.

Because I heap calumny on one poem, and immediately cover the next poem in an appreciative pile of roses, don't imagine that I am so easily a victim to my emotions that my opinions are little meditated. I like to spit at what I consider bad or unworthy (and much of what you sent me is unworthy of you), and I like to enthuse over what I consider sincere, real, and valuable. 'Béguinage' is all these three—not a Wordsworth model, or a

---

1 Amy Woodforde-Finden (1860–1919) set a sentimental poem by Laurence Hope (Adela Florence Nicolson, 1865–1904), 'Pale Hands I Loved', to music, to create a famous Victorian ballad. The 'garden' connection is in the poem's opening lines—'Pale hands I loved beside the Shalimar, / Where are you now', etc. The Shalimar (Royal Botanical) Gardens were across the river from Calcutta. Nicolson's husband was a British major serving in India.

chic adornment from the 'maison de Christina Rossetti', but an individual and highly successful production from the 'maison de P.H.J.'

Possession

See criticism one, especially the comment upon the poet and the poetess. 'Possession' is essentially a woman's poem. 'Béguinage' belongs to neither sex. It is a poem, and that is all and enough. 'Possession' is, metrically, quite good, but it is aimed at too low a standard.

Promenade Concert

Like the little girl with the curl over her forehead, when you are good you are very, very good, and when you are bad you are horrid. But even in your least inspired moments—and Sir Henry, Wood by name and Wood by nature,[1] seems to have had much effect upon your emotional and little upon your literary centres—good things rise out of the mediocrity as bubbles rise out of a marsh. There is, in the last stanza, an experience nakedly crystallized in a phrase:-

'clacking of applause, without even the compliment
Of an age-old second of silence.'

And that one experience compensates for the hysteria of the preceding lines. Your sincerity is always undeniable, and your hell-paving intentions *do* come out in such phrases as

'And the rivers of Eden
In the cold flute'.

But these are pearls surrounded not only by the pig's ear but by the whole of his bristling body. The 'burning triumph', the 'stinging pain', 'the singing and weeping for glory', are an exhibition (not in the sense of the Steyning highbrow) of emotion rather than a condensing, a torrent rather than a regulated fall, and as such is strictly out of place in a poem. It [is] as though a painter had flung a great mass of colours on to his canvas, and said to his critics, 'This is a landscape, for these are the colours that I see on the hills. The placing, dividing, and forming of those colours I leave to you.'

And while the colours would be bound to have some emotional significance, they no more make a painting than they do a stick of rock.

Tribute

A neat little advertisement, which might prove commercially saleable if 'Poetry' was changed to, say, 'Gibbs' Dentifrice'. One can write of mysticism without being a mystic; Wordsworth proved that. One can write of poetry, too.

Through The Night

Again, many of your merits and nearly all your faults come out in this. There is an obvious desire to say something and quite as obvious a reluctance to know what it is. There are *hints* of loneliness and the *statements* of verbosity. 'Drenched with rose', incidentally, is too reminiscent of de la Mare's 'Nod', in which the words 'dim with rose, and drenched with dew' appear. My dislike of the word 'burgeon' is a purely

1 Sir Henry Wood (1869–1944), conductor, closely identified with the Promenade Concerts.

personal one, as is my dislike of the word, 'primrose'. Unfortunately both appear in this poem (I hope you notice that I have used the 'poem' & 'verse' discriminately in these tiny criticisms) to test my boast of unbias.

'Each window pane shoots fire', is too quick, too impetuous an image to be satisfactory. There, again, you put down the emotional essence of what you wanted to say before you put your literary intelligence to work. I don't know how long you spent over 'Through The Night', but twice the time would have doubled its value, making it a consistently *good* poem, for it is good (careful word) in patches now. The imperative lines are very effective. So is the climax, notwithstanding the 'mother-of-pearl into pallid primrose', the type of line I can only call too easily pretty.

Up Train

Have I ever complimented you upon your command of conventional technique? If not, let me compliment you now, and also upon your ability to command the wider issues of form. 'Up Train' & 'The Symphony' are surprisingly effective in their set-out. Best of all, the form appears inevitable. 'Up Train' could have been written in no other way, the highest thing one can say of a technical experiment. 'Seed Nursery' has the simplicity of a nursery rhyme, set off by a remarkable diction, uninfluenced by any other diction I'm acquainted with.

> 'For the mad sweet-pea he rigs
> Pillories of little twigs'

gives me a most pleasant shock, a *physical* sensation. Few combinations of words have a physical effect upon me.

> 'And he sets between, for brushes,
> Meek and poodle-shaven bushes'.

This, too, and many other lines in this lovely little poem—'little' is the word, the littleness of a certain type of beauty, the littleness of ordered gardens, avenues, and a tidy sky—has the effect upon me of a curious and individual wine out of an old bottle marked with very colourful designs. And if these sentences are, in themselves, too rich and adjectival, blame your odd little muse & not me.

Symphony For Full Orchestra

When I read this first I wasn't sure whether its peculiar form was entirely necessary. But slowly the voices of the orchestra insisted, and the long, drawn-out question of the woodwind became inevitable, until, at the end, I wondered why the whole question, 'O Star In The Dark' was not repeated. Perhaps, if I read it again, I will see a good reason why it should be as it is. The one, sudden entrance of the timpani is remarkably effective. I can hear the harps glissando-ing (can you spell it?) over their strange phrases, the sudden, unharplike sound of the word 'cerements', the sibilant and treble 'Cease!' as they begin. And now any doubts I entertained as to the inevitability of the orchestral form are vanquished. Inevitably the violins say, 'These are his hands on your breast' and as inevitably the brass cry out and say, 'Return, star-crossed, The bloodshed morn is nigh.'

There is, as there was in 'Béguinage', only one phrase I object to.

'. . . Weave the straining clouds
Into maddened shrouds',

has too many words—& the wrong words—in it. The rhyme is a jingle. The adjectives add nothing. Polish up or remove that phrase, & I have no quarrel with the poem from beginning to end. In its limits, it is as lovely as anything I know.

And so what a strange, unequal selection of poems and verses you have sent me. You have sent me the sugariest custard, the cheapest port, & the most delicate white wine. I never remember before mixing my drinks so quickly, &, at the same time, so satisfyingly.

Never be pretty for the sake of being pretty. It's always in your power—and yours especially—to lift prettiness into your own sort of beauty. Whether it is the ultimate beauty I don't even care to guess; but much of it is what *I* understand to be beautiful. And that is all I can ever say.

But let me get off the point for a moment, and make what will probably be quite a futile attack upon your creed of simplicity. I admit that everything should be said as simply *as possible*, that meaning should never be smothered by conscious obscurity, that the most prized ornamentations of style and phrase have to go under when the meaning dictates it. But that *all* good poetry is necessarily simple seems to me very absurd. Because I can understand the English of Mrs. Beeton, there is no earthly reason why I should understand the English of Manley Hopkins—or W. H. Davies & W. H. Auden. I see no necessity why the greatest truths of the world, and the greatest variations of these truths, should be so simple that the most naive mind can understand them. There are things, and valuable things, so complicated that even he who writes of them does not comprehend what he is writing.

I admire the simplicity of Shakespeare, the easy language of Twelfth Night and the hard language of Coriolanus. I admire the simplicity of Mozart and the bewildering obscurity of the later Scriabin. Both had a great thing to say, and why the message of Mozart, because of its easiness to understand, is rated above the message of Scriabin, which is a separate message and the devil to follow, I shall never know. It is the simplicity of the human mind that believes the universal mind to be as simple.

Thank you for all you have said about the poems I've sent you. I profit by all criticism; yours is far from puerile, and though I am bound to disagree with much you say I agree heartily with most. With this letter I am enclosing two more poems. They are not typed, I'm afraid, but I hope that won't prevent you from reading and criticising them carefully. There is a sort of finality about the typewritten word which the written word lacks. Spare no compliment—I don't go all girlish; spare no condemnation—I am used to it and profit by it.

One day I want to send you ten thousand words of prose, 'Uncommon Genesis', a story set in no time or place, with only two characters, a man & a woman.[1] And the woman, of course, is not human. She wouldn't be. If

1 Later published as 'The Mouse and the Woman'.

you want it, I'll send it to you. If you don't, I won't.

Whatever you do to letters, story, or poems, don't give them the answer that so shocked the pundits of Steyning. If anyone said 'Sez You' after I had shown him or her a poem I think I should wither up. So, please, be genteel even if you must be condemnatory.

Laleham arrangement, though in the air, is oke by me,[1] and if there is any one expression worse than 'sez you' this is it. You are right, of course. December it is. Yes, I do paint, but very little, and the results are extraordinary.

I should have loved to reply to your hideous drawing with an equally hideous one of myself, but no ordinary pencil can do me justice. If I can find a photograph of myself when in the very far distance I will send it to you.

Dylan

P.S. Important. I shall be here (Llangain) until Saturday of this week. If you reply before I leave, and I hope you do, send the letter straight here. It can't go wrong.

MS: Buffalo

PAMELA HANSFORD JOHNSON
[card, postmarked 30 Oct 1933]
                                    5 Cwmdonkin Drive Uplands Swansea

Congratulations![2] A *very* long letter
will arrive in a few days—
probably by parcel post.
                    Dylan

MS: Buffalo

PAMELA HANSFORD JOHNSON
[early November 1933][3]   5 Cwmdonkin Drive Uplands Swansea

Excuses

I've taken a terribly long time to reply, I know, but, during the last week, I have been so utterly and suicidally morbid that my letter would have read like an excerpt from the Undertakers' Gazette. I hope, in the long week

---

1 Nancy and Haydn Taylor lived on the Chertsey houseboat in summer, but in winter moved to a cottage in the nearby village of Laleham.
2 The *Sunday Referee* announced on 29 October that it was to sponsor a book of poems by Johnson.
3 Thomas was sending his photograph (second paragraph); Johnson's diary for 6 November says, 'Letter from Dylan & photo'. His letters to her were often written over several days.

that has passed, you haven't forgotten my existence. And please don't be long in replying because *I* was. I look forward to a letter soon.

On receiving your photograph I went immediately to have my own likeness taken, there being no existent photograph of myself at this stage of decline. Either I proved too much for the delicate photographic plates, or else the photographer has gone, moaning, away, for I have had nothing from him. I don't want to hold the correspondence up any longer, so here is a very bad and uncomplimentary passport photograph taken two years ago. It's a poor return, but I shall send you a better and more recent photograph when, or if, it arrives. I do look something like the enclosed snap. Imagine the same face two years older, a bit thinner & more lined. The black shirt (strictly non-political) is the same. I am rarely as tidy or as well-groomed as that, and, pray God, I rarely have that cherub's expression. Still, it has its resemblance. Add a few shadows, draw in a cigarette & ruffle the hair: there I am, in my full glory.

Kind Action

I give you full authorisation to use this new letter form. You'll find it very useful. All you have to do is to write odd notes at different times—on whatever subject, & in whatever mood—and then bung them together under terse little headings. Go ahead, girl!

Congratulatory Hand and Helping Hand

Congratulations. Neuburg, for once, has not gone wrong. It is hardly possible to imagine that he could, for the choice was inevitable. I take as much interest in the publication of your poems as I do in the publication of my own. And if they were my own, I could not be more delighted to hear that your poems are to be published.

You will, I suppose, publish all you have written, but I do advise you to be careful in your editing of the earlier poems. There is no necessity at all why *one* of the printed poems should be bad, providing you use a blue pencil and a scissors with discrimination. If I can help you, in any way, to polish up the final drafts, or to do anything to help your book towards the success it is bound to be, let me know. I'll do my best, too, to advertise the book among those who do not believe Browning to be something to do with gravy. I'll want to buy a copy, too, and to receive a neatly autographed first edition. But don't forget: if there is anything, anything at all, you would like me to do, I should have the greatest possible pleasure in doing it.

Physiognomical Comment

You do look formidable, my Wilhelmina. I did not expect you to be so full and bright and strong, with such a British chin. What a dominant personality! Tut, girl, what a zest for life! And here I am, small, chinless, and like an emasculate Eton boy. Ah, the waves of self pity that engulf me as I gaze first upon your features and then upon mine (even though mine is two and a bit years old, and yours as recent as this morning's dew!) But, to pass from Jest to Earnest, let me thank you for sending your photograph.

You are very, very, pleasant to look at. There is meaning and strength in your face. I shall hang you in my room. This is certainly one of the things that could have been expressed better. All I have said is probably in the worst taste [*a line is deleted*: And as I seem to be verging on the edge of vulgarity, I shall] (I don't think I have sent an untidier letter. Excuse it.)

So now, if I look long upon your photograph, and you, looking upon mine, exercise your imagination in the details of age and cleanliness, we shan't be strangers to each other. From your photograph I know the lines of your face, from your poetry the lines of your mind. I'm not a physiognomist—I can't even spell the damned word—but I see how you bristle (images of a herd of porcupine) with individuality. Look like everybody else? No, no. But then I am biased.

Attack On Bats and Defence of Vermin

Believe me or not, the first two lines of 'Béguinage' are as bad as anything you've written. The image is smart and cheap; it falls too easily on the paper. And the attitude behind it is wrong, relying too much on a quick, admittedly vivid, visual impression, instead of upon a mentally digested experience. It is written from the mind's eye, not even from the mind's ear, for the sounds are unintentionally ugly. You have seized on a glimpse of what you wanted to express, and not on the still, slow scrutiny.

Your remark about the end of my Feverish poem is entirely justified. I plead guilty to bathos, but offer in excuse the fact that I copied out the poem as soon as I had written it, wanting to get it off to you and too hurried to worry about its conclusion. In the ordinary way I would never have passed it.

Leave me my 'hatching of the hair'.[1] It's verminous, I know, but isn't it lovely? And what is more refreshing than the smell of vermin? Hardy loved to sit beside a rotten sheep and see the flies make a banquet of it. A dark thought, but good and lively. One of the hardest and most beneficial kicks of life comes from the decaying foot of death. Uncover her face, she died young.

5. Defence of Poesie[2]

What you call ugly in my poetry is, in reality, nothing but the strong stressing of the physical. Nearly all my images, coming, as they do, from my solid and fluid world of flesh and blood, are set out in terms of their progenitors. To contrast a superficial beauty with a superficial ugliness, I do not contrast a tree with a pylon, or a bird with a weasel, but rather the human limbs with the human tripes. Deeply, of course, all these contrasting things are equally beautiful and equally ugly. Only by association is the refuse of the body more to be abhorred than the body

---

1 The poem, 'From love's first fever', has this phrase in the Notebook version (dated 14/17 October). In *Collected Poems* the phrase became 'the breaking of the hair'.

2 This section of the letter should be numbered '6' if it is to agree with its position after five headed sections. From this point, too, a different writing paper is used. But internal evidence suggests it belongs here.

itself. Standards have been set for us. What is little realised is that it was only chance that dictated these standards. It is polite to be seen at one's dining table, and impolite to be seen in one's lavatory. It might well have been decided, when the tumour of civilisation was first fostered, that celebrations should be held in the w.c., and that the mere mention of 'eating and drinking' would be the height of impropriety. It was decided by Adam and Eve, the first society lawmakers, that certain parts of the body should be hidden and certain be left uncovered. Again, it was chance that decided them to hide their genital organs, and not, say, their armpits or throats. While life is based upon such chance conventions and standards as these, it is little wonder that any poetry dealing impartially with the parts of the anatomy, (not quite impartially, perhaps, for the belly emphasises an abstruse point better than the Atlas-bone), and with the functions of the body, should be considered as something rather hideous, unnecessary, and, to say the least, indelicate. But I fail to see how the emphasising of the body can, in any way, be regarded as hideous. The body, its appearance, death, and diseases, is a fact, sure as the fact of a tree. It has its roots in the same earth as the tree. The greatest description I know of our own 'earthiness' is to be found in John Donne's Devotions, where he describes man as earth of the earth, his body earth, his hair a wild shrub growing out of the land. All thoughts and actions emanate from the body. Therefore the description of a thought or action—however abstruse it may be—can be beaten home by bringing it onto a physical level. Every idea, intuitive or intellectual, can be imaged and translated in terms of the body, its flesh, skin, blood, sinews, veins, glands, organs, cells, or senses.

Through my small, bonebound island I have learnt all I know, experienced all, and sensed all. All I write is inseparable from the island. As much as possible, therefore, I employ the scenery of the island to describe the scenery of my thoughts, the earthquakes of the body to describe the earthquakes of the heart.

Fatal selfconsciousness prevents me from carrying on in the same noble vein. (How about that idiom to help my argument?) It is typical of the physically weak to emphasise the strength of life (Nietzsche); of the apprehensive and complex-ridden to emphasise its naiveté and dark wholesomeness (D. H. Lawrence); of the naked-nerved and blood-timid to emphasise its brutality and horror (Me!)

There has been a great deal of nonsense in this poetical defence. There's some truth, too.

6. Refutation and Explanation

The 'dream' poem that you like is *not* the best I have sent you. Only superficially is it the most visionary. There is more in the poem, 'Before I Knocked',[1] more of what I consider to be of importance in my poetry. Please, this isn't boasting. I'm incurably pessimistic and eternally dissatisfied.

1 Dated 6 September in the Notebook.

So the poor old snail has wound his horn before. It is a long time since I read the Ode to Evening, so long that my memory refuses all responsibility.[1]

But surely you haven't missed one of the biggest warps in my poetry. My melting-pot is all sour. In two out of three of all the poems I have sent you, there has been a steady scheme of consonantal rhyming. The 'Eye of Sleep' is rhymed throughout. I never use a full rhyme, but nearly always a half rhyme.

Take the poem published in the Referee last Sunday[2] (did you like it?)

a	weather	a	earth	a	sings	a	flower	rocks
b	stars	b	head	b	land	b	trees	streams
xa	other	a	mouth	a	gangs	a	destroyer	wax
b	trees	a	death	a	wings	b	rose	veins
xa	feather	b	replied	b	fade	a	fever	sucks

and so on.   & so on.

I do not always keep to my rhyming schemes with complete faithfulness. As a rule, yes. But perhaps this elaborate explanation has been a waste of time. You may have noticed it all before, for it has a strange effect.

7. Patronising Remark

Certainly let friend Mednikoff read my poems, but don't show him the 'Eye of Sleep' alone. Show him the others, and tell me what he says, won't you, even if, with a sardonic Russian leer, he spits him of all the batch. From your meagre description of him he sounds most interesting, and I'm glad he waxed romantic over your 'Symphony'. But what 'circle' does he move in? The squared circle of the Geometrists? The fleshy circle of the Academicians?

8. Stop Press

The typewriter is still labouring over its 'Uncommon Genesis'. The story was written a year ago, but I have never typed it. The first—and probably the last,—typed copy is for you. It will be ready when I write to you next. I will keep my explanatory comments until then.

9. FORWARD THE VERSE BRIGADE!

I do not think that I have misunderstood your Creed of Simplicity. Perhaps I attacked it from the wrong angle. You were careful in your wording when you contrasted the beauty of simplicity and the beauty of

1 A poem called 'The eye of sleep' (5 October 1933 in the Notebook) has the line, 'Let fall the snail of time and wound his horn.' Johnson thought that this echoed a line in a William Collins poem, 'Or where the beetle winds his small but sullen horn.'
2 29 October. The poem was 'The force that through the green fuse drives the flower'.

obscurity, of light and dark, for if I think you a Wilhelmina (and I protest I don't; I think you a Pamela), you think of me as some Stygian cess-hound forever plumbing the intestinal emotions. You may be right, damn you, but all the words you use, 'beauty', 'simplicity', 'obscurity', mean different things to different people, are based upon individual preconceptions. 'Simplicity' to me is the best way of expressing a thing, and the ultimate expression may still be obscure as D. H. Lawrence's Heaven. 'Obscurity' is the worst way. I thought of a definition of beauty, but, like all such definitions, it is too limited. One of the greatest aspects of it is 'acquaintance plus wonder', but the expansion of this would lead me, through many vague pages, to the point where I started. Beauty, too, is the *sense of unity in diversity*. This needs no expansion.

And poetry need not appeal to the intelligent mind more than to the unintelligent. It is appreciated to the greatest extent by the unbiased mind. Each genuine poet has his own standards, his own codes of appreciation, his own aura. Reading a poet for the first time, one cannot be acquainted with him, & therefore, judging him by preconceived standards—however elastic those standards may be—one cannot fully appreciate him. One should take first an empty brain and a full heart to every poem one reads: an impossible task. The only possible way lies in the reading & re-reading, preferably aloud, of any new poem that strikes one as holding some and however little value.

The speaking of poetry should certainly be encouraged. I do hope you read aloud. I myself chant aloud in a sonorous voice every poem I read. The neighbours must know your poems by heart; they certainly know my own, and are bound to be acquainted with many passages of Macbeth, Death's Jester, and the Prophetic Books. I often think that baths were built especially for drowsy poets to lie in and there intone aloud amid the steam and boiling ripples.

10. A Potpourri of Original and Unoriginal Satire

> The Tharp that once through Neuburg's Halls
> The soul of humbug shed,
> Now hangs as mute upon your scrawls
> As if that soul had fled.
> So sleeps the vice of former days,
> So humbug's thrill is o'er,
> And hearts that once gave Tupper praise
> Now praise you all the more.[1]

I don't quite know what this means, but, apart from 'scrawls', which was brought in because it rhymed, it appears to be vaguely complimentary.

God help the Creative Arts Circle. I hope you won't. It would probably be something like this:

1 Thomas is parodying the Irish poet Thomas Moore (1779–1852), 'The Harp that once through Tara's Halls / The soul of music shed / . . .'

'"I will now call on Alberic Morphine to give a reading."
The rows of young women look up; their eyes glisten; they shiver
With the kind of emotion that's very misleading.
All have fine eyes, yellow faces, vile clothes & a liver.
They smoke a great deal, bath little, and wear no stays.'

or like this:

'You would meet Iris, she who lives serene
In the intense confusion of the obscene,
And drags her tea-time sex affair all fresh
To the dinner table, like a cat with flesh;[1]
Lesbia, whose outward form proclaims at least
Some variation on the normal beast;
Onan, recalling complexes before I speak,
His childhood roles of cad and sneak,
Youth's coprolytic loves and grosser fancies
Derive from reading Ernest Jone's romances.'[2]

You would meet Mrs. Murgatroyd Martin:

'She tells you of Pater and Pankhurst, of Tagore and Wilde,
Of man-made laws and the virtues of proteid peas,
Of Folk Song and Art and of sterilised milk for the child,
Of the joys of the Morris Dance and of Poetry Teas.'

You would hear a lot of nice things about Art, and lots of nice people would read your poems and say the nicest things, and you would go home and get sick on the mat.

But, as Ruskin once remarked to Carlyle, Please don't go all stiff-shirted on me. 'Doesn't any man or woman know exactly what sex means before life brings that great experience to them?' Yes, you wrote that, and it will need some explaining away at the gates of heaven where the phallus is taken as a fact and not as a peg upon which to hang one's little platitudes.

11. LOVE and HATE

Scoff at this enchanted Wood,
Ye who dare.

I wouldn't jibe at the old war-horse.[3] His hooves have beaten out time to nearly all the great orchestral pieces of the world. He introduced Schönberg to England. He arranged those stirring Sea Tunes that quicken the blood of every true-veined Englishman. What feet have not thumped to his conducting of the marches from Pomp & Circumcision. And I like his beard.

1 Thomas borrowed the first four lines from a poem by Edgell Rickword (1898–1982), 'The Encounter'. This appeared in a 1931 collection, *Twittingpan and Some Others*.
2 Ernest Jones (1879–1958), leading psychoanalyst and disciple of Sigmund Freud.
3 Sir Henry Wood.

There are only two men in England whom I hate with *all* my heart: Sir Edward Elgar and Mr. Geoffrey Grigson. One has inflicted more pedantic wind & blather upon a supine public than any man who has ever lived. The other edits New Verse. His place is already reserved in the lower regions where, for all eternity, he shall read the cantos of Ezra Pound to a company of red-hot devils.

12. My Life. A Touching Autobiography In One Paragraph

I first saw the light of day in a Glamorgan villa, and, amid the terrors of the Welsh accent and the smoke of the tinplate stacks, grew up to be a sweet baby, a precocious child, a rebellious boy, and a morbid youth. My father was a schoolmaster: a broader-minded man I have never known. My mother came from the agricultural depths of Carmarthenshire: a pettier woman I have never known. My only sister passed through the stages of longlegged schoolgirlishness, shortfrocked flappery and social snobbery into a comfortable married life. I was first introduced to Tobacco (the Boy Scouts' Enemy) when a small boy in a preparatory school, to Alcohol (the Demon King) when a senior member of a secondary school. Poetry (the Spinster's Friend) first unveiled herself to me when I was six or seven years old; she still remains, though sometimes her face is cracked across like an old saucer. For two years I was a newspaper reporter, making my daily call at the mortuaries, the houses of suicides—there's a lot of suicide in Wales—and Calvinistic 'capels'. Two years was enough. Now I do nothing but write, and occasionally make a few guineas out of my dramatic expositions of How Not To Act. A misanthropic doctor, who apparently did not like the way I did my eyebrows, has given me four years to live.[1] May I borrow that foul expression of yours—it isn't yours, really—and whisper Sez You into his ear.

13. A Touching Experience

After my last letter to you, written from the despondency of a Welsh hill cottage, I ran out of cigarettes and walked three miles to the nearest village, Llanstephan, to buy some.

It was a fool of a night. The clouds were asses' ears. The moon was ploughing up the Towy river as if he expected it to yield a crop of stars. And the stars themselves:—hundreds of bright-eyed urchins nudging each other over a celestial joke. It is a long road to Llanstephan, bounded by trees and farmers' boys pressed amorously upon the udders of their dairymaids. But the further I walked the more lonely it became. I found the madness of the night to be a false madness, and the vast horseplay of the sky to be a vaster symbol. It was as if the night were crying, crying out the terrible explanation of itself. On all sides of me, under my feet, above my head, the symbols moved, all waiting in vain to be translated. The trees that night were like prophet's fingers. What had been a fool in the sky was the wisest

---

1 In later years there were unreliable stories that a local practitioner—a Dr McKelvie or a Dr Flood—had warned Thomas that he was tuberculous.

cloud of all—a huge, musical ghost thumping out one, coded tune. It was a sage of a night, and made me forgive even my own foolishness.

There was, of course, no cigarette machine in Llanstephan.

14. A Rude Poem

Let me explain first that this was written in a violent mood when there seemed little to do but to insult someone. After reading his comments in the last Referee, I picked on Neuburg to be that someone. It's HARDLY CRICKET, I know, & I'm RATHER A CAD considering he is going to publish all your poems & has published a couple of mine, one very recently—but here it is:

> A Sunday paper did its best
> To build a Sunday singing nest
> Where poets from their shells could burst
> With trembling rhymes and do their worst
> To break the laws of man and metre
> By publishing their young excreta.

> A highfalutin little bloke
> Conducted (with an artichoke)
> The choir of birds who weekly piped
> From pages very neatly typed.
> Hail to the Referee all plastered
> With products of the pimp and bastard.

> With each prophetic phrase or clause
> Dropped from their educated jaws,
> The guts of Logic turn about,
> The swine of Bathos shows his snout.
> With every —— verse they print
> Their Muse develops a worse squint.

> Let all rejoice that Victor N
> Is far above the run of men.
> O new Messiah of the Muse
> Would that we could, like those old Jews,
> Place on thy head an ink-filled crown
> And crucify thee upside down.

15. A Piece of Sentiment

How long have I known you? I seem to have been writing these nonsensical letters of mine for ever, and for ever to have been receiving those letters of yours. But it can't have been for more than a few months. Yet I know you as well as I have ever known anybody in my life. Much of what I write to you is, I know, very silly, and much of it I've regretted as soon as I've posted the letters. But I have written what I wanted to write, I've got all sorts of things off my mind, and I have tried to be honest. I've found a poetess, and one, moreover, who likes *my* poems. I've found a very good friend. No, I refuse to become maudlin, but I'm glad that I've found you or, rather, that you've found me. I write to several people, but to none with the freedom that I adopt in my letters to you. You don't take offence when I become vulgar, as I so often do, or when I say unpleasant things about the poems of yours I don't like; you don't mind if I attack all the windmills in the world with a rusty pen; and, though you say you find much to laugh at in my letters, you don't, I know, laugh at what I am sincere, *really* sincere, in expressing. You like my letters. I hope our meeting, when it does take place, will not disappoint you. I won't run myself down any more; by this time you know as many of my faults and shortcomings as I do myself.

This is the first time, I think, that I've written like this, and it will be the last. I only wanted to tell you how much I appreciate you & your letters. Enough. Enough. Let the correspondence now continue as of yore, and still the postman bear into thy house and mine the brilliant products of the Battersea & Swansea Muse, and the dazzling correspondence of two diverse but well-attuned imaginations.

Dylan

This is not a modernist design but an afterthought on a particular glowing sentence. May it stir your curiosity.
[*Six lines are deleted*][1]

A Story For The Very Young[2]

Once upon a time there was a little girl. And this little girl, odd to say, was a po-et-ess. She was very ro-man-tic in her out-look, and wrote many nice ro-man-tic poems, using such words as, 'wings', 'melody', & 'breast', all of which was very nice. But she grew older, and vis-it-ors and rel-at-ives said, Oh, yes, she is a very nice girl, but what is she going to do? It was ob-vi-ous that she would be a po-et-ess always, or even something more im-moral. So she went on being a po-et-ess, and a kind man put her poems in a litt-le book. But one day she became ac-quaint-ed with a little poet, who was the funniest little poet you could imagine. And he wrote vul-gar poems about wombs and things. Well, dears, the po-et-ess and the little poet went on being ac-quaint-ed, and, at last, the po-et-ess took the Wrong Turning. She, too, wrote vul-gar poems, and it was nothing for her to use the horrible word 'Cancer' twice in one stan-za. And the little poet went all flower-faced, and wrote a lot of verses about the sun coming up and the moon going down. But the po-et-ess grew tired of her tu-ber-cular muse, and

1 Thomas had written:
   I am lying in bed now and
   I have just had a wonderful thought
   A lover [???] tell her how much he loves her.
   He thinks he loves her so much that he [?could change] into a tiny
   insect or fly, & that he could fly [?to where] she slept and go
   to sleep in her hair.
2 Having finished the letter, Thomas evidently restarted it. The preceding text covers both sides of six numbered pages. The text following is on a single page numbered '7'.

returned to her babb-ling brooks etc. And the little po-et burnt all his so-nice poems, and returned to his vomit and vul-gar-it-y. And they both lived happy ever after.

Moral   Let Cancer Be.

This seems rather a nasty and un-true story, and I don't know why I wrote it. But, then, this letter is such a terrible hotch-potch, written in odd places and at odd times, that the story fits in with the chaotic atmosphere.

Only half an hour ago I picked up the new Referee,[1] & read Mr. Vicky Bird's glowing article of praise. How it warms the cockles of the heart. Let me very boastfully say this: Take all his praise with a barrel of salt; take mine with none at all. I mean all I have sd about you & your poems; in his pretty little cage, God knows what the editing parrot means or does not mean.

And his infantile remark about 'never faltering in metre' or whatever he sd. It's as if a man sd of Wiley Post, 'What a marvellous flyer; one of the greatest things about his success is the skilful way in which he keeps up in the air!'[2] Oh God, oh Montreal! Oh Neuburg! Oh Jesus!

I agree with a lot he says, and I'll say a lot more in my next letter.

Dylan

Pardon all irrelevancies & inconsistencies, the bad grammar & the worse spelling. And take to heart, O Battersea Stick (remark the tonal value of the words) all I have sd from the depths of a tidal, though slightly corrupted, heart.

MS: Buffalo

PAMELA HANSFORD JOHNSON
[week of 11 November 1933][3]   Excuse the worse than usually
                                                    terrible writing!

Preface

In my untidy bedroom, surrounded with books and papers, full of the unhealthy smell of very bad tobacco, I sit and write. There is a beautiful winter sun outside, and by my side the oil-stove shines like a parhelion. On the wall immediately in front of me hangs my pastel drawing of the Two Brothers of Death; one is a syphilitic Christ, and the other a greenbearded Moses. Both have skin the colour of figs, and walk, for want of a better place, on a horizontal ladder of moons. The hot water pipes are swearing at me, and, despite the nearness of the stove, my tiny hands are frozen.

Last night I slept for the first time this month; today I am writing a poem

1 Sunday 5 November.
2 Wiley Post, a famous American airman of the time.
3 The letter was partly written on Saturday 11 November, but not completed for several days. Johnson's diary, 17 November: 'Letter from Darling Dylan, which was also morbid.'

in praise of sleep and the veronal that stained the ravelled sleeve. These twelve November nights have been twelve long centuries to me. Minute by minute through the eight hours of the dark I lay and looked up into the empty corners of this room. First I would seize upon some tiny thought, hug it close to me, turn it over and over in my brain, hoping, by such concentration, to find my senses dropping away into oblivion. But soon my lips would speak sentences aloud, and I listen to them.

'The man of substance never walks.' Then my lips say, 'He only wheels a truck', and, a thousand years later, I understand what I have spoken. Then I would repeat all the poetry I knew, but if I forgot a word I could never think of another to put in its place, unless it was a mad word and had no meaning. Then I would hear my heart beat, and count its beats, and hear their regularity.

And now, thanks to the God who looked with benevolent eye upon the antics of Lot's daughters, I have slept. Now I can reply to your letter and do my dance around your poems.

Some of the enclosed notes—I think this newspaper style we have adopted in our last letters suits our particular kinds of mentalities very well indeed—have been written during the last and letterless week. If half your notes are composed during the period between the sending off [of] your letter and the receiving of mine, then much valuable time (the adjective depends on you, of course) would not be lost. This, for me, is a statement of great common-sense, and having delivered myself of such a commonsensible idea, I shall probably be half-witted for the rest of the week.

The moods of the notes I leave to you. One, again, was written in the bath—a striking condemnation of those of my acquaintances who do not believe I ever take one—; one in the bus from Swansea to Trecynon (you have never heard of it, but it boasts a Little Theatre where I occasionally perform); and the rest in the privacy of my pensive and worm-ridden room.

Poisonal Accomplishments and Failings

What a terribly accomplished person you are! I can't sing, can't play any musical instrument, and can't draw. I paint a good deal, but quite untechnically, and the startling effects I sometimes do produce are owing to a diseased mentality and an entire lack of skill. O Wilhelmina Bernhardt! I apologise at once. I'm glad you're an actress, and I'm sure you're a good one. I've been acting on and off—mostly off—both as an amateur and as a vague professional since I was the size of your thumb. But I can't say I'm improved much since that time. My speciality is the playing of madmen, neurotics, nasty 'modern' young men and low comedians— quite straight acting. At the present time I—and the Little Theatre of Wales (it sounds good) are rehearsing 'Strange Orchestra'. Do you know it? I'm playing Val, if you do, and if you don't, I'll explain that Val is a nervous, unhappy writer of unpopular books, in love and yet frightened to be, full of bathetic and half-digested notions on Life with a Capital Letter. What sort of things do you play? Tell me you play hysterical young women with tumours, or erotic young things with Notions, and we'll go round together on the provincial music-halls playing Grand Guignol.

Talking of Grand Guignol, I met Eliot Crawshay Williams last week.[1] He's an old roué with a red face and wrong ideas.

Barter
For one 'jasmine' I will give you one 'belly'.
  "   "   'daffodil' "   "   "   "   "   'senna'.

But I'm damned if I'll swap my wormy wombs for all the fairy bubbles this side of St. Paul's. We're extremists, girl, one upstairs in our lady's chamber and the other downstairs in our lady's chamber-pot. Still, I will do my best to comb out the superfluous horrors in my beard on the one condition that you let Spring pass out next year without bestowing one single lavish spate upon its tomb.

The Publication Of a Book
I said that your book was bound to be successful, successful, that is, compared with any book of poetry recently published, and I repeat it. What harm can it do you? An unbiased reader does not expect a first book to be perfect. All he looks for are parts of promise and fragments of achievement. There have probably been no first poems ever published that have had more to offer than that. And there is certainly promise in all you've written. In two or three instances there has been undeniable and individual achievement. You are young, and can't expect any more than that. Even if you were withered and corseted into shape, there would be no need for you to expect more. Great reputations have been built upon much promise and small achievement.

You are, I know, capable of achieving perfection in a certain type of poetry, a poetry born out of Christina Rossetti and the Georgian and Poetry Bookshop Gang.[2] And you have failed, I know, in attempting a far higher thing—the creation of personal poetry, born out of Battersea, Mrs. Johnson and wide and haphazard reading. Really, your future as a poetess is capable of developing in one of two ways: along the hedgerows, littered with the PreRaphaelite and Georgian corpses, to a narrow but popular perfection, or in the middle of the road, scorning the hedges and the Referee ruts, towards a wide, unpopular and very splendid failure.

You yourself have to decide which way to go, but the literary people you will associate with will certainly help you to make up your mind. I know which way Neuburg wishes, and I hope to God that my sprawling letters will help you to take the other way. Fear Neuburg and all the Creative Lifers as you would fear the Boojum.

So speaks the Snark.[3]

1 Eliot Crawshay Williams (1879–1962), author, one-time Member of Parliament.
2 The Poetry Bookshop, founded 1912, encouraged the 'Georgian poetry' movement that was later frowned upon (not least by Thomas) for writing blandly about a comfortable, countrified England.
3 'For the Snark *was* a Boojum, you see'—a line from Lewis Carroll's nonsense poem, 'The Hunting of the Snark'.

Pawky (Your Word) Remarks

Why do you call your book Dayspring?[1] It isn't as if the poems in it had sprung out of natural associations. You don't snoop around the country lanes, looking for a ragwort to pour a bellyful of words on, or pimp in the recesses of the gasworks at the amours of stale and repetitive lovers, hoping to hear some words of love that you might jot down upon your pad of paper. Yours is a selfspring; everything comes out of yourself, and darkness, despite what you say, has infinitely more possibilities than day. There is too much *doing* in life, and not enough *being*. Proof of life lies in the answer to one question, and that question is not troubled with the mechanics of living, with the functions of living, or with the appearances of living—but with the vast verb, To Be. Age is not a matter of years, but of being. Man is pre-occupied with action, never believing Blake's 'Thought Is Action'. Dayspring! I may have missed the point of the title, and, anyway, God knows why I am so suddenly vehement.

Comment upon the Comments upon the Nastiness of the Present Writer

You ikkle bitch!

But seriously, it was the attitude behind what you said, rather than *what* you said, that called forth my singular nastiness. To call Sex the Great Experience is to call Birth the Great Adventure, and a prostitute the Lady of Dubious Morals. It is the escape of the coward-worded and the last resort of the prig-moralled journalist (neither of which applies to you). Do you remember Rampion in Point-Counter-Point?[2] He painted a wild picture of a naked man and woman. 'What do you call it?' he was asked. 'Some people call it love', he replied, 'And others call it——.'

It was not that you made your remarks—with which I thoroughly agree—too 'pretty'; I'm not corrupted enough to ask for the language of the gutter on every possible occasion. But there are only three vocabularies at your disposal when you talk of sex: the vocabulary of the clinic, of the gutter, & of the moralist. Of the three the last is by far the worst; it is compromise and the jargon of the prude. The clinic, at least, talks from knowledge of its subject, and the gutter talks from acquaintance. The moralist, with his half learnt knowledge and his frustrated or perverted acquaintance, cloaks everything in words & symbols. The naked man & woman remain.

Pathos (and forgive the pencil, for I've mislaid the ink)

Four years, my sweet. 1340 days & nights. And thank you for the optimistic remarks. I don't believe it either, but then it would be very odd if I did. You should hear me cough, though—a most pleasing sound, exactly like a sea-lion peeved.

No I don't think consumption has very much effect on what I write. (Oh,

---

1 Johnson's original title. It was published as *Symphony For Full Orchestra*.
2 In *Point Counter Point*, Aldous Huxley's novel of 1928, the character of Rampion is based on D. H. Lawrence.

my bravery with that not-quite-polite word.) I can't help what I write. It is part of me, however unpleasant a part it may be, and however necessary it should be to cauterize and castrate that part. Your belief in my power to write is one of the few things that makes me deny that twice-damned, diabetic doctor.[1] I have another believer—a communist grocer with a passion for obscurity & the Powys family. Both of you shall have a seat in heaven, or in my comfortable, but slightly wormy, hell.

Just after writing this, I received a rather disquieting note from Richard Rees[2] of the Adelphi, who, last week, asked me to send him some recent poems. He compliments me upon the high standard & the great originality exhibited, & said my technique was amazing (One Up for Formal Me), but accused me—not in quite so many words—of being in the grip of devils. 'The poems have an insubstantiality, a dreamlike quality', he writes, 'which non-plusses me.' He then goes on to say that the poems, as a whole, reminded him of automatic or trance-writing.

Automatic writing is worthless as literature, however interesting it may be to the psychologist & pathologist. So, perhaps, after all I am nothing but a literary oddity, a little freak of nature whose madness runs into print rather than into ravings and illusions. It may be, too, an illusion that keeps me writing, the illusion of myself as some misunderstood poet of talent. The note has depressed me more than the usual adverse criticism. It shows not dislike, or mere incomprehension, but confession of bewilderment, & almost fear, at the method by which I write my poetry.

But he is wrong, I swear it. My facility, as he calls it, is, in reality, tremendously hard work. I write at the speed of two lines an hour. I have written hundreds of poems, & each one has taken me a great many painful, brain-racking & sweaty hours.

If you like, pay little attention to the following criticisms of your poems, for they are based, as what I write is based, on my own peculiar standards, which may be the standards of a theorising failure & a bilious little crank.

I now stop turning over the dirty pages of my soul, lick my pencil, wipe my cold-filled nose, light a cigarette, & write

Some Frank Criticisms
Twenty To Twelve
Your ability to romanticise an atmosphere & to catch, with some considerable skill, the visual essences of a scene, is well displayed in this. But the whole thing is very slight, and would please the Refereaders more than it does me. It hangs between verse & poetry, and can either be called frail poetry or strong verse. I would prefer to call it the latter; it is a talented piece of versifying, facile, ornamental, & hung about with skilful

---

1 Perhaps a Swansea doctor, in Thomas's fantasy, who was supposed to have warned him of diabetes as well as tuberculosis.
2 Sir Richard Rees (1900–57) edited the *Adelphi*.

images. But it lacks subtlety; the images, striking as they are, are too patently obvious for the entire effect to stir much more than one's visual senses. There is no one line I can condemn; the thing is perfect, too perfect. This is more of an achievement than many other poems of yours, but the achievement is very limited. This is to me, the *wrong* direction. It is difficult to explain, in a short note, where the wrongness lies, but I do hope I have made myself clear. It has, apparently, nearly everything a poem needs—an experience, a fairly original diction, & an emotive appeal. Analysed more closely, it has nothing. You haven't given yourself enough to contend with. Knowing your own skill, you pick on something very easy to do, & do it, of course, skilfully & perfectly. Is it worth doing?

February (found the ink again)
The same thing applies. Are you going to be content with a narrow achievement or a wide promise? This, again, is pretty, skilful, and visual. And, I personally, don't care a damn for prettiness or skill, while the putting down of what the eyes have seen (plus a few literary affectations and one or two unusual literary words) has very little to do with poetry. Unless the spirit illuminates what the eyes have mirrored, then all the paraphernalia of the winter scene is as valueless as an Academy picture of Balmoral Castle.

Requiem for Spring
The same criticism applies, with the exception that in this even the skill is a little bowed at the knees.

> 'Of roses she bestows a lavish spate
> The hedgerows and the garden to bedizen'

is as bad as anything the Poet's Corner has ever printed. Indeed, every verse is. I'm glad you didn't send it for my benefit. And God help Neuburg's taste.
What was the matter with you when you wrote this?

Retrospect
All your skill and command of words, added, as you explain, to the cries of a halfmended (or is it fully mended?) heartbreak, make this a moderately good poem, with one or two touches of superlatively good writing. It is narrow, again, but its limits are the essential limits of the subject you impose on yourself.
'Brown into dust upon the morning sun' is an inevitably beautiful line, but the extraction of all the lovely phrases would mean quoting *nearly* every word. The pause in the last line is most effective.
Not perfect but promising. And if you've read all I've written before, (a sudden terrible thought that you show my letters to your mother), you'll know how complimentary this is.
One thing: phrases such as 'the mirage of eternity' are meaningless unless you qualify them.

Black Mess

No, I can't like it. I've tried very hard, but just as I'm beginning to say to myself, 'Oh well, this is quite all right,' along comes a revoltingly saccharine line, or some coy girlish sentiment, or a piece of very ordinary clumsiness.

> The lilies, the innocent lilies, are troubled,
> The trees rub their eyes awake,
> And the mice, the little mice that nibble the grasses,
> Crouch in the stones; their noses shiver with fear.

This is very pleasant; trivial, no doubt, but charmingly done; any moment a selfconscious Pan might come around the corner. Instead, that damned chorus starts again with all their 'silvered intaglio, livid seraglio' business. Occasionally I see something I like—rivers bisecting faces, 'they are surrounding the hills in a ring' (nice & simple), but far more often I see things that sicken me, the jimjackery and jugglebuggery of the *bad* and *pretentious* versifier. If you were bad and pretentious I wouldn't mind, but, as I've repeated so many times, you have nearly everything that contributes towards the make-up of an individual, original, & satisfying poet. If I didn't like you I wouldn't waste ten seconds over the Black Mass. I don't mean to be cruel, but there it is. I see, even in this *very* bad effort, the mentality that produced the Symphonic poem. But in this case you let your taste go down into the sugary vaults. Take a firm grip, for the Lord's sake, on your treacherous aptitudes for prettiness, pretty chaos, & word spinning.

The Morning Sun

By far the most curious poem you have sent me, this moves in a circle of words and feeling, disregarding itself, and falling, inevitably, into its own pattern. Even the touches I do not like do not fail in the general content, but only to the critical eye and ear that, after the first unqualifying response, pursue the ghosts of syllables into the deadends of the purist lanes. Re-reading what I have written I understand very little of it. The fault, dear Pamela, lies in your stars. Your stars are not mine; they twinkle in a different heaven, higher or lower than mine I cannot tell. Perhaps it would be as well if I contented myself with saying of this very individual poem, 'I understand and appreciate,' without bothering to go into the details of appreciation. But I cannot do that; I want you to go on writing like this, never whoring yourself to the fingers of prettiness or the charms of a cheap simile.

All your creeds of simplicity, that surely must comply with the dictates of the ballad form rather than with the long, spongy lines of the sonnet, are obeyed. Indeed, the poem opens on a ballad note, on a naive note thrilling with innumerable and subtle suggestions. The visual element is, again, very strong—I positively can see you, poor stranger in yourself, walking along the crowded pavements and gazing wonderingly down on your 'busy' hips (the perfect adjective)—but, this time, justifiably so. The language is economical and true, with a few exceptions, and the experience *is* a poetical one, and not merely the emotions of a self-confessed romanticist or the romances of a self denied sentimentalist.

Here are the exceptions: 'I think of sunlight & a pile of books.' Many bad poems, imitative of Rupert Brooke's bad poem, 'The Great Lover', include a catalogue of personal likes such as, 'Green apples in the morning sun,' 'The kiss of rain upon the rose,' and, inevitably, the more overpoweringly sentimental like—more overpowering because of its reversed sentimentality—of 'rough blankets on the skin' or 'the smell of tweeds.' The line of yours could easily be included in such a feminine catalogue. It is too sweet & reminds me too much of Percy Lubbock's 'Earlham.'[1] Alter it.

'Of brooks that gargle'

The associations are absurd, and the sound is ugly. You have said the same of phrases in *my* poems, but this is, strictly, such a beautiful thing that the intrusion of one discordant line must not spoil it.

'Will be forgotten as a twisted dream.' The adjective is wrong. You want a less sophisticated adjective, such as 'wicked' or even 'ugly', although I am not suggesting these. You will be able to find a better and more harmonious one.

For the rest I have no complaints.

> 'I feel the stocking pulling at my leg,
> And there is not a stranger in myself'

is severely and *mystically* physical, though many people won't see it. Write like this always, and I shan't grumble.

'Never strain after prettiness,' my first injunction, is now supplemented by, 'Never use your skill for the sake of skilfulness,' & 'Be yourself in your poetry as you are in your letters.' Morning Sun could have been written by no-one but yourself.

If you like, I will write more about this poem in my next letter. I have crowds of things to say about it, and some of what I say *may* help you.

Hymn of Despair and Hope

This is written on Armistice Day, 1933, when the war is no more than a memory of privations and the cutting down of the young. There was panic in the streets, we remember, and the food was bad, there were women who had 'lost' their sons, though where they had lost them and why they could [not] find them, we, who were children born out of blood into blood, could never tell. The state was a murderer, and every country in this rumour-ridden world, peopled by the unsuccessful suicides left over by the four mad years, is branded like Cain across the forehead. What was Christ in us was stuck with a bayonet to the sky, and what was Judas we fed and

---

1 Percy Lubbock (1879–1965), author and critic. *Earlham* is about his childhood.

sheltered, rewarding, at the end, with thirty hanks of flesh. Civilisation is a murderer. We, with the cross of a castrated Saviour cut on our brows, sink deeper and deeper with the days into the pit of the West. The head of Christ is to be inspected in the museum, dry as a mole's hand in its glass case. And all the dominions of heaven have their calculated limits; the stars move to man's arithmetic; and the sun, leering like a fool over the valleys of Europe, sinks as the drops in a test-tube dry and are gone.

This is a lament on the death of the West. Your bones and mine shall manure an empty island set in a waste sea. The stars shall shine over England, but the darkness of England, and the sarcophagus of a spoonfed nation, and the pitch in the slain souls of our children, will never be lit.

'And the earth was without form and void; and darkness was upon the face of the deep.' The old buffers of this world still cling to chaos, believing it to be Order. The day will come when the old Dis-Order changeth, yielding to a new Order. Genius is being strangled every day by the legion of old Buffers, by the last long line of the Edwardians, clinging, for God and capital, to an outgrown and decaying system. Light is being turned to darkness by the capitalists and industrialists. There is only one thing you and I, who are of this generation, must look forward to, must work for and pray for, and, because, as we fondly hope, we are poets and voicers not only of our personal selves but of our social selves, we must pray for it all the more vehemently. It is the Revolution. There is no need for it to be a revolution of blood. We do not ask that. All that we ask for is that the present Dis-Order, this medieval machine which is grinding into powder the bones and guts of the postwar generation, shall be broken in two, and that all that is in us of godliness and strength, of happiness and genius, shall be allowed to exult in the sun. We are said to be faithless, because our God is not a capitalist God, to be unpatriotic because we do not believe in the Tory Government. We are said to be immoral because we know that marriage is a dead institution, that the old rigid monogamous lifelong union of male and female—the exceptions are the exceptions of beauty—is a corrupted thought.

The hope of Revolution, even though all of us will not admit it, is uppermost in all our minds. If there were not that revolutionary spark within us, that faith in a new faith, and that belief in our power to squash the chaos surrounding us like a belt of weeds, we would turn on the tap of war and drown ourselves in its gases.

Everything is wrong that forbids the freedom of the individual. The governments are wrong, because they are the committees of prohibitors; the presses are wrong, because they feed us what they desire to feed us, and not what we desire to eat; the churches are wrong, because they standardize our gods, because they label our morals, because they laud the death of a vanished Christ, and fear the crying of the new Christ in the wilderness; the poets are wrong, because their vision is not a vision but a squint; they look at our world, and yet their eyes are staring back along the roads of the past centuries, never into the huge, electric promise of the future.

There is injustice, muddleheadedness, criminal ignorance, corrupted and inverted virtue, hypocrisy and stone blindness, in every sphere of life. If only for one moment the Western world could drop the veils that, ever since the Reformation, have clung around it like the films of a disease, and look, with lightened eyes, upon the cess it has created, on the greatness it has spilt & strangled, on the starvation it has fostered, on the perversions and ignorances it has taught, then it would die for shame. And we, who have not been long enough alive to be corrupted utterly, could build out of its manuring bones the base of an equal and sensible civilisation.

I will not bore you with any more propaganda, though why it should bore you God knows, for it is near to you as it is to me. Later, in another letter, I will give you a more reasoned outline of Revolution, the hard facts of communism—which is above communism for it holds the individual above everything else—and hope that you, too, may don your scarlet tie, and, striding into the Hampstead dens, scorch the Creative Lifers with an invective their poor bloody brains could never fathom.

But only if it does *not* bore you. The precious seeds of revolution must not be wasted, though I do not think they will be in you.

The Arty Party

The type of party you describe—and you describe it very well indeed—is a menace to art, much as I dislike the phrase. Wyndham (Tar) Lewis has struck them hard in 'Apes of God'; D. B. (Blue Moon) Lewis has poked them gently to see if they bite as well as bark;[1] Roy Campbell,[2] in his 'Georgiad', has trampled them down under the feet of his eighteenth-century charger; but still they flourish. Still do seedy things in their mothers' pyjamas, enthuse over some soon-to-be-forgotten lyricist, or some never-to-be-heard-of painter of nature in the raw and angular. Neuter men and lady tenors rub shoulders with 'the shams and shamans, the amateur hobo and homo of Bloomsbury W.C.1', while their hostess, clad in scarlet corduroy, drinks to their health in methylated spirits.

With a smattering, often incorrectly memorised, of encyclopedia learning, with the names of the transient stars of their decade on the tips of their tongues, with their men's breasts shaped with the aid of wadding, the young women speak on. Sodomhipped young men, with the inevitable sidewhiskers and cigarettes, the faulty livers and the stained teeth, reading Lawrence as an aphrodisiac and Marie Corelli in their infrequent baths, spew onto paper and canvas their ignorance and perversions, wetting the bed of their brains with discharges of fungoid verse. This is the art of to-

1 (Percy) Wyndham Lewis (1882–1957), writer and artist; *Tarr* (1918) was a novel. Dominic Bevan Wyndham Lewis (1894–1969), writer and satirist; *At the Sign of the Blue Moon* was a collection of humorous articles from the *Daily Mail*.
2 Roy Campbell (1901–57), South African-born poet, later a friend of Thomas.

day: posturing, shamming, cribbing, and all the artifice of a damned generation.

In the corner stands an emaciated female chanting that sentimental ballad, 'Proust A Song At Twilight'. From behind a divan rises a grisly laugh. Someone has made a joke about André Gide.

Seedy Young Thing Do you like Ibsen? *P.H.J.* No, I prefer Glauber.[1]

Oversight

Thank you for the detailed criticism of the '16 Poems'—a hell of a lot, really, to inflict on you in one dose—but as I haven't kept a copy of the little book I don't [know] which poems you are criticizing. It's terrible: I read 'This is a ghastly line', or 'this is very wormy', and I immediately want to look up the particular poem and agree with you. But I can't. In the next letter send me *all* the first lines with the numbers above them, will you? Don't forget.

On Skeletons

I was neither surprised or revolted at the sight of your little grinning skeleton. When you do sink you sink deep enough into the sugary pits to please all the Women's Friends in England. Don't you dare do it again.

I, too, have a wicked secret. I used to write articles for the Northcliffe Press on 'Do Novelists make Good Husbands?' and 'Are Poets Mad?' etc.— very literary, very James Douglas, very bloody.[2] I don't do that any more now: I ran the Northcliffe Press into a libel suit by calling Miss Nina Hamnett (she wrote the book called 'Laughing Torso', I don't know whether you remember it) insane. Apparently she wasn't, that was the trouble.

Epilogue

I've neglected to touch on several of the points I intended to, and I've left many of your comments unanswered. But five of these huge, tinily written sheets are enough to give you at a time. Write very soon, not in a week but in a few days; I'm giving you a whole week-end to compose your notes. Make them as long as these 'ere. I'm enclosing one poem, just finished.[3] It's quite my usual stuff, I'm afraid, & quite probably you won't like it. But, honestly, the one 'cancer' mentioned *is* necessary. And I will try to be good in future.

Dylan

Looking back over these notes I see many of them to be unusually aggressive & particularly humourless. Sorry!

And another thing before I forget it: If this letter is illegible—you haven't complained of my ugly writing once yet—tell me, & my next letter shall be done on the typewriter.

About the Chertsey trip. I'm terribly dubious at the moment about when I

---

1 Glauber salts, an old-fashioned purgative.
2 James Douglas, a clever bigot who edited the *Sunday Express* and wrote polemics about issues of the day.
3 Probably 'When once the twilight locks', dated 11 November in a notebook.

am coming up. I want a really good excuse first. I might be able to arrange a meeting with Middleton Murry—I met him this August in Chelsea. Or even with T. S. Eliot. (God 'elp me.) More about this, & other things, again.

MS: Buffalo

T. S. ELIOT[1]

[November 1933]   5 Cwmdonkin Drive   Uplands   Swansea

Dear Sir,

Richard Rees of the Adelphi has already, I believe, given a number of my poems to Mr Herbert Read who wrote to say that he, in his turn, was handing them over to you for your consideration.

Last week Richard Rees asked me to send him some more recent poems. I did so, and received the reply which I am enclosing along with a selection of recently written poems.

I do hope you will be able to find time to read them, if only to corroborate or contradict the suggestion of 'automatic' writing, the slightest idea of which is entirely unfounded. The fluency complained of is the result of extraordinarily hard work, and, in my opinion, the absence of 'knotty or bony passages' is again the result of much energetic labour—however misdirected—and of many painful hours spent over the smoothing and removing of the creakinesses of conflict.

Yours sincerely,
Dylan Thomas

PS: I hope you will not mind my sending the poems or the writing of such a troubled letter.

MS: Valerie Eliot

PAMELA HANSFORD JOHNSON
[early December 1933][2]

In The Bath

The water is lapping upon my abdominal shore, and a cigarette-end, slowly disintegrating, is being carried along by the steaming stream that runs, like a stream from the springs of hell, over my feet. No, this is not an abstraction; I am lying in the bath, smoking Woodbines, and staring, through hot mists, on to the paper that lies on my front. I cover the waterfront. The click, click of the geyser sounds like the distant champing

---

1 T. S. Eliot (1888–1965) was the director in charge of the poetry list at Faber.
2 The letter refers (page 80) to 'a literary party held in one's own little honour', and Johnson's diary for Saturday 25 November records, 'Party held in my honour by Victor and Runia'. The diary notes letters received from Thomas on 1 and 11 December.

of a lady tenor. All is very wet and white, giving rise to thoughts on life and love, on the impermanence of human emotions, the futility of personal effort, the dirty doings of Creative doctors, and the sudden alarming thought of Cinderella. Now it is hot and still. Peace, like an old hat, sits on me.

This is nonsense, of course, but it is a good opening to a letter; it tears down all formalities; it does away with many of the layers of bluff, double bluff, and self-doubt that so often prevent me from saying what I want to say; it is as intimate as the legs of the Pope's pyjamas.

But it is difficult, in this blasted bath, to know what to write about. In the ebullience of my youth and the limitless depths of my greenaged immodesty, I confess to having opinions on everything under the sun. The opinions are often immoderate, generally impetuous, and always verbose. But that matters very little. The great thing is to think, however wrongly.

What shall I regale you with: an attack on George Too Shaw To Be Good? a defence of Lesbia? a belief in vegetarianism? But no—George is clever but visionless; Lesbia is an aestiaboginous (I can't spell it)[1] island; and vegetarianism is inevitable.

Let me, instead, scrub the marks of the roads from my little feet, cough, spit, and whistle, pull up the plug, and retire, like an emaciated Cupid with pen for arrow, to a bleak, unmaidened bed.

In The Bed

Now that the drunkenness of a too-hot bath is wearing off a little, and the water of the bath has got into the ink, I shall write in pencil a few straightforward [*In the margin:* oh yeah?] facts.

THOMAS: HIS IDEAS

I am looking forward to what you've written—or are still writing—of the 'Woman Arisen'; I should love to add my few stanzas, or the ideas for the few stanzas (whichever you like), though my experience of waking with a woman at my side has been necessarily limited.

The medieval laws of this corrupted hemisphere have dictated a more or less compulsory virginity during the period of life when virginity should be regarded as a crime against the dictates of the body. During the period of adolescence, when the blood and seed of the growing flesh need, for the first time and more than ever again, communion and contact with the blood and seed of another flesh, sexual relationships are looked upon as being unnecessary and unclean. The body must be kept intact for marriage, which is rarely possible before the age of twenty; the physical expression of sex must be caged up for six or more years until, for the price of a ring, a licence, and a few hampering words, opportunity is presented with all the ceremony of a phallic religion. But so often the opportunity comes too late; the seed has soured; love has turned to lust, and lust to sadism; the mind

1 Neuburg popularised and probably coined the word 'ostrobogulous', using it to suggest the bawdy or bizarre (*OED Supplement*, Vol III, 1982, has an entry). This seems to be what Thomas intended.

has become covered and choked by the weeds of inhibition; and the union of two starved creatures, suddenly allowed the latitude of their sexes, is doomed from the start. The woman carries her marriage licence about with her as a bitch might carry the testimony of its liberated heat.

Such things may not be pleasant to talk about, but they do exist, and they are evil.

From the first months of puberty, girls & boys should be allowed to know their bodies (I am not trying to twist phrases, nor am I wishing to write down the bare words in all their ugliness). More than that, their sexual expression should be encouraged. It would be very nearly impossible for a young girl to live, permanently, with a young boy, especially if both were in school; they would not live together peaceably; they would have no money, and it would be difficult for them to earn. But the family of the girl should, for a certain time—the time of the mutual devotion of boy and girl—keep the boy in their house. And vice-versa. The lives of the boy and girl would continue individually—there would be school and school associations for both of them—but their domestic closeness and their sleeping together would blend the two individual lives in one, & would keep both brains & bodies perpetually clean. And both would grow up physically and mentally uncontaminated and refreshened.

Don't think I'm regaling you with some crank-ridden, pornographic notion. I really believe in what I say, and no argument has ever shifted my belief. It is not a theory, but an adjustment of the present corrupted facts to uncorrupted ideals. The issues of such an adjustment are, of course, tremendous; they attack the basis of established morals and the foundations of society. But are they wrong?* [*In the margin:* *This is a question to *you*.]

To expand the argument, let me point out that some sort of attraction or devotion would have to be the prelude of the association of the boy and girl. The two sexes, on reaching puberty, would not be lumped inconsiderately together; the honest friendship of boy & girl would be allowed entire freedom and culmination, that is all. There would be no binding agreements between the two families, and boy and girl could have as many lovers as they wished, until, eventually, they find a lover with whom they could [?live] for a longer time, or for ever.

After that—and pray God it didn't sound like Mr. Mybug in an inspired moment—let me return to the beginning. Send me the 'Woman Arises' with your next letter, and, conjuring up the emotions of husbandly love, I shall attempt to send it back—*with* additions—in *my* next.

But real collaboration has to be more than this. The poem *has to be born* in the presence of the two authors. And I hope that it won't be very long before that is possible.

Just a Word

You were very stern about the fragments of poems I sent you. They were written when I was fourteen, remember, and they damned well *had* to be bad.

Uncommon

Tomorrow, when this is posted, I shall send you my 'Uncommon Genesis', that much-promised story. I'm afraid it's rather long, and will take up a lot of your time. Do read it, though, won't you, and tell me exactly what you think of it. It was written just under a year ago, written straight off and never revised. When I was typing it, I saw all sorts of sentences that, had I been more careful, I should not have hesitated to correct or cut out altogether. Not being careful, I typed out good and bad. And here it is.

The passages in red type should really be in italics. You'll have to excuse the typing all along: in some places it's abominable. But I'm not very nimble-fingered at the best of times, and my machine, as you've noticed from the poems I've sent you, is moody and antique. It possesses all the French accents, but, unfortunately, I write in English.

'Uncommon Genesis' is an uncommon story (I'm sorry to preface it with so many absurd remarks), and you'll either like it, or dislike it very strongly. I'm hoping you'll like it. It has to be read with an unbiased mind, for it is written in a high and wordily romantic style that could, if the attention was shifted only momentarily off its meaning, be turned to bathos. But if you do really read it carefully & without prejudice, I don't think you will laugh. But you tell me all about it, if you will.

It's just struck me: Since we've been writing to one another I've loaded you with an immense quantity of my stuff; crowds of my poems accompany every letter; and now here comes over 20 closely typed sheets to add to the pile. Perhaps it would be better if I gave you a little rest—not from letter-writing, I'll be damned if I'll stop that—but from the inclusion of so much of my stuff. I know you honestly like it—just as I honestly like so much of the little I have seen of yours—but you can have too much of a good thing.

More about Luv

Thank you for telling me about your lost, but not forgotten, lovers, and if the pages did occasionally remind me of Ella M. Ruck, that composite novelist and poet, they were none the less sincere for that.[1]

And that was a horribly patronising remark, the remark of an introvertive crank on the extravertism (what a word!) of a far superior person. I'm very sorry. It probably took a great deal of courage for you to tell me about the frigid reader of newspapers upon whom you wasted such a lot of your affection. And who, by the navel of St. Francis, am I to comment on it? You paid me a compliment by telling me about him, & the G.N.L., & the British boy (your taste doesn't seem to lie in the direction of the arty & Poetical young men), & the emotional part of me thanks you very much. Never mind the intellectual part: that is nothing.

But why, if you fall in love again—& you are bound to at some time or another—will you not give again all that you gave before, not necessarily

1 The sentimental poet Ella Wheeler Wilcox and the romantic novelist Berta Ruck.

That Which Is Dearer etc., but all the energy of your youngness (youth, here, is the wrong word), your sweetness etc. (I evade saying everything, you know), your brightness & sulkiness and every other bloody mood and feeling you possess. I said your failing was the failing of loving too much. It is, and it always will be. So fasten your affections on some immaculately profiled young man, and love the swine to death. Love among the angels is a perpetual distemper.

(It didn't remind me of Ella M., really. I loved it, only I'm too xxxx selfconscious to say so, damn my rabbit's eyes!)

My Life. The Touching Autobiography Continued From the Last Letter But Three (or Four)

Gower is a very beautiful peninsula, some miles from this blowsy town, and so far the Tea-Shop philistines have not spoilt the more beautiful of its bays. Gower, as a matter of fact, is one of the loveliest sea-coast stretches in the whole of Britain, and some of its tiny villages are as obscure, as little inhabited, and as lovely as they were a hundred years ago.* [In the margin: *this sounds like a passage from a Tourists' Guide.]

I often go down in the mornings to the furthest point of Gower—the village of Rhossilli—and stay there until evening. The bay is the wildest, bleakest, and barrennest I know—four or five miles of yellow coldness going away into the distance of the sea. And the Worm* [In the margin: *Perhaps this accounts for my Complex], a seaworm of rock pointing into the channel, is the very promontory of depression. Nothing live on it but gulls and rats, the millionth generation of the winged and tailed families that screamed in the air and ran through the grass when the first sea thudded on the Rhossilli beach. There is one table of rock on the Worm's back that is covered with long yellow grass, and, walking on it, one [feels] like something out of the Tales of Mystery & Imagination treading, for a terrible eternity, on the long hairs of rats. Going over that grass is one of the strangest experiences; it gives under one's feet; it makes little sucking noises, & smells—and this to me is the most grisly smell in the world— like the fur of rabbits after rain.

When the tide comes in, the reef of needle rocks that leads to the base of the Worm, is covered under the water. I was trapped on the worm once. I had gone on it early in the afternoon with a book & a bag of food, and, going to the very, very end, had slept in the sun, with the gulls crying like mad over me. And when I woke the sun was going down. I ran over the rocks, over the abominable grass, and on to the ridge overlooking the little reef. The tide had come in. I stayed on that Worm from dusk till midnight, sitting on the top grass, frightened to go further in because of the rats and because of the things I am ashamed to be frightened of. Then the tips of the reef began to poke out of the water, &, perilously, I climbed along them on to the shore, with an 18 mile walk in front of me. It was a dark, entirely silent, entirely [?empty] road. I saw everything on that walk—from snails, lizards, glow worms & hares to diaphanous young ladies in white who vanished as I approached them.

One day, when I know you even better than I do now, you must come &
stay with me, some time in the summer. Swansea is a dingy hell, and my
mother is a vulgar humbug; but I'm not so bad, and Gower is as beautiful as
anywhere.

There is one bay almost too lovely to look at. You shall come & see it
with me; we shall both utter words of maudlin wonder, and swoon away on
the blasted heath.

My father was a master in the Swansea Grammar School, and still would
be, for he is not yet old enough to retire. But the last three months he has
spent in the London University Hospital, undergoing treatment for cancer
of the throat. He is home now, partially cured and exceedingly despondent.[1] His time limit is even shorter than mine (!). Ours is a nice 'ouse.*
There is one unintelligent dog, too, with the highly original name of Spot.
[In the margin: *All this doesn't sound very nice after an invitation,
however awkward, does it? I mean it, though.]

I will write more—not, fortunately for you, more of this depressing serial
autobiography—tomorrow. Now I am going to wash and shave, preparatory
to travelling to Gwaun-cae-Gurwen (I love introducing names like these),
where a spirited melodrama will be rendered by a talented cast. Thank
you.

Coplans (?) Comment

Why didn't someone kick that perverted doctor in the bottom? Aren't
any of the Creative Lifers men of action? Here in barbaric Wales, where
men are men, he would have been stoned to death by members of Y
Gobaith Cymru Wrdd.[2]

There's a charming incident in some novel—I can't remember which—
where a very narsty young man lies at the feet of a very nice young girl, &,
looking into her eyes, says, 'You remind me of cabbages and big brown
messes—I adore you'. It's much the same type of incident, with the
exception that I am sure you do not remind anybody of such things. But,
really, the astonishing part of that astonishing party—and it must be
pleasant to have a literary party held in one's own little honour*—was the
way in which the narsty doctor was tolerated for so long. Creative Lifer or
not, I should have bitten him severely in the calf. [In the margin: *Bah,
envy!]

Your aversion to him he most certainly will put down to inhibitions on
your part; perverted & unsuccessful lechers of his variety never believe
that their love-making (far too good a word) could appeal only to the base of
the stomach.

Interlude for Refreshments

No, I don't really spit in the piano, so there'll be no need to nail the top
down. And I certainly indulge in the singing of lewd roundelays. I shall

1 D. J. Thomas was treated in the hospital from 10 to 20 September, and from 10 to 24
October. The cancer (of the mouth) was eradicated by 1934, and he lived another
eighteen years.
2 Urdd Gobaith Cymru, the Welsh League of Youth. Dr Coplans: a friend of Johnson.

probably turn shy, & hide myself in the lavatory all day (up the stairs, first to the right).

My only real domestic vice is my indiscriminate sprinkling of cigarette ash over everything and everybody. Apart from this, I am not a particular nuisance, and I smell quite nice. I look about fourteen, and I have a large, round nose; nature gave it to me, but fate, and a weak banister, broke it; in cold weather it is sufficiently glossy to light up any room. When I am about on winter nights there is no need for the gas.

Cough! cough! cough! my death is marching on; the Venus in front of me cocks a marble eye in my direction, & the calendar, with a watercolour view of Lake Como, sways in the incredibly cold wind.

First Epilogue

I was sorry after sending those three sheets of socialism; they were nothing but facts, and facts, unvarnished, are always boring or bewildering. I am not going to indulge in any more propaganda in this letter; I shall keep two or three red hot notes—along with a note on W. H. Auden, the Poet of Revolution—& send them to you next time.

So the Tharp ranks oratory as one of the Fine Arts? I don't know about that, but the speaking of poetry is certainly one of them. You shall read some 'tweety' poems to me one day, &, rolling my Cymric r's, I shall reply.

Second Epilogue

This letter isn't as long as most of the letters I send you, but the long enclosed story does more than compensate. I'll write a *very* long letter next week; it will probably need a special postman to deliver it all by itself.

And if you don't reply very quickly & at great length, I shall turn myself, with considerable magic, into a winter fly, & come and die in your hair. This is the most terrible threat I know. Let it close the letter, along with an expression of bonhomie, and Old School affection.

Dylan

[*On the back of the sheet—two drawings of himself, cigarette dangling.*]

I'm sorry about this. It was on the back, & I didn't see it. I don't always draw like that, thank God.

MS: Buffalo

PAMELA HANSFORD JOHNSON
[about 21 December 1933][1]

Unwilling Reply

Nothing I can think of—including the personal delivery of Miss Garbo in a tin box—would please me so much as to spend Christmas with you, and to talk to you (though, really, I don't talk as much as all that) until Boxing

1 Johnson's diary notes receipt of a letter, 'with photo & book of poems from my little Dylan', 22 December.

Day. The towel and the jar of holly, especially the jar of holly, are terribly big temptations. But I must stand like a little martyr, denying the calls of the flesh (no, I don't mean that at all; it sounds as though you'd invited me to a pyjama party) and obeying, instead, the requests of a benighted family. My sister, brother-in-law and uncle will be down here for the holiday, and great fun will be had by all. Will it, hell! We'll all eat too much, I suppose, read the newspapers, sleep, and crack nuts. There will be no Yuletide festivity about it, and I, in an extra-black shirt, will brood over the fire, contemplating in the coals, the shapes of past Miseries and Follies.

I'm flattered to receive a Christmas invitation from you, from you who have known me for such a little time and in such unusual ways—more flattered (and terribly pleased) than I can tell you.

(By the way, I've discovered a new way of getting ill. You buy an ounce of Sailors' Plug Tobacco, a little machine for making cigarettes, and a packet of cigarette papers. Put a layer of Plug in the machine, put in the paper, turn round, draw out, and smoke the result. It's the worst taste I've ever known. I'm smoking one now.)

Your mother, I suppose, is in the charming invitation, too. Give her my Christmas greetings, and tell her to write separately and give me the low-down on her daughter (how the daughter is a champion ice-skater or steeple-chaser or Derby winner, how she likes Berta Ruck so much more than James Joyce, how she writes novels in her spare time and contributes to the, say to the 'Ladies' Chat' and 'Miriam's Weekly').

By the way, again, have you written any prose? If so, let me see it, won't you? I remember you told me something in a very longago letter about some stories you'd put on the fire. But aren't there *any* stories not used so harshly and, I'm sure, so needlessly? I think you should be able to write very good prose. But then, as I said before somewhere, I'm *very* biased.

I'd love to spend Christmas with you. Circumstances say otherwise, and my father is going up to Hospital in London in the first few days of January to have, as far as I know, several very necessary glands removed.

Three Poems

I don't honestly feel disposed to throw you a bone for your three most recent poems; you certainly deserve a whole puppy biscuit for the sixteen lines of 'Quest', and also, perhaps, a little bit of puppy food for the 'Motorists'. But you don't get a single mouthful for 'December Trees'.

'Quest' This is a very slight thing but quite successful in its limits, and the last five lines are attractive *because* of their slightness and simplicity. 'Weeps, just because of it', a rather whimsy line, might be improved by the deletion of the comma which makes, to me, a quite unessential pause. I haven't decided yet about the adjective 'unquiet'. As a rule I dislike such negative words, except in very especial instances. If a thing is not quiet there is no real need to say that it is not; it is much better to say what it is. 'Unquiet' doesn't *qualify* the mouse; I've told you of my belief as to the poetical function of the adjective before, haven't I?—'unquiet' doesn't add anything to the mouse. The thing to remember is that everyone has his different associations for every word; one person may, for some Freudian reason, associate 'mouse' with horrors and death's heads, another with a certain soft material and colour. So the poet who is going to put an adjective before 'mouse' must say to himself: I have two alternatives; either I can create such a tremendous and universal adjective that it will *embrace* every association built around the word—that is, it must be an adjective that complies with all the associations from horror to colour—; or I must create an adjective that will *break down* all associations, and make the 'mouse' a new thing with new associations. Does 'unquiet' satisfy either of those tests. I don't know. I rather think, despite my theories, that it is a very effective word. It must be one of those especial instances where such a negation can be used.

The Motorists   This is much the sort of thing that another (no, no, please, I don't mean that) of Neuburg's animals produces—one Harry Hodgkinson by name. The last four lines are, unfortunately, for they are good, spoilt for me by the fact that I know a very vulgar schoolboy poem in the same metre. The poem (the 'Motorists', not 'Eskimo Nell')[1] is bright and refreshing, but the sort of cheery poetry that makes me even more depressed than the 'City of Everlasting Night.'[2] That, again, is personal. As a rule I try to criticise your poems from a *pure* poetical standpoint, but various things prevent me from doing it with this. And down comes my omnipotent criticship with a bump. 'And scratch her great, brown face' is clumsy. Why the two bumpy little adjectives? Go on, tell me it's intentional.

December Trees   Just what you shouldn't write. Leave these 'Notes from a Rambler's Log Book', to other and far less talented young women. It's the easiest and least valuable form of valueless impressionism.

> 'December trees—
> Brown mists above the fields'

is the sort of opening one comes across on nearly every other page of 'The Best (or Worst) Poems of the Year,' which is a collection of the shattered pieces of sentimental romanticism swept up by that literary charwoman, Mr Thomas Moult.[3]

> 'October fields—
> A breath of wind about the sedge,
> A speckled rabbit in a hedge,
> And cold white snow.'

No, girl, no. This is terribly unworthy of you. Develop—and you *can* develop at a tremendous speed—along the lines of 'Quest' and 'I feel I am a stranger',

---

1 The bawdy 'Ballad of Eskimo Nell', also well known in the armed forces, may have originated in Canada.

2 'The City of Dreadful Night' is the melancholy poem by the alcoholic James Thomson (1834–82).

3 Thomas Moult (d. 1974) edited a long-running annual series, *The Best Poems of . . .*, on traditional lines.

that lovely poem that does and always will remain in my memory. Write out of yourself, and leave the hedgerows and the *visual* aspects of the countryside. And another thing: don't be afraid, at this stage of your development, to intellectualise more. Intellect alone never makes good poetry. You have the essential attributes of poetry, so can do no harm to yourself by letting your intellect have, now, a certain amount of freedom.

Hints for Recognition

The gradual shrinking you complain of is chiefly mental, for the more despondent I become the littler and weaker I feel.

Height—five foot six (about).

Weight—eight stone ten (about).

Hair—some sort of rat-coloured brown.

Eyes—big, brown and green (this sounds as though one were brown & the other green; the colours are mixed).

Distinguishing Marks—Three moles on right cheek, scar on arm and ankle, though as I generally wear socks you won't see the little mark there.

Sex—male, I think.

Voice—I suppose it would be called baritone, though sometimes it sweeps towards tenor and sometimes droops towards bass. Except in moments of hilarity, I believe I speak without an accent.

Size of Feet—five (this is not number).

Cigarettes—Players, forty a day stuck in centre of mouth.

Food—Hay.

This is neither very funny nor very illuminating, I admit, but I must, by any method possible, steer clear of the soulful outpouring that ended my last letter. I apologise, incidentally, for apologising for the overflow of feeling. I should have known how interesting such overflowing is, because the little, pulsating bits in your letters—when you defend your theism before a pack of negative-brained scoffers, or dwell, unhappily but unbrokenly, upon the passing of juvenile loves—are of immense interest to [me], who am also pleased by the fact that I have your confidence. My little Welsh ear is open for all secrets.

But the prospect of being comforted—insubstantially, it is true, but then the substance of life is and always will be to *me* less than the unreality—by a nice and slant-eyed shade, tempts me to indulge in even more abysmal desolations of the spirit.

From a letter to my Aunt, Discussing the Correct Approach to Modern Poetry.

> To you, my aunt, who would explore
> The literary Chankley Bore,
> The paths are hard for you are not
> A literary Hottentot

But just a kind and cultured dame
Who knows not Eliot (to her shame).
Fie on you, aunt, that you should see
No genius in David G.,
No elemental form and sound
In T.S.E. and Ezra Pound.
Fie on you, aunt! I'll show you how
To elevate your middle brow,
And how to scale and see the sights
From modernist Parnassian heights.

First buy a hat, no Paris model
what a line! But one the Swiss wear when they yodel,
A bowler thing with one or two
Feathers to conceal the view.
And then in sandals walk the street
(All modern painters use their feet
For painting, on their canvas strips,
Their wives or mothers minus hips.)
Then sport an open skirt and blouse,
For every arty thing allows
Her wretchèd bosom to be loosed
For men to see who talk of Proust.
Remember this at every table
Talk as rudely as you're able,
And never pass the peas with less
Than *one* remark on sexiness.

Your wardrobe done, (forget the rest,
The little things like drawers and vest),
You next must learn the tricks of speech
sorry! (Here nothing rhymes but 'Chelsea Reach').[1]
Learn to begin with words like these:
'Chiaroscuro', 'Bright's Disease',
'Timbre', 'soul', 'essential cheese',
'The social art', 'the rhomboid quip',
'The rhythmic works of Stink and Drip',
'The Joyce of Love', 'the D. H. 'Ell',
'The formal spheres of Little Nell'.
With such fine phrases on your tongue,
A knowledge of the old and Jung,
You can converse in any party
And keep the conversation arty.

Perhaps it would be best if you
Created something very new,

---

1 Johnson's first poem in the *Sunday Referee* (23 April 1933) was 'Chelsea Reach'.

A dirty novel done in Erse
Or written backwards in Welsh verse,
Or paintings on the backs of vests,
Or Sanskrit psalms on lepers' chests.
But if this proved imposs-i-bel
Perhaps it would be just as well,
For you could then write what you please,
And modern verse is done with ease.

Do not forget that 'limpet' rhymes
With 'strumpet' in these troubled times,
And commas are the worst of crimes;
Few understand the works of Cummings,
And few James Joyce's mental slummings,
And few young Auden's coded chatter;
But then it is the few that matter.
Never be lucid, never state,
If you would be regarded great,
The simplest thought or sentiment,
(For thought, we know, is decadent);
Never omit such vital words
As belly, genitals, and ——,
For these are things that play a part
(And what a part) in all good art.
Remember this: each rose is wormy,
And every lovely woman's germy;
Remember this: that love depends
On how the Gallic letter[1] bends;
Remember, too, that life is hell
And even heaven has a smell
Of putrefying angels who
Make deadly whoopee in the blue.
These things remembered, what can stop
A poet going to the top?
A final word: before you start
The convolutions of your art,
Remove your brains, take out your heart;
Minus these curses, you can be
A genius like David G.

Take courage, aunt, and send your stuff
To Geoffrey Grigson with my luff,
And may I yet live to admire
How well your poems light the fire.

---

1 Does 'Gallic letter' mean 'French letter', ie condom?

More Theorising

Only today, after reading for the hundredth time out of the 'Plumed Serpent',[1] have I come to make a valuation of Lawrence. And as nearly everyone today has some sort of set ideas upon that almost legendary figure, it may interest you to know what conclusions I—on the outskirts of the literary world, if any such world exists—have reached. I don't know whether you'll follow all of this note; anyway it isn't worth burrowing into the syntactical tunnels I so often lose myself in.

Lawrence was a moralist, a preacher, but his morals & his sermons were not progressive. He preached a doctrine of paganism and, to the best of his tubercular ability, attempted to lead a pagan life. But the more paganistic, sun-and-sex loving, one becomes, the less one feels the desire to write. A born writer is born scrofulous; his career is an accident dictated by physical or circumstantial disabilities. Lawrence preached paganism, and paganism, as the life by the body in the body for the body, is a doctrine that contents man with his lot. It defies the brain, and it is only through the brain that man can realise the chaos of civilisation and attempt to better it. Aldous Huxley, as his direct protagonist, preaches the sermon of the intellect; his god is cellular, and his heaven a socialist Towards. He would, as someone brighter than myself has said, condense the generative principle into a test-tube; Lawrence, on the other hand, would condense the world into the generative principle, and make his apostles decline not cogitare but copulare.

The young writer, if he would wish to label himself at all, must class himself under one of two headings: under the philosophy (for want of a better word) which declares the body to be all and the intellect nothing, and which would limit the desires of life, the perceptions and the creation of life, within the walls of the flesh; or under the philosophy which, declaring the intellect and the reason and the intelligence to be *all*, denies the warmth of the blood and the body's promise. You have to class yourself under one heading—the labels might overlap a *little*—for the equilibrium between flesh and not-flesh can never be reached by an individual. While the life of the body is, perhaps, more directly pleasant, it *is* terribly limited, and the life of the non-body, while physically unsatisfying, *is* capable of developing, of realising infinity, of getting somewhere, and of creating an artistic progeny.

Lawrence and his disease grew parallel, and one was nothing without the other. If he had had no disease, he would have been a pagan liver, and would never have written at all. As it was, weak and diseased, he wrote of the struggle of the ideas of the pagan strong. And his literature, therefore, however valuable, is a *lie* from start to finish.

Perhaps I haven't developed the argument sufficiently, and perhaps, O uncomplaining receiver of so many half-baked theories, I may be entirely wrong.

1 D. H. Lawrence's violent novel (1926), set in Mexico.

You get a rather beastly angle on Lawrence if you read, 'Lorenzo in Taos'.[1] And unless you want to regard the man as a vain, weakchinned, egocentric, domineering little charlatan, *don't* borrow the book.

Us Girls

How is 'Cinderella' going on? This is a really *interested* question, although it leads up to another personal statement. I've just started rehearsals for the 'Way of the World',[2] a play to be carted around the Welsh valleys where they won't understand one bawdy word from the beginning to the end. Do you know the play? (Of course you do.) I'm playing Witwoud, the second consecutive effeminate part. Much more of this type of playing, and I shall be becoming decidedly girlish.

Have you remarked upon the terrible young men of this generation, the willing-buttocked, celluloid-trousered, degenerates who are gradually taking the place of the bright young things of even five years ago? Or is the degeneracy, the almost unbelievable effeminacy, the product of the Welsh slums alone? In an hotel last night a boy, wearing a light green hat, white shirt, red tie, light green trousers and tightly fitting fawn overcoat, went up to the bar and said 'A whate port and a smale Ardathe, girlie'. I heard him. He was the most perfect example I've ever seen, the sort of thing one hears of in coarse stories but rarely encounters in the flesh (God deliver me from the flesh; the outer trappings are enough). I see more and more of them every day. They always existed, but in recent months—it seems months to me—they are coming, unashamedly, out into the open. I saw one with a drunken nigger last night.

It is the only vice, I think, that revolts me and makes me misanthropic. I can—theoretically—tolerate even incest (Tell me, have you read Leonhard Frank's 'Brother & Sister';[3] if not, get hold of it by some method and *do* read it; it's brilliant) and other domestic sins. But the sin of the boy with the nigger goes up like a rocketed scab to Heaven.

I'm trying to borrow that historical novel. Do you still keep up a correspondence with the author, or am I your only deliver[er] of long and literary—not always literary, either—letters?

Devils

Today I am starting on a new short story which will in a few weeks, I hope, be finished and good enough to send you. The theme of the story I dreamed in a nightmare. If successful, if the words fit to the thoughts, it will be one of the most ghastly short stories ever written. The action in it will be grisly enough, but—if it will come to pass—the tone of it will be so quiet that the horror should rise up like a clot of blood in the throat. 'I brought the broom for her to brush it into the wall', is the opening sentence

---

1 By Mabel Dodge Luhan (1933).
2 The comedy by William Congreve (1670–1729). Sir Wilfull Witwoud is an amiable buffoon.
3 First published in Germany, 1930; English translation by Cyrus Brooks the same year.

which, standing alone, is quite meaningless. But even alone it is horrible to me.

This is no despondency to-day. I feel like a dead man exulting in the company of his beetles, incarnadining the monstrous earth—words, words, words—with the blood of the worms (yes, worms again, my dear) that he breaks—as a housemaid crushes a flea—between the tips of his nails.

Sometimes I am very nice, but to-day I'm awful; I'm caught in my complexes, and they're giving me immense, if unholy, joy.

Do you know the experience of sitting in a corner of a darkened room, a little light coming in through the window, and staring, fixedly and unmovedly, at the face of another in an opposite corner, never taking the eyes off the lines of the other's face? Slowly the face changes, the jaw droops, the brow slips into the cheeks, and the face is one strange white circle, utter darkness around it. Then new features form on the face, a goat's mouth slides across the circle, eyes shine in the pits of the cheeks. Then there is nothing but the circle again, and from the darkness around it rises, perhaps, the antlers of a deer, or a cloven foot, or the fingers of a hand, or a thing no words can ever describe, a shape, not beautiful or horrible, but as deep as hell and as quiet as heaven.

If you don't know the experience, try it. It's all optical illusion, I suppose, but I always call it the invoking of devils. And, mark my grisly words, invoke the devils too much, and by God they will come.

I've got the devils to-day; little blue ones they are, with spats and bowlers and dentists' tweezers. So I'd better not write any more to you until tomorrow. This will delay the letter, I'm afraid, and it's been delayed, for various reasons, long enough already. But I don't want to write you— you of all people—a panegyric on the eyesockets of skeletons.

Words

A new poem accompanies this. I suppose it's my usual stuff again, and even a little more death-struck.[1] But don't be put off by my anatomical imagery, which I explained months ago. Because I so often write in terms of the body, of the death, disease, and breaking of the body, it doesn't necessarily mean that my Muse (*not* one of my favourite words) is a sadist. For the time at least, I believe in the writing of poetry from the flesh, and, generally, from the dead flesh. So many modern poets take the *living* flesh as their object, and, by their clever dissecting, turn it into a carcase. I prefer to take the *dead* flesh, and, by any positivity of faith and belief that is in me, build up a *living* flesh from it.

Talking of 'Muse', I read in an old John O'London (blast the tit-bitty paper)[2] several individual lists of favourite words, and was surprised to see

---

1 'See, says the lime', dated 13 December 1933 in a Notebook, fits the description. It wasn't published in Thomas's lifetime, but Daniel Jones included it in *The Poems*.

2 Thomas is deriding the modest literary pretensions of *John O'London's Weekly* by comparing it with *Tit-Bits*, a popular magazine of short articles and competitions.

that the choice depended almost entirely upon the associations of the words. 'Chime', 'melody', 'golden', 'silver', 'alive', etc. appeared in almost every list; 'chime', is, to me, the only word of that lot that can, intrinsically and minus its associations, be called beautiful. The greatest single word I know is 'drome' which, for some reason, nearly opens the doors of heaven for me. Say it yourself, out aloud, and see if you hear the golden gates swing backward as the last, long sound of the 'm' fades away.

'Drome', 'bone', 'dome', 'doom', 'province'; 'dwell', 'prove', 'dolomite'— these are only a few of my favourite words, which are insufferably beautiful to me. The first four words are visionary; God moves in a long 'o'. Have you any especial favourites? If so, now's your time, lidy.

Robeyism[1]

Thank you for giving a selection of my poems that might please the mighty Neuburg, but I don't know about the love poem; such a thing is so entirely out of my sphere that I'm frightened to think how bad it might be; I'll send it to the Referee next week, anyway. And thank you for taking all the callous things I said about 'May Day' without being at all annoyed, and for heeding my dogmatic tub-thumpery. Let me see, at the first opportunity, any new poems passed by the acid tests. I love the verses you put in your letters; they have many of the qualities I should like to see exhibited in your more serious work.

You must, you know, be an awfully entertaining little girl. Anyone who can be intelligently artistic, artistically intelligent, and downright vulgar *must* be nice. So your Resolution will be one you can't help fulfilling. It's remarkable how few of the moreorless cultivated young women one meets can be honestly vulgar. They talk, possibly, of matters which, a 100 years ago, were not supposed to exist, but they talk in a sly, subtle, sophisticated way, and their jokes—when they tell any—depend upon innuendoes. Now *you*, to your shame and credit, have a decidedly coarse wit, and your naughty verses about Gascoyne and his morbid preoccupations are little masterpieces in their way. I hope these compliments won't make your Correspondence Muse (a broad creature, not, on any account, to be confused with the slim, doe-eyed apparition of your green book) selfconscious. More power to her, and to you, sweet, Rabelaisian Pamela.

Dylan

Write soon; I *should* like to have a letter for Christmas; and write as long a letter as this. Don't complain of lack of material—these notes should be able to provide enough of that.

MS: Buffalo

1 George Robey was a music-hall comedian.

PAMELA HANSFORD JOHNSON
[25 December 1933][1]   5 Cwmdonkin Drive   Uplands   Swansea

*one of the many words I can't spell at all.

Another Aftermath: Christmas Day

Thank you for the cigarettes. The Christmas dinner over, and the memories of it—so far at least—more in the mouth than in the belly, I have been sprawling in an armchair, (yes, we possess one), smoking the first of your so very kind and unexpected present. While the family is collected around the wireless, listening to the voice of His Majesty, let me write a note to you to tell you how glad I was to read your last letter, and how horrified to think that you thought Robert Graves necessarilly* indicated the return of John Player.[2] The reference to my diabolical machine was not a hint to your generosity: I must assure you on that point, even though I have no doubt that the reading of my many letters has established this invisible personality of mine as one too honourable and Balliolic (not to say bucolic) for such an unmannerly action to be possible on my part. Play the game, you cads! And my style this gray December evening (a reference to robins will appear now any moment) is as heavy as the brandied pudding now rising in revolt, deep in the chambers of the intestines, against too much four-and-sixpenny port and vegetables.

Child: Mother, how many pips in a tangerine?
Mother: Shut up, you little bastard.

My gifts are arrayed in front of me: a startlingly yellow tie and a peculiar pair of string gloves from my sister; a cigarette case from my brother-in-law; ten cigars from my father; 50 cigarettes from an uncle; 50 cigarettes from a young woman in Battersea; a knitted thing from the manageress of the hotel near my Little Theatre; the complete Blake from another uncle; a new edition of the Koran from a friend who writes music (I'll tell you something *very* interesting about him one day); Mrs. Munro's 1923–1933 Anthology (including three poems by the Gascoyne), from a friend who writes communism; two James Joyce pamphlets from myself; while outside hangs a neat, but tight, black hat from my mother, who has despaired for some time of the curves and angles of a decrepit trilby. That is all; and though your gift will vanish far more quickly than some of the others, it will last far longer in my memory than any of them.

Now could I be more explicit than that.

I have been reading Blake's letters for the first time, and find, among other things, that his headings include: 'Dear leader of my angels', 'Dear sculptor of eternity', 'Dear friend of my angels', 'Dear friend of religion and order'—all of which, in this mellow mood, and with the possible exception of the last, I might apply to you.

1 Probably completed on New Year's Eve.
2 He sent her poems by Robert Graves; she sent him Player's cigarettes.

Over dinner I told, with no remarkable effect, the following story which I hope may benefit and amuse those of your friends to whom vulgarity, or at least the trimmings of it, is as amusing as it is to you.

A. My sister has just returned from a week's holiday in Paris, and, do you know, she didn't go to the Louvre once.
B. Good lord, change of food, I expect.

I hear the roofs of the ancestral house quake with your laughter. Do I? The story reads badly but speaks well. A story which reads better than it speaks is the story of the two goldfish swimming around in a bowl, one singing to the other that old song,

'No roes in all the world
Until you came.'

I have, as a rule, been averse to including such obvious rudery in my letters to you, but the sight of your crazy supplement (thank you for it), has quelled my aversion. If I could think of another funny story I'd tell you it, but the arms of Morpheus, along with the none-too-nimble fingers of Orpheus (damn that next door Chopin-er), are closing around me. Goodbye until to-morrow, when I hope that the heavy, academic idioms of this note will leave me lucid enough to write more and at more considerable length. The wireless is continually re-iterating the fact that Christmas is here, but Christmas, for me, is nearly over. How many more Christmases will these old eyes be blessed to see approach and vanish? Who knows: one far-off day I may gather my children (though a resolution denies it) around my spavined knee, tickle their chops, and tell them of the miracle of Christ and the devastating effect of too many nuts upon a young stomach.

.X.

A Tragic Conversation
A. Pity the philosophers, the specialists, and the careerists, for, being too acquainted with the fundaments of life or with a very small part of the mechanism of life, they have no time to look upon the vast panorama of social idiocy, of political wise-cracking and literary slapstick. Let us for once be superficial, pull a cracker and blow a whistle before the maggots play noughts and crosses on the delicate structure of our forms.
B. No, let us rather seize upon an aspect of this human tragedy, and pull it to bits, making it even more tragic. Let us walk in the lanes of an English county, remarking upon the futile stirrings of life in the hedges, and, taking out our inevitable notebooks, be vain enough to imagine that the words and rhymes we pen upon the pages are a sufficient excuse for the absurdity of our lives.
C. Pity the cynic and the man of letters, the two creatures in one of all God's creatures furthest removed from God.

Very Serious Question?
Am I mad?

Librarian's Corner
An ancient and immovable bias against Mr. Kipling, who stands for everything in this cankered world which I would wish were otherwise; an inexplicable dislike of Washington Irving, fostered by a clergical uncle whose favourite book, as he so often insists, is his Life of Mahomet; a hatred of Latin, fostered by a ridiculously inapt education; an appreciation of what f's can do in the place of s's (look at Graves's poem); a total ignorance of Lady Guff Gordon and Lady Longford; and a theoretical hatred of Byron, Keats, Shelley, and Wordsworth, do not assist me in admiring the Battersea shelves. Stella Gibbons I allow, though Cold Comfort Farm is not half as successful as it should be, owing to some carelessness in the development of the plot and the totally incredible and farcical climax; Gerfalcon I should allow if I knew it; and the Scarlet Letter is splendid. But where are yer moderns? (By the way, I have read, and don't like, most of Dreiser.[1] What he writes of is good and valuable, but he should learn *how* to write. After all, if a writer of English can only express himself awkwardly in that language, he should have a shot at German; as a matter of fact Dreiser's style is thoroughly Teutonic. And, by the way again, I read 'Look Homeward, Angel' a few years ago, and I thought it particularly good.)

Our books are divided into two sections, Dad's and mine. Dad has a room full of all the accepted stuff, from Chaucer to Henry James; all the encyclopedias and books of reference, all Saintsbury,[2] and innumerable books on the theory of literature. His library contains nearly everything that a respectable highbrow library should contain. My books, on the other hand, are nearly all poetry, and mostly modern at that. I have the collected poems of Manley Hopkins, Stephen Crane, Yeats, de la Mare, Osbert Sitwell, Wilfred Owen, W. H. Auden, & T. S. Eliot; volumes of poetry by Aldous Huxley, Sacheverell & Edith Sitwell, Edna St. Vincent Millay, D. H. Lawrence, Humbert Wolfe, Sassoon, and Harold Monro; most of the ghastly Best Poems of the Year; two of the Georgian Anthologies, one of the Imagist Anthologies, 'Whips & Scorpions' (modern satiric verse), the London Mercury Anthology, the Nineties Anthology (what Dowsonery!);[3] a volume of Cambridge Poetry & Oxford Undergraduate Poetry; most of Lawrence, most of Joyce, with the exception of Ulysses, all Gilbert Murray's Greek translations, some Shaw, a little Virginia Woolf, & some

---

1 Washington Irving (1783–1859), American author. *The Scarlet Letter*, novel by Nathaniel Hawthorne (1804–64). Theodore Dreiser (1871–1945), another American novelist.
2 George Saintsbury (1845–1933), writer and critic.
3 Another of Thomas's digs at the late Victorians, in the shape of Ernest Dowson (1867–1900), poet.

E. M. Forster. This is inadequate, really, but, added to Dad's, it makes a really comprehensive selection of literature. If any of the modern poets I've mentioned are not very well known to you I should truly, truly like to lend you them. All the ones I mentioned are worth knowing well. If you feel like reading, tell me which of the above you'd like to have & I'll lend them to you one by one. Will you?

Legend

What beautiful words are 'legend' & 'island'; they shall certainly go on my list. But Ruth is the loveliest name.

Enclosed is a note to your very kind mother. If you are a good girl you can read it. It doesn't say anything at all. But then what does? And which as well?

Up, Nero!

The last poem I sent you,[1] the one you didn't like, is *not* very good, and I'm glad you attacked it; thank you for the 'White Hope', and thank you, too, for expressing—in your remarks about the hiding of light and the running around in the same weary and minor track—much that I myself have felt and have never been able to express. On one point I disagree: the images are *not* mixed; they are severely physical all through; what gave you the impression of 'mixedness' was the conscious rapidity with which I changed the angles of the images. Yes, the 'iris' is a little bit too facile. But the poem (if you'll still allow me to call it that) is certainly not *mixed* in any way at all; it is on one level and one note, with one idea and one image, changed and transfigured as that image may be. But any bettering in my poetry won't come at one leap; it's going to be, (or it's not going to be, according to the depths of my moods), a very slow and ugly business; the 'hangman' has still a lot of work to do, and the anatomical imagery is not yet exhausted. But one day I hope to write something altogether out of the hangman's sphere, something larger, wider, more comprehensible, and less selfcentred; one day I may even come up to *your* expectations. And if I do, if ever I do, much of the credit will belong to a delightful (I *will* say it) young woman I have never seen.

Your 'Poem' is, at least, serious and simple, with many nice words and rhymes and a lovely little hop-skip-and-jump rhythm. The sentiment is agreeable, a straightforward expression of pantheism; and one or two lines almost transcend pantheistic thought (Jesus!) and hover about on the edges of mysticism. With two such words as 'mysticism' & 'pantheism' on my tongue I could go on for hours; but I'll spare you that.

A thing I have always noticed and always admired in your verses and poems is the directness of the opening lines; there is never any beating about; you say what you have to say as quickly and as simply as possible.

1 'See, says the lime'.

And you have never—as you said of me—put anything in to make it more difficult. The 'Poem' is so simple in thought and structure that it loses rather than gains by the repetition of the statement of your alliance with things as diverse as a swallow and a sod. 'Sod' when it rhymes with 'God' is, in itself, a most horrible cliché; whenever I see 'God' in line two of a bad poem I inevitably look down to line four to see how the poor old sod is dragged in there. And although this is not altogether a bad poem the too-close proximity of 'God', 'sod', 'heifer' & 'zephyr' *must* lead one to believe that the thought in which these words appear was dictated by the rhymes, and is therefore false. You started off with a very simple thought (I, for one, will never believe that the most valuable thoughts are, of necessity, simple); you confessed that you were one with the 'sparrow', and then, as a natural conclusion, went on to say that you were one with the 'arrow', too. If it comes to that, you can say you are one with the barrow as well. For you are, my dear, you certainly are. I'm not trying to be flippant; I'm merely trying to show you, by any method, how *essentially* false such writing is.

> I am one with the wind and one with the breezes,
> And one with the torrent that drowns the plain,
> I am one with the streams and one with the seas-es,
> And one with the maggot that snores in the grain.

A rhyming dictionary, a little selection of natural objects, and a halfpenny gift for stringing pretty words together, and one can write like this all day. 'My blood is drawn from the veins of the roses' is on an altogether different plane; here you have *added* to the by-now meaningless repetition of associations, and have contributed something quite lovely both to yourself and to the rose. Is this clear? It's something I'm always hammering at. The man who said, for the first time, '*I see the rose*', said nothing, but the man who said for the first time, '*The rose sees me*' uttered a very wonderful truth. There's little value in going on indefinitely saying,

> 'I am one with the steamship & one with the trolley,
> And one with the airedale & one with the collie';

there's too much 'Uncle Tom Collie & all' about that. Primarily, you see, the reader refuses to believe that *you* believe you are one with all these things; you have to prove it to him, and you most certainly won't by cataloguing a number of other things to which you *say* you are related. By the magic of words and images you must make it clear to him that the relationships are real. And only in, 'My blood is drawn from the veins of the roses', do you provide any proof. You gave the rose a human vein, and you gave your own vein the blood of the rose; now that *is* relationship. 'I am his son' means little compared with 'I am his flesh and blood.'

This is a final compression of what I want to say about the 'Poem', and what I do want you to read. As it is, the 16 lines are all separate, too separate; you could have written one, gone to sleep, woken up, and written the next. Though you talk all through of the relationship of yourself to other things, there is no relationship at all in the poem between the things you example. If you are one with the swallow & one with the rose, then the rose is one with the swallow. Link together these things you talk of; show, in your words & images, how *your* flesh covers the tree & the tree's flesh covers you. I see what you have done, of course—'I am one with the opposites', you say. You are, I know, but you must prove it to me by linking yourself to the opposites and by linking the opposites together. Only in the 'rose' line did you do it.

Is this all clear, or am I talking through my new black hat?

The Green Idyll of the Little Yellow God

Wagner moves me, too, but much in the same way as the final spectacular scene in a pantomime. I won't deny, for a moment, that he's a great composer, but his greatness lies in girth rather than in depth; it lacks humour and subtlety; he creates everything for you in a vast Cecil de Mille way; his orchestration is a perpetual 'close-up'; there is altogether too much showmanship and exhibitionism about him. His Valhalla is a very large and a very splendid place, but built in the style of a German baronial castle: the tapestries are too voluminous & highly coloured, there is too great a display of gold; while the gods that hold dominion over it are florid deities, puffed out with self-importance, wearing gaudy garments and angelic watch-chains.

You know the experience of walking through the palatial chambers at Windsor, admiring the wealth and the magnificence with an open mouth, and longing to sneak away into a small and quiet room where you can eat chips and drink mild beer in comfort. That is the experience which Wagner gives me; he reminds me of a huge and overblown profiteer, wallowing in fineries, over-exhibiting his monstrous paunch and purse, and drowning his ten-ton wife in a great orgy of jewels. Compare him with an aristocrat like Bach!

Still, I admire the way in which you admire him, and realise that it is only natural that Wagner should be one of your high gods. Whatever I can say about him, he is a big man, an overpowering man, a man with a vast personality and an overpowering voice, a dominant, arrogant, gestureful man forever in passion and turmoil over the turbulent, passionate universe. He's all that, I admit; parts of Tristan and Isolde are exquisite; and my sneers are the sneers of a pygmy at a dwarf, not even a David at a Goliath. Yes, he was bound to be the composer you admire, for the qualities (enumerated above) are the qualities that, artistically at any rate, seem to count most with you. You like the raucous, billowy, bawdy historical novel, the 'up-&-at-'em, kick-'em-in-the-belly, God's an Englishman shoutings of Mr. Kipling (though I do not, on any account, call you a hearty), the cloudy brawlings of Shelley, the virility of Washington Irving. If you like all these, how on earth do you like me—if you do? I'm little with no health at all, curled up in an old copy of the 'Funeral Gazette', sneering at the worm.

Neuburg

He didn't appear to like the poem I sent him last week; it was not very inspired, I admit, but it was so wonderfully comprehensible that I felt sure it would appeal to him. However. This week I'll send him that love poem. So your book is to be published in the spring now? Who by? And don't say you're going to call yourself Pamela Hansford Johnson; the three-name method is utterly American. If you do I shall call myself Dylan Marlais Thomas. So there!

Some Resolutions etc:

As this is the season of the year to make resolutions, I shall devote some of my time and, let it be hoped, some of yours, to the propounding of much idealistic nonsense to which it is my intention to adhere. This is such an ugly sentence that the brain naturally turns to the question of ugliness. Now there is nothing on God's earth that is, in itself, an ugly thing; it is the sickness of the mind that turns a thing sick and the dirtiness of the mind that turns a thing dirty. I do not speak of parliaments and committees, eternally ugly things, for they are composed of a collection of ugly minds; I speak of the pig and the popular conception of death. The pig is a particular animal and will eat only what is good for him; because what he eats is not good for us it does not follow that it is a messy food. The pig lies down in dung to sleep, because dung is warm and soft; he would probably think it a very dirty thing indeed to sleep on a sheet. Death is said to be ugly only because we entertain an ugly conception of the body. A live body is a building around the soul, and a dead body a building without it; without the soul a body breaks, but the broken pieces are beautiful and meaningful because the soul has made them so and has left its marks. Just as a live body has its rhythms and its pattern and its promise (promise is perhaps the greatest thing in the world), so has a dead body; and not only an abstract pattern but a physical one. A dead body promises the earth as a live body promises its mate; and the earth is our mate. Looking on one dead, we should say, Here lies beauty, for it has housed beauty, the soul being beautiful; just as, on looking on an empty house, we should say, Here stands strength (or anything else), for it has housed strength, strength being beautiful. What has this to do with a resolution? It leads me to resolve that I shall never take things for granted, but that I shall attempt to take them as they are, that nothing is ugly except what I make ugly, and that the lowest and the highest are level to the eyes of the air.

I resolve not to label the brain into separate compartments; that is, not to differentiate between what is in me that writes poetry and what is in me that says, Here comes one-o'clock; at this time I lunch. That is, again, a resolution not to differentiate between what is called rational and what is called irrational, but to attempt to create, or to let be created, one rationalism. It is said to be mad to write poetry and sane to lunch at one o'clock; but it is the other way about: Art is praise and it is sane to praise, for, praising, we praise the godliness that gives us sanity; the clock is a symbol of the limitation of time, and time is limitless: therefore it is wrong to obey the clock and right to eat not when the hands of the clock, but when the fingers of hunger, dictate. I resolve firstly to *make* poetry and, secondly, to write it; there is poetry in the hands of the clock if only I can realise that the clock is a limitation, and can express, in my poetry, the knowledge of that limitation and the knowledge of illimitability. I can learn, by such resolving, to say that nothing in this world is uninteresting. How can a thing have no interest that *is* in this world, that has the world around it, that has a past, a present & a future, that has all the associations of a million million minds engrained in it. A chunk of stone is as interesting as a cathedral, or even more interesting, for it is the cathedral in essence; it gave substance to the building of the cathedral and meaning to the meaning of the cathedral, for stones are sermons, as are all things. And if I can bring myself to know, not to think, that nothing is uninteresting, I can broaden my own outlook and believe once more, as I so passionately believed and so passionately *want* to believe, in the magic of this burning and bewildering universe, in the meaning and the power of symbols, in the miracle of myself & of all mortals, in the divinity that is so near us and so longing to be nearer, in the staggering, bloody, starry wonder of the sky I can see above and the sky I can think of below. When I learn that the stars I see *there* may be but the backs of the stars I see *there*, I am filled with the terror which is the beginning of love. They tell me space is endless and space curves. And I understand.

And now that I am started I can't stop; I've saddled a bright horse, and his brightness, not his body, keeps me bouncing up and down like a rubber star on his back. I have never raved to you before for as long as this, have I? But it really is a natural raving. Before one gets to a truth in one's own mind one has to cut through so many crusts of self-hypocrisy and doubt, self bluff and hypnotism; the polishing of phrases rubs off the sharp madness of the words and leaves only their blunt sanity. Here I am writing naturally; take it or leave it; this stream is yours if you want it, and can go on for as long as the teeth hold in the gums, for as long as (any image will do) the hairs of your head are as sweet as the ropes that hang down from the hands of the sky, hanging down to be pulled at—if one had the strength.

And to begin, I want to believe in dragons, not the windy, tank-like creature who quarrelled with St. George, but the vast and fiery legend, bearing half a planet on its shoulders, with hell in its nostrils and heaven in its scales, with a comet in the steaming socket of its eye, with a couple of dragon-lets at its side, with a grandmother at home knitting unbelievably large socks and finding counties in her hair.

I want to imagine a new colour, so much whiter than white that white is black.

I want to forget all that I have ever written and start again, informed with a new wonder, empty of all my old dreariness, and rid of the sophistication which is disease. How can I ever lie on my belly on the floor, turning a narrow thought over and over again on the tip of my tongue, crying in my wordy wilderness, mean of spirit, brooding over the death of my finger which lies straight in front of me? How can I, when I have news to scream up to heaven, and when heaven has news to scream down to me? I want to read the headlines in the sky: birth of a star, death of a comet. I want to believe, to believe forever, that heaven is *being*, a state of being, and that the only hell is the hell of myself. I want to burn hell with its own flames.

No, but my wants are not all cloudy as that; I want to live and love & be loved; I want to praise and be praised; I want to sleep and wake, and look upon my sleeping as only another waking; I want to live and die.

We don't worship nature; nature is what we wish it and worships us; we stop the sun, we tell the sun to go on.

'The universe is wild and full of marvels.' In the shape of a boy, and a funny boy at that, I have only a very short time to learn how mad and marvellous it is; I think in cells; one day I may think in rains. All around us, now and forever, a spirit is bearing and killing and resurrecting a body; I care not a damn for Christ, but only for his symbol, the symbol of death. But suicide is wrong; a man who commits suicide is like a man who longs for a gate to be opened and who cuts his throat before he reaches the gate.

There is an imp in your room, looking with my eyes at you.

Finale: the Hat talks

There is a foghorn crying out to the ships in the Bristol Channel as an albatross might have cried to the ancient mariner, over Shakespeare's multitudinous ocean on a deep, dark night. I should like to be somewhere very wet, preferably under the sea, green as a merman, with cyclamen crabs on my shoulders, and the skeleton of a commercial magnate floating, Desdemona-wise, past me; but I should like to be very much alive under the sea, so that the moon, shining through the crusts of the waves, would be a beautiful pea-green.

I am very often—especially in such fantastic frames of mind as have entertained me during the last few days—convinced that the angle of man is necessarily inconducive to the higher thoughts. Walking, as we do, at right angles with the earth, we are prevented from looking, as much as we should, at the legendary sky above us and the only-a-little-bit-more-possible ground under us. We can only (without effort) look in front of us and around us; we can look only at things that are between the earth and sky, and are much in the position of a reader of books who can look only at the middles of pages and never (without effort) at the tops and bottoms. We see what we imagine to be a tree, but we see only a part of the tree; what the insects under the earth see when they look upwards at the tree, & what the stars see when they look downwards at the tree, is left to our imagination. And perhaps the materialist can be called the man who believes only in the part of the tree he sees, & the spiritualist a man who believes in a lot more of the tree than is within his sight. Think how much wiser we would be if it were possible for us to change our angles of perspective as regularly as we change our vests: a certain period would be spent in propelling ourselves along on our backs, in order to see the sky properly and all the time; and another period in drifting belly-downwards through the air, in order to see the earth. As it is, this perpetual right-angle of ours leads to a prejudiced vision. Probably this was the divine plan, anyway; but I certainly intend to spend more time lying on my back, and will even, if circumstances permit, follow Mr. Chesterton's admirable advice, and spend as much time as possible standing on my head.

And so, for the present, I leave you, a short, ambiguous person in a runcible hat, feeling very lost in a big and magic universe, wishing you love and a healthy new year.

Dylan

MS: Buffalo

PAMELA HANSFORD JOHNSON
[early January 1934][1] [fragment]

It's a very bad sign when I have to put a little prologue before each letter, and it's some sort of a sign, too, that the letters are becoming heavier. But I don't know whether that's good or bad: it's O.K. by me.

The only reason for this prologue is: I'm sorry, but this isn't a particularly good letter; it's altogether too dogmatic & argumentative; and, reading it through after I'd finished copying the damned thing out, I confess it bored me stiff. Little scraps of it may not be dull as the rest, though: I advise you to find those little scraps, read them, & skip all the rest.

How the last 'Mutter' came to be included in an otherwise sane (too bloody sane & dull, that's the trouble) letter I really don't know; you'll have to pardon that, too.

My next letter, I promise, will be full of beans & epigrams, a highly journalistic affair with a couple of funny stories & a drawing.

Incidentally—a very important incident, too—I don't need to have any

---

1 This 'prologue' probably belongs to the next letter. Johnson wrote in her diary on 10 January: 'Long fulminating letter from Dylan giving the intriguing information that he'd met someone who knew & disliked me!' The 'someone' was Daniel Jones, who had found his way to Neuburg country, and in summer 1933 visited Steyning. Jones met Johnson there, 'and, I'm afraid', he wrote in 1977, 'was rather rude about her poems.'

maternal low-down on you; I know a young man who has met you & didn't like you. So there, ikkle Pam! Smile that off! I have you now on both hips! Three chairs for the mayor! Here's a toast to the invisible Pamela, now done dirt on by a friend of mine! Lift your glasses! Donk your schnozzles, boys, as Florence Nightingale once remarked.

Dylan

!! PROLOGUE !!

MS: *Buffalo*

PAMELA HANSFORD JOHNSON
[?early January 1934] [incomplete]   Swansea

Night and Day: A Provincial Rhythm

At half past nine there is a slight stirring in the Thomas body, an eyelid quivers, a limb trembles. At a quarter to ten, or thereabouts, breakfast, consisting of an apple, an orange, and a banana, is brought to the side of the bed and left there along with the Daily Telegraph. Some five minutes later the body raises itself, looks blindly around it, and, stretching out a weak arm, lifts the apple to its mouth. Waking is achieved between bites, and, over the now more-or-less clear scrutiny of the fruit, the webs of the last night dreams are remembered and disentangled. Then, still weakly but with increasing certainty of touch, the banana is peeled and the newspaper opened. At the last bite I have taken complete possession of the Thomas body, and read the criminal court cases on page three with great concentration. The orange, incidentally, is never touched until I get downstairs, the process of peeling and pipping being too cold and lengthy for such an hour of the morning. When the reports of rapes, frauds, and murders have been thoroughly digested, I light a cigarette, very slowly lay my head back on the pillow, and then, without any warning, leap suddenly out of bed, tear off my pyjamas, scramble into a vest and trousers, and run, as if the fiends of winter were at my heels, into the bathroom. There, holding the cigarette, I scrape the beard from my face and dab about with a futile sponge. And then downstairs where, after another cigarette, I seat myself in front of the fire and commence to read, to read anything that is near, poetry or prose, translations out of the Greek or the Film Pictorial, a new novel from Smith's,[1] a new book of criticism, or an old favourite like Grimm or George Herbert, anything in the world so long as it is printed. I read on until twelve or thereabouts, when perhaps I have read quarter of a novel, a couple of poems, a short story, an article on the keeping of bees in Upper Silesia, and a review by somebody I have never heard of on a play I never want to see. Then down the hill into the Uplands—a lowland

1 W. H. Smith, the booksellers and stationers, ran a lending library. New books could be borrowed for a small sum.

collection of crossroads and shops, for one (or perhaps two) pints of beer in the Uplands Hotel. Then home for lunch. After lunch, I retire again to the fire where perhaps I shall read all the afternoon—and read a great deal of everything, or continue on a poem or a story I have left unfinished, or to start another or to start drafting another, or to add a note to a letter to you, or to type something already completed, or merely to write—to write anything, just to let the words and ideas, the half remembered half forgotten images, tumble on the sheets of paper. Or perhaps I go out, & spend the afternoon in walking alone over the very desolate Gower cliffs, communing with the cold and the quietness. I call this taking my devils for an airing. This takes me to tea-time. After tea I read or write again, as haphazardly as before, until six-o-clock. I then go to Mumbles (remember the women of Mumbles Head),[1] a rather nice village, despite its name, right on the edge of the sea. First I call at the Marine, then the Antelope, and then the Mermaid. If there is a rehearsal I leave these at eight o'clock and find my way to the Little Theatre, conveniently situated between the Mermaid and the Antelope. If there is no rehearsal, I continue to commune with these two legendary creatures, and, more often than not, to conduct metaphysical arguments with a Chestertonian toper, (last night it was 'Existence or Being'), who apparently makes a good living out of designing scanty and dirty costumes for provincial revues. Then a three mile walk home to supper and perhaps more reading, to bed and certainly more writing. Thus drifts an average day. Not a very British day. Too much thinkin', too much talkin', too much alcohol.

We are both slaves to habit. I do not think that either of us are wide, and can never expect to be wide poets, (though, doubtlessly, you are a little wider physically than I am). We both have to concentrate on depth.

Another average day, recorded above, has passed. I am sitting up in bed, none too sober, with a blank sheet of paper on the eiderdown in front of me. But no words will come. The paper is covered with a divinity of thoughts, but it is as naked as the hand that holds it. The smoke of my cigarette reminds me of a lot of things.

I am going to put out the light, and think vain and absurd and never-to-be things until I fall to sleep.

Chestnut Saturday

Very unfortunately your mirth-provoking story of the mental Don Juan was familiar to me (and why my English doesn't permit me to say, 'I know the story about the man in the pub', I can't imagine). My best story is the very long one, spoken in the broadest of Welsh accents, about Marged Ann and the Vicar, but it's very vulgar and I'm afraid it loses nearly all the little point it has if it's written down. I'll keep that as a special treat to tell you, though again I can't imagine why it should be a special treat for you to hear a bawdy story told by a small Welshman in Anglo-Welsh.

1 'The Women of Mumbles Head' is a lugubrious poem by Clement Scott about an incident of 1883, when the lighthouse keeper's daughters saved a drowning sailor.

Just A Thought

Every thinking man—that is, every man who builds up, on a structure of tradition, the seeds of his own revolution—and every artist—that is, every man who expresses this revolution through an artistic medium—gradually form a series of laws for living, which he may or may not adhere to. Those laws are brought about slowly in the individual mind, are fostered by mental and physical experience. They do not enter the brain as laws but as the raw matter for thought; it is the brain that explores them, finds what is worthy in them, and then dogmatises them. And this is only right. I have theories on the art of poetry, and these theories—as you know, my poor sufferer of so much of my theoretical nonsense—are obviously dogmatic. Those theories entered the brain as impressions. On reading Wordsworth, I was given the impression that, although he talked of mysticism, he was not a mystic but only a moraliser. Later I stabilised this impression as a dogma, or rather as two dogmas: Morals are the *imposed* trimmings around *inherent* doubt, and: A mystic is a man who takes things literally. All theories are made in that way. And that, too, is only right, for by this method alone can the individual have any hand in the shaping of his own spiritual & mental life. I dislike meat, I dislike killing, therefore I make my own law: It is wrong to eat meat. Thus all the laws in the world have been made. The words Jesus said were only his impressions erected into laws. Rémy de Gourmont[1] has called such an erection the principle of criticism, and, here again, I am in agreement, for Jesus was himself a critic more than anything else; he was given God to read, he read God, understood Him, appreciated Him, and then, stern in his duty as a critic, decided it was his mission in life to explain the meaning of God to his fellows.

God is the country of the spirit, and each of us is given a little holding of ground in that country; it is our duty to explore that holding, to gain certain impressions by such exploring, to stabilise as laws the most valuable of these impressions, and, as far as we can, to abide by them. It is our duty to criticise, for criticism is the personal explanation of appreciation. Though a man may hate the world he still appreciates it, and his hate is as valuable as my love; he may hate it for its madness, as I love it for that; he may hate the whole of humanity as I hate the social system that is pulling it to buggery; he may hate pain, as I believe in pain. But we are both critics of life, however misguided. The man who hates & the man who loves are all right; but there is no room in the country of the spirit for the man who accepts, or does not accept, without hate or love.

Hate and love, after all, are nearly one; a blow can be a kiss out of heaven, and a kiss a blow out of hell.

I am writing this at the window. Outside in the cold I see the structure of the sky. Yes, the structure of the sky, the vast grey erection from the edge of here to the edge of nowhere. Yes, the erection of the sky, for the sky is no more than a godly dogma made out of a heavenly impression.

1 Rémy de Gourmont (1858–1915), French novelist and poet.

'And if thou wilt, remember,
And if thou wilt, forget.'[1]

Your latest poem has made one thing certain to me: your alliance with the PreRaphaelite school of poets and with Christina Rossetti, the best PreRaphaelite of the whole bunch, in particular. But perhaps you will take the word 'alliance' uncomplimentarily, so let me suggest—and this is most certainly a compliment—that you are the only writer I know today who can be said to be in the true PreRaphaelite descent. Again, this is not to say that anything in your work is not your own, for, above all, it is a personal expression; but the merits of that particular, unfashionable, and mis-judged school are shown very clearly in your poems. And, added to those merits, is your own undeniable gusto (a word I hope you won't take exception to), your joy in living and in expressing, and your continual fecundity of natural emotions. Your verse is narrow, but it seems to be a deliberate narrowness, and does not destroy any of its intensity. It is, I am sure, in increased subtlety and elusiveness that you are certain to develop. Christina Rossetti is too little known, [except] by some of her moralistic verses; she had a most delicate command of rhythm, as you have when you take the trouble, a delicate sense of the sounds of words, and a highly competent technical ability which never appeared laboured because of its simplicity; you have all those, too. But it is her perspective of life that interests me most: sweet, small, & narrow, delicate to the point of elusion. Those are four of your qualities, but whereas she was so often caught in semi-theological arguments, was probably too virginal to look at herself in the mirror, and was, on her own admission, disgusted by the sound of laughter, you have a startling sense of humour (I'm not piling on compliments, please, I'm trying to make some sort of a valuation), and a vitality which that other very charming lady never possessed. Walter de la Mare owes much to Christina, and, if there is any labelling to be done, I would put you & de la Mare, that questioning poet, in the same compartment & mark it 'Subtlety and Sensitivity. Perishable. With Care.' You are young, young enough to become subtler and more sensitive, to trust your own sense of harmony much further, and to produce poetry that will stand out far above the singing of even the best lyricists of to-day.

I do not think 'The King Dies' is a good poem, but it is a promising poem; it is not subtle enough, either in rhythm or in the play of vowels; but it is a poem in what I consider to be the right direction for you; it points towards the progress that you are bound to make. I prefer you when you are more personal than this, when you have no guiding thought behind you, but rather when you are in the process of selection—selecting your images to suit your particular moods, selecting your *thoughts* to fit those *images*.

1 From 'When I am Dead, my Dearest' by Christina Rossetti (1830–94).

The substance of your poetry is always slight, and in 'The King Dies' the slightness is too little redeemed by subtlety of expression. I don't think there is any necessity for me to go into it in detail; all I have to say I've said in this note, and I may appear to have said nothing. That is why I very modestly prefaced the note with a quotation from the Rossetti itself.

Leave the lambkins alone, or never, at least, use them unless you can then take them literally, that is rid of all their associations, or unless you can build new & worth-while associations around 'em. But don't worry about that at the moment; go on writing but more carefully still; submit every syllable to a thorough test; never be afraid of subtlety, even though it may lead you to obscurity (dangerous advice to some, but not to you). And show me all you write.

A Complaint

This method of letter writing, this selection of odd notes, is very satisfying, but it's a swine in some ways. I write the notes for my letters to you at odd times & in pencil on bits of paper. It takes me a hell of a time to copy them all out on these mammoth sheets.

Put this in your Pipe — and if you haven't got one, I'll lend you mine; it reeks.

Ha, child, I was as crafty as you. I confess that my reference to your love of Kipling was no more than a highly titivating bait. Of course you don't like his flagflapping, for you know as well as I do that patriotism is a publicity ramp organised by holders of excess armament shares; you know that the Union Jack is only a national loin-cloth to hide the decaying organs of a diseased social system; you know that the Great War was purposely protracted in order for financiers to make more money; that had it not been for the shares in the armament firms the War would have ended in three weeks; that at one period of the War French and German were shelling each other with ammunition provided by the same firm, a firm in which English clergymen and politicians, French ambassadors and German business men, all had a great deal of money invested; that Kipling, rejected by the army because of weak physique, is nevertheless a 'I gave my son' militarist; that the country which he lauds and eulogises is a country that supports a system by which men are starved, and fish, wheat and coffee are burnt by the hundreds of tons; a system by which men are not allowed to work, to marry, to have children; by which they are driven mad daily; by which children are brought into the world scrofulous; by which the church is allowed to prevent the prevention of sexual diseases;[1] a system so just

---

1 Thomas was talking about contraception. The 'respectable' argument for letting the unmarried use condoms, that they reduced the risk of venereal infection, cut no ice with opponents. Although no one could 'prevent' the sale of condoms, already widespread, the churches (and authority in general) still deplored their use outside, and sometimes inside, marriage.

that a man is arrested on Chritmas Day for arrears of rates, when his wife is expecting a baby & his children are dying of typhoid fever caused through the eating of bad fish supplied by a profiteering tradesman. Woah! England, my England. And Kipling still flaps his belly for it, and it is easier to bribe a politician than it is to bribe a costermonger.

And what's all this about the 'delicacy of a silver-point drawing' in the five weak lines you quoted from 'The Way Through the Wood'.[1]

MS: Buffalo

PAMELA HANSFORD JOHNSON
[?1934] [fragment]

For some forsaken reason someone I have never heard of—Professor Somebody—has written a long article about me. Most of it deals with the fact that I am a better actor than Irving and a greater orator than Disraeli. The excerpts I send you show that I'm a greater poet than Blake.

That article is apt to do an awful lot of harm. I'll be jeered at even more. 'Relating the elemental forces of Earth, Humanity, & the Universe'. 'My philosophy'. Jesus!!

I'm sending it to you to show that someone thinks I *am* good; what if he is nuts? That doesn't matter.

MS: Buffalo

PAMELA HANSFORD JOHNSON
[?1934] [fragment][2]

But enough of this. It sounds, and is not, an alcoholic remorse, the self-pity of gin, the result of constipation. Let me talk to you of rats, or rather of *a* rat with whom I have become acquainted. I was sitting in the porch of the Pwlldu Inn on a cold, sunny afternoon, eating an unnaturally large sandwich and sipping at a quart mug—both sandwich and mug were almost as large as me. In the midst of my meal I heard a loud stamping (that is the only honest word to describe it), and, looking up, saw a rat

---

1 The surviving MS ends here.
2 The MS is not at Buffalo. Pamela Hansford Johnson must have had it in 1953—which was before she disposed of her Thomas letters—because she wanted to use it in a valedictory article she was writing about Thomas for the magazine *Adam*. She described it when she wrote to the Dylan Thomas Trustees (5 December 1953), saying it was 'an excerpt from a letter'. The Trustees refused permission to publish. In 1965 it was quoted in FitzGibbon's biography of Thomas, and in 1969 appeared in *Dylan Thomas. Twelve More Letters* (Turret Books, copyright of letters retained by the Thomas Trust). After that it seems to have disappeared.

standing immediately in front of me, his eyes fixed on mine. A rat? This was a rat with a capital R, a vast iron-gray animal as big as a big cat, with long, drooping white whiskers and a tail like an old frayed whip. Normally I am frightened to death by rats, even by mice, and certainly by moths, but this monstrosity of a creature did not alarm me at all. He couldn't move quickly anyway, he was much too fat. He merely stood there in front of me until I threw him a piece of cheese. He sniffed it, swallowed it, and stamped away. Again 'stamped' is the only word: he went away like a fat old soldier from a canteen. Thinking of him when he had gone, I came to the conclusion that he must be the Father of all Rats, the First Rat, the Rat Progenitive, the Rat Divine.

Only source: Twelve More Letters

TREVOR HUGHES
[early January 1934][1]

Ever since I left you alone on the deserted railway platform, waving a last, forlorn handkerchief as the train rushed me onwards to Chelsea and Sir Richard Rees, I have been meaning to write you a long letter. Sometimes the monstrous shape of the Rayner's Lane illuminated sign[2] has risen up in my dreams like the advertisement of my conscience, and I have sworn to jump out of bed the next morning, grab pencil and paper, and write until darkness fell again upon the emptiness of Wales with an accustomed clatter. But the mornings have been cold, the pencil has not been near enough, the paper has been too virgin to deflower, and my own incorrigible laziness has made me postpone, time upon time, the pleasure of continuing our correspondence. Once I can start, then everything's all right; the words, God knows, come easily enough, too easily for some as I will tell you later. But the inspiration to begin has not knocked in the blood nor fingered the fingers. Now—with divine help—this letter can go on for some time. I was with you in September; now Christmas has gone, and the only letters between us during that period have been short and almost business-like in tone. Did I thank you for sending back my story? I know I never sent the new poems as I promised. Let this be my repentance, and may I join you, if only for a little while, in your single wilderness.

You seem no cheerier than when I last saw you, and indeed I would be surprised if you were. Living in Metroland with a crippled mother—and please don't imagine for a moment that these words are flippant in any way—is not conducive to the Higher Optimism, nor, in the midst of such respectability and subservience to the office clock, to the unrespectable

1 A letter from Hughes of 13 January 1934, at Buffalo, is probably a reply to this letter.
2 The sign of the Underground rail station near Hughes's home.

creation of literature. I remember advising you to climb out of your morbidity, little realising then, perhaps, that you were not the Jonah swallowed by your own whale, but the whale—I have faith in your ability to write—swallowed by the Jonah of circumstance. And either this is a deeper tortuity than it appears, or it has no meaning at all. Now I understand a little, but only a little, of the circumstance that has played so hard with you, and if it has not swallowed me it is because of my self-centredness, my islandic egoism which allows few of the day's waves to touch it. Soon after I left you, my father went to the University College Hospital to be operated upon for cancer of the throat; today he went back to school, weak and uncured.[1] And only a little while ago I learnt the truth of my own health. But the statement of Dad's disease and the warning of mine have left me horridly unmoved; I become a greater introvert day by day, though, day by day again, I am conscious of more external wonders in the world. It is my aim as an artist—that, too, has been denied, but not by the pontifical Eliot—to bring those wonders into myself, to prove beyond doubt to myself that the flesh that covers me is the flesh that covers the sun, that the blood in my lungs is the blood that goes up and down in a tree. It is the simplicity of religion. Artists, as far as I can gather, have set out, however unconsciously, to prove one of two things: either that they are mad in a sane world, or that they are sane in a mad world. It has been given to few to make a perfect fusion of madness and sanity, and all is sane except what we make mad, and all is mad except what we make sane.

No, the great Eliot has not damned me, but he has been cautious. Rees, on the other hand, though printing two poems of mine and taking a peculiar interest in all I write, has made one very startling accusation: that much of what I write is not written consciously, that any talent I may have is clairvoyant, and my fecundity is accounted for by 'automatic writing'. Charles Williams of the Oxford University Press, and author, as you know, of several mystic books,[2] has read many of my poems but confesses that he does not understand them; they cannot be 'pooh-poohed' but he could not say that he liked them. And so we go on, meeting nothing but courtesy and interest, and nothing but a rather bewildered refusal to print. I am sending you a few recent poems to criticize, not in the pedantic way of the professors but by your own and far more valuable methods. Be as honest as I am with you. They are, I admit, unpretty things, with their imagery almost totally anatomical. But I defend the diction, the perhaps wearisome succession of blood and bones, the neverending similes of the streams in the veins and the lights in the eyes, by saying that, for the time at least, I realise that it is impossible for me to raise myself to the altitude of the stars, and that I am forced, therefore, to bring down the stars to my own level and to incorporate them in my own physical universe.

1 The treatment worked. Jack Thomas was cured.
2 Charles Williams (1886–1945) wrote poetry and criticism as well as supernatural thrillers.

Prose and Verse is a sad story, and postponed as often as my letter. Only a little while ago it was budding into light, creeping up even through my lethargy; now it has sunk down again, and is no more than a legend for old men to tell their children: Once upon a time there was a boy who had Literary Pretensions, not only for himself but also for those of his friends who, too, burdened the editors of England with their sad expostulations. And the boy decided to produce a periodical in which he himself and the other unfortunate young men might express the vicissitudes of their spirits in great detail; he advertised it and interested in it many of the leading Intellectuals of his Philistine town. But something happened; one friend went to London, and another to a university, both very big and bewildering places, while the boy was left with a few equally bewildering contributions upon his hands. Time passed, and a new Intellectual arose who, hearing of the boy's frustrated plans, resolved to see that, at long last, those plans should come to fruition. Again something happened, or, to tell the truth, two things happened, and one was the fault of the boy and the other was the fault of the intellectual. The boy, very suddenly, became disgusted with the mental disease of his country, the warped apathy of his countrymen, and of the essentially freakish nature of himself. And the Intellectual became lazy. So again the periodical was buried under the mists of the mind, and again were the boy's friends done dirt on. But one day 'Prose and Verse' will arise in all its splendour, and be published not out of the bowels of dirty Wales but from the heart of the metropolis. And he and his friends will be older and wiser, and their contributions may even be better than they were before. Yes, 'Prose and Verse' is buried but not forgotten. It shall be published, that I promise. And that some of it, at least, shall be good, you yourself shall see to.

It may be a day or two before this letter is completed for, intent as I am upon writing it, I seem to become busier with every new idle day. In the mornings and afternoons I find I have more and more to write, and the fact that what I write may be valueless does not alter the fact of the time it takes; my evenings are given to rehearsals and performances at the Little Theatre, or to the steady but increasingly copious sinking of drink. Remember, too, that the scrappiness of this letter is owing entirely to the odd minutes I am devoting to it, and not, as it might appear, to such a startlingly untidy brain.

This new year has brought back to my mind the sense of magic that was lost—irretrievably, I thought—so long ago. I am conscious, if not of the probability of the impossible, at least of its possibility, and the paradox has clothed itself like a fairy. It needed courage to say that 'like a fairy', for the young pantomime ladies, gallivanting in gossamer nudity, have robbed the fairy of all but her woman's body. A fairy is not supernatural; she is the most natural thing in the world. How much easier it is to believe in her, in her magnificent transformations, in her wings and wonder, than it is to believe in the invulnerability of the pope, the genius of Bernard Shaw, and the Loch Ness monster. Not that I doubt the existence of the latter, but those who see him look upon him wrongly. A man who perceives a particularly unbelievable sunrise or sunset does not phone the news to the papers; if he sees—as all of us have seen—a firebreathing centaur in the shapes of the clouds he does not take a photograph of it so that his friends might be impressed with its reality. He says, Very wonderful, and he goes on his way. So it should be with the monster in the Loch; the villagers should see it, if it is to be seen, remark upon the legendary curves of its trunk and the horns on its head, then go home quietly to their beds. 'I saw the monster,' they would say to their wives. 'Go on, do you believe that?' 'I don't know about believing it,' would be the reply, 'But I saw it all right, and very unbelievable it was.' There the matter would drop.

Superstition is a moral vice, but a man who believes in the supernatural is a man who takes things literally. It is the aim of the church—that embodiment of a medieval moral—to do away with man's sense of the literal. How much better to say that God is big than that he is 'all-pervading'.

There is no vice (a deliberate contradiction); what we know as vices are social crimes; it is the fault of society that it will not adjust itself so as to make those crimes either uncriminal or unthinkable. But society to adjust itself has to break itself; society should accommodate man, not hinder him; but it has grown up rotten with its capitalist child, and only revolutionary socialism can clean it up. Capitalism is a system made for a time of scarcity, and the truth of today is the truth of fertility. All that renounces fertility is a lie.

The trouble, of course, with preoccupation with the roots and the substance of magic is the frequency with which the devil and his forked apprentices inhabit the mind of the believer; despondency can so easily be put down, not to an organic disturbance or to self-insufficiency or to a misanthropic philosophy, but to the bedevilled paradoxes of the brain; the faults in oneself can be too easily blamed on the things that go squawk in the night; Satanism is too easy a synonym for sadism. The most terrifying figure in history is, to me, the French abbé who became, through some sexual stringency or latitude, a connoisseur of the grave and a worshipper of his sister Worm. He would not lie with a woman unless she dressed herself in a shroud, painted her face as the face of a corpse, and lay as stiff and unbreathing as though she were in the clasp of her last lover. The abbé was probably a gentleman and kind to dogs, but his view on the living was through the lenses of the dead—there is a delightful image somewhere which pictures each blade of grass as the periscope of a dead man—and this, despite my own morbid system of aesthetics, strikes me as an unpardonable fault. The most beautiful thing in the world to Poe was a woman dead; Poe is not to be challenged on the grounds of taste but on those of accuracy, for a woman dead is not a woman at all, the spirit that made her a woman being fled and already metamorphosed. To love a dead woman does not appear to me to be necessarily unhealthy, but it is a love too onesided to be pure. Love is onesided, I admit, for it lies more in what you put into a woman—and for once I am not speaking anatomically—than in what you take out of her. The cynic would say that it is the other way about; but then the cynic is a dead man, and, despite the fact that I consider paganism to be the most evil of doctrines, the body was given to live as much as the stars were given to live up to.

You said once in one of your valuable letters that still, incidentally have a prominent place on my desk, that your troubles at my age encompassed the whole of womanhood, while mine—little toper that I am bound to become—could be circled by the limits of a half pint measure. While disagreeing thoroughly that my adolescent troubles could be confined to a short and bewildered acquaintance with drink, I confess that woman as a generalisation, even as a physical generalisation, has never worried me at all. The actual leaping in my blood has always been caused through the memory of, or the contact with, some particular and actual person. It is also my pleasure or misfortune to confess to a lean and suspicious creator of pathological literature that I am in love. What is more it [is] not an unnaturally onesided love. Laugh as much as you like, though I don't think you will. Will you?

Have you been reading as much as usual, or has that hindered inspiration of yours at last burst out of the womb of the pen? I am looking forward to the reading of your promised story, and am hoping, too, that you are satisfied with it. You know your own faults as well as I know my own, and while I am spending more and more time on the shapes of paragraphs, the slow formation of sentences, and the deletion of commas, it would still be probably advisable for you to spend less and less time on remodelling and more on the redhot creation of your prose. Much is against you, I know, but I find it hard to say whether adverse circumstances are a hindrance or not. The best in a man comes out in suffering; there is a prophet in pain, and an oracle in the agony of the mind. Such things are easy to say; it is easier to recognize the prophet than to heed him; if only I could say with Blake, Death to me is no more than going into another room. How easy, too, it is to say that; there is as much charlatanism in a poet as there is in an astrologer, and it may be that the genuineness and the value of the one is the genuineness and the value of the other; both have a love and an awe of the miraculous world, and both are conscious of horizons.

Does one need 'New styles of architecture, a change of heart'? Does one not need a new consciousness of the old universal architecture and a tearing away from the old heart of the things that have clogged it? Still our minds are hovering too much about our testicles, complaining

> ... In delicate and exhausted metres
> That the twitching of three abdominal nerves
> Is incapable of producing a lasting Nirvana.

We look upon a thing a thousand times; perhaps we shall have to look upon it a million times before we see it for the first time. Centuries of problematical progress have blinded us to the literal world; each bright and naked object is shrouded around with a thick, peasoup mist of associations; no single word in all our poetical vocabulary is a virgin word, ready for our first love, willing to be what we make it. Each word has been wooed and gotten by a vast procession of dead littérateurs who put their coins in the plate of a procuring Muse, entered at the brothel doors of a divine language, and whored the syllables of Milton and the Bible.

But consciousness of such prostitution need not lead us, as it has led James Joyce, into the inventing of new words; it need not make us, as it has made Gertrude Stein,[1] repeat our simplicities over and over again in intricate and abstract patterns so that the meaning shall be lost and only the bare and beautiful shells of the words remain. All we need do is to rid our minds of the humbug of words, to scorn the prearranged leaping together of words, to make by our own judicious and, let it be prayed for, artistic selection, new associations for each word. Each word should be a basin for us to cough into, to cough our individual diseases, and not a vessel full already of others' and past diseases for us to play about with as a juggler plays with puddings.

> Stands Harrow steeple where it did
> When Horace Vachell[2] was a kid?
> And does the Sign stand like a sinner?
> And is there still too much for dinner?
> Lie my old poems unremoved?
> And is your mother's health improved?
> And other questions I've no time
> Or inclination, too, to rhyme,
> And questions better left unsaid
> Till next I sleep in Trevor's bed.

Now the sooner you write the sooner I shall reply—and I certainly want to—and the more of your work you send me the more shall I be pleased. Write as much as you like, or even more, and I promise that my next letter will be longer than this one and will have much more to say. I hope to be coming up to stay with my sister in the next three or four weeks; no definite date is arranged yet, but I'll let you know as soon as it is; and, if nothing else, we can spend a few hours together in the Fitzroy Tavern.[3] But I hope I'll be able to see you longer than that.

Goodbye and God bless you.

Dylan

MS: Buffalo

---

1 Gertrude Stein, American avant-garde writer, who lived in Paris.
2 Horace Vachell (1861–1955), novelist.
3 The Fitzroy Tavern in Charlotte Street, then a landmark for London's bohemians, gave the 'Fitzrovia' district its rather self-conscious name.

*PAMELA HANSFORD JOHNSON

[January 1934][1]

Spajma and Salnady
or
Who Shot the Emu?

---

a one act play never to be presented

(It ought, perhaps, to be explained that the names of the two principal characters—Spajma Oh-no-nel and Salnady Moth—are anagrams upon the respective names of the present reader and author.)

Scene One:

(The scene is set in a large hall, curtained in red and puce; there are scarlet bananas painted all over the ceiling, and the skins of dead lepers cover the floor; all the doors are the wrong way up and have no knobs, an oversight made up for by the fact that there are knobs on nearly everything else; in the corners can be seen the garrotted bodies of old herbalists, the left arms of postmen, and the complete works of Galsworthy. When the curtain rises the scene is in darkness. After the third hour of darkness, a very small voice is heard saying, 'For Christ's sake put on the light, Albert.' The lights go up, and the Spirit of Poetry—a stout, middle-aged woman clad in a fireman's costume—is seen to be brooding in the middle of the stage.)

Spirit of Poetry Life is like that; it always reminds me of Scarlatti, for fugue people know how to enjoy it. How can *I* be possibly expected to be unmiserable when, like a professed midwife or a smalltown whoremaster, I am knocked and called up at all hours of the day and night? Day after day, week after week, pale young people come up to me, and, with hardly a smile or a goodmorning, ask for a quick half pound of inspiration all about pimps and gasworks. And probably at that very moment I am making up a private verse of my own concerning the beauty of the gum-trees in Radnorshire. But of course I always oblige 'em; I give them their half pound, with a couple of drains thrown in, and then ...

(A Startled Young Poet with peas in his hair suddenly thrusts his head round one of the curtains)

Startled Young Poet Give me a rhyme for 'pimp', quick.

Spirit of Poetry 'Limp', you bloody fool.

[1] Johnson noted its receipt in her diary on 17 January. The letter has no salutation.

(The S.Y.P. cackles and retires)

There you are, you see what I was telling you. It's like that all day. And the things I've got to provide: everything from traction-engines for the Realists to anemones for the Kiplings or Kiplets. Oh, why wasn't I the Spirit of Carpentry; carpenters need such small vocabularies.

(Enter a Pale Realist in spats)

Pale Realist Quick, give me a rhyme for 'gasworks'.

Spirit of Poetry I can't, there isn't one.

Pale Realist Oh, yes there is.

Spirit of Poetry Oh, no there isn't.

Pale Realist Oh, yes there is.

(This argument would go on for some considerable time, but it is broken by the entrance of Spajma Oh-no-nel, the poetess; bearing her famous torso proudly in front of her—a couple of very old publishers are hiding in it, by the way—she steps between the combatants)

Spajma Stop!

(They stop)

Spirit of Poetry Oh Gawd, you here again?

(The Pale Realist sees her, makes a noise in his teeth, and vanishes)

Spajma I want half a pound of the usual, please.

Spirit of Poetry All right, all right, don't hurry me. Where's the other swine?

Spajma What other swine?

Spirit of Poetry You know.

Spajma Oh, Salnady Moth, you mean?

Spirit of Poetry Of course that's who I mean. Where is he? I gave him a stanza too much yesterday, and the day before he stole a short story when I wasn't looking. You can't trust those Metaphysicians: they'd steal the eggstains from the corners of your mouth. What did you say you wanted?

Spajma Half a pound of the usual, please, and a rhyme for 'navel'.

Spirit of Poetry 'Navel'? No, no, you don't mean 'navel' my dear; that's the wrong word for your school; you probably mean 'grovel'.

Spajma No I don't; 'navel' I want; and tomorrow I'll want six 'bellies' and a 'senna-pod'.

Spirit of Poetry I knew it; it's that dreadful Moth creature; he's corrupting you.

(Enter Salnady Moth, with a leer.)

Salnady Good morning. A quick womb, please, two milks, a hangman, a dash of sleep, and a pint of wax.

(With a scream, the poor Spirit makes her exit, doubtlessly going in the direction of the Metaphysical Stores. Our hero and heroine are left alone.)

Salnady Nice weather we're having. What have you been doing lately?

Spajma I've been to see John Barrymore on the films. Don't you love his moustache?

Salnady I'm afraid I very rarely go to the pictures. The vast majority of films is atrociously bad, but that is not the reason which prevents me from going. My diurnal round—with which, from our last conversation, you are acquainted—allows little time for me to sit, holding a greasy hand in mine, to swoon before the magnified image of a platinum blonde, or to wonder how much worse that mountebank of an actor, John Barrymore, can possibly be in his next film. A good description of him is: a bunch of mannerisms and a profile. Among the few films I have enjoyed are: the Cabinet of Dr Caligari, Atalanta, Student of Prague, Edge of the World, Vaudeville, Waxworks, the Street, M, & Blue Angel (all German); Sur les Toits de Paris; Potemkin (Russian); The Gold Rush, the Three Little Pigs, & the Marx Brother comedies (American). The 'Bill of Divorcement' was not a film at all, but a screened play very badly & very theatrically acted, with the exception of the girl; the plot was disastrously altered, and the introduction of that wretched 'unfinished sonata' reached the depths of bathos.[1]

Spajma Don't you like Norma Shearer, Lionel Barrymore, Clark Gable, George Raft, Joan Crawford, & Uncle Tom Navarro and all?

Salnady No. I like abstruse poetry, symbolical fiction, discordant music, & beer. Oh, yes, I like you, too, by the way.

Spajma (coyly) Wait till you know me proper, flesh and all.

Salnady Don't be pornographic. I said I like you, and I do. When I know you better I shall like you better. I know. It's I'm the trouble. There's the great possibility, or even probability, that you won't like me at all.

Spajma I agree. But tell me, who was that burner of boats who has been playing ducks and drakes with the lily of my reputation?

Salnady To translate: you mean who was it who said that he had met you and did not like you?

---

1 Thomas liked horror and thriller movies, and the German titles he mentions include some of the best-known. *A Bill of Divorcement* (1932) was adapted from the 1921 play by Clemence Dane (pseudonym of Winifred Ashton) about a deranged father.

Spajma Yes.

Salnady It was the Arty Young Person who met you—only for an hour or two—in Steyning, where, in the company of a tall thing and a limping girl, he had come to have tea and argue with Victor Neuburg. You were there, so he tells me, lying in a hammock or some such thing and looking very bored at his conversational efforts. Neuburg showed him your poems, and he did not like them. In his own words 'she' (you) 'had a nice body but a bloody brain'. He made another couple of rude remarks, too, but I'm too much of a gentleman to repeat them. Beneath my black shirt beats a white heart.

Spajma And that's all.

Salnady That is all. I think I'm Pretty Decent to tell you. I could have kept you curious for ages. But then the incident is very little in itself. He liked what he saw of the body but didn't like what he saw of the mind; I like what I've seen of the mind and haven't seen any of the body. But I like both.

Spajma I hated him, anyway. Or didn't I?

(At this enigmatic point, the two agèd publishers leap out of Spajma's capacious torso where they have been hiding and eavesdropping—eavesdropping in the torsoes of lady poets is still, incidentally, a much practised recreation in many parts of Shropshire—and execute a nimble dance around the handsome, if pygmy, couple.)

First Publisher I wanted to publish your book but I didn't like the title.

Second Publisher I wanted to publish your book but the title gave me the pip.

Salnady What was the title?

Both Publishers Symphony for Full Orchestra . . .

(And with a howl they vanish under one another's beards.)

Spajma This comes as a surprise to me. Don't *you* like the title?

Salnady Not I. I like it less than 'Dayspring'. You won't take offence, I know, when I tell you what impression such a title might give one. It sounds rather presumptuous, I'm afraid, as if your undoubted talents had reached their full maturity. If I were a cynical reviewer, I might be tempted to say: 'Miss Johnson is a gifted composer—for the picolo.' You don't mind my saying I don't like the title, do you? I'd much prefer just 'Poems' or 'Thirty Poems' or even 'First Poems'. Still, I am very much looking forward to my signed Presentation Copy from the author.

(For the first time Spajma perceives that her companion is walking—though, of course, he is not walking at the moment—with a hobble and a stick.)

Spajma (with interest) Why are you limping?

Salnady   I have sprained my ankle, and very painful it is, too. It happened like this: (Spajma looks very bored but he continues) On Sunday nights it is my custom to go to my Mermaid hotel—you can't have an official drink in Wales on a Sunday, of course—creep up the stairs & into the manageress's room where, in the company of the manageress herself—a stout, charming, middle-aged girl with red hair and a thirst—a dim barmaid, & my dress-designing toper, I consume too much out of too many bottles, argue on obscure religious points, & listen to a gramophone. Last Sunday I stayed longer than usual, and, in attempting to go downstairs to the bar, slipped and fell a considerable way. My ankle went up like a balloon & I retired to bed, the manageress's bandages, sympathetic stories from the toper, and more beer. There was slight annoyance when I arrived home in time for dinner the next day. The untidiness of my speech is due to the fact that I am still in great pain.

Spajma   There's a pity, you sot. But you're too young for all this ladishness, aren't you? You probably think it's very smart & wicked of you. It's just childish.

Salnady   Possibly. But it must be drink or drug, you know.

Spajma   Yah! Haven't you any ambitions?

Salnady   (with a subtle leer) Yes, to learn German.

(This remark is greeted with derisive laughter from the 147 dumb Jews who have just come in)

Spajma   No, real ambitions, not laughable ones like that.

Salnady   That was real. But I should like to see a crippled yoddler throwing almanacks from the top of the Matterhorn; I should like to see a Bulgarian spy eat spinach with a violin bow; I should like to see a bankrupt teacher of eurythmics stealing the dental plate from a Yukon trapper; I should like to stand on an ice-floe and teach Rameau to a class of conies; and I should like to learn German.

Spajma   And you think you're funny.

(She joins in the general Jewish laughter and spits elegantly at the approaching figure of the Spirit of Poetry).

Spirit of Poetry   It's no good; I've run out of all you want. Mr Moth, you have used up all the available milk, wombs, wax, hangmen, and sleep. Miss Oh-no-nel, there's none of your usual left: you've used it all up, all your bliss and rowan hedges, your half-forgotten loves and tired trees, your absent Pucks, your Titania-lidded roses.

Spajma & Salnady   Then what on earth are we to do?

Spirit of Poetry   Nothing on earth, my children. Neither in hangmen nor roses will you find what you want. You must go and look far away. Both of you are too limited.

Salnady Oh, but I wrote an awfully good story called 'The Tree'.

Spajma Well, I liked it anyway, though other people probably won't. And I wrote two awfully good poems; one was called 'Phoenix', & I didn't have a title for the other one.

Salnady Yes, I liked them. But I'll tell you all about them in detail the next time we meet.

Spirit of Poetry Yes, and this mutual admiration pleases *me* very much. But there's nothing left of your old stuff, and what there is is in the bargain basement of the Metaphysical Stores. This hall is very big, but it becomes very stuffy at times. And I don't like the way these 147 dumb Jews keep popping in and out.

Spajma Who are they?

Spirit of Poetry Oh, they are the Philistines of the world; they always hang around the doors of this building. When anybody asks me for something particularly absurd or eccentric, or when the same person asks me for the same things all the time, or when anybody makes a more than usually silly remark, they all charge in and jeer. They're probably not so dumb as we think. Now don't hang about here any more, there's good children. Go away, it's much bigger and brighter outside. Parnassus—& pardon the cliché, me dears, is always outside; you know that, don't you? Out you go, and do a bit of climbing.

(The Startled Young Poet, the Pale Realist, and many thousands of young women in hand painted sandals suddenly burst through the door & shout at the Spirit. Spajma and Salnady go out together. The Jews see them go, but for once they do not jeer.)

Scene Two:

(The scene is changed. The hall has given place to a great stretch of mountains, and the ceiling to the stretch of a mad and star-covered sky. It is dark. Spajma and Salnady are standing motionless upon the lowland, looking up at the lean tops of the mountains. Though it is too dark to see their faces, we know that they are despairing. Though their dark bodies are faded into the dark body of the night, we know that they are weak and tired. There are voices heard or there are no voices heard. It might be the silence that speaks, or the speakers themselves may be silent. But we who stand at a great distance hear those voices say: 'What a little way you have come and yet how tired you are. Joseph leading the Virgin on an ass's back was no tireder than you.' We hear:)

First Mountain I am the mountain at the beginning, a suffering thing of a hill. Milk runs over me. There is blood in my hands. You cannot help but climb me.

(And we do not know whether the sighing is the sighing of Spajma &

Salnady as they climb up the milky rocks, or the suffering sighing of the hill. We hear:]

Second Mountain I am a blind, hot hill, hungry for the food of the stars, to whom this musical world around me is as white and as kind as a breast. You cannot help but climb me.

Salnady Unmilk me of this mothering hill.

Second Mountain Take my blind life. Rebel and rabble, take the wind of my food, let it blow in your spaces.

A Great Voice There is a hole in space.

(And all the time we see Salnady's darkness, we see the darkness of Spajma, climbing the sides of the rocks. We hear:]

Third Mountain I am a happy hill. (We see a contented lightning light him up like a match. We hear:] There is laughter in my green, there are sheep on my sides, there is piping in my shades. (And all the hills echo. We see that the sky is an old man. We hear:] You cannot help but climb me.

Fourth Mountain I am a strange, new hill, blacker and whiter than all the boys' bones under the sea, than all the girls' bones in their unhallowed acres. (The old man has gone, and the sky is naked. She has unbuttoned her stars. We see the faces in the flesh of her breasts. We hear the music in the chiming of her wrists and the stream of her tickling hair. We hear:] Climb me, you cannot help but climb me. I burn like a fat in the fire, I lie cool like a nail in the grass. I am what you will have me, weak or strong, light or dark, warm as ice, cold as flame. I burn, I burn. When you leave me, I go out. You cannot help but climb me.

(We see Salnady's brightness, the lightness of Spajma, illuminated against the hill. There are colours on the nakedness of the sky. Now the sky is a woman, now the sky is a man, unbuttoned of the stars. He is hot, she is cold, she is hot, he is cold. He wrinkles and ages, she is younger than her blood, he is an infant, she is a mother. We hear:]

Spajma and Salnady Where are the others, the other climbers?

A Great Voice For one there is no other. There are no others. There is a hole in space.

(We see the ghosts at the lever of the curtains. We expect to see the climbers climb higher and higher as the invisible hands bring down the sky. But they are motionless. There is another scene. There is an interval, stranger than the play itself. We go out and have a drink in the interval, and are served by young and old. There is a star in our cup. And, drinking, we remember how our two players had been left, low on the fringes of the fourth mountain, looking up at a sky, looking down at a sky. 'Tell us', we ask a critic, 'What is the dramatist going to do with Sanaldy [sic], what is he going to do with Spajma? Will they move, will they stay, one move, one stay?' But he cannot tell us, the interval is long, and the star has the tail of a comet hanging like the wick of a witch's candle over our one cup.

––––––––
––––––––

And in the distance, Pamela, I think I can hear the baying of the 147 Jews. Forgive much. Write soon.

Dylan

Epilogue[1]

I shall be coming up to stay with my sister during the next few weeks, but the sister is merely an excuse. There are only two reasons for my visit: one is to see you, & the other is to look for a job. I have suddenly decided that I must earn money. If not I shall very soon be on the streets. I am going to look for a job in a publisher's office, though God knows what I have to offer any publisher in return for a living wage.

I hope I won't cut my throat before this reaches you. If I do cut it, I shall start with a meat-saw at the side & cut through & through till my head is hanging down my back.

MS: Buffalo

GLYN JONES

Glyn Jones (1905–95), poet and novelist in English, although brought up in a Welsh-speaking household, was a Cardiff schoolmaster when he read Thomas's poem 'The Woman Speaks' in the *Adelphi*, March 1934.

[March 1934]   5 Cwmdonkin Drive   Uplands   Swansea

Thank you for your appreciation of my *two* poems in the Adelphi. The 'Woman Speaks' but the young man writes, and your doubt as to my sex was quite complimentary, proving (or was it merely my uncommon name?) that I do not employ too masculine a pen.

You ask me to tell you about myself, but my life is so uneventful it is not worth recording. I am a writer of poems and stories (a story of mine is appearing in the Adelphi quite soon)[2] who is trying—quite vainly—to dispute Murry's contention that the object, in which the artist experiences the joy of losing himself, is no longer a recognised exchange for bread-and-butter, shelter, light, and warmth. On the economic level, I have no function.

1 The sheet containing the 'Epilogue' is not attached to 'Spajma and Salnady', but probably belongs here. It refers to Thomas's proposed visit to London. In her diary on 17 January Johnson wrote, 'Darling letter—in play form—from Dylan who is coming up soon!' Their first meeting was on Friday 23 February.
2 'The Tree', published December 1934.

At the moment I am attempting to form an anthology of English poems and stories written by contemporary Welshmen. So far I have decided nothing definite; but if, sometime in the near future, you wish to contribute to this anthology, I should be delighted to see some of your work. What is this 'Tiger Bay'?[1] Prose or poetry?

If you are ever in Swansea, do call up here. I shall be very pleased to see you. And if you have half an hour to spare, then I hope you'll send me along a letter.

Dylan Thomas

MS: Carbondale

GLYN JONES
[about 14 March 1934]   5 Cwmdonkin Drive   Uplands   Swansea

If you are not coming to Swansea for some time, why not send me a few of your poems—poems, preferably, that have not been published? If possible, I want only unpublished material for my anthology which, with the grace of God, may be brought out sometime this year. You needn't worry about the poems that I shall accept; W. H. Davies, and all his little nancy parasites, are banned. I don't care so much about the 'hardness' and the 'stiffness' of the poems, so long as they are, in the best sense, modern, and so long as there has been a genuine necessity for writing them. As a matter of fact, I hope that some good 'fluid' verse will find its way to me. There seems to be an aversion today to poems which flow quite evenly along the pages; readers are always looking for knobbly, gristly bits of conflict in modern poems, apparently not realising that a poem can express the most complex of conflicts and yet show none of the actual conflicting gristle. I would really like to see some of the things you write. Are you—I hope you aren't—an admirer of Grigson's 'New Verse', and of the (usually) unutterable bosh that Ross-Williamson prints in his 'Bookman'.[2] You are, I suppose, a good Socialist. As a Socialist myself, though a very unconventional one, I like to read good propaganda, but the most recent poems of Auden and Day-Lewis seem to me to be neither good poetry nor propaganda. A good propagandist needs little intellectual appeal; and the emotional appeal in Auden wouldn't raise a corresponding emotion in a tick. Are you obscure? But, yes, all good modern poetry is bound to be obscure. Remember Eliot: 'The chief use of the "meaning" of a poem, in the ordinary sense, may be to satisfy one habit of the reader, to keep his mind diverted and quiet, while the poem does its work upon him.' And

---

1 A poem by Glyn Jones, published in the *Adelphi* under a pseudonym in April 1934. Tiger Bay was the cosmopolitan docks district of Cardiff.
2 Hugh Ross Williamson (1901–78), author and journalist, was trying to modernise the old-fashioned magazine *Bookman*.

again: 'Some poets, assuming that there are other minds like their own, become impatient of this "meaning" which seems superfluous, and perceive possibilities of intensity through its elimination.' (If you know these quotations, I am sorry.) The fact that a good poem is obscure *does* mean that it is obscure to most people, and its author is therefore— contrary to his own ideas, for every poet thinks that he writes for an universal audience—appealing to a limited public. None of us today want to read poems which we can understand as easily as the front page of the Express, but we all want to get out of the poems twice as much as we ourselves put into them. It would be possible to catalogue most of the reasons for modern obscurity. Some poets, like Gertrude Stein and the French-American Transitionists of Eugene Jolas,[1] have evolved a mathematically precise method of removing the associations from words, and giving language, or attempting to give language, its *literal* sound, so that the word 'cat' becomes no more than a one-syllabled word with a hard consonantal ending; others, like Joyce, have magnified words, lengthened and animated them with contrary inferences, and built around them a vast structure of unexpected and often inexplicable associations; others, like Auden, have taken their public too much for granted, and have cut out all words that seem to themselves unnecessary, leaving their poems at the end written in an imaginative shorthand; others, again, like Rimbaud, have introduced exclusively personal symbols and associations, so that reading him and his satellites, we feel as though we were intruding into a private party in which nearly every sentence has a family meaning that escapes us; others, like Eliot, have become so aware of the huge mechanism of the past that their poems read like a scholarly conglomeration of a century's wisdom, and are difficult to follow unless we have an intimate knowledge of Dante, the Golden Bough, and the weather-reports in Sanskrit; others, like Graves and Riding,[2] have something intellectually new to inform us, and indulge in a logical game of acrostics. Then there are the Cummings,[3] so very often short, who, obsessed by the idea of form, chop up their poems into little strips and pin them horizontally, diagonally, & upside-down on the pages. My own obscurity is quite an unfashionable one, based, as it is, on a preconceived symbolism derived, (I'm afraid all this sounds very woolly and pretentious), from the cosmic significance of the human anatomy. And I think that is about enough of that.

If this letter sounds too annoyingly dogmatic, send me a picture postcard of the National Museum, will you? (I shall know what to do with it.) No, but I should like to see your work very much, not for the sake of pinning it down and labelling it like a butterfly, as I appear to have done above, but merely to enjoy, or not to enjoy, it.

1 Eugene Jolas was a founder (in 1923) of the Paris periodical *transition*. It published work by Thomas in 1936.
2 Robert Graves (1895–1985), writer. Laura Riding/Laura (Riding) Jackson (1901–91), American poet and critic.
3 E. E. Cummings (1894–1962), American poet, fond of typographical experiment.

Now to answer a few questions. I am in the very early twenties. I was self-educated at the local Grammar School where I did no work at all and failed all examinations. I did not go to a university. I am not unemployed for the reason that I have never been employed. I have done nothing but write, though it is only recently that I have tried to have some things published. I have had two poems in the Adelphi, several in the Sunday Referee (a paper you should take), some stories & poems (there is one story in this week's issue) in the New English Weekly,[1] some poems in the Listener, (I have a very obscure one in this week's, too),[2] many things in an atrocious rag called the 'Herald of Wales', a poem in John O'London's, while the Adelphi, the New English Weekly & other papers including, I hope, the Criterion, are going to print some things in the fairly near future. And that's about all. Not a very formidable list. Oh, I forgot, a poem of mine was read over the wireless from London last year.[3] I believe I am going to live in London soon, but as, so far at least, no-one has offered me suitable employment, living is rather an ambiguous word. I shall probably manage to exist, and possibly to starve. Until quite recently there has been no need for me to do anything but sit, read and write (I have written a great deal, by the way), but now it is essential that I go out into the bleak and inhospitable world with my erotic manuscripts thrown over my shoulder in a sack. If you know any kind people who want a clean young man with a fairly extensive knowledge of morbid literature, a ready pen, and no responsibilities, do let me know. Oh, would the days of literary Patronage were back again!

Write me a letter, and send along some poems. Tell me about yourself. I'm too lazy to ask questions. And if you do really want an obscure poem, invest threepence on a copy of this week's Listener. Even if you don't like my poem there's a good Latin crossword.

Dylan Thomas

MS: Carbondale

STEPHEN SPENDER

In 1934 Stephen Spender (1909–95) was a member of W. H. Auden's 'Gang' of politically minded poets with upper-middle-class backgrounds and left-wing sympathies. His first book of poems appeared that year.

[mid March 1934]　　　　5 Cwmdonkin Drive　Uplands　Swansea

Dear Mr. Spender,

I'm very glad you wrote and very pleased that you like the poems of mine which you have seen. I'm glad in more ways than one that you wrote to

---

1 'After the Fair', issue dated 15 March.
2 'Light breaks where no sun shines.' It was Thomas's first poem in the *Listener*.
3 'The Romantic Isle', submitted for a poetry competition, and read on the BBC's National Programme, 28 June 1933. The poem is lost.

me, for I have been trying during the last few weeks to write to *you* and tell you how much I liked your last poem in New Verse. Your poems in New Verse, and the last one especially, seem to me to be by far the most valuable things that have been printed there. I hope you won't think I am saying this merely because you have been so kind about my own poems.

Here, in this worst of provincial towns, I am so utterly removed from any intellectual life at all, that it is a great pleasure for me to receive even the shortest congratulatory letter. The fact that I am unemployed helps, too, to add to my natural hatred of Wales.

Mr. Grigson has asked me, through the Listener, to send him a few poems with a view to having them printed in New Verse. But I don't think he'll like what I sent him. What periodicals are there that publish the sort of verse I am trying to write? I have been printed in the Adelphi, the New English Weekly, the Listener, & the Referee. Do you know of any other papers—or rather, would it be too much trouble for you to write and tell me—which might publish my poems? This is asking rather a lot, I'm afraid. If you're too busy to write, perhaps I could see you in London when I come up next—just after Easter.

Thank you again.

Yours Sincerely,
Dylan Thomas

MS: Houghton

T. S. ELIOT

[mid March 1934]   5 Cwmdonkin Drive   Uplands   Swansea

Dear Sir,

Some months ago I sent you a few poems for your consideration, but have heard nothing from you since. I am wondering if the poems ever reached you, or whether you have not yet had time to read them.

I enclose a return envelope.

Dylan Thomas

MS: Valerie Eliot

T. S. ELIOT

[about 21 March 1934]   5 Cwmdonkin Drive   Uplands   Swansea

Dear Sir,

Thank you very much for your note. I am more pleased than I can say to think that you found something to like in my poems. Most of the poems you saw were written just about two years ago, when I was eighteen, and I think that my work has improved quite a lot since then.

I will be up in town from Easter Monday,[1] or before, until the end of the week. I wonder whether it would be possible for me to bring you some more recent poems to see?

Thank you again for your kindness.

Yours Sincerely,
Dylan Thomas

MS: Valerie Eliot

PAMELA HANSFORD JOHNSON
Round about 21 March '34

Apology & Regret

I apologise for having delayed this letter so long; usually I write my letters very quickly & then forget to post them, but this time it's quite different. I've been too ill to write, to do anything but sit fatalistically by the fire, sip Turkish tobacco out of a most exotic pipe, and scribble small conceits on the backs of postcards. Which shows you how very ill I must have been. Now I am regaining vitality, and will have to write at a hell of a speed in order that you may receive my honeyed words before the end of the week. I shall also endeavour to keep clear of the emotional element. I still regret that now famous letter with all the conviction of my murky conscience. And I do regret having hurt you, as you said, in my last outpouring. I *do* regret that letter.[2] It gives me a pain where I eat and where I sit down. And the pathos of the second folio is equally regrettable. Of course I know that nothing has, or ever can be, spoilt. Of course . . . I . . . know . . . of course . . . I . . . know! The sub-editor can go out of business, and the woolly reporter of the soul regain his position.

Health

The nicest thing that has ever been said to me you put at the foot of the first page of your letter. You won't remember what it was, and I'm not going to tell you. But I shall fight the Spectre of Disease with all my puny powers and grow as pinguid as your melancholy satyr himself, if only to live up to those so many words. And when at last the Great Cricketer disturbs my bails, I shall go serenely back into the Heavenly Pavilion, talking of you & Alma Mater to the enthusiastic crowd, & conscious that my Innings had not let down the prestige you so beneficently granted. This sounds like Mr. Baldwin's humour, but it's deadly true.[3] You alone know how True-Blue I really am, & what a collection of old school ties my vest conceals.

1 2 April.
2 No surviving letter fits the description. But Johnson's diary for 8 March, three days after Thomas went back to Wales following their first meeting, says: 'Received letter this morning from darling Dylan telling me he loved me. Oh it *is* so difficult to reply!'
3 Stanley Baldwin (1867–1947), Conservative politician, three times Prime Minister.

Beyond the Agates[1]

I'm so glad your pantomime was a success; it deserved to be; I, from my prophetic couch, willed that it would be so. Mind, I allow *you* a little congratulation for the success; you wrote it and acted it, I admit; but I had an awful lot to do with it, too. But why say it didn't amuse me? It struck me as being very good. It's not the sort of humour that makes me laugh uproariously & bite my neighbour's ears, but that's my fault & not yours. Wit is something entirely out of my comprehension. I can understand slapstick, rude stories, lunacy & modern verse. And that's about all. Oscar and his little epigrams would have left me as cold as an Eskimo during the breeding season. This is the sort of humour I like & understand (I hope you haven't heard it; you can't stop me, anyway):

A man attended a large Society banquet, & was placed in the next seat to his hostess. When the spinach was brought on to the table, he immediately put his hands into the bowl & rubbed a great deal of spinach into his hair. Sensation. 'Do you *always* rub spinach into your hair at dinner?' enquired his hostess in an icy tone. The man looked flabbergasted. 'What a terrible mistake', he said. 'I thought it was cabbage.'

I find that that story is very rarely successful. But—if it has not already done so—Battersea Rise should roll & retch with its prodigious laughter.

Yes, when we quarrel, your solid Ted shall come & watch us; it should be a very good lesson for him. Do you fling things? When I used to quarrel with friend Jones we used to take it in turns to sit on each other's heads. We might adopt that slightly eccentric method. Had enough? says one. Yes, says the other in an agonised voice. Then the positions are changed. And eventually, tired & hurt, the two arguers sit hiccuping on the floor & wonder what the argument was about.

Your poems are changing, and for the better. The change, not the fulfilment, is quite evident in the poem you sent me. 'Pinguid' *is* a lovely word, but it is also an affected word. It means fat, doesn't it, & is an obvious Latinization. Your first line would be vastly improved if you changed it to its English equivalent. Or even said 'A gray, old satyr, lying in the shade.' Anything like that, the more naive the better. I see that the females who now adorn your poems are a very athletic lot. One woman *would* keep leaping on to vines (probably an alcoholic complex), & now you have a girl who leaps about so indiscriminately that she is called the 'leaping' girl and left at that. I'm not laughing at this sudden introduction of the sporting element. Far from it. I'm just writing a lot of nonsense while I try to define my reactions to the 'Poem' as a whole. The motif—let me have my jargon—is good, and 'curling' into the womb is just the sort of

---

1 When he was in London with Pamela Hansford Johnson at the end of February, they went to see Sean O'Casey's play *Within the Gates*. His side-heading in the letter echoes the title and introduces his comments on a pantomime that she had written for a local performance. Then he goes on to criticise her poems, and 'Agates' suggests James Agate, a prolific critic of the day.

juicy anatomical conceit I love. I can't like the second line of the last stanza. I fail to see *why* she should bite her lip, or change colour like a piece of litmus paper. She should have been more subtle in her—what is it?—her loathing, though neither that nor the crossed-off word are the ones I mean. She needn't have gone to the trouble of gnawing her own anatomy. The old boy, pinguid as ever, could merely have looked into her eyes, & seen there, hidden, deeply away, the reason for his letting her go. Which would be much better psychologically, and would probably result in a better poetical line.

The two prose-poems (I'll allow you that) are very uneven. Much of the writing is, for you, almost criminally wrong, being just what you can do so well but shouldn't. You can lavish the best lavishers in the country off their spates when you want to. But don't you dare do it. But what the hell's the good of me talking if you listen with one ear & with the other catch the modulations of the bagpipe and the rippling rill? Piece One is remarkable for the number of entirely meaningless & affected words you have managed to drag in. 'Dulcimer', 'Drumdeep', 'Cohorts', & 'Silken Shadowy Girls'. All the damned abracadabra of the Poet's Corner, and as gutless as a filleted herring. What does it mean, anyway, this coy questioning of the heart (a few centuries ago it would have been the liver, a far better emotional prophet) as to whether you shall, or shall not, do a bit of 'arping? This asking your heart to browse, like a cow, in the lilies? This semi-devotional-mystical voodoo of Saint John and the Seven Candlesticks? What does it mean: I don't want a message; I believe that poetry can have only one message. My latest definition of poetry is 'The expression of the unchanging spirit in the changing flesh' (I may have told it to you before). But I want something more than this insipid uncertainty, this amorous insistence on the 'silk' in girls, this squeaking of 'dulcimers' when the dulcimer is an out-dated and useless thing. In this Piece you adopt the same attitude that makes a person call a poet a 'troubadour'. Why 'cohorts'. Ah. I know the reason. 'Cohorts' is a pretty word, with a lot of nice, dim, tapestry associations. But, my dear, you aren't doing a piece of embroidery. You're writing a poem. And the whole trouble is, of course, that you aren't. This Piece should never have been straggled out as prose. You shd have written them in metre, and they would have been bloody still.

I will knock this romanticist warbling of yours out of your head. I've got a lot to say to you, but I'll wait till I *see* you. Then I can tell you really what I mean. 'The blood-wet rags of the beggar' is good, and so are little patches—I keep coming back, however unconsciously, to embroidery images—in 'Fear', which is, as a whole, almost worse. One of my troubles in slating these is my conscious feeling that the *emotion* in both *is* worth expressing. But, far from there being too little, there is too much 'peace in your pen'. It flows—that's the word—far too quickly & fluidly.

More about these—& a far saner criticism—when I see you. I want you to write *very* well, because I know you can. And, blast my gizzard, I'll do my best to make you drop this willowage and lilery.

I'm sorry Jack Common refused your poems.[1] I advise you to try Squire of the 'Mercury', but I wish you'd let me select them. I know the ones he'll accept.

[*At head of page:* I couldn't—just *couldn't*—finish the poem I told you about. Very caddishly I used the dolphins in another poem which I'm enclosing.]

I've had a few poems in papers lately (New English Weekly, Listener, & John O'London), but I've been frightfully lucky in other ways.[2] After my poem was printed in 'The Listener', Stephen Spender wrote me a letter, saying that he liked it, & offering me some review work on a few good periodicals. I'm going to meet him & have dinner with him when I come up. He might be able to do something for me. Geoffrey Grigson, too, wrote a letter, asking me if I'd like to have some poems printed in New Verse. And, best of all, T. S. Eliot wants me to call & see him. He was, for him, quite complimentary. From a literary point of view this has been a very good week. From every [?other] point it's been terrible. I've been feeling ill, and I've wanted to have you to talk to. Now I'm better, and I'm coming up to town next Thursday. I *will* come to your place on Saturday. Don't say you have visitors or anything like that, will you? (Anyway you asked me, & I know you want me to come).

I'm not going to write any more. This is probably the worst letter I've ever sent you. But I want you to get it before the weekend. Write to me before Thursday, & reassure me.

> Love,
> Dylan

I'm sending you two poems—one very simple—& a bad short story. The story is included only because it will give you an opportunity to give me the bird as ferociously (what a curious idiom, especially with that adjective) as I gave it to you over the Prose Things. I'm almost frightened that it's whimsy, God deliver me.

> Love again
> Dylan

MS: Buffalo

STEPHEN SPENDER
[late March 1934]   5 Cwmdonkin Drive   Uplands   Swansea

Dear Mr. Spender,

Thank you very much for the trouble you have taken in sending me the names and addresses of those papers. I have already sent half a dozen poems to the Spectator, and have mentioned your name. (Even if I sent

1 Jack Common was a left-wing writer associated with the *Adelphi*.
2 *New English Weekly* printed stories, not poems, in January and March 1934. *John O'London's Weekly* printed a poem, but not until 5 May.

poems to every periodical you mention, I would still have enough left over to light all the fires in Wales.) I haven't seen the Spectator recently, but isn't it rather—conservative?

Since your letter I have come across Mrs Munro's 23-33 Anthology for the first time,[1] and again I thought your poems the most valuable there. But who is Gascoyne? I saw a geometrical effort of his in one New Verse, and also a poem in which he boasted of the ocarina in his belly. Is he much subtler or much more absurd than I imagine? It is his sheer incompetence that strikes me more than anything else. (I don't really know why I am writing this, which can be of little interest to you, but his poems seem particularly false by the side of 'Byzantium' and 'After They Have Tired'.)

T. S. Eliot, to whom Richard Rees of the Adelphi showed a few of my poems some months ago, wrote me a very nice note this week, asking me to send him some more recent things. I may still use your name when I write to him, mayn't I?

And yes, I certainly would like to do some reviewing. I need all the money I can possibly get. I shall be very grateful to you if you can get me a little to do. I am coming to town next week for one reason alone: to attempt to make some unsuspecting editor see that, without my assistance, his paper is bound to fail; the point will probably take a lot of seeing.

I shall be in London next Friday, and will stay for a few days. Either the 2nd or the 3rd will suit me perfectly. Would the best thing be for me to give you a ring on one of those days, or could I meet you at some place in town?

Thank you again for your letters and your advice.

Yours Sincerely,
Dylan Thomas

MS: Houghton

GEOFFREY GRIGSON
[late March 1934]   5 Cwmdonkin Drive   Uplands   Swansea

Dear Mr. Grigson,

Thank you very much. I am glad you are going to print the two poems I sent you. I am enclosing a new poem, just completed, which may be some good to you.[2] I shall send you some more poems later, if I may.

I shall be up in London from Easter Saturday until the end of the following week, and am visiting Hampstead during that time to see some friends. Could I call & see you?

Yours sincerely,
Dylan Thomas

1 Thomas had been given the anthology for Christmas, as he wrote on 25 December.
2 The next two issues of New Verse contained three Thomas poems: 'Our eunuch dreams' (April); 'When once the twilight locks' and 'I see the boys of summer' (June).

P.S. I have been reading over again my poem starting 'Our eunuch dreams . . .', and am struck more forcibly than before by what might seem to be the jarring optimism of the first six lines of the fourth part. I suggest that this revised stanza sounds far less false:

> This is the world: the lying likeness of
> Our strips of stuff that tatter as we move
> Loving from rag to bone;
> The dream that kicks the buried from their sack
> And lets their trash be honoured as the quick.
> Suffer this world to spin.[1]

But, of course, it's entirely in your hands. If you think this revised version to be better in any way, I do hope you'll use it.

Dylan Thomas

MS: Buffalo

PAMELA HANSFORD JOHNSON
[late March 1934]

My dear Pamela (I may call you that, mayn't I?)

So glad to have your letter. What a nice hand you have. You must write to me again some time. I do *so* love receiving *intellectual* letters, don't you? It gives you a sort of—how shall I put it—a sort of stimulus, don't you find? And when one is plucking one's own little flowers from the Garden of Poesy (such a lovely phrase, don't you think. It was told to me by a Mr. Wheeble), it helps, nay invigorates one to fresh horticultural efforts, to know that far away from one is yet another soul scarching for Beauty ('Truth is Beauty', you know, as Keats so aptly put it) in those Evergreen Haunts.

And, my dear, how can I tell you in words—words! ah, frail words! such gossamer cups they be!—the emotions your prosepoems inspired in my bosom. (I have often thought, haven't you, that whereas the Upper Classes have bosoms the Working Classes almost invariably have breasts.) Those dainty pieces smacked—ah, false pen! See how you play your gay little tricks with me!—of a loveliness which even I, humble in

---

1 Thomas was revising two lines: line 3, which previously read 'Loving and being loth', and line 6, previously 'This is the world. Have faith'. The changes were not made, and the unamended version survives in *CP*.

my devotion to the Great God Pan (Elizabeth Browning, you remember) have sought after through many sunny hours. So sweetly indeed did they fall upon my ears (Shakespeare, I think, but if Sir Walter Scott I stand corrected) that I have arranged with Mrs. Grimmfluf that you address our next weekly meeting of the Ladies Culture Guild on 'Inspirations I Have Received'. Is this too personal a title? Perhaps I could arrange for you to speak on 'The Sexual Habits of Moths'. Our Guild is *so* entranced with Natural History. *Do* write to me again. Who knows, maybe I shall let you see my little volume of verse. I call it, 'Thru' Hull with the Muses'.

Yours,
Sinfonietta Bradshaw (Miss)

Kind Lady,
    Hearin yew ar a poitess and travel on the tramz I hav beene wonderin if you would care to spare me a 2/6. I have a mutual perculeirity with yew, kind lady; I, too, travel on the tramz, though, being a bachelor of sum 57 years I am no poitess. By perfession I am a Female Impersonator, and I were silk nex to my skin.
    Thankin yew for the 2/6, I hope,

I am,
Lesley Pough

Dear Sir,
    We are sorry but we must return your poem. You are, we assume, under a misapprehension. Our offices are the offices of the London Mercury-Manufacturers Association, & not of the Mercury Periodical edited, we believe, by Sir John Sitwell.

Yours Faithfully,
Rod, Pole, & Perch Ltd

Dear Madam,
    Will you do us the honour of accepting this small Rhyming Dictionary, a tribute of our sincerest admiration. (Move up the car, please!)
From,
The L.C.C. Tramway Workers Union

Thank God, now I can get a word in.[1] You'll be interested to know that the B.B.C. have banned my poetry. After my poem in the Listener ('Light

---

1 At this point a new sheet begins. The remainder of the text probably belongs here.

Breaks Where No Sun Shines')[1] the editor received a host of letters, all complaining of the disgusting obscenity in two of the verses. One of the bits they made a fuss about was:

> 'Nor fenced, nor staked, the *gushers* of the sky
> *Spout* to the *rod* divining in a smile
> The *oil* of tears.'[2]

The little smut-hounds thought I was writing a copulatory anthem. In reality, of course, it was a metaphysical image of rain & grief. I shall never darken Sir John Reith's[3] doors again, for all my denials of obscenity were disregarded. Jesus, what are we up against, Pam?

The poem you didn't like,[4] along with 'When the galactic sea was sucked', & a new poem which I'm sending you, is to be printed in the April New Verse.[5] That particular poem isn't as bad as you think. There is no reason at all why I should not write of gunmen, cinemas & pylons if what I have to say necessitates it. Those words & images were essential. Just as some have a complex in regard to lambs & will never mention them even though lambs are necessary for their thought, you, my Christina, refuse to look a pylon in the face. I wasn't conceding anything. I wanted gunmen, and, shatter my hams (your oath, but such a wonderful one that you mustn't be allowed to have it all for yourself) I bloody well had them. Ha!

I'll be up as early as possible on Saturday, but don't hold anything up (I don't mean hold up a flag or an old man's adenoids in a bottle: you know what I mean), because I mayn't be able to leave Swansea until Friday night. More than probably I shall, of course, but I'm telling you this in case. . . . It's no good me saying I'm looking forward to seeing you again. You know how much I am.

What are we going to do? Smile darkly over the fire?

I want to see Congreve's 'Love for Love' at Sadler's Wells, if it's still on. Will you come? Or is there something else you'd prefer to see. There's the 'Country Wife'; that should bring out your best bawdy laugh. Find out if 'Juno & the Paycock'[6] is still running. It isn't in the West End, I know, but it may be in some obscure theatre.

What a chatty little letter this. Nothing but facts. It must be—it is—the effect of this pedantic day. The sky looks like the graph of a heavenly calculation.

---

1 *The Listener* was founded six years earlier as the BBC's literary weekly.
2 Thomas is misquoting himself. Line 2 should end with 'rod', line 3 begins with 'Divining'.
3 John Reith (1889–1971), Baron Reith of Stonehaven, autocratic Director-General of the BBC.
4 'Our eunuch dreams'.
5 'When the galactic sea' = 'When once the twilight locks'. See page 129.
6 By Sean O'Casey.

No, I haven't been doing anything I shouldn't. I have smoked only two cigarettes since I last saw you. You can't—yes, you can—realise how terrible it has been to give them up. I've chain-smoked for nearly five years; which must have done me a lot of good. I am allowed a pipe—mild tobacco, not too much. That keeps me alive, though I hate it like hell. I take walks in the morning and pretend there's a sun in these disappointed skies. I even go without a coat (sometimes) in this cold weather, & tread be-jumpered over the sheepy fields.

I've told you, I think, about the coughing sheep that plague my life. In front of my nice little villa is a field where bankrupt farmers pasture their animals before the time of the slaughter house. It's hard to believe how many of those doomed creatures are consumptive. Good old meat-eaters. In a week that particularly diseased sheep that keeps me awake half the night with its centenarian coughs will be done to death, cut up in various saleable lengths, and hung on hooks in butchers' windows. Some sweet little child will develop a sore throat one of these days, or suddenly his lung will break up like a plate (not a Bell plate). So much for the carnivorous. One day I shall undoubtedly turn into a potato. You won't like me then. And, on that day of Transformation, I certainly shan't like you, salt rasher of bacon!

I like to be tidy-minded, but I so rarely am. Now the threads of halfremembered ideas, the fragments of halfremembered facts, blow about in my head. I can write to-day only awkwardly & uneasily, nib akimbo. And I want to write so differently: in glowing, unaffected prose: with all the heat of my heart, or, if that is cold, with all the clear intellectual heat of the head.

There were no shear-marks visible in my last letter for the reason that I had cut out nothing. I never shall in my letters, though the uncut material may, when I think back on it, hurt me very much. And how horribly easy it is to be hurt. I am being hurt all day, & hurt by the tiniest & most subtle things. So on goes the everyday armour, and the self, even the wounded self, is hidden from so many. If I pull down the metals, don't shoot, dear. Not even with a smile or a pleasant smile or a rehearsed smile. (Like a speech from a Russian drama. Look, little Ivanivitch, there are bodies in the Volga. One is your little aunt Pamela. Go give her a snow-cold kiss. No, O little wretch, that is a dead postman. That is your auntie, the one with the poem in her teeth.)

What a biased child! 'Dolphined' is *your* word. Nothing shall take it away from you. All my words are your words (cue). The only reason I never finished the poem in which *your* word originally appeared was because I failed utterly to make it good enough. You are with me when I write (cue).

And now I shall rise from the lovely fire, jam my hat hard & painfully on my head, & go out into the grey day. I am strong, strong as a circus horse. I am going to walk, alone and stern, over the miles of grey hills at the top of this my hill. I shall call at a public house & drink beer with Welshspeaking labourers. Then I shall walk back over the hills again, alone & stern, covering up a *devastating* melancholy & a tugging, tugging weakness with a look of fierce & even Outpost-of-the-Empire determination & a seven-league stride. Strength! (And I'm damned if I want to go out at all. I want to play discords on the piano, write silly letters or sillier verses, sit down under the piano & cry Jesus to the mice.)

If *I* had money I would go round the world, looking for somewhere where the sun was always shining, beautiful & near to the sea. And there I should build me a house as splendid as Keawe's, so that people should call it the house of light. All day there should be music, and olive-skinned virgins, bearing wine in lotus-coloured bowls, should wait on my littlest want. Women with the voices of harps should read to me all day long. And one day, leaping up from my scented couch, I should cry, 'For Christ's sake give me a tram'.

MS: Buffalo

*PERCY SMART
[late March 1934]   5 Cwmdonkin Drive   Uplands   Swansea

All literary back-chat postponed till I see you!

Dear Percy,
    I was very pleased to have your note this morning. I have been meaning to write you at length ever since you broke a six-months silence by sending me your two-part letter. But somehow my resolution was never carried out, and whenever I think of the Grammar School I think of you, and whenever I think of you my conscience ups and gives me one in the neck.
    I have, too, a very shameful thing to confess: Since you wrote last I have been up to town several times, and not once have I let you know, or dropped, unexpectedly, on to the Smart threshold. I meant to, of course, but Muswell Hill is such a hell of a way out, and anyway I don't know where it is. Not that that is any excuse at all. Now I want to make up for past delinquencies, not by writing a usual (or now, unusual) wordy letter, but by seeing you in person and personally offering you all my apologies. I will be in London from next Saturday (Easter Saturday) until the end of the following week. I hope you aren't too busy, and will be able to spend at least one evening with me. Do write and let me know where, and at what time and date, I'll be able to see you. What about Tuesday or Wednesday evening? Don't forget. I'll be in town nearly all the time & can see you anywhere. Or shall I struggle to your digs?
                                                        Dylan

MS: National Library of Wales

PAMELA HANSFORD JOHNSON
April 15th Sunday [1934][1]

Soliloquy. Morning

The worms are doing very nicely today. Sunday in Wales. The Sunday-walkers have slunk out of the warrens in which they sleep and breed all the unholy week, have put on their black suits, reddest eyes, & meanest expressions, and are now marching up the hill past my window. Fathers are pointing out the view to their stiff-collared whelps. I'd like a big green stick with a pike on the end. Mothers are resting their bellies on pram-handles; little girls are telling each other their harmless stories of affectionate Sunday School mistresses; boys with pomaded scalps are thinking of picture shows and lingerie; and all the starch, the thin pink blood, the hot salty longings, and the respectable cream on the top of the suburban scum, run down the stones, like a river end up in the Sabbath well where the corpses of strangled preachers, promising all their days a heaven they don't believe in to people who won't go there, float and hide truth. Life passes the windows, and I hate it more minute by minute. I see the rehearsed gestures, the correct smiles, the grey cells revolving around nothing under the godly bowlers. I see the unborn children struggling up the hill in their mothers, beating on the jailing slab of the womb, little realising what a snugger prison they wish to leap into, how the eyes of men are abused by the town light, how the gasoline has crept under their nostrils like the smell of a new mechanical flower, how the stars have been counted for us, how the smiles of Moon, the seventh planetary god, have been translated to the shapes of hills & shores on which, from the first marking of time, the atomed tides of light break and make no sound, how the God of our image, gloved, hatted, & white, sits no longer playing with his stars but curving his Infinite length to the limits of a Jew's theory, and how, each Easter dawn, the sun moves back a finger's length into the East, rising, to satisfy the Christian convictions of the astrologers, in the sign of Aries, the sign of the Lamb.[2]

I wish I could see these passing men and women as ghosts only, and look on their cheap shapes and substances as the own cheapness of my mind clothing itself, for a minute's maggot, in all these diversities. But I see them solid and brutal; if there are ghosts, *I* am turnip and sawdust, and you are the longest shadow that ever fell under the sun. I wish I could see them as the pagan houses of flesh and blood, as creature-boned and sky-sexed, as the beings that have grown like a bug from a bug out of the garden of Eden, as the fleshes that need no brains but only the conscience of their fleshes

---

1 Thomas had returned to Wales from his Easter visit on 9 April.
2 Thomas evidently knew some astrology. At the vernal equinox, 21 March, the Sun enters the imaginary zone of Aries, the sign of the Ram (not the Lamb). The Christian Easter was adapted from a pagan festival held at the equinox.

and the consciousness of their fleshes and the freedom and the Mexican splendour. If I, incorrigibly romantic, could see them as a Yucatan people, call them to a cat-drinking ceremony, and know their names as childish Nazul, Tilim, & Yum-Chas, my Sunday worm would disappear like a Japanese mouse in a flash of green light—you remember the story—and my letter would be as loving as I wish it. Loving it is now, but recondite and scaly as the zodiacal Scorpion.

I wish I could see these passing men and women in the sun as the motes of virtues, this little fellow as a sunny Fidelity, this corsetted hank as Mother-Love, this abusing lout as the Spirit of Youth, & this eminently beatable child in what was once a party frock as the walking embodiment of Innocence. But I can't. The passers are dreadful. I see all their little horrors.

I wish I could see them as the pitiable products of a capitalist system, wage-slaves, economic eunuchs, mass-systemised, the capitally lettered Workers that Sir Richard Rees, & men who need do no work, are so intent upon making the martyrs of their own intellectual Inquisition. Again I can't. What are these Workers to me? Isn't every thought, every lift of the lids, every smile, every kiss, a Work that no creature but this divine, this rational, meat-eating man can accomplish? Man himself is a work. Today he is a dirty piece of work. But tomorrow he may sprout wings under his serge shoulders, be faced and sided like Aquarius, who is the first sign of the vital year. He may be a bluff, white Tsar, ordering the insects of the earth, the slugs & beetles, the preachers and gangsters, the lovers & lepers, & even the little, loving letter-writers like ourselves, on the maddest missions all over this altering earth. He may be as benevolent as the Alhambra, or gloomy as the Gate.[1] Today he is bloody, and that is a bloody nuff for me.

Comment. Night

I read over what I wrote this morning. All is silly, but why should I cross it out or throw away. It's just a little more me for you to grapple with. Which sounds even more conceited than many of the other things I've put in my letters to you. I've often wondered—I thought of asking you, but am always so vastly happy with you that I don't like introducing morbid & egotistic subjects—whether you think me as conceited a little young man as I often think you must do. I'm not, really; profoundly the other way. But I've noticed that when, for example, you—quite honestly and often misguidedly—run down your poetry, I never retaliate, as every true-blue poet should, by saying how very unsuccessful my own poetry is, too. I never say it, but not because I don't think it. I *know* it. And when you say, of a poem of mine, 'that's bad', & I try to argue & show you how good it

---

1 The original Alhambra was a music-hall in Leicester Square, the name used by extension for music-halls in general. The Gate was one of London's avant-garde theatres.

really is—that, too, must sound conceit. Darling, it isn't. I'd hate you to think that I was all self-contented, self-centred, self-satisfied in regard to—well, only one little thing, the things I write. Because I'm not. And I'm not half as brave, dogmatic & collected in the company of Literary persons as I might have led you to believe.

Thank God it's dark. Now I can't see the people outside. I might be in a world of my own, owing nothing but the seeds of hate to all the dark passers scuttling to the rub-a-dub-dub in the bebatted belfries of the stinking churches, scuttling homewards again or out on their half-frustrated amatory expeditions after the sin of love has been emphasised by St. Paul & his pimply apostles. I'm going to put on the light; the bad water-colours on the walls will be meaningless, Lake Como a lake of the brain, & even the naked Greek dart-throwers as human as the lumps of stone that clutter up the back garden. I don't want to see my books; a library is a sanatorium of sick minds; I don't want to see my papers all over the floor; why should I take my bed in the sanatorium? There's nothing better now but sitting in a circle of darkness, watching the shape of the body be shapeless, & hearing the intimate rustlings of the room louder & louder. Why aren't you here with me, in my little circle, holding my hand & braving the wicked world with me? Don't tell me—I know. The world is so wickedly wicked it won't let you brave it with me. I have just to go on hoping & waiting. I can make a shape of you to sit with me in this circle; I love the shape, but the shape isn't enough. I try to think of you marooned on your own dark island. Make room, darling. I'm as lean as Ugulino, I don't take much room.[1] There, I'm comfortable now.

Avaunt, you worm-faced fellows of the night. Pamela & me, on one circled island, sit & poke our fingers at you.

Comment. Tuesday Morning

Monday was a dead day, the hole in space you talk of, such a deep, damp hole as I must have fallen into when I last left you. I can hardly remember a thing about Monday, certainly not the rising & setting of the day. I don't think I read or wrote. I remember lifting up a cushion to see if you were underneath. You weren't. That was early in the morning, & it was after that, I believe, that I fell with a great clatter into space. After all, when you pick up a cushion to find nothing underneath—that's a terrible surprise. Of course it would have been rather a surprise if you had been there. But I haven't got over the idea yet that if I open a cupboard door *very* quickly, I might see you sitting & beaming inside. If you open a furnace door quickly, you'll see the devil, leering on a coal. But you have to shut the door even more quickly. And if, perhaps, you were in the pantry when I opened it one

---

1 Count Ugolino of Pisa, imprisoned with his sons and starved to death, 1289. In Dante's *Inferno*.

day, the shape of you I saw might—& would be, I think—no more than a very devilish trick. And when I touched you, as I undoubtedly would, I would not be surprised to see you change colour as rapidly as though I were a pinguid satyr, & disappear in an acrid flame through the holes of the cheese.

Monday was dead. I know I wanted to write another section of this letter, & tell you in great detail how much I love you. But I died about ten o'clock, & I think you died with me.

Now Tuesday, today, is quite a different sort of day. It's so abominably warm & bright that I shall have to satisfy my conscience, which, like most other things, is bound up in you, by taking a bus to Gower & walking over the cliffs. I shall hate it because I shall be so lonely. But it shall be done; all your commandments shall be obeyed. I am writing this in a deck-chair under the clothes-line. This should really be a very sexy note (it's not going to be), for above me & around me all the disembodied underclothes of this respectable Drive are doing a very naughty dance. Not so disembodied, though. Those spindle-shanked pants, two lines away, have their own airy limbs; a spring demon has inhabited them: O inhabited pants! And that little vest, (mine, I think) is breathing up & down as though the Carnera[1] wind were developing its chest beneath it.

Lunch. After lunch I go out to do my duty & your commands on the rocky fastnesses of Wales. And, late in the evening, I will finish this letter. Goodbye,——. I left the blank because I can't think of anything lovely enough to call you. Goodbye, darling. And I put such an inflection into the word that it sounds almost as lovely a word as I want to call you.

My latest song: 'Come into the garden, bawd.'

Wednesday Morning

I couldn't write last night, was too tired after my medicinal walk which led me into the village of Llangennith,[2] miles from anywhere, very near nowhere. Now, quite early on another bright blue day, I am sitting in the untidiest room you ever saw, writing the last few pages. I have just finished an incompetent drawing in pastels of a negro riding on a leopard down the clouds, & although it has made me feel in one of the most airy & unearthly moods, I'll try to answer your question.

I told you the answer over lunch one day, when you were misting the walls near our table with your long breaths of misery. I told you that however much I loved you I would still be able to say 'Lousy' to anything that you wrote, & to tell you to take up raffia work if I thought that your poems had, and could have, no value at all. And I would. I've said 'lousy' to many of your poems, and will undoubtedly do so again, just as you have spat you of my angularities & my blonde bones. But, right deep down in the

1 Primo Carnera was a heavyweight boxer.
2 A Gower village at the north-western corner of the peninsula.

pit of my belly, I know that you can be good, that you have been good, & that all the little lice in your Muse's ear will one day get up & depart. I can't enthuse over your poetry as yet, & you would know that I was wrong if I did. But I can say, honestly & honestly, that there is a thing in your poetry, in your Lotus Women, Symphonies, Lullabies, & Morning Suns, that is the thing of all true poetry. And if I can't name that thing, it is my fault & not yours. You couldn't give up writing, you know you couldn't. It would be criminal if you did. You have been given certain talents & facilities for the writing of poetry which you must, for the sake of all you believe in, love and live up to. What is wrong is your attitude, or, at least, much of your attitude, towards those talents. Because the talent, which is very easy to see in twenty out of the twenty-four pages of your book, is not enough by itself; the work-woman in your poetess, the intellectual, the thinking craftswoman, has not had half enough to do. You must work at the talent as a sculptor works at stone, chiselling, plotting, rounding, edging & making perfect. You told me, too, over the same lunch, that you hadn't got the time & energy to do all this. My dear, I know; I know you haven't; and I know that it's wrong, as wrong as anything under the sun, that you have to work in a dull, methodical office all the day, all the long, wild & wonderful day that waits for you and can never have you. But instead of going home in the evenings &, after dinner, sitting down to write a poem or two, why not sit down to write perhaps no more than three perfected lines? Instead of three or four mediocre poems, each with a line, a phrase, or a hint of beauty in it, you would, eventually, have *one* poem, or one stanza of a poem, that had all those *collected* lines, phrases & hints in it. You told me that the Lotus Woman was written very quickly, even though I thought it the best thing you had done. I still think so, but I liked it for no more than two lines & two phrases: the rest was ordinary. If, over that same poem, you had spent as many hours as you spent minutes, each line would be one I'd like, & each separate phrase. This advice is easy to give & hard to carry out. But I want you to try to carry it out. You mustn't waste your little bit of genius. You mustn't read bad poetry, must forget your Tennyson & even your Housman. You must pack your poems tight, work at them every spare moment you have. Whatever you do, I believe in you. I believe in you at your worst & your best. Send periodicals & reviews to hell. Work at your poems. And send me every line you write. As long as I have you at the back of me I'm going to be good. And so are you, with me behind you. And I'm going to be behind you & with you always.

Wednesday afternoon Soliloquy

You are my only friend. I say quite seriously that I have never really spoken to any other human being, & that you are the clear point of faith with which the psalmist lifted his eyes to the hills. When I went away from you, it seemed you had abandoned me to myself. And when I was with you, after all these years of pursuit, we were face to face, alone. And you were a tiny spirit floating around the room, flying faster and faster till you came invisible, & I could hear only your wings. It was a very quiet, monotonous sound, and came from a tail-less, mangy dog which limped across the room. I raised my foot to kick it, but it was the toe of a giant who reached up to take the stars in clusters. Then you were behind me, whispering, 'Juggle with these. Juggle, I say. Go on'.

I wish I knew what that soliloquy meant. It means something very big, but I can't understand it. I know you weren't the mangy dog, dear. But who was? That's the worst of writing without thinking: you write more than you think. I must have been the mangy dog, but I don't feel at all self-pitiful today. Damn the nonsense. Forget it. I seem very, very near to you this afternoon. And being near you is worth all the nonsense in the world.

I'm going to drink some coffee now, & then finish this page. You'll have my letter tomorrow morning. Write over the week-end to me, so that I get your letter by Monday. Coffee. Even coffee has become a symbolical rite. The composition of my own letter and—best of all—the having of yours, has become the greatest event of my week, holier than the ritual of the bath, than the linking of sweet airs & phrases, than the night and its dreams. No more moujik, stomachic depression. No more worm for either of us, or if there must be a worm in our letters let it be the jolly, red-bellied one you told me about & not the grey-whiskered journeyman of the tomb.

> Fathom the wavy caverns of all stars,
> Know every side of every sand in earth,
> And hold in little all the lore of man
> As a dew's drop doth miniature the sun.
> But never hope to learn the alphabet,
> In which the hieroglyphic human soul
> Most changeably is painted, than the rainbow
> Upon the cloudy pages of a shower,
> Whose hinges a wild wind doth turn.
> Know all of each! when each doth shift his thought
> More often in a minute, than the air
> Dust on a summer path.

That's my great Beddoes.[1] I wish to God we were lying by the side of the fire, reading his lovely gloom to one another ere the Spider make a thinne curtaine for our Epitaphes.[2]

---

1 The quotation is from Thomas Lovell Beddoes's play *Death's Jest Book*.
2 John Webster, *The White Devil* (1612):

> 'O men
> That lie upon your death-beds, and are haunted
> With howling wives, ne'er trust them,—they'll re-marry
> Ere worm pierce your winding-sheet: ere the spider
> Make a thin curtain for your epitaphs'.

Oh we are not at home in this December world,
Cold sirs & madams.

Shall we live on an island, somewhere in the Mediterranean, writing & reading, loving & sleeping, singing our sweet, rude rhymes to the seals? I love you, darling. Goodbye.

Dylan
X

MS: Buffalo

GLYN JONES
[mid April 1934]   5 Cwmdonkin Drive   Uplands   Swansea

I must really apologise for not having written before, but I have been spending the last fortnight in town, and have had very little time to do any of the things I had intended. I hope your throat is better, and that you will soon be able to come down and see me. Perhaps, if you are well enough, you might feel like coming down this coming Saturday, or the Saturday after, and spending the week-end here.

I read your 'Tiger Bay' in the Adelphi. I didn't like it very much, but then I am biased against that sort of thing. I liked the 'hooks of her hair', though, and the 'guts' of the thing were undeniable.

If you can in Cardiff, buy a copy of 'New Verse', which will be out in a few days. I have two or three poems in it.[1]

Let me know when you can come down. Any week-end you like, and the sooner the better. Your poetry, &, probably, your theories of poetry, are so opposed to mine that we should have plenty to discuss.

Dylan Thomas

MS: Carbondale

GLYN JONES
[mid April 1934]   5 Cwmdonkin Drive   Uplands   Swansea

I shall expect you on Saturday.

I refuse on paper to quarrel with you about obscurity, fluid verse, T. S. Eliot, Walt Whitman, Worker's Poetry, my own anatomic slap-stick, and other controversial points mentioned in your letter, especially as you're coming down. (I would far rather be Eliot than Whitman, if only because Eliot has a very splendid sense of form.)

And as for the Workers! People have been trying to write to them for years. And they still don't care a damn. The trouble is that in attempting to

1 Only 'Our eunuch dreams' appeared in the April issue.

write for the Workers one generally writes *down*. The thing to do is to bring the Workers *up* to what one is writing. (And, there, I'm starting to argue already.)

MS: *Carbondale*

GEOFFREY GRIGSON
[mid April 1934]   5 Cwmdonkin Drive   Uplands   Swansea

Dear Grigson,

Thank you very much for writing. I'm sorry we could not meet for lunch, but your illness was a very real excuse. I shall be in London in about a month's time when I hope we can meet again. I'll let you know when I'm coming up.

I wonder whether it would be possible for you, when you are fit and about again, to see whether there is any chance for me to do some review work. I hope you won't mind me asking you this, but things are not going too well with me at present and I'd welcome any sort of journalistic work at all.

New Verse was awfully good this month, and I was pleased to see Carlos Williams given one in the eye.[1]

1 The April issue, reviewing Williams's *Collected Poems, 1921–31*.

The poem you said you'd read and tell me about is incomplete in the version you have. I enclose the complete poem.

Yours Sincerely,
Dylan Thomas

MS: Texas

PAMELA HANSFORD JOHNSON
Wed April 25th '34 [incomplete]

Introduction

When I received your mammoth envelope, I had no idea what it contained and began to wonder whether you had sent me your life-story in detail. I was quite expecting to see your letter open with, 'I was born on a cold and lousy May day in a garret in Park Lane', or something of the sort. Instead, of course, you gave me enough literary material to fill a book, and how on earth I'll be able to criticize it all by Thursday I've no idea. You see I'm writing this on Wednesday morning, although I received all those evidences of your teeming brain by the second Post on Monday. I should have started writing before, but I've really been busy—what with my damnable walks (I'm awfully glad you've taken to them, too), rehearsals for a play (I don't know why I keep on doing this), drawing the drawings for the play (it's an arty piece of Coward),[1] typing and revising stuff for Vicky, & attempting, quite uselessly, to finish a fairly long short story that I wanted to send you. So now I have only a very few hours in which to tell all the little that's been happening to me, to tell you once more that I love you and think of you all the time, and to do my best with your stories and poems.

Times Literary Blurblement

I agree: it was a gentlemanly criticism, but hokum for all that.[2] The offices of that disgusting paper, as you know, are peopled with very old gentlemen who carry no literary credentials but a pocket Tennyson and a long ruler—the ruler to rap all originality over the knuckles, & the Tennyson as an infallible criterion by which to test everything they review, from 'Chaucer to Ezra Pound'. They were particularly unfair with you; your book, in spite of its little horrors and 'Helens' & 'Black Masses' & 'Possessions', was worth more than the few niggardly lines they devoted to it, & the few patronising remarks about 'youthful freshness' & 'the uncomplicated daring of youth'. 'Lack of experience' had to come out, of course, it's a wonderful fall-back. But even in detail the so-called criticism was hopeless: what 'impulsive mannerism' is there in that very pleasant

---

1 A revival of *Hay Fever*, the 1925 play by Noël Coward (1899–1973).
2 *Symphony for Full Orchestra*, just published, had been reviewed in *The Times Literary Supplement*.

phrase 'grandly frail', which is an ordinary figure of speech (I can't remember the name) to be found in any English textbook. The dig at Mr. Newbury was justified, of course, it was a very easy dig to make; but the anonymous review certainly didn't do you justice. My Dad read your book & liked it very much. He thought it was nearly all fresh and lovely. 'Graceful skimming' was his phrase, I think, &, on the whole, it's very apt. But you aren't going to skim any more. Today's poems—at least they are today's poems to me—are incomparably better. I wish they could have been printed, too.

MS: Buffalo

TREVOR HUGHES
[?spring 1934][1]   5 Cwmdonkin Drive

Dear Trevor,

I have the villain of a headache, my eyes are two piss holes in the sand, my tongue is fish-and-chip paper. Dan Jones is staying here for a few days, and last night and the night before we wasted our substances and distended our bellies with low company. It's difficult to write, because the bending of the head hurts like fury. And my hand ain't what she was. Oh, woe, woe, woe, unto Mumbles and the oystered beer. Dan is playing very weak music. I wish I loved the human race, but ghouls, vampires, women-rippers, deflowerers of weeny infants, warted soaks, pimps, and financiers pass by the window, going God knows where or why, in a dream up and down the hill. It isn't a silly face, it's a purposeful face, with a big vein of rottenness, an almighty canker, growing under the nose. The horrid moustaches of the human face: dripping with last twelvemonth's tears and beer, stained with egg, cows' kisses, udder-rubbings, and night custard.[2] The teeth, the werewolf's teeth, big as gob-stoppers, windy teeth, full of holes, just like Ramsay MacDonald,[3] crunching on the Paste and Putty of Our Hearts—what utter snobs we are to imagine that the card-shapes under our waistcoats hold more of beauty and sensitivity than the little cupid abortions of gelatine beating under a whore's shirt. Look at the notices in tram cars: Spitting on Christ prohibited. In the parks: Do not walk on God. What shall it be? Jew's mucus or gentile's praise? Ripeness is all—all balls. We're over-ripe, we night-walkers, cunt-stalkers, wall-chalkers. The women of the world, perpetually out of perspective, cry, Focus, Focus. Is it our fault that we misinterpret them? Perhaps we've got to be superstitious, natural, supernatural, all one huge satanic process. Our words—'give me a half-pint, a Hovis, a book by Paul de Kock,[4] and thou,

---

1 A phrase near the end of the letter, 'froth on the park trees', suggests April or May.
2 Thomas had a long-running fantasy about this imaginary beverage, whose properties were both magical and obscene.
3 James Ramsay MacDonald, Labour Prime Minister of the National Government, 1931–5.
4 Charles Paul de Kok (1794–1871), French writer, supposedly indecent.

thou old lavatory chain'—are spells to drag up the personified Domdaniel pleasure.[1] Everything we do drags up a devil. Last night, Dan and I, none too brightly, for the womb of the Mermaid was empty, and the radio-gram blaring, discovered we had too little feeling. We almost lost our tempers, proving how unfeeling we were. The petty emotions, hates, loves, and spites, we said grandly, were nothing to us. We were artistic Ishmaels, and we scorned with a ha and a ho the lusts that shot up bushes, burning like cantharides, all over the waterless places. Sex was an instrument to annoy women with, and the anachronistic loyalties, faithfulnesses, holy-desires, gratitudes, mercies and charities were no more than words to cover over the evil intentions of our inferiors. (Because they are inferior, these blubbery-eyed old men, stiff-dickied, these shop-assistants with their ingrown virginities priced at 1 11¾², these frigging boys, these wailing mothers, & disappointed communists; and God help our godheads if we can't play Christ, and Christ was always the white sheep among the black, the superior, the natty gent in a tramps' ward.) We started to remember old cruelties, the purposeful raising of desires in girls we knew & the purposeful unsatisfying of them, the tongue-cuts, the embarrassments, the ungrateful things we had done, the muck we'd uttered with our tongues in our cheeks. Our lowest feelings, when we sit drunk-maudlin, holding a whore's hand, are the highest feelings of the maggoty men around us. Artists don't have to die etc. They crucify themselves etc. All the old bullshit.

Why am I writing this? Is it to show the futility of effort? Are you playing Freud to me as I tell you that, like Havelock Ellis, I bore holes in the floor to piss through[3] or cut a pigeon's throat as I copulate? I don't know why or what, but last night we, who had no feelings, spoke passionately, waving our arms in the air, saying, Desire is Nothing, as we stroked her buttocks, saying, Hunger is Vanity, as we swilled and wallowed, damning the conventions as we took a bus home and lied when we got there. Why I am writing this is uselessness. Stop it. I can't shout, like Lawrence, of the red sea of the living blood. Why can't I put a message in a parcel? There's muck in the soul of man, and a devil in his loins. God was deposed years ago, before the loin-cloth in the garden. Now the Old Boy reigns, with a red-hot pincers for a penis. Here's to him. But the sun's shining, there's a froth on the park trees, mother has made welshcakes, I've got a large Players, & my shoes are off. Take now content, no longer posturing as raped and reaped, the final emblem. Very contented, I promise to write again soon. And soon I'll be seeing you. Sadder than ever before, with a cough and a headache, I

---

1 Daniel Dom, an apocalyptic figure in early Thomas writings, notably in the story 'Prologue to an Adventure'.
2 One shilling, eleven pence and three farthings in pre-decimal notation.
3 Dr Havelock Ellis (1859–1939), English author of the classic *Studies in the Psychology of Sex*. An admirer of Freud, Ellis's personal tastes included urolagnia, which in turn amused (or interested) Thomas. See pages 199, 251 and 253.

say, Goodbye, Trevor, mind Anna & the blue trees. Like a devil, too, I wave my pincers at the stars.

Dylan

MS: Buffalo

GEOFFREY GRIGSON
[late April 1934]   5 Cwmdonkin Drive   Uplands   Swansea

Dear Grigson,

Thank you for your letter, and for the promise of the books for review.

I am enclosing a new poem which I hope you will be able to read, and which I hope will interest you. I think it is a little better than the others you have of mine. I will be very interested to see what you say about them.

I will be up in London at the end of May. I hope we'll be able to meet then.

Yours Sincerely,
Dylan Thomas

MS: Texas

PAMELA HANSFORD JOHNSON
Wednesday May 2 [1934]

<u>Very Early</u>

I have decided not to get up today, to lie serene in my bed and write of the things that go round me, the shapes of shadows on my mountainous knees, the curving of my immaculate breast and the life in my ever-scribbling fingers. I have put on nice new pyjamas, so this is going to be a pleasant day, and perhaps I shall not think of worms at all but only of the sun that I'm sure is shining in the curious world outside, and of other equally lazy people who, too, from the white islands of their beds are writing to oncs they love on the commercial sea. In peril on the commercial sea. What is this death, this birth and apparent pain, this glib love, this rush to the head of so many extraneous creatures of the air that crowd my words and never let me stop a sentence at a nice, rhythmic stop? Don't tell me.

Which I think is about as nice an opening to a letter as any as I can think of. And having told you that I intend to spend the whole day in bed, I now contradict my own slothful intention and pull the sheets back. I shall go out immediately and commune with the sun—yes, I have established the fact: the sun is shining most strongly—or, on second thoughts, retire into a blowsy world of papers and pencils and write weak odes to a literary parhelion.

Now it's very obvious that I shouldn't begin to write so early. Half in, half out of sleep, I can't possibly write anything but a lot of high-falutin nonsense. Most words are Boojums at eight o'clock. And I can never say, 'Hark, hark the Snark' until at least after breakfast.

Well, why am I writing now? *You* have already risen and are staring, not very intelligently, at the stories of sudden death in the Express. Or perhaps it may be later than I think, and you are buying your cigarettes at the shop where the girl who thinks me jolly would be very much surprised if, tousled and red-eyed, livered and lachrymose, I was to walk in now. Or perhaps you are sitting in the bus, passing Chelsea or Kronsky, and wondering what the hell rhymes with piano. And here *I* lie, in a lukewarm bath of half-slumber, with the unpolished taps of words turned full on. Yes, why? I wanted to tell you the most remarkable dream I dreamed last night, in which I was climbing ladders all the time and waving to Pamela-faced horses on the top of asylum towers. But when I started to put the dream in order, it sounded Double Dutch, or, at least, Double Hatch, to me.

After Breakfast

It is still too early to be intelligent. Sometimes I think it always is, and that about fourteen o'clock I might really get up and say something brilliant. But anyway you wouldn't like me if I did, and the hankering after cleverness is the hobby (wrong word introduced for the sake of the alliteration) that, theoretically, I most abhor. I should like to indulge in a rapid rifle rattle of Oscar wit—not necessarily concerning Oscardom (Pouff is the sweetest thing)—and say new clever things about sex and moths and hipbaths and all other luxuries in this breadandbutter world.

The mention of Oscar reminds me of Oscar Browning, that divinely blueblooded snob of the Oxford nineties. The last incident about him I read yesterday—I wish I could say I'd read it Gomorrah—in a book called 'Swan's Milk' by Louis Marlow.[1] I'll repeat the very simple story, but first explain that Oscar was a little, very old, bald don, of the sort who always stops—in hopes—to read the writing on public lavatory walls. Oscar and another man were sitting on a mountain side, talking. 'What is the difference between a bob and a shingle?' the old don enquired. 'There's not much difference, only a shingled head looks like a boy's, behind.' 'A boy's behind,' roared Oscar, 'A boy's behind. How can I sit here and listen to your obscene observation. A boy's behind. I've never wanted to see a boy's behind. Any other simile. But a boy's. . . .' And in sheer joy he kicked a little dog who happened to be near them right over.

That's all. And that's enough for an hour. I want to read the crime page in the Telegraph. And I have, too, a violent desire to draw pin-men.

Noon

Or, at least, somewhere near noon. It's the word that attracted me. Have I ever told you of the theory of how all writers either work towards or away from words? Even if I have, I'll tell it to you again because it's true. Any

---

1 Louis Marlow (1881–1966). Some of his books were written under his real name, Louis Wilkinson.

poet or novelist you like to think of—he either works *out of* words or in the *direction of* them. The realistic novelist—Bennett,[1] for instance—sees things, hears things, imagines things, (& all things of the material world or the materially cerebral world), & then goes toward words as the most suitable medium through which to express these experiences. A romanticist like Shelley, on the other hand, is his medium first, & expresses out of his medium what he sees, hears, thinks, & imagines.

A nice, true chunk of dogmatism, superbly inapt on such a May morning.

I have noticed in my last few letters—you are guiltless, as usual—a tendency to write a lot of immaterial matter, and then lump in all the actual replies at the end. So that half of your pages go uncommented though never, my darling, unread. Let me be a model letter-writer for once, & reply to your letter page by page in strict order.

Our Future

I believe with all my heart that we'll live together one day as happily as two lobsters in a saucepan, two bugs on a muscle, one smile, though never to vanish, on the Cheshire face. But I will never exhaust *my* flow of pessimism, for, sadistically, it gives me a delight, or a pain and a delight mixed in one, to imagine the most dreadful things happening to us, to imagine a long future of bewilderment and disillusionment ending in Tax Collectors (I never want to hear their bloody names again) matchselling, and sterile periods of the production of cracker-rhymes that we, in our hopeless megalomania, will imagine as the disregarded fruits of genius. That one day you will vomit at the sight of my face, and I at the tones of your voice. That I go nuts and you go gaga. So let me occasionally chime in with a deep chord of misery, & throw myself over an abyss of hopeless and quite unnatural speculations as to the future of two small and harmless persons who, in accordance with everything god has said or has been said to say since the beginning of the world, love and want each other.

May 29

Is a date that has become very important on the calendar. I will, unless everything goes wrong and the winds of circumstance blow me helter-skelter in my pyjamas over the Adriatic or the Caribbean, be seeing you then, and the twenty odd days to go will be more turtle footed than any twenty days have ever been.

When I said that I must have something definite in mind when I come up, I did not mean that, otherwise, I should be starving all the miserable day in the bewidgeoned park. Those days are not yet; they're just held in store. No, what I meant was the utter boredom I'd endure between the times of goodbye and halloa to you. So something definite there must be—

1 Arnold Bennett (1867–1931), a chronicler of 'ordinary lives'.

Vicky's proud party, or a futile interview with an uncaring [*word omitted*], or even a few luncheon appointments with bad poets. I'll write and arrange something with somebody, and probably the result will be as vague as that.

Trouble at home. What a mild, mad phrase. No, no, there's none, or, at least, none that matters. But my father & mother are going to leave here about the end of June & go to live in the country, God-knows-where.[1] I won't go to the country. I'll come to town. And it will need a very philanthropic deity, indeed, to tell me what I do or where I sleep or even— if it wasn't for you—why, why. I won't stay with my sister, either. I am going to find a high, conventional garret, there to invoke the sadistic Muses, get a little drunk on air, and wave my hand to you over the Dome.

Your Stories
'Headline' was good. 'Buried Treasure' was good. And there's a big bit that's good in 'A Man Had A Monkey'. Obviously I like it less than the other two, but the theme is pretty, and the working out, with the exception of a part of the Divine Comedy at the end, sufficient. A very guarded opinion that I at once upset by saying, in my most fruity manner, how, after even the first rough reading, the lump rose obediently in the throat. My objections to the end are these—objections, quite unusually, concerned with the matter and not the treatment. Your God (in the story) is, admittedly, the God of the myth and the fairystory, but there is no reason to make him a silly God, or to make Gabriel a bad book-keeper. All the details of the sentimental murder of the monkey would be known in heaven. God proclaimed sentence on the monkey-keeper in a most unjust & ungodly way. If the monkey hadn't been within earshot, the most terrible things might have happened to the man. And there is never a miscarriage of justice in the heaven of the fairy books. The monkey should leap on to God's throne and pull at His sleeve *before* sentence was pronounced. Otherwise, it's silly, & God is even sillier. '. . . and he was dreadfully afraid. But suddenly there was a clashing in the branches . . . etc.' O.K.

And the other thing: no elephant could deafen Gabriel unless he was a white one. I understand why you wrote the passage about Gabriel stopping his ears. But it won't do.

With pruning & the removal of some of the too many & too emotional adjectives ('Silver' clashing, for instance, in my first objected-to paragraphs) the story might easily be as lovely as Anatole France's 'My Lady's Juggler', a story that, in no way disparagingly, it at once brings to mind.

On points of writing alone, I have a few more things to quarrel with, & especially the very first paragraph of all which is written most carelessly and incompetently. Your 'he's' & 'them's' are terribly misleading. The

---

1 It was 1937 before Jack and Florence Thomas left Cwmdonkin Drive for a village outside the town.

punctuation doesn't help, either. *Who* earned enough money? Napoleon & Charlie Chaplin? . . . so that people would laugh at *whom*? The tail, the beast, the *pollened* head? Or the man & his monkey? To collect pennies for *whom*? I understand it, of course, but it's most clumsily ambiguous.

'Pollened' is pretty unnecessary. 'Its head on his breast' is enough. And surely the man is an Italian. Even if he wasn't, he wouldn't say 'Old chap' to the monkey—You seem very fond of putting these prep-school endearments & colloquialisms in the mouths of nearly all your characters. I remember the little Annie who called her husband 'a silly ass', & the father in the Tallboy Terror who said the most unspeakably Poonah[1] things.

Oh, my dear, their 'hairy nudity'. How *can* you speak of such things. Why not 'the hirsute appendages on their ungarmented forms'? or something equally as dreadful.—'Where his friends chattered together & swung on the trees, untrammelled by velvet jackets & hateful gold braid'. I'm not suggesting that as a substitute for your too heavily adjectived paragraph, only removing a few of the adjectives to let you see for yourself how much better it sounds & looks when it is more simple & unaffected.

The monkey's 'brittle' bones are not wanted either. The monkey's bones are enough by themselves.

'Impart' is a bad word. Be simple, dear, with a simple story, & let the monkey try to 'give' his warmth to the man.

'That was deeper than the forest trouble' is too easy & conversational. 'That was deeper than the troubles of the forest' . . . that isn't good, I know, but it isn't as slipshod. You'll find a better phrase than that.

'Old chap' appears again on page 3. So does 'beastly'. I think he'd say 'nasty clothes', just as if he were talking to a very little child.

'Old chap' again at the foot of the same page. Bai Jove, old horse, this bally diction is enough to put you under the weather, what?

'Winnowed like mustard seed' is too flowery. It's out of the very appealing naiveté of the rest.

The rest is slight and lovely. I have no complaints. I can only sit back & read it & like it very much, & envy you for a gift of sweetness in writing that is more valuable in the end than all the loud & strident sournesses of the rest of us.

I'll read this again. This is, perhaps, the first prose piece of yours that I would willingly print in any prose anthology—with the adjectives, or some of the adjectives, removed, & the heavenly injustice rectified. Yes, you *are* going to write good stories, very good stories. You've written one now, slight as it is. But it's no slighter than 'My Lady's Juggler'. And that's a story that will last, as yours might last. Go on, my Pam, go on. The sky's the limit.

---

1 'Poonah' described the supposed character of stiff-necked British army officers in India, and could be extended to mean snobbish self-importance.

Referee Poets. No. 2[1]

Thank you for your abortive list of poems. I disagreed heartily with you. 'We See Rise The Secret Wind', 'In Me Ten Paradoxes', 'The Eye of Sleep' & 'Thy Breath Was Shed' are all very bad indeed.[2] I have rewritten 'The Eye of Sleep' almost entirely, and it is now a little better, though still shaky on its rhythms and very woolly as to its intention (if any). But I know how hard it is to make any sort of comprehensive list for anyone else.

I am going to include some poems which have been printed, so 'Boys of Summer', though altered & double the length, is to open the book. Other poems are:

'Light Breaks Where No Sun Shines'. 'Before I Knocked And Flesh Let Enter'. 'No Food Suffices' (revised). 'When Once The Twilight Locks' (revised). 'Our Eunuch Dreams'. 'A Process In the Weather'. 'The Force that through the Green Fuse'. 'Where Once the Waters Of Your Face'. 'That The Sum Sanity' (revised). 'Not Forever Shall the Lord of the Red Hail' (revised).[3] And about six or seven others I am still in the process of pruning and cutting about. You say Vicky's obstinate. Well you know I am, too. And nothing that I don't want goes in.

Red Book[4]

So that's where I left it. I was despairing of it. You are an angel not to read it. I confess that if you had left your book somewhere, & told me implicitly not to touch it, the first thing I would do when your back was turned would be to peep, with a nasty, aren't-I-a-lad expression, into the pages. But I believe you, and I am glad you haven't read it because it contains more nonsense to the square inch than most wards in a home for people who imagine they are Bath buns or postage stamps or maypoles etc.

I wish I could have disguised myself as an Old Girl—pince-nez, warts, & thin vowels are essential, I suppose—and come to hear your impassioned reading. Did you read your Symphony? If you intend to some other time, a good idea would be to cultivate—if that is [the word] and I'm sure it isn't,— a violent indigestion before beginning. Think how easy the timpani would be then. But I'm afraid you want artificial teeth to do full justice to the harp. What is it like, really, reading your own poems to a set of polite people who, in all probability, imagine a trochee to be a new sort of lawn game? Were you nervous? I hope you were, you bitch, for you shouldn't read poems to Old Girls. I've a good time [mind] to ferret an Old Boys' Society, & read them the waxiest & wombiest efforts that I've got.

1 Thomas was the second of the *Referee*'s prize poets, with publication of his book guaranteed. It appeared at the end of 1934 as *18 Poems*.
2 Of these four Notebook poems, only 'The Eye of Sleep', rewritten as 'I fellowed sleep', appeared in *18 Poems*.
3 Of the ten poems in this group, three were not used in *18 Poems*: 'No Food Suffices', 'Not Forever Shall the Lord of the Red Hail' and 'That The Sum Sanity'. The last is a distant echo of Thomas's first *Sunday Referee* poem, 'That sanity be kept'; in its revised form it was printed in the *Swansea and West Wales Guardian*, 8 June 1934.
4 Probably the 'red notebook' containing stories, now at Buffalo.

Answers. And Tit Bits[1]

Play was 'Strange Orchestra', which we've done before.[2] I played, as usual, a degenerate artist. But my drawings were good. One was a large abstract, done mainly in furniture varnish, titled from the Revelations: 'The Star Called Wormwood'. And the other two were early Victorian pastels of nude women rolling about in fields.[3] A few of the audience were quite horrified, the con-Genital idiots!

I can't think what plays *we* could do, but I think we'd be funniest as the Macbeths. But in our prospective society, I refuse to play incestuous fathers *all* the time. Let me have a change now and then, and play a homosexual butler. You, my dear, shall play whores & whores only. 'Sex', by Mae West, may be a good Starring Vehicle for us, though I refuse to appear without my trousers in more than two acts out of the three.[4]

Would you like to play Mrs Alving in 'Ghosts'. I'd love to play Oswald, even though he is your son. We'd give them neurosis with a capital F.[5]

I'll look up some plays, & show them to you when I come up. I'm enclosing a poem[6] and a story. Darling, will you type the story for me so that I can send it to Lovat Dickinson's.[7] Perhaps you won't like it very much, but I refuse to anticipate that. Tell me what you think of it. Damn the details; just tell whether, as a whole, it's at all successful.

The poem is, I think, the best I've written—I've said that to you about a lot of mine, including all sorts of wormy beasts. It may be obscure, I don't know, but it honestly was not meant to be. It's too—I can't think of the word—for any thing but New Verse to print. I'll get Grigson to do it. But it isn't Grigson's opinion I want. It's yours. And what are these 'new standards' you've arrived at. I hope they aren't too high.

Only about an hour ago, a boy of fate, disguised as a telegraph messenger, came with a wire from 'New Stories' accepting my 'Enemies'.[8] It was accepted by another paper a month or two ago, but refused at the last moment because of the word 'copulation' on the last page. Now 'New Stories', has it, copulation & all, & is to print it next month.

1 *Answers*, which imitated the George Newnes magazine *Tit-Bits*, was founded by Alfred Harmsworth in 1888 as *Answers to Correspondents*, to begin what became the Northcliffe publishing empire.
2 A slip or a deception—the play was *Hay Fever* (see letter of 25 April). Earlier in the year Thomas had been dismissed from the leading role in a Little Theatre play, *Martine*, because at the dress rehearsal he slipped out to the pub once too often. Thereafter he did little acting.
3 In *Hay Fever*, Act I, a housekeeper is shocked by a painting—'I don't know if it's quite the thing—lots of pink, naked women rolling about in a field.'
4 Mae West, bawdy film star of the 1930s.
5 In Ibsen's once-scandalous play, the 'ghosts' are those of past lies and sexual hypocrisy that haunt Mrs Alving.
6 'If I was ['were' as published] tickled by the rub of love', dated 'April 30, '34' in a Notebook.
7 Lovat Dickson, author and publisher, was managing director of Lovat Dickson Ltd, publishers, 1932–8. The story was 'The Visitor'; Johnson's diary notes that she typed it on 6 May.
8 Published in *New Stories*, June/July 1934.

Try 'New Stories', 118 Banbury Road, Oxford. Address it to E. J. O'Brien—of the 'Best Short Stories of the Year'.

Money

Short stories of the sort I write hardly make anything. 'New Stories', for instance, perhaps the best story journal of the lot, doesn't pay at all. And poetry wouldn't keep a goldfinch alive. Novels and popular, narrative stories are the things. I'm damned if I'm going to write for the Strand,[1] even if I could, which I very much doubt, and novels are a long and arduous business. Besides, it's no use writing a novel merely for the sake of writing one. You have to have something to say that only the novel can express. My novel—I've done the first chapter—will be, when and if I finish it, no more than the hotch-potch of a strayed poet, or the linking together of several short story sequences. I shall scrap it in a few days. No, novels aren't for me—yet. So what's the alternative? Six months ago I'd have suggested the docks or the oven with the greatest equanimity. But now I've got to live. It's when I'm with other people more than when I'm by myself that I realise how much I want you and how very far away you are from me. I'm willing to work. I do work, but in an almost anti-mercenary direction. Which is no good at all for you or me. Something has to be done, but Christ knows what it is. And Vicky can't help. He can do little more than keep himself alive, & that not very comfortably. And the arty people I know are almost as broke as I am. There are all sorts of things I could do. I could get in with a bad repertory company in Coventry, or some place like that—I forget the exact place. But that's as far away from you as ever & quite futile. A man wants to take me for a long trip up the Mediterranean, and I could go to Russia with a Welsh Communist organisation. All very nice, but what the hell's the good? I might have a fairly good time, but I'd make no money at all, and if I thought about you when I was standing on the dockside at Odessa I'd break my heart. So something has to be done. And with that nice, comfortable platitude, I sink back into a usual lethargy and continue to write of my uncommercial maggots.

Percy Droppeth Again[2]

No more Percy again. I haven't got the time. This has got to go by the Last Post. Percy, the ubiquitous, the inscrutable, & the entirely bafty, will have to wait. But he'll come. What a profoundly unamusing book we might make out of him. I wonder how much madness the British reader takes to his ounce of nonsense. Can you imagine the Times Supplement reviewing 'The Quality of Percy'? 'This bafty book . . .' 'Conglomeration of youthful horseplay, senile smut, & lunatic obscurity'. Mr. Gerald Gould . . . 'Hotcha!'. No, I can't imagine it, either.

---

1 The *Strand Magazine*, owned by Newnes, published topical articles as well as fiction, much of which was ephemeral, but included stories by the likes of H. G. Wells and P. G. Wodehouse.
2 The 'Rev Percy' began as a character in games of fantasy that Dylan Thomas and Dan Jones played.

By the way, raw carrots are splendid. But raw potatoes are bloody. I've given them up, anyway, and had breadandmilk for supper last night. It tasted pretty loathsome, but I got it down somehow & pretended it was good. No more yapping at my diet. My darling Pam, you don't eat half enough yourself. I won't be satisfied until we play a rousing game of hockey together. And, after the match, we'll retire into the woodshed—where all dirty things happen—& commit fel-o-de-se.

Again I haven't replied to half your letter, & again I've left too many things unsaid. I don't think that I've said I love you. But I do. Oh I do. Goodbye, Pamela, & write soon, very soon.

Dylan XXXXXXX
a magic number, dear

MS: Buffalo

PAMELA HANSFORD JOHNSON
May 9 '34

Yesterday I received from Southampton a small, round tin of Tooth Powder, enclosed, in an explanatory note, at the request of a Mrs. Johnson of Battersea Rise. 'Eucryl destroys germs in every part of the mouth.' Was that the intention of your mother's much-to-be-thanked request? Or perhaps you sent it after my ringworm poem,[1] in order that I may clean my mouth out with great thoroughness? Give my love to your mother, and thank her for the Powder. Whether it will destroy the germs or not, I cannot possibly say. I hope not. I admire germs. And, if I remember, I shall bring a few more than usually bawdy paragraphs into this letter to satisfy their lecherous itches.

And, while I remember, too, let me raise one nasty growl about your unparalleled bitchiness in pinching my letter to the Neuburg. I wrote a stony, non-committal letter to him, received your pathetic appeal, and immediately tore the old effusion up and posted off a charming, Micawberish affair. And don't you go about jeering at my Old School Tie. I hate Old School Ties. I haven't got one. I shall now attempt to light a Russian cigarette in a most rakish manner, and look all sexy at the mantelpiece. But it doesn't work. I am fated to be British under my Russian exterior. But don't always point at my Tie. Just pretend it isn't there. Anyway, it was a sweet letter, and, if nothing else, I meant what I said about Pamela Johnson, though if I had had any idea that she would see the letter, I would have introduced a long and dirty paragraph all about her nasty little moist-nosed muse.

Again I am unwell. Melodramatic introduction, reminiscent of some wheezy Shylock, to a page of remorse and self pity. But no, it shall not be. Even more melodramatic. Sir Jasper Murgatroyd enters through the

---

1 'If I were tickled by the rub of love'.

trapdoor with a snarl, and immediately opens his waistcoat and distributes, from his navel, Empire Marketing Board pamphlets on 'The Caul of the Colonies'. To put it plainly—it is an intellectual impossibility to put anything plainly—I feel about as much use [*seven words are deleted, the last two of them* Nudist Colony] (a sudden puritanism makes me delete this. Very indecent). (I am trying very hard to deny the Tooth Powder, and to devote all my bawdy and soul to the composition of Old Tin Kettle innuendoes. But it fails. This May morning is un-naturally church. The birds sing the Ave Maria. My germs tell me that Ave Maria sounds like a sexual disease. I whisper 'Poonah' to them, and display an invisible gout. They vanish.) But I am ill, ill as hell. I have had a headache for a fortnight, and haven't slept for longer than that. I've lost all hope of ever going to sleep again. I lie in the dark and think. I think of God and Death and Triangles. I think of you a lot. But neither You nor the Triangles can make me sleep. I've drugged myself up to the eyelids. I have a little box of tablets with an instruction on the cover not to take, on any account, more than three. I take nine, and still I remain awake. I have tried everything. I have tried getting drunk. I have tried keeping sober. I have counted sheep and bathchairs. I have read till I can't see any more. I have tried completely under the bedclothes & on top of the bedclothes, right way up, wrong way up, with pyjamas, without pyjamas. A good idea, of course, is to gas yourself just a *little* bit. But I can't think how that's going to be done.

No more. Darling, send me to sleep. No more. Perpetually pathetic, these daft little notes of mine can serve no purpose but to show you, again and again, how much I need you.

And no Mediterranean for me. I'd love the sun, and I'd love the places the sun would take me to. But it's all useless, for, when I came back, I'd be just where I was before I went away—a little less pale perhaps, but as green as ever as to what I must do in this dull, grey country, & how one little colour must be made out of you and me. The chromosomes, the colour bodies that build towards the cells of these walking bodies, have a god in them that doesn't care a damn for the howls of our brains. He's a wise, organic god, moving in a seasonable cycle in the flesh, always setting and putting right what our howls at the astrologers' stars and the destiny of the sun leads us on to. If we listen to him, we're O.K. And he tells me, 'Don't you go away now. You stick to your un-amiable writings and your never-to-be-popular morbidities. You stick as near as you can to what you love.' So no trampsteamer up a blue sea for me. Give me Pamela & a Chatterton attic.[1] Enough for the likes of me, and too much, too, for God knows why she loves this idiot writing & writing, precious as a herring, on this Old School paper.

---

1 Thomas Chatterton (1752–70), precocious and impoverished poet, whom Wordsworth called 'the marvellous Boy'. He committed suicide.

It must be this ecclesiastical morning that drives me into such stagey melancholia. And so, by cunningly sitting in a room looking over the east of Swansea chimney pots, I avoid the sun and all the priestcraft of May. I sit and devour the brick walls with my eyes, hoping to draw out a little of the masons' opium that, hot from their foul pipes, cemented these breeding huts together. But the room is stuffy, filled with the tobacco smoke it shouldn't be filled with & my naughty thoughts that leap, like Tom Warner's,[1] from clinical observatories in Vienna to syphilitic cabarets in Buenos Aires, from Builth Wells to Chimborazo, from the altitudes of poetical ideals to the rhyming of 'catalepsy' and 'autopsy'.

I shall have nothing to send you. The old fertile days are gone, and now a poem is the hardest and most thankless act of creation. I have written a poem since my last letter, but it is so entirely obscure that I dare not let it out even unto the eyes of such a kind and commiserating world as yours. I am getting more obscure day by day. It gives me now a *physical* pain to write poetry. I feel all my muscles contract as I try to drag out, from the whirlpooling words around my everlasting ideas of the importance of death on the living, some connected words that will explain how the starry system of the dead is seen, ordered as in the grave's sky, along the orbit of a foot or a flower. But when the words do come, I pick them so thoroughly of their *live* associations that only the *death* in the words remains. And I could scream, with real, physical pain, when a line of mine is seen naked on paper & seen to be as meaningless as a Sanskrit limerick. I shall never be understood. I think I shall send no more poetry away, but write stories alone. All day yesterday I was working, as hard as a navvy, on six lines of a poem. I finished them, but had, in the labour of them, picked and cleaned them so much that nothing but their barbaric sounds remained. Or if I did write a line, 'My dead upon the orbit of a rose', I saw that 'dead' did not mean 'dead', 'orbit' not 'orbit' & 'rose' most certainly not 'rose'. Even 'upon' was a syllable too many, lengthened for the inhibited reason of rhythm. My lines, *all* my lines, are of the tenth intensity. They are not the words that express what I want to express; they are the only words I can find that come near to expressing a half. And that's no good. I'm a freak user of words, not a poet. That's really the truth. No self-pity there. A freak *user* of words, not a poet. That's terribly true.

> 'I'll not be a fool like the nightingale
> Who sits up till midnight without any ale,
> Making a noise with his nose,'

is a quotation I write down for no reason at all. Neither do I feel it to be correct. For I'll be a fool like the hyena, sitting up till dawn without any pleasure, making a noise with his guts.

---

1 A Swansea friend, later a musician.

This is out of mood with the day. I should be writing some sunny paragraphs, imagining in the words for you a green and blue expanse of Welsh country where the cattle, in accordance with all conventions, 'low', where the lambs 'frisk', and the glassy streams 'babble' or 'tumble' according to the rhyme. I'll walk this afternoon, and, perhaps, in the late night, when I write to you again, the nearsummer loveliness will have gone into me so deeply that all the clowning and the pretentious stomachraking of the last two pages will be nothing but an echo that refuses to 'ring' in your ears or an odour that refuses to 'waft' to your nose.

But, before I go out, very lonely and quite twice as pale & haggard as usual—I hardly weigh anything at all, eight stone or under now—, into my Gower bays, there are several matter of fact things in your last letter which I want to answer.

Now Orage,[1] though a very pleasant and a very sincere man, is known to be almost entirely lacking in taste. He runs the literary sections of the New English Weekly by a system of filing. He has in his office literally hundreds of poems and short sketches and stories. Most of them are bad, but that doesn't matter. It's quantity with him, not quality, that counts. And week by week one or two of those stories and poems are taken down from their dusty shelves and printed. You just wait your turn, and then in you go. So there's really very little satisfaction in having anything printed in Orage's paper. He doesn't pay *at all*, and the standard he sets is so low that it's hardly flattering to be accepted by him. He goes in for mediocrity. 'Headline', whatever its faults—and I begin to suspect that its main faults, at the moment, may be my fault—is not mediocre, and not original enough—in subject, at least,—to startle him into an acceptance. I've no idea where you can plant 'Headline'. Its matter, I should imagine, would be too ordinary for 'New Stories', which deals with rather out-of-the-way affairs. 'The London Mercury' might like 'A Man Had A Monkey', though I believe they keep you waiting rather a long time before they reply. The 'Everyman' prints stories. So does 'John O'London'; but, for the last, the more conventional the better. I'll have a look at some more of the magazines littered about the house. I can't remember the name of the story, but the one about the watch, the little girl, and the nasty old gentleman, is more of a *commercial* effort than any I can think of of yours. And, though you'll probably squeal to heaven at the suggestion, you might do worse than send it to a paper such as 'Nash's'. There are scores of papers like that, above the standard of the 'Strand' & 'Pearsons', that *might* stretch their standards of taste sufficiently to allow admittance to your cheery little story. And have you sent any poems to J. C. Squire? And have you sent to Harriet Monroe?[2] And what about a mild (very mild) poem to

---

1 A. R. Orage (b. 1873) edited the *New English Weekly* until his death in November 1934.
2 Harriet Monroe founded *Poetry* (Chicago) in 1912 and edited it until her death in 1935.

Frank Kendon, of John O'London's. He printed a terribly weak, watery little thing of mine—I've never shown it to you—last week (Saturday May 5).[1] These do seem dreadfully lowbrow suggestions. But they're not derogatory. Far from it. But you've struck such a curious *medium* in your poetry lately that publication becomes very difficult; there are so few medium papers left. By that I don't mean 'middlebrow' or anything like that. But you've brought 'conventional' poetry, descendent from Tennyson & the middle Victorians, to a point of near-perfection, and any modern, even any *alive* influence, is absent. So that editors of most periodicals are rather troubled at your poetry, for most of the editors (&, unfortunately, the editresses) look at the influences first and the individuality afterwards. If a poem, in the John Donne descendency, is fairly good, they print it; if very good, in the Tennyson descendency, they refuse to. What they never realise—they cannot, of course, being, principally, caterers for the fashionable taste of the moment, and a taste which has spat Tennyson out & sucked up the good & the bad of John Donne in large mouthfuls—is that the convention, the heredity, of the poem doesn't matter a farthing. It's the individuality of the poet, an individuality that owes nothing to the Jacobeans or the Victorians, that really matters. If you, still (& inevitably) retaining the old Johnson individuality, were to tack on to your poems the conscious influence of Donne, Tourneur, Traherne or Manley Hopkins, you'd get published all over the place & be the moment's wow in every public salon. But you're not going to do that, because you realise that it's worthless, & that what Jack Common (entirely ignorant of everything outside intellectual socialism) refused for the Adelphi is far more valuable than most of the Donne-fathered babies he lets discharge inside his nice yellow covers.

I like your new poem, very much as the Toothy Beth (what happy little jingles you could write about a Toothy Beth) would like it. I like it, but can't say much more about it. There is usually some phrase, or simile, or line, or even stanza to which I object, or in which I find sometimes a purposely rough image I imagine to be unsuccessful because it is not smooth enough & sometimes a little gush-bubble that a rude snarl of mine can prick to nothing & sometimes a precious word (a 'burgeon' or a 'pinguid') which revolts against my waxy ear and my urny taste. But, in 'Sarcophagus', I can find nothing except a desire to be liked. And I fall to desire, as always, liking it with a toothed inarticulateness. It's a bit harmless, a little bit thin, I think. I see no vast reason why it should have been written. But written it is, and read it have been, and like it I do. I'm not usually as dumb as this over a poem of yours. But, really, I've nothing at all to say about it. It's there, just there, and I like it. For which brilliant

---

1 'Dare I?', a shortened version of a Notebook poem that later had its missing stanza restored, became 'Ears in the turrets hear', and survived to reach *CP*.

piece of criticism I shall be awarded the Neuburg biscuit—a weekly prize for the longest nothing in the vaguest words.

H. Corby seems a dirty boy.[1] But you're too old a bird to be stoned by him. I think I should like to quarrel with H. Corby about the Justification of The Phallus In Architecture, or The Influence of Sodomy On Wickerwork. What a perverted time we boys would have.

Is, by the way, the Babs of the skyblue jumper the same Babs Ross who sometimes decorates the Poet's Corner with her sweet little name? Anybody who can write a poem & put Babs under it deserves a pat on the back. I lift my hat. Three moths and a woodpigeon, one calling your name, fly out. Ach, it is always the same. These woodpigeons. . . . !

And now, before I get any archer, & start to crack very weak jokes about plums, let me go out for my much-talked of walk. Goodbye till tonight, my dear.

Morning. Sunday 13.

But the night never comes. And two loose days have passed since I wrote those last ink words. They were loose days, and I accept the reprimand—before it comes—with a bowed head and a dim, canary mouth. I don't know why I do it. It's silly and childish, but somehow inevitable, especially on a sunny Saturday evening in a seaside village where, most of the afternoon, I had lain in the sun, trying to colour my face and look out-of-doors.

I hate the little, minor disturbances of the world—the forgetting of letters, the losing of papers, the tiny falls, mishaps & disappointments which crop up, regular as the suicidal wish, each gassy day. Last night, in the deserted smokeroom of a seaside pub, I found myself suddenly cornered by three repulsive looking young men with coloured shirts, who asked me, in a most polite & Turpin way, for my cigarettes. Since they all looked *exactly* like Wallace Beery in one of his less debonair moments, I gave them my cigarettes and enough money to buy three pints of beer.[2] They then smiled—or rather showed me about ten (or less) broken teeth (between them)—and persisted in drinking their illgotten beer in front of me & making rude remarks about the length of my hair. Now, I don't mind their communist ideas, or even the practice of them. But why *my* cigarettes, *my* beer, & *my* funny hair? It's little incidents like that that make one feel very weak & small in a country full of strong barbarians. Before they left me—probably to intimidate another lonely little person—they told me what was apparently a dirty story in Welsh. That was the last straw, & later the sun went out.

This morning, looking at Vicky's noncommittal remarks about Dylan

---

1 Herbert W. Corby was another of the *Sunday Referee*'s poets. He also wrote articles for the paper.
2 Dick Turpin, eighteenth-century highwayman. Wallace Beery, twentieth-century tough guy in Hollywood movies.

Thomas, the experimentalist, I found myself wondering who this sad-named poet was, & whether he had any separate existence from the sadder person, of the night before, bullied out of his lawful cigarettes by three strongmen & falling back, in the event of his comic cowardice, on to a stony pile of words. And why should this experimentalist be given so many lines in a national newspaper, & my Beery-mouthed desperadoes be consigned to the mortality of a letter page?

Anyway, I'm not an experimentalist & never will be. I write in the only way I can write, & my warped, crabbed & cabinned stuff is not the result of theorising but of pure incapability to express my needless tortuities in any other way. Vicky's article was nonsense. If you see him, tell him I am not modest, not experimental, do not write of the Present, and have very little command of rhythm. My Pegasus, too, is much, much more spavined than that of A. L. Basham,[1] who is too selfconscious, or Pamela Johnson, whose latest published 'Poem' is sweet, girlish drivel.

Tell him, too, that I don't know anything about life-rhythm. Tell him I write of worms and corruption, because I like worms and corruption. Tell him I believe in the fundamental wickedness and worthlessness of man, & in the rot in life. Tell him I am all for cancers. And tell him, too, that I loathe poetry. I'd prefer to be an anatomist or the keeper of a morgue any day. Tell him I live exclusively on toenails and tumours. I sleep in a coffin too, and a wormy shroud is my summer suit.

> 'I dreamed the genesis of mildew John
> Who struggled from his spiders in the grave'

is the opening of my new poem. So there. But I don't like words either. I like things like 'ungum' & 'casabookch'. XXX, for you, my bleeder.

All of which, I think, must be owing to the condition of the liver. But never forget that the heart took the liver's place.

My novel, tentatively, very tentatively, titled 'A Doom On The Sun' is progressing, three chapters of it already completed. So far it is rather terrible, a kind of warped fable in which Lust, Greed, Cruelty, Spite etc., appear all the time as old gentlemen in the background of the story. I wrote a little bit of it early this morning—a charming incident in which Mr. Stipe, Mr. Edger, Mr. Stull, Mr. Thade and Mr. Strich watch a dog dying of poison. I'm a nice little soul, and my book is going to be as nice as me.[2]

New story about Mae West: Mae West visited a farm while on a tour through the West States, & was taken around the farm by a handsome young farmhand. They came across a bull making love to a cow. 'Tell me,' said Mae West, 'How does the bull know exactly when the cow is—sort

---

1 A. L. Basham was the third and last *Referee* poet to have a book sponsored.

2 Some of these characters with anagrammatic names occur in Thomas's story 'The Holy Six'. See, in the letter of (about) 21 May, Thomas's description of 'my novel of the Jarvis valley'.

of—wanting to be made love to?' 'Waal,' sd the farmhand, 'It's all a matter of smell with these here animals.' Later they came across a ram and a ewe, also in a Lawrencian attitude. And on asking the same question, Mae West received the same answer. As the farmhand saw her to her car, she turned round & said: 'This has been a real swell day. Say, you must come up and see me sometime—when your catarrh's better.'

Which leads me, quite naturally, to the end of this ridiculous letter. [*Some words are deleted*.] (Sorry. Had to cross this out. It was indecent.) I love you, Pamela, more every day, think of you more every day, and want to be with you more every day. Don't take much notice of my rantings and rumblings, and less of that horrid poem I sent you last week. I love you and love you. I only believe in you. Nice, round Pamela, I love you. All the time. Always will, too. Write very soon and keep me alive. Sorry for all my letter. I'm not too well—perhaps it's that. You don't mind how daft the letter, do you? If it's the mask I know, never lift it, my twiceblessed. Love, & the crosses I can't write because there's not room enough. P.S. What do you want for your birthday? Books? Rings? Wurlitzer Organ?

[*On a separate sheet*:]¹

And now goodbye. I seem to be getting back into my old letter mood, and don't really want to stop writing. But I have to stop sometime, and I've already delayed this letter longer than I wanted to. Reply in a very few days, will you. And do be honest. Remember, I'm very fond of birds (Damn, that again!). Yes, do write back soon. Wave your hand to your mother for me, and kiss yourself goodmorning and goodnight.

Dylan

MS: Buffalo

HAMISH MILES
[?May 1934] [draft]²

Dear Mr. Miles,

Thank you for your note. I'm sorry to have been so long replying. The poem in your possession is printed in this month's New Verse. I had no idea at all it was going to be, as Geoffrey Grigson told me that he didn't like it very much.

I'm enclosing three poems, all very similar in subject & approach. The one beginning 'I dreamed my genesis' is more or less based on Welsh

---

1 The final paragraph may belong to another letter.
2 Written in a notebook where Thomas and Dan Jones composed alternate-line poems. Hamish Miles, the likely addressee, was an editor at Cape, the publishers, and also helped to edit *New Stories*. The 'Welsh rhythms' remark is in contrast to Thomas's later denials of Welsh-language influence, eg in a letter to Spender of 9 December 1952.

rhythms, & may seem, rhythmically, a bit [?strange] at first. I do hope you'll like one of them, though I admit their constant anatomical symbols can't be to the taste of many, & are, quite often, not even to the taste of myself.

I am coming up to town sometime next week. May I call & see you then?

Yours Sincerely,
Dylan Thomas

MS: Texas

PAMELA HANSFORD JOHNSON
May [about 21, 1934]   Laugharne

I am spending Whitsun in the strangest town in Wales. Laugharne, with a population of four hundred, has a townhall, a castle, and a portreeve.[1] The people speak with a broad English accent, although on all sides they are surrounded by hundreds of miles of Welsh county. The neutral sea lies at the foot of the town, and Richard Hughes writes his cosmopolitan stories in the castle.[2]

I am staying with Glyn Gower Jones.[3] You remember I showed you one of his bad poems in the Adelphi. He is a nice, handsome young man with no vices. He neither smokes, drinks, nor whores. He looks very nastily at me down his aristocratic nose if I have more than one Guinness at lunch, and is very suspicious when I go out by myself. I believe he thinks that I sit on Mr. Hughes' castle walls with a bottle of rye whiskey, or revel in the sweet confusion of a broadflanked fisherwoman.

Incidentally, I showed him some of your poems, your latest poems. And he couldn't understand them at all. An ardent admirer of the Criterion, he fails to understand you. And it's quite true. You are getting pleasantly obscure, and much of what you write at the moment must seem quite mazy and difficult to almost anyone except myself. But then the reason is obvious. I, too, am mazy and difficult. We both are in our fleshly lives. And let me remind you that you will find my body damnably difficult to dispose of. 'That particular one' (your Bluebeard words) has found a widow. I will never find anyone except you. The only solution will be a little poison in my cup. Even then there would be the phantom Thomas, head under arm, three mackintoshed, weakchinned and blowsy, seeking you out and groaning his disembodied bawderies in your ear. Or, of course, you could garotte me as I nibble at my vermicelli.

(Rose plot,
Fringed pool,
Ferned garotte.)

I seem always to be complaining that I cannot fit the mood of my letters

1 Laugharne is an ancient borough, and its mayor is called a portreeve.
2 See page 215.
3 Glyn Jones at that time used the pseudonym 'M. G. Gower'.

into the mood of the weathered world that surrounds me. Today I complain again, for a hell-mouthed mist is blowing over the Laugharne ferry, and the clouds lie over the chiming sky—what a conceit—like the dustsheets over a piano. Let me, O oracle in the lead of the pencil, drop this customary clowning, and sprinkle some sweetheart words over the paper, (paper torn slyly from an exercise book of the landlady's small daughter). Wishes, always wishes. Never a fulfilment of action, flesh. The consummation of dreams is a poor substitute for the breathlessness at the end of the proper windy gallop, bedriding, musical flight into the Welsh heavens after a little, discordant brooding over the national dungtip.

My novel of the Jarvis valley is slower than ever.[1] I have already scrapped two chapters of it. It is as ambitious as the Divine Comedy, with a chorus of deadly sins, anagrammatised as old gentlemen, with the incarnated figures of Love & Death, an Ulyssean page of thought for the minds of the two anagrammatical spinsters, Miss P. & Miss R. Sion-Rees, an Immaculate Conception, a baldheaded girl, a celestial tramp, a mock Christ, & the Holy Ghost.

I am a Symbol Simon. My book will be full of footlights & Stylites, & puns as bad as that. Kiss me Hardy? Dewy love me? Tranter body ask? I'll Laugharne this bloody place for being wet. I'll pun so frequently and so ferociously that the rain will spring backward on an ambiguous impulse, & the sun leap out to light the cracks of this saw world.

But I won't tell you my puns, for they run over reason, and I want you to think of me today not as a bewildered little boy writing an idiot letter on the muddy edge of a ferry, watching the birds & wondering which among them is the 'sinister necked' wild duck & which the 'terrible' cormorant, but as a strong-shouldered fellow polluting the air with the smell of his eightpenny tobacco and his Harris tweeds, striding, golf-footed, over the hills and singing as loudly as Beachcomber in a world rid of Prodnose. There he goes, that imaginary figure, over the blowing mountain where the goats all look like Ramsay MacDonald, down the crags and the rat-hiding holes in the sides of the hill, on to the mud flats that go on for miles in the direction of the sea. There he stops for a loud & jocular pint, tickles the serving wench where serving wenches are always tickled, laughs with the landlord at the boatman's wit, ('The wind he be a rare one he be. He blows up the petticoats of they visiting ladies for the likes of we. And a rare thirst he give you. Pray fill the flowing bowl, landlord, with another many magnums of your delectable liquor. Aye, aye, zor'. And so on), and hurries on, still singing, into the mouth of the coming darkness. Or he hies him manfully to the Hikers' Hostel, removes his pimples with a bread knife, and sprinkles a little iodine over the one and forty bats that ring the changes in the Hikers' belfries.[2]

But the eye of truth, tired of romancing, turns back with a material

1 The imaginary 'Jarvis hills' and 'Jarvis valley' occur in early stories. The novel was never written.
2 'Hiking' as an earnest group activity (the Germans were keen on it) was becoming a vogue, both admired and laughed at.

squint on my self, and marks the torture in my too-bony hand and the electric livingness in the bodies of the goldfish I carry in the lining of my hat. Pamela, never trust the goldfish in the lining. They dribble lead over the nice, new felt. And their molten excreta drops, with the noise of the drums in Berlioz, on to the open skull.

I am tortured to-day by every doubt and misgiving that an hereditarily twisted imagination, an hereditary thirst and a commercial quenching, a craving for a body not my own, a chequered education and too much egocentric poetry, and a wild, wet day in a tided town, are capable of conjuring up out of their helly deeps. Helly deeps. There is torture in words, torture in their linking & spelling, in the snail of their course on stolen paper, in their sound that the four winds double, and in my knowledge of their inadequacy. With a priggish weight on the end, the sentence falls. All sentences fall when the weight of the mind is distributed unevenly along the holy consonants & vowels. In the beginning was a word I can't spell, not a reversed Dog, or a physical light, but a word as long as Glastonbury and as short as pith. Nor does it lisp like the last word, break wind like Balzac through a calligraphied window, but speaks out sharp & everlasting with the intonations of death and doom on the magnificent syllables. I wonder whether I love your word, the word of your hair,—by loving hair I reject all Oscardom, for homosexuality is as bald as a coot—, the word of your voice, the word of your flesh, & the word of your presence. However good, I can never love you as earth. The good earth of your blood is always there, under the skin I love, but it is two words. There must be only half a word tangible, audible, & visible to the illiterate. And is that the better half? Or is it the wholly ghostly part? And does the oneeyed ferryman, who cannot read a printed word, row over a river of words, where the syllables of the fish dart out & are caught on his rhyming hook, or feel himself a total ghost in a world that's as matter-of-fact as a stone? If these were the only questions, I could be happy, for they are answered quickly with a twisting of sense into the old metaphysics. But there are other and more dreadful questions I am frightened to answer.

I am whimsy enough today to imagine that the oyster-catchers flying over the pearlless mudbanks are questioning all the time. I know the question and the answer, but I'm going to tell you neither, for it would make you sad to know how easily the answer drops off the tip of the brain. Fill up the pan of the skull with millet seed. Each seed shall be a grain of truth, & the mating grains pop forth an answer. (Bugger me black.)

I wish I could describe what I am looking on. But no words could tell you what a *hopeless*, fallen angel of a day it is. In the very far distance, near the line of the sky, three women & a man are gathering cockles. The oyster-catchers are protesting in hundreds around them. Quite near me, too, a crowd of silent women are scraping the damp, gray sand with the torn-off handles of jugs, & cleaning the cockles in the drab little pools of water that stare up out the weeds & long for the sun. But you see that I am making it a literary day again. I can never do justice [*the words* in my precious prose *are deleted*] to the miles and miles and miles of mud and gray sand, to the un-nerving silence of the fisherwomen, & the mean-souled cries of the gulls & the herons, to the shapes of the fisherwomen's breasts that drop, big as barrels, over the stained tops of their overalls as they bend over the sand, to the cows in the fields that lie north of the sea, and to the near breaking of the heart as the sun comes out for a minute from its cloud & lights up the raggèd sails of a fisherman's boat. These things look ordinary enough on paper. One sees them as shapeless, literary things, & the sea is a sea of words, and the little fishing boat lies still on a tenth rate canvas. I can't give actuality to these things. Yet they are as alive as I. Each muscle in the cocklers' legs is as big as a hill, and each crude footstep in the wretchedly tinted sand is deep as hell. These women are sweating the oil of life out of the pores of their stupid bodies, and sweating away what brains they had so that their children might eat, be married and ravished, conceive in their wombs that are stamped with the herring, &, themselves, bring up another race of thickhipped fools to sweat their strength away on these *unutterably* deadly sands.

But now a piece of sun comes out again. I am happy, or, at least, free from this morning's tortures. Glyn has gone fishing, and in another half hour the 'Three Mariners' will have undone their waistcoats. I shall drink beer with the portreeve, & no crimping pussyfoot shall say me nay.

I forgot to bring your letter with me. It lies locked at home in the Pamela drawer. Its memory makes Laugharne a bit brighter—but still not bright enough—and it closed with the only words that should ever close a letter. But I can't remember many of its details. I'll reply to them again, or perhaps they can wait till I see you again. I shall look out for your tail-less story. I forgot to bring 'Anna' too. It is the best story you have written. You are becoming very competent, dear, and your stories are all your own. There are many things for me to say about 'Anna', but they, too, must wait.

Oh hell to the wind as it blows these pages about. I have no Rimbaud for a book or paper rest, but only a neat, brown rock upon which I have drawn three very ferocious travesties of your face—one eyeless, one toothless, & all entirely bloodless. Oh hell to the wind as it blows my hair over my forehead. And woe on the sun that he bloody well shines not.

Soon I see you. Soon I kiss you hullo.

It's getting cold, too cold to write. I haven't got a vest on, and the wind is blowing around the Bristol Channel. I agree with Buddha that the essence of life is evil. Apart from not being born at all, it is best to die young. I agree with Schopenhauer (he, in his philosophic dust, would turn with pleasure at my agreement) that life has no pattern & no purpose, but that a twisted vein of evil, like the poison in a drinker's glass, coils up from the pit to the top of the hemlocked world. Or at least I might do. But some things there are that are better than others. The tiny, scarlet ants that crawl from the holes in the rock on to my busy hand. The shapes of the rocks, carved in chaos by a tiddly sea. The three broken masts, like three nails in the breast of a wooden Messiah, that stick up in the far distance from a stranded ship. The voice of a snotty-nostrilled child sitting in a pool and putting shellfish in her drawers. The hundreds and hundreds of rabbits I saw last night as I lay, incorrigibly romantic, in a field of buttercups, & wrote of death. The jawbone of a sheep that I wish would fit into my pocket. The tiny lives that go slowly & liquidly on in the cold pools near my hands. The brown worms in beer. All these, like Rupert Brooke, I love because they remind me of you. Yes, even the red ants, the dead jawbone, & the hapless chemical. Even the rabbits, buttercups, & nailing masts.

Soon I see you. Write by the end of this week.

Darling, I love you.
XXXX

MS: Buffalo

PAMELA HANSFORD JOHNSON
Sunday morning [27 May 1934][1]   in Bed

Question One.   I can't come up
        Two.   I'm sleeping no better
Question Three. 'No' I've done everything that's wrong
        Four.   I daren't see the doctor
Question 5.   Yes I love you

I'm in a dreadful mess now. I can hardly hold the pencil or see the paper. This has been coming for weeks. And the last four days have completed it. I'm absolutely at the point of breaking now. You remember how I was when I said goodbye to you for the first time. In the Kardomah[2] when I loved you so much and was too shy to tell you. Well imagine me one hundred times worse than that with my nerves oh darling absolutely at the point of breaking in little bits. I can't think and I don't know what I'm doing   When I speak I don't know if I'm shouting or whispering and that's a terrible sign. It's *all* nerves & no more   But I've never imagined anything as bad.

And it's all my own fault too. As well as I can I'll tell you the honest, honest truth. I never want to lie to you. You'll be terribly angry with me I know and you'll never write to me again perhaps   But darling you want me to tell you the truth don't you

I left Laugharne on Wednesday morning and went down to a bungalow in Gower. I drank a lot in Laugharne & was feeling a bit funny even then. I stayed in Gower with Cliff, who was a friend of mine in the waster days of

1 Johnson's diary for 28 May records 'appalling distressing letter from Dylan'. The letter is scrawled in pencil; everything about it seems designed for maximum effect. The housewife who was the likeliest candidate for the part of scarlet woman said years later that it was nonsense.
2 Kardomah Ltd ran a chain of cafés.

the reporter's office. On Wednesday evening Billie his fiancée came down. She was tall & thin and dark with a loose red mouth & a harsh sort of laugh. Later we all went out & got drunk. She tried to make love to me all the way home. I told her to shut up because she was drunk   When we got back she still tried to make love to me wildly like an idiot in front of Cliff. She went to bed and Cliff and I drank some more and then very modernly he decided to go & sleep with her. But as soon as he got in bed with her she screamed & ran into mine

I slept with her that night & for the next three nights   We were terribly drunk day & night   Now I can see all sorts of things. I think I've got them.

Oh darling, it hurts me to tell you this but I've got to tell you because I always want to tell you the truth about me. And I never want to share   It's you & me or nobody, you & me & nobody. But I've been a bloody fool & I'm going to bed for a week   I'm just on the borders of DTs darling, and I've wasted some of my tremendous love for you on a lank redmouthed girl with a reputation like a hell. I don't love her a bit   I love you Pamela always & always   But she's a pain on the nerves. For Christ knows why she loves me   Yesterday morning she gave her ring back to Cliff.

I've got to put a 100 miles between her & me

I must leave Wales forever & never see her

I see bits of you in her all the time & tack on to those bits   I've got to be drunk to tack on to them

I love you Pamela & *must have* you   As soon as all this is over I'm coming straight up. If you'll let me. No, but better or worse I'll come up next week if you'll have me. Don't be too cross or too angry   What the hell am I to do? And what the hell are you going to say to me? Darling I love you & think of you all the time. Write by return   And don't break my heart by telling me I mustn't come up to London to you becos I'm such a bloody fool.[1] XXXX Darling. Oh Darling.

MS: Buffalo

TREVOR HUGHES
[7 June 1934]

Dear Trevor,

One day, with all the provocation in the world, you will spurn forever my unorthodox and unpunctual advances and break up into a million fragments the friendship that still lies between our spasmodic bursts of correspondence. For I am the most unreliable friend that ever was, but, far

1 Thomas went to London on 13 June, stayed two weeks, and was forgiven.

from glorying in my conventional disregard of the decent limits and conventions of friendship, I am heartily ashamed of it and make an effort now to stir out of stupor and to write what I hope—unfortunately I remember saying this before—will be the first of a new and protracted series of confessionals.

The last time I wrote to you was soon, though not soon enough, after our parting at the Lyons' Café of the Clerkly Slaves and the appointment, which, of course, I failed to keep, at the Tavern of the Long Hair and the Flowing Tie. And in that letter, I remember, was a frank, though perhaps misguided, criticism of your story, a number of weak apologies, and a promise to write again directly upon receipt of your answering letter. Your letter came, and only today, on the seventh of June, do I prepare to reply. Postpone again the spurning and breaking, and do please regard the shortness of this letter as nothing but a timid fear upon my part that my name at the foot of the page will no longer hold its accustomed magic in the dens and quagmires of your abominable Lane.

Now, Trevor my lad, how is the world misusing you, and are your metaphysics still, like mine, neatly and surgically wrapped in a wadding of darkness? Here there is still no light, only a new mile of suffering murk added to the horizon, and a fresh acre of wonder at this rotten state that might easily and sweetly be changed into the last long acre where the dead breathe for the first time. But how goes it with you? Is there an arc of light over St. Paul's, a new-gutted twinkling in the stars of the electric sign, a stronger tide of words, or a repeated sea more dismal than the Sargasso, more heavenly sounding than the Bosphorus? Here I am getting older and no wiser, and have lately become entangled with an erotic girl with whom I indulge in unrepeatable displays of carnality. In *your* tight-tided little island, does the hank of bone and the curled slit play its hot, customary part?[1] You—who said once that you should have been canonized in accordance with your principles—are you lately become a celibate to whom the lifting of skirts is no more than the lifting of skirts? I am looking forward to the day when Mr and Mrs Hughes, in their two backed beast, face the double faced world. That way, perhaps, lies your salvation and mine, though I doubt whether I, personally, could remain sober and faithful for more than a week on end.

Such is our weakness, comrade. In our anatomical creature, we see the creature of the material world as weak and struggling as ourselves. But, day by day, I realize more that, together, we could work out our separate providences, and reach, at least some kind of heaven up a ladder of words.

---

1 Explicit sexual detail is rare in Thomas's letters. Perhaps he had been sexually involved for the first time. 'If I were tickled by the rub of love' (30 April 1934 in a Notebook) observes,

> 'This world is half the devil's and my own,
> Daft with the drug that's smoking in a girl
> And curling round the bud that forks her eye.'

So write soon to me, before I see you on my next visit to London which will be in the next week or two.

I will not apologise again for all that needs apology, but will content myself with knowing that, to me and, I hope, to you, the mere composition of this letter means more than all the apologetic stupidities I could put together for somebody else.

Dylan

MS: Buffalo

EDITOR, SWANSEA AND WEST WALES GUARDIAN[1]
June 8 1934

TELLING THE TRUTH TO THE PUBLIC
EXPOSE HUMBUG AND SMUG RESPECTABILITY

Sir—In this overpeopled breeding box of ours, this ugly contradiction of a town for ever compromised between the stacks and the littered bays, the Philistines exercise an inevitable dictatorship and regard the first glimmerings of a social intelligence and the first signs of a godly abhorrence of the parochial diseases much as the black man must have first regarded the features of his lily-faced brother.

You have most worthily demonstrated the fact that a local newspaper need not exclusively confine itself to the printing of photographs of our more bovine notabilities; the detailed reports of crimes which, in a less criminal state of society, would be unnecessary; insipid gossipings on the topographical positions of vanished streets and the references in bad novels to our God-chosen town; the retelling of old jokes; running commentaries on the gradual break down of the parish pump; and the useless quibblings between Christ-denying Christians, irrational Rationalists, and the white-spatted representatives of a social system that has, for too many years, used its bowler hat for the one purpose of keeping its ears apart.

But the colour of a shirt counts little to the man who has no shirt on his back, and the musical heaven after death harped on by the gentlemen with the harmonium is a poor substitute for the man whose heaven on earth—warmth, clothes, food, a woman, and may be, children—is denied him on all sides. You can do more than merely allow the amateur and professional politicians of the town to display their bad manners in public. It is within your power to force up to the very limits of censorship, upon all your readers some little consciousness of the immoral restrictions placed upon them, of the humbug and smug respectability that works behind them all their handcuffed days, and to do this, not from any political bias, but from the undeniable conviction that the divinity of man is not to be trifled with,

1 A weekly newspaper, more radical than most, that survived for a few years in Swansea. Thomas was under the influence of Bert Trick, the left-wing grocer.

that the manna of God is not the lukewarm soup and starch of the chapels, but the redhot grains of love and life distributed equally and impartially among us all, and that at our roots of being lies not the greed for property or money, but the desire, large as a universe, to express ourselves freely and to the utmost limits of our individual capabilities.

Fascism would sprout to life like a flower through a coffin's cracks, watered by the excreta of the dead, the droppings of the political dead, the spittle of the Anti-Christs who have crucified Him and His children since the kiss of a man who wanted thirty pieces of silver in order, perhaps, to bribe one of the councillors of Jerusalem with a sack of coal or a cask of wine, or, as a member of the Jerusalem Road Improvement Committee, to buy a row of houses that the committee had decided to knock down for extension purposes. It would still stink of the weeds of this decomposing system of society, and all the tails of all the black shirts in the world would not wipe away the mud and the black and blue bruises from the well kicked bottom of the British public.

That we know. The shirts are changed, but the masks remain, hiding the riddle faces of those to whom the beauty of the tangible world approximates to the individual leisure for observing it. To them there is no world that is not to be touched and felt or sensed by the ambiguous senses of the maltreated body. To them the individual is a factor towards a state, and still an intricate machine for work that sells its sweat and muscle or else starves and is broken down. To them the individual is not a world, a structure of bone, blood, nerves and flesh, all made miraculous by the miracle of the mind, but a creature that works for the profit of its fellow creatures so that it may drag out its days and eat what is provided it and be buried at its own expense.

Fascism would clear the working man's house of bugs and attempt to provide him with a little more of what he should never have been deprived of; the divine right to live, regardless of his own working capacity.

Fascism would do this and more, so that he might work the harder and be dragged deeper into a false state of security and a blasphemous content, with his position at the very bottom of an anti-religious world of class.

That we know. It is within your power to force the consciousness, of that, and the hate of that, upon a thousand brains, and to show, through the medium of that consciousness, that the beautiful world has been made foul by the men who have worked against men, by the devil in man which has worked against the God in man.

Teach to hate, and then to believe in the antithesis of what is hated.

Yours etc.

Swansea   DYLAN THOMAS

EDITORIAL NOTE.—Mr. Dylan Thomas is a contributor of literary articles and reviews to the 'Morning Post' and the 'Listener' (the official organ of the BBC), and is also a contributor to 'New Verse' and 'New

Stories'. A volume of his poems will shortly be published. He is a Swansea man and a member of the Little Theatre.

GLYN JONES
[?early July 1934]   5 Cwmdonkin Drive   Uplands   Swansea

I have no possible excuse this time; no yellow letter weeks old in my pocket to pardon—in some respect, at least—the interminable time I have taken in replying to your letter, thanking you for the returned manuscript of 'Uncommon Genesis', and commenting upon our double show in the recent New Verse.[1] No excuse except that of laziness, a thing I would be heartily ashamed of if it were not for the summer weather, the pressure of commissioned prose, and the state of torpor which, as you know, is inevitably the rest [?result] of a London visit.

I had three weeks in town, saw Richard Rees again, and many other editorial gentlemen who, so far, have been unable to comply with my very reasonable—& soon very necessary—desire for congenial employment. I had a certain amount of good luck though, planted some poems, found an agent[2] who will take all my prose, and was commissioned—money, unfortunately, on delivery—to write a long novel all about my Jarvis valley. I've done a few thousand words already. About a 100,000 are needed. Work for the winter.

After reading your poem in New Verse I came to the very vain and boastful conclusion that it was strongly influenced by myself. Other people noticed it, too, though whether wrongly or rightly I cannot say. I didn't like it very much. I didn't like my own poems either. Do tell me if I was more conceited than usual in imagining the poem of Glyn Jones to be indebted—indebted, probably, for its worse points—to Dylan Thomas.

Have you written to the Rhondda woman yet?[3] If not, let me see the letter before you send it, will you? I might want to add a pathetic appeal for a job at the end of it. I'd take a job anywhere now, because, although I have plenty of work to keep me infernally busy for months, there is no immediate money in it. My dad is retiring at the end of this term, and after that I face the bitter world alone.[4] Are there any possibilities in Cardiff? I'd do anything, but am unfit for most things, my only qualifications being a Heart of Gold and a willing and discursive pencil.

'Uncommon Genesis' I have cut by at least half. It is now quite good. My agent—God, that sounds good—has it now.

When are you coming down to see me? Any Saturday will suit me

1 The June issue.
2 The firm of Curtis Brown.
3 Probably Margaret Haig, Lady Rhondda (1883–1941), proprietor and editor of the weekly magazine *Time and Tide*.
4 D. J. Thomas didn't retire until December 1936.

perfectly, and I'll be really delighted to see you. What about this Saturday? The arrangements are in your hands entirely. Bring down one of your more arty friends if you want to. As far as Hart goes, this is Liberty All.

Dylan

Write soon, tell me when you're coming down, and do please understand that laziness is the only reason I haven't written many times & at much greater length than this.

MS: Carbondale

PAMELA HANSFORD JOHNSON
[about 3 July 1934]

Good morning. I hope it is morning with you. If not, good morning still. The sun in my heart comes up like a Javanese orange:—for similar images compare any poem in the Poet's Corner. I am at my open window again, looking out now on boys with red hair playing cricket. As always at this magically, *and* dirtily, casemented window, I am happy and aloof. Yes, I can think of you doing your usual things in your usual house, imagine your [?tottering] up the Rise and your burning Minor in the bus.[1] But I, to you, move in a fabulous, Celtic land, surrounded by castles, tall black hats, the ghosts of accents, and eternal Eisteddfodau.[2] Come down to see *me*, but come, my love, in the summer when we can move from this North London stuffiness near to the sea, and lie about on large cliffs by small villages, and fix my moustache not on a rolling, public bowl but on the edge of each private wave. To compensate for my disadvantage over you, here is an ambiguous, and totally inadequate, outline of my house and district. G.W.R. station. Shabby, badly built streets. Unutterable melancholy blowing along the tramlines. Quarter of an hour's tram ride up a long, treed road. A square, a handful of shops, a pub. Up a treed hill, field on one side, houses on the other. Near the top of the hill a small, not very well painted, gateless house. Large room, smaller room, study, kitchen. Four bedrooms, w.c., lavatory. Space at back sufficiently large for wash-house, clothes line, deck-chair and three sparrows. Private school in field opposite. Nice field. Tennis court above. Very nice, very respectable. Not much traffic. Lot of sparrows. My own room is a tiny, renovated bedroom, all papers and books, cigarette ends, hardly any light. *Very* tiny. I really have to go out to turn round. Cut atmosphere with book-knife. No red cushion. No cushion at all. Hard chair. Smelly. Painful. Hot water pipes very near. Gurgle all the time. Nearly go mad. Nice view of wall through window. Pretty park nearby. Sea half a mile off. Better sea four or five miles off. Lunatic asylum

---

1 De Reszke Minor was a brand of cheap cigarette.
2 An eisteddfod is a Welsh musical and literary gathering; 'eisteddfodau' is the plural.

mile off. Workhouse half a mile off. All this sounds depressing, but you must come down. And come down soon, as soon as you can. If it's hot and summery we *can* have a wonderful time.[1] And if it rains, we can fug all day and all night with the greatest pleasure in the world.[2]

You asked about Dad. He's no better, and has to see his London doctor even more often. My mother is weak but still garrulous. You won't like her. She talks too much, too often, and too unintelligently for it to be possible for you to like her. But she's very kind and would love to see you. So explore this Welsh darkness, my darling. I may even take you to Laugharne, which is the nearest approach under the sun to a Stygian borough.

Is This Political Work?

If you read the newspapers, you'll see that Swansea is the centre of all revolutionary activities this week. It is the week of the trial of Tom Mann and Harry Pollitt, whose trial has been framed-up by the police and the local authorities.[3] I have just left the Socialist Party, and offered my services to the Communists. I *was* in time for Mosley's meeting,[4] and was thrown down the stairs. No harm done, however. I have just completed a seditious article attacking the shirted gentleman, having discovered, quite by accident, that he is the biggest owner of slum property in Birmingham. Cha!

Old Stiffened Bowels-Gore is a dirty but comic boy.[5] Don't choke him off yet. There must be a certain amount of pleasure for him in chattering about genital organs to unknown and invisible young ladies. He's far enough away. Tell him he can write as freely as he likes—the dirt-box—and enjoy his little bit of Stockport filth. Then, when the letters grow too verminous, write back and tell him what he can do with his book on Lawrence. Or tell him to devote his phallic energy to poor old Hannah. Still, his letter is a nasty piece of work. He's the [?best] example of an 'in-and-in' I've ever heard of.

Your poem is good, and promising. It is careful, well modulated, and, fortunately, neither too sweet nor too simple. I don't know about the sixth line of the first verse, which sounds something like the opening line in a

1 Johnson eventually went (with her mother) to stay in Swansea from 15 to 29 September that year. While she was there her 'nerves went smash', according to her diary, and she had to see a doctor. Their love affair, which apparently was unconsummated, was over before the end of 1934.

2 To fug = to stay indoors in a stuffy atmosphere. Perhaps Thomas was making sly homophonic use of the word.

3 Harry Pollitt, general secretary of the Communist Party of Great Britain, and Tom Mann, a veteran Party member, appeared at Swansea Assizes on 3 July charged with making seditious speeches in the South Wales coalfield. They were found not guilty next day.

4 Sir Oswald Mosley, the British fascist leader, held a rally at the Plaza Cinema, Swansea, on Sunday 1 July. Thomas was not thrown down the stairs.

5 Johnson had received (she wrote in her diary) a 'peculiar letter from a curious poet' in the north of England, whose name Thomas parodied as 'Stiffened Bowels-Gore'.

London Mercury sonnet.[1] And the seventh and eighth line of the second verse are quite bad. The poem is intelligent, and has many beautiful phrases. 'The blood was love.' 'The funnel of the tempers.' The lost Atlantis line is a successful surprise. On the whole, it's one of your best poems. Obviously much care has been taken with it, and if these remarks do sound un-naturally guarded it is because your poetry is changing so definitely in attitude, and is becoming so much more intense and muscular, that I am frightened to say much for fear of interrupting its progress. I always knew you had a splendid poetry in you; now it's forming itself. My influence, obvious mainly in lines five, ten, and thirteen, and, perhaps, in the construction of a few other phrases, will drop away and leave your verse naked and itself. Progress from this, but don't, as in the lines of the 'stucco wall' & the 'line of lamplight', sink to an easy, impressionist objectiveness. Both these lines could have appeared in Rupert Brooke's 'Great Lover' catalogue, and have no place in a poem such as this. Not much of a comment on the poem, I'm afraid. But what it promises is so good that I daren't say anything more. Go on, work on from this. Condense even more. Oh, I forgot, line nine is bad, too. Another item in the Rupert catalogue. The rest—too good for me to spoil, and an incalculable improvement on nearly all that is printed in 'Symphony'.

I admire the Obituary, too. You could write in many directions. This is a good piece of impromptu writing. Thank God, in your Poem you've found the one direction for you. Go ahead, lidy. All the juiciest coconuts is at the top.

Your story is as lovely as all the last stories you've sent me. You've got a style and a matter of your own. Little as they are, I can't think of anyone's stories printed today that are better. You are bloody good, you know. I'm sending the story back, just a little bit sub-edited, but I want you to send it back to me again. Reasons for sub-editing: 'Returned the pressure' is far too cold a phrase. 'Quick' is unnecessary and spoils the sound of the sentence. 'Broken the ice' is very hackneyed, &, again, doesn't add anything. 'Blade of grass' is simpler & more effective than a 'green blade.' The descriptive sentence isn't needed, and I don't like fruit on the sky. 'The man's' sleeve is false. So is 'Hell'. You know what's wrong with 'choking bliss'. I don't know why, but, really, the name of the boy is unimportant. Obviously she won't go to see him again. He comes & he goes, &, as it's the girl's story, it's better that his shadow should be nameless. 'Fretting' is one of your blasted words I can't bear; 'quieten his fingers' is good. Of course he looked at his watch, & not at his boot. Why mention it? 'Defensive fury etc'— either Ethel M.[2] or David H., I don't know which. To shout 'something' is rather slack, & an avoidance of an issue. Who cares about the bus-conductor? 'Darkness' & 'aloneness' in one sentence sounds horrible. 'The man,' drat him, again. 'From the darkness of a forgotten past' sounds like Corby & his scientific skull. What part of the woman's anatomy is her

---

1 Under Squire's editorship, the magazine was not keen on 'modernist' verse.
2 The novelist Ethel M. Dell? Or the novelist Ethel Mannin?

'bed'. She kissed the woman on the bed. I don't like sentences that have the slightest suggestion of ambiguity.

Now, my dear, what are you going to do with this and with the rest of your really splendid stories? Either buck your agent up, or take them away from him. Anyway 'Procession' & this are entirely your own property. Send them to Hamish Miles, & ask him to consider them either for Life and Letters or New Stories.[1] Both these are stories as good as any I've read for years. You've got nearly everything that Katherine Mansfield possessed, & a good deal more. Again let me remind you of the position of the coconuts. Go on, go on, my darling lady.

All the editing in 'Suddenly A Woman' *is* worth abiding by. Just with those few phrases—the phrases & words I have blackened—thrown out, the story is *perfect*. O.K., love.

I have just finished a review for the Adelphi. God, some tripe is published. Out of seven books sent by Rees only two are worth anything. The other four are unbelievably bad. Excerpt from 'The Selected Poems of Charles King':

'Thou camest from the Paradise of Love,
A fondling in the dew-drops, out of Time,
When far in Being's arcane Hesperid-grove
Strayed Monna Lisa with her Prince of Rhyme.'

Excerpt from Frank Kendon's 'Tristram'.

'The thirsty greyhound drew his leash
Tighter about Sir Tristram's wrist;
He heard a noise of rising water:
The dog should wet its thirst, at least.'

Excerpt from 'Singing Waters' by Ian Dall:

'As might a butterfly when first
It from the dark cocoon does burst,
He rises from the rippled ring
To joy of rhythmic uttering.'

And a poem by Sydney Salt, one of the highbrows of Majorca:

Seeing Goya.

'Goya shot a few bullets through the sky.
So did Dostoevsky—who else?
Hungry men these, who knew the meaning of lean.'

What a life is the life of a hack reviewer. Thank God the others, William Soutar & William Montgomerie (Squared Circle) are very traditional & very competent. Sydney is nuts.

---

1 Miles was also editing 'Life and Letters Today'.

I'm enclosing a short story. I've been a bit tired, & this is a recreation story. Don't be too hard on it, & if there's any merit in it all perhaps you'll type it out for me darling? I'll have a poem to send you next time. It's too hot to be very fertile. I don't know how you manage it. I think I must be very lazy.

In my next letter, too,—it should, I know, be in this, but I've put the damned papers very carefully away and can't remember where—I'll send the rest of 'No More Canary Wine'. It's highly mannered, but will grow out of that, and should be a rattling good story.

Is the finger better? Have it cut off if it hurts much more. I should love you with only four fingers on one hand.

I miss you. I miss you terribly. I think of you, love you, and look at your picture which I've taken out of my little locked drawer and put on the ledge over my table. Oh, darling, darling, you're such a long way away. I should like to be sticking my moustache on every milestone between us.

XXX

It won't, it can't, be long.
Send me Pietà.
Tell me how goes my Son of Kong?[1]
Give my love to your mother.
And take *all* my love for yourself.

XXX

And if you talk again of the beastly young men who have been in love with you as 'the others', I shall do something hideous & horrid with the sharp insides of grandfather clocks.

X

MS: Buffalo

EDITOR, *SWANSEA AND WEST WALES GUARDIAN*
July 6 1934

THE REAL CHRIST—AND THE FALSE
Peculiar Heavens
CREATED BY LITTLE ORATORS

Mr. Dylan Thomas, the literary critic and poet, writes:
Since my last letter, when, with as much forceful imagery as the law of censorship allows me, I spoke of the party to which Mr. Mainwaring Hughes[2] lends, if nothing else, a sense of humour and a clean dickey, I

1 The 1933 film *King Kong* was much talked about. In Pamela's diary [20 August 1934], Dylan was 'Baby Kong'.
2 Mainwaring Hughes, a coal merchant and town councillor, was a leading local member of the British Union of Fascists.

have listened to a Christian orator promising his audience a celestial mansion on the condition that they give themselves to Christ, and asking them to be content, while on the earth, with any sort of insanitary hovel, ragged garments, and bad and meagre food that the powers of the land feel it fit to provide them.

While admiring the sincerity of the orator, and envying his mastery of the accordion, I could not help wishing that he would utilize his power of expressing such morbid convictions, his clear diction, and very effective histrionics, for the purpose of providing his Christ with a flat-iron instead of a harp, and for impressing upon those who sniggered around him the fact that the essence of Christianity is a product of good, red, living vitamins rather than of a sticky balsam for embalming the bodies of the dead.

For his Christ is clothed in a shroud. The wounds are still bleeding, the cry of despair and abnegation still on his colourless lips. His Christ, like an ethereal sexton, sits waiting in the clouds for man to die. The orator, and his bannered boys, forget that the boulders at the gate of the tomb were thrown aside, and that the raised and living Christ came out like a man from anaesthetic, a symbol of life, a reawakened, revolutionary force, not a walking corpse with the words of a dead message stale and yellow on his mouth.

Michael Angelo's Christ of the Last Supper is full-mouthed, with a bellyful of wine and chicken. (It is very pleasant to reflect that he would be ineligible for the British Union of Fascists.) The orator's Christ is a pussyfoot and a vegetarian, and what is more, a Deity superbly indifferent to the crimes of His children against His children, to the blasphemous blackening of the air as an English Bishop buys foreign controlled armament shares, as men of culture and integrity are thrown penniless out of their own land by a megalomaniac drunk on words and blood, as Sir John Simon[1] pulls another feather from the Angel of Peace.

Can this timid emblem of suffering stare around at our contemporary world, and, sickened of the waste and murder, the obscene hypocrisy of those war-mongers and slave-drivers who venerate His name and void their contagious rheum upon the first principle of His gospel, afford no more proof of His living energy and His Messiahdom than the mere offer of a heavenly accommodation (h. and c., cherubs, every godly convenience) at the end of this giddy life?

The heaven of the capitalist is best described by Richard Aldington:[2]

'It was like a crematorium
Or rather a cadaver factory,
Where every day
Millions of people were consumed to smoke.
Out of ten thousand towering chimneys
Gushed black greasy smoke

1 Sir John Simon (1873–1954) was British Foreign Secretary, 1931–5.
2 Richard Aldington (1892–1962), poet, novelist and editor. The poem Thomas quotes (in a condensed version) is a section from 'A Fool i' the Forest'.

That whitened to a cloud of bank notes.
All the angels drove to work in tanks.
Far above them the mystic symbol,
Made of dazzling electric lights,
Ran about the sky and changed its colours:
More and more and more for ever,
Holy, Blessed, Glorious, Mass Production.'

UNIFORMED ANGELS

In the heaven of the Fascists the uniformed angels parade every morning, making the customary salute, before the golden throne. The humbler angels are kept serenely in their places. There are no intellectual angels. The black Jehovah, very naturally, distrusts intellect. And only the Best Books are read. There are organised sports, and even the cherubim are forced to show, by their prowess in swinging on the parallel bars and in improvising knuckle-dusters with three pennies, how eminently qualified they are to organise the paradisaical rank and file. The anthem of their heaven is, of course, a setting of that famous poem:

'How odd
Of God
To choose
The Jews.'

But the heaven of the religious orators is more infernal still, a sublimated charnel-house, foul as a morgue set at the end of a slum near the parade of policemen, unsavoury old women, and drinkers of methylated spirits, a dismal place full of young men singing Welsh hymns in suspiciously high voices, and blind old men dabbling their hands in the blood of the crosses that stand up all over the place like so many scarlet pylons.

Which is the heaven of the living men. We shall not for the promised residence in any of those cloudy regions, bow down contentedly before the twisting makers of laws and moneys that provide us with the fag ends of existence on the earth. It's heaven on earth or no heaven. Neither a Christ of cloud nor a Deity that the moths have been at, is a Saviour for us. Our symbol of faith must be a naked life, not a pale cross of death done up in a mummy blanket and surrounded by the Pyramid walls of an established stupidity.

DYLAN THOMAS

Swansea

JOHN LEHMANN

From the 1930s, John Lehmann (b. 1907) was a leading figure in literary London, as poet and editor. He was one of the editors of *The Year's Poetry* for 1934 (which contained Thomas's 'Light breaks'); for 1935 ('Especially when the October wind'), and for 1936 (three further Thomas poems).

[about 10 July 1934]   5 Cwmdonkin Drive   Uplands   Swansea

Dear Mr. Lehmann,

Thanks very much for the note and the letter. I enclose three poems. The first, beginning, 'I see the boys of summer', was published in the June New Verse. The other two are unpublished. I send you these three as they more or less go together, being based on something of the same idea and in chronological order. I am having a book of poems brought out in a few months, and, I suppose, the first two of these poems, at least, will be printed in that book. If you like the poems at all, I hope that fact won't prevent you from possibly accepting them.

I was asked to mention the names of some of the periodicals I've contributed to during the last twelve months: Adelphi, New English Weekly, New Verse, Sunday Referee, John O'London's, Listener, and a few Welsh papers which aren't of much literary interest.

I could, if you wish, send you some more poems. I do hope you'll let me know.

Yours Sincerely,
Dylan Thomas

MS: Location unknown

GEOFFREY GRIGSON
[mid July 1934]   5 Cwmdonkin Drive   Uplands   Swansea

Dear Grigson,

Thanks for the note.

I have no poems at all at the present moment, or at least no poems which I should care for you to see. I hope in a few days to be able to send you two new poems, though.

I enclose my answers to the questionnaire.[1] I'm afraid they sound rather priggish in places, but I couldn't avoid it. They make me sound, too, very contented with my work, which I am certainly not. If they are not what you want, or are too long, I'll be quite willing to do another set of answers.

You asked me to remind you, some time ago, about the books for review. I've been doing a certain amount of reviewing lately, & would be very pleased if you could, as you promised, send a few volumes along.

1 Published in New Verse, October 1934, as 'Answers to an Enquiry'. Thomas said his poetry was 'the record of my individual struggle from darkness towards some measure of light'.

I'm sorry to have no poems ready. I'll send you some during the week, if I may.

Sincerely,
Dylan Thomas

I hope to be in London about the middle of August. I was up a little time ago, but heard that you were away on holiday. I was sorry to miss seeing you.

MS: Texas

PAMELA HANSFORD JOHNSON
July 20 '34

Your letter made me very happy, too. I am listening to Monteverdi's Ballet of the Ungracious Ladies. And that is very happy music, in spite of Pluto and a coloratura Venus. I have only just finished reading 'The Stranger' of Algernon Blackwood—a very happy story, in spite of the ghost.[1] I am smoking a good Turkish cigarette, and have pinched a glass of invalid port from my mother's bedside. Your letter is on the table in front of me, and, later in the night, Comrade Trick is coming to take me to a Fascist demonstration. Nothing much could be better. Your presence would make everything all right. Through the body of words I tickle you a courteous salute under the chin. You now have a long white beard, and I find myself tickling General Booth of the Salvation Army. But these little snags of vision are to be expected. Yesterday I divined the position of a garden slug. There, under that particular tuft, that small square of soil (I said) lies a fat slug. I dug up the tuft, and there the slug lay, smiling like Mona Lisa. I now add to my list of recondite & entirely uncommercial attainments that of being able to unearth slugs at any given moment. If we ever possess a parrot or a canary, my gift will be distinctly useful. If not, it can still be used as a method of bridging over any awkward pause in the conversation. 'Find a slug for the gentleman.' 'Certainly, my dear.' And, so saying, I produce from the potato bed a black, juicy specimen with a long mane.

Your pun on the first line of James Joyce's little lyric has been very much appreciated by a select section of my friends. How very apt that the book from which that particular lyric (this sentence I challenge you to beat for literary coyness) is culled, should be called Chamber Music. Can *I* be vulgar for a moment, too?[2] I heard a funny story yesterday about a man with three testicles. This man, this very odd man, went into a public house and called a drink. Then, after a few drinks, he turned round to the

---

1 Algernon Blackwood (1869–1951), writer, especially of short stories.
2 'Chamber' was a euphemism for the much-joked-about chamber-pot, used as a bedroom urinal in houses without indoor lavatories, of which there were plenty in the 1930s.

company in the bar and said: 'I bet you a pound note that me and any other bloke here have got five testicles between us.' At this, of course, there was much merriment, and the bet was taken on. 'Him and me,' said the very odd man, pointing to a little fellow in the corner. 'Now we'll go into the other room, and then you can come in one by one & see that what I've said is true.' Just as he reached the door of the other room, the little fellow from the corner followed him & whispered softly in his ear, 'I say, mate, I hope you've got four. I've only got one.' I think that's a very funny joke. It doesn't look very funny written down, but just you try it on the right company!

Back to the land now. No more talk of gangrene and sexual aberrations. I'm enclosing a new story, 'The Vest'[1] which will provide all that is needed of violence and general nastiness (General Nastiness of the Fifth Buffs).

Your Stories

Neither of them are as good as the last few you've sent me. 'The Old Mrs' is rather badly written all through, although the theme and the working out of it is good. Incidentally, the punctuation in both stories is abominable, and makes nonsense of many, too many, of the sentences. But all I said in my last letter about the merits & the attitude of your stories applies to 'The Old Mrs' & 'Magnificat'. Everything in them, except the actual writing, is as good as in 'Pietà', 'Anna', & 'Suddenly A Woman'. I've hacked them about a bit, as usual, though not in the Old Mrs, at least, with very much effect. In 'The Old Mrs' you are frequently very slipshod in expression. 'Anyway', 'To be literal', 'Metaphorically speaking', 'For all that', 'The Devil to pay' and other abominations of style are littered along the pages. The story is too realistic, too human in a John Bull sense, for me to be able to criticise it as thoroughly, or, rather, with as much possible insight, as a story that is more severely psychological—'Suddenly A Woman'—or more fanciful & mysterious—'Anna'. I don't know much about human beings. Only the exceptions interest me. I dislike people as a whole, & the Man in the Street is evil when you take him out of the Street. So, biased and not very competent, I do not find the 'Old Mrs' half as interesting a story as 'The Two Gardeners', or as fascinating—in a literary sense—a character as our little Minnie or our ugly Clara. But from the point of view of *writing* alone, there's a lot to quarrel with in this domestic tragedy.

Reason for Quarrel & Pencilling

First pencilling. The opening sentence had to be altered to get over the wretched paragraph on page three: 'She arose, preparatory to . . . sleep.'
Second Cliché. Unwarranted cliché too.
Third I've protested before at your habit of making a very simple operation, such as this, into a vague colloquialism. 'As she was dried' is what you meant & what you should have put.

1 First published in *Yellowjacket*, May 1939.

Fourth 'Shrivelled' is too decorative, too descriptive, an adjective. 'Empty' is literal.

Fifth Colloquialism, again.

Sixth Horrible. 'To be literal'. Chk! Chk!

Seventh One of your damned colloquial 'anyways' again.

Eighth Precious affectation. Bad Viola Price.

Ninth This is purely a suggestion. The Harmonium, as the dead husband's musical instrument, seems to me a truer choice than the piano.

Tenth No reason to mention this at all.

Eleventh I like 'Aces'. You shouldn't have cut it out. It links together the actions of seeing the girl & buying from the girl.

Twelfth Not 'dived', darling. The poor gentleman wasn't a performing seal.

Thirteenth Ugly word. The rather frigid correction I've made seems to be more in keeping with the impersonal, &, itself, rather frigid, nature of Maggie's romance.

Fourteenth 'She blushed' is enough. You don't blush 'coldly', & 'hotly' is a real Ethel M-ism.

Fifteenth The slice of Mrs Leach's life is not essential. I still don't like your efforts at the colloquial speech of the Lower Classes.

Sixteenth Just to get over the cutting out of Mrs Leach's monologue.

Seventeenth Horrible. 'Metaphorically speaking.' Chk! Chk!

Eighteenth See reason number Eight. When you decide to write badly, then . . .

Nineteenth Bloody colloquialism that looks, & is, cheap & hindering.

Twentieth Just another suggestion. 'You be careful, that's all' seems to me to be enough. It implies the mysteriousness with which old ladies—as far as my very little knowledge of old ladies goes—invest the most ordinary platitude.

Twenty First The ironic 'rather beautifully', is obvious in the rest of her conversation. You needn't comment. (That's a nasty thing to say, too.)

Twenty Second Clumsy sentence. And marred, as you so often mar a sentence, by that infernal dash '—' of yours. The dash, except in very special cases, is a sign of carelessness, or of ignorance of punctuation. In your case it's just damned carelessness. And there are dashes all over the story.

Twenty Third Exactly the same reason. It's so simply avoided by a full stop & another capital letter.

Twenty Fourth Untrue psychologically. I hate idiomatic speech of this sort.

Twenty Fifth An Ethel M. trick. Very much unworthy of you even in your most pedestrian—or, if you like, realistic moments.

Twenty Sixth I've altered the last sentence to get over the obviously necessary deletion of the clumsy 'that, though she was showing etc' sentence.

And that's a hell of a lot of hacking, isn't it? But I'm sure it's justified. As you'll see, I've done my best, too, to do something with the punctuation.

Have a look, when you're typing the story again, at the commas I've introduced. You'll be able to correct them a bit. At the moment they're not too good, as I've got a special punctuation of my own. But your commas in this story are planted just where you like & not where the sense or the construction dictates.

Go carefully through the punctuation, do cut the worst of the things I've mentioned, stick to the last sentence, &, if you like, prune the whole thing even a little more. *Then* send it to your agents. It will probably be good. Emotionally, it's good even now. And the motive is *remarkably* good. But in places it's shoddy, definitely shoddy, a very second-rate example of your work. It is, perhaps, more saleable a story than 'Anna' or 'Pietà'. But it hasn't got as much of the you—the literary you, now, not the flesh & blood—that I love.

In case I haven't told you before: I love the other *you* too. I love you, my darling.

Magnificat is, to my mind, a better story, but that is, perhaps, because it is less real than the other—less real, that is, than the world of regular appointments & cafés & cinema foyers, a world that I, caught between two foyers, regard as *less* real (& so do you) than that of divine madnesses, milk-suckled dolls, & petty crucifixions. The main fault of the story lies, again, in the actual writing. I don't know, but perhaps you are writing too fast. Not too much—no-one can ever write too much, & it's an absurd lie to say that by writing 'too much' it is possible to write oneself out—but too quickly. The theme, the motive, is again very effective. Clara is a dramatic figure of some importance, and Mr. Calder is a good symbol. But there are patches of shoddiness, and far too many sentences, badly punctuated sentences, too, of the same construction. But this, in spite of the things I'll point out & which you are really fully aware of, is a true story in that it is a story that is true to yourself. Even if you are truly despicable, the truly despicable writing of your stories is worth-while & very essential. As it is, you are lovely (I'm awfully biased in that respect), & *each*, each single, unlovely sentence (by unlovely I do not mean conventionally ugly or anything at all like that) is a lie to your loveliness & is unworthy of you. Don't say I expect too much of you. I expect only what I know you are capable of producing. This applies all ways. Now to the story. I won't, as in the criticism of the 'Old Mrs', give a detailed list, but only point out some of the more obvious & the more debatable things. To begin with, Clara wasn't a daily help, because she 'slept in'. 'Architects paraphernalia' I object to for the same reason that I objected to 'the drying business' in the other story. The *fact*, the fact that Mr. Calder did keep architectural implements in the top room, is mentioned towards the end of the story. 'Sullen Clara was' is a magazineish inversion. Almost a perversion. So 'one day Clara found herself a young man', did she? What a horrible transformation of sex! 'Jealousy was a ball of flesh in her throat' is a good example of figurative language gone wrong. In this tale, anyway, figurative language is *not* wanted. Not f.l. of this sort, at least. 'She mottled with anger' reminds me of another character of yours who also attempted to imitate the Big Bad Wolf. The dashes—the damned dashes that I'm employing now—I won't comment on. I don't like the idea of Kitty meeting her father at the bottom, but that's because I've got a nasty mind. The trouble is that so many other readers have. The picture of Mr. Calder sucking his cold pipe (Clara, apparently, had put the matches in the soup) brings to mind the picture of the Poona father in the 'Tallboy'. It's just such a damned foolish, &, as regards the story, unnecessary thing, that that old war-horse would have done. And Mr. Calder, apart from that, & in spite of the very little time & space you devote to him is by way of being a genuine creation. Now I'm very dubious about the end of the story. It's right that a star *should* fall, & it's pretty certain that a star *did* fall. But should you mention it? Yes, perhaps you should. I've suggested an alternative end sentence, cutting out the possibly melodramatic touch of the 'rattling windows'. It's only a suggestion, but have a look at it. If nothing else, it might suggest a better end to your mind.

This is what I meant by too many similarly-constructed sentences: 'She bent down and, scraping her fingers under the dresser, examined it closely.' 'She would run up to her room and, burying her face in the pillow, dream of her wedding day.' 'The preacher told the story once again and, as Clara heard of the sorrows etc, she felt the tears fall on to her folded hands.' And so on, right through the story. Use that construction if you like, but *do* put a comma after the first 'and'. Always. Otherwise the sentence doesn't make any sense.

You do work, darling, don't you? You're going to be prodigiously prolific one day. And I shall smart with shame as I produce one obscure line to your twenty equally obscure & equally good lines, & one story to your seven. Go on working. Produce as much as you like but don't work too fast. And heed your Uncle Dylan when he points out the obvious faults, even though he himself goes on writing stories like 'The Vest'. 'The Vest', by the way, you mightn't like at all. Tell me what you think of it, & don't spit at it at once because it's nasty. There's a lot of nastiness in the world, and I must use my dung-fork now & then. By my next letter I hope to have another story ready to send you. If you can, type out 'The Vest' for me. Don't hurry about it, though. I've got agents now, too—theirs are the last few letters you've re-directed to me—& they want some stories of mine. Curtis Brown. They seem very good.

I'm going to write to Neuburg to-day, Sunday, asking him about my bloody book. I won't be very rude, I promise you. He is a little swine, though, isn't he? I can understand why he doesn't love me any more. But surely he hasn't given up loving you. He mustn't do that, he's such a nice little badger. (I've read a book on the life of the mole. You wouldn't believe! He's a horribly lecherous little thing. O Mole Mio.)

'Flower', by the way, in my 'All all and all'[1] (Bradawl, Nuttall, & Bugger-all) is a two-syllabled word.

1 'All all and all the dry worlds lever', soon to appear in *18 Poems*.

Ha! 'Teredo' is an old one on me. I wrote a poem in 1933 beginning

> 'Half is remembered since your halfhands' knocking,
> And ten teredo fingers bored the womb'

Why don't you call your cat 'Egypt'? This is good Shakespeare, & good felinology. Or why not 'Dda', in memory of Hywel Dda,[1] a Welsh prince, who introduced the first law for the protection of cats? The rest of the names that I can think of are inevitably bawdy.

More (for no reason at all) of my long-postponed Political Corners*

An economic system (he barked) must have an ethical sanction. If it can be forced home on the consciousness of people that the present economic system is ethically bad, the seed has been planted that may in time grow into a fine revolutionary flower. Convince people that a thing is bad, and they are ready to listen to a reasonable plan for its overthrow. There is and always must be a stream of revolutionary energy generated when society is composed, at top and bottom, of financial careerists and a proletarian army of dispossessed. Out of the negation of the negation must rise the new synthesis. The new synthesis must be a classless society. But there is no great future for a political party based solely on the claims of the workers, as human labour in industry is almost obsolescent. The negation has emerged, & the future of politics must be in the synthesis of production & consumption. There is no use in the ownership of a national plant unless, there is sufficient financial credit to make it function. The control of money—that is banking, credit, consumption—is the only key to the communal State. Industry is capable of giving the community a high standard of living, and it is only a faulty monetary system which prevents industry from delivering the goods. Aggregate prices are higher than the aggregate of communal incomes & wages. The monetary & credit system is only a system of book-keeping or accountancy. What is required is not a bloody revolution but an intellectual one. Alternatively, there is the confiscation of property by force. The revolutionary political parties are not in common agreement on that point. The Communist Party, with the faint endorsement of the I.L.P., advocates force to reach power. The Socialist League, the New Socialist Party, the orthodox Labour party believe in first attaining constitutional power and then putting their policies into practice. If constitutional government cannot, in the space of a year after the next General Election, fulfil their policies, then a united front must be made, the army and the police force must be subdued, and property be taken by force.[2]

* I'm very fair, anyway. I mark this section so that you can skip it.

1 'Hywel the Good', a Welsh king of the tenth century.
2 A Labour Government, beset by economic crisis in 1931, had given way to a National Government, in effect a coalition, which cut unemployment benefit and angered socialists. The next election was due in 1936 at the latest. The far Left talked about revolution; Bert Trick's voice can be heard.

No-one can be neutral, neither worker, intellectual, nor reactionary, for the composition of the classes has changed. The class-struggle is primarily the intellectual struggle, and, however remote it may seem from the economic process, it is nevertheless conditioned by it. All that matters is the right and the wherewithal to live, and all that remains is to discover, not by hypothecating, but by the trial experiment of constitutionalism, & then, if that fails, of force, the most scientific way to introduce the new society. The governing principle must be that of consumption. The worker is only a factor in production, & nearly an obsolete factor at that. But a consumer is a perpetual factor in any society. All society ceases to be class-ridden when treated purely as a primary body of consumers. The most efficient and just organisation is under the direct control of the State. Those controlling the State shall earn, in consumer-credit, no more than the worker who controls the drains of the State. Private profit must end. Reserves against depreciation must be the only charge on industry.

The release of humanity from toil is overdue. Long hours & low wages are anachronistic. The whip of poverty can only flog a dead horse. The shout of the ring-master is a dead language. Our heritage is machine-made leisure. We have the desire, the means, & the opportunity, but not the common & united front that is not frightened, if the ballot and the pressure of constitutional government fails, to advocate, & practise, the last reserve of communal force.

The State of the future is not to be an economic despotism or a Christian utopia. It is the state of Functional Anarchy.

And a fol dol dol and a reel of cotton. So much for that. I'm preparing a paper on Functional Anarchy from which, with the permission of my readers, I shall quote in my next open letter to the constituents of the Battersea ward.

This is a mess of a letter, too. It dribbles and mouths all over the place like Maurice Chevalier.[1] I'll blame it on the weather which is an unhealthy mixture of blues and grays. As soon as I finish this letter, I'm going to sit in the sun and watch a county cricket match. Even degenerates like myself have that old True-Blue urge which naught can vanquish. I am looking for my School Tie which is, I believe, acting as a sort of strap around a pile of pornographic literature lent to me some months ago by a small man on the sands. I am also practising, in a low voice, how to say, 'Well played, sir,' & 'Demmed bed luck' when a ball hits the wicket-keeper in the pelvis. Happy, funny, bloody, wicked, dirty, beautiful world o'mine. Oh why aren't I with you, my darling?

And of course I'll see you before your holidays. I'll be up in August. And don't forget about Wales.

Write soon and write much. Tell me again you love me. I love you so much. Tell me all there is to tell. Go on working hard. Don't draw

1 Maurice Chevalier (1888–1972), French singer and entertainer, a film star by the 1930s.

moustaches on my photograph. Give my love to your mother. Do make another burn-mark in the Chelsea Bells.[1] Have a drink for me. And kiss me good morning before I gird up my loins and go. All possible love whateffer. Do call your cat 'Egypt'.

Dylan

XXX. Sometime in August. (I think I shall have someone to sit (again) on my face so that, meeting, you won't recognise me, and we can start being in love again. A dirty desire.) I love you. Bloody-face loves you.

MS: Buffalo

JOHN LEHMANN
[about 24 July 1934]   5 Cwmdonkin Drive   Uplands   Swansea

Dear Mr. Lehmann,
   Thanks very much. I am glad that you are going to use a poem of mine. 'Light' was, as probably you know, printed in the 'Listener', to whom the only acknowledgement belongs. I do not want my age to be published, of course. For purposes of arrangement *only*, I was born on October 27, 1913.[2]
   I shall be in London for the August Holiday Week, and, perhaps, for a little longer. If you are not away during that time, would it be possible for me to meet you? Perhaps we could have lunch together?

Yours Sincerely,
Dylan Thomas

MS: Texas

GLYN JONES
[?late July 1934]   5 Cwmdonkin Drive   Uplands   Swansea

Nearly every note I scribble to you seems to start off with an apology. I'm becoming fatalistic, and have given up excuses. But I'll make an exception in your case, and hasten to assure you (*not* one of my favourite idioms) that I only received your letter today. I've been away off & on for the last week, & everything has become rather jumbled. I *am* going up to London very soon, but, at the moment, I can't tell the exact date—whether it will be towards the end of this week or at the beginning of next or what. When— definitely—are you going up? Write soon and tell me, won't you? Even if

---

1 The Six Bells, a Chelsea pub.
2 Thomas was adding a year to his age. His mother, too, sometimes said he was born in 1913.

our days of departure can't be fitted in any way, we'll both be in town some time next week. Now give me the name of your Gower-st hotel or boarding house, so that I shan't miss you. In return I'll give you my telephone number (I've forgotten it for the moment) *at* the house *at* which I shall be staying for some of my visit.

A perfectly bloody note, I admit. Don't take any notice, or not much notice, of the Pateresque idiom[1] employed throughout. Write soon & tell me your plans. We'll have, if nothing else, a few days together anyway. I want to see the Covent Garden Ballet? Do you?

Dylan

P.T.O.

I nearly forgot to tell you: I was severely rated by my family after you left at the end of your door-step visit some weeks ago, and am commanded to write a public apology (it's a bloody funny world, I never seem to do anything right, and what I do do right I forget) for my apparent, but totally unintended rudeness in not extending an invitation to your people to come in & have tea. It didn't matter if they'd had tea, or didn't want tea, or didn't want to come in, or were anxious to get home—I should have asked you to ask them. This isn't the commanded apology. This is quite private & sincere. Your car had gone half way down the hill before I realised. I was awfully muddled at the time, trying to think out a rhyme for 'badger'— with one result, a vulgar half-rhyme.

Give my regards to your people. And when you're all in Swansea again, you damn well have to come in and nibble a bit of bun even if you're all crammed up to the eyes with food and looking for a place to get sick.

So long.

Dylan

MS: Carbondale

PAMELA HANSFORD JOHNSON
2nd August[2] [1934]

Excuses

This letter is short and late for two reasons. First, I have been waiting until today for a reply from Gertrude Stein, hoping, that as a result of her letter, I should be able to come to town very soon, and with a good, if futile, excuse. Second, I turned out for a cricket team on Tuesday evening, finished with the remarkable analysis of 34 overs 60 odd runs & 3 wickets, 1 innings 0 runs, 2 dropped catches, & have been a physical wreck ever

---

1 Walter Pater was sometimes ridiculed, like other members of the 'aesthetic move-ment', for his mannerisms—not for banality, which is what Thomas seems to be talking about.
2 Thomas wrote '2nd July' in error.

since, tortured with rheumatism & a stiff right arm. The Stein letter arrived this morning. To all intent it was quite bloody, but it furnishes an excuse of sorts, and I shall be in London on Wednesday or Thursday of next week. The Stein has, apparently, nothing to do with the bicycles which are owned by a Mr. Magnus Cohen.[1] There's nothing in it for me, of course, but I'll have a peep at him, &, perhaps, sing a few snatches of the Horst Wessel song outside his office door. I have given up my cricketing career, & can now cheat at Mah Jong with a dexterity worthy of Mr. Arthur Waley himself.[2]

Agents

What a beautiful word, too. Think of Rodin's 'Pinker', and the natural annoyance following their mistake in not attempting to *make* saleable what is only unsaleable to a mind counterfeited with slush magazine stories will fade into a proper perspective. As it is it's all right. Pinkers[3] will sell 'Headline' & the poem for you, & *you*, eventually, will sell the rest. That's the worst of being 'classy'. You have to look awfully high all the time. You won't ever be *very* popular, but, dear! dear! you will be loved. Curtis Brown's don't like me very much either. I think they've got morbid minds, for the first two stories they are sending out are 'Martha' & 'The Vest'. Now if they want smutty stories . . .

Jokes

The mongoose was appreciated. Have you heard of Mae West's Trunk Crime? 'Come up & saw me sometime.' Isn't Baffy a lovely word? It's a better name than Taffy for your cat.

Virginity

A criticism not a physical discussion, although the criticism is dreadfully short. I can't do justice to it in a few lines. Further nagging will follow. Yes, I don't like Kensington. The story's too human for me. It's very clever but it's too feminine. It's a minor affair in every sense of the word, and the actual writing appears rather too casual. The theme, again, is good. All your themes are. And there's a very strong end. But it is—it has to be, I suppose—too commonplace for me to like it as much as your others. I hope the next story will be a little more imaginative. The nature of language, not the language of nature, for you! 'Anna'. 'The Gardeners'. Even 'Hidden Treasure' (with some alterations) are all truer to you because they are bothered less with the actions of human feet & hands & more with the action of the imagination.

Vicky

Ironically following Virginity. I'm glad he still loves us. I'm glad, too, that he hasn't been able as yet to get my book published, for I want to cut some of the poems out & substitute some of the later ones. He *is* the King of the Poet's Corner. Those six poems of his contained all the faults &

1 Some joke or fantasy concerning a non-literary Stein seems to be intended.
2 Arthur Waley (1889–1966) was an authority on Chinese literature.
3 A literary agency, founded in New York by James Brand Pinker.

merits of his literary 'brats'. In those six poems he showed himself as he really is. Good for him.

Entertainment

I'll be in time for the first Prom.[1] I know you don't like the first Proms, but they're playing some of the Planet music. Till Eulenspiegel, & two Bach string preludes. Let's go, shall we? I like the noise & the tobacco smoke & the young men with beards & the young women with the London Mercury under their arms.

Heil!

Of course. Young Freddy is the ideal Fascist novitiate. I should have seen that. He's perfect. I suppose we will go to Vicky's one evening? I hope he'll be there. I'm doing a new series for the local socialist paper: a series on Intellectual Revolution. I've got some lovely articles to come: on 'Censorship', 'Sex Ethics', 'Blood & Force', 'The Marxian Brothers' 'State Nurseries', & 'The Sin of Patriotism'. You should see the letters I'm receiving. I had one from 'Mother Of a Boy Scout'.

Beer

It wasn't a very good parody, was it? It certainly made me laugh though, and some of Herr Mittelbrau's lines were better than the originals. I've written a reply, but I've lost it. If I find it, I'll bring it up & you can give it to Kalie to give to him. 'Light', incidentally, is to be published in 'Poems of the Year', an anthology brought out by the Bodley Head in opposition to Thomas Moult's horrible 'Best Poems'.

New Poem

I enclose my new poem. I hope you'll like it. It's going in New Verse this month.[2] I took a long time over it, &, at the moment, anyway, I'm a little bit pleased with it. Not much—just a little bit.

The Sweetest Thing

I do love you, Pam, but I'm not going to tell you in this letter. I'm to see you in a few days. I'm so happy to think of that that my rheumatism vanishes. X

Cruelty

Have you seen the Spectator review of 'Symphony'. In case you haven't, I enclose it. Good God is all one can possibly say. Vicky deserves every word of it, of course. But you don't, my darling, & Vicky shd be publicly horsewhipped for insulting your book as he did with his asinine compounds & his lack of tact. Now, my darling, don't let the review annoy or worry you. Show it to Vicky, & I hope it annoys & worries *him*. I know you worry like hell when someone—not me, of course, for I am a privileged

1 The Promenade Concert was on Saturday 11 August.
2 'If I were tickled by the rub of love' appeared in the August *New Verse*. But Thomas had already sent her that poem. This one may have been 'Half of the fellow father as he doubles' (retitled 'My world is pyramid' for *18 Poems*), which *New Verse* published December 1934.

person—slates you. But who cares? It doesn't matter. I think it's a very funny review, anyway. He must have enjoyed himself writing it.

And now goodbye. Write to me by Monday or Tuesday. Give my love to your mother, & do thank her for the trouble she has taken in the cyclists' cause.

I'll be with you so soon.[1] Goodbye & all the love in the world.

XXX Dylan

MS: Buffalo

GLYN JONES
[? early August 1934]   5 Cwmdonkin Drive Uplands Swansea

I have been waiting, and am still waiting, for a letter from London that will definitely decide my day and hour of departure. The letter has not yet come. If it does not arrive by Monday or Tuesday, I shall be leaving G.W.R. Swansea at 7 a.m. If the letter does arrive after this note is posted, I may be going up any time between now & then. All horribly vague, & insufficient excuse for you to return to Cardiff. You carry on from North Wales, Glyn, and I'll give a ring to the Garth Hotel early on Thursday morning—about nine o'clock, before you go out. I'm sorry but I don't know what the devil my phone number is, & shan't know now until I reach town. But a ring at nine o'clock Thursday morning to the Garth Hotel will find you, won't it? I'll be seeing you. Is there going to be anybody with you? I'll be alone all the day time every day. I will, as I said before, be seeing you. Good luck to your North Wales trip.

Dylan

MS: Carbondale

GEOFFREY GRIGSON
[about 5 August 1934]   5 Cwmdonkin Drive Uplands Swansea

Dear Grigson,

Here are the two poems I said I'd send you. I hope it's not too late. More especially, I hope you like the poems. They are both very recently written. Do let me know if it is too late, as I may be able to do something else with the poems. But I hope, again, that you'll like them and be able to print them.

I'm coming up to town at the end of this week. Will you be away then?

Sincerely,
Dylan Thomas

MS: Texas

1 Thomas arrived in London on Friday 10 August.

*ITHEL DAVIES[1]
[envelope postmarked 8 August 1934]   5 Cwmdonkin Drive   Uplands
                                                             Swansea

Dear Mr Ithel Davies,
    We are informed that you are an official of the No More War Movement.
If that is so, we would like to have details of membership, because we
believe the present militarist trend of national politics makes it imperative
that those who object to War in any shape or form should actively identify
themselves with the Movement.
    If membership is open to us, we wish to enrol ourselves, not merely as
nominal members but as active propagandists. That the work of the No
More War Movement is, at least locally, little known to many confirmed
objectors, seems to be a matter of concern. We would wish to propagate,
through the columns of all the journals at our disposal, the urgency of
bringing together into a common front those who hold similar views to
ourselves.
    May we congratulate you upon your articles, and hope that you will be
able to reply soon to this letter.
                                        Yours Sincerely,
                                        Dylan Thomas
                                        A. E. Trick (Twentieth Century)
MS: Jonathan Fryer

TREVOR HUGHES
Wednesday [?15 August 1934]   53 Battersea Rise   London   SW3[2]

Dear Trevor,
    All the apologies in the world would be, I know, quite unavailing. It
wasn't until this evening that I realised what a prize bugger I have been. I
stayed in the Fitzroy until about half-past seven this evening, saw no sign
of you, wondered why on earth you hadn't arrived, for you are, as a rule, as
punctual & as conscientious as I am not, & then was conscious of a faint
and rather terrible suspicion. Was I too early, too late? No, that wasn't it:

1 A solicitor (later a barrister) practising in Swansea, who had written articles for the
   Swansea and West Wales Guardian, Davies was a lifelong pacifist, and went to prison
   in the First World War for his principles. The letter, typewritten, was sent to Davies c/o
   the newspaper.
2 The Johnsons' house in south London (the postal district was SW11; SW3 is Chelsea).
   Thomas was in London, staying with Pamela and her mother most of the time, from 10
   August to 15 September, when the Johnsons returned with him to Swansea, and stayed
   at the Mermaid Hotel for two weeks. In London, Thomas is known to have met Trevor
   Hughes on Monday 20 August. So—if he was not telling the truth about 'going home
   Tuesday'—this letter may have been written the previous Wednesday, 15 August.

six it was all right. Then I took a disconsolate & suspicious bus-ride back to Battersea. Then Pamela, who acts in a vaguely sardonic secretarial capacity to me, distrusting me—in that sense, at least—as much as you do, looked up her little diary & found—as I had been vaguely terrified—that *Tuesday was the night. Will* you accept the apology? It's damnably true, & I know what hell it is sticking lonely in the Fitzroy for an hour—I've done it myself. I know. Do please accept it. I wanted like hell to meet you & to drink bad beer with you & be as scatter-brained & egotistic as ever to your burning silence. I'm going home Tuesday. I think. Will you meet me Monday. *Not* in the Fitzroy. We daren't trust that again. *I'll* come to meet you outside Baker Street at six. Monday. If you feel it worth it, do write and confirm it. Pamela sends you her love. She likes you almost as much as I do.

Dylan

MS: Buffalo

GEOFFREY GRIGSON
[27 August 1934][1]   53 Battersea Rise (at the moment) SW11

Dear Grigson,
 I know you'll excuse this note, but it is quite essential that I take advantage of the offer you made, I think seriously, last week. I can't go back to Wales yet, for even the foundations of the Old Home seem to be crumbling. If I had realised at tea yesterday that things were really as bad as they are, I wouldn't have had to trouble you with this undignified note. My world of good, dying fathers and bad, female poets is proving affectionately unstable. I don't mind the Garret and Crust at all, but I'd much prefer to borrow some money and to postpone such a conventionality. Again I apologise for the substance and the mood of this.
 Five o'clock, Wednesday?

Very sincerely,
Dylan Thomas

MS: Texas

GLYN JONES
[September 1934]   5 Cwmdonkin Drive Uplands Swansea

Dear Glyn,
 As usual I am apologising, &, as usual, there is every excuse for my delay in writing to you. I only arrived home from London a few days ago; I had been up there ever since I was there with you—a long and, comparatively,

1 Johnson's diary, Sunday 26 August: '. . . he left me to go to Grigson's for tea & didn't come back [till 1.10 am]. So dispiriting.'

worth-while stay. Mother had forgotten to readdress your last letter, & it was waiting, all virgin & unopened, for me.

Yes, certainly let's go to see Caradoc,[1] & the sooner the better, as I intend returning to London—permanently, then—in about a month. By the way, Geoffrey Grigson is very interested in you and your poetry. When are you going up to town again? He wants to meet you and to introduce you to some others of the New Verse people.

And what about coming down to Swansea on Saturday? Can you manage this Saturday? If you can't, let me know when you can come down. I hope it'll be soon. The Aberystwyth date depends, of course, on you.

Write soon, explaining your Caradoc &, don't forget, your Swansea plans. And don't be too
annoyed at the
(really) unavoidable
delay in writing.

Dylan
(Good for New Stories. When?)

MS: Carbondale

PAMELA HANSFORD JOHNSON
[late October 1934]

P.S. Jumper at end of week (mother).

Book It And See

First of all, to reply to the short letter marked Bloody private and confidential. Runia seems to have given you a fairly correct summary of the correspondence between us. Another letter—written by Neuburg & Runia in collaboration, actually in different sorts of ink—came later, explaining very carefully a number of things that I can't understand at all, and asking—as you intimated—for a poem for this Sunday's Referee. Why, do you know? I suspect vaguely Caponeish[2] measures. Vicky is, I believe, putting me on the spot, though what spot, & why, God alone knows. My letters, as perhaps Runia told you, demanded the return of my book.[3] But I'm no more likely to get it than I am to find Gibbon's History of Christianity in my navel. Only force remains. No, I can't seriously adopt the idea of a second selection of even more immature & unsatisfactory

---

1 Caradoc Evans (1878–1945), who outraged the Welsh establishment with his novels and stories. When Jones and Thomas visited him in Aberystwyth that autumn, he gave them tea and friendly conversation.

2 The American gangster from Naples, Al Capone, was no longer at large, having been gaoled for tax evasion three years earlier.

3 Thomas was disenchanted with the Sunday Referee over his forthcoming book of poems. The newspaper wanted a publisher to share the cost, but was having difficulty finding one. Johnson's diary, Friday 19 October: 'Worrying calls from Runia [Tharp] re Dylan's book which necessitated me writing him a second letter.'

poems. I find, after reading them through again, that the poems in Vicky's confounded possession are a poor lot, on the whole, with many thin lines, many oafish sentiments, several pieces of twopenny Christ, several unintentional comicalities, & much highfalutin nonsense expressed in a soft, a truly soft language. I've got to get nearer to the bones of words, & to a Matthew Arnold's hell with the convention of meaning & sense. Not that it matters, anyway. Life is only waves, wireless waves, & electric vibrations.[1] Does it matter, my little radio programme from Battersea, that the high or the low tension runs down? I have, of course, in the weakness of my spirit, sent some clumsy poem for the Referee.[2] But, blast, I will be firm, & the October date still stands. Much thanks for the Bloody private low-down. Yah for Neuburg & his literary thieves' kitchen.

House Lend A Little Chairful

In reference to my prospective studio. Janes[3] and I will be coming up definitely about the second week of November, by car fortunately, bearing with us typewriters, easels, bedclothes, brassières for lady models, & plumcakes for Nelson's lions—a cherry or two for Eros, a copy of the London Mercury for Nurse Cavell. We want a room about fifteen shillings per week: it must be as large as possible, larger if possible, unfurnished, with good light. Preferably gas: electric is bad for our sensitive eyes & complexions. But don't worry about looking for one: we will procure one, even if it is a little out of Chelsea. But you might keep your eye open; one eye. Have you a mattress & a chair either to give or sell to two poor, unrecognised geniuses? I don't want to take a mattress up, it's too big, & I don't want to buy one because I'm frightened of getting rabies or ringworm. Don't throw any old furniture over the neighbours' walls. It would be vitally useful to us. If you have a fairly large & dirty table you don't intend taking with you, store it somewhere, & I'll buy it from you. Don't forget, my prospectively philanthropic clother & furnisher of the artistic poor! Table, mattress, chair! I don't want to buy them from a second-hand shop, owing to the possibility of disease; I would, if you had them, like to purchase them from No. 53 (going—gone) Battersea Rise.[4]

The Hart, My Lord

Your letter does read as though your nerves had been chewn by a dog. Why, o neurotic, this sudden tremble? Don't tell me. The wholesale effect of years' official labour. The reaction of liberty.[5] And so on through all the

1 Early in October a six-day international physics conference in London and Cambridge had prompted newspaper articles about the mysteries of the atom, including (to quote *The Times*) the fact that sub-atomic matter could 'behave both as particles or as waves'.

2 'Foster the light' appeared in the *Sunday Referee* on 28 October.

3 Alfred Janes (1911–99), the Swansea painter, first met Dylan Thomas through Dan Jones, and was a lifelong friend. In 1934 he had just left the Royal Academy Schools and taken a room in Redcliffe Street, near the Fulham Road. He and Thomas moved in on 13 November.

4 The Johnsons were to move across the Thames to a flat in Chelsea.

5 Johnson had left her job at the bank and was writing her first novel.

psychological text phrases to an unenviable end. Condole with your mother for me; if her nose troubles her, remove it. It would not be uncharitable to say that she would not miss it. Nevertheless, condole; read her 'Pursuit' in a baritone voice; put my letters in her tea. And, for yourself, Take The Philosophic View. Look at the gallons of stars, the London infinity, & what is an over-pumping heart? (These things are easy to say: I have just spilt the ink on my hand, & am cursing God.) Be better, darling, but don't worry about being better. If we die, here are two nice epitaphs:

> Here lies the body of Pamela J.
> You can kick in her ribs, there's nothing to pay.
> Here lies the body of Dylan M. T.
> You can trample his balls. He don't care a d—.

Cruel, you aver? But then, but then, isn't the world cruel, Mrs. Matthews?

(Here too lies the body of Meriel Right,
With teeth in her buttocks, & serve her right.)
But she's a nice girl, & that serves her right, too.

Pursuit
   Well, I wouldn't chase it. I'd let the damned thing go. Blood on the raspberry to it, for all I care. I think it's lousy, just lousy. There's no merit in it at all: it's coy, it's turgid, it's affected, it's nauseating. I cannot, I am afraid, approve of the New Manner, which seems to me to be a bloodier way than ever of linking together Old Mannerisms. No, I mean, you just *can't* go on like that. It's criminal. I know you're not well, but you can't blame the poor thing on a too-rapid heart. Sorry to be so rude. I can't give any constructive criticism.

On A Testicle Made For Two
   Your insertion of the word 'testicles' at the foot of a page entitled 'Blast & Fugger' has rather puzzled me. I don't know whether you were being merely low, (come out of the wood, girl, if you are, & let's be really indecent), or whether you were using that very nice word merely as a swear-word (If so, I congratulate you. I'd never thought of it) or whether there was some deeper, & more sinister, significance. I'd rather believe in the second theory (testicles as a term of disapprobation). The first theory belies your dainty character, & the third gives rise (ha, phallic!) in my mind to many disturbing ideas: you aren't, by any chance, turning male, are you? I do hope not. I've always wondered why you won't come to bed with me; it just seems silly to me, but now I am beginning to wonder. What with these sinister references (Did you know that in Ancient Mexico there was a Court Dignitary Called the Keeper Of The Imperial Balls? I didn't) & the

nail-cum-penis dream that perplexed you so much some time ago, who knows? Tell me the dreadful truth. I'm sure I don't like little boys in That Way.

John O'London's Circumcision[1]

A definite success. There were thirty five people in the audience, that's all, and thirty of them were women. But what women! All of a dim, uncertain age, most of them virgins, & all with some smattering of Freud & Lawrence. The chairman, a big-bellied bore, introduced me as a Young Revolutionary (I was becomingly clad in red) who was tackling A Difficult & Courageous Task. I then gave them the works. At the beginning there was a frozen & horrified silence, but eventually I induced a few titters, &, at last, real, undeniable interest. A glassy look came into the eyes of the spinsters. I put in several wise-cracks, & ended with 'Let Copulation Thrive'. Then the ladies, in one solid mass, bombarded me with questions. In the Communist Erewhon[2] I had dealt with, would there be no perversions? What we consider as perversions, I replied, (excuse the novelette form of this report) are, for the most part, healthy & natural bypaths of sexual life. How could a woman defend her honour in such a State? Tin drawers, I replied with Ready Humour. Do you believe in preventatives? The day, I replied, that legalised birthcontrol & clinical abortion come into practice, will go down as a French Letter day in the annals of history. And so on for two hours, until middle-aged ladies, who, before that night, would have blushed or been horrified at the mention of pyjamas, were talking gaily about whirling-sprays, Lesbianism, sanitary towels, latrines, fornication & other everyday & normal things. Trick made a nice little speech about the inevitability of Revolution, a gentleman defended repression with a very blood-shot eye, Janes made a joke about gallstones, & the meeting closed. God knows what we've done to those ardent & earnest ladies, but I hope it hurts. The more I see of Wales the more I think it's a land entirely peopled by perverts. I don't exclude myself, who obtain a high & soulful pleasure from telling women, old enough to be my mother, why they dream of two-headed warthogs in a field of semen. (I heard, later, that a committee meeting has been held, & that care must be taken in the future as to who is invited to lecture. Those bloody women woke up in the cold light of morning, & regretted those few hours of—if nothing else—verbal freedom.)

---

1 The John O'London's was a literary society in Swansea. Trick left an unpublished account of the proceedings which says there was a 'stunned silence'. Thomas's subject was allegedly 'Pornography and the nineteenth-century novel'.
2 *Erewhon*, the imaginary land of Samuel Butler's satire (1872). It is an anagram of 'nowhere'.

Last week-end I spent in Aberystwyth with Caradoc Evans. He's a great fellow. We made a tour of the pubs in the evening, drinking to the eternal damnation of the Almighty & the soon-to-be-hoped-for destruction of the tin Bethels. The university students love Caradoc, & pelt him with stones whenever he goes out.

I have nothing to send you (except a pound of love), but have nearly finished a short story. I am working very hard on a poem: it is going to be a very long poem; I've completed fifty lines so far; it is by far the best thing I've done; I don't suppose I'll have finished it even when I see you; but you shall read what there is of it then.[1]

How much more of your novel? Of course, I want to see it all before Pinkers have it.

Now love & goodbye, more love than goodbye, for I'll see you soon. But write soon & much, & do, my darling, get better for me. I don't like to think of you ill. (And you, very naturally, don't like being ill.) Don't forget any old furniture—especially mattress, table, & chair. Give my love to your mother.
    Love again, & a terrible lot of it. XXXXXX

                                                                Dylan

MS: Buffalo

GEOFFREY GRIGSON
[early November 1934]   5 Cwmdonkin Drive   Uplands   Swansea

Dear Geoffrey,
    I've been meaning to write to you for the last month, and was awfully glad to get your letter. In answer to your questions: (a) I am in Wales, (b) I'm coming to London in about ten days, (c) I *have* been on the Balearic Islands occasionally,[2] (d) I've died once or twice, too, (e) I am never lascivious. Penniless I retreated from London, and penniless I return. I've been staying all over the place, with Caradoc Evans in Aberystwyth, with an indulgent but ailing mother, as now, with a large lady and her hotel on

---

1 'When, like a running grave' has exactly fifty lines.
2 Not true.

the Gower Peninsula, and in a cottage in Carmarthenshire, glorying in the name of Blaen Cwm, where I lived on carrots, (no, that's not quite true, I had onions as well). But in ten days or less I'll be taking a room with another bloated aristocrat in town. I hope I'll see you and Norman[1] very soon.

Have you seen Pope Eliot lately. He's doing funny things with my book. Three or four days ago his secretary sent me a letter by express post—I don't quite know what express post means, but you have to pay sixpence to the boy at the door—asking me to make *no* arrangements until I had heard from the Pope himself who was writing that evening. What earthly arrangements could I make? And I'm damned if he's written. I remember somebody telling me once that she had used a poem of mine as a sort of funnel to put in a bottle, as a sadistic doctor wanted a sample of her urine. Do try to find out if the entire staff of Faber and Faber are doing similar things with my twenty poems.

Of course you can use any poems of mine you want to. I've written a new one—bit better than the others, I think—which I enclose.[2] Perhaps you'd like to use that too, or instead.

Thanks very much for the promise of the books. But it's hardly worth sending them if I'm coming up in ten days, is it? Do let me have some then, though. I'm relying on reviews to ensure the carrots and onions.

Yours,
Dylan

Do you think it would be better if the enclosed poem were *not* divided into stanzas? I've tried it that way, but it seemed more obscure.

Ross-Williamson of the Bookman has given me some reviews. Do you think Janet Adam Smith[3] would too if I wrote her a nice, cooing letter?

MS: Texas

ERICA WRIGHT (T. S. Eliot's secretary)
Sunday [4 November 1934]

Dear Miss Wright,

Thanks for your two letters. In reply to the first: I intend coming up to London in about ten days' time. And, for the second, I can only say that the arrangements are, very unfortunately, out of my hands.[4] A wire was sent to me on Saturday, saying that a publisher was to start—whatever 'start'

---

1 Norman Cameron (1905–53), poet and advertising copywriter. A friend of Grigson, he kept a disapproving eye on Thomas during the latter's first years in London.
2 Perhaps 'Should lanterns shine', printed in *New Verse*, December 1935.
3 Janet Adam Smith (1905–99), author and journalist, was assistant editor of the *Listener*.
4 Miss Wright wrote on 1 November to say Eliot 'hopes that you will not make any decision about the publication of your poems before hearing from him'.

means—on Monday, if Mr Eliot was still undecided.[1] I'm writing back today to say what you told me. And that's all I know about it. Mr Eliot hasn't written yet, but I expect I may hear from him [*Thomas typed 'Him', then overtyped a lower-case 'h'*] tomorrow. I wish I knew more about all this than I do. I'll try, anyway, to stop whatever mysterious decisions *are* being made.

Yours very truly,
Dylan Thomas

MS: Valerie Eliot

DENYS KILHAM ROBERTS[2]
[November 1934]   5 Cwmdonkin Drive   Uplands   Swansea

Dear Mr. Roberts,
    Herewith is the proof of my poem—all correct except for the one singular instead of plural in line [*number missing*] of the verse, which I have corrected.

Dylan Thomas

I suppose I will be notified when the anthology is to appear.

MS: Texas

1 The *Sunday Referee*, afraid of losing their prize poet, moved at last. As a result, Eliot returned Thomas's poems to Neuburg on 5 November, 'with great regret that you are unable to allow us to keep [them] for further consideration'. Eliot said later that he regretted having been 'so fussy' about Thomas's work—'one ought to have accepted the inferior with the first-rate'.
2 One of the editors of *The Year's Poetry*. The poem was 'Light breaks'.

Success and Marriage
1934–9

The publication of *18 Poems* in an edition of 250 copies, just before Christmas 1934, caused sufficient stir in the narrow-drawn literary circles of the time to make Dylan Thomas noticed by a few influential critics and readers. Two years later *Twenty-five Poems*, though more guardedly received, added to his reputation. Much of this time was spent in London, but he rarely had a fixed address, and his parents' house in Swansea remained his real base. His tiny earnings for stories and poems, supplemented by borrowing, with Cwmdonkin Drive available as a refuge, enabled him to lead the casual life he desired. In the spring of 1937, following D. J. Thomas's retirement, his parents moved to a smaller house, and shortly afterwards, Thomas married Caitlin Macnamara, whom he had met the previous year. They lived either at her mother's house in the New Forest or in the small town of Laugharne, on the coast of West Wales. Their first child, Llewelyn, was born in 1939. Poverty had become a practical problem, rather than an appropriate condition for a poet. Thomas was beginning to earn a little more from his writing. But it was a precarious existence.

A. E. TRICK
[December 1934]   5 Redcliffe Street   London   SW10

Dear Bert,

This seems a nice and suitable time to write the letter that I know I should have written at least a week ago. The Sunday Referee has done us both quite proud, although personally I do not think that Neuburg chose the most flattering passages of either your letter or comrade Thompson's. Your criticism was good, and naturally I agreed with every word of it: it contained, expressed in a beautifully condensed way, what you and I have discussed for so many hours. And win the prize—what is the prize, by the way?—it bloody well should. Comrade Thompson wrote at far greater length than you, explaining subtleties in my bad poem that I was and still am not aware of. And your Oxford cum Vanoc[1] letter was just as good; I heard two anarchistic gentlemen arguing vigorously over it in a café last night.

There is no news, or there is all news. The city goes on, myself now a very insignificant part of it. I live, with Janes, just off the Fulham Road, on the borders of Chelsea, Fulham, South Kensington, and Brompton, in a large room with a bathroom and sort of inferior wash up adjoining. This is the quarter of the pseudo-artists, of the beards, the naughty expressions of an entirely outmoded period of artistic importance, and of the most boring Bohemian parties I have ever thought possible. Slightly drunk, slightly dirty, slightly wicked, slightly crazed, we repeat our platitudes on Gauguin and Van Gogh as though they were the most original things in the world. There are, of course, scores of better people that I do meet, but these little maggots are my companions for most of the time. I think I shall change my digs quite soon.

Another Swansea boy—hark, hark the parish pump—lives in the room above us. He is Mervyn Levy,[2] a small and cunning Jew who does small and cunning drawings, and, at the present, does not work in the Royal College, Kensington. This bloody land is full of Welshmen, and, day by day as I feast my eyes upon their mean and ungenerous countenances, I feel

1 A letter from an H. Thompson was mentioned in the Poet's Corner on 11 November. On 25 November the *Sunday Referee* published a letter from Trick, in reply to an article about pacifism by the political correspondent, 'Vanoc II'.
2 Mervyn Levy, artist and entrepreneur, was at school with Thomas and remained a friend. His drawings of Thomas are in the National Portrait Gallery and the National Library of Wales.

more like Caradoc whose books are, in a small circle at least, becoming a highbrow success owing to my uninterrupted praise of them.

I am not at the moment working very hard; I find it difficult to concentrate in a room as muddled and messy as ours is nearly all the time; for yards around me I can see nothing but poems, poems, poems, butter, eggs and mashed potatoes mashed among my stories and Janes's canvases. One day we will have to wash up, and then, perhaps, I can really begin to work. As it is, most of the more recent stuff that I brought up with me has been accepted in various periodicals. A new, very highbrow magazine called, very originally, 'Art' is to print my 'Burning Baby'[1] in its first quarterly number, January 1935, the Adelphi is printing my 'Tree' this December, the next 'Criterion' is printing my 'The Visitor'—that is in the middle of this month—New Verse is printing a long poem[2] which you have in your cuttings book and also a review, slating, of Spender's new poem 'Vienna', and my book of poems will be out before Xmas.[3] I have hopes, too, of a publisher, probably Boriswood,[4] publishing my stories in the spring. To continue this egoistic survey, I have met a number of new notabilities including Henry Moore, the sculptor, Edwin and Willa Muir, Wyndham Lewis, and, certainly not least, Betty May.[5]

Betty May is, as you probably know, an artist's model who has posed— perhaps that is not the most correct word—for John, Epstein and the rest of the racketeers. She wrote a book, too, describing herself as 'The Tiger Woman of Paris'. At least she didn't write the book, she sponsored it; it was written really by Gilbert Armitage[6] for the sum of £40. I am going to write an article for her, under her name, for the News of the World. My payment will not be monetary, but, and although she is now not as young as she was, that will not matter.

Now how does your world go? Has the Guardian reformed and started to print your nasty little nigglings again? And what are you doing all these long winter nights: writing propaganda? propagandish poems? indignant and abusive letters? or reading more of those damnable facts that you manage to extract from all sorts of seditious quarters? I kept the Daily

1 'The Burning Baby' was inspired by the nineteenth-century eccentric, Dr William Price, who in 1883 cremated the body of his infant son using coal and paraffin on a South Wales hillside. He was prosecuted unsuccessfully; cremation was soon accepted as lawful. Thomas's story was published in issue No. 1 of a small-circulation magazine, *Contemporary Poetry and Prose*, May 1936. It used the anagrammatic joke-name, 'Llareggub', for the first time.
2 'My world is pyramid', December 1934.
3 David Archer of the Parton Bookshop had put up £20, the *Sunday Referee* £30, and the book came out on or about 18 December 1934.
4 Publishers went in fear of prosecution for obscenity, and many of Thomas's early stories were too explicit for all but small, expensive literary magazines to handle. Boriswood, a publishing firm that dabbled in 'dangerous' books, was a forlorn hope. It had just brought out an edition of James Hanley's risky novel *Boy*, but emasculated it with asterisks. (The hero talks to a prostitute: 'Swing *** ***. Now *** ***. Oh God! *** ***.')
5 Edwin Muir (1887–1959), writer and critic. Betty May, the so-called 'Tiger Woman', artists' model and one-time friend of Aleister Crowley.
6 Armitage was a well-connected literary journalist.

Worker Princess Marina Supplement for you, but, as usual with all such things, I went and lost it. It was a special and particularly seditious pamphlet abusing the whole of the Royal Family and exhibiting almost bawdy cartoons of our 'Enemy the King'.[1] Very good. London was hell on the day of that Royal Ramp, the streets crowded enough to be almost impossible to walk in, the whole of the traffic disorganised and the pubs open to eleven all over the city. There were women and their babies—I saw them—who waited all night outside the Abbey, keeping those perishing children in the cold and fog for at least forty hours. I told Norman Cameron about it and said that they all should be put in lunatic asylums. He said that there was no necessity; all that needs be done is to keep them in England. Isn't this letter well typed?

Write to me soon, telling me all that you know I would like to know, all about the Guardian and sedition in general. As this is the first letter it must not, according to the rules of etiquette, be too long. There, you liar, it isn't etiquette I'm worrying about, it's just sheer laziness.

Give my regards to Mrs. Trick junior and senior and to Miss Trick whose poems, so Vicky tells me, are by far the best and the most sincere that he receives.

Write soon. And don't forget: all the news.

Dylan

I came across yesterday, in the possession of a fellow whom I don't know & can't borrow from, the first *real* literature of Fascism & Nazism. It is called 'Might is Right' & was printed in Australia in the 1890's. The author is called Ragnor Redbeard. If you can by any method, get hold of it.

MS: Ohio State University

GLYN JONES
[December 1934]   5 Redcliffe Street   London   SW10

Many thanks for the letter, and many apologies that you should have had to write the first letter since I came up to town about a month ago. I seem to have been very busy and have written only two letters home during the whole time. I haven't written to any friends at all, and hope that they know me well enough by this time to realise that it's no more than a lazy carelessness on my part—though a lazy carelessness is bad enough, God knows.

Very, very glad to hear that you are coming to London about Christmas. I am looking forward to seeing you and to introduce you to Grigson. I am, as I think I told you when, during the famous Caradoc expedition, we last met, staying with a painter called Janes. We possess one large room in a quiet street in South Kensington—in South Kensington, that is officially,

1 Princess Marina married the Duke of Kent, 29 November 1934.

but we are near Chelsea, Fulham and Brompton. Everything is in rather a mess, but if you don't mind that, and I don't somehow think you do, then I do really wish you would sleep with us. Janes spends most of his time indoors and cooks his own meals, but I have most of my scanty meals in cafés—scanty not for the reason of utter penury, although I have had and do have and am having at the moment a particularly lean period, but for the sake of the demon alcohol who has become a little too close and heavy a friend for some time now. Pile in with us, will you? We shall also have the greatest pleasure in providing quite nice breakfasts free of all charge. Does that induce you? Yes, of course it does. So when are you definitely coming up? I'm not, I don't think so at the moment at least, going home for Christmas. My book of poems is coming out then, and I hope to make just sufficient money to keep me happy for the few most important days of the holiday.

So you've been reviewing Edith Sitwell's latest piece of virgin dung, have you?[1] Isn't she a poisonous thing of a woman, lying, concealing, flipping, plagiarising, misquoting, and being as clever a crooked literary publicist as ever. I do hope you pointed out in your review the real points against the book (you did, I know, but I like being dogmatic)? The majority of the book was cribbed from Herbert Read and Leavis,[2] actually and criminally cribbed. She has misquoted Hopkins at least twenty times, reprinted many poems without the permission of publisher or poet. Yes, that was my poem all right, reproduced without my name, misquoted at the end, and absurdly criticised. I duly sent my protest to Gerald Duckworth and he replied to the effect that so many protests of a similar sort had been received, that he could as yet do nothing about it. It is being hoped that he will have to withdraw the book. I *would* like to see your review of it.

What news there is can wait until I see you. Let it be soon, and don't forget to let us know when that will be. You stay with us, of course.

Dylan

Excuse me typing this, but I have only just found my pen & ink.

MS: Carbondale

GLYN JONES
[26 December 1934]   5 Cwmdonkin Drive   Uplands   Swansea

Dear Glyn,
    I'm so bloody sick of apologising to you in every one of the too few letters that I write you that today I refuse to So Humble myself. Ach!
    Now this is the position: I, unfortunately, have to stay in Swansea until

---

1 Sitwell's book *Aspects of Modern Poetry*, published by Duckworth, was savagely critical of *New Verse*, and used Thomas's poem 'Our eunuch dreams' as one of its bad examples. She added insult to injury by not mentioning Thomas by name.
2 F. R. Leavis (1895–1978), the rigorous literary critic.

Saturday, as then my sister & brother-in-law are returning to London & will give me a commodious and entirely inexpensive ride. I suggest—& I have already explained it to Janes, my partner—that you stay the nights you are in London—the nights I am not—in 5 REDCLIFFE St; there will be an entirely empty & quite pleasant bedroom at your disposal, & Janes will see to your little wants & to your larger wants, such as breakfast etc. You'll find him a very nice chap, &, of course, expecting you. I'll see you, then, on Saturday evening. To get to REDCLIFFE St, you take a 14 bus from Piccadilly (marked Putney), which goes up the Brompton Road, the Fulham Road, & stops outside the Redcliffe Arms at the corner of Redcliffe Gardens. Walk up Redcliffe Gardens on your right, & there, after a few street turnings, lies the ancient baroque architecture of my residence. Don't forget—No. 5. Now do be an angel, & do what I say. On Sunday we'll go to the Grigsons' house in Hampstead.

(I've lost your home address, & only hope that the vague marks I have made on this envelope will be satisfactory to the postman.)

Cheers.

Dylan

MS: Carbondale

GLYN JONES
[about 28 December 1934]   5 Cwmdonkin Drive   Uplands   Swansea

Dear Glyn,

This, at the moment, is how the position stands: I wrote you a letter on Wednesday night, addressed, probably, to a legendary street in Cardiff, I having lost your last letter, and in that letter of mine I explained that I was home for Christmas & would be unable to see you before Saturday. Now, I am afraid, the date is Monday, as my sister can't travel before Sunday afternoon. I asked you—in the letter that you probably won't ever receive—to call at 5 Redcliffe Street, S.W.10, where my partner, Janes, would be expecting you; my bedroom is empty & welcome to you, & comrade Janes will see to your home comforts etc. Everything's in a devil of a mess, isn't it? If this letter gets you before Monday, *do* follow my instructions & sleep in Redcliffe St. Directions to reach my habitation: Take the 14 bus from Piccadilly, up Brompton Road & Fulham Road to the Redcliffe Arms at the corner of Redcliffe Gardens. Walk straight up Redcliffe Gardens, & my street is about the fourth or fifth on the right.

Now, if this letter gets you *on* Monday, please do 'phone me immediately: This is my phone number: FLAXMAN 1644. We can then meet, arrange sleeping & accommodation details, & see everyone we can see together. But don't forget: unless I see you before, *do* go to Redcliffe St & let Janes put you up. He's a very nice chap. Anyway, above is my number. Don't forget it. Monday, then, if not before.

Talk to you about everything then.
The usual apologies
for slackness

Dylan

MS: Carbondale

CHARLES FISHER[1]
[early 1935]   5 Redcliffe Street   SW10

Dear Comrade Fisher,
Thank you very much for your letter to which I would have replied sooner had it not been for about twenty reasons: the abominable cold cramping the fingers, elongating the sweet hours of bed, and forcing, eventually, the tired half sleeper to erect a small fire in an insufficient grate; the sin of laziness, cancelling the positive virtue that regards sin and virtue lazily, equally and equably; the lack of ink, my tame harridan having, bless her breasts, spilt the contents of a full bottle on the linoleum; the worries of a life that consists, for the most part, in building the brain on paper and pulling down the body, the too small and too weak body to stand either the erection of a paper brain or the rubbing of saloon counters; the pressure of words; the lack of stamps; flu in embryo, a snotty, chicken-faced foetus swimming, very red, behind the nose; and another twelve reasons, all too complicated to go into at the moment. The ink still staining the linoleum, and my harridan asleep, I have to type this letter. The keys are cold.
You asked me to tell you about my theory of poetry. Really I haven't got one. I like things that are difficult to write and difficult to understand; I like 'redeeming the contraries' with secretive images; I like contradicting my images, saying two things at once in one word, four in two words and one in six. But what I like isn't a theory, even if I do stabilise into dogma my own personal affections. Poetry, heavy in tare though nimble, should be as orgiastic and organic as copulation, dividing and unifying, personal but not private, propagating the individual in the mass and the mass in the individual. I think it should work from words, from the substance of words and the rhythm of substantial words set together, not towards words. Poetry is a medium, not a stigmata on paper. Man should be two tooled, and a poet's middle leg is his pencil. If his phallic pencil turns into an electric drill, breaking up the tar and the concrete of language worn thin by the tricycle tyres of nature poets and the heavy six wheels of the academic sirs, so much the better; and it's work that counts, madam, genius so often being an infinite capacity for aching pains.

1 A colleague and close friend of Thomas on the *South Wales Evening Post,* Fisher was later a journalist in Canada.

About manuscripts. I'm very pleased and glad that you do want a manuscript of some poem of mine, and I'll try to let you have what you want. But my method is this: I write a poem on innumerable sheets of scrap paper, write it on both sides of the paper, often upside down and criss cross ways, unpunctuated, surrounded by drawings of lamp posts and boiled eggs, in a very dirty mess; bit by bit I copy out the slowly developing poem into an exercise book; and, when it is completed, I type it out. The scrap sheets I burn, for there are such a lot of them that they clutter up my room and get mixed in the beer and butter. Now what can I send you? A typed copy? Shall I write some out for you? or preserve from the waiting fire the next batch of almost illegible sheets? Anything you like. I am at your service.

Write again soon. I write so few letters, and like writing them, even if my style is a little too heavy footed. Give my regards to Mr. Job; prevent Mr. Hatcher from taking too many Woolworth waitresses to the cinema and from inviting little girls up dark lanes to show them his stamp album; plant a rose in Reuben's hair; remember me to Bill Latham and to Tom Lucy; and tell Eric that Henekey's devastating cider now costs two pence halfpenny a glass.[1]

Dylan

PS. The manuscript, whatever it will be, I'll send on to you when you tell me what you want. I can't give you the exercise books, for they contain the only copies I possess.

PPS. What are *you* doing with yourself? Do you write at all now, that is apart from the daily hack work?

MS: the recipient

MORTON ZABEL[2]
[late January 1935]   5 Redcliffe Street   London   SW10

Dear Mr. Zabel,

Thank you for your letter which was sent on to me by the 'Criterion'.

I'm afraid I can't suggest titles for the two poems you've decided to keep for publication. Would it be possible to use the first lines as titles?

You very kindly asked me to let you see some more poems. Here are three very new ones.

Sincerely yours,
Dylan Thomas

1 Bill Hatcher, Bill Latham and Tom Lucy were reporters on the *Evening Post*.
2 Morton Dawen Zabel was editor of *Poetry* (Chicago). The letter is annotated in another hand, 'Feb 9/35 retd new mss'. The magazine published no poems by Thomas until 1937.

PS. If you like the new poems, and decide to keep them, perhaps the first lines, as in the case of the other two, had better be used as titles.

D.T.

MS: University of Chicago

A. E. TRICK
Tuesday [?mid February 1935]   5 Redcliffe Gardens   London   SW10

Dear Bert,

This is only the second letter I've written since I came to this very Big City, and it should have been at least the tenth; I've had such a lot that I wanted to say to you, and, now that I do sit down and attempt to tell you, I can't remember a damned thing. Before I try to remember, anyway, thanks for the review in the Guardian and for your Trickish letters in the Post. What a swine Hughes is, isn't he? have you ever read such mannered blarney in your life?[1] Bud and blossom be ――. What's he think I am? Something in a vase or a horticultural exhibition? I liked your review immensely, but then I'd seen it before; but who *is* responsible for the proof correcting? And what did the last sentence mean? Who is the crowner of hacks? By the way, what did you think of Vaughan Thomas's article?[2] It was quite, or even very, flattering, and, I suppose consequently, I liked it. It appeared pretty intelligent, too; I'm meeting him one day this week, or rather one evening, when we intend to have a peep, in our country cousin way, at the Literary Great in the Cafe Royal. Thanks for sending Mewis's letter along; I haven't replied yet, and haven't had time either to write something smutty for his sensational speech in the J.O.L. meeting. He told me that you, from the depths of an abusive and economic imagination, conjured up several wisecracks for the Social Menace and the Dowdy Lady ('I got a son at sea', you remember) to writhe at and object to. I hope they had more crack in them than wisdom; be a dynamitard, if that's spelt correctly, and blow the retired sea captain, Weeping Willy, and the ingrown virgins sky high and with as much rude and illbred noise as possible. I still think of that evening with a faint glow of 'something attempted obscenely, something dung', and remember your muddly boots with pride. Have you attended one of those highbrow salons again? No, of course you haven't; I was forgetting that there is now probably a subdivision of the Society called 'The Anti-Thomas And Trick League', presided over by a backbiting eunuch and a couple of embodied maidenheads.

London is good; Porth[3] is better; and the nostalgia of open and grassy

1 Thomas was offended by a fulsome review that Trevor Hughes had written of *18 Poems*.
2 A. Spender Vaughan-Thomas reviewed *18 Poems* in the *Herald of Wales*, 12 January 1935.
3 A mining town in South Wales, at the foot of the Rhondda Valleys, seen as a centre of industrial militancy in the 1930s.

spaces is, as they say in sentimental diaries or even dairies, strong upon me. I go my way, and the rest of London go theirs. All London is out of step, except me. My book is selling well. A few complimentary reviews have appeared, and Edwin Muir is to write another in the Listener in about a week or a fortnight's time. My chest, he complained, is bad, and my nose runs. Janes has got a rash. There are mice in my room. Work is sporadic. Two and two are still, to my disordered muse, five or even six, and algebra is the study of curves. I'm working on a story to be called 'The Lemon' which will probably be given the raspberry by every self or public-respecting editor in London; and I have just finished two poems which are, I hope, to appear in the new New Verse, Uncle Geoffrey permitting. Some rude reviews of mine you'll see in the Feb Adelphi, and also a review of my own book (what a thrill of pride overcame me when I put those long wished for words on paper) by Rayner Heppenstall[1] who is a nice little Yorkshireman with an aptitude, even an obsession, for singing Yorkshire songs about the Seven Immoral Joys of the Holy Mary—at least he sings them when he's drunk, and drunk he was when I first met him.

Celebrities I meet often and too often, they being a lousy set on the whole, or off it. Herbert Read, Grigson, Cameron, the Muirs, and Heppenstall are the best. Racketeering abounds, and the only racket a comparatively honest person such as myself can belong to is that of the squash racket; squash 'em right, and left, that's the motter.

'The Duchess of Malfi'[2] is now on in town, and this evening, Wednesday, I am to see it for the second time. You remember how much you liked it when you read it first; well, it's a hundred times more thrilling and more beautiful on the stage, and, although the London production is rather thin blooded and Bloomsbury aesthetish, the play comes over and survives all sorts of bad acting; it's the greatest tragedy since Shakespeare—no, but perhaps Webster's White Devil is better still; I believe people are negotiating to have that put on eventually in the Embassy, Hampstead.

If these films come your way do see them: Morgenrot, the German Nazi propaganda film about submarine warfare, The Forbidden Territory, a sort of Boys' Own Paper version of an anti Soviet message, The Thin Man, which has probably been to Swansea and is the best American film I think I've seen, and any of the new Walt Disney's, especially 'The Orphans' Benefit'.

Since I've been in London I've come into contact on a number of occasions with intellectual communism and communists, with A. L. Morton, editor of the Daily Worker, Cockburn, proprietor, with a youthful notoriety, Esmond Romilly, editor of the schoolboys' communist monthly,

1 Rayner Heppenstall (1911-81), novelist and poet; after 1945 a radio producer.
2 The play by John Webster (?1578-?1632).

Out of Bounds, and with all the pseudo-revolutionaries such as John Lehmann, John Pudney etc.[1] And I dislike all of them. Not so much as persons; most of them, I'm sure, would be quite kind to dumb animals; but *as* revolutionaries and as communists, for, born in fairly wealthy middle-class or upper middle class homes, educated at expensive prep schools, public schools, and universities, they have no idea at all of what they priggishly call 'the class struggle' and no contact at all with either any of the real motives or the real protagonists of that class struggle. They are bogus from skull to navel; finding no subjects for their escapist poetry, they pin on a vague sense of propagating the immediate necessity of a social conscience rather than the clear sense of expressing their own un, pro, or anti social consciousnesses. The individual in the mass and the mass in the individual can be made poetically important only when the status and the position of both mass and individual are considered by that part of the consciousness which is outside both. I shall never, I hope, be mixed up in any political ramifications of literary, or pseudo literary London; honest writing does *not* mix with it; you can't be true to party *and* poetry; one must suffer, and, historically, poetry is the social and the economic creed that endures. I think I'll be able to send you some more inflammable literature during the week.

Yes, on deep consideration, Porth *is* better. Some people have invited me to spend part of the summer with them in the hills of Derbyshire, and I think of accepting.[2] Conditions have more to do with writing than I realised; it may seem affected, but I do really need hills around me before I can do my best with either stories or poems; the world here is so flat and unpunctuated, like a bad poem by K. J. Raine.[3] I'm moving from be-artised (in two senses) Chelsea soon anyway, and will let you know my change of address. There are all sorts of plans in my head: Derbyshire, Ireland, East End tenement, Richard Hughes in Laugharne (he's invited me), and even a short tramping existence around England. And I don't know what's going to happen yet.

This is a Me letter; so let yours be a Your letter, telling me all about your political naggings etc. What are you reading now? If possible, get hold of Fontamara,[4] by whom I don't know, which is a very good novel of the

---

1 A. L. Morton wrote for, not edited, the *Daily Worker*; Claud Cockburn was the paper's diplomatic correspondent, not its proprietor; Romilly had run away from his public school the previous year, aged fifteen, to campaign against private education. John Pudney (1909–77), novelist and poet, in 1935 on the staff of the BBC.

2 Thomas stayed for a month with the young historian A. J. P. Taylor (who thought him a sponger, and loathed him) and his wife Margaret (who became a devotee and patron), in their cottage at Higher Disley, on the rural edge of Manchester. It is not quite in Derbyshire.

3 Kathleen Raine, poet and critic.

4 *Fontamara*, by the Communist Ignazio Silone, first published in Britain in 1934, is about the ravages of Fascism in an Italian village.

kind you like. Bernard Brett's 'The Irreconcilables' is quite good, too. Have you bought a copy of my poems yet, you dog? I haven't got a copy to send you, although, God knows, you deserve one as much as, more than, almost anybody. I might have a new book this year, but I don't know yet. Tell me what people in Swansea think of the poems, if they think anything at all.

How is Mrs. Trick junior? And Mrs. Trick senior? Remember me to Pamela,[1] and tell her that Uncle Neuburg considers her the brightest and the most originally promising of all his juvenile poets and poetesses. He wants a poem from her soon.

Don't be as long in writing a letter as I am. I'll really be expecting one next week. Make it as long as you like, or as long as I like, which is even longer.

Dylan

MS: *Ohio State University*

GLYN JONES
[March 1935]   5 Cwmdonkin Drive   Uplands   Swansea

Dear Glyn,

As you see, the trials of life have proved too much for me, the courts have found me guilty, and, rather hollow eyed and with little real work to my credit, I've returned home for a few weeks' holiday. I'm leaving, I believe, in the first week of April, but for the country then, and not for London—: Surrey, Cheshire, Derbyshire, I don't know which. It's very lonely here in Swansea, and the few old friends I have spend their days in work and their evenings in indulging in habits which I've had quite enough of—at least temporarily. As it is, I'm working on some short stories, but I don't know whether they're any good, and I would like you to have a look at them. Do you feel like coming down one Saturday before I go? There are crowds of things for us to talk about, and far more peace and comfort than we had in the pubs & that wretched room of mine in London.

How are you getting on? Have you sent any poems to Geoffrey G. yet? What about your story of the workman shitting over the cliff? The Adelphi hasn't printed the other story yet, has it? Has Pope Eliot replied? And all sorts of other questions.

And now I remember one of the main points of this letter. Some weeks ago in the gossip column of the South Wales Evening Post, there was a paragraph to the effect that Richard Hughes, in a long conversation with the gossip-writer about modern poetry, had said how much he admired my

---

1 Trick's daughter Pamela was five years old, and had a vivid turn of speech. A phrase in Thomas's poem 'My world is pyramid', 'What colour is glory?', is said to be hers.

poems.[1] That definitely gives us an introduction to him, doesn't it? What do you say if I write him a note, asking whether we could call & see him in his Castle one week-end? If your car is still alive, we could run down to Laugharne, visit him & his beard, & then either return to our homes— these things could be settled later—or stay with our relations around Llanstephan. I think we'd have an interesting time. I won't write to him, of course, until I hear from you.

Levy, by the way, who now has very fierce black whiskers almost down to his middle, sends his greetings to you, & is going to try to get hold of you when he goes back to Cardiff at Easter. Will you be there then? *His* address is still 5 Redcliffe Street.

Drop me a line soon. I feel quite keen about visiting Richard Hughes.

Yours,

Dylan

P.S. Roger Roughton[2] also wishes to be remembered to you. He's just left for America.

MS: Carbondale

PAMELA HANSFORD JOHNSON
[?early March 1935][3] 5 Cwmdonkin Drive Uplands Swansea

I've retired home, after a ragged life, for a few weeks' rest before I go to the country for the summer. I should have written what's much too long a time ago, because there's so much to explain and so much that, perhaps, will, and should, never be explained—it means such a lot of belly rubbing and really tearful apologies on my blasted part. But never mind that. Britons never will be slaves, and I'm a rat. I saw Janes before I left London, and he told me that he had had tea with you and that you were working hard on your new novel. He said, though, that you were having rather a lot of trouble with it. Would you like me to go through, in my usual nagging way, what you've written so far? You know—to say, 'No, no, no, this can't be, too lush, too lush', & 'This is impossible', & 'Cut, cut, cut'. Etc. I'd really like to; you write better when you've got someone to stand behind

---

1 9 January 1935.
2 Roger Roughton, Communist and literary journalist, edited *Contemporary Poetry and Prose*, 1936–7. He committed suicide in 1941.
3 Johnson wrote in her diary on 7 March: 'Letter—of all Things, from Dylan, who is in Wales & repentant. I wish he hadn't written.' Their relationship cooled quickly once Thomas was living in London. In January 1935 she had written in the diary: 'Says he loves me but can't resist Comrade Bottle.' But Thomas continued to visit her and to write, intermittently, for another year.

your shoulder sneering when you go purple & using a cruel pencil over your choicest peacock-greys. Would you like me to repeat my usual & my 'This Bed' sub-editing?[1] If you would, and you still aren't too angry with me for all the silly and careless things I've done, send the MSS to me at home, & I'll send it back very soon & very carefully gone-through.

Love to your mother and—always—to you.

Dylan

MS: Buffalo

RICHARD HUGHES

Richard Hughes (1900–76) was already an established author. He lived in some style at Laugharne Castle, a house adjoining the ruins, overlooking the estuary.

[early April 1935]   5 Cwmdonkin Drive Uplands Swansea

Dear Mr. Richard Hughes,

As I'm going to spend this coming week-end in Llanstephan, I wonder whether I could call and see you some time on Saturday (6th)?[2] Only a few days ago I was shown an old cutting from a local newspaper in which you said that you'd read some of my poems. That does give me some sort of introduction, doesn't it, however vague? I was in Laugharne in the late summer, but the ferryman, who knows everything, told me you were away, and so I didn't batter at the Castle gates. I do hope I'll be able to see you this time.

Sincerely,
Dylan Thomas

MS: Indiana

MICHAEL ROBERTS[3]
Sunday 7th [envelope postmarked 8 April 1935]
5 Cwmdonkin Drive Uplands Swansea

Dear Michael Roberts,

Sorry I haven't been able to reply sooner, but the Parton Bookshop redirected your letter to me only a few days ago.

---

1 Pamela Hansford Johnson's novel, *This Bed Thy Centre* (the title suggested by Thomas), was published in 1935, followed the next year by *Blessed Above Women*.
2 'Saturday 6 April' fits the calendar.
3 Poet and journalist (1902–48). He edited *The Faber Book of Modern Verse*, 1936, which included two Thomas poems.

Very pleased you intend including me in the anthology. No, the American rights haven't been sold, of course.

Is the anthology coming out soon? I'll be sent proofs, I suppose? Thanks very much again.

Sincerely,
Dylan Thomas

MS: Berg

DESMOND HAWKINS

Hawkins (1908–99), later novelist, critic and broadcaster, reviewed Thomas's *18 Poems* for the magazine *Time & Tide*. When he became literary editor of *Purpose*, he wrote to Thomas, inviting him to contribute.

15.5.35   Three Gates   Higher Disley   Cheshire[1]

Dear Desmond Hawkins,

Thank you so much for your letter. Of course I remember you well. And thank you for your criticism in Time and Tide. I've been so unwell during the last month or two that I haven't been able to write to you about it, but I do appreciate all the kind things you said. On the whole the literary weeklies have treated that book of mine in a very gentlemanly way, but, apart from your review and one other, there were no constructive comments. Those privately coded blocks of feeling, derived from personal, unpoetical, or even anti-poetical, complexes must certainly be done away with before I write any more—or, at least, before I write any better. And I must do something about my policeman rhythms.

I'm so glad to hear that you've got the opportunity of publishing uncommercial and 'tolerably specialised' criticism, and I'd be awfully pleased to do anything I could. I don't know whether I'm capable of even a 'tolerable' specialisation. Poetry, Jacobean and Metaphysical, and music, minus the more intricate technicalities, mysticism (honest), and psychology (abnormal for preference) are, for Purpose's purpose, about the only things I appreciate sufficiently. Perhaps I can do something for you on those lines?

I'm staying in Cheshire until the end of the week, and then returning to London for some days. Somebody told me you were living in the country, but, if you happen to be in town when I am, perhaps we could meet somewhere—'somewhere' inevitably means a pub—and talk over things. If that's not possible, will you let me know before Monday?

1 See n.2, page 212.

And of course I'd be delighted to send you or, preferably to give you, some poems.

Sincerely,
Dylan Thomas

MS: National Library of Wales

A. E. TRICK
[summer 1935]   Glen Lough   Co. Donegal   Meenacross   Lifford

Dear Bert,

Is it any good telling you that, for the last three months or more, I've been meaning and meaning to write a long letter to you, a sort of self-explanatory monologue and travelogue, an unnecessary lecture on the ways of a Welsh poet in the amazing world? I've been meaning to ask Twentieth Century all about the economic ruptures, and whether the Guardian had managed to invent a truss for them yet, to learn about the new Vanocs of Socialism and the bollocks of the old gang, to inquire, very politely and sincerely, into the questions of health, work, and happiness. But I'm never very hot on meaning: it's the sound of meaning that I like, and so the long letter remained unwritten, the months moved on, and I shifted from the Derbyshire peaks to the London saloons, from the upper reaches of the Thames to the edge of the Atlantic without saying hallo or goodbye to you. How is the family? How is the small world? (It's the big world, really.) What have you been reading and doing? Does John J. still dance with the skeleton? Has the corpse of Mainwaring H. sprouted rhubarb yet?[1] How many times have you lectured on 'The Syphilisation of Man' to the ingrown virginities of the prig-squared Circle? Tell me all about everything. I'm ten miles from the nearest human being (with the exception of the deaf farmer who gives me food), and, in spite of the sea and the lakes and my papers and my books and my cigarettes (though they're damned hard to get, and I've few left of them) and my increasing obsession with the things under the skin, I'm lonely as Christ sometimes and can't even speak to my Father on an ethereal wave-length. I came here—'here' is a cottage studio, once owned by an American artist, perched in a field on a hill facing a lot of wild Atlantic—with Geoffrey G., but he's gone back to town.[2] And here is a wild, unlettered and unfrenchlettered country, too far from Ardara, a village you can't be too far from. Here are gannets and seals and puffins flying and puffing and playing a quarter of a mile outside my window where there are great rocks petrified like the old fates and

1 Mainwaring Hughes of Swansea, a local politician.
2 The studio, formerly a donkey-shed, had been used by the American artist Rockwell Kent. Grigson took Thomas there for a rest cure, and stayed a couple of weeks. When Thomas left, he walked off without paying the farmer, Dan Ward, which offended Grigson and may have begun their estrangement.

destinies of Ireland & smooth, white pebbles under and around them like the souls of the dead Irish. There's a hill with a huge echo; you shout, and the dead Irish answer from behind the hill. I've forced them into confessing that they are sad, grey, lost, forgotten, dead and damned forever. There are St. Bridget Shapes crossed in the rafters of my cottage, and these Shapes are to keep away what and who should be kept away. You are superstitious here or mad, whimsy or barmy, and the blood sports are bloody sports, but I can break a trout's neck now as skilfully as Geoffrey (who gave me the killing rod) but with more conscience. My days these days are planned out carefully, or at least conveniently, to the clock I haven't got (if time is the tick of a clock, I'm living in a funny dimension, in an hourless house): I rise at nine, I breakfast and clean up till ten, I read or write from ten till one, I lunch at one, then I walk over the cliffs to the sea and stay or walk about there till half past three or four, then tea, after tea I write until the early dusk, then I climb over the hills to the high lakes and fish there until dark. Back. Supper. Bed. I have a little illegal poteen whiskey with my supper, and I smoke black shag in a bad pipe. One day a week I shall walk ten miles to Glendrumatie where there is a shop and a porter bar. It rains and it rains. All the damned seagulls are fallen angels. Frogs and storms and squids and clegs and mutton-birds and midges and killing beetles. Dead sheep in the bracken.

But this is by no means a despondent letter. Words are coming nicely, and the rain can't get in through the roof. I have a blazing turf fire, and the only sound is the sea's on the million stones. I have a beard, too, a curly, ginger growth, neatly irregular, sweetly disorderly. I'll keep it for good, I think, or long enough, anyway, for the Tricks & the Thomases & my Mumbles Mermaid (bless her hair and her tail) to admire and finger it. I have my homesicknesses, but they vanish all right, like all the thoughts of permanency, and the Uplands and the Park go up in a wet smoke. In my sicker moments I think of me writing by my gas-fire opposite the tall, Greek nudes, of walking past your shop to the trainstop, and rattling along to a beery and fleshly Oystermouth,[1] of walking to your house in the Sunday rain and sitting by the fire until we've set the whole world straight, and the whole Welsh world is dark. But I wouldn't be at home if I were at home.[2] Everywhere I find myself seems to be nothing but a resting place between places that become resting places themselves. This is an essential state of being, an abstraction as concrete as a horsefly that's always worrying the back of your neck, plaguing and bothering before it draws blood. I'm at home when the blood's spilt, but only until the pricked vein heals up again, and my water and sugar turn red again, and the body and

---

1 Oystermouth is part of the Mumbles.
2 John Clare (1793–1864), wrote in 'Journey out of Essex'—which described his wanderings after he escaped from a lunatic asylum in 1841—'so here I am, homeless at home and half gratified to feel that I can be happy anywhere'. Thomas had reviewed Clare's poems for the Adelphi in June.

the brain, all the centres of movement, must shift or die. It may be a primary loneliness that makes me out-of-home. It may be this or that, & this and that is enough for to-day. Poor Dylan, poor him, poor me.

I wish I could provide you with notes on the financial, political, economic, industrial, and agricultural conditions of this lazy and vocal land, but my powers of natural observation, never very clear, would gain me less Marx every day. I find I can't see a landscape; scenery is just scenery to me; botany is bottomy or Bottomley, Horatio obliqua;[1] little He wotted[2] when he made the trees & the flowers how one of his Welsh chosen would pass them by, not even knowing that they were there. My own eyes, I know, squint inwards; when, and if, I look at the exterior world I see nothing or me; I should like very much to say that I see *everything* through the inner eye, but all I see is darkness, naked and not very nice. What can be done about it? The birds of the air peck my moustache. Idly I shoo them aside, engrossed in thoughts concerning the spiritual anatomy of the worms of Donegal. This is a poor, dirty land, and the pigs rut and scrabble in the parlours. There are few political feelings in the West, though most people seem to favour a mild Republicanism. My deaf farmer believes in fairies, and burns a red lamp under a religious magazine reproduction of somebody's hideous head of Christ; even his calendars are Christian: I always expect to find a cross in the soup, or find a chicken crucified by skewers to a fatty plate.

Have you heard from Fred Janes? He's living higgledy piggledy in a ruin and a riot of a Kensington studio with Levy, the bearded, and a couple of other irresponsible and wildly conventional painters. He might be returning to Swansea soon; London's lousy in the hot weather, and Fred loves Gower like a Rhossilli rabbit. He might, too, bring Scott,[3] a little beard, with him. That'll be nice; Scott's well worth knowing, and Fred is more seriously *and* comically metaphysical than ever.

I've stayed with Dan Jones in Harrow for a few days. He reads all the time, and is cleverer than ever. But his mind's in a mess, for he doesn't know any direction, he isn't sure either of music or writing, though he does both competently and often brilliantly. I wouldn't be surprised to see him turn into a first-rate literary critic, producing a standard study of 'A Comparison of European Literatures'. He has all that Jamieson had, with more wit, more sensibility, and, within his time limits, a far more comprehensive erudition. He's a prig, a snob, & a boor, but I like him.

Trevor Hughes, of the undiluted letters, is no nearer the looney bin, but the smell of the padded cells is floating about his nostrils. He has lately

---

1 Horatio Bottomley (d. 1933), journalist, MP and fraud. Thomas, who rarely employed a Latinism, seems to be using this one to suggest deviousness.

2 'My Garden' by the schoolmaster poet T. E. Brown (1830–97) has the much-parodied line, 'A garden is a lovesome thing, God wot!'

3 The painter William Scott lived with Thomas, Janes and Levy at a new address, Coleherne Road.

become a friend, counsellor, & admirer of Pamela J., who has spurned me as a small, but gifted, Welshman, of unsocial tendencies & definitely immoral habits. Her last novel has sold well, & is now in a fifth edition. Her next honourable addition to the shelves of libraries & the welfare of widow wombs is to be called 'Blessed Among Women'.

The rest of my acquaintances are very much as usual, thank you. Geoffrey G. has a small daughter, Caroline, & a new hedgehog. Norman Cameron has a book of poems appearing very soon. And my next poems will be published by Dent.[1] Now the news fades, the rain is coming heavily, and I'm going to make myself some creamy tea. I'll write more, & more interestingly I hope, after the creamy tea. Good-bye, as is said, (and that's a foul thing to say), for now.

For now was a long now, and it's morning again, with the wind sweeping up from the sea, and a straight mist above the hills. I've had breakfast, built a tiny stone bridge over the stream by my front door, fallen twice in the muddy gutters by the side of the stream, and banged my thumb with a hammer. In half an hour or less I'm going to work on my new story, 'Daniel Dom'. Did I tell you about it when I saw you last? It's based on the Pilgrim's Progress, but tells of the adventures of Anti-Christian in his travels from the City of Zion to the City of Destruction.[2] I've been commissioned to write it, but I won't be given any money until the first half a dozen parts or chapters are completed. The agents are rather frightened of blasphemous obscenity (and well they might be), and want to see how clean the half dozen chapters are before they advance me anything. The poor fish don't realise that I shall cut out the objectionable bits when I send them the synopsis & first chapters, & then put them immediately back. I've finished John's story, too; it's called, 'Cora, The Vampire'. I'll send it to you to show to John once I've had it typed. Do you still take New Verse? A long poem of mine will be in the next one—(consternation!).[3]

I don't know how long I shall be here; it all depends on how the silence and the loneliness attack me. I had thought of staying here until September, but the hot months are long months, and, though I can't say I like my fellows very much, and though my social conscience is becoming more flea-bitten every day, I can't indefinitely regard my own face in the mirror as the only face in the world, my beard as the only beard, my undisciplined thoughts as the only thoughts that matter under the sun, or the lack of light, and as the thoughts that revolve the egg-shaped earth. I

1 After some ups and downs, the firm of J. M. Dent published *Twenty-five Poems* in September 1936.
2 The story never amounted to more than a few manuscript pages, published as 'Prologue to an Adventure'.
3 August/September issue, 'A Poem in Three Parts' (later called 'I, in my intricate image').

will want more than an echo, sad, grey, lost, forgotten, & damned forever, to answer me in August, & more than the contaminated sheep to rodger on the high cliffs. But, if I can, I'll stay here until September, come home for a few weeks, & then return to London; when the season commences, I hope to have a certain amount of dramatic criticism, or, if that sounds too pompous, a little free entertainment on the stage & a little free love off stage from any publicity-seeking actresses I can find. It's fairly honest to be a dishonest critic of a corrupted, commercial theatre—as the best socialists suck all they can from the jaundiced arseholes of an anti-socialist state.

Before I say goodbye, I must tell you about Vicky Neuburg. He's got a new residence in North London, a crazy room full of books, kippers & warming-pans, a hot-as-hell conservatory with a fountain pool full of goldfish, & a jungled garden where members of a strange Neuburgian clan, The Circle (I think) of Creative Art & Life, meet, talk, jibber, froth, prowl, & presumably do their poetical best to fornicate, among the rushes and wormy ferns. The Creature himself—I must tell you one day, if I haven't told you before, the story of how Aleister Crowley turned Vicky into a camel—is a nineteenth-century crank with mental gangrene, lousier than ever before, a product of a Jewish nuts-factory, an Oscar Tamed. Runia Tharp is a believer in the voice of nature, and cages a fart in the bath under the fond delusion that it resembles, in pitch & tone, the voice of some Wordsworthian spirit invoking a horsefly. Rest In Purgatory.

Write soon & at great length, telling me all there is to tell of everything in which you know I'm interested—personal things, impersonal things, local politics, news, views, & all the etceteras you can think of.

Give my love to everybody—even Mrs. Waldron. (I saw a seal like Mrs. Waldron yesterday.)

Yours,
Dylan

MS: Ohio State University

JOHN LEHMANN
3.8.35 Glen Lough Meenacross Lifford Co Donegal

Dear Mr. Lehmann,
So sorry not to have replied before. I've been moving around rather a lot, and my letters have got muddled. I haven't written very many poems lately; the problems of where on earth to live, and, even more important, how on earth to live anywhere, have been too difficult; but I'm enclosing six fairly recent ones, one of them a hundred lines long,[1] you might think it better to choose from than from any of those in my book. You'll have to

---

1 'I, in my intricate image'.

cxcuse my handwriting; I don't think there's a typewriter nearer than Belfast.

Would it—I don't suppose for a moment it would—be possible that the publishers might advance me my payment *before* publication, *soon*? I need it like hell, and more urgently.

Anyway, here are the poems. And apologies again for delay.

Sincerely yours,
Dylan Thomas

MS: Victoria

JOHN LEHMANN

14.8.35   Glen Lough   Meenacross   Lifford   Co Donegal

Dear John Lehmann,

Thank you very, very much indeed. I doubted the possibility of an advance from Lane, and I certainly didn't expect you to advance anything on your own account.[1] It was very, very kind and thoughtful of you. I needed the money urgently—to pay my debts here and return to England. Thank you again. I hope to pay you back quite soon.

A letter was forwarded to me yesterday from Kilham Roberts, explaining that you hadn't been able to get hold of me, and telling me again about the Year's Poetry.[2] You'll be letting him know, I suppose, that you've got my address.

I shall be here only a few weeks more, but anything addressed to me c/o Norman Cameron, 49c British Grove, will always be forwarded on.

If you don't like the poems I've sent you, I could let you have one or two more.

Very sincerely yours,
Dylan Thomas

MS: Victoria

DANIEL JONES

Tuesday August 14 1935   Glen Lough   Meenacross
            nr. Glencolumkille   Lifford   Co Donegal   Irish Free State

Addressed, unavoidably, to Fred [Janes].
And to be read either late at night or
when at least *half* tipsy.

This is the first long letter I've ever written to you. I'm not much good at

1 John Lane of the Bodley Head published *The Year's Poetry*, to which the previous letter also refers.
2 Lehmann and Kilham Roberts were still co-editors of *The Year's Poetry*.

writing letters, I can't strike the, if I may coin a phrase, happy medium between trying to be funny, not trying to be funny, and trying not to be funny. I can't write as I talk—thank God I can't talk as I write, either—and I get highflown and flyblown and flyfaultin [?error for flyfalutin] if I try very consciously not to be self-conscious. Take me as I come—sounds like Onan—and remember the dear dead days that had to have a gallon or two of nonsense (often awfully good nonsense) or parch. This is written for two main reasons: first, because I've been socially rude, (you can't talk), and Goat has probably shown her horns and Bear has growled and the jealous Hook[1] been haughty as wadding ever since I said, 'Yes, ten o'clock outside the Queen's Hall,' and then, doom on my roving scrotum, found a Jewess with thighs like boiled string and got drunk and woke up with a headache and a halfpenny and a button. It was, if I may coin a phrase, the same old story. You, I know, didn't care a seal or a fig when I flouted (that's a word I haven't used for years, have you?) the conventions and didn't even apologise. My excuse for not apologising is that you're so hard to get hold of, Harrow's will-of-the-wisp, Pinner's Sibelius (I'm still the Swan of Tawe). Give what is proper to give, anyway, to Goat and Hook and Bear, and tell Jumbo, 'There is an indiarubber police-force in Archix.'[2] Make up what story you can to explain my sins away; they won't believe it; on the last morning-after, Bear said 'whiskey' in a clear voice, and then leered. The second, and the most important reason for my writing is: I never can believe that the Warmley[3] days are over—('just a song at twilight when the lights Marlowe and the Flecker Beddoes Bailey Donne and Poe')[4]— that there should be no more twittering, no more nose-on-window-pressing and howling at the streets, no more walks with vampire cries, and standing over the world, no more hold-a-writing-table for the longest, and wrong adjectives; I can't believe that Percy, who droppeth gently, can have dropped out of the world, that the 'Badger Beneath My Vest' and 'Homage to Admiral Beatty' are a song and a boat of the past; that Miguel-y-Bradshaw, Waldo Carpet, Xmas Pulpit, Paul America, Winter Vaux, Tonenbach, and Bram, all that miscellaneous colony of geniuses, our little men, can have died on us; that the one-legged grandmother—remember the panama-hat-shaped birds, from the Suez Canal, who pecked at her atlas-bone—doesn't still take photographs of Birmingham; that the queer, Swansea world, a world, thank Christ that was self-sufficient, can't stand on its bow legs in a smoky city full of snobs and quacks. I'm surer of nothing than that that world, Percy's world in Warmley, was, and still is, the only one that has any claims to permanence; I mean that this long, out-of-doored world isn't much good really, that it's only the setting, is only

1 Goat, Bear, Hook: fantasy-names for members of Jones's family.
2 Jumbo was Jim Jones, Dan Jones's elder brother. Archix was an imaginary country.
3 Dan Jones's house in Swansea, before the family moved to London.
4 Thomas is parodying 'Love's Old Sweet Song', a popular late-Victorian lyric (Molloy and Brigham, 1884) that lingered on into his childhood: 'Just a song at twilight/When the lights are low,/And the flick'ring shadows/Softly come and go'.

supposed to be the setting, for a world of your own—in our cases, a world of our own—from which we can interpret nearly everything that's worth. And the only world worth is the world of our own that has its independent people, people like Percy, so much, much more real than your father or my mother, my Jewess or your girl on the roof, places and things and qualities and standards, and symbols much bigger than the exterior solidities, all of its own. Didn't we work better, weren't poems and music better, weren't we happier in being unhappy, out of that world, than in—not even out of— this unlocal, uncentral world where the pubs are bad and the people are sly and the only places to go are the places to go to? I think it is the same with you, though it's so long since I've seen you, dry months, too, that you may be, though you couldn't be, all different, all older, in your cat's lights more learnèd, even Harrowed to some sort of contentment, never regretting for one moment the almost-going of Percy's celestial circle. No, that couldn't be; that world *does* remain, in spite of London, the Academy, and a tuppenny, half-highbrow success. I never thought that localities meant so much, nor the genius of places, nor anything like that. I thought that the soul went round like a Gladstone bag, never caring a damn for any particular station-rack or hotel-cloakroom; that gestures and genius made the same gestures in Cockett and Cockfosters;[1] didn't we look at our geniuses and say, 'We're taking you somewhere else to live, but we won't part.' I placed my hand upon my heart and said that we would never part; I wonder what I would have said had I placed it on my head. So on and on; like an unborn child in the city I want to get born and go to the outskirts. Here in Ireland I'm further away than ever from the permanent world, the one real world in a house or a room, very much peopled, with the exterior, wrong world—wrong because it's never understood out of the interior world—looking in through the windows. This sort of nostalgia isn't escapist by any means, you know that; just as the only politics for a conscientious artist—that's you and me—must be left-wing under a right-wing government, communist *under* capitalism, so the only world for that WARMDANDYLANLEY-MAN must be the WARMDANDYLANLEY-WORLD under the world-of-the-others. How could it be escapism? It's the only contact there is between yourself and yourselves, what's social in you and what isn't—though, God knows, I could shake Bram's intangible hand as seriously as the hand of Dean Inge, and with far greater sense of reality. Even surrealism, which seemed to have hopes and promise, preaches the decay of reality and the importance, and eventual dominance, (I don't like those words however much I try to look on them coldly), of unreality, as though the two could be put in two boxes: isn't Percy flesh, bone, and blood, isn't Evangeline Booth a shadow, isn't Percy a shadow, isn't Evangeline flesh, bone, & blood, isn't Percy flesh-bone-& blood-shadow, isn't Evangeline flesh-bone-and-blood-shadow, isn't Percy-Evangeline flesh bone and blood?—and so on and on. I'm not going to read this letter over afterwards to see what it reads like; let it go on, that's all, you don't mind

1 Suburbs of Swansea and London.

the dashes and the hyphens and the bits of dogma and the brackets and the bits of dog-eaten self-consciousness and the sentimentality because I'm writing by candlelight all alone in a cottage facing the Atlantic. From the WARMDANDYLANLEY-WORLD I'd no more think of writing this letter than of using words like 'Proust' and 'flounce' and 'akimbo' and 'schedule' and 'urge' when talking in that W-W; I wouldn't have or need to; this is only covering old ground in words and phrases and thoughts and idioms that are all part of that world; it's only because, now, here in this terribly out-of-the way and lonely place, I feel the need for that world, the necessity for its going on, and the fear that it might be dying to you, that I'm trying to resurrect my bit of it, and make you realise again what you realise already; the importance of that world because it's the only one, the importance of us, too, and the fact that our poems and music won't and can't be anything without it. Soon I'm going out for a walk in the dark by myself; that'll make me happy as hell; I'll think of the almost-but-never-going-gone, and remember the cries of the Bulgarian scouts as I hear that damned sea rolling, and remember the first world—where do they pretend it is, Waunarllwyd?[1]—as I stand under an absurdly high hill—much too high, our world has its hills just the proper, the *nice*, length (I'm arching my index-finger & thumb and joining them tastefully)—and shout to it, 'Go on, you big shit, WARMDANDYLANLEY-WORLD has a hill twice as beautiful and with a ribbon and bell on it, & a piece of boiled string on the top, if the WARMDANDYLANLEY-MAN wants it like that'. And I'll finish this when I come back.

[*New page.*] But it was so late when I came back that I padlocked out the wild Irish night, looked through the window and saw Count Antigarlic, a strange Hungarian gentleman who has been scraping an acquaintance (take that literally) with me lately, coming down the hill in a cloak lined with spiders, and, suddenly very frightened, I hurried to bed. This is written in the cold of the next morning, the Count is nowhere to be seen, and it is only the thin mouth-print of blood on the window pane, and the dry mouse on the sill, that brings the night back. It's hard to pick up the night threads; they lead, quite impossibly, into the socket of a one-eyed woman, the rectums of crucified sparrows, the tunnels of coloured badgers reading morbid literature in the dark, and very small bulls, the size of thimbles, mooing in a clavichord. At least, they lead to absurd things. Where was I last night? Feeding my father with hay? offering Hook a newt in a bluebag? I was talking about worlds. We must, when our affairs are settled, when music and poetry are arranged so that we can still live, love, and drink beer, go back to Uplands or Sketty and found there, for good and for all, a permanent colony; living there until we are old gentlemen, with occasional visits to London and Paris, we shall lead the lives of small-town anti-society, and entertain any of the other members of the WARMDANDYLAN-LEY-WORLD who happen to visit the town; Fred will be a greengrocer, painting over his shop, Tom an armyman with many holidays, Thornley a

1 Waunarlwydd (the correct spelling) is another district of Swansea.

nearby vicar, Trick a nearby grocer, Stevens a bankmanager with holidays, Smart a bankmanager with holidays, and the rest of our vague WARMLIES this and that all over the wrong world.[1] Mumbles, and the best saloon bars in Britain, will be open for us all night. And Percy will come drooping slow there. Yeats never moves out of his own town in Galway, Sibelius never out of Helsingfors. So Jones and Thomas, that well-known firm of family provisioners, shall not move out of their town. So be it.

But now of course all the things are different; we must peck on and snoot away in an unlovely city until we can manage our own fates to a Walesward advantage. If you and the menagerie stay on in Harrow, I shall, in the winter, come and lodge near there, too, and go up to town only once or twice a week. We shall twitter. That, at least, is practicable. And Harrow, hell with such a nice name, shall shine like a star, and the maidenheads fall like rain.

I am working hard here, and have got lots of new poems. I want you to see them, I want you to tell me a lot about them before my new book[2] comes out at Christmas.

Write before I leave here on the thirtieth of August, a long, careless letter.

All the love of one WARMDANDYLANLEY-MAN to the other one.

MS: Texas

ROBERT HERRING[3]
[summer 1935]   Glen Lough   Meenacross   Lifford   Co Donegal

Dear Mr. Herring,
Very many thanks. I'm glad you liked the poem,[4] and hope that the story will prove printable, too.

As to payment, it would really suit me better if a cheque could be sent on earlier than is usual. You did mention that possibility, although I quite understand that nothing definite can be arranged yet.[5]

Thanks for the good wishes. I hope I'll be allowed to contribute again.
                                          Yours sincerely,
                                          Dylan Thomas

1 Fred Janes's father was a greengrocer. Thornley Jones wrote music. Alan Stevens worked for a bank, as did Percy Smart, Thomas's correspondent of a few years earlier.
2 It was 1936 before *Twenty-five Poems* appeared.
3 Robert Herring (1903–75) edited the magazine *Life and Letters Today* from 1935 to 1950. In December 1935 it printed the first seven sections of the 'Altarwise by owl-light' sequence, which Thomas had been working on in Ireland. The Spring 1936 issue carried his story 'The Lemon'. See letter to Desmond Hawkins, page 230.
4 Probably 'A grief ago'.
5 The letter is annotated in another hand: '£5 for Story & Poem'.

From September on, my address will be 5 Cwmdonkin Drive, Uplands, Swansea. It will, at least, always find me.

MS: Carbondale

DESMOND HAWKINS
16th Sep '35   5 Cwmdonkin Drive   Uplands   Swansea

Dear Desmond,

Are you annoyed at not hearing from me? The truth is that from the time I left you until the day before yesterday, when I arrived home, I've been on the blindest blind in the world and didn't know what day it was or what week or anything, lost most of my little property, including many, to me, valuable papers, and, what is worse for me, my job on the Morning Post.[1] I can only excuse myself by pretending that it was practice for the more alcoholic pages of our King's Canary.[2]

I don't remember whether you gave me the completed list of names of characters or not, and if you did I lost them. So, before I can begin my part, do send the full list along. I'll be able tomorrow, when my hand doesn't shake so much, to work on the opening pages but I can't do much without all the Chapfork Benders etc. So send 'em soon. We must—and the lord knows it's my fault alone—get to work.

What about the poems? Have you, as I thought you might, decided that the shorter one is better for your purpose?

Write & tell me anyway. And I'm so sorry for the delay.

Yours,
Dylan

P.S. Do you remember Fluffy, the chorus-girl with glasses? It was mostly her fault, the nice, nice bitch.[3]

MS: National Library of Wales

GEOFFREY GRIGSON
[?September 1935]   5 Cwmdonkin Drive   Uplands   Swansea

Dear Geoffrey,

I'm an old twicer, aren't I? Here I lie, lily-faced between the sheets, looking like Shelley and the Three Little Pigs rolled into one, very pretty in my white pyjamas, with a droshki cough. Thanks so much for your letter,

1 Thomas had been reviewing thrillers for the strait-laced *Morning Post* since Geoffrey Grigson, its literary editor, hired him at the start of the year.
2 *The Murder* (or *Death*) *of the King's Canary* was to be a satirical detective story, poking fun both at the genre and at thinly disguised literary figures. The 'Canary' was the Poet Laureate. Over the years Thomas had different collaborators for this laborious joke. In the second paragraph, 'Chapfork Bender' = Stephen Spender.
3 Thomas and Hawkins had met her at one of their haunts, The Marquis of Granby.

dear Doctor, and I'm so glad the Morning Post has taken me back without a scolding.[1] I promised to explain to you what happened and why after I left you in London, but now I try to I can't. I drank the night custard of the gods, but they must have been the wrong gods, and I woke up every morning feeling like hell in somebody else's bedsitting room with concealed washbasin. This morning I have battled with a venomous doctor who wanted me to go places with him and do things, but, old Terry,[2] I won by a short lung. I have to stay indoors for six or eight weeks, during which time I feel sure I'll be able to work hard and well. So do send me thrillers, and I promise the most satisfactory reviews. But, for the love of the great grey cunt of the world, don't tell the details of my present indisposition to anyone but Norman the Nagger: they might ruin my lecherous chances.[3] No, I shan't begin dying yet. I've lived a bit quicker than lots of people, so I *can* begin five years under the scheduled time. But that gives me nearly ten years, and, lo there Sadokiel[4] (tell Normal that, it's nice to be quoted), that embryo you told me about is going to produce many strange and good things.

So send the thrillers and love to you, Doctor Terry.

Love to Normal, too. I'll be writing to him.

Carlos

MS: Texas

RICHARD CHURCH

Church (1893–1972) was a poet and novelist who worked as a civil servant before joining J. M. Dent as poetry editor in 1933. Letters from him to Thomas showed him trying to be fair to poems which were not to his taste.

8th October '35   5 Cwmdonkin Drive   Uplands   Swansea

Dear Richard Church,

Thank you for your letter.

I shan't be in town until the first week of November. Shall I call in and have a talk with you then? I'd be up sooner, but this wretched illness of

---

1 This sounds like the reviewing job that Thomas thought he had lost when he wrote to Hawkins on 16 September. But he may have been sacked and re-hired more than once, and the date of this letter to Grigson is uncertain.

2 'Dr Terry' was one of Thomas's nicknames for Grigson.

3 'Norman the Nagger', 'Normal' on other occasions, was Norman Cameron, whose attitude to Thomas was equivocal, as in his poem that Thomas's enemies like to quote, 'The Dirty Little Accuser' ('When he quitted a sofa, he left behind him a smear./My wife says he even tried to paw her about'). Whether Thomas was really suffering from gonorrhoea, as he implies to Grigson, is unknown.

4 Thomas is quoting from a poem by Cameron, 'The Successor', about a high priest, Sadokiel.

mine keeps me indoors. I'd have replied sooner, too, but I don't seem to be able to concentrate. These are passing troubles, and in a very few days, I hope, I can get down to sub-editing my poems.

Here, anyway, are most of the manuscripts. I haven't titled any of them. The first poem, divided into six parts of fourteen lines each, (each to be printed on a separate page, for, although the poem as a whole is to be a poem in, and by, itself, the separate parts can be regarded as individual poems) is so far incomplete; there will be at least another four parts.[1]

I hope you'll like this poem, incomplete as it is, and the others. I'll be able to type out & revise the rest quite soon.

Cameron has just sent me a copy of his book.[2] It is awfully good, isn't it?

I'm looking forward to seeing you at the beginning of November when we can talk over most of the details.

Yours sincerely,
Dylan Thomas

MS: (J. M. Dent)

NANCY AND HAYDN TAYLOR[3]
October 27th 1935 [Thomas's 21st birthday]

Dear Nancy and Haydn,

Thank you both very much. It is nice to be remembered, especially at such an important, if I may coin a phrase, cross-road in life's journey.

The family lawyers, Paff, Grabpole and Paff have just departed; there's been a little bother, you know, over the transferring of the estate. Later on this evening I'm going down to the Marlais Head to give a formal address to the tenants. They're to present me, I believe, with a platinum walking-stick, complete with bell. Lord Hunt-Ball has given me a glass-tube for holding tiny flannel shirts. Lady Utterly has presented me with a wooden leg.

Thanks again for the present. I bought a grey hat and a book of ballads. I also have a tweed suit covered in coloured spots, a new mackintosh, new shoes, a book, new trousers, a pullover, & no hope for the future.

There's no news. I'm working moderately hard, and Dad has a very painful throat.

I'm coming to town for three days in the first week of November, and am already preparing my small jar of red paint.

The tenants are clamouring. I must go.

Love,
Dylan

MS: Estate of Haydn Taylor

1 'Altarwise by owl-light', which eventually had ten sections.
2 *The Winter House.*
3 Thomas's sister and brother-in-law.

DENYS KILHAM ROBERTS
28.10.35   5 Cwmdonkin Drive   Uplands   Swansea

Dear Mr. Roberts,
    Here are the corrected proofs.
    Poem was printed in New Verse and in my Eighteen Poems, (Parton Press).
    Poem In October[1] was printed in the Listener and in Eighteen Poems.
    I was born 27th October, 1914.

                                                Yours truly,
                                                Dylan Thomas

MS: Texas

DESMOND HAWKINS
I.II.35   5 Cwmdonkin Drive   Uplands   Swansea

Dear Desmond,
    A very short note. How are you? Thanks for last letter.
    Can you come and have a drink next week? A morning drink if possible—say 12 o'clock in the Marquis on Tuesday or Wednesday morning? I'm up for about four days. We can discuss much belated Canary then. I've done a first bit but it's lousy, and I'm rewriting it. May have it ready. Hope so.
    Now as to the poem for Purpose. Do for sweet Christ's sake use the one beginning Foster the Light, nor veil the cunt-shaped moon. The fact is: I was having a poem done in the coming Life & Letters, & had a letter from R. Herring to-day saying the poem had just been printed, owing to my abominable carelessness, in the Oxford Programme. As Life & Letters is just going to press, he wants another poem pronto.[2] All I have are passages of that long thing I gave you beginning, Altarwise by owl light in the bleeding house. So do, do, Desmond, use the Foster rather than the Altar. (That is, of course, if you'd intended using either). After all, you see, L & L have paid me a fiver already for the poem they now can't print. What an existence. Excuse haste & violence.
    Drop me a card, if you can, by Monday first post saying whether you're going to meet &—& when.

                                                Yrs Dylan

1 'Poem in October' (= 'Especially when the October wind', not the piece now known as 'Poem in October', written nine years later) was included in *The Year's Poetry, 1935* when it appeared in December. The unidentified 'Poem' was not. Kilham Roberts, who was a practising barrister and also secretary of the Society of Authors, excluded it at the last minute because 'several lawyers' agreed it was technically obscene and might have led to a prosecution for obscenity. The offending poem was probably 'If I were tickled by the rub of love'. See page 168,n.
2 *Programme* had published 'How soon the servant sun' and 'A grief ago' in issue No. 9, 23 October 1935. *Purpose* didn't publish 'Foster the light'.

Nice poem in S. Bookman. What shall we call him: Writhing Codd, Ruthven God?[1]

MS: National Library of Wales

ROBERT HERRING
[November 1935] [incomplete][2]

[. . .] I'm enclosing it—or them—in the hope that you will like it, despite its obscurity & incompleteness. It's the first passages of what's going to be a very long poem indeed, but each section is a more-or-less self-contained short poem; if you think they're nice, you can use one, or two, or all, or whatever you like of them—calling them 'Passages Towards a Poem' or 'Poems for a Poem', whichever seems to you least precious [. . .]

I've just looked at the ms I'm sending you. It's smudgy & smells of all sorts of things. Sorry. And there are review scraps on the back. Can't be helped.[3]

MS: Location unknown

RICHARD CHURCH
9 12 35   5 Cwmdonkin Drive   Uplands   Swansea

Dear Richard Church,
    Thank you for your letter, and for the candid criticism of my poems.[4] I do appreciate the trouble you have taken to make your attitude towards these poems quite clear, and am glad that you value my work highly enough to condemn it when you find it—though wrongly, I believe—to be influenced by such a 'pernicious' experiment as surrealism. Far from resenting your criticism, I welcome it very much indeed, although, to be equally candid, I think you have misinterpreted the poems and have been

1 Ruthven Todd, poet and journalist. After Dylan Thomas's death he was commissioned to write the official biography, but never did.
2 The text is taken from a dealer's catalogue, where it is abridged as shown.
3 See previous letter.
4 Church had written (26 November): 'I believe that poetry should be simple as well as sensuous and beautiful . . . It should be the expression of the poet's personality after the conflict and not during the conflict . . . With these axioms, I look upon surrealism in poetry with abhorrence . . . I am distressed to see its pernicious effect in your work, because I believe you to be outstanding amongst your generation . . .'

misled as to their purpose. I am not, never have been, never will be, or could be for that matter, a surrealist, and for a number of reasons: I have very little idea what surrealism is; until quite recently I had never heard of it; I have never, to my knowledge, read even a paragraph of surrealist literature; my acquaintance with French is still limited to 'the pen of my aunt'; I have not read any French poetry, either in the original or in translation, since I attempted to translate Victor Hugo in a provincial Grammar School examination, and failed. All of which exposes my lamentable ignorance of contemporary poetry, but, surely, does disprove your accusations. As for being 'caught up in the delirium of intellectual fashion of the moment', I must confess that I read regrettably little modern poetry, and what 'fashionable' poetry I do come across appears to be more or less communist propaganda. I am not a communist.

I hope you won't object, but I took the liberty, soon after receiving your letter, of writing to a very sound friend of mine and asking him what surrealism was, explaining, at the same time, that a critic whose work we both knew and admired had said that my own poems were themselves surrealist. In his reply he told me what he thought the principal ideas of surrealism were, and said that surrealist writing need not have any 'meaning at all'. (He quoted some dreadful definition about 'the satanic juxtaposition of irrelevant objects etc'.) I think I do know what some of the main faults of my writing are: immature violence, rhythmic monotony, frequent muddleheadedness, and a very much overweighted imagery that leads too often to incoherence. But every line *is* meant to be understood; the reader *is* meant to understand every poem by thinking and feeling about it, not by sucking it in through his pores, or whatever he is meant to do with surrealist writing. Neither is the new group on which I'm working influenced, in any way, by an experiment with which I am totally unfamiliar. You have, and no doubt rightly, found many things to object to in these new poems; all I wish to do is to assure you that those faults are due neither to a delirious following of intellectual fashion nor to the imitation of what, to my ignorance, appears a purposely 'unreasonable' experiment inimical to poetry.

In conclusion, I have quite a number of poems simple as the three you liked, poems, to my mind, not half as good as the ones you cannot stand for. Do you wish me to send those on to you, or would you rather me wait until we can discuss everything when I come to town in the early new year?

Again, I trust you will not find this letter pretentious or impudent. I have thought a great deal about what you said in your letter, and my only excuse for the possible pretentiousness of my reply is that I really do want [you] to realise that you have—my obscurity is to blame—misinterpreted the purpose of my obviously immature poetry, and attributed to it experimental absurdities I hardly knew existed.

Yours sincerely,
Dylan Thomas

MS: (J. M. Dent)

PAMELA HANSFORD JOHNSON
[?December 1935][1]

Hullo Pam,

I haven't written to you for such a long time that I'm tired of waiting for your reply; and neither has mother, catering for her invalids, including Arthur now, the pleasant uncle,[2] answered your nice letter to her, and dad only answers bills. What a family. We all have our little aches, we moan, we plug ourselves with patent medicines. Dad has a new pain (isn't this lovely ink, it's called Quink) in the eye, mother has indigestion, Arthur has rheumatism and a cold, I cough. When *you* wrote last you were dying, almost cuddling the long, black guardian worm who is the exclusive death-property of the Johnsons. Are you better, my rose, my own? And you aren't cross with me? No, of course you aren't, my mole, my badger, my little blood-brown Eve. (That's how I feel.) But this is a shoddy letter and I'm not going to finish it—just to spite myself. I haven't written a word—except for incompetent thriller reviews—since I came home. Not even a letter. I feel too weak and too tired.

But here's a true story: Tom Warner is learning short-hand. On Monday he wrote the word 'egg' all day. On Tuesday he wrote the word 'kick' all day. On Wednesday he decided to revise Monday's work, sat down, and wrote 'eck'.

Tom plays the piano for Heather on Friday nights. It's driving him mad. He has to play Ketèlbey and Irving Berlin and selections from talkies.

It's no good. I can't write. I shall put this in an envelope and then sit looking at the fire. I love you. I am a blue-green buzzard and my name is Dylan.

MS: Estate of Pamela Hansford Johnson

---

1 Thomas wrote occasionally throughout 1935 and into 1936, and this letter may be the one whose receipt was noted on 11 December 1935. But it could be earlier or even later. It is one of two letters (the other dated 6 August 1937) that came to light among the papers of Lady Snow (her second marriage was to the writer Lord (C. P.) Snow) in 1984.
2 Arthur, a brother of D. J. Thomas, worked for the Great Western Railway, as their father had done.

RAYNER HEPPENSTALL[1]
31st December 1935   5 Cwmdonkin Drive   Uplands   Swansea

I owe you a lot of apologies, five shillings, and a long letter. I haven't got enough news to make a long letter, I certainly haven't five shillings, but I do apologise for my delay in answering your letter, quite half of which I nearly understood. Green ink makes everything illegible, anyway, but your handwriting makes even a simple address look like a nice Sanskrit poem. From what I could gather, you'd come back either from the Rectory or the Fitzroy and were gassed hard. Purposely you were in a strong, and came out only for impudent purposes. What a time you've been having. But thanks again, I'm frightfully glad to hear from you. I never think of cider without thinking of black eyes, and the mere mention of Clerkenwell brings back the years like the smell of old violents (what I meant to type was old violets, but I'm damned if I'm going to cross anything out). Now, on the last day of the year, I am sitting more or less seriously down to type you a long delayed, but now most seasonable, letter. I'm typing because my own handwriting is bloody and my hand shakes.

As, with lynx eyes, you'll spot, I'm taking a rest at home far from the beards and bow ties, and will be here until the end of January. Let's meet when I come back to town and, over beer, roar our poems at each other like little Bellocs, and stamp up Bloomsbury, waving our cocks.

I had a letter a little time ago from Oswell Blakeston,[2] and he said he'd met you and a new black eye of yours in, I think, the Café Royal. He said that you had said you were now entirely tamed and pugnacious no longer. But do be pugnacious once more, just once more, and attack G.E.G.[3] like a bloodhound. I like him as a chap, but he's a mean little, cheap little, ostentatiously vulgar little, thumb-to-my-nose little runt when he tries to be funny at the back of New Verse. I've never read such a hideous, ineffective piece of invectory, malicious, Beachcomberish balderdash as his ten nasty lines about your poems.[4] They were really disgusting, and nobody could have any patience with them. How is the book doing, by the way? I don't read many periodicals now and have seen very few reviews. I see you're writing for Oswell's supplement in Caravel, too. Do you know anything about Caravel? I've never, in my ignorance, heard of it before.[5]

I spent most of the summer in Donegal and did a lot of good work there, but a wave of rather alcoholic laziness has set in since and I am only just beginning to put words together again. The poetry machine is so well oiled now it should work without a hitch until my next intellectually ruinous visit to the bowels of London. I want to go abroad this summer but I don't know where. Do you know anything about Spain? Can you get along

1 See n. 1, page 211.
2 Oswell Blakeston (1907–85), writer and painter.
3 Geoffrey Grigson.
4 *First Poems*.
5 A short-lived magazine, 1934–6, published in Majorca. It printed Thomas's poem 'Hold hard, these ancient minutes' in March 1936.

without Spanish and without money? (The same applies to any country and I'll probably end up in a bedsitting room off the Fulham Road.)

But why Kilburn, Rayner, of all places? Why not a much cheaper place in the East End? If you don't object to vermin you can get a palace of a flat near London Bridge for about [?12 shillings; *Thomas typed* L2 shillins] a week. Come and live in Limehouse with me, and write books like Thomas Burke.[1]

I told you there was no news. I live a comfortable, sheltered, and, now, only occasionally boozy life in Swansea, along with Fred Janes. I'm writing a very long poem—so are you, if I read your letter correctly—and a number of dream stories, very mixed, very violent. There is much to be said, if I may coin a phrase, for leading the conventional life. (But when I think of it, I always have, for the shabby drunkenness of upper Chelsea was even more conventional than this.)

Write a letter sometime and tell me what you're doing.

Good luck, and plug Grigson.

Yours,

Dylan

MS: Texas

FREDERIC PROKOSCH[2]

[?winter 1935/6] 5 Cwmdonkin Drive   Uplands   Swansea   South Wales

Dear Frederic Prokosch,

I should have replied months sooner, but I've been ill and away. Thank you so much for writing. I've put down the first things I could think of in the book you sent me. I'm glad you liked some of the poems in it. I liked your poem in New Verse immensely. Don't forget you promised in your letter that you'd send me a copy of your novel when it appeared.

I think the first and the eleventh are the best poems in my book.[3] I don't care much for the last one, the one you said you liked; it's a mechanical thing, and there are lots of near-Swinburne in it. Dent's are bringing out some more poems in the spring. I'll ask them to send you a copy.

Thanks again for writing. Did you get my address through David Gascoyne?—his name's on the envelope. And do you ever come to England?

Sincerely,

Dylan Thomas

The book's in a separate envelope.

MS: Texas

1 Thomas Burke (1886–1945) wrote *Limehouse Nights*.
2 American poet and novelist.
3 'I see the boys of summer' and 'When, like a running grave'.

OSWELL BLAKESTON
[?early January 1936]   Cwmdonkin Drive   Uplands   Swansea

Dearest mouse my dear,[1] You're awfully lucky, you and the little whisker friends, all smug and slimy, listening to Cocteau & Burns and Naylor & Allen behind the skirtingboard.[2] Nobody ever heard of a Mouse Menace, you are not a national danger, and people write poems about you and call you slinkie and nice and velvet. You'd be safe even in Chicago, where they'd give me a fifth leg. Every year sixteen thousand London brothers & sisters cornered caged and killed. They brought out an Act to destroy me in nineteen nineteen, when I was only five years old. But they give me a week! I haven't seen you for so long, not since we spent an evening in not going to the Queen's Hall, and not since I left you, outside the Café Rat, very rudely for a sillie. I'm coming back, travelling under the seat all the way, nibbling brown paper, at the beginning of next month. Will you meet me? And this time I'll promise not to be bad; I'll powder my snout and not run after hen-rats. And will you send me more of my fan-mail sometimes? I'm so unpopular these days, whenever I switch on the wireless, it's an interval.[3] I was abominable about the B.B.C. But I'll get what's coming to me: when I die I'll go to hell; and it'll be Rat Week always.
        Much love to you, very much, Oswell.

                                              From
                        [*the letter is signed with a self-caricature*]

MS: Texas

RAYNER HEPPENSTALL
January 6th 36   5 Cwmdonkin Drive   Uplands   Swansea

Thanks for letter. I'll write a good reply in a few days. For the moment excuse this nasty little note, but I've got to tell you immediately what I forgot to tell you before. When I wrote to you I meant to say: Don't be cross because I've used your name in some letters from the West Wales and Swansea Guardian to London publishers. I was asked a few weeks ago to run a weekly book column for the W.W.G.,[4] and I thought it would be a

1 Both Blakeston and his partner Max Chapman, painter, described brief sexual encounters with Thomas in the early London days. Rodents obsessed Thomas, and were part of some shared fantasy.
2 Gramophone records: Jean Cocteau reciting poetry; George Burns and Gracie Allen, American husband-and-wife comedians; Naylor, an astrologer, reading horoscopes.
3 'Intervals'—deliberate silences between programmes—were a feature of early British radio.
4 Thomas introduced a column called 'Books and People' in the *Swansea and West Wales Guardian* on 17 January, and contributed to it once thereafter.

Good Thing if I managed to delude publishers, when writing to them and asking them for review books, by telling them that some literary blokes with Names would be possible or/and occasional contributors to the column. So, most illegally, I used your name and Blakeston's. I let Blakeston know yesterday, and you today—I should have let you both know days ago, of course, before the publishers could ring you up and find out my little lies. But I forgot. You don't mind, do you? It can't do you any harm, and it might do me some good. I didn't, of course, expect you to review for this unknown paper, and used your name only as a Bluff. So, again, don't be cross. Actually, if you ever want a couple of books, I'll do my best to get hold of them for you.

Best wishes etc, and I'll be writing.

Dylan

Where is Mortimer Market?
And the East End is on, as far as I'm concerned.

[*There is a small drawing of Thomas, arms spread. From his mouth emerges a balloon with the words, 'Don't lock me up, Messrs Cape'.*]

MS: Texas

EDITH SITWELL

The poet and critic Edith Sitwell (1887–1964), having savaged Thomas in a book in 1934 (see n. 1, page 206), had changed her mind. Her belated review of *18 Poems*—and of the poem 'A grief ago', published in *Programme*, October 1935—was to appear in the *London Mercury* for February 1936.

17th January 1936   5 Cwmdonkin Drive   Uplands   Swansea   S. Wales

Dear Miss Sitwell,

I wouldn't be able to thank you enough for your letter, so I won't try, but I loved it and appreciated it, and I'll owe you a lot always for your encouragement. No, of course, I don't care a damn for an audience, or for 'success', but it *is* exciting—I suppose it's the only external reward—to have things liked for the reasons one writes them, to be believed in by someone one believes in who's right outside the nasty schools and the clever things one (me) doesn't want to understand, like surrealism and Cambridge quarterlies and Communism and the Pope of Rome. And yes God does permit everything, and health's only a little thing, and to the devil anyway with 'personal troubles' which *are* the devil—(mine are only the indescribably mean naggings of having absolutely no money at all, for I live on my few poems and stories and you know what that means, and a few rowdy habits, and the very insignificant melancholies of 'things not coming right' etc, and really nothing very much more). I'm a very happy sort of bird, and I don't care much.

How I would like you to be able to do something about those new poems of mine, because there are quite enough to make a small book and I would like to have nothing more to do with Richard Church. I've a contract for poems with Dent's, but if Church dislikes my surrealist imitations so strongly that he'll be willing to break the contract—and I think he does hate them and will be willing—could I let you know then and would you help me? It *is* kind of you to suggest wanting to help them be published.

I don't think I should have mentioned that I was eighteen when I wrote that Welsh-starch-itch-trash poem;[1] it sounded like an excuse, but it wasn't because I'm twenty one and the same excuse would apply to every line I write. I know, though, that you didn't take it as an excuse—and anyway why should I talk about that silly poem? Why, by the way, Miss Sitwell, are people of my age—and I would say that when I know that age doesn't matter a bit in poetry, (does it?)—so terribly frightened, in their talk and letters, of being solemn and earnest for one moment? I know I am.

And I'm going back to London in the middle of February (I shall beard the Church then) and will try my *hardest* to manage to stay there until the first few days of March, because I want so much to meet you. My address is Swansea until about the seventeenth of next month.

Again, I won't try to thank you, because I couldn't enough, for your advice and help and encouragement.

Yours very sincerely,
Dylan Thomas

MS: Berg

DESMOND HAWKINS
18th January '36[2]   5 Cwmdonkin Drive   Uplands   Swansea

Dear Desmond,

I should have answered you such a long, long time ago that, in spite of my natural good manners, it's hardly worth apologising, is it? I am sorry, anyway, and I'm not dead—(I had my suspicions yesterday morning, though).

Thanks for Purpose; I liked the reviews and I'm so glad you said a few words about Cameron's poems—his book's been horribly neglected from what I can see from the periodicals that come into my Swansea retreat, ('retreat' it is, from the onslaught of my London enemies, from that ghoul of a Marquis—though here, admittedly, there's the very devil of a Mermaid). And I always like Porteus, don't you?[3] (Though G.E.G.[4] isn't all that good.)

---

1 'Our eunuch dreams', the poem that Sitwell castigated. He must have written her a previous letter.
2 Thomas wrote '18th February' by mistake.
3 Hugh Gordon Porteus, writer and critic.
4 Geoffrey Grigson.

Going to soak the Bookman for a guinea? I don't know if it'll like advanced young men now that Ruthven Todd's been given the push. He (Todd) is probably nice and is coming to London some time this month. I'm nice, too, but I won't be back until the middle of February—for a couple of weeks or more then, so let's meet. Let's meet in a pub like the Plough, or even somewhere in the East, but not in that bunch of Charlotte-street baNinas.[1]

You did tell me—I mean, I didn't dream it, though thank God my dreams of that Papal paper are very rare—that you were going to do a fiction review for the Criterion, didn't you?[2] That's fine. I must write a novel quickly for you to review it. (And the King's Canary shall *not* die. We'll have a shot at it, blast us we will.)

About poems: I don't know that I've got anything much good at the moment, but I probably will have by the time I see you. I'm working hard enough but so slowly, & a lot of my time for the last week or two has been spent in preparing a smug paper for the L.C.C. Institute of Education. You're not in a vast hurry for poems, are you? I'll be in town not later than February 17, & will send you a postcard, with dates for you to pick from— as many as you like—a week before that.

Best wishes
Dylan

Remember me to Porteus if you see him. I'd like to meet him again very much. Couldn't we arrange a mild, or a bitter, night out all together?

MS: National Library of Wales

EDITH SITWELL
24th January '36   5 Cwmdonkin Drive   Uplands   Swansea

Dear Miss Sitwell,

This is horrid paper; I had some Sweet Nell of Old Drury Bond but I've lost her. Thank you so much for your letter, and of course I'd love to dine with you on the 18th at your club and come to your party. It's kind of you and nice of you to ask me. The one person I know, and only slightly, is David Higham[3] who arranged the Dent's contract for me. I'm looking forward a lot to being taken round to Duckworth and Bumpus. (No, I don't know Mr. Wilson.)[4] Are you sure you really don't mind taking all this

---

1 A word-play on Nina Hamnett.
2 T. S. ('Pope') Eliot edited the *Criterion*.
3 David Higham led an exodus from the firm of Curtis Brown in 1935 and set up a new literary agency, Pearn, Pollinger & Higham. Thomas was wobbling between the old firm and the new.
4 J. G. Wilson ran Bumpus, the booksellers.

trouble? I'm so very grateful to you. You must have listened to a great deal of the woes of young poets. And to take a regular job is the most sensible suggestion in the world. I would willingly and gladly, but have, apart from the little writing, reviewing, hack journalism, and oddjobbery I've done, hardly any qualifications. But you shall have all my confidences when we meet. They look depressed on paper, and I'm not. (If there's been too much talk of 'the woes' in my letters, it's because it's been raining every time I've written to you. It always rains in Swansea.) I do hope your arrangements won't fail you, and that I shall meet you on the 18th & the 19th.

Yours very sincerely,
Dylan Thomas

MS: Berg

ROBERT HERRING
30.1.36   5 Cwmdonkin Drive   Uplands   Swansea

Dear Robert Herring,
I'm sure the worst will happen; it always does; I shall get blind. So let's meet, shall we, on my first day in town? the 10th. Shall we meet somewhere in the evening: I mayn't be up for lunch. You can tell me all about Miss S. She isn't very frightening, is she? I saw a photograph of her once, in medieval costume. And thanks a lot: I'd like very much to dine on the 20th. Don't bother to write, unless, of course, you *aren't* free on the 10th. I'll ring you in the afternoon to fix the time and pub. I shan't wear a gardenia but I am short with bulging eyes, a broken tooth, curly hair and a cigarette. Otherwise I am respectable enough even to go into Oddenino's (That's not a suggestion for a meeting place, but the Café Royal is, I believe, barred to me, and anyway I prefer places with things to spit in). Do you ever see Oswell Blakeston by the way? If you do, wave your hand at him for me. I hope to have a drink with him next month. And if you *aren't* free, then do suggest any other day after the 10th.

Yours sincerely,
Dylan Thomas

MS: Texas

DESMOND HAWKINS
1.2.36   5 Cwmdonkin Drive   Uplands   Swansea

I'm coming to town on the 10th, this Monday week. What about meeting Tuesday the 11th, Wednesday 12th or Thursday 13th morning in—say—

the Plough[1] between 11.30 a.m. and mid-day? Drop me a card & tell me: and if you know a better pub around the district—O.K. Discuss everything then. Sorry to scribble such a tiny note but I *must* have a shit.

Yours,
Dylan

MS: National Library of Wales

DANIEL JONES
6.2.36 [on the envelope: 'oh so urgent']   5 Cwmdonkin Drive

RA. On this most significant notepaper[2] I write to Warmley's Bigwig for the first time since August 1935. There wasn't any need for me to write and say 'Ra, Maestro' when you carried off the Musical Biscuit of the Year, because you knew I wasn't exactly displeased about it.[3] I'm coming up to London on Monday (the 10th). How do I get hold of you? Write quickly & tell me. We must meet (we most certainly must meet. There are 350 things I want to tell you). Tom is here with me at the moment, cutting a horn lesson to make 3/- illegally. Can't write. Notes between Warmlies are barmy. Great Men (and the whole point is, of course, that we mean it) must *meet*. And soon. Don't forget. Write before Monday.

Love,
Dylan

MS: Texas

RAYNER HEPPENSTALL
6.2.36   5 Cwmdonkin Drive   Uplands   Swansea

I do hope this finds you, because when you wrote last you said you might be sacked from your Soho home at any moment. You wrote a nice, sad letter, do you remember, just after that Blairy man had let into you with a metal shooting stick?[4] And you had a cold and were hard up and hadn't got any food—only lots of stamps. When I read the letter I had a cold and a hangover and rheumatism in the elbow, 3/1d between me and a big place

---

1 The Plough was near the British Museum. Writers and editors drank there.
2 The paper has heavy horizontal lines.
3 Jones had won the Mendelssohn Travelling Scholarship.
4 The writer George Orwell (1903–50), whose real name was Eric Arthur Blair. Heppenstall, who shared a flat with him, said that Orwell came back drunk one night and attacked him.

quite near called Tawe Lodge;[1] and I couldn't write seriously, and I didn't want to see Shirley Temple, and all my friends were dead. And aw what the hell anyway was just what I felt. Now I'm better, no hangover, no cold, no rheumatism, 3/2d, and a short story—called most beautifully 'The Phosphorescent Nephew' finished, typed, and accepted by a half-doped American editor.[2]

I'm coming to town on the 10th, this coming Monday. Do let's meet during the week. And let's make it the morning, shall we, because I think I've found a small, fluffy thing and I want it in the evenings. What about Wednesday morning—provisionally? But you make the date. Where shall we meet? Shall I ring your bell (if you've got a bell), or what about a clean pub with no beards in it? Let me know before Monday if possible. I haven't seen you for months. Are you clean-shaven? Looking forward etc.

Yours,
Dylan

MS: *Texas*

ERIC WALTER WHITE[3]
8.iii.36   5 Cwmdonkin Drive   Uplands   Swansea

Dear Eric Walter White,

I am, by accident not by nature, so abominably rude and unreliable that I have to spend the best part of the first week after my regular short visits to town in writing frantic letters of apology. Before these regular short visits, I work out my plans in the most pleasant detail: almost every day is arranged so that something nice happens in it. And then, when I do come to town, bang go my plans in a horrid alcoholic explosion that scatters all my good intentions like bits of limbs and clothes over the doorsteps and into the saloon bars of the tawdriest pubs in London. I *was* looking forward to meeting you and to being taken to hear music; but minor nastiness followed rudeness (ringing you up, for example, and then not appearing) and I heard no music at all and I failed to meet you. It would bore you to death to hear all the reasons, but I do really and deeply apologise for my behaviour.[4]

I'm returning to town in about a fortnight, before I go into the country to

---

1 The Swansea municipal 'workhouse', for paupers.
2 The story has not been identified.
3 Eric Walter White, arts administrator and writer.
4 They were supposed to meet on 20 February at the Reform Club, after Thomas had been to a cocktail party at Edith Sitwell's. He didn't turn up, but telephoned to suggest they meet at a restaurant instead. He didn't turn up there either.

work, and nothing so silly shall happen again. Will you have a meal with me then and let me apologise personally? Do say yes.

Yours very sincerely,
Dylan Thomas

MS: *(the recipient)*

WYN HENDERSON

Mrs Henderson (1896–1976), occasional journalist and publisher, was the friend of many artists and poets, and quite often their lover: as she was, briefly, Dylan Thomas's. Later in life she was close to Caitlin Thomas.

9.3.36   5 Cwmdonkin Drive   Uplands   Swansea

Darling (Dylan) Darling (Dylan again) Wyn, and Oswell (if he's about),

How nice of you to purr about me after dinner, two fed, sleek cats rubbing against the table legs and thinking about a scrubby Welshman, with a three-weeks-accumulated hangover and a heart full of love and nerves full of alcohol, moping over his papers in a mortgaged villa in an upper-class professional row (next to the coroner's house) facing another row (less upper) and a dis-used tennis court. It was a lovely rolling letter, out of the depths of dinner, and a winy mantle of love hung over it, and thank you a lot, Wyn and Oswell.

Wyn privately: As your mascot and very welcome guest, I'd love to come to Cornwall more than anything else: it sounds just what I want it to be, and I can write poems, and stories about vampire sextons deflowering their daughters with very tiny scythes, and draw rude little pictures of three-balled clergymen, and go [to] pubs and walks with you.[1] It's all too lovely to be good; and I'd enjoy it so much. I'm coming to town in about a fortnight: I've got to meet a few publishers and try to get money from them as I haven't any, and, I believe, to read some poems over the wireless. That won't take long: the publishers will (probably) pretend to be deaf, and the wireless will break down. If you are gone by then, chugging into Cornwall, shall I follow you and will you meet me, me lost, me with beer in my belly and straws in my hair? And if you haven't chugged away, but are still rampaging in Bloomsbury (or wherever you rampage mostly) we can go together, can't we? And that will be nicer still. (This letter, Wyn dear, is too excellently phrased. But I've just finished writing a story called The Phosphorescent Nephew; and whatever I do now, bugger me it's literary.)

So thanks, Wyn, for the invitation. I do hope you won't be gone when I come back to London—even though you have to go away and leave me

1 Henderson had a cottage near Land's End. Thomas met her through Oswell Blakeston. It was probably Norman Cameron's idea that he take refuge in the country.

there temporarily—because there are lots of little things to talk about.
Much love to you, (and to old Slime, the State Parasite).

Dylan

MS: Texas

ERIC WALTER WHITE
March 13th 36   5 Cwmdonkin Drive   Uplands   Swansea

Dear Eric Walter White,
   Of course I wasn't appalled, I was awfully pleased to get your letter and
forgiveness so soon. I hope you're feeling better and are out of bed.
   Yes, it was rather risky fixing an appointment immediately after a party,
though E. Sitwell's party was very sedate and had more dukes than drinks.
I'm so sorry the reference to my 'explosion' made you feel old and sad, but
with most members I know of the generation before mine, it seems mostly
to be a matter of constitution rather than inclination, and Norman
Cameron, with whom I stay when in town, and whom you probably know,
is always telling me, 'Just wait till *you're* past twenty five.'
   And the Fitzroy and the Running Sore shall be barred; I know a good pub
in the Bayswater Road and one in Paddington, but the ones more central
seem nearly all spoilt now. There used to be that lovely one in Wapping,
looking over the river, until the beards went there. I think the Plough's safe
these days, and the one Younger's house in Mayfair is quite clean up until
about 8-30. Anyway, we'll see, shall we?
   Here's one of the two copies left (to my knowledge) of my poems. A chap
here was keeping them in the vain hope that they would one day reach a fabulous price, but I told him not to be silly, and he gave me this one back quite
willingly—he hadn't read it anyway. Thanks a lot for wanting it, though
three-quarters of the poems are awfully young and awkward as you'll see.
   I hope to see you soon.

Best wishes,
Dylan Thomas

MS: (the recipient)

DESMOND HAWKINS
[March 1936]   [Swansea]

Dear Desmond,
   It's funny about ram. Once I looked up an old dictionary and found it
meant red, but now I can't find it in any dictionary at all. I wanted ram in
the poem to mean red *and* male *and* horny *and* driving *and* all its usual
meanings. Blast it, why doesn't it mean red? Do look up and see for me.[1]

1 Hawkins planned to publish 'Find meat on bones', but wanted to know what 'ram'
   meant, in Stanza 3: 'A merry girl took me for man,/I laid her down and told her sin,/
   And put beside her a ram rose.' The poem appeared in *Purpose*, April/June issue, 1936.

I'll be in town for about four or five days from the week-end of March 28 on. Monday's the 30th: what about our beer party Monday, Tuesday, or Wednesday? Do you think you could arrange it? I'll be going, on Thursday I believe, to Cornwall for the spring. (We moneyed poets. And do I get half a guinea for my ram-rose?)

I hope the Pope consents: I've never seen him human, only in his office telling me 'And what is more, surrealism is a dead horse'.[1]

What happened in Church?

Yours,
Dylan

MS: National Library of Wales.

RICHARD CHURCH
17th March 1936   5 Cwmdonkin Drive   Uplands   Swansea

Dear Richard Church,

I'm so sorry to have delayed sending my poems to you.[2]

I have been thinking about them a good deal, and about what we said when we last met. I promised to send two lots of poems, one lot containing the recent things, most of which you've already seen, and one of more-or-less simple, unambiguous poems. But I don't think now that that's a very wise plan—or, to my present way of thinking, a very honest one. Just as you, as you said, would consider it almost dishonest to publish poems you could not explain to those people who might buy them, so I feel it would be dishonest of me to attempt to get published a complete book of 'simple poems': I shall always go on trying to write simple, unambiguous things, but they can only be a very little part of my work ('my work' sounds awful, but it can't be helped). What I want to do is to include a certain number of these 'simple poems' in each collection of new poems I, God willing, might publish in future years. The same with this present collection.[3] As you'll see, most of the poems are the very recent ones you have, in the past, objected to—along with ones much less difficult. I should not like the simples or the not-so-simples to be published separately: after all, they were written more or less at the same time and do, together, represent my 'work' for the past year and more.

1 Thomas was introduced to T. S. Eliot at one of the beery Plough lunches later that month. H. G. Porteus, another of the circle, who was present, says that Thomas and Eliot 'then both departed, fairly tanked up', for the lunch described in Thomas's first letter to Vernon Watkins.

2 A form letter from Dent dated 19 March acknowledged receipt of 'the manuscript entitled TWENTY-THREE POEMS'.

3 *Twenty-five Poems* (1936) contained seven poems that could be called 'simple'. Six of these were written between March and August 1933, *before* the group of 'anatomical' poems that formed the core of *18 Poems* (1934). What appealed to Church was a style that Thomas had already abandoned.

If, after this final reading—and believe me I'm not being snooty at all—you come to the conclusion you could not honestly print them in your series, am I at liberty to try to have them published elsewhere? I hope, of course, most sincerely, that you will be able to publish them: if not, the day *may* come when none of my poems will be indecently obscure or fashionably difficult.

Yours sincerely,
Dylan Thomas

MS: (J. M. Dent)

GEOFFREY GRIGSON
Sunday [?March 1936]   Cwmdonkin Drive   Uplands   Swansea

Dear Geoffrey,
Thanks so much for the books. I'm coming up to town tomorrow, for about 3 days, before going to Cornwall. 3 days with N, of course.

Shall I ring you up? I haven't seen you for months. Can't we have a drink together, and grieve?

About books, too. I'm a good chap now, and will always do them regularly, pronto, and properly, for as long as you want me to.

And has Fanny left you for ever and ever? Going to tell Terry about it.

Thanks about books—again.

Love to you Doc.

MS: Texas

RICHARD CHURCH
[April 1936]   Polgigga   Porthcurno   Penzance   Cornwall[1]

Dear Richard Church,
I am so sorry that I failed to call in and see you when I was in town, but I was there only a very few days and then not feeling particularly well or editorworthy. I'm hoping to recover some of my lost good health in the country and to do some serious work.

So far I'm afraid I've no other poems to add to the ones already in your possession, or none, at least, with which I am pleased enough as yet.

Have you come to any decision as to the fate of the poems? I do apologise for my delay in writing, and hope that you'll let me know some time the result of your re-reading.

Yours sincerely,
Dylan Thomas

MS: (J. M. Dent)

1 Wyn Henderson's cottage was in the village of Polgigga.

DESMOND HAWKINS
Sunday April 11th [1936]

Dear Desmond,
    Address above. It's sunny all day here, and rat to your nasty grey London. So sorry you couldn't make it last Monday; we might have got so pleasantly pissed and played darts again. See you when I come back in about seven weeks' time. Do send that ten bob on: I've finally let the M. Post down, and have nothing to live on now. Curse.[1]

> Yours
> Dylan

Address isn't above, it's below: here:
Polgigga, Porthcurno, Penzance, Cornwall. That isn't three places, it really is my address.

MS: National Library of Wales

T. S. ELIOT
12th April 1936   Polgigga   Porthcurno   Penzance   Cornwall

Dear Mr Eliot,
    Thank you so much for the note. I should have replied before, but I've been trying to settle down here and, after being so messy in London, it takes a long time.
    I've got some new poems, but I'm not really certain about them, and don't at the moment think they're good enough to send you. Anyway, I'm going to work hard on them and see what happens. I've been writing quite a lot of stories lately. Would you care to see the very latest one? It's called 'The Orchards', and I'm enclosing it. Perhaps you won't like it at all; nobody's seen it to tell me anything about it, and it may be all wrong. I do hope it isn't because I've spent a long, long time working on it. Even if you can't use it—and I hope you will be able to—a lot—would you tell me something about it?
    I'm looking forward to another little beer party with Hawkins and Porteus. Are you coming along?

> Yours sincerely,
> Dylan Thomas

MS: Valerie Eliot

---

1 The newspaper printed a review article by Thomas on 27 March, then nothing more until it carried two final articles, 28 August and 11 September.

VERNON WATKINS

Thomas's friendship with the poet Vernon Watkins (1906–67) began in 1935, when Watkins, who lived near Swansea on the Gower Peninsula, read *18 Poems* and went to see him. Watkins, eight years older than Thomas, had published nothing at the time (his first book, *Ballad of the Mari Lwyd*, appeared in 1941). After a mental breakdown in 1927—he revisited his old school, attacked the headmaster and was held in a nursing home for a considerable period—he worked as a bank clerk in Swansea for the rest of his days, a literary and intellectual fish out of water. Both Dylan and Caitlin, misinterpreting his gentle air, thought he had homosexual inclinations, and were surprised when he married. His widow Gwen Watkins, who saw Thomas as a ruthless exploiter of his friends, has written of her husband: 'Dylan was his *alter ego*: when he supported, protected, admired Dylan it was because of the life he had never lived himself.'

Monday [postmarked 20 April 1936]
Polgigga   Porthcurno   Penzance   Cornwall

Dear Vernon,
Perhaps it's a bit late to say Sorry for not having let you know I couldn't come to see you that particular Sunday—whenever it was—and to tell you how much I missed you and the unwonted walk and the toasted things for tea and the poetry after it; but I want to say Sorry, and I hope you'll forgive me, and I hope, though that's the wrong way of putting it, that you missed your hearty, Britain-chested, cliff-striding companion as much as I did. I had crowds of silly, important things to do: pack, write formal letters, gather papers, and catch the Sunday night train; and I didn't get out of bed until all those things had to be scamped through. Now in a hundred ways I wish I hadn't come away; I'm full of nostalgia and a frightful cold; here the out-of-doors is very beautiful, but it's a strange country to me, all scenery and landscape, and I'd rather the bound slope of a suburban hill, the Elms, the Acacias, Rookery Nook, Curlew Avenue, to all these miles of green fields and flowery cliffs and dull sea going on and on, and cows lying down and down. I'm not a country man; I stand for, if anything, the aspidistra, the provincial drive, the morning café, the evening pub; I'd like to believe in the wide open spaces as the wrapping around walls, the windy boredom between house and house, hotel and cinema, bookshop and tubestation; man made his house to keep the world and the weather out, making his own weathery world inside; that's the trouble with the country: there's too much public world between private ones. And living in your own private, four-walled world as exclusively as possible isn't escapism, I'm sure; it isn't the Ivory Tower, and, even if it were, you secluded in your Tower know and learn more of the world outside than the outside-man who is mixed up so personally and inextricably with the mud and the unlovely people—(sorry, old Christian)—and the four bloody muddy winds.
I was in London for just over a week, and the same things happened there that always happen: I kept roughly a half of my appointments, met half the people I wanted to, met lots of other people, desirable and otherwise, and

fully lived up to the conventions of Life No. 13: promiscuity, booze, coloured shirts, too much talk, too little work. I had Nights Out with those I always have Nights Out with: Porteus, Cameron, Blakeston, Grigson, and old Bill Empson[1] and all—(Empson, by the way, has been very kind to me in print, in a review of the Faber anthology, saying, quite incorrectly, though than which etc. there could be nothing nicer for my momentary vanity, that little or nothing of importance, except for Owen and Eliot, comes between Eliot and ME. Ho! Ha!) Also I had lunch with Pope Eliot, as I said I would have; he *was* charming, a great man, I think, utterly unaffected; I had a spot of rheumatism that day, and nearly the whole time was spent in discussing various methods of curing it, ('I think it was in 1927 I had my worst bout, and I tried Easu Ointment' etc). I left London with Life No. Thirteen's headache, liver, and general seediness, and have by this time thoroughly recovered.

Polgigga is a tiny place two miles or less from Land's End, and very near Penzance and Mousehole (really the loveliest village in England). We live here in a cottage in a field, with a garden full of ferrets and bees. Every time you go to the garden lavatory you are in danger of being stung or bitten. My hostess, or what you like, has unfortunately read too many books of psychology, and talks about my ego over breakfast; her conversation is littered with phrases like narcissist fixation and homosexual transference; she is a very simple person who tries to cure her simplicity by a science which, in its turn, tries to cure the disease it suffers from. I don't think that's my phrase, but here in this Freudian house[2] it's truer than hell. One day, though never in a letter, I must tell you the whole silly, strange story behind all this—this most irregular, unequal Cornwall partnership; I don't think for a moment that you'll enjoy it, and I know that you'll agree with me how wrong, if there can be any values here, I was to begin it. But I *shall* tell you, probably when I see you in the summer—a summer I'm looking forward to a lot. The one thing that's saving me—saving me, I mean, not from any melodramatic issues but just from sheer unhappiness—is lots and lots of work. I'm half way through another story, and have more or less finished a poem which I want to send you when I'm better pleased with it. But here again I'm not free; perhaps, as you said once, I should stop writing altogether for some time; now I'm almost afraid of all the once-necessary artifices and obscurities, and can't, for the life or the death of me, get any real liberation, any diffusion or dilution or anything, into the churning bulk of the words; I seem, more than ever, to be tightly packing away everything I have and know into a mad-doctor's bag, and then locking it up: all you can see is the bag, all you can know is that it's full to the clasp, all you have to trust is that the invisible and intangible things packed away are—if they *could* only be seen and touched—worth quite a lot. I don't really know why I should be unloading any of this on you, and probably

1 The poet William Empson (1906–84).
2 Wyn Henderson had been psychoanalysed.

boring you—no, that's wrong, you couldn't be one of the bored ones of the world—at the same time. But you are—even if only momentarily—the one happy person I know, the one who, contrary to facts and, in a certain way, to circumstances, seems to be almost entirely uncomplicated: not, either, the uncomplication of a beginning person, but that of a person who has worked through all the beginnings and finds himself a new beginning in the middle—I hope, for your today's happiness,—a beginning at the end. That's not clear, of course. You might, and would, I know, if you could, help me by talking to me. I don't fear—we talked about it, do you remember—any sudden cessation or drying-up, any coming to the end, any (sentimentally speaking) putting out of the fires; what I do fear is an ingrowing, the impulse growing like a toenail into the artifice. Talk to me about it, will you—it's probably a terrible task I'm trying to drag you into— in any way, any words. And tell me what you're doing and writing. I'll write you again soon, a clearer letter, less face-in-the-earth, less eye-in-a-sling.

Yours always,
Dylan

God, I almost forgot.

Are you rich temporarily? Would you like to lend me some money, a pound or, at the very most, two pounds? I have a beastly, vital debt—rather a lot— to pay in the next few days; I've got together most of it, but not quite all, and all has to be paid. I can—if you *are* penniful temporarily, and, if you're not, do forget it and go on writing the long letter you're going to write to me—let you have it back next week certainly. Of course, you don't mind me asking you, but if you're broke or holiday-saving, I can get a few pounds elsewhere—though not, Mr. Watkins, with such lack of embarrassment as I can ask you for it.

Yours always again,
D.

[*Pencil P.S.*]

Did the snaps—I bet they didn't—come out well, or at all?

MS: British Library

ELFRIEDE CAMERON[1]

25th April [1936]   Polgigga   Porthcurno   Penzance   Cornwall

Dear Elfriede,

Wyn is not quite my cup of nightcustard:—(difficult English idiom, cup of tea). When we booze it's all right, but when we don't she talks about Books and Havelock Ellis and the frustrated ego. (Then I'd like to slap her

1 Norman Cameron's first wife.

across the tittie with a hard-boiled ego.) I'm enclosing a little drawing (very refined line) of her & me. But I do manage to do a little work, and I'm sending you a poem I've written here, a poem about the same Long Gentleman (you ask Norman) who shared his bed with grapefruit and windscreens and everything,[1] I'm going to do a story too—a nice one you'll like, with no worms or bellies, but all about a man who was unanimously elected by the Board of Skeletons to act as referee for three seasons in the cricket matches of the dead: they play with bits of each other in Dead Cricket, with shin-bone and eye-ball, and all. I'm going to try to write it anyway, if Wyn doesn't take me out too much to introduce me to busmen. I know I don't need much encouragement to whack the bottle bang, but I should always try to stay, when away from the intellect-ruining city, in company that gives me no encouragement at all: then I have only myself to blame when I'm a Bad One. That's very commonsense; I wish I hadn't come here; this is a little London, even though the Out-of-Doors is lovely and there's lots of Nature about. I don't like the big, natural spaces between houses much, but Cornwall's a nice, nice county as the exterior world goes, and Mousehole is the best village. I want to live there (Mousehole), not with our Wyn but cosy and cheaply with something dumb and lovely of my own choice, with a woman who hasn't been psycho-analysed or rodgered by celebrities. Wyn at her best's at her booziest, when she sings her simple song about the Sparrow:

> There was a bloody sparrow
> Flew up a bloody spout,
> Came a bloody thunderstorm
> And blew the bugger out.

I think that's awfully good; I say it about twice a day and laugh and laugh; but perhaps it's not so funny.

How are you? Get better soon, won't you, and full of health and unwheezy. Are you still red in bed, or pale and lazy downstairs, or making a German beast of yourself in the country—striding all over the awful Out-of-Doors in creaky-leather shoes? Are you going to write to me, and tell me about yourself? I don't think I've got any news or gossip or dirt—apart from lots of silly stories about Havelock Ellis, about what scent he uses on his handkerchief and why he makes his female visitors drink so many cups of tea. And David Archer[2] is leaving London; his mother has given him a riding jacket to go to Durham in, but he has not arrived there yet. People, apparently, are coming quite openly now with handcarts to take away the few remaining books from his shop; David is furious because somebody has the idea of turning the shop into a café. He, David, told me in a letter that

1 Sonnet IX of 'Altarwise by owl-light'.
2 David Archer, d. 1971, once described as 'a left-wing Bertie Wooster', came from a well-to-do Wiltshire family, spent his inheritance running the Parton Bookshop, and so helped publish *18 Poems*, and died penniless. He published other poets besides Thomas, among them David Gascoyne, George Barker and W. S. Graham.

Gladstone used to come to the shop, but I think that he was boasting a little. It rains here all day, even better excuse for Wyn to take me fugging in the Logan Inn (where Norman is a most attractive person, very drunk, very Fascist, and who wishes to be remembered to you). I have met the Mousehole people, the whimsy Veronica with her lame leg called Gilbert, & the bloated McColls, and the self-eaten postmaster, and I hate them all.[1] Wyn has a new dog aged ten weeks which I hate more than anybody: last night late, it jumped on to my bed, sat on my face, pissed on my chest, and bit my belly. I am going to kill it with a little axe. Get all well again quickly, Elfriede. Am I going to stay with you some time? Sorry this is a dull letter, but I've got bees in the brain because I was Bad yesterday.

All my love,
Dylan

MS: Theodore Brinckman

DESMOND HAWKINS
25th April [1936]   Polgigga   Porthcurno   Penzance   Cornwall

Dear Corkpins,

Did you get my letter? I've been expecting to hear from you. Don't the firm of Daniel send their contributors copies of their journals? Or do they just send them a bag of healthy nuts and a dirty post card in Basic English? The Editor knows where to ram my rose. And *Purpose* owes me twenty pints.[2]

Are there any *Purpose* books for me to review? My Morning Post is broken; now I stand naked in Cornwall with no Conservative erection.[3] Have you any books on Music or Magic you'd like to give me? Have you reviewed Harry Price? (He sounds like *Purpose*'s cup of tea). Would you like some ha ha dirt on Beverley Nichols's Gods and Public Anemones?[4]

And do you remember talking to me about Time and Tide? Would it be wise for me to write to them for reviews, mentioning old Corkpins? Or could you do some back-stairs work? I used to sleep in Lady Rhondda's

---

1 Veronica Sibthorp (previously McColl, later Armstrong: she was married three times) (1908–73) came from a wealthy family, as did Archie McColl, her first husband. John Waldo Sibthorp, whom she married about 1932, was a printer, and had been one of Wyn Henderson's lovers. Veronica had a crippled leg, which she referred to as 'Gilbert'. At about the time of this letter she was having an affair with Thomas, as was Wyn Henderson. Her third husband, the painter John Armstrong, is said to have made her destroy letters from Thomas; two that survive are in this collection, but they were not written until 1939.

2 In the 'Canary' fantasy 'A. Desmond Hawkins' became 'B. Osmond Corkpins'. *Purpose* was published by C. W. Daniel & Co.

3 The *Morning Post*, later merged with the *Daily Telegraph*, supported the Conservative Party.

4 Harry Price (1881–1948), occult author. Beverley Nichols (1898–1983), popular author.

Valley.[1] Really I do need review work more than ever before. Has the Literary Review any books for me? And is it to print my story?

Do write and answer soon. I want books, books, books, any sort from anywhere. Books, books. (God, I'll have to learn to read. I wish you could review books by stars alone.)

Seen David Archer? Roger R.[2] tells me that David's mother has sent him a riding-coat to go to Durham in, but that he hasn't arrived there yet; that people are now coming quite openly with handcarts to remove all his books; that he says Gladstone used to call at his shop: (but nobody believes that, that's boasting).

If we ever—and we must—write The Canary, I've got some nice true stories for it about Havelick Pelvis.[3] I met a woman down here who used to stay in his house a lot; she says that every morning of the first few weeks of her first visit he came into her bedroom with a cup of tea; when she'd finished it, he gave her another and asked her, '*Now* do you want to make water?' Then he'd give her another cup of tea and ask her, 'Surely *now* you want to make water.' Then he'd give her another cup of tea and hold the chamber pot up invitingly and say, 'Now surely you must make water *now*.'

Don't forget: do write and tell me about reviews.

> Yours,
> Dylan

MS: National Library of Wales

RICHARD CHURCH
1st May 1936   Polgigga Porthcurno Penzance Cornwall

Dear Richard Church,

I am so very, very glad that you are going to publish my poems.[4] Knowing how you feel about their obscurity and (occasional) wilful eccentricity, and about your own obligations, both as a publisher and a poet, to the public you have already created by bringing out the work of so many of the more Intelligible Boys, I do appreciate your decision to let me and that public 'face each other'. I can only hope that the poems will, in some little way, justify the faith you have in them—a faith, perhaps, that goes against judgement.

In less than a month I shall probably be able to let you have the other

1 Lady Rhondda, who owned *Time and Tide*, was the daughter of D. A. Thomas of Merthyr Vale, the coal king, ennobled as Viscount Rhondda. The ambiguous reference to sleeping in her valley is a joke.
2 Roger Roughton
3 = Havelock Ellis, student of urolagnia.
4 Church had written on 28 April: '... Still I cannot understand the meaning of the poems, but in this matter I have decided to put myself aside and to let you and the public face each other.' Church asked for half a dozen more poems to 'add to the bulk'.

half dozen poems you need: two new ones, completing the long poem of which you have the first eight sections, and four younger ones selected and revised.

I'm very glad too that you liked my story in *Comment*.[1] I've had quite a lot of stories of more or less the same kind published lately, and have got together enough to make a book. I know you don't publish short stories at all; if you did, I should certainly have sent the book to you to look sternly upon. (I'm afraid I can't make good sentences on a typewriter.) At the moment I'm vainly squinting around for some innocent publisher who doesn't mind losing money on twenty difficult and violent tales.

One day I hope, as you suggest, to write a story about my earlier world; but I don't feel sure enough of myself to attempt it yet in the form of a novel. What I have been thinking of lately is a book about Wales with a slender central theme of make-belief, a certain amount of autobiography, and also a factual Journey of the more popular kind (the Bad Companion's English Journey, Muir's Scottish one, etc).[2] It's difficult to write about this in a letter, but I should, when I come back to town in a month's time, like to talk it over with you. Could we arrange to have a meal together? I'll let you know the exact date of my return. I'm sure that if you would be kind enough to talk over this Welsh idea with me, it would clear up nearly all the vaguenesses and leave me something practical and (almost) commercial to work upon.

Do excuse this very loosely written letter.

And thank you again for all your encouragement.

Yours sincerely,
Dylan Thomas

MS: (J. M. Dent)

OSWELL BLAKESTON
May 4th [1936]   Polgigga

Darling Slime,

I'm out of circulation too, with a swollen throat and a pint-sized headache, a jumping hand and not half enough air in my lungs. I'm not sober either, or at least not so much that you'd point after me in the street and say, There goes a sober man. I think you are the nicest person in the world, and I think I'm the wickedest rat in the wrong world too. I've been here weeks, in this little London to me, and I haven't said Hullo to you: I've heard you're swollen and ill and I haven't even had the Welsh, the worst, decency to say Sorry, so sorry, to you; to say, Oswell, nice, you know how

1 'The Dress'. *Comment* ('Incorporating Poet's Corner') had been started by Victor Neuburg and Runia Tharp; the *Sunday Referee*'s poetry period was over.
2 J. B. Priestley, whose novel *The Good Companions* appeared in 1929, published his travelogue *English Journey* in 1934. Edwin Muir's *Scottish Journey* was published in 1935.

much I do like you, you know what a Bad One I try to be and what a Good One I am really. Thank you for the Nott letter. I think of you a lot, more than you know old dirty, but I never seem to try to tell you that I do. Spit on me because I'm awful. This is Dylan Sacrifice Day. And how are you now, poor poisoned and bottom-burned Oswell, Simon, & Dewsbury,[1] king girl, friend of all boozy poets (and me too)? Do get better soon; mus Slimus shan't become extinct; get better and healthy and pretty again; you mustn't swell. I know you want to know if I'm happy with Wyn, and I am in some ways because Adie is good and gentle, (Wyn sent her away to stay with the beery and nice McColls, but asked her to come back because I missed her such a lot), and because the country, as open-air goes, is very grand. And Wyn, when she boozes, is a person I like, but, when she's drinkless, she's booky. Now she's taken a hill house in Mousehole, and we move there in a fortnight. Then I'm coming back to London for a very tiny time before returning for the summer. Meet me, won't you, and we'll both be stronger and better and we'll rampage everywhere. Get well. My love to you, Dylan.

MS: Texas

T. S. ELIOT
6th May 1936   Polgigga Porthcurno Penzance Cornwall

Dear Mr Eliot,

I am so very glad that you were interested in my story and that you're going to print it.[2] If I have some poems during the next few weeks, may I send those as well for you to read? I'm able—so far—to work hard and regularly here, and should certainly have something to show you in a short time.

I know this is very irregular, and I know that English periodicals never pay on acceptance but only on publication. But do you think it would be possible for me to be paid for my story in advance, or, failing that, to be paid *something*, however little? I feel rather silly and nervous asking this, but it really is extremely urgent to me. I've never been in a worse fix for money than I am now—and that means a lot, because I live by the poems and stories I write and am consequently nearly always penniless. But this time I have to find money somewhere, and in a very few days. The only way I can think of is to try to obtain in advance payment for the few recent things of mine that have been accepted but not yet printed.

I do hope you don't mind me asking this. I'll quite understand, of course, if the Criterion isn't able to pay any contributor in advance; though I really hope it is.

1 Pseudonyms that Blakeston was using.
2 The *Criterion* published 'The Orchards' in July 1936.

Again, I'm so sorry about this letter; honestly I wouldn't have written hadn't it been so terribly important to me.

Yours very sincerely,
Dylan Thomas

MS: Valerie Eliot

FABER & FABER
14th May 1936   The Queech   Raginnis Hill   Mousehole   Cornwall

Dear Madam,
    Thank you for your letter. I am returning to town next week, and shall be delighted to accept Mr Eliot's invitation to the Criterion Evening.

Yours faithfully
Dylan Thomas

MS: Valerie Eliot

DESMOND HAWKINS
[June 1936]   5 Cwmdonkin Drive

Dear Desmond,
    A thousand, if I may coin a phrase, apologies. I've only just reached home.
    These are the only pomes I seem to have. Hope I'm not too late, & that one of them will prove (see 'if I may' at the top) satisfactory.
    I'll write a letter very soon.

Yrs
Dylan

MS: National Library of Wales

GEORGE REAVEY[1]
17th June [1936] [postcard]   5 Cwmdonkin Drive   Uplands   Swansea

I didn't see you (I think) at the Surrealist party to ask you about the Poetry Reading on the 26th.[2] I see my name's down on the little notice. That means I'm definitely invited to read, doesn't it? I'd love to, of course. I

1 George Reavey (d. 1976), critic, poet and translator. He was connected with the Europa Press, and spent much of his time in Paris.
2 The International Surrealist Exhibition was held in London at the New Burlington Galleries, 11 June–4 July, attracting much publicity and derision. The associated reading featured Paul Eluard reading his poems in French; translations of his poems by, among others, Samuel Beckett, Reavey and David Gascoyne; and poems by assorted non-surrealist writers, including Thomas.

don't quite know what stuff to choose, though. I'm coming up to town on the Friday morning (for the weekend). Could you spare half-an-hour sometime that day—before the reading—to look through some stuff with me? You'll know what'll go down best. I've got a little chunk of prose & a new poem [that] might do. But we'll see—if you *can* spare that half hour. Let me know all about it, won't you? Best wishes, Dylan.

P.S. I owe you a whole £.

MS: Houghton

JOHN JOHNSON[1]
June 18th 1936   5 Cwmdonkin Drive   Uplands   Swansea

Dear John Johnson,
   I'm so sorry I haven't replied to your letter before this. I was in London some days ago, but had unfortunately left your address behind, and I didn't know any quick way of getting hold of it. I shall be back in town for the weekend of the 26th of this month. Could we have lunch, or a lunchtime drink, together on Saturday 27th, or on Monday? Do let me know, won't you?
   Thanks for writing, and for the nice things you said. We can talk about plays and things when we meet—if, as I hope, we do.
Yours sincerely,
Dylan Thomas

From a typescript. MS location unknown

RICHARD CHURCH
22nd June 1936   5 Cwmdonkin Drive   Uplands   Swansea

Dear Richard Church,
   All my apologies. I *am* so sorry about this very rude delay. I found that my housekeeper in London had forgotten to send the poems along to you that evening before our last meeting; and I looked through them again and thought them lousy. Now I've polished them up and worked hard at them, though two I had to scrap entirely. I'm enclosing five: four you haven't seen before, and the fifth is a slightly altered version of a poem you already have.
   For purposes of acknowledgement: The poem beginning 'And death shall have no dominion' was printed in the New English Weekly; the ones beginning 'Today, this insect, and the world I breathe' and 'Then was my neophyte' are to be printed next month in Purpose; and the last two

1 John Johnson, later a literary agent, was then assistant editor of *Life and Letters Today*.

sections, IX & X, of my long poem are to be printed next month in Contemporary Prose and Poetry.

Do forgive me for being so long in sending them. I haven't, actually, been at all well, and am about to go into the country again—the only place for me, I think: cities are death.

By the way: after reading my long letter indignantly denying certain of your critical charges, you'll be amused to know that I'm reading some poems to the Surrealist Exhibition on the 26th of this month—(though I haven't discovered why I am).

Sincerely yours,
Dylan Thomas

MS: (J. M. Dent)

JOHN JOHNSON
[card, postmarked 23 June 1936] 5 Cwmdonkin Drive Uplands Swansea

That's fine: Saturday 27th; Vianis, 1.15. You'll recognise me easily. I'm short with lots of hair. Sincerely,

Dylan Thomas

MS: Jim Martin

J. M. DENT & CO
1st July 1936   5 Cwmdonkin Drive   Uplands   Swansea

Dear Sir,

I agree that the simpler form of the acknowledgement of the periodicals in which my poems were printed is advisable.

As to the other matter: if you omit the numbering of the poems, are you going to use the first line of each poem as its title (as I did, for what I thought would be reasons of convenience, in the list of contents)? I have not otherwise titled any of the poems, and would not like to have to do so. If you think the method of first-line titling would be best, then of course it's o.k. with me.

As I've taken out some of the poems from the first collection Mr. Church saw, and put in others, the book can't be called Poems In Sequence any longer. I want it called by the number of poems there are in the book: 30 Poems (or whatever it is; I've lost count, having reshuffled them such a lot).

There are, incidentally, now ten sections of the work in progress which makes the last poem in the book, and not eight as you said on the sheet which I am returning.

Yours truly,
Dylan Thomas

MS: (J. M. Dent)

RICHARD CHURCH
1st July [1936]   5 Cwmdonkin Drive   Uplands   Swansea

Dear Richard Church,

I shouldn't be sending you this I know but I've lost the letter
accompanying the enclosed form. I'm afraid it's awfully unsatisfactory, but
I really can't put anything else down. And the title can't be Poems in
Sequence any longer, as I've reshuffled all the poems, taken a few out and
put a few more in, before I suggested that title. I want it to be called, as I
think I mentioned when I saw you, just the number of poems there are in
the book (another thing I don't know, as I've sent the poems in batches and
in such a muddly way).

Yours sincerely,
Dylan Thomas

MS: (J. M. Dent)

NIGEL HENDERSON[1]
7th July 1936   5 Cwmdonkin Drive   Uplands   Swansea

Dear Nigel,

Thank you so much for the papers; I've been working on the poems and
I've burned the indiscretions. I should have written and said thanks weeks
ago, but I mislaid your address, and the letter you wrote has been chasing
me all over the place; it arrived this morning. Sorry you didn't give me a
nudge at the exhibition; it wasn't earnest conversation really; probably
little jokes.

About the Group Theatre: I had some drinks with John Johnson about
ten days ago, but hadn't anything much to offer him. I've been thinking of
doing a Horrible play, mostly in prose with verse choruses and have got
bits of the story mapped out; but I would like to meet Doone[2] before I get
down to it, as, without *some* sort of promise that it will be performed, I
don't feel like devoting a lot of time to it at the moment—I can't as a
matter of fact, because I've to review lots of crime stories in order to buy
beer and shirts and cigarettes.

I'm coming up to town at the beginning of August. If you're about then,
perhaps we could fix a Doone, you and me meeting? And if you've got a
green hat of mine, do be an angel and send it along; it rains here all the
time, and my brim's coming off.

---

1 Wyn Henderson's younger son. He was connected with the fashionable Group Theatre,
  which produced 'committed' plays.
2 Rupert Doone, instrumental in founding the Group Theatre in 1932, was responsible
  for most of its productions.

I'll drop you a line as soon as I know definite London dates.

Thanks again,
Yours,
Dylan

Only source: SL

RICHARD CHURCH
10th July 1936   5 Cwmdonkin Drive   Uplands   Swansea

Dear Richard Church,
   Thank you for your note. I'm glad you think the first line method of indexing is satisfactory.
   But I don't really like POEMS IN PROGRESS as a title; I don't think I understand what it means anyway. The last incomplete poem in the book, consisting of 10 separate poems, is in itself a work in progress; to call the whole book POEMS IN PROGRESS would rather complicate things wouldn't it? I rather like the uniformity of 18 POEMS as a first book and 30 POEMS (or whatever it is) as a second. If you don't like a numerical title, I personally should prefer just POEMS or NEW POEMS, however dull that may sound. But it's 30 POEMS (or whatever it is) that I'm fondest of. However, you know best, and I leave things to you. I hope you don't use POEMS IN PROGRESS though.

Yours sincerely,
Dylan Thomas

   [*A drawn line connects the words* NEW POEMS *with this postscript.*]

which, of course, sounds too important

MS: (J. M. Dent)

RICHARD HUGHES
14th July 1936   Cwmdonkin Drive   Uplands   Swansea

Dear Richard Hughes,
   I'm going to Fishguard by car tomorrow, and passing awfully near Laugharne. I do hope you'll be there because we—that's painter Alfred Janes and me—would like very much to call on you.[1] We shall, shall we, some time in the afternoon? Hope I shan't miss you as I did last time.

Yours sincerely,
Dylan Thomas

MS: Indiana

1 Alfred Janes was driving his father's car, and the ostensible reason for the journey was an exhibition of paintings at Fishguard that Augustus John was to judge.

JOHN JOHNSON
15th July 1936   5 Cwmdonkin Drive   Uplands   Swansea

Dear John Johnson,
    Thanks for your letter. I was very sorry, too, that we didn't have more time together, but it was—this is my weekly sorry day—all my fault really. I should have had a proper lunch with you, not a few bolted drinks with Betty Boop.[1] I always find Lunch in London a deliberate lie; next time we meet, let's make it Drinks.
    I hope I'll be able to start a play quite soon; and I realise, of course, that there can't be a guarantee of production. So glad, though, that you're going to help make things easier.
    I'll send you the stories, sixteen of them. Four or five of them sentimental and possibly worthless—I hope not, because I think they are readable at least—, at the beginning of next week. I'm going away this morning to stay very richly with Richard Hughes in a castle, otherwise I could send them off earlier. Hope this isn't too long a delay. And thanks so much for wanting to take this trouble over them. But I doubt if an established, commercially established, publisher would be very keen; some people consider the stories dirty and, occasionally, blasphemous—which they probably are. But you shall see anyway, and thanks again for wanting to.
    I think I'll be in town some time in August; let you know beforehand and we'll have some drinks.
                                        Yours,
                                        Dylan Thomas
MS: *Jim Martin*

*CAITLIN MACNAMARA

Dylan Thomas's future wife (1913–94) was born in London of Protestant Irish parents; her mother was half French. One of three sisters, she had a brief stage career as a dancer, and lived with a painter in Paris before meeting Dylan in spring 1936. She was forthright, high-spirited and brazen, and men fell for her in droves. The first syllable of her name rhymes with 'Cat', not 'Kate'.

Friday morning 17th, I think.
[17 July 1936]   Cwmdonkin Drive   Uplands   Swansea

Caitlin darling darling, I caught lots of buses and went to sleep in them and

---

1 Betty Boop was a nubile film-cartoon character, created (1930) to publicise the Boop-Boopa-Doop song. According to Johnson, Thomas meant Caitlin Macnamara, whom he had met in London that spring.

ate wine gums in the train and got here awfully late in a sort of thunder storm.[1] This morning I can't do anything but sit with my headache and my liver in a higgledy piggledy room looking out on the rain, and now I'm trying to keep my hand steady to write a neat letter to you that isn't all miserable because I'm not with you in Laugharne or in London or in Ringwood[2] or whatever daft place you're in without me. I dreamed all sorts of funny dreams in my big respectable feather bed—which is much much better than a battlement bed full of spiders—dreams with you in them all the time, and terrible ticking clocks, and vampires, and ladies with long arms putting out the light, and intimate black dogs just sitting on us. I love you Caitlin. I love you more than anybody in the world. And yesterday—though it may be lots of yesterdays ago to you when this wobbly letter reaches you—was the best day in the world, in spite of dogs, and Augustus woofing, and being miserable because it had to stop. I love you for millions and millions of things, clocks and vampires and dirty nails and squiggly paintings and lovely hair and being dizzy and falling dreams. I want you to be with me; you can have all the spaces between the houses, and I can have a room with no windows; we'll make a halfway house; you can teach me to walk in the air and I'll teach you to make nice noises on the piano without any music; we'll have a bed in a bar, as we said we would, and we shan't have any money at all and we'll live on other people's, which they won't like a bit. The room's full of they now, but I don't care, I don't care for anybody. I want to be with you because I love you. I don't know what I love you means, except that I do. [*four words are deleted*] (I crossed that out. It was, 'In 21 messy years', but I don't know what I was going to say). Write to me soon, very very soon, and tell me you really meant the things you said about you loving me too; if you don't I shall cut my throat or go to the pictures.

I'm here in a nest of schoolmasters and vicars, majors, lawyers, doctors, maiden aunts; and you're lord knows where, in the country, miles and miles from me, painting barmy ivy. Now I'm sad, I'm sad as hell, and I'll have to go to a pub by myself & sit in the corner and mope. I'm going to mope about you and then I'm going to have a bath and I'm going to mope about you in the bath. Damn all this anyway; I only want to tell you all the time and over & over again that I love you and that I'm sad because you've gone away and that I'm not going to lose you and that I'm going to see you

1 The outing to Fishguard (letter of 14 July) was engineered by Thomas. He knew that Caitlin was at Richard Hughes's house in Laugharne with Augustus John, whose lover she had been, on and off, for years. John gave his wife Dorelia a version of the episode in a letter of 20 July: 'I drove down to Wales taking Caitlin who wanted to see Dylan Thomas. We stayed at Laugharne Castle & the next day by a strange coincidence Dylan turned up out of the blue! He had [an] artist called Jane[s] with him. I drove them to Fishguard Caitlin and Dylan osculating assiduously in the back of the car.' The sequence of events on 15–17 July isn't clear, but Dylan and Caitlin were together much of the time, and the episode was the real beginning of their love-affair.
2 Caitlin's mother, Mary ('Yvonne') Macnamara, whose husband Francis abandoned her when the children were small, brought up her family in the hamlet of Blashford, Hampshire, on the edge of the New Forest. Ringwood was the nearest town.

soon and that I want us to get married once we can and that you said yes
you wanted to too. And write to me when you get this, or before you do,
only write and tell me all there is to tell me. And I'll write to tell you when
I'll be in London, and then we'll meet, however much they try to stop us,
and then I'll be happy again and I'll try to make you happy by not being a
half wit. All my love for as long as forever & ever is Dylan

XX

MS: Andrew MacAdie

*KEIDRYCH RHYS

An influential, if eccentric, journalist and poet, Rhys (1915–87) founded the magazine *Wales*
in 1937, the first publication of any significance to cater for Welsh writers in English: the so-
called 'Anglo-Welsh'. His real name was William Ronald Rees Jones.

23rd July [1936]   Cwmdonkin Drive   Uplands   Swansea

Dear Keidrych Rhys,
   Thank you for writing. I was very interested in this idea of an Anglo-
Welsh anthology when I first heard of it, and still agree with you that it's
got lots of possibilities. Faber's, I believe, are interested, aren't they?
Somebody I forget now on the Faber staff mentioned it, and your name, to
me—some time before Sylvia Gough appeared with your address.
   I shall be in town on Thursday, July 30, just for the day, and shall spend
licensed hours in the Wheatsheaf.[1] If you're still in town, why not come
along there round lunch-time? It's much easier to talk these things over
than to write about them, isn't it? Perhaps you would send me a line, if you
are free lunch-time next Thursday? I'm afraid that's the only day I'll have
in London until the early winter—it gives me the willies.

Yours sincerely,
Dylan Thomas

MS: National Library of Wales

DENYS KILHAM ROBERTS
[?summer 1936]

   Here are lots of poems for you to see.
   The one beginning, 'A Grief Ago' was printed in 'Oxford Programme'.
   The one beginning, 'Hold hard, these ancient minutes' in 'Caravel',
Majorca.
   The one beginning 'Foster The Light' in 'Contemporary Prose & Poetry'.

1 A pub in 'Fitzrovia'.

The one beginning, 'Do you Not Father Me?' in the 'Scottish Bookman' (now dead, I think).

The one beginning, 'Ears In The Turrets Hear' in John O'London's Weekly. (Don't I get around?)

The one beginning, 'Today, this insect', & the one beginning, 'Then Was The Neophyte' are to be printed in 'Purpose'.

The first seven poems (each *quite* complete by itself) from 'Poems For a Poem', were, as you see, printed in 'Life & Letters To-Day'. The last three have been, or will be, printed in 'Contemporary Prose & Poetry'.

I've had several fairly recently in New Verse, but I expect you've got all the New Verses: I haven't any copies.

I do hope you'll be able to use one or some of these.

I hope, really, you'll like one or two of the 'Poems For A Poem'; though they are linked together by a certain obscure narrative, they're entirely self-contained.

Yours sincerely,
Dylan Thomas

MS: Texas

JOHN LEHMANN
17th August 36   Cwmdonkin Drive   Uplands   Swansea

Dear John Lehmann,

I'm sorry about the delay in answering your card: it wasn't readdressed here until today, as the fellow with whom I share my London address has been away on holiday.

I agree, of course, about your printing the poems. I do hope, though, that all the Editors decide on printing either 'A grief Ago' or 'Then was The Neophyte', as I think the other poem they have in mind, 'From Love's First Fever', is awful.[1] However, anything's all right with me.

Yours sincerely
Dylan Thomas

TS: Victoria

DESMOND HAWKINS
21st August 1936   Cwmdonkin Drive   Uplands   Swansea

Dear Desmond,

I'm not dead or poxed—much—or paralysed or mute; just depressed as hell by this chronic, hellish lack of money; it's the most nagging depression, and is always with me; night and day in my little room high

1 *The Year's Poetry, 1936*, published 'A grief ago', 'From love's first fever' and 'Where once the waters of your face'.

above the traffic's boom I think of it,[1] of possessing it in great milky wads to spend on flashy clothes and cunt and gramophone records and white wine and doctors and white wine again and a very vague young Irish woman whom I love in a grand, real way but will have to lose because of money money money money.[2]

I was in London three weeks ago, over the bankholiday, behaving so normally that I'm still recovering; I knew it was useless trying to get hold of you in holiday time; I stayed out of the silly neighbourhood, in Chelsea with my Ireland. I may be coming back in September.

No, no titles, (though I like Sunset Over Nigeria, and you can use that if you like, or Necrophilia in Mumbles).[3]

Betty? Pfff. She gives *me* a pain in the appendix. (And is it only appendix?)[4]

Remember me to your baby. I'll write it a dirty poem when it's older.

Love, Dylan

MS: National Library of Wales

DESMOND HAWKINS
27th August 36   Cwmdonkin Drive   Uplands   Swansea

Dear Desmond,

Look, have you still got a copy of that story of mine about the looney-bin: Uncommon Genesis it was called, but I want to rename it just The Woman And The Mouse. I've lost my manuscript copy, and I must include the story in a collection I'm hoping to get published soon.[5] If you have, will you send it along as soon as you can? You shall have it back, for whatever curious purposes of your own, as soon as I've typed it out again.

I'm hoping to be in London for a few days next week: mainly to sit for a drawing for a frontispiece for a book for which I've been for half commissioned for. [sic][6] But it all depends on m

o
n
e
y,

money, [*a line is deleted*]

---

1 An echo of Cole Porter's 'Night and Day' (1932)—'In the roaring traffic's boom,/In the silence of my lonely room,/I think of you, night and day'.
2 Caitlin Macnamara.
3 Hawkins had asked for something better than first-line titles.
4 A West End shopgirl, briefly on the scene.
5 Published in the quarterly review *transition*, Fall 1936, as 'The Mouse and the Woman'.
6 See the letter to Church, page 254.

Could P. pay me a quid for those two poems *now*?

Soon I'll really have to make a horrid little law of my own that all poems by me, Rat Thomas, have to be paid for on acceptance, not on publication. [*a line is deleted*]. No, but cross my chest, for anybody's sake see if P. *will* pay me now. It's absolutely essential—if you like words like that—that I do get enough money by the beginning of next week to take me up to town and keep me there for 2 or 3 days. When this drawing is done, I'm sure my proposed book—Welsh Journey—will be immediately commissioned. I'm writing little belly-whine notes to all the few editors (including Corkpins himself) who owe me pennies for stuff of mine they've accepted but not yet printed. And unless these editors (including Corkpins) fork out, I shall have to cancel my visit, my drawing, and any prospects I may have of being given enough by a trusting publisher to undertake at once my Celtic Totter. So do have a shot to get me that quid, or whatever it is. If all the few editors will do their short share, I'll be able to buy a pretty ticket and come right up. Looking forward to almost seeing you.

Dylan

MS: National Library of Wales

OSWELL BLAKESTON
27th [?August 1936]   5 Cwmdonkin Drive   Uplands   Swansea

[*the head of the letter has four ragged circles, inscribed respectively*: 'original genuine rat print' '& this' '& this' '& this']

Hullo dear Oswell,

I *am* glad you've let me know you are back in London again and so much better. I didn't know where you'd been mousing, or I'd have inked a whisker and written to you, sniffed all my little sewer newses and included a cheese-eye view of my Swansea nest; I'd have told you how an awful lot of my family (all looking exactly like me, very dirty, broken-toothed, smelling of armpits and yesterday's poems and things) had taken a summer cruise to Tristan da Cunha; & how other members of the family (from the black branch) had invaded London, drunk all the inkpots dry in some East-End warehouse-offices, and lived for a long time on brown paper: this was reported in the Daily Telegraph last week, and I've pasted it in our album. And about our album: we get a lot of fan-mail; there was a letter from a Retired Lieutenant in the Daily Telegraph a few days ago, advising some agricultural correspondent not to get rid of all the Rats in his farm-fields as, as soon as the Rats have been stamped out, enter Adders in hundreds. So if you ever cast me out, you'll have a dreadful snake in my place, all puff and hiss.

Where have you been? And who's who now? I don't like your young men very much; I think you'll be able to write a naughty book and call it slime and punishment.

If I can, if money allows me, I want to come up to town next week; I must come up to see about a book, a Journey through Wales, I want to, and think I shall be, commissioned to write; and to have a frontispiece drawing of me done by old Augustus (type Moose) which will, shifty agents tell me, almost ensure that publishers will kiss my ears and drown me in milk and pounds. If you have a green-backed drop of milk you could, or would like to, spare me, I think I'd be able to rat my way about and claw up a little more and buy a ticket to London, and bite through the skirting-boards into the publisher's little room and frighten him into giving me a nice commission—which would mean drinks and taxis and ridiculous food for you and me and other needy animals. But if you can't and haven't, don't worry a bit. You aren't an inadequate mouse. You're the best mouse: rats are dirtier and uglier and live on the little balls of fluff and dust between their toes. *If* I can manage, by some means or another, to come up to town next week, shall we—one night—get helplessly drunk?

Love
Dylan

P.S. I've got nothing to send *you*:—only a little piece of cheddar left over from tea.

MS: Texas

JOHN HADFIELD (Publicity Dept, J. M. Dent)
1st September 1936   5 Cwmdonkin Drive   Uplands   Swansea

Dear Sir,
    I'm enclosing a fairly recent photograph of myself as you asked me to. Would you, I wonder, send it back to the address behind the photograph—when you've finished with it.

Yours faithfully
Dylan Thomas

MS: (J. M. Dent)

EDITH SITWELL
2nd September 1936   Cwmdonkin Drive   Uplands   Swansea

Dear Miss Sitwell,
    I know I couldn't have expected you to answer my letter of so many months ago. I was dreadfully rude, not turning up and everything, and I do understand about your not answering my silly letter of apology. But I hope

you aren't cross with me really, and I really do want you to believe that I regret—as much as anything in the world—not having continued the friendship I think we began. Will you meet me again, in spite of things? You're still a great encouragement to me—& always will be—& I do appreciate it.

Yours very sincerely,
Dylan Thomas

MS: National Library of Wales

GEOFFREY GRIGSON
[September 1936]

Dear G.

Thanks again for the books.

I can't send any new poems now, as Dent has brought out my book—which had unpublished ones I wanted you to see—unexpectedly.[1]

I liked the German poem. I'm trying to learn a little German myself. Here's something I made of it: I found it awfully hard, & had to paraphrase in bits. But all the meaning & the flatness and the metre & things are there.[2]

Love,
Dylan

MS: Texas

DESMOND HAWKINS
[September 1936]

Dear D,

Look: Dent has just brought out my book—unexpectedly. I didn't think it was coming out for weeks. It contains the two poems you've got to print in Purpose, I mean that you're going to print in Purpose. What does [a] careful editor do about things like that, do you know?

Love,
Dylan

MS: National Library of Wales

1 *Twenty-five Poems* was published on 10 September 1936. It was hardly unexpected.
2 The poem was by Wilhelm Busch, the 'German Edward Lear'. Thomas's translation, made from a literal crib supplied by Grigson, consisted of twelve couplets, beginning, 'The Elephant one sees afar/Goes for a walk in Africa.' On the back of it Grigson has scrawled 'DYLAN, MY GOD'.

CAITLIN MACNAMARA
Sunday [card, postmarked 19 October 1936]

Darling, thank you for your long lovely letter and the handkerchief which isn't a handkerchief at all but my very very favourite scarf which I wear all the time—and for the photograph. I like you when you climb,[1] but I'm awfully prejudiced, I like you when you do anything, (and that's quite separate from loving you altogether). This squiggle is only to tell you that I've almost finished a letter for you and a nice story, but that I won't be able to send them off until tomorrow: I have an ill father who's horribly fond of talking about death, so I sit and read to him. I love you, it's almost too wonderful (to me) to say; but I want to say it and I want to say it and I am saying it—: I love you; and we'll always keep each other alive. We can never do nothing at all now but that both of us know all about it. You can do anything & be anything, so long as it's with me. This, as you might gather Miss Macnamara, is from Dylan—& God, he must be with you soon XXXXXXXXXXXXXXXXXXXXXXXXXXXXXX

[*typed in the margin at right angles to the text are the words*: The Elephant. *Beside them is written*: This hasn't got anything to do with anything: it was typed on the card when I bought it. That's silly.]

MS: Texas

DESMOND HAWKINS
22nd October 1936   5 Cwmdonkin Drive   Uplands   Swansea

Dear Desmond,
    YOU PURPOSE PEAPOTS OWE ME A QUID FOR THOSE TWO POEMS. How are you? Try to remember to keep some lunch dates free for me when I come up to town in about a fortnight's time. I've got some new poems and some new jokes and some new diseases, I'm feeling fine.
    A WHOLE POUND YOU PEAPOTS. IN THE HUMAN INTEREST[2]—MY EYE. MONEY, TINKLY MONEY, FOR GOD'S SAKE.
    I'll let you know exactly when I come up more or less TINKLE
                                                        Dylan

(From Dylan Thomas, author of Two Poems in the September–December 1936 issue of Purpose, C. W. DANIEL & Co)

MS: National Library of Wales

1 One of Caitlin's sisters, Nicolette, had a photograph dated 1936 of Caitlin in a tree at Blashford.
2 W. Symons, editor and proprietor, wrote his editorial under this heading.

E. AND J. MUNRO[1]
10th November [?1936]

Are you coming along tomorrow night? I'm dim, but I hope so.

Dylan

MS: Location unknown

JULIAN SYMONS[2]
10.11.36 [postcard]   5 Cwmdonkin Drive   Uplands   Swansea

Thanks for writing; it's nice to hear that you're bringing out a magazine, and I'll be delighted to send you something. I haven't got a poem at the moment; I expect that I'll have one finished in a week or ten days; by the end of this month certainly. That's not too late, is it? I'll send it along as soon as possible.

Yours sincerely,
Dylan Thomas

MS: Texas

JULIAN SYMONS
16 11 36 [postcard]   Cwmdonkin Drive   Uplands   Swansea

Glad to hear the end of the month isn't too late for a poem; and very pleased you're going to review my book: I do hope you like it.[3] I've had the oddest set of reviews, and I've been called everything from a literary Marx Brother to a Roman Catholic.

I'd rather not review Auden; I'm not close enough to him, he's not sufficiently my cup of tea, for me to enjoy his new poems very much or to talk about them constructively (with a few exceptions, especially the prologue); and I know he's far, far too good for me of all people to attempt to be destructive. But thanks very much.

Best wishes,
Dylan Thomas

MS: Texas

1 Unidentified correspondents.
2 Julian Symons (1912–94), novelist and poet. The magazine was *Twentieth-Century Verse*, first published January 1937. Thomas contributed 'It is the sinners' dust-tongued bell'.
3 *Twenty-five Poems.*

CAITLIN MACNAMARA
[November or December 1936]

Nice, lovely, faraway Caitlin my darling,

Are you better, and please God you aren't too miserable in the horrible hospital?[1] Tell me everything, when you'll be out again, where you'll be at Christmas, and that you think of me and love me. And when you're in the world again, we'll both be useful if you like, trot round, do things, compromise with the They people, find a place with a bath and no bugs in Bloomsbury, and be happy there. It's that—the *thought* of the few, simple things we want and the *knowledge* that we're going to get them in spite of you know Who and His spites and tempers—that keeps us living I think. It keeps *me* living. I don't want you for a day (though I'd sell my toes to see you now my dear, only for a minute, to kiss you once, and make a funny face at you): a day is the length of a gnat's life: I want you for the lifetime of a big, mad animal, like an elephant. I've been indoors all this week, with a wicked cold, coughing and snivelling, too full of phlegm and aspirins to write to a girl in hospital, because my letter would be sad and despairing, & even the ink would carry sadness & influenza. Should I make you sad, darling, when you're in bed with rice pudding in Marlborough Ward? I want so very much to look at you again; I love you; you're weeks older now; is your hair grey? have you put your hair up, and do you look like a real adult person, not at all anymore beautiful and barmy like the proper daughters of God? You mustn't look too grown-up, because you'd look older than me; and you'll never, I'll never let you, grow wise, and I'll never, you shall never let me, grow wise, and we'll always be young and unwise together. There is, I suppose, in the eyes of the They, a sort of sweet madness about you and me, a sort of mad bewilderment and astonishment oblivious to the Nasties and the Meanies; you're the only person, of course you're the only person from here to Aldebaran and back, with whom I'm free entirely; and I think it's because you're as innocent as me. Oh I know we're not saints or virgins or lunatics; we know all the lust and lavatory jokes, and most of the dirty people; we can catch buses and count our change and cross the roads and talk real sentences. But our innocence goes awfully deep, and our discreditable secret is that we don't know anything at all, and our horrid *inner* secret is that we don't care that we don't. I've just read an Irish book called Rory and Bran, and it's a bad charming book: innocent Rory falls in love with innocent Oriana, and, though they're both whimsy and talk about the secret of the language of the hills and though Rory worships the moon and Oriana glides about in her garden listening to the legendary birds, they're not as mad as we are, nor as innocent. I love you so much I'll never be able to tell you; I'm frightened to tell you. I can always feel your heart. Dance tunes are always right: I love you body and soul:—and I

---

1 Caitlin, reminiscing in old age, said she had caught gonorrhoea from a man at a party. Conceivably she was suffering the after-effects of an abortion, which would explain Dylan's remark at the end, 'You're not empty, empty still now, are you?'

suppose body means that I want to touch you & be in bed with you, & I suppose soul means that I can hear you & see you & love you in every single, single thing in the whole world asleep or awake.

Dylan X

I wanted this to be a letter full of news, but there isn't any yet. It's just a letter full of what I think about you and me. You're not empty, empty still now, are you? Have you got love to send me?[1]

MS: Maurice Neville

GLYN JONES
[December 1936]   5 Cwmdonkin Drive   Uplands   Swansea

Dear Glyn,

I was very glad to hear from you; it's been such a long time; and, though I knew more-or-less that a letter to your school address would still find you, I was for some reason really dubious about writing: you seemed to have vanished so successfully into Cardiff and marriage that I wondered whether you were cross with me in some vague way about a vaguer something or other that I may have said or done. I'm awfully pleased to know it's nothing like that; I think we both must have been just careless. How are you? I see you quite a lot in the Adelphi, but have you given up Grigson's paper and the rest? I hadn't heard about the book of stories: that's grand. What's it going to be called? I believe I've met Hamish Miles once. (bald?)

And about the review:[2] of course I didn't think it was unfair; it's about the best I've seen of the book, and it helped me a lot; it really *was* constructive; I never knew, for instance, that I was such a numerical demon. And I agree with what you said about some of the poems being 'tidy enough' but so weak in contrast with some of the earlier bits of explosive bombast; that's true, and perhaps I was silly in allowing those 'tidy' poems to appear more as a concession to obscurity-decriers than anything else. You're the only reviewer, I think, who *has* commented on my attempts to get away from those rhythmic and thematic dead ends, that physical blank wall, those wombs, and full-stop worms, by all sorts of methods—so many unsuccessful. But I'm not sorry that, in that Work in Progress thing,[3] I did carry 'certain features to their logical conclusion'. It had, I think, to be done; the result had to be, in many of the lines & verses anyway, mad parody; and I'm glad that *I* parodied those features so soon after making them, & that I didn't leave it to anyone else.

But, personally, I'm sorry you didn't mention the one particular poem in the book—'Then Was My Neophyte'—which I consider the best. Nobody's

1 Caitlin, uncertain about her future, went to Ireland, where she spent several months working as a barmaid and writing poetry at her father's hotel in Ennistymon, Co Clare.
2 In the *Adelphi*, December 1936.
3 The 'Altarwise by owl-light' group.

mentioned it; perhaps it's bad; I only know that, to me, it is clearer and more definite, & that it holds more possibilities of progress, than anything else I've done. But thanks a great, great deal for your review. I'm afraid I shan't be in London on the 12th; I've been home here for nearly two months, & shan't be returning until the middle of next week. *If* you're still up, my address will be 27 St. Peter's Square, Hammersmith, W.6. I don't know the telephone number but you can get it from Directory Enquiry; it's Cameron's flat, but, as he's just moved in, I don't suppose his name will be in the book. And anyway, if you *won't* be up then, could you come down & see me for the day in the New Year? I'll be home most of January. Or could I come up & see you? I'm looking forward to either—very much.

Yours,
Dylan

MS: Carbondale

T. A. SINCLAIR
20th January 1937   Cwmdonkin Drive   Uplands   Swansea

Dear Sir,
    Thank you so much for asking J. M. Dent whether the line 'Once in this *wind*' was not a misprint for 'once in this *wine*'.[1] Of course it is, though no-one at all, including myself, spotted it. I'm letting Dent's know at once. Thanks again. I *do* appreciate the fact that someone has read my poems so carefully.

Yours sincerely,
Dylan Thomas

I apologise for the delay in answering you: I've been away, and most of my letters were unavoidably not forwarded to me.

MS: Texas

*EMILY HOLMES COLEMAN

American novelist and poet, 1899–1974. Her best-known fiction, *The Shutter of Snow* (1930), draws on her experience of madness following the birth of her child in 1924. After living in Paris, where she contributed to *transition*, she was in London in the 1930s.[2]

28 & 29 January, 1937   Cwmdonkin Drive   Uplands   Swansea

darling Emily dear, dear Emily darling, Emily Emily dear Emily,
    I think of you so much. I think of us, and all the funny, nice things we've

1 In 'This bread I break'.
2 The envelope is addressed to 'Mrs Emily Holmes Coleman   7 Oakley Street   Chelsea London, S.W.3.' On the flap of the envelope is: '*PS* Say hello, for me, to Bob, & John Somerfield. *PSS* This is a very bad letter: a better one'.

done, and all the nicer things we're going to do. I think of nice places and people, and, when I think of them, you're always there, always tall and death-mouthed and big-eyed and no-voiced, with a collegiate ribbon or a phallic hat. I think of us in pubs and clubs and cinemas and beds. I think I love you.

What little beast told you I didn't leave on the Taffy train that night? I left, my God I left, and the train took seven hours instead of four, stopping at every single station while the guard told dirty stories to the station-master and naked porters danced among the milk-churns and the ticket-collector abused himself over his punching-machine and the driver buggered the fireman on the footplate. I didn't look out of the window, but I knew what was happening: I had psychic claustrophobia, and could tell by each reverberation and roar of the rails exactly what position the fireman was in. The train smelt of lust and armpits and lava-bread.[1] I was home at half-past-eight in the morning, very weak, very vague, and I slept for two days. I grew very friendly, by the way, with the drunken man we found asleep: his name was Duck, he was fifty two years old, he had a son my age who was a commercial traveller, he himself was a coal-exporter and he said he had met Greta Garbo in Tunbridge Wells. I think he was a liar, but he was a nice man too and he invited me to stay with his family any time I liked. I'm not going to, though: I may see Wallace Beery in Gloucester. Mr Duck was a life-long subscriber to the Film Weekly, the Picturegoer, Film Fun, The Cinema Weekly, and the Film Gazette. He liked films.

What are you doing? Have you retired to your kitten and temple? I'm in my bowlerland again, hemmed in by vicars, but it's only to-day, just over a week since I left you, dear, that I've started to work. After two days' sleep I was like a little bull, a little spotty bull, and I endured without alcohol. Brainlessly, I cut out drink, and only my sane mother saved my sanity, driving me out to the pubs with a stern but sad demand to drink myself steady. Now I am fit again, though scabious, and my three pints a night—from nine-o'-clock until ten—are a legitimate heaven. This morning I started on a story that I dreamed about a blind horse[2] and a wooden woman, and this evening, like a fallen cherub at my window facing the park, I'm writing to you, to Emily, to my darling, inaudible, scabious, American Emily. I love you.

Don't worry your head about Norman's[3] venereal warning; he's timid and jealous. Shall I give you a lecture on Norman? Norman is good, but too much of him is made personally interesting and interestingly eccentric

1 Laverbread, an alleged Welsh delicacy. It consists of the fronds of a seaweed, *Porphyra umbilicalis*, boiled and then fried.
2 The image of a blinded horse begins the Thomas poem 'Because the pleasure-bird whistles', first published 1939. Vernon Watkins said that it came from a dream of Thomas's, in which a horse stood in a cage of wires that became red-hot. A bystander said, 'He sings better now.'
3 Norman Cameron again.

through financial invulnerability. His brusqueness and rudeness, even his intolerance of shams, wouldn't be half so effective—wouldn't, perhaps, be at all—if he weren't entirely immune from the attacks of money and the lack of it. He is able to maintain his literary honesty through the dishonesty of property, his social honesty through (to me) the unsociability of a private income. He will never have a real friend until he realises that; real friendship is built up on mutual need—need for everything, pooled love, pooled possessions, pooled lack of possessions, pooled contacts, pooled miseries—while all that Norman needs from a friend is friendship, and friendship, to him, is only acquaintanceship that has gone on for sufficiently long. He has so many friends because he can turn easily from one to another, asking little from each but companionship. He has never *tried* a friend's friendship to the full, is ignorant of the extent to which real friendship *can* be tried; and, therefore, when his own friendship is tried, it fails. It fails through his lack of experience: he can open his heart to let lots of people in, but he can't open it out altogether for one person: he covers his heart with half-friends to conceal its nakedness from the advances of a whole friend: he doesn't understand that a real friend is always naked, that a real friend doesn't have to undress but that he just has no clothes to wear in front of him. Norman understands nothing of the reasons that bind people together; from a man, 'Love thy neighbour' is, to him, homosexual; he can't understand that people are bound together because of what they *give out* to each other, not because of what they offer to each other:—(and a companion is always offering, offering anecdotes, intimacies, hospitalities, while a friend is giving out all the real, warm things that lie so very deep underneath all those material offerings). And he can't understand—just because he has, inside himself, had no experience of it—that, though a single little match can set the world on fire, altering its appearance, the things that made up that world, all the causes and forces and bases of the world, can never alter. I mean he understands people so little that, when their *appearances* alter under altering circumstances, he is confronted by them as by strangers. He looks for a rigid conformity in the hearts of his friends; even if he found it he would not know it, for he doesn't understand that the only conformity is that of Affection, that the heart moves but does not alter, that even when the heart has moved a universe away from him it remains, in what it originally *gave out*, unalterable for ever. A wind from anywhere can blow anything about willy-nilly, but any shape that anything once had is static; you can pull the moon down, but the moon always remains in exactly the same shape and position as when you saw it clearly for the first time. This is all frightfully clumsy, but it's true. It's something that old Norman must learn through himself; otherwise, he will suffer and die through an ingrowing heart.

What funny people we know. Antonia[1] too. I've been thinking about her. I think Antonia will never recover from once having been mad. She

---

1 Antonia White (1899–1980), novelist. Her autobiographical *Frost in May* was published in 1933. Like Holmes Coleman, she had been mentally ill and institutionalised.

was a tame cat in a cage who always, much against her waking will, was dreaming of liberty; and then, one waking day, obsessed by those dreams, she escaped into liberty, a liberty that for her—necessarily because of her long, tame imprisonment—was far more terrifying than the safety behind the suburban-zoo bars. So at last she crawled back to the zoo, through a million strange and frightening places full of human wild animals, and now she is done for, done for ever perhaps. She wants to be tame again, but she's been let loose once. Now tame companions are no good for her, and wild companions frighten her; the only companions she feels comfortable with now are those, like herself, who have been brought up tame and dream of a wild liberty, but those, at the same time, who have never got beyond dreaming of it and who therefore have few of her own fears. Mr Gascoyne, conscientiously pursuing his Richmond sanity right to the gates of the insane institutions, has always been too careful to try to unlock the gates: a poetical surrealist in a looney-bin is a literary freak, but a surrealist who hangs around outside, pimping through the bars at the looney-logical activities of the inmates, can always be a man-of-letters and an acknowledged authority on the dark bits of the brain. So Antonia is comfortable with him, because he is a tame animal striving very hard to enjoy his zealously cultivated half-liberty; she, poor dear, was a tame animal forced through dreams into an unwelcome liberty, and is now a wild animal wanting so very very hard to enjoy the lack of liberty which she welcomed. That's all clumsy too, and it's true too I think. I don't know Peggy at all, otherwise I'd give a speech about *her*. And Phyllis doesn't seem to me to be complicated at all: she's just a good guy.

I don't really know about Caitlin. I don't know how tough my Caitlin is, how powerful her vagueness is, whether the sweet oblivion in which she moves about is proof against the little tiny hurts that can eat through a mountain while the big hurts just batter against it. I know she hasn't got much feeling about *physical* pain: she once wanted to boil a lobster but hadn't got a saucepan big enough, so she found a small saucepan and boiled the thing bit by bit while it screamed like a frog or a baby and drove us howling out.[1] I know she's done away with most of the natural sense of surprise; nothing, I think, can shock her except squeamishness; and she can blush like a naked schoolgirl too. Of course I shall sleep with her; she's bound up with me, just as you are; one day I shall marry her very much—(no money, quite drunk, no future, no faithfulness)—and that'll be a funny thing.

I've been writing most of this—this probably too moral nonsense—in my aunts' house in Carmarthen,[2] where I often stay, and I came back this Thursday morning to find your little telegram letter waiting. I know, my dear dear, that I should have written before, but time, since London, has been such a humourless muddle of headaching days and lonely heartaching

---

1 In *Double Drink Story*, published posthumously (1997), Caitlin wrote of her delight at throwing a live flat-fish into a hot frying pan and eating it half raw: a victim devoured.
2 Probably the cottages at Blaen Cwm, Llangain, outside Carmarthen.

nights packed to the skull and ceiling with great, blind, fleshlike, over-familiar dreams that fight and destroy themselves in the dark; there doesn't seem to have been any regular succession of hours, and half-past-nine has followed midnight, and almost the moon has risen at midday. And I didn't want to write, either, until my brain was cool; I wanted a true, honest letter, not the hysterical hangover I should certainly have suffered on paper had I written before this. My hands still shake, but I know my head now: and my head says 'Hullo, Emily', and inquires after your health, and hopes you aren't too unhappy, and tells you I love you. I know my heart too, but that's dumb as a red egg and is silent even when it breaks (I'm told).

FRIDAY I'm finishing this on the floor of my bedroom in front of a gasfire on which water is boiling to make me some nourishing tea. It's been snowing all night and is still snowing: my very special field is quiet and padded, it looks like white rubber: I didn't know before that snow had such a rubbery kick: my field's a springboard, and the barmy birds who are searching for snow-worms are shot up and down in the air like ping-pong balls on a fountain. It's half past ten in the morning: are you asleep? I wish I was fast asleep by your side, very warm, dreaming about the milk-white birds of Eden and the blue goats of Gehenna; and I wish, (at this moment in time that will never never be again until time stops and then works backwards from Resurrection to Genesis, the last Trumpet note to the first Word, from the darkness of Judgement to Light), that I was waking up by your side, turning round slowly to see your face in the first of the shining, snowy morning. I wish I was with you. Never care what people say, my darling: Peggy's 'He won't write', & Antonia's 'He doesn't love you' and Norman's 'Beware, beware!' I shall always write to you, and always love you, & never hurt you purposely: never hurt you at all, you're a very rare and expensive animal, and Christ knows I'm a lucky little man to love you & have you loving me. I'd write lots more, but my fingers are decomposing, and I must keep enough strength to shudder my way outside and give bread to the starlings. Will you write me a letter very soon, please? Tell me everything you want to tell me; tell me what you're doing and what you're thinking; tell me about boozy Bob and stallion D'arcy and red leg-opening Phyllis, and tidy Tony, and that intolerable pouf your cat. Tell me tell me tell me tell me . . .

And don't be cross that I've been so long writing.

Dylan

I'm coming back to town, only for a few days, about *February 14*, before going to Oxford to lecture; then I'm going home & coming up again about *March 4*, for a few days, before going to Cambridge to lecture.[1] Shall I see you then? Let's do everything in the world—(though I know what we'll do, of course: just go to pubs and bed. And what could be lovelier, anyway? I'm always happy with you.)

1 Thomas gave Coleman different details in his letter of (probably) 11 February.

Give my love to anybody you see. But keep most of it. (And don't give any to James Travers: it would be mental necrophily).

[*At the foot of the letter is a drawing of a ship with* SS Emily *on the side, perhaps sinking. Alongside it is a small figure in a rowing boat. Underneath Thomas has written* The Welsh Sea]

MS: *Delaware*

DAVID HIGHAM
9th February [1937]   5 Cwmdonkin Drive   Uplands   Swansea

Dear Higham,
    I do, really and deeply, apologise for my rudeness in not replying to your last letters. I've been ill, off and on, but not ill enough, I admit, to excuse my rudeness. I think the real reason why I haven't answered you before is that I felt—and still feel—ashamed, ashamed, that is, about all this nonsensically careless business of my book of short stories. It's quite true what you heard: that Spenser Curtis Brown had my stories, sent them to Church (who, incidentally, was forced to refuse them), and has now given them to Frank Morley.[1] It came about in—my fault, of course—a vague and weak way: Curtis Brown wrote to me quite a time ago, enquiring about my stories and asking me to send them to him. I sent them, more or less without thinking, though obviously I should have—and should greatly have preferred to—let you have them once they were ready. My capacity for even the simplest business undertaking is negligible; it sounds as though I'm trying to plead the notorious vagueness of the Dreamy Poet Type B classified by Punch, but really I'm a complete nitwit when it comes to replying to people, organising anything, making any sort of deal, keeping my tiny affairs in order, and even, in this shame-making case, just sending to *one* agent the very little, and very uncommercial, work I do. None of that vagueness is a respectable excuse, I know; but my new resolutions are for Punctuality and Order, and I *will* keep them.
    As for this project that I should do a book about Wales:—I am very keen about it, and feel pretty sure that I could make a good job of it too. What I wanted to do was a Welsh Journey, from the top of the agricultural North to the Rhondda Valley, a Journey suggested by Priestley's and Muir's though, of course, owing nothing to their method of approach, being far more personal and intimate: not a series of generalisations about Wales, or a survey of its position today, or a Nationalist tirade, or a naturalists' rambling-tour, or an historical textbook about harps and castles, but an intimate chronicle of my personal Journey among people and places. I should want to do the Journey alone, some times on foot, sometimes by

1 A director of Faber.

bus or train, having a more-or-less definite route but being at liberty any time to interrupt it when any especially interesting incident, or people, or place, appeared. That is, I should map out for myself a set number of towns or villages on the Journey from North to South, which I'd regard as my brief headquarters; what route I would take between those headquarters would be decided by what incidents arose, what people told me stories, what pleasant or unpleasant or curious things etcetera I encountered in the little-known villages among the lesser-known people. This is all very vague, and is meant to be. I purposely do not want a too-definite or binding plan to be put before a publisher; I want the Journey to be individual and informal; neither quite a picaresque travel book nor a personal journey, but a mixture of both; and certainly not a Journey that blusters about the Open Road. It's difficult to explain, but somehow I feel certain it can have a commercial interest for publishers. (Augustus John will do a frontispiece for it—a portrait of me—and, if I can make him, some drawings. But the frontispiece is certain. I know lots of newspaper people in Wales, too, and can get as many photographs as are needed.) What I had in mind was that I should be paid expenses, preferably weekly, for the length of time the journey takes—expenses enough to pay my travel and accommodation bills (£5?)—which should be anything from two to three months. I realise that even a publisher favourably inclined might hedge a bit at undertaking to dole out expenses like this on a project which I am able to describe only so vaguely; and it occurred to me that perhaps he would pay my expenses for, say, *one* month, give me time to write up fully the chronicle of that one month's Journey, and then read it and see whether it's good enough to warrant him going on paying expenses for the rest of the time needed to complete the book. (I don't know whether I'm making myself clear; I know I'm writing very clumsily today.) Naturally I'd rather that some nice publisher would guarantee to pay expenses for the whole 2 to 3 months; but I know absolutely nothing about how far publishers allow themselves to go on a thing like this. I could, if necessary, draft out a rough map of the route I'd like to take. I intended calling on—and, in some cases, staying with a number of Welsh and anglo-Welsh writers and painters who live in Wales—Richard Hughes and Caradoc Evans for instance—and of getting some Welsh sketches from Cedric Morris, the painter.[1] I can't think of anything else at the moment.

I shall be in town next week for some days. Perhaps, if we met, I might be able to explain this Welsh project a little more clearly; at least I can try. Do let me know whether you'll be able to see me then, any time during the week, and whether this Journey business is, as I ignorantly believe it to be, of some practical value.

And, before I forget, Simon and Schuster of New York say they are interested in my work. Do you think it advisable to get in touch with them about 25 Poems?

1 Cedric Morris (1889–1982), of Swansea, came from the family of industrialists that gave its name to the district of Morriston. He travelled widely but did much of his painting in Wales.

Sincere apologies again for my rudeness and carelessness.

Yours sincerely,
Dylan Thomas

MS: Texas

DAVID HIGHAM

11 2 37   5 Cwmdonkin Drive   Uplands   Swansea

Dear Higham,

Thank you for taking my long delayed letter so nicely. I'm coming up to London tomorrow, but will be there only a few hours before going on to Cambridge; I'm returning to London on Wednesday: could we meet sometime in the morning? I'll ring you up anyway on that morning, and find out. I wish it would be possible for us to meet somewhere outside; I get more terrified of offices every day. But, again, I'll find out when I ring you. And I do hope there'll be something a bit definite about the Welsh book.

Yours,
Dylan Thomas

MS: Texas

*UNKNOWN RECIPIENT

[?1937]
Fraser's Bookshop 12.a.m.

Dear Peter,

So sorry about not calling this morning to do a Richards with you. I've got the filthiest feeling in the head, & I had another Prairie Oyster made with H.P. sauce & it made me feel worse. I really can't face anything, and I shall be sitting in the Baron pub. Do come along if you can.

Love,
Dylan

MS: Robert Williams

*KEIDRYCH RHYS

[?February 1937]   [?Swansea]

[*The first sheet is missing. The manuscript, written on both sides of a single sheet, is headed '2'.*]

committee etcetera. But you let me know what you think about it.

When do you intend bringing the first number out? I can let you have a little pile of stories & poems, my own & other people's, whenever you like. But it would first of all be best, I think, to establish, quite firmly, the intentions of the magazine: is it 'advanced'? is [it] to contain, if possible, the work of older and more certainly 'arrived' writers? Is there to be a definite line drawn between the traditional & the experimental? And, too: what size is [it] to be, that is *how many* stories & poems, & of what length etcetera, *can* it contain? At what intervals will it be produced? Are contributors to be paid? Are there advertisements? Is it possible to reproduce drawings? (I know most of the Welsh artists, in & out of Wales. I might, some time, be able to get John[1] to do something: he has promised me some drawings for a thing of my own.) Or will that be too expensive? These, again, are simple questions, but they may as well be settled at once. I know that those details are, really, nothing to do with me; but I should like to know about them all the same: they give the phantom magazine some commercial actuality.

You say, in your letter, that you're looking to me for a lead. I find it difficult to suggest anything without first of all knowing what ideas you have already formed. But this I *can* put forward even now, as my own opinion (& an opinion, obviously, that is quite open to correction or argument): I think the magazine should be entirely restricted to creative work; I think this work should be, nearly all of it, of young men, though occasionally, whenever possible, the introduction of some established writer (like Davies) would be valuable; I think that, with the exception of these few Davies, the contents should be, in the best sense, 'contemporary', new and alive and original; I do not think it should be stridently Welsh in tone or approach—that is that Welsh politics, for example, should not enter into it; I think that Keidrych Rhys should be Editor, and should appear on the title page as sole Editor, and that Dylan Thomas should be some variety of a literary advisor, going through all the mss with Mr. Rhys; I think that the title should be simple & direct, like say 'Welsh Writers';[2] I think that a notice should be drawn up as soon as possible, & circulated among all likely people, certainly among all Welsh Universities; I think each number should be fairly large. And that's about all, for the moment, that I *do* think about it; apart, of course, from thinking it a really grand idea, & hoping to the Welsh Lord that it is not going to be still-born.

Forgive this barrage of questions, & the rather didactic tone I've taken. Write & let me know things as soon as you can, won't you? And don't forget to see if, if possible, you can lend me a tiny piece of money which I shall give you back at the end of the month when I am returning to London to lecture. Best of luck, anyway, for yourself & the magazine.

Yrs, Dylan T.

MS: National Library of Wales

1 Augustus John.
2 Rhys called it *Wales*.

*EMILY HOLMES COLEMAN
Thursday [?11 February 1937]   Swansea

Emily darling,
    It's good that you write to me: I like your letters like whiskey and
cherries and smoke and honey, and always I understand at least half of the
handwriting. Now this is just a very short note to tell you things; I'm up to
my eyes in lecturese, and anyway all the things I could want to write to
you I'll be telling you soon. I have to give two lectures to the Cambridge
something-or-other on Saturday & Sunday (13th, I think, and 14th), and in
order to arrive there with a clear tongue I shan't stop in London before; I'll
go to Cambridge straight from here, and then return some time on
Monday.[1] I'll ring you immediately. We'll have a million celebration
drinks, and cover the English night with a Welsh American glory. And yes:
I got rid of my spots for 2 days, then they returned to me, crying out Daddy.
So I'll have to start all over again, (with you), though my hands are like
lilies now. Monday then. I've missed you terribly.
                                                                        XX
                                                                        Dylan

MS: Delaware

*KEIDRYCH RHYS
26th [March 1937]   'Marston' Bishopston near Swansea

Dear Keidrych,
    Sorry about delay. My family has just moved to this new address,[2]
which meant an awful lot of bother, and my mother has been, & is,
seriously ill.
    I'm going away—on that Welsh Journey business I've told you about—on
April 3rd. Would it be possible for you to come to Swansea before that—I
could meet you in a pub any morning, afternoon, or evening you like. If you
can't manage it, do drop me a line about it, & I'll send you on the
contributions I've got together & what few practical suggestions I have to
offer. But it would be best, wouldn't it, if we could meet?
                                                                        Yours,
                                                                        Dylan

MS: National Library of Wales

---

1 According to J. C. Wyn Lewis, quoted by Gwen Watkins in *Portrait of a Friend*,
  Thomas was in Cambridge on 12 February 1937 to address the Literary Society at St
  John's College, and spent several days in the town.
2 D. J. Thomas had retired. Bishopston is a village a few miles west of Swansea, by a
  valley running down to the sea.

*EMILY HOLMES COLEMAN
Easter Monday [29 March 1937]   'Marston' Bishopston Glamorgan

Emily darling,

We've moved to a small house—lawn, miniature drive, garage and mortgage—in the country by the sea, five minutes' walk from the cliffs of Pwllddu and Brandy Cove; and the weather's blue and soft, with a fine chill wind to make edges; and old men plough up and down among the cabbages behind the house, and seagulls complain to the scarecrows, and sheep and cows and trippers leave manure and sandwiches regularly in the foreground of our well-mown view; and I can stretch my legs to the Joiners' Arms, and do a lyric straddling on a stile, and hear in the near distance the voices of the Valley girls cry rape and resignation. I would have written to you sooner had not my mother been so seriously ill; she still is ill, with acute neuralgia in the roots of the nerves of her face, is weak as a moth, can't move at all in bed, and worries the daylight out of the window. I loved your wire and letter; remember me very much to Phyllis Jones: has she met the map of Ireland yet? she deserves the nicest man in London, all for herself; and would he appreciate that lovely, lean favourite? I have made some new old friends; I am, if you read Dickens, Dylan Veneering.[1] The only democratic conception of human equality is that all men are tragic and comic: we die; we have noses. We are not united by our drabness and smallness, but by our heroisms; the common things are wonderful; the drab things are those that are not common. And I am inequal to a woman (for an unnecessary example) only in the sense that I am not so womanly. It's only among poor failures that I find the people I like best: the rich can, as a generalisation, achieve originality only by becoming a little insane. Cyril Connolly[2] (an example chosen for no reason I can think of) is small because he has continually to be *proving*; the great character is his own proof of everything: he is not successful, because he is too busy: the glory of the world is narrow: he is too big for it. And it's the grossness of folly I love. (I love you too, but that's a happening, not, I think, a basis for events as is my love for Mr Fork, the crippled woodwork master, Mr Plane, the darting waiter, Mr Dish, the drunken clerk, the ham actor, the faded beauty, the assistant assistant film-producer.) It's a Welsh bank-holiday, a very social day, and soon I shall join the cold picnic-parties on the cliffs, drink beer in the 'bus-depôt, find a tripper's knicker in the gully, be a pocket Chesterton on the rolling, inn-roads.[3] Of all days I like these crowded days the best; I'm sitting at the window, not to miss a motor or a tandem or a hiking shop-assistant, not to miss one shout or back-fire, one squabbling little boy, one lanky schoolgirl full of candles and tomorrow, one yesterday's market-gardener remembering the Easter fairs at Neath and Oystermouth

---

1 The Veneerings, in Dickens's *Our Mutual Friend*, are social upstarts.
2 Cyril Connolly (1903–74), critic and editor, notably of the magazine *Horizon*, 1939–50.
3 'The Rolling English Road' is a poem by G. K. Chesterton.

before the great West died.[1] And on Thursday I'm going to North Wales with a haversack and a flapped cap.

My only news is nonsense. If you can get to a wireless, try to listen to the Western Region on the twenty first of April: I'm reading some poems: Auden's Ballad, John Short's Carol, one of my own. Caitlin has knitted me a sweater out of raw brown sheeps' wool, and I look like a London shepherd in 1890. Fred Janes is painting the portrait of a lump of paper. My story about the burning of the sea is smouldering on: 'There was a sore procession driven down the waters of the Bristol Channel, loud-toothed and tailed, with a sharp trumpet full of fishes and an emerald, soaked drum, towards the high cliff on which she stood that afternoon before the misadventures that befell the sea and country, the first catastrophe, the blinding of the horse and the self-destruction of the dead, the flight of the woodpeckers and the burning of all the navigable world'. There's hardly anything to say; I miss you deeply, and want to come back to London soon; I remember everything, and it's all good to remember. You are very, very near to me.

Now I'm going out to make or break my social links with the bright, chapped Easter world.

Love to you my dear, now & always,

Dylan

I'll write a longer letter on my daft Journey, full of facts and dreams and lectures and little drawings.

MS: Delaware

GEORGE BARKER[2]
4th April [?1937]   Marston   Bishopston   Glamorgan

Dear Barker,

It was nice to get your letter. For some reason we never seem to have met—I saw you in Archer's once, and at a boozy party—but I hope we'll be able to when we're both in London. I hardly know any verse-writers at all; I know the one who looks as if he'd had an unfortunate sexual experience under the sea; and the one with little red pig eyes and a private income; and Norman Cameron and Desmond Hawkins of whom I'm very fond. But all my friends are failures, I think the glories of the world are mingy, and the people I know and like best—hack Fleet streeters, assistant assistant film-producers, professional drunks, strays and outlaws, who are always, & always will be, just about to write their autobiographies—are too big to

---

1 In his story 'Prologue to an Adventure', soon to be published in *Wales*, Thomas uses the phrase, 'that winter night before the West died'.
2 George Barker, 1913–91, poet.

want them or to get them. I'm only saying this, in a first letter to you, because I liked very much the idea of an exchange of verse epistles between us, and I think it would be amusing to begin by talking about ourselves and our friends. Who'll start? I wish *you* would: an epistle about where you live, what you do, all the why's, objects & near people. And what about the form? Wouldn't it, don't you think, be best for us both to use the same form, blank verse or some variety of stanza? I can see a lot of good, pleasant things coming out of this. We might publish them? Anyway, do write & tell me things, tell me whether *you'll* start the exchange. I go away walking tomorrow, but your letter will be forwarded from this address. And I'll be in town in June.

Best wishes,
Dylan Thomas

MS: Texas

*EMILY HOLMES COLEMAN
[telegram, 6 April 1937, 7.31 pm, Machynlleth][1]

LETTER ARRIVING I'M IN GODS KNOWS WHERE ON ADJECTIVAL JOURNEY ALL LOVE DYLAN

Original: Delaware

CAITLIN MACNAMARA
Wednesday [early May 1937]   59 Gt. Ormond St W1 (HOL7701)[2]

Caitlin Caitlin my love I love you, I can't tell you how much, I miss you until it hurts me terribly. Can you come up to London before I go to Wales again, because I think I shall have to be in Wales a long time, a couple of months almost; I've been in a nursing home with bronchitis and laryngitis or something, no voice at all, no will, all weakness and croaking and spitting and feeling hot and then feeling cold, and I'm about now but quavery and convalescent and I must see you. I haven't seen or written to

---

1 A small town on the north-west coast of Wales. Caitlin, who was returning from Ireland via Holyhead at about this time, after being away for several months, may have been Thomas's real reason for being in north Wales.
2 This was the Sibthorp address; Thomas remained friendly with Veronica, the woman he had met in Cornwall, and in later years she let it be known that he had wanted to marry *her*. Caitlin had returned from Ireland after Easter, and the love affair with Dylan was under way again by 13 April, when David Gascoyne saw them together in London. He wrote in his journal, 'Yesterday or the day before, [Dylan] confronted [Emily Coleman] with Caitlin M., whom he announced his intention of marrying almost at once.'

you or let you know I'm alive—which, at the moment, and remembering neurasthenically my days of almost-death, I don't think I was—since Wednesday, the 21st of April, when I lost you in the morning, found money, and shouted on the wireless.[1] Darling, you mustn't have been angry with me for not writing my love, my love which can't ever move but is growing always; you must not have disbelieved, for one little split hair of the day or night, that day and night I think of you, love you, remember everything all the time, and know forever that we'll be together again—& Christ knows where—because it must be like that. But I don't want to write words words words to you: I must see you and hear you; it's hell writing to you now: it's lifting you up, (though I'm sure I'm not strong enough), and thinking you are really my flesh-&-blood Caitlin whom I love more than anyone has loved anyone else, & then finding a wooden Caitlin like a doll or a long thin Caitlin like a fountain pen or a mummy Caitlin made before the bible, very old and blowable-away. I want you. When you're away from me, it's absolutely a physical removal, insupportable & irreparable: no, not irreparable: if I lost a hand when you weren't with me, when you came back it would grow again, stronger & longer than ever. That's my cock words again, though all it means is true as heaven: that it's nonsense me living without you, you without me: the world is unbalanced unless, in the very centre of it, we little muts stand together all the time in a hairy, golden, more-or-less unintelligible haze of daftness. And that's more words, but I love and love you. Only love, and true love. Caitlin Caitlin this is unbearable. Will you forgive me again—for being ill and too willy-minded & weak and full of useless (no God, not useless) love for you, love that couldn't bear writing even if it could, to write & say, I'm dying perhaps, come & see me quickly, now, with some gooseberries and kisses for me. I'm not dying now, much. If you're where I'm writing to—please everything you are—can you telephone here? And come up? & be with me somewhere, if only for an only I don't know how long? Please, Caitlin my dear.

XXXXXX
Caitlin

Dylan X Caitlin

Dylan

I have to be abstemious.

MS: Maurice Neville

1 Thomas was booked to make his first radio broadcast, from the BBC studios in Swansea, reading poems and discussing 'Life and the Modern Poet'. At the last minute he asked to do it from London instead, then vanished from the studio without leaving a script for their files: 'a very serious matter', the BBC kept telling him.

D. J. AND FLORENCE THOMAS (his parents)
June 10 [1937]   c/o J W Sibthorp Mousehole Cornwall

Important Letter

Dear Mother & Dad,

There's no doubt whatever that I've been a careless, callous, and quite unreasonable person as regards letting you know about myself since I left you at the beginning of April, and, as usual, I've no excuse, and you know me well enough to realise that if I did genuinely have one I wouldn't be long in explaining and elaborating it. Since I last wrote, and that was much too long ago, I've been working hard, but not too productively, have secured a little, but not extravagantly much, money on advance for the Welsh masterpiece, and have—I'm not sure how much of a shock this might be to you—during the last three days moved on to Cornwall for a little—I can't actually call it a holiday—change of sorts and of weather and of companions. I intend, things which I want to explain permitting, to stay here until the end of June, and then return home for a while—to see mother and you—before continuing the rest of this daft & postponed journey of mine. I'm staying here with Caitlin Macnamara (whose writing on the envelope mother'll probably recognise) in a cottage lent to me by a man called Sibthorp; the address isn't really Mousehole, but, as the postal system here is so bad, I've been told that a Mousehole address is far easier & quicker to write to. The cottage is in Lamorna Cove, a beautiful little place full of good fishermen and indifferent visitors. I suppose that I'm piling on the shocks and surprises in this very late letter, but I must tell you too that Caitlin and I are going to be married next week by special licence (I think that's what they call it) in the Penzance registry office.[1] This isn't thought of—I've told mother about it many times—speedily or sillily; we've been meaning to for a long time, & think we should carry it out at once. Everything will be entirely quiet & undemonstrative, two of the villagers here will be witnesses, and neither of us, of course, has a penny apart from the three pounds which we have carefully hidden in order to pay for the licence. We'll stay on here until the end of the month, then for a time Caitlin will go home to Hampshire & I'll come back to Wales until I can make just exactly enough money to keep us going until I make just exactly enough money again. It may, & possibly does, sound a rash and mad scheme, but it satisfies us and it's all we ask for. I do hope it won't hurt you; though I know I'm a thoughtless letter-writer & (this sounds like a novelette, doesn't it?) a pretty worthless son. I want you to know now &

1 Dylan and Caitlin were not married until 11 July, a Sunday, when the Penzance register office was persuaded to open. It's unclear why they spent money on a licence—a method used by people in a hurry—when they had been thinking about marriage for a month. In June, Jack Thomas had asked his son-in-law, Haydn Taylor, to see if the wedding could be stopped, but by 25 June he was writing to Taylor, resigned to 'the mad scheme' since 'the young irresponsibles are bent on their supreme act of folly'.

forever that I think about you every day and night, deeply & sincerely, and that I have tried to keep myself, (& have succeeded) straight & reasonable during the time I've been away from you: a time that seems years, so much has happened. I'm completely happy at the moment, well-fed, well-washed, & well looked-after. It's a superb place—the haunt, unfortunately, of aged R.A.s and presidents of West Country Poets' Rambling Clubs—and a delightful cottage, and weather full of sun and breeze, and I'm so glad mother's being well again, & I send her all my love. Do you mind, but I've got to ask you to do a few things for me, simple things and, to me, very necessary ones: could you send on some clothes, my green suit, a shirt or two, one of the pairs of shoes I've left, & those dark gym-shoes. I've had to buy an extra pair of flannel trousers, but I'm still a little short of clean and changeable things. Is it too much to ask, on top of all I ask you—& on top of what so rudely I rarely acknowledge? I would be so grateful, & I mean that with all my heart. I'll write again tomorrow, because then I'll know the exact Penzance date. I'm terribly terribly without money, so can't phone or get up to Penzance to find out: Rayner Heppenstall, who's staying with his wife a few miles away, is going to lend me a few shillings tomorrow, & I can then see to the few essential things.

Please write to me quickly; I would appreciate, so very much, you sending clothes & letters; and I'll try to be much more explicit & less (I should imagine) sensationally full of Dylan-life-altering news when I write tomorrow.

All my love, apologies, & hopes,

Dylan X

MS: Estate of Haydn Taylor

DAVID HIGHAM
14th June [1937] for the moment at Oriental Cottage   Lamorna   Cornwall

Dear Higham,
Letters only just this moment forwarded; I've been honeymooning I think, and haven't yet done enough mss to send you. It's getting too personal & not enough Welsh: I've had to scrap lots. But it's coming, dear God, it's coming, & I faithfully promise you shl have it very soon. I *do* want money too, so I *must* work hard.

Yes, happy thank you, sunburned & steady-handed.

Sincerely,
Dylan Thomas

MS: Texas

*KEIDRYCH RHYS
Monday [June 1937]

Oriental Cottage   Lamorna Cove
nr Penzance   Cornwall

Dear Keidrych,

Thanks for the contributions.[1] You say the problem is how to get shot of things without offending. Surely that's simple: just bung them back with an editorial nothing-doing, or, in the case of friends or acquaintances, with a private note about space and suitability.

I admit that what I've seen of Heseltine[2] I've disliked intensely, and would, perhaps, find it a little awkward to say of anything he had written, 'This is perfectly bloody', without suspecting myself of prejudice; luckily 'The Drunk' is so worthless from every aspect, so transparently an adolescent fake without either the excuse of adolescence or the intelligence to be even moderately accomplished charlatanism, that it doesn't matter at all; it can't matter, because it isn't there; there's nothing there except the knock-kneed and bilious shadow of weak bad-taste indifferently cultivated; and it's not worth the trouble of thinking about or of wasting such invective as could, with more justice, be expended on the pretentious & ingrown-virginal hysteria of what Margiad Evans believes to be a review. You couldn't, even through what I've always thought to be an unnecessarily vehement affection for her novels, contemplate using an article in which, just as one example, almost every reference to Glyn Jones' book is grotesquely & obscenely on the edge of libel & is written as though Miss Evans were, in the process of reviewing, being fucked with literary skill and Celtic ardour on the Blue Bed itself.[3]

The other two stories are, I think, well worth doing something with. 'King Pantygwydr' seems as good as most stories in the accepted magazines; & Glyn Roberts' story, with a little pruning, would be an effective job of reporting. I don't want my comments to sound high-hat or handed, but, really, any magazine that cd print the review or that unmentionable story is murdered at birth.

I'm looking forward to the first number very much. But what do you mean by: 'I am told I should print poems by Etc . . .' who told you? Keidrych, my Welshman, you're the editor, and if, by Christ, things like Heseltine's (& there must be a lot of that sort of thing being excreted) are going to go in, it's about time Something Was Done. Nobody like you or

1 Material intended for *Wales* No. 2 ('August 1937').
2 Nigel Heseltine, b. 1916, who was seen (if not by Thomas) as a promising young writer of the period, published stories and verse, and helped edit some issues of *Wales*. Later he worked overseas as an economist. His father, Philip Heseltine, was the composer Peter Warlock. *Wales* No. 1 printed six of his poems, but nothing called 'The Drunk'.
3 The novelist and short-story writer Margiad Evans (Peggy Eileen Whistler; 1909–58) was English, but had Welsh forbears called Evans. Her review of Glyn Jones's first collection of short stories, *The Blue Bed*, appeared in the second issue of Wales. 'It touched me again and again with the ague of ecstasy', she wrote. Glyn Jones himself was pleased with the review.

me's going to be associated with a periodical producing *undisguised* hooey. Not me anyway. And why you? It's so difficult trying to see eye to eye when we never see each other. Do let me have a look at the first no. when it appears, & let me know more about the such very vague plans for the second. You say in 1938 you'll bequeath the responsibility to me; as yet, I don't know what that responsibility is; if it's only to chuck away the few bits of filth & nonsense I've seen, (always excepting Glyn Jones, Etheridge, Pritchard, Watkins),[1] it's pretty easy. But I know nothing.

Best wishes, & write soon.
Dylan

Since writing that, I've had the first number of 'Wales', and, everything accepted—haste, etc—what a good number it is. It looks good & neat, too, doesn't it? Again, I think it's Heseltine who's responsible for the only really no-good contribution. Didn't Watkins's longer poem[2] look well? I see you made no mention of yourself as editor, but merely referred to yourself as Secretary. Are you going to stick to that in future numbers? Let me know how everything goes, won't you? Remember, I know nowt about your plans for circulation etc. Do you believe Smith's will handle it? It's got some very dubious passages, expecially my references to pessaries, damaroids, & gamarouches?[3]

And do you want the things you sent me back soon? I haven't, incidentally, got a copy of Pritchard's other story, but I'm almost sure it's too long & not half as good as the present one.

Are you paying contributors?

MS: National Library of Wales

NANCY AND HAYDN TAYLOR
Sunday [postmarked 20 June 1937; no stamp]
Oriental Cottage   Lamorna Cove   Nr Penzance   Cornwall

Dear Nancy and Haydn,
I heard from my late London address that you had been ringing up during the last week to try to get hold of me, and that you'd heard—from father, I suppose—of my plans for a pleasant and eccentric marriage. The people in

1 Ken Etheridge (1911–81) wrote plays and poetry. John Prichard (1916–88), from Swansea, wrote promising stories when younger; he was a friend of Thomas, who usually misspelt his name. 'King Pantygwydr,' mentioned earlier in the letter, was by Prichard, and appeared in the third issue of *Wales*, Autumn 1937.
2 'Griefs of the Sea'.
3 Thomas's contribution was a surreal story, 'Prologue to an Adventure', set in a 'strange city' which has a 'Pessary Court', a 'Gamarouche Mews' and a 'Damaroid Alley'. (Damaroids were under-the-counter pills containing damiana, a plant alleged to be aphrodisiac.)

the London address told me that they had carefully been evasive in their replies to your questions about my whereabouts as they didn't know whether or not I wished them, for whatever strange reasons I might have had, to be broadcast. Father may have told you my Cornwall address, but, in case he didn't, here it is. It's a borrowed cottage with a jungle garden and three lavatories, and is only a few miles from where I stayed last year. But I don't imagine that that's of any interest. I lead a most mysterious life, on the surface; actually, it is the almost inevitable life of any penniless drifter with a liking for odd places and odder people, very few regrets about anything and no responsibilities. You mightn't agree with 'no responsibilities', considering that I'm so very nearly married, but Caitlin is—whether that's a fortunate thing or not in the opinion of others—sufficiently like myself to care little or nothing for proprietary interests and *absolutely* nothing for the responsibilities of husbandly provision. It will not yet, of course, be possible for us to live together all the time, & we'll go away whenever we feel like it or—& this will be, until the days of our comparative prosperity, which still would mean a genuine but never-yet wretched poverty, more frequent—whenever it is, from the point of view of money or/and accommodation, essential. (I'm sorry about these tortuous phrases, but I've just been reviewing, with unction, cunning, & entire literary dishonesty, a book on Social Credit & the Economic War.) Incidentally, I'd like to explain about my not returning home the day after Nancy and I met at Paddington Station: the lent pound note I gave back to the original lenders, my own expected cheque did not arrive for several days, & by that time I was again in debt for almost the complete worth of the cheque. It was unfortunate in some ways, but good in others, as, had I not been in London when I shd officially have been working at home, this lovely three-lavatoried cottage would never have been mine for the summer, Caitlin & I would not have come to a decision so quickly, and (perhaps, but I think it unlikely, bloody unlikely) another social catastrophe would have been averted. So much for that. I'm sending this letter of explanation to your Laleham cottage, as I haven't had any news about your moving. I hope it reaches you. As a gesture, Christian, gentlemanly, ladylike, sisterly, in-law-brotherly, friendly, & (in face of your obvious distrust of what could be, & has, by father, been called 'this lunatic course of action') congratulatorily from a married couple of some years' standing to two younger persons about to embark on the voyage of legal matrimony, would you like to slip me a couple of quid? I'm afraid the last few words are a sorry come-down after the grandiloquence of my previous circumlocution, but I do, actually, want to buy a hell of a lot of things almost at once, &, though father's been desperately kind & sent me five pounds last week with sort of resigned wishes for my happiness, I'm still really short of the bare amount I need. This is a letter of apology, explanation, defence (though not apologetic) and cadgery. I'll always be grateful if the cadgery succeeds, honestly grateful. Anyway, write to me very soon: I'll pay every intention to the advice etcetera that I anticipate from so many family counsellors & despairers. But in seriousness, you could help me with very little. And with less than very little, I now put down my pen and hope this leaves you. Forgive this ill, & too-often facetious letter; the best thing that can be said about it is that none of it is blarney.

Love to you both,
Dylan

MS: Estate of Haydn Taylor

DAVID HIGHAM
Friday [2 July 1937]   Oriental Cottage Lamorna Cornwall

Dear Higham,

I'm glad the Curtis Brown business is over at last. When Faber has finished looking through my MS, could you return it to me just for a few days? There are several details I want to correct, etc.

More personally: do you think it would be possible for you to get a little money—however little—out of Dent for me almost immediately? That may sound rather startling, perhaps, considering that I haven't supplied any of the required words yet; the book's in a hell of a mess, disheartening me, but I know it will come all right. But the trouble is that I have no money at all—literally none, no cigarettes, too little food on a diminishing credit—to live anywhere at all to continue writing. It's almost impossible to knock this stuff into shape—a book, that will eventually, I'm afraid, not contain many references to Wales—with all these mingy worries nagging on all sides.[1] If I can't obtain some money by early next week, I'll have to move from here to nowhere: and in nowhere I can obviously do nothing. Do please try to raise me a little money, even five pounds, from Dent. I'd be more than grateful, it would, cheaply here in the country, keep me going for some time, and I could again, I'm sure, work hard and well. Sorry for the wheedling, slightly desperate, note, but it can't be avoided.

I hope you can write quickly.

Yours,
Dylan Thomas

P.S. The Best Short Stories people are printing a story of mine in this year's collection. It wouldn't, I suppose, be possible for you to get me paid by them in advance? Not that I'm hopeful.

MS: Texas

1 The 'Welsh journey' book was never written.

DAVID HIGHAM
Tuesday [6 July 1937]   The Lobster Pot[1] Mousehole Cornwall

Dear Higham,
   So glad Faber want the story for their Welsh book. And of course I accept.
   I hope you've received my pathetic, and now even more disastrously important, letter. As you see from the address above, I've had to move from Lamorna, and I shan't be able to stay here long without some almost immediate money. It's hard to work at all under these conditions.
   'The Orchards' is going to appear in the Faber Book of Modern Stories, too, isn't it?[2]

Yours,
Dylan Thomas

MS: Texas

DAVID HIGHAM
Tuesday [13 July 1937]   Lobster Pot Mousehole Cornwall

Dear Higham,
   Thanks very much indeed for getting hold of all that money for me so promptly. Dent's *are* good to me. Those cheques did a lot of good, and have temporarily made us safe.
   I'm afraid that, owing to the muddle about my changing addresses so often, my acknowledgement of O'Brien's letter—Best Short Stories—didn't reach him until the book had gone to press. So that's three guineas I won't be having. Nelson, however, are doing an anthology of poetry very soon, & have agreed to pay me a few guineas for one from my first book. They might, do you think, hand over the money to you beforehand?
   I'll let you have back the book of short stories manuscript not more than a week after I receive it.
   Thanks again.

Yours,
Dylan Thomas

MS: Texas

1 The Lobster Pot was a restaurant and guest-house, run jointly by Wyn Henderson and Max Chapman. There was an adjoining cottage; Dylan and Caitlin lived in it before and after their marriage.
2 Faber published *Welsh Short Stories* and *The Faber Book of Short Stories* in 1937. 'The Orchards' appeared in both.

VERNON WATKINS

15th July [1937]   Lobster Pot   Mousehole   Cornwall

I'm sorry that this is such a short & inadequate
letter: I'll do much better next time.

Dear Vernon,

If, in some weeks' time, you see a dog-like shape with a torn tail and a
spaniel eye, its tail between its legs, come cringing and snuffling up
Heatherslade gravel,[1] it will be me; look carefully at its smarmy rump
that asks to be kicked, its trembling, penholding paw that scribbles, 'kick
me', in the dust. It will deserve your anger. But, really, the Grief of the
Sea[2] was this: I was fooling about with a copy of the poem, playing the
pleasant, time-wasting game of altering, unasked-for, somebody else's work;
and then, when I met Keidrych with the manuscripts I had collected, blindly
and carelessly I must have included among them the for-my-own-benefit,
not-to-be-shown copy instead of the original. I hope you forgive me: that's the
truth. I was worried when I saw the first number of Wales, with that
Thowdlerized version in it, and should, anyway, in a few days have sent off an
explanation to you. Further than that I Cannot Go, but you may still kick me
when we meet in Pennard again—and I'm hoping that will be soon.

Yes I thought 'Wales' was good, too. I had actually very little myself to
do with the editing, though when Keidrych goes up to Cambridge next year
I shall probably—and with you as colleague, or whatever it is, if you'd be—
take it all over. And no more Nigel Heseltine when we do: he can crawl
back into the woodwork, or lift up his stone again. And wait until you see a
review by Margiad Evans of Glyn Jones's stories in the next number: I told
Keidrych, quite truthfully, that it read as though Miss Evans were being
raped in the Blue Bed as she wrote the review.

My own news is very big and simple. I was married three days ago; to
Caitlin Macnamara; in Penzance registry office; with no money, no prospect
of money, no attendant friends or relatives, and in complete happiness.
We've been meaning to from the first day we met, and now we
are free and glad. We're moving next week—for how long depends on
several things, but mostly on one—to a studio some miles away, in
Newlyn, a studio above a fish-market & where gulls fly in to breakfast. But
I shall be trying to come home soon for at least a few days, along with
Caitlin: I think you'll like [her] very much, she looks like the princess on
the top of a Christmas Tree, or like a stage Wendy; but, for God's sake,
don't tell her that.

Write as soon as you can, and bless me.
Love to all the family.

Yours always,
Dylan

MS: British Library

1 Watkins lived with his parents on the Gower coast, above the little bay called
  Heatherslade.
2 Thomas had made slight alterations to 'Griefs of the Sea' in manuscript.

PAMELA HANSFORD JOHNSON
6th August 1937   Fradgan Studios[1] Newlyn   Penzance   Cornwall

It was very very nice of you to write, I'd been wanting to hear from you. I'm a long way from everywhere, in a 'high huge haystack of a studio over the harbour, full of worries and happiness lazing away all the writeable days, writing an occasional bad love poem of the sort that begins, 'It was not love until you came', drinking scaly beer in the pubs near the Fish Market, counting Caitlin's change—if any, fighting with primus-stoves, spending the rent. Caitlin can only cook one thing, and that is Irish bread which requires a very special type of oven, unobtainable in England; she drinks a lot though, so we eat in the morning as we're too unsteady in the evening to open the tins. (That isn't altogether true: I've managed to finish two stories which are unlike anything I've ever seen, and a satanic Horliquin-ade[2] just like something I never want to see.) I can now light old Etna, the primus, without burning more than two fingers and an eyelash, and can be left alone with the methylated spirits. If I'm reformed, it isn't noticeable. Newlyn is famous for its fleas and Dod Proctor:[3] I go to bed with the former, and could with the latter. Caitlin was very rude yesterday to the Proctor woman who's thin and red-tipped and shiny. As we were leaving her house, the Proctor said, 'Wait a minute, I must powder my nose'. And Caitlin said, 'Why don't you put it in a bag?' There has been a young rash of poets, lately; you can buy a surrealist in Mousehole—an artists' village full of fishermen—for a couple of whiting; Rayner Heppenstall, very nice man, newly married, came down for a religious gloom; Oswell Blakeston, coming out of the well to work, has done little more than sit about on his headquarters; Philip Henderson has gone rugged in a wee wee Wendy bungalow next to a bird-hospital run by a marionette-maker. There are Teas, Christian Science & literary, and folk dancing and punch-&-judy shows for adults. A young man living in Truro, got hold of my address somehow & invited himself over. I couldn't read his signature, & when I opened the door at tea-time there was a bright brand-new pig standing there who said his name was Thuel Roskelly.[4] There weren't any acorns so we gave him whiskey and it made him drunk and after he'd snorted a lot and rubbed his back—covered, undoubtedly, with short stiff hairs—he said he was a poet, that he wrote in Comment, had met Victor B & thought him conventional, said he himself couldn't write very well but that he was practising hard and would in time be able to fart in tune. He was very odd. He slept on the sofa after that, so we tip-toed off and left him shaking himself like a cocktail, with snores and hiccups. When we came back, he'd

---

1 Max Chapman had a studio there.
2 Presumably a pun on 'Horlicks', the bedtime drink.
3 Mrs Dod Procter (1892–1972), painter, who lived in Newlyn for many years.
4 Thuel Roskelly was a young poet and journalist.

gone. The air here is very invigorating and there is a splendid view of the English Channel.

Last week, a man [called] Mulk Raj Anand[1] made a big curry for everybody about. The first course was beans, little ones. I ate two and couldn't speak. A little man called Wallace B. Nichols,[2] who has made a small fortune out of writing epic poems on people like Cromwell and Nelson and Mrs Elsie Guddy, took a whole mouthful and was assisted out. He writes for the Cornhill. After the main dish, which was so unbelievably hot that everyone, except the Indian, was crying like Shirley Temple, a woman, Mrs Henderson, looked down on to her plate & saw, lying at one corner of it, a curious rubbery thing that looked like a red, discarded french letter. In interest, she picked it up and found it was the entire skin from her tongue.

It's terribly hard, Pamela dear, to thank you for all the nice things you said in your letter. All I can say is that I'm happy, very happy indeed. We are poor as the mice that live in our clothes cupboard, and have no prospects of anything but a short, irresponsible, & happy life of poverty. That's sententious.

I'm so glad you're happy too. And there's nothing again for me to say about that. We know each other very well. I'll call with Caitlin as soon as we get back to town, and we'll all get plastered. You said you wanted to send us something: that's lovely. I asked Caitlin, & she doesn't know what. We live day-by-day, buying just enough food to last the day, buying a new towel, if we can, when the old one gets talkative, buying soap when we offend each other. What we want to do, & have been unable to do, is to buy a bigger lot of small things so that they'll be there when we want them. So, if you can & if you like, you can send me a pound with a long newsy letter. That is not the correct thing to ask, I suppose, but it's the thing everybody forgets. You can't eat cut glass or drink decanters or wash with a silver spoon. Very incorrect, but we know each other very well. If you can, too. But the newsy letter, *yes!* My love to Mrs J. Say, 'Well, old man, we both asked for it, eh?' to Neil[3] for me. And love & happiness to you.

Dylan

MS: Estate of Pamela Hansford Johnson

1 Mulk Raj Anand, Indian novelist.
2 Wallace B. Nichols (b. 1888), novelist and poet.
3 Johnson married Gordon Neil Stewart in 1936.

EDITH SITWELL
20th August 1937   Fradgan Studios Newlyn Penzance Cornwall

Dear Miss Sitwell,

Before anything else, I want to thank you with all my heart for your great generosity and graciousness. Caitlin and I thank you for the lovely present with which we bought all sorts of things we wanted, from knives and towels to a Garbo picture, and paid off the clamourers. And to the man who gave me the present you enclosed, all I can say is thank you. I shan't ever be impertinent about his name, but I shall always think of him with gratitude. He must be a kind, splendid person.

And now I want to apologise for this apparently very rude and disrespectful delay in answering and acknowledging your present and letters. I'm awfully bad with letters, I know, but I couldn't be unmannerly, or unappreciative, enough to let a reply like this linger on through slackness or carelessness. For the last ten days I've been in and out on the Newlyn fishing-boats, making a little money, and have hardly been on shore at all during the daytime. I've just been snatching a few hours of sleep when I can, too utterly tired in head and every limb to write even the shortest sentence of gratitude for all you've done and are doing for me. This sounds weak, but it honestly is true. Sometimes over twelve hours, on a rough sea, in a twelve-foot boat. My job's over now, and I can start thinking again, not moving all the time in a kind of fish-eyed daze.[1]

It's wonderful of you to take all this trouble about trying to get me some work. I'm sure, aren't you, that something must come out of it. Almost above all, I should like some connection with the BBC. I've done one broadcast, of my own poems and of a few poems by Ransom[2] and Auden, on the West Regional programme, and I was told that it went down quite well. That was late in April this year, but no-one's got in touch with me since. I love reading poems aloud, and I do hope Mr. Maine will succeed in making the BBC interested enough to let me read some more. Oh those little ninny five-minute readings with a death at the end of each line. I wouldn't mince, anyway. I should enjoy very much reading some of Sacheverell Sitwell's poems, if the BBC, & he, some time allowed me: it's great and grand aloud, isn't it? pillars and columns and great striding figures through a microphone. I'm writing today to Peter Quennell,[3] though I know him very slightly from parties, and I'll send Miss Reynolds my three or four new poems. A friend of mine is typing my new story, and, as soon as it's finished, I'll send it to you along with the poems. I do so much want you to read them; I'm not sure of them at all; I hope you'll tell me all about them; sometimes I'm afraid they caricature themselves.

---

1 The fishing trips were a fantasy. So was the 'sailing around to North Devon' later in the letter.
2 John Crowe Ransom (1888–1974).
3 Peter Quennell (1905–93), author and historian.

Life here has at last become too much, even for us who don't demand grand comforts. With smells from the fishmarket in front of us and dust from the coal-yard below us and flies from the dump behind us, we might as well live in the street. Our studio's haunted, too, and last month the landscape painter next door hanged himself from the rafters. So we're going to go to Wales for some time, to my mother's house, sailing around to North Devon in fishing-boats & working our way, as best we can, across to Swansea. It shouldn't take us more than a week. We start about September 1st. I do hope this change of address won't be awkward if any of the people you've asked to help me want to get in touch immediately. My mother's address is MARSTON, BISHOPSTON, near SWANSEA, Glamorgan.

It's impossible for me to tell you how deeply I appreciate your kindness, and value your friendship. I'll always remember it. Caitlin thanks you very much for your message. She's looking forward to meeting you. I hope we all can meet in London, soon. And I hope sincerely that your friend in Paris will get better.

All my gratefulness &
apologies,
Yours very sincerely,
Dylan Thomas

MS: Texas

GEOFFREY GRIGSON
September 7 [1937]   Marston   Bishopston   Glamorgan

Dear Geoffrey,
Here are the hundred words, though I don't know if it's the sort of thing you want.[1]
No, I haven't gone back into the grass. I spent the summer in Cornwall, and was married there. I'll give you a ring, if you like, when we're in town at the end of the month and we can meet and make a noise. If you like.

Dylan

Good luck to Auden on his seventieth birthday.

MS: Texas

1 *New Verse* for November was an 'Auden Double Number'. Thomas contributed one of 'Sixteen Comments' ('I think he is a wide and deep poet ... He makes Mr Yeats' isolation guilty as a trance'). 'Seventieth birthday' was a Thomas joke: Auden was thirty.

DESMOND HAWKINS
[September 1937]   Marston   Bishopston   Glamorgan

Dear Desmond,

I haven't seen you for a year, or perhaps more. Where are you living now and how are you? I'm coming to London at, I think, the beginning of next month. We must meet, there must be such a load of gossip for us both, and stories, and intimate literary secrets. I've been in Cornwall all the summer, met Blakeston there who said you were turning up to stay outside Penzance. You didn't though, or did you? I'm beautifully married, and how's your daughter? Let me know your town days, I'm looking forward to a big beery lunch with you. If you want a poem or a dirty crack, you've come to the right shop.

Love,
Dylan

MS: National Library of Wales

DESMOND HAWKINS
[September 1937]   Marston   Bishopston   Glamorgan

Dear Desmond, progenitive man of letters,

My wife is Irish and French, you haven't met her, she is two months younger than I am,[1] has seas of golden hair, two blue eyes, two brown arms, two dancing legs, is untidy and vague and un-reclamatory. I am lost in love and poverty, and my work is shocking. I can let you have one longish and very good poem, unprinted, for an immediate guinea. It is this week's masterpiece, it took two months to write, and I want to drink it.[2]

I'm a bumpkin, too, and my news is stale as New Verse. I haven't been in town since May, but I'm going up next week to try to write some quick advertisements for petrol and make enough money to buy my wife a ping-pong table.[3] We competed, the week before last, in the Swansea Croquet Tournament, and only lost by one hoop.

If you want that poem, it's yours for a pound. I've come down one shilling, and it's forty lines.

Can you be in town Friday, Saturday, Sunday, or Monday of next week? Goodbye & good luck, cradle-filler.[4]

Dylan

MS: National Library of Wales

1 Caitlin was ten months older.
2 An early version of 'I make this in a warring absence'. The poem eventually appeared in *Twentieth Century Verse*, January/February 1938.
3 Norman Cameron, an advertising copywriter, may have found some freelance work for Thomas.
4 Mrs Hawkins was expecting a second child.

*KEIDRYCH RHYS
[October 1937]   Marston Bishopston nr Swansea

Dear Keidrych,

How about everything? Is Wales coming out soon?[1] Is the list of contents the same we drafted together in Swansea? When are you coming here to have a drink? I think we're going back to London in about a week's time; can you come to Swansea before then? It would be nice to meet, wouldn't it? I can get hold of John Prichard, & Vernon if you like. Anyway, let me know things.

Dylan

MS: *National Library of Wales*

*KEIDRYCH RHYS
21st October [1937]   Blashford Ringwood Hants

Dear Keidrych,

Rudely, I didn't answer your last letter or acknowledge the ballads. Everything's been uncertain: shelter, money, prospects, destination. We left Swansea just over a week ago; now staying in another relation's house,[2] on charity & sufferance; for how long, I don't know; and cold London's waiting. (I'll instruct my mother to send ballads on to you. I liked the near-bawdy one best, I can't remember its name. Some, I suppose, you'll print.)

In the letter I (rudely) didn't answer—this vagueness of marital position isn't an excuse—you said 'Wales' was nearly ready, and that the proofs had been returned. Please don't forget to send me a copy: I've met an old fellow here who's rolling in money and pretention, and who might, if I treat him properly, that is dishonestly, enough might help considerably in financing it. He's not a Welshman: art is international to him: but he likes young poets so much. I want him to read 'Wales'.

Also in your unanswered letter, you said you'd like to give us something little (necessarily) for a wedding-present. That's lovely of you, we're so despairingly penniless. If you really meant what you said—& obviously you did or you wouldn't have said it—you might send us a tiny cheque (maximum, one guinea, minimum one penny). Anyway, write very soon & do send 'Wales'. I have real hopes of this old poet-lover.

Dylan

MS: *National Library of Wales*

1 Issue No. 3 of Wales, 'Autumn 1937'.
2 The 'other relation' was Thomas's mother-in-law, Yvonne Macnamara. He didn't get on with her.

JULIAN SYMONS
22 October [1937]   Blashford   Ringwood   Hants

Dear Julian Symons,
    When does the next number of 20th Century Verse appear? I can send you a longish poem in about a week. So sorry not to have answered your last letter: I've been changing addresses so often & so quickly I haven't been able to attend to anything.
    And can you let me have Ruthven Todd's address?

Sincerely,
Dylan Thomas

MS: Texas

VERNON WATKINS
[postmarked 25 October 1937]   Blashford   Ringwood   Hants

Dear Vernon,
    Thank you for the poems. I like them all. My respect for them is always increased when I read them again, and in typescript. 'Mana' is magnificent, especially the fourth verse. At the moment, I think it's your best short poem. I still don't like the first line. Perhaps I never mentioned it, but from the beginning, from the first time I saw the poem shaping, I've felt the line to be wrong, disliked 'fabled'—not because it is used as a verb, but because of its position—and felt uneasy about the rhythm. The rhythm is one that I myself have used to death, and my feeling against it is perhaps over-personal. The line is so stridently an opening line: tum tum tum, all the wheels and drums are put in motion: a poem is about to begin. I see the workman's clothes, I hear the whistle blowing in the poem-factory. And one other line I think is bad: 'Laid in the long grey shadow of our weeping thought'. This, to me, has far too many weak words. They are weak alone, & weaker when added together. They do not cancel each other out, though, but elongate a thin nothing: a long, grey, weeping sausage. But that's fancy talk. What I mean is, the whole line seems a kind of tired indrawing of breath between loud & strong utterances. And I've always disliked the weak line. I admit that readers of complicated poetry do need a breather every now and then, but I don't think the poetry should give it to them. When they want one, they should take it and then go on.
    I don't know yet what I'll read at the Cardiff lecture, but I'll let you know beforehand: the Ballad certainly, After Sunset probably, one or two of the lyrics in 'Wales', and, perhaps, either Mana or Griefs of the Sea. And an Auden, a Ransom, maybe Prokosch.
    This is a very lovely place. Caitlin & I ride into the New Forest every day, into Bluebell Wood or onto Cuckoo Hill.[1] There's no-one else about;

1 'Bluebell Wood' and 'Cuckoo Hill' were childhood inventions by Caitlin and her sisters.

Caitlin's mother is away; we are quiet and small and cigarette-stained and very young. I've read two dozen thrillers, the whole of Jane Austen, a new Wodehouse, some old Powys, a book of Turgenev, 3 lines by Gertrude Stein, & an anthology of Pure Poetry by George Moore. There are only about 2,000 books left in the house.

My poem is continuing. You shall have it next week. Regards to your mother & father. Remember me to Francis[1]—to whom I *must* write. And have a nice week-end.

Dylan

[*four lines of verse are deleted*]

This was a quotation from the new verse of my poem, which I've thought better about.

MS: British Library

*KEIDRYCH RHYS
28th October 1937   Blashford   Ringwood   Hants

Dear Keidrych,

It was very very nice of you to send that present; thanks and gratitude. We bought cigarettes and beer and a new shirt. I'm smoking the cigarettes now, with affection for you, & I'm full of beer and wearing the bright green shirt.

No, I don't blame the world that doesn't give me (and Saunders Lewis)[2] money. I think poets are treated well enough; no-one beats them with a little whip; they can walk safely in the streets. The only trouble is that a bad poet is treated as well as a good one. I think Spender should be kicked in his headquarters once a week, regularly & officially. And Day-Lewis should be hissed in public, and have his balls beaten with a toffee hammer. After all, it's a coming thing to be a poet; we should be treated with more flippancy. I want money, not as a poet, but as a hungry & thirsty man; a poet doesn't want meat & drink, only paper. God help those who have no bowels, only consonants & vowels. What would happen if there was a poet's strike? I'd love to stand on picket-duty in Barker's scribbling-room, and cosh him for every half-rhyme. 'Unless we're paid three pounds ten a week, we won't write another bloody poem'. That'll set the dogs barking. We'd come to an agreement with the critics: fifty per cent of every article about us. Hear Mr Leavis cackle! There goes Day-Lewis, ratting to the London Mercury! Apes on strike! Down tools in Bloomsbury! (a bankrupt Grigson offers 25%).

---

1 Francis Dufau-Labeyrie, a French friend of Watkins. Later he translated Thomas's *Portrait of the Artist as a Young Dog.*
2 Saunders Lewis, 1893–1985, Welsh writer, scholar and nationalist, and a major figure in Welsh-language literature.

I'm enclosing the Gower ballads. I found I had them with my papers here. (My papers! Old, soiled poems, going at half price; unanswered letters; world-shattering, unfinished masterpieces that wouldn't shake a flea's ear).

V. Watkins wrote to-day, saying you wanted E. Sitwell to review 'Wales' somewhere. If I manage to get to London next week, I'll be seeing her & I'll ask her.

Thanks again, very much. Hope to see you soon. And don't forget to send me 'W' when it comes out.

Dylan

PS Third number[1] just arrived. I'll write later. It looks good.

MS: National Library of Wales

JULIAN SYMONS
28th October 1937   Blashford   Ringwood   Hants

Dear Julian Symons,
Thank you for Todd's address. I'll let you have the poem very shortly; and no, of course I don't mind it being held over until December.

I'm afraid I couldn't write anything about Lewis;[2] I haven't read enough, and I'm not an admirer. I'm looking forward to reading the number, though.

That sounds a splendid idea—the stories by poets. I hope it comes off, and I'd like you to use a story of mine very much.

Sincerely,
Dylan Thomas

MS: Texas

DESMOND HAWKINS
30th October '37   Blashford   Ringwood   Hants

Dear Desmond,
No, my goodness, I had no letter from you. No-one can have forwarded it from Wales. I am staying here near the New Forest, and am too broke to move. By crook I got from Wales, as I told you I would, but not to London. Here I feel planted for ever, or until next week. As soon as we're in London, I'll let you know. Thank you very much for the week-end invitation. I

---

1 Contents included Thomas's poem 'We lying by seasand' and his story 'The Map of Love'.
2 (Percy) Wyndham Lewis, the novelist; similarly in the next letter.

accept with pomp. The poem I have to revise. I thought it was perfectly correct—as to detail—before I read it again early one morning. Then I saw that the third verse, which dealt with the faults and mistakes of death, had a brilliant and moving description of a suicide's grave as 'a chamber of errors'.[1] I'm now working hard on the poem, and it should be complete in some days.

Lately, I've been receiving strange requests from magazines: first, for a kind of obituary notice, for New Verse, on Auden, or perhaps a tribute on his seventieth birthday; second, for a valuation (Symons's word) of Wyndham Lewis, for 20th Century Verse; third, for a description of my most recent trauma, with, if possible, ancestral symbols, for 'Transition'; & last for a contribution to a special number of Henry Miller's 'The Booster', 'completely devoted to The Womb'.[2] Do you think this means, at last, that I'm a man of letters? The only contribution to give Mr Miller, anyway, is a typewritten reply to the effect that I too am, passionately, devoted to the womb. And you, Mrs Dyer. Looking forward to seeing you.

Love, Dylan

MS: National Library of Wales

VERNON WATKINS
13th November '37   Blashford Ringwood Hants

Dear Vernon,
    Thank you for the new version of 'Mana'. I think it's very right now, don't you? I never really care to suggest actual, detailed alterations in anyone else's poem, (in spite of the apparently contradictory evidence of 'Griefs of the Sea'), but I'm glad you did alter the first line—(here-it-comes-boys)—and that line in the middle—(now-boys-take-a-deep-breath).

    Here, after so long, is my own new poem.[3] I hope you'll like it. I've used 'molten', as you suggested, but kept 'priest's grave foot', which is not, I'm sure, really ugly. In the last line of the seventh verse, you'll notice—'a man is tangled'. It was weeks after writing that line that I remembered Prokosch's 'man-entangled sea':[4] but I don't think any apologies are necessary, anyway. Lines 4 & 5 of the last verse might, perhaps, sound too fluent: I mean, they might sound as though they came too easily in a

1 'I make this in a warring absence', Stanza 6, has the phrase, 'the room of errors'.
2 The writer Henry Miller (1891–1980) was invited to help run *The Booster*, formerly the magazine of the American Country Club in Paris. Later it was renamed *Delta* and had a brief life as a literary journal.
3 'I make this in a warring absence', also called 'Poem (for Caitlin)' on first publication. A note in *VW* calls it 'Poem to Caitlin'. This is confusing, since a different piece, 'Unluckily for a death', had the title 'Poem (to Caitlin)' on first publication. Thomas gave convoluted explanations of 'I make this'—see pages 313 and 449. In fact it is about his sexual jealousy.
4 In Frederic Prokosch's poem 'The Baltic Shore'.

manner I have done my best to discard, but they say exactly what I mean them to. Are they clear? Once upon a time, before my death & resurrection, before the 'terrible' world had shown itself to me (however lyingly, as lines 6 & 7 of the last verse might indicate) as not so terrible after all, a wind had blown that had frightened everything & created the first ice & the first frost by frightening the falling snow so much that the blood of each flake froze. This is probably clear, but, even to me, the lines skip (almost) along so that they are taken in too quickly, & then mainly by the eye.

I wonder if you would type a couple of copies of the poem for me—there's no typewriter within miles—and let me have them as quickly as you can. I must get the poem off, and soon, because I need, terribly urgently, the little money it will get me.

News, though not much, when I write again. And I'll write when I send off the poem to Eliot—(I want the Criterion to do it). Don't forget, will you? And much love to you.

Dylan

P.S. It's a full stop after 'ice' in the last verse.
P.P.S. If I come to Cardiff to lecture—which is financially improbable—I'll try to spend the night at Swansea. And see you, of course.
P.P.S. Since writing this, I've done another little poem:[1] nothing at all important, or even (probably,) much good: just a curious thought said quickly. I think it will be good for me to write some short poems, not bothering about them too much, between my long exhausters.

MS: British Library

VERNON WATKINS
[Postmarked 20 November 1937]   [Blashford]

Dear Vernon,
Thank you so much for the typewritten poems. I agree with you entirely as to the (apparently) hurried ending of my sixty-line-year's work, and will alter the middle lines of the last verse.[2] This should take me until Christmas, and my present to you will be, inedibly, the revised and final copy. About go-cripple-come-Michaelmas I'll write next time. It looks & smells good. At the moment, though, I have another favour to ask. In ten days' time I am to give a reading in the London University, reading alone with no commentary. I scrapped the Cardiff lecture, as I had prepared no grave speech and did not feel like travelling 200 miles just to recite, in my fruity voice, poems that would not be appreciated & could, anyway, be read in books. The London affair, however, is at the request of a vague friend, &

1 'The spire cranes', also enclosed with the letter.
2 'I make this in a warring absence.'

will have to be fulfilled. I shall read you, me, Auden, Ransom, Prokosch, Yeats. I have plenty of me at hand, several of you, & enough Auden. Will you assist me, tremendously too, by telling me what of Yeats to read and— this is the favour, the tiresome favour—copy out for me the poems you choose?

This house is stacked with books, but all prose, and I have brought nothing with me but a few Penguin Shakespeares and a pocket dictionary. I know it's a bother for you, but if you could type for me—say, half a dozen Yeats (middle & late, including, if you think it as good as others, the one ending 'A terrible beauty is born',[1] & the ones I know so little & that one you have read me)—it would be kind and splendid. It's too much to ask you also to copy out one Prokosch, but, if you have some spare minutes, could you do it? I want the reading to be of poems not *too* well known—with Yeats's exception, & Prokosch, I believe, is still only known as a dilettante name—outside the Criterion & one or two other papers of an established snob-appeal. The programme, roughly, I have in mind is: 'Dead Boy' & either 'Captain Carpenter' or 'Judith'—of Ransom; 'Prologue' & 'Ballad' of Auden; one good Prokosch; at least three Yeats; that tiny poem by Antonia White; John Short's Carol; Gavin Ewart's[2] 'sexual insignia' poem; your Ballad of the Rough Sea, Griefs of the Sea, & Mana; my new poem, & two of the poems at the end of my last book. I shall read for, probably, 3/4 of an hour, explaining, of course, that my reading is not supposed to prove anything, and that my selection is based on nothing but a personal liking. The details of the programme I may alter. Anyway, do try to copy out those things as quickly as possible. I began this letter two days ago, & then, owing to the arrival of all sorts of odd people here, put off sending it until to-day. Now the time I have before the reading is alarmingly short; I've just realized the date to be the 27th. This is rudely rushing you, but could you type the Yeats—&, I hope very much, a Prokosch by about Wednesday. It's blackmail to say I'm relying on you, but I crookedly am. I respect your judgement, & your typing. Love & admiration as always.

Dylan

MS: British Library

HERMANN PESCHMANN[3]

21st Nov 1937   Blashford   Ringwood   Hants

Dear Mr. Peschmann,

Thanks for the letter. I'm sorry it isn't possible for me to speak to your Society this year: the worst of having such frequently changed, & always indefinite, addresses is that all one's letters go astray. I should be glad to

---

1 'Easter 1916'.
2 Satirical poet (1916–95), for many years an advertising copywriter.
3 Critic and anthologist, after an earlier career in business. An extra-mural tutor in literature, he ran a poetry club at Goldsmith's College, 1936–9.

come along one Monday or Wednesday early in January: perhaps we can fix a definite date some time soon.

And thank you very much for forwarding my letter to Anna Wickham.[1]

Yours sincerely,

Dylan Thomas

MS: *Philip Skelsey*

*KEIDRYCH RHYS
Monday 20th December 37
68 Parliament Hill
Hampstead NW3[2]

Dear Keidrych,

Sorry not to have written before, with news and poem; my excuse is that there's been neither. As you see, we're staying, for the time, in Anna's house; and you know what that is. I think we'll even have to spend Christmas in London, and here too; so think of us with your comfortable puddings.

I enclose a very short poem,[3] which is yours for some shillings: the number of shillings I leave to 'Wales', but I do hope it will buy one tot of rum in the snow.

Winnie Barham doesn't speak too well of the paper's business, says the price should be reduced by half. How much are you charging for the 24-page number? And do let me know what's going in.

All my best wishes; & please try to let me buy that snow-tot in honour of you & Wales: at Christmas.

Dylan

MS: *National Library of Wales*

JULIAN SYMONS
[?about 1 January 1938]
Blashford Ringwood Hants

Dear Symons,

Your urgent note has just been forwarded here. I can't think what became of the poem I sent. Anyway, here is another copy, which

1 Anna Wickham (Edith Alice Mary Harper) (1884–1947), poet, feminist, bohemian; she committed suicide. A notice in the hall of her house in Hampstead said, 'Saddle your Pegasus here'.
2 Anna Wickham's address.
3 'The spire cranes' (11 lines) appeared in *Wales* No. 4, March 1938.

I do hope isn't too late, perhaps the original copy has arrived by this time.

> Happy New Year,
> Dylan Thomas

MS: Texas

HERMANN PESCHMANN
January 3 1938   Blashford   Ringwood   Hants

Dear Mr. Peschmann,
   I'm sincerely sorry not to have answered your letter before this. I've been in town recently, & all my papers have been left here, so I couldn't get your address as there was no-one to forward anything. And even now—I do hope you'll excuse my vagueness and carelessness—I can't find the particular letter of yours in which you suggested a reading date for January. I seem to remember it was the 27th(?). Would you be so kind—in spite of this rude delay of mine—as to tell me on what date you had invited me to read, & whether the invitation is still open. I'll be in town from the end of next week on.

> Apologies again,
> Your sincerely,
> Dylan Thomas

MS: Texas

GEORGE REAVEY
January 3 1938   Blashford   Ringwood   Hants

Dear George,
   I shan't be in London until the end of next week. We were, as you know, staying with Anna Wickham, but a difference of lack of opinion made us return to the country. I'm afraid I can't yet find a copy of 'The Orchards'. It was printed in the Criterion, & reprinted in The Faber Book of Modern Stories & Welsh Short Stories (also published by Faber). I haven't a copy of any of these books, otherwise I'd tear the story out. I'm writing today to my home in Wales, asking if there is, by any chance, a copy there. That's the best I can do: I never manage to keep the manuscripts of anything I write.
   I'm enclosing a list of names to send to about the guinea edition.[1]

---

1 George Reavey and the Europa Press were supposed to be publishing a collection of stories by Thomas, *The Burning Baby*, in both a limited and a popular edition. After many tribulations, the book failed to appear.

Something should definitely come from some of them. I'll write you if I think of any others.

Is it possible for you to write about the details of the book you mentioned in your note & on the telephone? Or would you prefer to leave it until I come back to town? Anyway, do let me know.

Yours,
Dylan

MS: Houghton

LAWRENCE DURRELL[1]
[?early January 1938]   Blashford   Ringwood   Hants

Dear Lawrence Durrell,

I would like to have seen you too, after that first short meeting in Anna's house, in a clean pub with an evening before us and pockets jingling and lots of fire and spit and loud, grand affectations and conceits of Atlases and London coiling and humming: but Caitlin and I went away in a pantomime snow, thrown out at midnight, and we spent the night very coldly and trained back without tickets to charity in the morning. Now *this* warmth is ending, and we'll train back without tickets to London and live there in a bad convention. I think that England is the very place for a fluent and fiery writer. The highest hymns of the sun are written in the dark. I like the grey country. A bucket of Greek sun would drown in one colour the crowds of colours I like trying to mix for myself out of a grey, flat, insular mud. If I went to the sun I'd just sit in the sun; that would be very pleasant, but I'm not doing it, and the only necessary things I do are the things I am doing. Unless by accidents, and my life is planned by them, I shall be nearer Bournemouth than Corfu this summer. It will need a nice accident for us to live anywhere; we are stages beyond poverty; completely possessionless; and we are willing but angry; we can take it, but we don't want it. I liked your Stygian prose very very much, it's the best I've read for years. Don't let the Greek sun blur your pages, as you said it did. You use words like stones, throwing, rockerying, mossing, churning, sharpening, bloodsucking, melting, and a hard firewater flows and rolls through them all the time. . . . And it's so brave too; you used the sudden image of Christ with incredible courage. I mean to borrow the typescript of the Black Book as soon as I get to London.

But I wonder what Anna will make of Miller's books. I know her well. Morals are her cup of tea, and books are just beer: she swallows them down without discrimination of taste or body or brew, and judges them by the effect they have on her bowels. For her a good book produces a bad poem

---

1 Lawrence Durrell (1912–90), not then established as a novelist, lived outside England, mainly in Paris and the eastern Mediterranean.

from her, containing an independent moral judgement, but the poem could really have been written without the book. And I think it insulting to books to take them as a purgative in order to void material which, with a little constriction of the muscles, could have been voided anyway.

My own book isn't nearly ready. I am keeping it aside, unfinished, and writing off, now, the things that would be detrimental to it if I were to continue. You said on the back of the envelope that you wanted a poem for a special number;[1] I have one I can send, but Miller, in his letter, said he did not know when the two prose pieces of mine would appear, owing to some unexplained difficulties, and it's rather silly, isn't it, sending you stuff to keep and not to print. But do tell me; I'd love to send you the poem of course.

Sincerely,
Dylan Thomas

MS: Carbondale

GEORGE BARKER
January 6 1938   Blashford   Ringwood   Hants

Dear George Barker,
Do you feel like forgiving me for the months and months delay in answering your letter and acknowledging your poem? I've got hundreds of excuses, most of them genuine, and I'll tell you them all if you want me to or are forgiving enough to listen. But what I want to know is: are you in Dorset now, & would you be in to me if I came across from here with Augustus John, with whom I'm staying? This week-end or some-time, or early next week? I should very much like to see you, apologise, & talk more about the epistles.

Best wishes,
Dylan Thomas

MS: Texas

DAVID HIGHAM
8 January 1938   Blashford   Ringwood   Hants

Dear Higham,
I'm glad Reavey's been reasonable. Yes, £20 was what was paid to me, I remember now.[2] Formally, I approve that the rights revert to me provided that should the book be published elsewhere Reavey be repaid. Is that correct?

1 The reference is to *Booster*, later *Delta*, which Durrell helped Miller to edit. Two Thomas poems and a prose piece appeared in *Delta* in 1938 and 1939.
2 Apparently a payment for *The Burning Baby*.

With regard to the book & Church. I should rather like to select the stories to include in the new book myself, but perhaps Church should be sounded on this. Will you find out *exactly* how many stories he requires to make the new book the required size? I suggest five.[1]

Augustus John suggests that the portrait frontispiece should be done in colour.[2] This is quite an expensive process, of course, but wouldn't it be worth it? It would sound, and look, good. Will you mention it to Church when you talk to him about the other things?

I hope the Oxford Press will stump up soon. Everything's getting dreadful again.

What there is of my family is well & strong.

Yours,
Dylan Thomas

MS: Texas

REV. KENNETH THOMPSON[3]

13 I 38   Blashford Ringwood Hants

Dear Mr. Thompson,

Thank you for writing. I believe I should apologise to you, too, for I don't think I answered your last letter, a long time ago. I'm really sorry if I didn't: I had no means of getting in touch with you, as I'd unfortunately lost your address: Earl's Court was all I could remember.

And thank you for telling me about Hartcup. I wrote to him today, asking him if he'd like to send me some poems. I hope he will.

And I hope, too, that we'll be able to meet some time again, in Swansea or in London.

Best wishes,
Yours sincerely,
Dylan Thomas

MS: Bodleian Library

GEORGE REAVEY

[mid January 1938]   Blashford Ringwood Hants

Dear George,

Sorry not to have written before. I've been away, and neither did I know about the A. John portrait. The very good one he did, like a bloody fool he burnt while drying it in front of the fire for a final sitting, and he's only just

---

1 A second book, to include prose and verse, was planned by Dent. This became *The Map of Love*, published 1939.
2 The promised painting was taking a long time to arrive.
3 Unknown correspondent.

finished another one. He's taking it with him to London today. His address is: Park Studio, Pelham St, South Kensington. He will have a good man he knows to photograph it, but knows nothing about how to get a block made. Will you get in touch with him about it? He'll autograph 50 copies. What sort of blurb do you want me to do? Is it necessary to have a blurb at all? Wouldn't just, 'This is the first collection of prose by D.T.' do as well as anything? I don't like the usual sort of inadequate and misleading summary that appears; I myself am obviously not going to write a eulogy; and it isn't for me to write any sort of critical preface. I'd much prefer the stories to speak for themselves. You asked about reviewers. The papers that have noticed my work at length have been New Statesman (Stonier), New English Weekly, Times Lit Sup, Observer (Henry Warren), Criterion, Time and Tide, Spectator, Western Mail, Cardiff, South Wales Evening Post, Listener, Telegraph, Life and Letters, all of whom should obviously be sent review copies. But I suppose you know all about that. Anyway, do send some to Welsh papers too. Oh yes, and to Seamus O'Sullivan of the Dublin Review: that's got a good circulation I think. I can't think of any more names; actually, the list I gave you was of people who might be persuaded to buy the limited edition. Henry Miller wants a copy, and says he'll show it to lots of people and try to make them buy it: but I wouldn't know about that.

You wanted excerpts from reviews. Here are some. There are lots more but I haven't got them. Perhaps you can find some knocking about in old papers. Do write to me soon and tell me how things are progressing.

Yours,
Dylan

MS: Texas

DAVID HIGHAM

January 19 1938   Blashford   Ringwood   Hants

Dear Higham,

Thank you very much for managing to get hold of the O.U.P. money so soon; it was very kind of Charles Williams.

I'm enclosing the gramophone 'agreements'.

Hope you can get the short stories along to me soon.

Yours,
Dylan Thomas

MS: Texas

JULIAN SYMONS
20 January 1938 Saturday[1]   Blashford   Ringwood   Hants

Dear Julian Symons,
    I'll be able to let you have a poem by the end of next week. Is that too
late? Poem of abt 40 lines.

                                        Sincerely,
                                        Dylan Thomas

MS: Texas

HERMANN PESCHMANN
Feb 1 '38   Blashford   Ringwood   Hants

Dear Mr Peschmann,
    Thank you for the letter. I'm glad my visit went so well, & hope I'll be
able to come again.
    You say you want to know what the poem (in Twentieth Century Verse)
is 'about'.[2] There I *can* help you, I can give you a very rough idea of the
'plot'. But, of course, it's bound to be a most superficial, &, perhaps,
misleading, idea, because the 'plot' is told in images, & the images *are*
what they say, not what they stand for. Still, I hope this is of some
assistance, even if not especially for your review. (Could you, by the way,
send me a copy of that New English Weekly? I'd be very grateful, because
I'm out of touch with everything here.)

                                        Sincerely,
                                        Dylan Thomas

            The poem is, in the first place, supposed to be a document, or
            narrative, of all the emotional events between the coming and
            going, the creation and dissipation, of jealousy, jealousy born
            from pride and killed by pride, between the absence and the
            return of the crucial character (or heroine) of the narrative,
            between the war of her absence and the armistice of her pre-
Stanza 1   sence. The 'I', the hero, begins his narrative at the departure of
            the heroine, at the time he feels that her pride in him and in
Stanza 2   their proud, sexual world has been discarded. All that keen
            pride seems, to him, to have vanished, drawn back, perhaps, to

---

1 The letter is misdated: 20 January 1938 was a Thursday. No 40-line poem by Thomas
   ever appeared in Symons's *Twentieth Century Verse*. The letter could belong to early
   1939, but there is still no day/date fit.
2 'I make this in a warring absence'—in the January/February 1938 issue as 'Poem (for
   Caitlin)'.

Stanzas 3 the blind womb from which it came. He sees her as a woman
& 4 made of contraries, innocent in guilt & guilty in innocence, ravaged in virginity, virgin in ravishment, and a woman who, out of a weak coldness, reduces to nothing the great sexual
Stanza 5 strengths, heats, & prides of the world. Crying his visions aloud, he makes war upon her absence, attacks and kills her absent heart, then falls, himself, into ruin at the moment of
Stanza 6 that murder of love. He falls into the grave; in his shroud he lies, empty of visions & legends; he feels undead love at his
Stanza 7 heart. The surrounding dead in the grave describe to him one manner of death and resurrection: the womb, the origin of love, forks its child down to the dark grave, dips it in dust, then forks
Stanza 8 it back into light again. And once in the light, the resurrected hero sees the world with penetrating, altered eyes; the world that was wild is now mild to him, revenge has changed into
Stanza 9 pardon. He sees his love walk in the world, bearing none of the murderous wounds he gave her. Forgiven by her, he ends his narrative in forgiveness:—but he sees and knows that all that has happened will happen again, tomorrow and tomorrow.

MS: Texas

VERNON WATKINS
7th February [1938]   Blashford   Ringwood   Hants

Dear Vernon,

I haven't written to you for such a long time. I don't know, even, if I thanked you for the typewriting of those Yeats, Prokosch, & Watkins poems. If I didn't, I'm ashamed. And, ashamed or not, thank you very much. And for the jack-in-the-box at Christmas: it frightened us all: we opened it late at night, when we were very delicate, and leapt to the ceiling like Fred Astaire.

I was in London last week, and read some poems to night-students of the university. I didn't like the people at all; some looked like lemons, and all spoke with the voices of puddings. I detest the humility I should have, and am angry when I am humble. I appreciate the social arrogance I have in the face of my humility. I bow before shit, seeing the family likeness in the old familiar faeces, but I will not manure the genealogical tree. Your poems, Ballad, Mana, Griefs, Sunset, were more successful—from the point of controversy afterwards—than any I read. By a few, your poems in 'Wales' have been admired: The Sunbather, in particular, got them on their backs. Will you send me any new poems there are? I shall probably be addressing, from my canonical chair, more earnest suckers next month; & I'd prefer them to suck up something valuable.

I've been writing some poems, but they're away, in the house of an enemy, being typed. They're matter-of-fact poems, & illogical naturally: except by a process it's too naturally obvious to misexplain. Rhymes are coming to me naturally, too, which I distrust; I like looking for connections, not finding them tabulated in stations. A sense of humour is, I hope, about to be lost: but not quite yet: the self-drama continues: bluff after bluff until I see myself as one: then again the deadly humour. But don't bother about this understated difficulty. Send me poems, & I'll send you some. Mine—not through humility or knowledge of less competence—will be more unsatisfactory. At the moment I am, in action, a person of words, & not as I should be: a person of words in action.

Here's a photograph, taken by a woman near us.[1] It's one of many: this is the toughest. Why I want you to think of me—photographically, when I'm not about—as a tough, I don't know. Anyway, it's very big; you can write a poem on the back, or draw whiskers on it, or advertise Kensitas[2] in the front window.

My love to you, my regards to your family, & write soon. I hope to see you before the summer. Caitlin is well, happy, & dancing.[3] I miss you.

Dylan

MS: British Library

HENRY TREECE

Poet and critic (1911–66), an enthusiastic exponent of the romantic 'Apocalyptic' movement, which was a muddled reaction against politics in poetry that developed towards the end of the 1930s. With J. F. Hendry (1912–86) he edited *The White Horseman*, a collection published in 1941. His modest study of Thomas, *Dylan Thomas. 'Dog Among the Fairies'*, was not published until 1949.

[early February 1938]   Blashford Ringwood Hants

Dear Mr. Treece,

Thank you for your letter. Reavey told me, when I was in town last month, that you were writing a book about my poetry, and that he believed

1 The photograph, which shows Thomas scowling at his cupped hand as he applies match to cigarette, was reproduced as a frontispiece in *LVW*. It was taken by Nora Summers, a painter and photographer who lived with her wealthy husband six miles from Blashford. Many of the extant 1930s photographs of both Dylan and Caitlin were taken by Mrs Summers, who was a frequent visitor, being engaged in a long sexual affair with Caitlin's mother.
2 Kensitas cigarettes.
3 Caitlin, a dancer *manquée*, liked to dance by herself, to gramophone records if possible, claiming that it gave her both aesthetic and erotic pleasure.

a section of it had been printed; but he was vague about names and dates, and I had no means of getting in touch with you. I think the information actually surprised me more than it must have surprised Richard Church[1] who is, without due respect, a cliché-riddled humbug and pie-fingering hack, a man who has said to me, when I told him I was starving, that a genuine artist scorns monetary gain, and who later confessed, with a self-deprecatory shrug and a half-wishful smile that has brought tears to many a literary society, to a slight jealousy—'we're not so young as we were, you know'—of the vitality of modern youth. He thinks like a Sunday paper. I can see him telling you, with that pale, gentle, professional charmer's smile, placing together the tips of his thumb and index finger, as if to express some precise subtlety, 'It is perhaps just a *little* too early, don't you think?' If the information had been less surprising, I would have felt ashamed, it was not a thing I expected, then or ever; two small books of verse have never, to my knowledge, produced, in their writer's lifetime, a book of explanation and assessment by another writer, nor has such an adequately small reputation as mine needed an analysis of it to make it bigger. But this is not to say that I personally consider it inadvisable to write such a book as yours, and it would be unnatural of me not to be pleased and grateful. I am very much pleased, and I hope you *will* finish the book. Whether there is a place for it, and whether this is the time to place it, I can't be expected to know. I should think a publisher might be induced to take it, and I've no doubt that all the papers and magazines that have reviewed or discussed my books will take good notice of it; also a small book would be brought out cheaply, and a number of people, I should think, would get hold of it if only in order to attack the idea of such a book being written. That is, I don't quite mean that the idea of the book will be unpopular, but many of the Church-minded fogies will, with kindly condescension, 'regret' its appearance so early—I can hear them peep-peeping—in a young man's career. Will you send me a copy of the first chapter in the New English Weekly?[2] I'd be very grateful. I can't make any real, practical suggestions yet, for obvious reasons; but I should like to read some of what you've already done, and then, if you'd let me, I'd like to write at length. I could send you all the new work I have, and other sorts of material. And I'll see, of course, that you're sent a copy of my short-story book next month. Do write soon, as I will be changing my address. And do please understand that I myself think the book a grand idea, but that it should be continued only if *you* yourself, scorning the pooh-poohers and youth-talkers, the hedging ill-wishers and gassy jealous-mongers, think it interesting and advisable. It isn't for me to say anything but thank you, to promise you wholeheartedly all the assistance you may want of me, and to repeat my own belief in the eventual success of such a book:—(This, again,

1 When Treece approached Church, the publisher suggested that a book-length study of Thomas might be premature.
2 28 October 1937, 'The Poetry of Dylan Thomas. An Assessment'.

is no more than natural conceit; my opinion as to the advisability of having a book written about my own work is bound to be too prejudiced to be of worth to you.) Best wishes, and

Yours sincerely,
Dylan Thomas

MS: Buffalo

CHARLES FISHER
11th February 1938   Blashford   Ringwood   Hants

Dear Charles,

This is mostly to ask you if you could find out Dan's address for me. Tom, I suppose, knows it. I've been in London a lot since I saw you last, and meant to have a nostalgic re-union with Dan, but all I knew was that he lived in Sherwood Ho., Harrow, which didn't seem right. I'm going back to town at the end of next week, so could you let me have the address quickly? It would be very nice of you, and I'll leave you a sycamore tree in my will as soon as I've uprooted it from my wife's mother's garden. I miss our old meetings. Here, apart from Caitlin and a few very immediate people, there's no-one to talk to easily except Augustus J., who can't hear. Swansea is still the best place: tell Fred he's right.[1] When somebody else's ship comes home I'll set up in Swansea in a neat villa full of drinks and pianos and lawn-mowers and dumb-bells and canvases for all of us, and the villa shall be called Percy Villa. I have been writing quite a lot, being locked in a room every morning with beer & cigarettes and the implements of my trade. I've been lecturing, too, to classes of London University. My stories are appearing next month, under the title of 'The Burning Baby: 16 Stories', published by the Europa Press of Paris & London, and in 2 editions—a general one, and a limited signed one, dear me. And my next book will be that reversed version of Pilgrim's Progress, & will appear with the Obelisk Press, Paris.[2] Publicity over. Give my love to the boys—I can't write to them, because I don't know their numbers or roads—& when you write tell me how they are & what they're doing, & what you're doing and how you are. Don't forget the address, will you?

Love,
Dylan

MS: the recipient

1 Unless otherwise indicated, 'Fred' in a Thomas letter is always Alfred Janes, as 'Dan' is Daniel Jones, 'Tom' is Tom Warner and 'Vernon' Vernon Watkins.
2 'Prologue to an Adventure', which remained a short story. The Obelisk Press, set up in the 1930s, specialised in erotica and avant-garde novels (often the same thing) that weren't acceptable in London.

JAMES LAUGHLIN

James Laughlin (1914–97) was the founding editor and president of New Directions Publishing Co. in the U.S., which in 1936 (to the alarm of his wealthy family) set out to publish young writers. Laughlin also wrote poetry of his own. He remained Thomas's American publisher to the end.

15 February 1938   Blashford   Ringwood   Hants

Dear Mr. Laughlin,
Thank you for writing, and for offering to send me a copy of the last New Directions Collection, which I would very much appreciate. No, I haven't as yet an American publisher, but I have an agent here who is, I believe, in touch with one in connection with my two volumes of poems, 18 and 25. Next month a volume of my stories, 'The Burning Baby', is to be brought out by the Europa Press of London and Paris. Would you be interested in that volume for America? If so, do let me know when you send along the Collection. I have also a number of new poems that have appeared only in some English magazines, not in a book of mine. Would you care to see those? I should like to get them printed in America, but do not know what periodicals to send to.
                                            Yours sincerely,
                                            Dylan Thomas

MS: Houghton

*KEIDRYCH RHYS
[?February 1938]   Blashford   Ringwood   Hants

Dear Keidrych,
I'm afraid I can't supply those nine lines about In Parenthesis;[1] my knowledge of the book isn't too sure—I've only read it once—& there's no copy of it here. I'm sorry, and sorrier not to have written before. We left Anna Wickham's in turmoil, and haven't yet settled ourselves again.
Here's the opening of the long story I'm working on. I hope there's time for you to print it in number 4.[2] If there is, be careful of the punctuation, won't you? I've written it out—my borrowed typewriter's in London—as carefully as I can.
John[3] is away for a week or two, so I haven't been able to ask him for a blurb. I know he'll say something nice, & I'll get it ready for next time.
My stories—called 'The Burning Baby: Sixteen Stories'—are to be

1 An allegory of the First World War, the first work to be published by the London-Welsh writer and painter David Jones (1895–1974).
2 *Wales* No. 4, March 1938, carried Thomas's surreal story 'In the Direction of the Beginning'. An ornate piece in his 'prose-poem' style, it consists of one very long paragraph and was published as 'fragment of a work in progress'. But Thomas got on with his autobiographical stories and left it unfinished.
3 Augustus John.

published very soon, by, unfortunately, the Europa Press. I've just returned the proofs. They'll be out in a few weeks.

I do really hope 'Wales' will live; it will be scandalous if it dies. Have you tried Mrs Byng-Stamper, Manorbier Castle, for support?[1]

Write soon. Hope this fragment will be O.K. It's all I've got at the moment. I'd obviously give you every single thing I do, but I've *got* to be paid sometimes.

> Love,
> Dylan

MS: National Library of Wales

DENYS KILHAM ROBERTS
26 February 1938   Blashford   Ringwood   Hants

Dear Mr Kilham Roberts,

Of course you have my permission to include *Where once the Waters* and *The Force that through the Green Fuse* in the Penguin anthology. You needn't write to ask them, but acknowledgement to the Parton Press—who published my *18 Poems* in which these two poems appeared—should also be made.

> Yours sincerely,
> Dylan Thomas

MS: Texas

JULIAN SYMONS
[early March 1938]   Blashford   Ringwood   Hants

Dear Julian Symons,

It's in order, isn't it, for my Poem (for Caitlin) to be printed in a Paris periodical? I want it to appear in the Booster, which hasn't any English circulation. I'll see, of course, that an acknowledgement is made.

I've just been sent a couple of poems by Meurig Walters,[2] & hear you've got some of his. I do hope you'll be able to print one. I think they're very strong & original, don't you?

> Yours,
> Dylan Thomas

MS: Texas

---

1 Frances Byng-Stamper, a wealthy patron of the arts, lived at Manorbier Castle in Pembrokeshire. Augustus John knew her.
2 See next letter.

*KEIDRYCH RHYS

March 10 [1938]   [headed paper: Blashford   Ringwood   Hants]

Dear Keidrych,

Thank you for the answers. There are still some questions. Why Herring?[1] Who is Mair Evans (you?)[2] Do you agree to refuse to publish Heseltine in future? (I do not want to scram his eyes out. I do not fight with chickens, but neither do I want their messes wrapped up in paper). I'm afraid I *did* reply nastily to W. H. Reese;[3] reading his letter again, I found it overwhelmingly impudent, not so much to myself as to a stranger; I did not realise his red nonconformity, but I doubt if it would have made much difference. I wrote to Symons[4] about Meurig Walters[5]—will you forward this letter to him, by the way?—and he said he was printing some of his poems soon. I don't know whether I'll send anything for the Welsh number of 20th Century Verse. I *must* have money for what I write; and Symons paid me one tiny guinea for the last, long, serious poem of mine he printed[6]—which took 3 months to do.

I'm leaving here next week, for nowhere; I want to be in Wales, but it offers me nothing at all; I'd take any job in Wales, because I like living there best. (The paper 'Wales' is different, of course; so long as it'll print me I'll write for it, though I could do with a shilling from it now & then).

Now there's nothing, nothing at all; I'm facing starvation, which is a pity. Sorry to hear about your arm, & hope it's better now. Have you got much for the next number yet? I'll send a few short poems, if I'm still in the land of the bad-living. I've written to Cameron,[7] but have had no reply, & I'm going to write to MacNeice.

Write soon, with news.

Love
Dylan

The two prose-pieces of mine that you've printed are to appear in Henry Miller's 'Booster' in Paris.[8] That's OK, isn't it? Acknowledgement will be made. DT.

MS: National Library of Wales

1 Robert Herring.
2 *Wales* No. 4 carried an item by 'Mair Evans', 'Tradition and the Faber Stories'.
3 William Herbert Reese (1908–97), Welsh-language poet.
4 Julian Symons, of *Twentieth Century Verse*.
5 Meurig Walters (1915–88), a Presbyterian minister, wrote poetry in English and Welsh. Thomas admired his work.
6 'I make this in a warring absence'.
7 Norman Cameron.
8 One story, 'Prologue to an Adventure', and one poem, 'I make this in a warring absence', appeared in 1938 issues of *Delta*, successor to *The Booster*.

MEURIG WALTERS
March 10 1938   Blashford   Ringwood   Hants

Dear Meurig Walters,

I only want to say how much I liked your 'Rhondda Poem' in the last number of 'Wales', and how very good I think it is. I wrote to Julian Symons, of '20th Century Verse', about it, asking him whether he'd seen it and, if so, didn't he agree that he should get in touch and ask you whether you'd contribute to his paper. And he told me he had some poems of yours already, and is going to print them soon. I'm looking forward to them with great interest.

My admiration for that one poem and for all [that it?][1] promises, for its energy and roughness, its freedom from the traditional corruptions of 'taste' and 'beauty', and from that holy trinity of the English writer, memory, evocation, and nostalgia, is very genuine, and I just had to write and 'congratulate' you—a word I do not really like using—on the liveliest contribution that has appeared in 'Wales' and one that proves yet again its indispensable function.

> Sincerely,
> Dylan Thomas

MS: National Library of Wales

GEORGE REAVEY
Sunday [March 1938]   ·   Blashford   Ringwood   Hants

Dear George,

About the American negotiating: James Laughlin IV, of New Directions, wrote to me last week; he wants to be my publisher in America, and do all my future books as well. I'm going to sign a contract with him some time. But about the 'Burning Baby': Laughlin had heard that the Europa Press was doing it, & asked me to suggest to you right away that you consider printing 500 sheets for him. Laughlin was leaving America last week, & can be got hold of c/o American Express Co. Paris. I think, don't you, it's a good idea to get done by 'New Directions'? They've published Cocteau, Miller, Stein, Saroyan etc., & make nice books. (Laughlin sd he wanted to get in touch with the Europa Press quickly; he wants to bring out *a* book of mine this year.) In the event of New Directions doing the 'Burning Baby', I get, don't I—and that, for me, is the most important thing, because I am penniless—a separate advance royalty from them? I'm going to, anyway: I just have to.

I hope there's not going to be too much complication about getting the John portrait; I know it's in his London studio, but he's terribly careless. I

1 The page is creased.

suppose, if the worst comes, the book can come out quite well without him.[1] I shall probably be seeing him in a few days, & I'll try to get things straight then: but I know that he's going to leave all the business of photographing, block-making etc. to you.

Film rights? Yes, of course you can handle them for me, but, Christ, how could *those* stories be filmed? Shirley Temple as the Burning Baby?

Don't forget the Laughlin.

> Yours,
> Dylan

MS: Houghton

GEORGE REAVEY
14 March [1938]   Blashford   Ringwood   Hants

Dear George,
   Keidrych Rhys tells me you've sent him circulars about the book. What about sending me a few to post around? Did you get my last note? Have you got in touch with John?

> Yours,
> Dylan T

MS: Houghton

CHARLES FISHER
March 16 '38   Blashford   Ringwood   Hants

> I'm very busy writing, & I'd like to
> send you my new poem when it's
> finished—next week. Send me
> something you've done.

Dear Charles,
   Thank you for the news, and the address, and the fact that you all miss me a bit. I've been in London, but only for a short time, and couldn't get in touch with Dan. And since I returned I've been very busy failing to make money. I may get a job on the BBC: it all depends on the BBC. It was nice to hear of your play, and Fred's fishes, and Tom's sonata. You talk, by the way, about Ifor Davies as though I knew him. I don't. Wish him a symphony for me. Murder of the King's Canary: I'd very much like to do it with you because I've got lots of new ideas which I'm too lazy to tell you at the moment. Will it go as a radio play? I'd like to make it, with you, into a novel, make it the detective story to end detective stories, introduce

---

1 Augustus John's painting of Thomas was eventually used for *The Map of Love*.

blatantly every character & situation—inevitable Chinaman, secret passages etc—that no respectable writer would dare use now, drag hundreds of red herrings, false clues, withheld evidences into the story, falsify every issue, make many chapters deliberate parodies, full of clichés, of other detective-writers. It could be the best fun, & would make us drinking-money for a year. Write some time & tell me how you feel about it; I hope to be somewhere about Swansea in the early summer, and we can discuss it properly then.[1]

Love to all the boys, & to yourself.

Dylan

MS: the recipient

DESMOND HAWKINS
March 16 1938 — Blashford Ringwood Hants

Dear Desmond,

It was very very nice to hear from you, and very wicked of me not to have congratulated you on your safe delivery. I have just been reading a book by Dr. Carlos Wms, D.D., B.O., full of medical details, and I know what you must have suffered. In your sweet mirth, as T. E. Brown says in my favourite poem, God spied occasion for a birth;[2] and who knows what little Hitler rocks dreamily at your feet as you, at your littered desk, sit destroying a reputation with one critical hand and tossing off your Grigson-pipe with the other.[3]

The poem that was meant for your stupendous number—there isn't, I suppose, a spare copy?—died, twisted in its mysteries and I am trying now to bury it in another poem which, when completed, I shall send to you along with a photograph of Caitlin and myself breeding a Welsh Rimbaud on a bed of old purposes and new directions.

Answering your questions:

The Europa Press belongs to George Reavey, that sandy, bandy, polite, lockjawed, French-lettered, i-dotted, Russian t'd, non-committal, B.A.'d, V.D.'d, mock-barmy, smarmy, chance-his-army tick of a piddling crook who lives in his own armpit; he diddled and swindled me, the awful man; I will get him to send you a review copy, *and* a photograph of his headquarters if he isn't sitting on them.

---

1 Fisher had succeeded Desmond Hawkins as the *Canary* collaborator.
2 Another dig at T. E. Brown, this time for his poem 'Between Our Folding Lips':
'. . . We love, God makes: in our sweet mirth
God spies occasion for a birth.
Then is it His, or is it ours?
I know not—He is fond of flowers.'
3 Hawkins thought that this obscure joke might have had something to do with Geoffrey Grigson's alleged dislike of pipe-smoking. But 'tossing off' means masturbation.

I am staying here charitably until next week when we go to London again with a pick and axe for the gold pavements. I am working busily on some new stories; I want to write a whole lot, like that one you liked about Grandpa, stories of Swansea and me.[1] I don't, by the way, think that that story is better than the one in the Faber book, or than others in my Europa mistake:[2] these stories are more than 'free fantasy': they do mean a lot, and are full of work.

Croquet is over; it's all shovehalfpenny & skittling squireachy now; we've a rolling road here & an old inn[3] and a wind on the heath. To heel, to hounds, to hell.

Do you ever see the little quarterly, 'Wales'? There's good writing in it. You might drop it a poem, care of me; it prints those English outsiders as well; and it pays nothing, on publication.

Shall we ever see you in London? Perhaps, later, when your moving's over, you'll invite us for a week-end? We are quite good, and hate babies.

Write soon; I'll send you a pretty poem; 'tell me about your novel'.

The art on these pages are sections of a large, & utterly filthy, drawing which got a blob of ink in the middle and is now lost to the peepers of posterity.[4] But there's plenty more dirt where these came from, and I am collecting together a whole album of studies of unnatural history.

Love,
Dylan

MS: National Library of Wales

ROLAND PENROSE[5]
21 March 1938   Blashford   Ringwood   Hants

Dear Roland,

Of course you may count on my support, and I'll send you a story or a poem when it's needed. I don't, I suppose, get paid for a contribution? That sounds extremely mean, but I write so slowly and produce so little that it's essential—considering the fact that I try, though always without success, to exist on my writing—I have a little money for anything of mine that is published. I really am in a very bad, distressing position now, living on

1 'A Visit to Grandpa's' had just appeared in *New English Weekly*, of which Hawkins was now literary editor. It was the first to be written of ten stories, conceived as a book (eventually *Portrait of the Artist as a Young Dog*), which Thomas worked on in 1938 and 1939. He saw it as a 'provincial autobiography'.
2 The projected 'Burning Baby' book.
3 New Inn House, where Thomas's mother-in-law lived, was a former pub.
4 Two fragments of the 'filthy drawing', well executed in ink, have been pasted in, one at the beginning of the two-page letter, the other at the end; the text fits around them. In the first, a cave-man figure is contemplating a worried-looking dog. In the second, a naked negroid figure with a prominent erection chases a naked woman.
5 Roland Penrose (1900–84), authority on art; in 1938 a surrealist painter.

charity, unable to buy for myself even the smallest necessary luxuries, and having little peace of mind from those most small and nagging worries to work as well and carefully as I should like. I may have to stop writing altogether very soon—for writing is obviously full-time or not at all—and try to obtain some little, sure work. I'm sorry to write as meanly and wretchedly as this, but the way in which I'm forced to live has begun to colour everything. But, of course, if the Gallery Bulletin[1] *can't* pay, I'll still be very pleased to send you a poem or some prose. Best wishes,

Yours ever,
Dylan T

From a typescript. MS location unknown

VERNON WATKINS
[postmarked 21st March 1938]   Blashford   Ringwood   Hants

Dear Vernon,

Many thanks for your letter, and for the poems before. We are not going to Ireland, and we will try to be in Gower some time in the summer. The reason I haven't written for such a time is not because I found nothing to say about your new poems, but because I have been in London, in penury, and in doubt: In London, because money lives and breeds there; in penury, because it doesn't; and in doubt as to whether I should continue as an outlaw or take my fate for a walk in the straight and bowler-treed paths. The conceit of outlaws is a wonderful thing; they think they can join the ranks of regularly-conducted society whenever they like. You hear young artists talk glibly about, 'God, I've a good mind to chuck this perilous, unsatisfactory, moniless business of art and go into the City & make money'. But who wants them in the City? If you are a money-&-success-maker, you make it in whatever you do. And young artists are always annoyed and indignant if they hear a City-man say, 'God, I've a good mind to chuck this safe, monotonous business of money-making & go into the wilderness and make poems'.

Poems. I liked the three you sent me. There is something very unsatisfactory, though, about 'All mists, all thoughts' which seems—using the vaguest words—to lack a central strength. All the words are lovely, but they seem so *chosen*, not struck out. I can see the sensitive picking of words, but none of the strong, inevitable pulling that makes a poem an event, a happening, an action perhaps, not a still-life or an experience *put down*, placed, regulated; the introduction of mist, legend, time's weir, grief's bell, & such things as 'which held, but knew not her', the whole of the 13th line, 'all griefs that we suppose', seem to me 'literary', not living. They seem, as indeed the whole poem seems, to come out of the nostalgia

1 The magazine of the English surrealists.

of literature; the growth is not, like, say, Rossetti's, a hothouse growth, but one that has been seeded from a flower placed, long ago in the smelling and blowing and growing past, between pages. A motive has been rarefied; it should be made common. I don't ask you for vulgarity, though I miss it; I think I ask you for a little creative destruction, destructive creation: 'I build a flying tower, and I pull it down'. Neither—a phrase we used once, do you remember?—could I call this an 'indoor' poem; one doesn't need the sun in a poem to make it hot. But—though this [is] silly—it is a poem so obviously written in words; I want my sentimental blood: not Roy Campbell's blood, which is a red & noisy adjective in a transparent vein, but the blood of leaves, wells, weirs, fonts, shells, echoes, rainbows, olives, bells, oracles, sorrows. Of course I can't explain my feelings about the poem, except, sentimentally speaking again, to say that I want a poem to do more than just to have the appearance of 'having been created'. I think, of the poem, that the words are chosen, & then lie down contented with your choice.

'Was that a grief' has a lot more vulgarity in it, breaches of the nostalgic etiquette. There are, too, I think, stalenesses: 'a later threnody', 'in the years to be'; awkwardnesses: 'Next from blood's side, with poppy's nonchalance'; weaknesses: 'Their fingers frail as tendrils of light's flower'. Stale, because the words come, not quite without thinking, but without fresh imagining: down they go, the germ of what you want & what is yours ready-folded in a phrase not yours and that you don't need. The awkwardness of 'poppy's nonchalance' is obvious: it sounds like a man with a lisp & a stutter trying to gargle. And weak, because that particular alliterative line is too easily-taken, a 'breather-between' energies. But I like the poem greatly, your 'grand lines' in the 4th verse are as grand as they could be. And all of it has your own peculiar power of minute concentration: the immense, momentous scrawl on the leaf.[1]

I've always liked your ballads very much, & so far—inevitably—the ballads & lyrics mean more to me than the long & complicated poems. Will you let me send the Collier ballad to Robert Herring?

Here are 4 poems, two short simple ones, done fairly quickly, a conventional sonnet, and one I have spent a great deal of time on.[2] The typewriter I generally use has been taken from me. Could you type these out for me? I very much want to send them away some-time at the end of this week and sell them for a mouse's ransom.

I haven't finished the World story[3] yet, but I'm working on a series of short, straightforward stories about Swansea. One has been finished &

---

1 The Watkins poems that Thomas is discussing were later published with the titles 'Call It All Names, But Do Not Call It Rest', 'The Windows' and 'The Collier'.
2 Watkins said in *VW* that the four poems were 'O make me a mask', 'Not from this anger', the first part of 'After the funeral' and 'How shall my animal'. But none of these is a 'conventional sonnet' so Thomas must have included 'When all my five and country senses see', which is.
3 'In the Direction of the Beginning'.

published, & I'll send you a copy when I have one: which will [be] in a few days.

Don't be too harsh to these poems until they're typed; I always think typescript lends some sort of certainty: at least, if the things are bad then, they appear to be bad with conviction; in ordinary mss. they look as though they might be altered at any moment.

Write soon & send a poem.

Love,
Dylan

P.S. About 'blowing' light in the last verse.[1] Can you think of anything better? Do try.

MS: British Library

HENRY TREECE

23 3 38 Blashford Ringwood Hants

Dear Henry Treece,

I wanted to write as soon as I had your long, explanatory letter and the first chapter of the book, but I suddenly became very busy trying to make enough money to let me be busy in peace. Now, having failed utterly to rake in or stave off, surrounded by the noises of disruption and ejection, at last and again on the doorstep, facing a butterless future, I can reply to you at ease.

Do you, I wonder and hope not, know what it is to live outlegally on the extreme fringe of society, to bear all the responsibilities of possessionlessness—which are more and heavier than is thought, for great demands are made of the parasite, and charity, though soon enough you can learn to slip it on with a pathetic feeling of comfort, is a mountain to take—and to live from your neighbour's hand to your mouth? I have achieved poverty with distinction, but never poverty with dignity; the best I can manage is dignity with poverty, and I would sooner smarm like a fart-licking spaniel than starve in a world of fat bones. A poem, obviously, cannot be begun with the strength and singlemindedness it demands and deserves unless there is enough money behind it to assure its completion: by the second verse the writer, old-fashioned fool, may need food and drink. I know I will be paid— and how well, how well—for a poem when it is finished; but I do not know how I am going to live until it *is* finished. If I am going to live on writing any longer, I shall have to give up living; or write in a vacuum. Now I go without cigarettes, the tubular, white ants, in a smoking, swarming country. I feel in the position of the professor who was seen far out in the

---

1 In *CP*, the penultimate line of 'How shall my animal' is 'You have kicked from a dark den, leaped up the whinnying light'.

sea, spluttering, struggling, waving his arms and crying, 'I'm thinking, I'm thinking'. People on the beach, who knew he was always thinking, did nothing; and he sank.

Yes, I have seen my poetry called 'considerable' and 'important', and so it is to me. I am not really modest at all, because, putting little trust in most of the poetry being written today, I put a great deal in mine. Today the Brotherhood of Man—love thy neighbour and, if possible, covet his arse—seems a disappointing school-society, and I cannot accept Auden as head-prefect. I think MacNeice[1] is thin and conventionally-minded, lacking imagination, and not sound in the ear; flop Day-Lewis;[2] and Spender, Rupert Brooke of the Depression,[3] condemns his slight, lyrical, nostalgic talent to a clumsy and rhetorical death; I find his communism unreal: before a poet can get into contact with society he must, surely, be able to get into contact with himself, and Spender has only tickled his own outside with a feather. And who is there? George Barker, perhaps, with his hysterical persecutions and after-midnight revulsions? Gascoyne, with his Man's Life Is This Meat, and needing a new butcher, with his lobster on a bald head and his indigestible Dreams of Isis and peachmelbas? You mention Cameron and Madge.[4] Cameron's verse has no greater admirer than myself, and I respect Madge's verse, though with complete lack of affection. But when you say that I have not Cameron's or Madge's 'concentric movement round a central image', you are not accounting for the fact that it consciously is not my method to move concentrically round a central image. A poem by Cameron *needs* no more than one image; it moves around one idea, from one logical point to another, making a full circle. A poem by myself *needs* a host of images, because its centre is a host of images. I make one image,—though 'make' is not the word, I let, perhaps, an image be 'made' emotionally in me and then apply to it what intellectual & critical forces I possess—let it breed another, let that image contradict the first, make, of the third image bred out of the other two together, a fourth contradictory image, and let them all, within my imposed formal limits, conflict. Each image holds within it the seed of its own destruction, and my dialectical method, as I understand it, is a constant building up and breaking down of the images that come out of the central seed, which is itself destructive and constructive at the same time.

Reading back over that, I agree it looks preciously like nonsense. To say that I 'let' my images breed and conflict is to deny my critical part in the business. But what I want to try to explain—and it's necessarily vague to me—is that the *life* in any poem of mine cannot move concentrically round a central image; the life must come out of the centre; an image must be born and die in another; and any sequence of my images must be a

---

1 Louis MacNeice (1907–63), poet and radio playwright. Thomas invariably wrote 'Macneice'.
2 Cecil Day-Lewis (1904–72), poet and novelist.
3 Norman Cameron is said to have coined the phrase.
4 Charles Madge (1912–96), poet and sociologist.

sequence of creations, recreations, destructions, contradictions. I cannot, either—as Cameron does, and as others do, and this primarily explains his and their writing round the central image—make a poem out of a single, motivating experience; I believe in the single thread of action through a poem, but that is an intellectual thing aimed at lucidity through narrative. My object is, as you say, conventionally to 'get things straight'. Out of the inevitable conflict of images—inevitable, because of the creative, recrea- tive, destructive, and contradictory nature of the motivating centre, the womb of war—I try to make that momentary peace which is a poem. I do not want a poem of mine to be, nor can it be, a circular piece of experience placed neatly outside the living stream of time from which it came; a poem of mine is, or should be, a watertight section of the stream that is flowing all ways; all warring images within it should be reconciled for that small stop of time. I agree that each of my earlier poems might appear to constitute a section from one long poem; that is because I was not successful in making a momentary peace with my images at the correct moment; images were left dangling over the formal limits, and dragged the poem into another; the warring stream ran on over the insecure barriers, the fullstop armistice was pulled & twisted raggedly on into a conflicting series of dots and dashes.

All this, of course, is not a comment on your chapter, but only a most unsuccessful attempt, again, at 'getting things straight' for myself. As for helpful comments, I'm afraid I have none. I shall be very interested to read your chapter on Hopkins's influence, because I have read him only in the most lackadaisical way; I certainly haven't studied him, or, I regret, any other poet. The comparison with the Surrealists should give you a lot of scope, especially if, as I'm sure you do, you think it little more than a highbrow parlour game. I haven't, by the way, ever read a proper surrealist poem, one, that is, in French from the Breton boys. I've seen some translations by Gascoyne, but they were worthless.

Before I forget: New Directions, America, is going to publish both my books of verse and my book of stories, and also the long story I have been working on lately.[1] It's the intention of New Directions to 'build' me in America; advanced writing apparently sells very well over there, they're such culture-snobs; and I should think that, in some little time, the end of this year perhaps after my books are published, there would be no difficulty at all in finding a small, snob publisher to do your book: it could later be done in England. I really think it would be more successful, to begin with, brought out that way.

I want to send you the dozen or so new poems I've written and a bundle of reviews, but I will have to wait until they are forwarded to me from my last lodgings. Here, however, is one very new poem, which I consider—at the moment—to be more satisfactory as a whole than anything I've done. I hope you can understand the handwriting, I've no typewriter.

1 The first New Directions book of Thomas's writings was published in 1939. In 1938 *New Directions in Poetry and Prose*, an annual anthology edited by Laughlin, published the 'In the Direction of the Beginning' fragment.

I'm sorry I can't suggest anything; if I do think of anything helpful I'll write it down and send it to you immediately; and the other manuscripts won't, I hope, be long coming. My book of stories has been delayed, owing to the printers turning shy and calling certain paragraphs obscene; I understand new printers now have it in hand, and it is to appear on the 1st of April. I'll send you a copy, of course.

I have, suddenly, thought of a very little something, but it is a point, probably, that you have touched on, or are going to touch on, incidentally: the question of religion and the supernatural in my poetry. I know there is something I should like to write you about those questions: shall I?

I am sorry not to be able to stamp this letter. My wife and I are here completely alone, and have no food and no money at all. Neither shall we have any until the end of next month. Until then, quite honestly, we starve. That is easy to write, but all the world's hells to know.

Yours very sincerely,
Dylan Thomas

MS: Buffalo

*GEORGE DILLON[1]

25 March 1938   Blashford   Ringwood   Hants

Dear Mr Dillon,
I'm glad you're going to print the four poems I sent you,[2] and I certainly hope to send you some more soon.

No, none of the poems will appear anywhere else before May.

Here is the note about myself that you asked for.

Yrs sincerely,
Dylan Thomas

PS A letter to this address will always be forwarded to me immediately.

MS: Chicago

HENRY TREECE

[late March 1938]   Blashford   Ringwood   Hants

Dear Henry Treece,
This is to thank you, deeply, for your presents; for I shan't regard them as anything else. I, too, will send you a present one day, and may you

---

1 Editor of *Poetry* (Chicago) from 1936.
2 'When all my five and country senses see', 'O make me a mask', 'Not from this anger' and 'The spire cranes'.

welcome it as gratefully as I did yours. The cigarettes tasted better than any I've ever had; I am, by preference, a chainsmoker, though usually all the links are missing. I am not hurt, I do not lift the nose, nor call you Boy Scout: Thank you very much for sending me two such very nice things; and I am grateful to you always. (It is more than a romantic fallacy to say that only a garret-poet can produce the immortal line; it's a realistic lie. One can write on bare nerves, but not on an empty stomach; the 'impulse' of a poet is not affected by hunger & squalor, but the 'craft' needs time and concentration which a man nagged by hunger cannot afford to give it.)

I'll write *very* soon with, if possible, more suggestions & mss. Please don't bother to return anything I send you. Do you want the chapter back?

This is only a note of thanks, but the word is not 'only'.

Sincerely,
Dylan T

MS: Texas

JAMES LAUGHLIN
March 28 1938   Blashford   Ringwood   Hants

Dear Mr. Laughlin,

Thank you for writing, and for sending me the books; they interested me very much indeed, and I thought they were splendidly produced. I appreciate deeply the kind things you said about my work. I have, of course, no hesitation at all in accepting your offer of American publication, and in letting you have not only the books I have published in England but also the books that I am writing and shall write in the future. I should like you, that is, to be my American publisher for good and all.

About the books of mine that have been printed over here: my first, 'Eighteen Poems', which had a considerable success in its way, was brought out by the Parton Press; the copyright is mine, and you can have the book whenever you like. (Details about sheets—and some, I think, may have been printed already, in preparation—can be gone into later, can't they?)

My second book, 'Twenty Five Poems', was published by J. M. Dent. I did not, by the way, know I had any American agents; in fact, I have not, and I have never heard of Ann Watkins Inc. The agent in England who handled my 'Twenty Five Poems' was David Higham, of Higham, Pollinger, and Pearn, 6 Norfolk St, Strand, London; Watkins Inc. *may* do their work in America; I just don't know.[1] Neither have I heard from Watkins Inc. about your publication terms. Will you get in touch with Higham? I am writing to him by this post. I am quite sure there will be no

1 Ann Watkins & Co, a New York agency associated with Pearn, Pollinger and Higham.

possible difficulty in getting them to arrange for you the American rights, etc. of the Dent-published book. Dent has not, of course, any claim to the American copyright; my contract with them is for the British Empire alone.

My third book, 'The Burning Baby: Sixteen Stories', will appear on the first of May—it should have appeared sooner, but there was some unavoidable delay owing to the printers turning shy of some particularly harmless passages—from the Europa Press.[1] I have already written to George Reavey, of that Press, telling him to correspond with you immediately, and suggesting to him, as you said in your letter, that he should, right away, print 500 sheets for you. That matter should be easily settled. Reavey's address is: Europa Press, 7 Great Ormond St, London W.C.1.

Now comes the most difficult, and to me the most desperately important, part of this letter. I must say, straight away, that I *must* have some money, and have it immediately. I live entirely by my writing; it can be printed only in a small number of advanced periodicals, and they pay next to nothing, usually nothing. I was married recently—against all sense, but with all happiness, which is obviously more sensible—and we are completely penniless. I do not mean that we just live poorly; I mean that we go without food, without proper clothes, have shelter on charity, and very very soon will not have even that shelter. I have now less than a shilling; there is no more to come; we have nothing to sell, nothing to fall back upon. If I can be tided over for a little time, I think I will be able to work hard enough to produce poems and stories that will provide some kind of food and shelter. If not, there is no hope at all. I apologise for this recital, but every one of my hopes is based on the possibility that New Directions may be able to give me an advance on royalties: on royalties, perhaps, for books to come as well as for the books already published and which are, apart from certain arrangements, outside my province, with Reavey and my agent Higham, already yours. I will, of course, sign a contract with you stating that *all* my books, past, present, and future, are to be published by you—if you want them—in America. If New Directions cannot see its way clear—and it's all extremely irregular, I know, and must be very annoying to you—to give me an advance on royalties now, before even the books have been published in America, I am more than willing to dispense with my future royalties and take whatever sum you can give me for the complete American copyright of all books I shall write. For what I need now, and more urgently than I can tell you, is money to continue living. And, unfortunately, money *at once*: that is the important thing. I hope to finish a long prose work soon, perhaps next month—that is, if I can procure lodgings and buy necessities, for we must leave this address the moment we can buy a railway ticket to anywhere—and have it published in London in the autumn. That book, too, I can deliver, and will deliver, to

1 The printer decided the text was obscene. See page 351.

you quickly as some further exchange for the advance I hope to the lord you will be able to forward me when you receive this letter, this unavoidably miserable letter for which I again apologise. I had hoped to write all this in a businesslike manner, but I failed. I failed because, although I know nothing about the business of publishing or the agreements that can be made between publisher and author, I know enough to realise that my most sincere appeal for an immediate advance on the work you wish to publish is unorthodox and, possibly, insolent. I am sorry I had to write this, but I am forced to do away with dignity and formality, and ask you this question: Can you, at once, give me money for which, in return, I promise you all the work I have done and will do? I wish very much to be published by you. I hope, beyond all things, that you will answer me. I'll try to make my next letter to you a less wretched affair than this.

Yours very sincerely,
Dylan Thomas

MS: Houghton

MEURIG WALTERS
28 March 1938   Blashford   Ringwood   Hants

Dear Meurig Walters,

I was glad to hear from you that you were glad to hear from me; it was kind of you to talk so kindly about my letter which was, after all, the very smallest tribute I could pay to a poem that immediately struck me as one of the most original I had read for a long time; and it was encouraging to me to know that my encouragement to you was not misinterpreted as an act of senile condescension but taken simply for what it was: the congratulations and best wishes of one young man who writes a lot of poetry to another young man who writes little—on his own statement—but who is going, I hope, to write a lot more.

Glyn Jones—I haven't seen him for 2 years—was biographically correct: I am 23, married, from Swansea, and without property. I have been living out of Wales now for about a year, but not through choice; I hope at Easter to be somewhere near Swansea. We must arrange to meet.

I have just written to Keidrych Rhys suggesting that a mass-poem—though that's an ugly name—should be written by all the contributors to 'Wales'. That is, that each person should write a verse-report of his own particular town, village, or district, and that all the reports, gathered together, should be made, not by alteration but by arrangement, into one long poem. The poem would be called Wales, & wd take a whole number of the paper. The poem would be written by *all* the writers concerned, &

not by individuals. If the idea comes to anything, I hope you will take charge of the Rhondda report.[1]

Please do write again. I shall be very glad to see any poems of yours, new or old.

Sincerely,
Dylan Thomas

MS: *National Library of Wales*

MERVYN PEAKE[2]
[?March 1938][3]   Blashford   Ringwood   Hants

Dear Mervyn:
Do excuse this delay: my addresses are in a muddle, as always, and I never know what charitable home I may be trying to park myself in next. I hope your show went well, and I wish very much I could have seen it: I saw some splendid notices. Nothing we planned seems to have gone right, that visit to Wales for instance, and it is all my fault; I feel I can't go on with the idea of a Welsh travel book; for one thing, Rhys Davies has just done it, and a feeble job it was.[4] But I'm trying to do a series of stories about Welsh people,[5] and I'd like to show you one or two of them when we can get together in London—which I hope will be very soon—for you to see if you could, or would like to, do anything about drawings for them some time.

And the crazy book, yes, yes, of course. I *do* wish I could have seen the new drawings. I'm looking forward a lot to getting down to that book—though, now, I have no idea of what the story would be. Have you?

And have you seen a little quarterly called 'Wales' that prints poems & stories, fairly experimental, by Welsh people writing in English? Have you got a poem you could send me for it: I'm a kind of literary adviser to the thing. I hope you have.

I'll ring you as soon as I get to town.

Yours,
Dylan

MS: *University College, London*

1 The Mass-Observation movement, described at the time as 'a technique for obtaining objective statements about human behaviour', had a bizarre offshoot in attempts to write poetry by committee. Charles Madge, a founder of M-O in 1937, organised the 'Oxford Collective Poem', which took twelve undergraduates a month to research and write. *New Verse* published it in May 1937. *Wales*'s reply was never written.
2 Mervyn Peake (1911–68), writer and painter.
3 Peake's 'show', referred to in the letter, was an exhibition of line drawings at the Calmann Gallery. Maeve Gilmore, then married to Peake, wrote in *A World Away* (1970) that, on the day of the private view, 'Hitler marched into, oh God, was it Czechoslovakia? or was it Vienna?' Only Austria was properly invaded in 1938. Hitler entered Vienna on 13 March.
4 Rhys Davies (1903–78), novelist, published the descriptive *My Wales* in 1937.
5 *Portrait of the Artist as a Young Dog.*

*MERVYN [?PEAKE]¹
[?1938]

Mervyn dear Merve
   Will you please lend me coat and trousers for a day. Any coat & trousers so long as they aren't my own. I am supposed to speak on a public platform tomorrow Sunday just after lunch. May I call early morning say eleven.
                                             Love,
                                                Dylan
PTO
   I must, unfortunately, call for coat & trousers—doesn't matter that M is taller than D—before eleven. Say, 10.30.

[Below the text Thomas has drawn a horizontal self-caricature]

MS: University College, London

*JOHN PRICHARD²
April 1 [1938]   [headed paper: Blashford   Ringwood   Hants]

Dear John,
   I really believe Keidrych himself has your story; I thought he was going to print it in the last number—he told me he was, though that was some time ago—and I thought, therefore, that the copy must be with him. Will you find out? Anyway, I'm writing to my mother today and I'll ask her to look among the papers I've left there; if I have the story, she'll find it and send it on to you. I'm sorry about this bother, but very glad that you can get the story printed; I'm sure Herring would do it too: it's one of the best stories I've read for years. Are you working hard? I'd be very glad to see some new stuff if you felt like sending it; and I promise to return it carefully. Are you putting something in the new number of 'Wales'. I've got an idea for a collective Welsh poem which I'll tell you about when—as we hope—we come back for Easter; it might be a good idea, & wd need Vernon, you, Glyn Jones, Keidrych, Meurig Walters (did you like his Rhondda poem?) and a few others to work on it.
                                             Yours,
                                                Dylan

I've got 'Mr Sanbow's Rose' here. Do you want that back?

MS: National Library of Wales

1 University College Library believes the recipient was Mervyn Peake. Perhaps it was the amiable Mervyn Levy, on whom Thomas could rely for small favours. In any case the date is guesswork, and might be years earlier.
2 See page 290.

VERNON WATKINS
April 1 38   [Blashford]

Dear V:

The mouse is released, the cheesy bandits have nibbled off, there are squeaks of jubilation, and whiskers glint in the sun. Thank you very much indeed for the present; it came when we had no tubular white ants to smoke, when we needed them passionately; now we've got antheaps, and this evening we go to the pictures, and your closeup shall be brighter than any.

I liked your two words, and am keeping both. I'm as sure now as you are of the 'lionhead', and 'whinnying' is certainly far better than my word and may—I am coming to think it is—be the best.[1] I'm so glad you liked the poem, I had worked on it for months. The opossums are unsatisfactory, I know.[2] Before your letter came, I had cut out the ubiquitous 'weather' from the anticlimatic poem, and am revising it all; I will conquer 'rebellion in'; and 'eyed' tongue shall, momentarily, become 'lashed'.[3] The poem in memory of Anne Jones[4] I am completely rewriting; and again the 'weather' shall drop out: I'm making it longer and, I hope, better than any of my recent simple poems.

In one thing you are still wrong: 'poppy's nonchalance' is bad; it cannot be anything *but* bad; and I refute *your* criticism from the bottom of my catarrh. 'In the years to be' should, of course, stand; I was silly, and perhaps priggish, to call it a catchphrase; there is no reason why it shouldn't be and no reason that you should not revitalize it if it were; I've got one of those very youthfully-made phrases, too, that often comes to my mind & which one day I shall use: 'When I woke, the dawn spoke'.[5] You are right to write poems of all kinds; I only write poems of allsorts, and, like the liquorice sweets, they all taste the same.

I've just read a poem in an American paper, that I think's very good: Evening Prayer:

[*by Robert Fitzgerald, later collected in* In the Rose of Time. *Omitted here*]

I'm looking forward very much to seeing you.

And thanks again,

Love, Dylan & Caitlin

MS: British Library

1 In *CP*, 'lionhead' occurs in 'How shall my animal' ('That melts the lionhead's heel'), as does 'whinnying'; see postscript and note, page 327.
2 Watkins had referred to the one long and three shorter poems sent by Thomas (letter postmarked 21 March) as an 'opus' and three 'opossums'.
3 In *CP*, 'O make me a mask' has 'The bayonet tongue'. But the words 'rebellion in' were not changed.
4 'After the funeral'.
5 A later poem by Thomas begins, 'When I woke, the town spoke'.

VERNON WATKINS
[?April 1938]   Blashford   Ringwood   Hants

Dear Vernon,

In haste. Thank you for the letter & the revised poem; I shall write tomorrow evening—so that perhaps our letters cross—about this & the Broken Net. Now here is the Anne Jones poem, & now I think it is more of a poem; will you type it for me?[1] I knew it was feeble as it stood before, & the end of it—that is the part that becomes the new brackets—was too facile &, almost, grandiosely sentimental. (By the way, when you type it, will you spell Anne as Ann: I just remember that's the right way: she was an ancient peasant aunt.) I think there are some good lines, but don't know abt the thing as a whole.

News—I have a little—& criticisms etc in tomorrow's long letter. You don't mind typing for me, do you? I'm looking forward to what you say about the poem. But—again—don't read it till it's typed.

The 38th line may seem weak, but I think I wanted it like that. Anyway. . . .

Love to you
Dylan

MS: British Library

JAMES LAUGHLIN
[early April 1938]   Blashford   Ringwood   Hants

Dear Laughlin,

Thank you very very much for the twenty dollars. I'm glad you told me how things are with you. This will get me and my wife to Wales, where I come from; there I hope we can live cheaply in the deep country; and next month's twenty dollars—it's good of you to spare and promise so much when you're near broke yourself—should keep us going if we eat and drink carefully. I must get to London to meet you in May. Yes, I know I'll never make much money if I stay honest, but then I don't need much; I like money, I like the way it crinkles, I like good food and too much drink; but what I really want is just enough to keep me warm and living so that I can go on with poems and stories.

I've written to the Europa Press about those sheets, but Reavey is somewhere in Paris and won't be back until after Easter. I'll write to you as soon as I hear from you, *and* get him to write. How long will you be in

---

1 'Broken Net' was a Watkins poem. 'Ann(e) Jones', i.e. 'After the funeral', was nearing its final form.

England, and where, if anywhere, do you intend staying? You might care to find a temporary place with me. But that can wait too. Don't get butchered before we meet; two pals of mine are lost in Spain already.[1] Thanks again; now we can eat.

Dylan T

MS: Houghton

RICHARD HUGHES
[early April 1938]   Blashford Ringwood Hants

Dear Richard Hughes,
    Caitlin and I are spending Easter in Wales, and some time of it near Llanstephan. Will you be at Laugharne then? And if so, may we call and see you?
    We are hoping very much to rent a cottage for the summer, somewhere in Carmarthenshire. Do you know of any likely places cheap enough for us? If you do happen to know of anywhere, or know anyone who might know, we'd be very grateful if you'd tell us, when—as we hope—we can meet you again.

Sincerely,
Dylan Thomas

MS: Indiana

JAMES LAUGHLIN
April 25 1938   Marston Bishopston Glamorgan South Wales

Dear Laughlin,
    Have you heard yet from the Europa Press? Reavey has not written to me. He is probably in Paris, being tasteful, noncommittal, and useless.
    I hope next month to be able to move to a cottage in a Welsh fishermen's village. It will be completely peaceful there, and I should be able to work without these bloody nagging worries that make any sort of concentration impossible. But of course my moving there, and my living & working, depends on what money I can scrape up, or have scraped up for me. I do hope to God that you can keep to your promise of sending me some, soon, early in May. I'm reckoning entirely on it. The rent for the cottage is nearly a pound a week, that is, nearly 5 dollars. Food is cheap there, & we'll be

1 If two of Thomas's friends were killed in the Spanish civil war, he kept very quiet about it.

able, I hope, to buy enough. But the rent, without your help, is right out of our reach. I'm sorry to have to rely on you so much, especially as you've had no work of mine yet; but, as you know, you can have all I'll do; & I *must* be paid immediately for it: some advance, I mean. It's a pity I've got to write to you like this.

When you write, do tell me when you are arriving in London. I should very much like to be there to meet you; actually it's rather important that we should meet for arrangements etc. But now all that matters to me is moving to that little village & trying to live there.

Henry Miller, himself a poor chap, is getting some of my new prose printed in France, but I shall make nothing out of it.[1]

I hope I'll be hearing from you very soon.

Sincerely (& with apologies
for all this money talk; but it *is*
urgent, & I do hope as heartily as
you do that steel begins to boom)[2]
Dylan Thomas

MS: Houghton

MEURIG WALTERS
26th April 1938   Marston Bishopston near Swansea Glam

Dear Meurig Walters,

Thank you for the letter and the poems. I want to write a long letter about it and them, but this is only a hasty note. I've just arrived here, and I shall stay until May 1st. Then I'm going to Laugharne—do you know it? It's between Pendine and St. Clears, ten miles or more from Carmarthen— for the summer. I wonder when we could meet. I can't come to the Rhondda, I'm afraid, because I never have any money. But if you can come to Swansea before May 1st, or to Laugharne (which is far more out of the way) any time after, I'd like to meet you very much. Do let me know. Perhaps we *could* see each other in Swansea? Any pub or place. If that can't be managed, I'll write my long letter sooner.

Yours,
Dylan Thomas

P.S. Several other contributors to 'Wales' live in Swansea, & we could meet them: Vernon Watkins, John Prichard, Charles Fisher, etc.

MS: National Library of Wales

---

1 The Parisian *Delta* published 'Prologue to an Adventure' in the Christmas 1938 issue.
2 The Laughlin family's money came from steel-making.

JAMES LAUGHLIN
May 7th 1938   Gosport Street   Laugharne   Carmarthenshire   Wales

Dear Laughlin,

Thank you for the cheque. Your letter was forwarded rather late. It will help me a great lot. I've managed, as I think I told you in my last note, to get a fisherman's cottage, furnished, here in a very odd town; and if I can raise enough regular money to live on I should be happy and contented. This is a good place, undiscovered by painters, and, because the sea is mostly mud and nobody knows when the water will come in or go out or where it comes from anyway, with few sprinkling trippers or picnickers. It's a sociable place too, and I like that, with good pubs and little law[1] and no respect. I hope you can come here to see me. There's a spare bedroom for you. I too hate London, and it would be better in every way for us to meet here. If you can manage it, I'll tell you, in my next letter, how to get here. It won't cost much to come down from London.

About my book of stories and their commercial possibility in America. The stories aren't as esoteric as you might imagine. Some of them are pretty straightforward, & I think one or two, God help me, are straightforward pretty. I know it's not a very good book, but it's got things moving and happening, it isn't dead meat, it isn't dished-up Joyce, it's not heavy or soulful. Reavey is printing about a 1000 copies for England, but I don't believe he knows how to sell anything except a false personality. He's tucked up under his own armpit & looks at the world around him through a moist clump of ginger hair. He does *admit* bad taste, he's above commerce (but not so far above that he can't swindle his authors, who are a puny lot anyway and cultivate their wet dreams). The dark, struggling world with its riches, hostilities, bitches, unjustices, obscene middle-age, is a tasteless joke to him: 'oh, *must* you bring up the world again? that living dodo?': a deprecatory hem, a slight, supercilious Cambridge titter, a ringed and dainty gesture copied from some famous cosmopolitan bumboy, a deadfish smile, a tinkle in a sherry glass that is never filled up more than once, a drawing of well-decorated blinds, a discreet itch in the cock, a little bed-niggling, a short sleep with carefully surrealist dreams, & the stupidity, poverty, insanity, enmity, of the great world that holds the world of Reavey like a flea's shit in a whalebed, is dismissed again for ever, counted as nothing. (Though I don't know why I should trouble to write all that.)

And yes yes what a grand, comic heroism it is, this glandular, neural importance of ours, this fighting and entering, denial, acknowledgement, and annihilation. How I hate those words. How I hate to know what we're doing—Don't show my V.C. to the visitors, Willie,—to put down immodestly the facts of our own naked heroism. And every time we're given a

---

1 Laugharne, which was off the beaten track, had a reputation for tough characters, family feuds and fist-fights. A police constable was stationed there and dispensed rough justice.

little medal for it we nearly get sick with glory and hate and *shame*. But I know I shan't go down; I've got that heroism, too, and badly. I think that this *churning* matters, I shall go on writing what's wanted even though it won't ever be. We all may be wrong, but it's still the charge of the light brigade, the Battle of the Boys of the Light. Oh the lovely melodramatic heroes. On, on, money to right of them, fame to the left, an income, a new suit, a special party, 'Tell me Mr. Gluepot how did you start writing? do you believe in the feminine verse-ending? is Europe at the Crossroads?', lobster for tea, champagne every night, a niche in Letters, and an everlasting hole in the earth.

You say I will find you sentimental, grossly contrived, & blundering. You will find me sentimental too, vague, conceited, cowardly, proud, very ordinary, all appetite & no belly. I'll tell you all about the things in New Directions, with arrogance, vehemence, but don't believe me. I'm very sincere but I rarely know what I mean, & my attitude is a loud mixture of great tolerance & great intolerance.

No, I can't translate. I'm without education, I left a smalltown school when I was 15 or so. I do some hack reviewing occasionally, but either slate or praise the books too much for my reviews to be used regularly. The standard of reviewing is mediocrity, and—tum tum the Boys of Light—I refuse to judge by it.

I'll try to get a copy of my 2nd book of poems for you. And I'll write a letter to Reavey's armpit and tell it that the wide world outside wants to know about sheets.

Here's a new poem, just finished.[1] I'm sorry not to be able to type it. Before you read it properly, will you type it out yourself? I think typescript gives a manuscript some finality and completion.

And don't forget: try to come here after Pound.[2]

Thank you again, very much.

Dylan Thomas

MS: Houghton

KEIDRYCH RHYS
May 8th 1938   Gosport Street   Laugharne   Carmarthenshire

Dear Keidrych,

We've taken a fisherman's cottage here for the summer. Hope you'll come and see us sometime soon. Together we might make an attack on Squire Hughes and get him to put up some money.[3] I'm afraid I can't, at the moment, raise anything. Is it true that the Parton Bookshop has gone bust? And have you really lost £80?

I'm not going to do a review of Heseltine's nonsense. It's just a Violent

1 'How shall my animal'.
2 Laughlin, who published Ezra Pound, was on his way to see him in Italy.
3 Richard Hughes was a potential source of extra finance for *Wales*.

Rain in the neck to me.[1] If people were making a great blather about Heseltine, saying that these poems were good or anything like that, I'd like to say, in print, that I think them bad; but as no-one cares a bit, why should I bother. I'll send the pamphlet back, if you like, for someone else to do.

Heseltine should receive the recognition due to him: complete silence. I'm not going to mention him again ever in a letter to you.

What did the Criterion say about *Wales*?

I had a sweet letter from Meurig Walters. He said that he knew his poems weren't very hot yet, but, after all, he'd only written about 10 and he couldn't expect to be perfect.

What are you doing in Leeds? Do you want a Wales contribution from me? Write soon, & don't forget to look us up & stay a bit.

Love,
Dylan

MS: Carbondale

GEORGE REAVEY

[May 1938]   Gosport Street   Laugharne   Carmarthenshire   Wales

Dear George,

This is my new address. How is the book getting on? Any proofs coming soon? James Laughlin asked me to tell you not to forget about the sheets. *Let me know a few things.*

Sorry to have missed your party for Beckett[2] & the other man (That's the painter, isn't it, whose work we liked so much?). We haven't been in London together since we last saw [*sic*], & it isn't likely I'll be up before my book comes out: I'll be up then for a drink with you.

Regards to your wife.

Yours,
Dylan

MS: Houghton

HENRY TREECE

16th May 1938   Gosport Street   Laugharne   Carmarthenshire

Dear Henry Treece,

I've been moving house. That is, I've left, with trunks and disappointment, one charitable institution after another and have found and am now occupying, to the peril of my inside and out, my rheumatic joints, my fallen chest, my modern nerves, my fluttering knitted pocket, a small,

1 *Violent Rain* was Nigel Heseltine's first book of poems.
2 Samuel Beckett (1906–89), whose novel *Murphy* appeared in 1938, was not yet a playwright with a large following.

damp fisherman's furnished cottage—green rot sprouts through the florid scarlet forests of the wallpaper, sneeze and the chairs crack, the double-bed is a swing band with coffin, oompah, slush-pump, gob-stick, and almost wakes the deaf, syphilitic neighbours—by the side of an estuary in a remote village. (The village also contains bearded Richard High-Wind Hughes,[1] but we move, in five hundred yards, in two or more different worlds: he owns the local castle, no roof and all, and lives in a grand mansion by its side and has a palace in Morocco: these legendary possessions were acquired half by whimsy, half by influence. I could beat out an elfin cadence with the best, be naughty, delightful, naive, adult, shrewd, bewitching and pawky about children—'He has the fairy alchemy':—H. Wolfe[2]—but all the influence I could raise wouldn't buy me a paper-bag of trippers' shit from Merlin's cave.) And that is my excuse for not writing, for not thanking you for the Hopkins chapter[3] or enclosing the mss I promised. It's taken such a time to settle down and up. I hope you'll forgive me. I was much impressed by the Hopkins chapter, which means I enjoyed it and thought much of it was true. What a lot of work you've put in. I never realised the influence he must have had on me. As I told you before, I have read him only slightly. I have read far more Francis Thompson. I've never been conscious of Hopkins' influence. As a boy of 15 or 16, writing in all sorts of ways false to myself, composing all sorts of academic imitations, borrowing sometimes shamelessly and sometimes with the well-suppressed knowledge of a pretence to originality, I find—from looking over many hundreds of those very early poems— that there was, and still is, to me, not a sign of Hopkins anywhere. (And I *had* read him then, as I had read a great deal of poetry, good and bad; or, rather, I had read *through* his book.) The people most to be found in those early poems were, I think, the Elizabethans and George Peele, Webster and, later, Beddoes, some Clare (his hard, country sonnets), Lawrence (animal poems, and the verse extracts from the Plumed Serpent), a bit of Tennyson, some very bad Flecker and, of course, a lot of bits from whatever fashionable poetry—Imagists, Sitwells—I'd been reading lately. But out of all that muddle, some poem-sections of which I enclose unaltered, I see no Hopkins. You might see it; you've already proved several things to me in that extraordinary chapter. Sometimes, I think, the influence of Swinburne is more obvious than that of Hopkins in a couple of the quotations from my poetry that you use: 'All all and all the dry worlds couple',[4] for instance. This is rhythmically true, at least.

Very much of my poetry is, I know an enquiry and a terror of fearful expectation, a discovery and facing of fear. I hold a beast, an angel, and a

1 Richard Hughes made his name with *A High Wind in Jamaica* (1929), a novel about children captured by pirates.
2 Humbert Wolfe (1885–1940), poet and civil servant.
3 Chapter 5 of Treece's book about Thomas was called 'The debt to [Gerard Manley] Hopkins'.
4 The poem is 'All all and all the dry worlds lever', but 'lever' becomes 'couple' in the third stanza.

madman in me, and my enquiry is as to their working, and my problem is their subjugation and victory, downthrow & upheaval, and my effort is their self-expression. The new poem I enclose, 'How Shall My Animal', is a detailed enquiry; and the poem too is the result of the enquiry, and is the furthest I can, at present, reach or hope for. The poem is, as all poems are, its own question and answer, its own contradiction, its own agreement. I ask only that my poetry should be taken literally. The aim of a poem is the mark that the poem itself makes; it's the bullet and the bullseye; the knife, the growth, and the patient. A poem moves only towards its own end, which is the last line. Anything further than that is the problematical stuff of poetry, not of the poem. That's my one critical argument, if it can be called that; the rest is a poetical argument, and can only be worked out in poems.

I've been looking through some old reviews, hoping to find some vague material for you. Desmond Hawkins' review of 25 Poems in the Spectator was one of the best, I remember, but I haven't a copy of it. He said several very good, clear things. Here are a few reviews which might give you some opportunities for remarks etc. There's no point in sending you ordinary, straightforward damning or congratulatory reviews, is there—This is great, This is punk. Stephen Spender, by the way, said in a review of the year's poetry some time ago—in the Daily Worker—'The truth is that Thomas's poetry is turned on like a tap; it is just poetic stuff with no beginning nor end, shape, or intelligent and intelligible control'. Do you think that's worth mentioning and refuting? It's a belief held by many fancy poets like Spender. (I should like to know, too, how much that complete bit of nonsense was caused by a review I once wrote for New Verse of Spender's 'Vienna' operetta. Have you a copy of that review?) I know that you wouldn't want to introduce into your book any particular bickering, but Spender's remark is really the exact opposite of what is true. My poems *are* formed, they are not turned on like a tap at all, they are 'watertight compartments'. Much of the obscurity is due to rigorous compression; the last thing they do is to flow; they are much rather hewn. Now Spender himself has no idea of form; his poetry is so much like poetry, & so remote from poems, that I think most of his work will become almost as unreadable as the worst of the Georgians—& very soon.

Another remark I came across in a review—by Julian Symons of Hart Crane[1] in 20th C. Verse—is: 'No modern poet except Thomas is, for me, more affecting, more able to twist words to the shape of the reader's tears.' Are you going to mention Hart Crane? Three or four years ago, when I first knew Norman Cameron, he told me that the most obvious modern influence in my poetry *was* Crane, a friend of his. And he was astonished, and at first unbelieving, when I told him that I had never heard of Crane before. He showed me some of his poems then, and I could certainly see what he meant: there were, indeed, two or three almost identical bits of phrasing, and much of the actual sound seemed similar. Since then I've

1 Hart Crane (1899–1932), American poet; he committed suicide.

read all Crane's poems, and though now I see the resemblance between his poetry and mine to be very slight, I can understand that some people might still think I had come under his influence.

You ask me about the Middle Ages. I know nothing about them. You must remember I've had no education—I left a provincial secondary school when I was 15 or so—and I've never read anything except in Modern English. Also, I can't read French, although I've often been called an imitator of the surrealists etc. I'm looking forward to the chapter on surrealism, and the 'straight' poems.

I want to let you have this very inadequate letter straight away. There's been too much delay between our writing, but it was all my fault and now I'm settled, however precariously, once again. I'm not enclosing in this letter a selection of very early poems; I'll try to get them typed tomorrow & will then send them off straight away. I haven't forgotten about religion & the supernatural, but it seems to me now like an essay that has to be written so it will be better if I say what I think about it, at random, informally, from time to time. One of the times will be when I send off the typed poems, tomorrow or the day after. Again, forgive me. I've got a lot of material about—reviews, about 10 exercise books full of poems,[1] a few articles on poetry etc.—and they only need a little weeding & cutting before I can let you have them. If you've got any questions that might have arisen from the chapters you've done or from the plan for the rest of the book, do let me know.

All Best Wishes,
Dylan T

MS: Buffalo

JAMES LAUGHLIN

May 17 1938   Gosport St Laugharne Carmarthenshire Wales

Dear Laughlin,

Very glad to hear that you will come down to Wales to see me. I suppose it will be early in June.

And glad that you liked the poem I sent you. I enclose two others. When is the 1938 New Directions[2] to appear? I haven't much new stuff yet, apart from the 3 poems you now have of mine. 4 short poems are coming out in Poetry, Chicago—not because I like the paper but because it pays.[3] If your number comes out late in the year, I should have one or two poems and some prose by then. I write extremely slowly: a poem may often take 2 months.

Auden is, I think, 31. I am 23. I don't know Auden, but I think he sounds

1 Only four exercise books, containing about 200 poems, are known to exist; they are at Buffalo.
2 *New Directions in Poetry and Prose.*
3 The poems were the four named in note 2, page 330.

bad: the heavy, jocular prefect, the boy bushranger, the school wag, the 6th form debater, the homosexual clique-joker. I think he sometimes writes with great power: 'O Love, the interest itself in thoughtless heaven, Make simpler daily the beating of man's heart.'[1] I can't agree he's as bad as MacLeish.[2] He's overpraised of course. I've added my own little dollop of praise in a number of New Verse devoted entirely, with albino portrait and manuscript, to gush and pomp about him. He's exactly what the English literary public think a modern English poet should be. He's perfectly educated (& expensively) but still delightfully eccentric. He's a rebel (i.e. an official communist) but boys will be boys so he is awarded the King's Medal; he's got a great sense of Humour; he's not one of those old-fashioned, escapist Bohemians (which means he doesn't get drunk in public, that he dresses like a public school-master not like a 'silly artist'); he follows his own ideas truly of the brotherhood of man, 'Love thy neighbour and, if possible, covet his arse', but there's no hanky-panky about him; he's a man's man. He's just what he should be: let him rant his old communism, it's only a young man's natural rebelliousness, (& besides, it doesn't convert anybody: the awarding of conservative prizes to anti-conservatives who are found to be socially harmless is a fine, soothing palliative, & a shrewd gesture. And, incidentally too, the rich minority can always calm down a crier of 'Equality For All' by giving him *individual* equality with themselves).

About Higham. I am writing to him. He has handled only one poetry book for me, '25 Poems', which Dent published. He has had nothing to do with the handling etc. of either my first book of poems or my book of stories. I shall be telling him that—apart from '25 Poems', for which he still manages the *minute* royalty arrangements between me & Dent (about 10 shillings every quarter)—I don't require any more the services of an agent. Neither do I. I shan't, whatever Higham hopes, be producing a novel, now or at any other time: only obscure poems & imaginative prose, & over those, as he well knows, he needn't bother a bit.

Looking forward to seeing you soon.

Dylan T

MS: Houghton

*JOHN PRICHARD
May 20 1938   Gosport St Laugharne Carmarthenshire

Dear John,

Thank you for giving *Black Spring* to Fred to bring to me. Did you read it?

And congratulations on your *Bachelors Three*. I enjoyed it very very

1 The opening lines of W. H. Auden's poem 'Prologue'.
2 Archibald MacLeish (1892–1982), American poet.

much, quite as much as the promenade story: perhaps even better. It made me laugh out loud. A man called Montgomery Butchart is soon to start a publishing firm, & wants mss. I gave him your name, and he will get in touch with you. Even though you haven't enough stories for a book, he may do something about an advance on the amount you have. I don't know how much money he has, but he's worth going after. Have you sent anything to Miller's paper, 'Delta'? If not, will you send me something to send him: I'm writing to him this week. I know he'll accept. Not too long a story, if prose. But what about sending me The Green Skulled Crews & a few others to send him? The fact that it's been printed in Wales doesn't matter a bit. Do write me in a day or two. I have Mr Sanbow's Rose here. Shall I lend it to Hughes or send it back to you?

About *Bachelors Three*. I think the *complete* success of the story—though it's grand now—is marred by two or three small phrases: 'at these courts carnal, holden . . .' I do think that that's out-of-place. I do *know* it is; it pulled me sharply, & irritatingly, in the middle of my enjoyment. It's too much of a facetious trick. The trick came off in one passage in the prom. story, but not here: 'these carnal courts, held' is right. And another phrase: 'the broken sundial which shall tell no more hours that are golden' is, to me, clumsily 'literary'. If you must have it at all, why not 'no more golden hours'. But I think the sentence is best, & the climax of the story more effective, if it stops at 'broken sundial'.

Shout if you don't like these tiny criticisms. I swear both those phrases are wrong, from the depth of my catarrh.

Don't forget to write very soon about Sanbow & things for Miller.

Dylan

PS wish you could come down here for a day or two, or a weekend. Hughes, (whom we see very little of, by the way, he's such a wet stick) would like to see you, too. And that might be good policy.

MS: National Library of Wales

HENRY TREECE
June 1st [1938]   Gosport Street   Laugharne   Carmarthenshire

Dear Henry Treece,

I think Edith Sitwell would be very pleased to read the book. I don't know if she likes me, personally, now, or not. I have the idea she's offended, but this may be incorrect. I wrote her some two months ago at her Paris address, but have had no answer; perhaps she's away, perhaps the letter hasn't been forwarded, perhaps the address is dead, perhaps she has been insulted by my very long delay in replying to her letters, perhaps she too has gone lazy or bad-mannered (this I doubt extremely). Anyway, she still likes my work and she'll undoubtedly like yours, and her London address, which won't be dead unless this Girton & county and deaf middle-aged ladies' institution has been raided, is care of The Sesame Club, 49 Grosvenor St., W.1. The Paris address is 129 Rue Saint-Dominique, VII. About her review, & the subsequent letters, in the Sunday Times,[1] some of which you said you might mention or include:—She makes a few interesting misreadings, or, rather, half-readings. She says the 'country-handed grave' in my poem A Grief Ago is 'that simple nurse of grief, that countryman growing flowers and corn'. My image, principally, did not make the grave a gentle cultivator but a tough possessor, a warring and complicated raper rather than a simple nurse or an innocent gardener. I meant that the grave had a country for each hand, that it raised those hands up and 'boxed' the hero of my poem into love. 'Boxed' has the coffin and the pug-glove in it.

Edith Sitwell's analysis, in a letter to the Times, of the lines 'The atlas-eater with a jaw for news/Bit out the mandrake with tomorrow's scream,' seems to me very vague and Sunday-journalish. She says the lines refer to 'the violent speed and the sensation-loving, horror-loving craze of modern life'. She doesn't take the literal meaning: that a world-devouring ghost creature bit out the horror of tomorrow from a gentleman's loins. A 'jaw for news' is an obvious variation of a 'nose for news', & means that the mouth of the creature can taste already the horror that has not yet come or can sense it coming, can thrust its tongue into news that has not yet been made, can savour the enormity of the progeny before the seed stirs, can realise the crumbling of dead flesh before the opening of the womb that delivers that flesh to tomorrow. What is this creature? It's the dog among the fairies, the rip and cur among the myths, the snapper at demons, the scarer of ghosts, the wizard's heel-chaser. This poem is a particular incident in a particular adventure, not a general, elliptical deprecation of this 'horrible, crazy, speedy life'.

You say you intend showing the book to Michael Roberts who will be 'sympathetic towards us'. You are not treading on my corns when you call Roberts a good Thinker, but I personally can do without his condescension. He commented in the London Mercury that 'it is a pity D. T. should sometimes give the impression of using a large & personal vocabulary merely to make a schoolboy exhibition'. The phrase I object to is not 'a schoolboy exhibition', for I'm not afraid of showing-off or throwing my cap in the air, but 'It's a pity'. What function has this patronising 'pity' in criticism? Do I need a critic to weep over my errors of taste? Let him point them out, tell me, if he likes, how to rectify them; but, for Christ's sake, not sympathise.

Yes, I should certainly write to James Laughlin of New Directions (Norfolk, Connecticut). I've had a lot of letters from him lately about plans for publicity for my stories and poems in America, & I know he'll be very interested in your book. He seems genial & very earnest and has been

---

1 Sitwell's review appeared on 15 November 1936.

giving me small sums of money regularly, though now they've ceased. He talks about 'his' poets; and takes an avuncular interest in obscurity.

I wonder whether you've considered writing anything—perhaps only a few paragraphs—about the Welsh-ness of my poetry:—this is often being mentioned in reviews and criticisms, and I've never understood it. I mean, I've never understood this racial talk, 'his Irish talent', 'undoubtedly Scotch inspiration', apart from whiskey. Keidrych Rhys—editor of the very good little magazine 'Wales'—always has a lot to say about it. He's an ardent nationalist, and a believer in all the stuff about racial inspiration etc. If you felt like it, you might drop him a line (c/o J. F. Hendry, 20 Vernon Road, Leeds) & tell him about your book and ask him what he thinks about the Welsh in my work. Anyway you'll get back a long & interesting letter: he's the best sort of crank.

I know little Dyment.[1] He's a harmless twig, not worth shaking off.

Yes, the oompah *is* a swing-band term. I enclose a glossary from a story in a swing magazine: Black Trumpet.

And Hughes is still a jive-man. His stories, I think, are mediocre: his verse negligible: his demon, whimsy (see any conversation in H. W. in Jamaica, & especially the last sentence in the book). Of course I get more out of life than he does. My envy may be rancid, but my faith is the best butter.

I think the method you adopted in the Surrealist chapter—the clearing away of superficial misconceptions by attack and contrast of quotations— is the only effective one, and I thought the whole chapter extremely well argued & formed. You know Gascoyne's poem in a very early number of New Verse, that begins something like 'White curtains of tortured destiny'? There are some lines in that I feel sure you could make use of, lines far more engaging and precociously lunatic than any in his Magritte poem. I've nothing to argue about in this chapter, &, apart from that Gascoyne poem for quotation, no suggestions. It's a fine piece of work, & has convinced me once again that my own sane bee in the bonnet can never be a pal of that French wasp forever stinging itself to a loud and undignified death with a tail of boiled string.

Did you tell me, in an early letter, that you might spend some of your summer holiday in Wales? Why not come & see us here? There's room for you, & food.

Yours,
Dylan T.

I'm looking forward to the other chapters, & will try to let you have the poems I promised you—early ones—very soon. They're not being as easy to arrange as I imagined.

MS: Buffalo

1 Clifford Dyment, poet (see page 1017). Richard Church was fond of his work, and published his first book of poems, *First Day*, in the same series as Thomas's *Twenty-five Poems*.

JAMES LAUGHLIN
June 1 1938   Gosport Street Laugharne Carmarthenshire S Wales

Dear Laughlin,
   Delighted to hear you're in England. Yes, do please come down for the
weekend—& for as long as you care to stay. We've a poky cottage, but
there's room for you, & extremely welcome.
   You take a train from Paddington to Carmarthen and then take a 'bus
from Carmarthen to Laugharne. (The 'buses run every hour.) Or else you
take a train from Paddington to St. Clears (just beyond Carmarthen) & taxi
from there. But I advise the first: to Carmarthen & then 'bus. When you get
to Laugharne, go into Brown's Hotel—anybody will tell you where that is—
& enquire our whereabouts. It's very easy.
   It's about 5 hours, I think, altogether from London to Carmarthen, &
then about $\frac{1}{2}$ hour from Carmarthen to Laugharne.
   Looking forward very much to seeing you. We expect you Saturday. Start
in the morning, early as possible.
                                             Yours,
                                             Dylan T.

MS: Houghton

*JOHN PRICHARD
[about Wednesday 1 June 1938]   Gosport Street   Laugharne

Dear John,
   Glad to hear you can come down.
   The American publisher man, James Laughlin who runs New Directions,
is also coming down to see me this week-end. You can stay with us—we've
only a tiny place, as you know—& Laughlin can stay in the pub; or,
alternatively, you can stay with Hughes[1] & Laughlin here. I'll see Hughes
tonight & find out. Anyway, whatever is arranged, there's room for you.
And the arrangement will probably be that you stay with us, which will be
nicer.
   You know how to get to Laugharne don't you? A 'bus from Carmarthen
Guildhall Square. Drop in at Brown's Hotel & buy a Felinfoel[2] and ask
where we live: they know.
                                             Dylan

MS: National Library of Wales

1 Richard Hughes.
2 A beer brewed at Felinfoel, Llanelli.

D. S. SAVAGE[1]
10 June [1938]   Gosport Street   Laugharne   Carmarthenshire   S Wales

Dear D. S. Savage,
   Just had your note about the Partisan Review. I'll be delighted to send a couple of poems, in a few days when they've been typed. It doesn't matter if the poems have been printed before, recently, in English magazines, does it?

With best wishes,
Yrs truly
Dylan Thomas

MS: Texas

GEORGE REAVEY
16th June 1938   Gosport Street   Laugharne   Carmarthenshire

Dear George,
   I am sorry to hear about the complications; I rather thought it was some stupidity on the part of the printers that had caused this delay. Will you tell me which are the stories, or sections of stories, to which most objection is taken? The only story I can think of which might cause a few people a small and really unnecessary alarm is The Prologue To An Adventure; this I could cut out from the book, and substitute a story about my grandfather who was a very clean old man.[2] If, however, objection is taken to the book as a whole, then your suggestion of publication first in Paris seems very sensible. I was approached by Lawrence Durrell, for the Obelisk Press, some time ago, and I am pretty confident that, through Durrell and Miller, it would publish the book. That is, unless you have other Paris plans. To publish first in America doesn't seem so good to me, as Laughlin does not want to bring the book out there until a book of my poems has been published and until he has managed to establish for me a small American reputation. I don't think either that a collection of opinions from 'responsible' people should be used except as a very last chance. As to your suggestion of publishing the first edition at a guinea, I know nothing: is the alleged obscenity any less harmful at a guinea?[3] and would a guinea book sell at all?

---

1 Derek Stanley Savage (b. 1917), poet and author. Savage contributed to the American magazine *Partisan Review*, and in 1938 compiled a 'little anthology' of British poets for it. The other poets he chose were Roy Fuller, Julian Symons, Keidrych Rhys, David Gascoyne and George Barker.
2 'A Visit to Grandpa's'.
3 A high-priced book was less likely to be prosecuted for obscenity than a cheap one. The authorities assumed that the well-off were less corruptible than the poor. Publishers followed this unwritten rule.

I had a letter from John this morning. What a muddler he is. He says now that he is dissatisfied with his portrait of me, & would like to do another:— we may as well wait until the Religious Tract Society offers to publish The Burning Baby. But I'll find out what I can from him when he comes down here next week.

There is no contract between me & the Parton Press as to my 18 Poems. The book, as you know, was published by David Archer, then in charge of the Press, & the copyright is mine. I lost badly on that book, owing to my ignorance & Archer's vagueness: I was given, in small irregular sums just about the time of publication, no more than £4 or £5, & have not received a halfpenny royalty although the book, for poetry, has sold, since 1934, remarkably well. The profits of the book—at the beginning at least, when reviews would sell it—just went straight to help Archer's personal debts. Since then, although many copies have been sold, I know, I have heard & had nothing at all. So if new arrangements are to be made, I think I should be given a fair lucrative deal. Are you prepared to give me money? When, & how much? I think the book, given some new publicity, wd sell quite well again. Auden's first poems in their new, stiff-covered edition went, as you remember, splendidly: & that was before he was the comparative best-seller he is today.

I won't be in London for some time, as I cannot afford the fare. Let me know news (if any) about the book, & (very soon if possible) about the 18 Poems. Unless I can manage to cut out the offence in my stories, Paris publication seems to me best, though I am getting heartily fed-up with all the bother and can't, at the present moment, see why I should extend your publishing rights to 2 years; if you fail to do anything with it in the stipulated time, I may as well have a shot at it myself. I want the book published soon, because I need urgently the little it will make me. This is not a definite refusal of your suggestion for extension, but is certainly what I feel like now.

Sincerely,
Dylan T

MS: Houghton

HENRY TREECE
16 June 1938   Gosport Street   Laugharne   Carmarthenshire

Dear Henry Treece,
I'm very glad indeed that you both will come and spend some time with us in the summer; any time, for any time. I warn you that our cottage is pokey and ugly, four rooms like stained boxes in a workman's and fisherman's row, with a garden leading down to mud and sea, that our living & cooking is rough, that you bathe or go dirty; you will find my wife extremely nice, me small, argumentative, goodtempered, lazy, fumbling,

boozy as possible, 'lower middle class' in attitude and reaction; a dirty tongue; a silly young man. I hope you like drinking, because I do very much and when I have money I don't stop. There are three good pubs here, the best bottled mild in England, and no prohibitive drinking hours; there are walks, & boats, and nets to pull, and colossal liars to listen to. There is a double bed in one room, two single beds in the other; you can sleep in the double bed, or in the two beds, or sandwiched in a single one. There is an earth lavatory and it smells like a shithouse. Welcome; & let me know when. (By the way, what do I call you? Throw your Treece away.)

This is a bad time for me again, and I can't buy a stamp for you. I haven't a single penny, or halfpenny, or filed French slot-coin. Smokeless and breadless, we face a bad weekend. We wait for shillings which we have no right to expect. Bitter, cruel Laugharne; my pipe is full of buttends from the grate, my table crowded with the dead ends of poems, my head full of nonsense. The sun is shining on the mud, my wife is out cockling, I am writing to a critic in Northumberland, a little girl has called with buns, I say, 'No buns', though all my everlasting soul shouts for them and my belly is turned by the sight in the kitchen of two poor dabs we caught, two out of all the breeding monsters in the sea, with a broken net yesterday. Last week I finished a long story about my true childhood, and here's a letter from Life & Letters saying they will print it and pay for it in September.[1]

> O Chatterton and others in the attic
> Linked in one gas bracket
> Taking Jeyes' fluid as narcotic;
> Drink from the earth's teats,
> Life neat's a better poison than in bottle,
> A better venom seethes in spittle
> Than one could probe out of a serpent's guts;
> Each new sensation emits
> A new vinegar;
> Be a regular
> Fellow with saw at the jugular.
> On giddy nights when slap on the moon's mask
> A madman with a brush has slapped a face
> I pick a stick of celery from the valley
> I find a tripper's knicker in the gully
> And take another nibble at my flask.
> What meaning, voices, in the straight-ruled grass,
> Meaning in hot sock soil? A little cuss
> Can't read sense in the rain that willy nilly
> Soaks to the vest old dominies and drunks.
> Dissect that statement, voices, on the slabs.
> Love's a decision of 3 nerves

1 'The Peaches', another of the *Portrait of the Artist* pieces. It appeared in October.

And Up or Down love's questions ask;
On giddy nights I slap a few drunk curves
Slap on the drunk moon's mask.
Rape gulp and be merry, he also serves
Who only drinks his profits
And would a-wooing go around the graves.
Celibate I sit and see
Women figures round my cell,
Women figures on the wall
Point their little breasts at me;
I must wait for a woman's smile
Not in the sun but in the dark;
The two words stallion and sterile
Stand in a question mark.
The smiling woman is a mad story,
Wipe it away, wipe a crumb
From the preacher's table.
I offer you women, not woman,
A home and a dowry:
3 little lusts shall your dowry be,
And your home in a centaur's stable.

That's better; but the trouble is I can quite easily feel like that these days, & when I said my head was full of nonsense I meant it. I'm an expert at aping my own moods; now I could wear Dowson's invisible hat, & my throat can encompass Chesterton's dead rattle; John Gawsworth's[1] sanitary towels float down the air like red snow.

When I mentioned Life & Letters, I thought that that paper might easily be interested in any chapters of yours you might like printed separately. Herring's a friend of mine, more or less, & why not write to him? And do tell me what poem, or piece of poem, you'd like me, for a footnote, to analyse in detail? I'll send you some things very soon, & try to answer your questions. You might send me the 'straight' chapter some time. Apologies for muddled letter, for the lack of a stamp.

Dylan Th

MS: Buffalo

D. S. SAVAGE
28 June [1938]   Gosport St   Laugharne   Carmarthenshire

Dear D. S. Savage,
    Here's one of the poems I promised.
    When I wrote before, I forgot that I had promised to New Directions nearly all my new poems:—N.D. is going to publish my two poem books in

1 John Gawsworth (T. I. F. Armstrong) (1912–70), writer and eccentric.

the U.S.—for that yearly anthology of theirs. So this is the only one I can spare. It hasn't been published anywhere in England yet, & if it is it will only be in some small, non-U.S.-sale paper like 20th Century Verse.

But I think you said that contributions weren't too late by August 1, and if I finish a new poem before then, shall I send it along?

Sincerely,
Dylan Thomas

MS: Texas

JAMES LAUGHLIN

28 June [1938] Gosport Street Laugharne Carmarthenshire

Dear Laughlin,

I was extremely sorry you could not come to Wales; our cottage was brushed and cleaned and lardered; I wore a fresh shirt and red trousers.

I received an order from Miss Swan; she is very kind, and must be charming.[1] There was difficulty over her address, and though I have written to several addresses there has either been no answer or the letters have returned 'unknown'. Would you forward this letter to her as soon as possible? I do not, on any account, want her to think me ungrateful for her generosity and the nice things she said about my poems. I have asked her if she would send me her poems, and if she would like to see mine. You won't forget this letter, will you? A little regular assistance is almost more than I can hope for, but I still do hope.

You ask me if I have been published in America? Only in transition (when it had, as it still may have for all I know, an American address) & in Poetry. I have been asked for a poem for an English number of the Partisan Review, and shall send them one. There will still be over half a dozen poems—not counting those in preparation—for the New Directions anthology when they are needed. 'Poetry' published a poem of mine in their English number, edited by Auden and Michael Roberts, last year, & were supposed to have printed in their May number (as I think I told you) 4 short new poems you haven't seen. Whether the poems appeared in the May number or not I don't know.[2]

I have no new poems completed yet, but will let you have them in time. And I am now more than halfway through that long piece of prose I mentioned to you in a previous letter; it would do best, I think, as a separate pamphlet, but you shall see & tell me what you think.

Do I leave the editing of my 2 books—the selection of 30 of the best poems—to you? I'm quite prepared to, of course.

---

1 Emma Swan, of New York City, who sent Thomas money over the years. New Directions published her poetry.
2 See n.2, page 345, and n.2, page 360.

Reavey—do let me know what you think of him, especially after my malicious analysis—wrote a few days ago to say that he was having trouble with the printers over my stories, and that he has been warned by a solicitor not to think of publishing them, as they stand, in England. I replied and told him that if the alleged offence was contained only in isolated passages I wouldn't have any honest qualms about cutting them out. But the little weazel hasn't answered me, & might be cooking up all sorts of plans. You said it was not honest of me to conceal from you the fact that Reavey had the American rights of my stories; I was not *concealing* it from you because I didn't know the fact existed: the contract was rushed through and gabbled over, Reavey taking quick advantage of my vagueness and stupidity. I'm not in the habit of concealing, dishonestly, facts about my small & uncommercial work; usually I'm cheated myself.

I hope your publicity campaign's getting under way; & I'm looking forward to the contracts that you said you would soon be drawing up. I'll write and tell you when anything happens, & keep you posted with my new work. If there are any other questions, do please ask me. Apologies for the long delay.

Best wishes,
Dylan T

Please remember Emma Swan's letter.

MS: Houghton

CHARLES FISHER

Friday [June or July 1938]   Gosport St Laugharne Carmarthenshire

Dear Charles,

We ½ expected you on Saturday, & on Tuesday too. Sorry we weren't awake and up personally to see to breakfast and your departure. Hope you'll come again, and spend the night. Hughes is back now, & we may all go up there for dinner & pull his beard. Also we must get started on the Canary. Dorothy Parker called *her* canary Onan. See you perhaps tomorrow? We were run up to Swansea last night to see the fight,[1] but you

---

1 There is no obvious candidate. Ronnie James, a Swansea lightweight boxer, fought Freddie Miller, former world featherweight champion, in Swansea, on 27 June 1938. But that was a Monday, and can't be the event referred to, unless Thomas got the day of the week wrong. Conceivably the reference is to Joe Louis v. Max Schmeling in New York (see n.1, page 359) on 23 June. News film of this famous fight could have been shown at British cinemas weeks later. But it ended in the first round, so there wouldn't have been much to see.

weren't—as you probably know—in the Singleton. Have you heard anything about the wireless set? We've found a large room now for Caitlin to dance in, & all she needs is music. Don't forget, will you? If you *can* come down tomorrow, don't bother to inform us beforehand: we'll be around.

Love,
Dylan

MS: the recipient

VERNON WATKINS
5th July [1938]   Gosport St   Laugharne   Carms

Dear Vernon,
    When are you and Francis,[1] or you or Francis, coming here again? Come soon. My mother wrote to tell me that she'd seen you, & that you told her you hoped we weren't too tired when you arrived that Sunday. Of course we weren't. It's always lovely to see you. I've nearly finished my story,[2] & you must see it & read it in detail & tell me where I am too extravagant.
    Harvard University wrote to ask me for something for their special magazine in honour of Eliot—just a paragraph or two of what I think of him, his writing, his religion, his influence, etc. I've written a heap of notes, none of which seems really satisfactory. Do please tell me a few things, just as you helped with that little Auden appreciation. Just a few comments or notes.
    Don't forget to come soon.

Love,
Dylan

MS: British Library

HENRY TREECE
6th or 7th July [1938]   Gosport Street   Laugharne   Carmarthenshire

Dear Henry,
    I should have written ten days ago and acknowledged your kind and welcome bungift, six days ago and acknowledged the chapters, and should have answered immediately your short note about August 2. But rudely I've put all off, wanting time to read the chapters carefully, to write about them, to analyse a poem, to answer your questions, so that I could send one long, full letter. Even now, when I do write at last, these ambitions are only partly realised and still full of holes, and the analysis, Freud help it, must

1 Francis Dufau-Labeyrie.
2 'One Warm Saturday', according to Watkins.

wait until next time. I'm working, hard for me, though there's very little to show for it: some incomplete prose about a dwindling woman, a tame poem, a taste of nice words in the head.

I'm especially glad you can come to stay for August week, as this is the week of great celebration here: a carnival with queen, a regatta with prizes, a dance with soaks. Laugharne—pronounced Larn—will be almost gay and certainly crowded. The High Wind blows its trumpet, few that can walk from their houses will walk back, there will be speechmaking, drunkmaking, sickmaking, Mr Watts the draper will undoubtedly shit his trousers, and we must all dress up. Perhaps it won't be like that at all, but it is a good week for a visit anyway. I'd been hoping that, by the time you arrived, we would have been in our new house, but that's unlikely now. I don't know how you get from here to Harlech, but I know you can quite easily; North Wales is just a bit further on, one way or the other. And I don't know how you get to Laugharne from Northumberland; somehow, I do know, you must get to Carmarthen or to Tenby: we lie about midway. From London it's easy (but unhelpful): Paddington to Carmarthen direct: half an hour's busride from there. There is no railway station here, but we have a nice townhall. From where will you travel? (And no, before I forget, I wasn't in Baker-St. Post Office Christmas 1936. Were you in the Knitted Buoy department of Llantrisant Naval Museum on Mother's Day? Why Baker-St?)

I thought the Straight-Poems chapter was convincing and concise. Do I understand, from your Eliot quotation at the head of the chapter,[1] that the poetry in these straight poems is a calculated escape from the personality-parade of my loud and complex poems? I don't know if they are at all, and I really don't see how they could be; I wrote them, most of them anyway, quite a long time before the other poems in the 25 volume. The straight poems in '25' were, indeed, with a very few exceptions—I'll be able to show you all dates when we meet, but I can't now remember the exceptions because I haven't got copies of the two books—written before most of the poems in the '18' volume. But I don't want to muddle things now; we can go together over all my manuscripts (if you care to, of course) and see properly how these poems do genealogically work. It might have very curious results. Both books contain poems written over about 8 years; there is no definite sequence. I have a great deal of material still, in mss books, to shape into proper poems; and these I will include, quite vaguely, (that is: without considering an easily marked, planned, critical 'progress') in future published books. But we can talk about this. (Those above are teastains.)

I was interested in what you said about my lack, except in that little finger-poem,[2] of any social awareness. I suppose I am, broadly, (as opposed

1 'The progress of an artist is a continual self-sacrifice, a continual extinction of personality . . . Poetry is not a turning loose of emotion, but an escape from emotion; it is not the expression of personality, but an escape from personality.' (T. S. Eliot, *The Sacred Wood*.)
2 'The hand that signed the paper', perhaps written with Hitler in mind.

to regimented thinkers and poets in uniform) antisocial, but I am extremely sociable. But, surely it is evasive to say that my poetry has no social awareness—no evidence of contact with society—while quite a good number of my images come from the cinema & the gramophone and the newspaper, while I use contemporary slang, cliché, and pun. You meant, I know, that my poetry isn't concerned with politics (supposedly the science of achieving and 'administrating' human happiness) but with poetry (which is unsentimental revelation, and to which happiness is no more important—or any other word—than misery):—(I'll elaborate that, if you'd like me to. Not that it's obscure, but it may, in some way, be helpful to add to it.) But the idea you gave me was that you actually consider me unaware of my surroundings, out-of-contact with the society from which I am necessarily outlaw. You are right when you suggest that I think a squirrel stumbling at least of equal importance as Hitler's invasions, murder in Spain, the Garbo-Stokowski romance, royalty, Horlick's, lynchlaw, pit disasters, Joe Louis, wicked capitalists, saintly communists, democracy, the Ashes, the Church of England, birthcontrol, Yeats' voice, the machines of the world I tick and revolve in, pub-baby-weather-government-football-youthandage-speed-lipstick, all small tyrannies, means tests, the fascist anger, the daily, momentary lightnings, eruptions, farts, dampsquibs, barrelorgans, tinwhistles, howitzers, tiny death-rattles, volcanic whimpers of the world I eat, drink, love, work, hate and delight in—but I *am* aware of these things as well.[1]

Another very small criticism: in your Introduction you say that I 'do not, like other poets of (my) age, lean over gates, seeking kinship with daffodils & sheep'. Do you mean other poets of my age-in-years, of my generation, or of my century? I ask you, what other poets of my age—excluding people like Gawsworth, who are not poets at all but just bearded boils in the dead armpit of the nineties—*do* lean over gates? It's a crack at young Georgians, not at New-Versers, intellectual muckpots leaning on a theory, post-surrealists & orgasmists, tit-in-the-night whistlers and Barkers, Empson leaning over his teeth to stare down an ice-cold throat at the mathematical mystery of his doom-treading boots, Grigson leaning over his rackets to look at his balls, Cameron riding on the back of neat graves. And, actually, 'seeking kinship', with everything, daffodils, sheep, shoehorns, saints, bees, and uncles is exactly what I *do* do. I think, with all due lack of respect, that it's a futile crack anyway.

It's nearly post-time and I've done almost nothing except get noisy about very little matters. I think I'm putting most of my comments & criticisms

1 Hitler's invasions: Austria had been taken over, unopposed, in March. Spain: the civil war, republicans v. fascists, was still going on. Romance: the film star Greta Garbo and the conductor Leopold Stokowski were having a well-publicised love affair. Horlicks was propelled to fame in the 1930s by an advertising campaign that invented the concept of 'night starvation', for which the product was the cure. Joe Louis: the American boxer had defeated the German Max Schmeling to win the world heavyweight title two weeks earlier. Means test: the much-hated system, introduced in the 1930s, of auditing a family's income and savings to see if it was poor enough to receive unemployment benefit.

off until August. But I'll write soon, properly soon, with more about these chapters: I took several notes which need only a little filling-out to make a long, vulgar, enthusiastic, argumentative letter proving nothing at all. Write when you can. I'm returning the Introduction.

Yours,
Dylan T

I haven't, of course, read the chapters you've sent me in any order, but, from what I have read, it seems to me that you've quoted that make-it-clean-boys part of my Answers to an Enquiry about $\frac{1}{2}$ dozen times.[1] This is probably due to the irregular way I've read. How does the plan of the book stand now? I'll certainly let you have a poem-analysis for a footnote, and more material you'd care to use may come out of our future joint examination of piles of mss.

Dylan

MS: Buffalo

*GEORGE DILLON
8th July 1938   Gosport   Laugharne   Carmarthenshire   S. Wales

Dear Mr Dillon,
    Early in April, or perhaps late in March, you accepted four poems of mine, and said that you thought they would appear in your May number. Have they appeared yet? Or, are they going to be printed in 'Poetry' some time in the near future?[2] I am anxious to know because, if you have now decided *not* to use them, I should like to have them printed in England so that I can get a little money for them. I am very poor.

Yours sincerely,
Dylan Thomas

MS: Chicago

WYN HENDERSON
13 July 1938   Gosport   Laugharne   Carmarthenshire

Darling Wyn,
    Norman[3] and his new Dutch girl—there's a nice girl too, perhaps—came down last weekend, full of love and London chatter and drink and money. Norman told me that you were working hard for my book of

1 In the *New Verse* 'Answers to an Enquiry' (October 1934), Thomas wrote, 'Whatever is hidden should be made naked. To be stripped of darkness is to be clean', in answering 'Yes' to the question, 'Have you been influenced by Freud and how do you regard him?'
2 The poems (see page 330) were published in the August issue.
3 Norman Cameron.

stories. I'd been worrying about them, wondering what was happening and going to happen, fearing the subterranean, and sub-human, activities of ginger George;[1] but now, to me, everything's grand. Thank you very very much; why didn't I ask you about the stories in the first place; thank you for working for them; I do hope you succeed in making the meanies realise I'm not a smuthound. Norman also said that you had, or were trying to get, a lawyer's list of words, phrases, or sentences to which objection is taken. I wrote to mangy George, asked him to get a list, told him I was willing, within reason, to cut anything out, that I deprecated Paris publication; but filthy, armpit-loving, rude-eyed George never replied. The only thing to excuse him would be a business head, for he has no gifts, no charm, no merit; but he's apparently learned only trick A: how to cheat poor young men of pennies, piss in cripples' trays. Are you working independently? Can I help in any way? I wish you could write to me. I should have written to you a long time ago.

Soon, in the beginning of August, we hope to move from this ugly, furnished fisherman's cottage to a tall and dignified house at the posh end of this small town, and are busy trying to collect, piece by piece, po[2] by washstand, furniture from friends & relatives. Rent is a mystery certainly, food is a luxury almost. Caitlin—who sends much love to you—is going to have a baby: most likely in January: it's a very nice mistake, and neither of us worries at all.

Norman said you were busy these days? What else do you do? Write soon. Give our love to Ian & Nigel,[3] and of course to yourself: lots. And thank you again.

Dylan
& Caitlin

MS: Texas

GEORGE REAVEY

[July 1938]   Laugharne   Carmarthenshire   S Wales

Dear George,

I've been expecting to hear from you.

I was told that Wyn Henderson has been interesting herself in the welfare of my stories. I wrote to her; she said she was compiling, for my benefit, a list of legally objectionable phrases etc. Also that you now definitely intended publishing, first of all, a small, expensive, signed edition in Paris. Is that true? And then a bowdlerised English version. I'd be

---

1 George Reavey.
2 A 'po' was a chamber-pot.
3 Wyn Henderson's sons.

pleased, and surprised, to be told something about this: before the book comes out, if possible.

Augustus John says that a portrait of me is now ready. You can get a photograph of it, if you care, without difficulty.

Henry Miller says the Obelisk Press is keen to get the stories. He'd like to know if, when, & how.

Dylan T

MS: Houghton

VERNON WATKINS
Wednesday [postmarked 14 July 1938]   Gosport St   Laugharne

Dear Vernon,
We'll be able to come up to Bishopston this weekend.
Is Francis coming here on Thursday? We've had no word yet.
News when we meet. Think about Eliot for me.
Are you listening-in tonight?

Love,
Dylan

MS: British Library

HENRY TREECE
24th July [1938]   Laugharne   Carmarthenshire

Dear Henry,
Thank you for the cutting. I disagree that it's a great pity Roberts[1] gossips to newspapers: it's very revealing, he loves all that sort of publicity (though he'd chuckle at it in public) and I think it shows him up beautifully. He certainly is not the popular conception of a poet, nor any other conception either; he's a professional prig, and dry as dust in the place where he isn't damp. I heard him once sneering at the 'childish' idea of poets wearing long hair and corduroy trousers; and if that's not childish, what is? He said Eliot, who was a good poet, dressed and looked like a business man; of course Eliot does, because Eliot is a business-man, and a prosperous one. Empson, Bottrall[2], MacNeice, & others have professional jobs, & dress to fit them; other poets (or not) are advertising writers (Quennell, Cameron, Tessimond),[3] reporters like Madge, booksellers, clerks; they all wear the uniform of the work that pays them. I like very

1 Michael Roberts.
2 Ronald Bottrall, poet and administrator.
3 A. S. J. Tessimond, poet and advertising copywriter.

much the idea of poets dressing professionally, if they are poets alone. I dislike 'he's a poet but he dresses like an ordinary chap'; I like, 'he's an ordinary chap but he dresses like a poet'.

Am I sensitive about my age—in years? (I'm not, by the way, younger than Chatterton when he died: he was 18). I don't really feel sensitive at all about it; and the only thing that, naturally, annoys me is the gossip of another generation: I belong to my own, generation and gossip. Myself in 10 years bores me now, but then I suppose I shall be just as interested. The best moment, & the one it is least possible to realise, is this: 5 to 12 on Sunday morning, 24th July 1938. I'm sensitive, & hackle-raising, only, perhaps about every moment, younger or older, that isn't this.

The drawing of yourself has a very big nose. But in your letter you said you were keeping it to the grindstone. No drawing of my own could do justice to my particular baby bulbousness; I look like an Aryan Harpo bitten by wasps, and the moths have been at my teeth.

I'm glad that Laughlin, in spite of his 'premature' babbling, will do your book in America. He is running some sort of a small publicity racket out there now: advertisements & readings on the radio etc. He should, he tells me, be ready to do your book next summer.

Keidrych Rhys came here a few days ago; I asked him about your letter to him, but he said he'd never received it. I've asked him anyway to write to you.

Yes, I know the London Bulletin. Reavey's announcement of my stories for June is incorrect. He's had a lot of trouble with solicitors or lawyers, & it is now impossible to print the stories in England in their present form. A small, expensive edition will be done in Paris first, then a purged one here. I hate the Paris idea, but Reavey bought out my copyright.

We're looking forward to your visit on August 2nd. When you write again, before that, address the letter just to Laugharne, no special address, as we are moving into another house during the next few days & I'm not quite sure what it's called. Just 'Laugharne' will reach me.

Best wishes,
Dylan

MS: Buffalo

D. S. SAVAGE

Sunday [July 1938]   Gosport St   Laugharne   Carmarthenshire

Dear D. S. Savage,

Sorry to bother you, but it's about that poem of mine for the Partisan Review. Do you remember I told you that New Directions was going to publish several new poems of mine this year? Well, I've just had a letter from them & they say *they're* going to use the poem—'How shall my animal'—that I sent to you. Is it too late to ask you to change the poem in your possession for another, the one I enclose?[1] If it is too late, do let me know quickly and I shall write to New Directions telling them not to use the poem. That, however, takes time, so I thought it best to write first to you, hoping you'll be able to change the poems.

This is a lot of bother about a very small matter, but it's no fault of mine. Sorry.

Yours sincerely
Dylan Thomas

MS: Texas

JAMES LAUGHLIN
July 27 1938   Sea View[2]   Laugharne   Carmarthenshire   S Wales

Dear Laughlin,

Before anything else: Would you mind substituting this enclosed poem for 'How shall my animal', which you were going to use in the new New Directions.[3] It's a livelier poem anyway, but I find too that it's one the Partisan Review is going to use: and they, unfortunately, had the poem before I sent it to you. It's a pity our very first bit of business together, however simple, should be complicated like this, however simply. I only hope this request for substitution isn't too late. If it is, nothing fatal has happened—there is still time to explain to the Partisan people—but I'll be glad if I am in time. I'm an unbusinesslike bugger but getting better.

And now: I can't properly understand all the contracts. One I do understand, & have signed and enclosed it. I'll fire along to you everything I do, right away. But the long contract, about me being the author and proprietor of a work entitled 'Poems', isn't clear to me. I'm author and, I gather, proprietor too, of the '18 Poems', but am I proprietor of the '25 Poems'? I don't know. I've lost the contract between me & Messrs. J. M. Dent: if I ever read it. I know Dent's haven't got any American rights to my book, but can I call myself proprietor? Have you, by the way, ever written to David Higham, of Higham, Pollinger & Pearn, London, who was, for that book, '25 Poems', alone, my agent? Until I get a little elucidation, from you or him, I can't clearly sign that contract. Or the other contract either. All the contracts please me, except as to that one detail: I promise you all future books etc. All that I agree to. But I must know whether I am the proprietor of that one book. And too, if Higham must still be my agent, *everywhere*, for that book. I've tried, in previous letters, to make this clear to you: that

---

1 The substitute poem, 'It is the sinners' dust-tongued bell', appeared in *Partisan Review*, Fall 1938.
2 A thin six-roomed house, rented from the Williams family, who more or less ran Laugharne.
3 *New Directions in Poetry and Prose*, 1938 published three Thomas poems: 'How shall my animal', 'In memory of Ann Jones' and 'I make this in a warring absence'.

I'm not clear at all about '25 Poems'. I'll sign, of course, because I want you to publish in America everything I do & have done. But I'm not intelligent about things like this, & they must be explained to me simply. Sorry again about this bother, but I obviously can't—as I did once—sign without understanding. Neither can I, *yet*, send back signed those receipts for the £8, or 40 dollars, you sent me: because they say you have the right to publish *all* my books in America, & I don't know—I know there are no American rights, but nothing else—about the '25 Poems'. Do write soon.

Glad everything else is going well: propaganda etc. And I hope the broadcasting is a success. You're getting on well for me; I wish I was better, and clearer.

Reavey is talking now about a Paris edition first of my stories, followed by a bowdlerised English version. There again I know nothing: he sends me cryptic notes & no explanations.

Best wishes. Thank you for forwarding the letter to Emma Swan. She has again sent me a little money.

Dylan T

P.S. I'll have some new stuff to send you soon.
P.P.S. Are you going to try to get published in American magazines all my stories? and poems? I mean the stories & poems in your possession, that have been published in English magazines? That's fine.

MS: Houghton

JAMES LAUGHLIN
28 July 1938   Sea View   Laugharne   Carmarthenshire   S Wales

Dear Laughlin,
In yesterday's letter I forgot to enclose this (I hope) substitution poem. Here it is now. Does my probable stupidity as to your contract annoy you? I look forward to you writing.

Best wishes,
Dylan T

Henry Treece tells me that you were quite keen about his book about me. He's coming down to spend a holiday with me next week: he's a total stranger to me, by the way.

MS: Houghton

CHARLES FISHER
Thursday [late July 1938]   Sea View Laugharne Carmarthenshire

Dear Charles,

We've moved house & tilted our noses. Our previous house, once a palace, is now that cottage. How we ever existed there is beyond us. Here we could have two bedrooms each, which is quite useless.

Will you give Tom this note.

When are you coming to see us. Henry Treece is down next week to stay. Come along & meet him? Bring some poems.

Love,
Dylan

MS: the recipient

CHARLES FISHER
Monday August 8 1938   Sea View Laugharne Carmarthenshire

Dear Charles,

Sorry—we all were—that you couldn't come down on Saturday. Treece and his abominable girl are going away tomorrow morning, but can you still visit us Tuesday? We'll expect you. Bring Fred if you can. But bring yourself and poems, jokes, & bits of play.

Love,
Dylan

MS: the recipient

T. S. ELIOT
23 August 1938   Sea View Laugharne Carmarthenshire

Dear Mr Eliot,

I am applying to the Royal Literary Fund[1] for a grant of money because of my present desperate position and because my wife is soon going to have a baby. We have no support at all apart from my earnings as a writer, which are extremely little, and I hope the Fund will see that my cause is deserving. I'm told that in my application I should give the names of two or three well known writers who will say a word for me. Could I please use your name, which would be of very great help? As far as I can gather, all you would have to do—if you did agree to help me in this way—would be to answer the enquiries of the Fund trustees and to say that, in your opinion, I was deserving of their charity. Without some such immediate grant I will have to give up the house that with difficulty we rented and

1 See page 368.

furnished here & take again to lodgings and running from debts and instability and less and less opportunities for doing my own work. But above all I have to consider the welfare of my wife and her baby, and I do very much hope that you will allow me to use your name.

Yours sincerely,
Dylan Thomas

MS: Valerie Eliot

JOHN DAVENPORT

John Davenport (1908–66) was a pugnacious critic and literary figure, subject of many anecdotes, who lives on as a character in other writers' reminiscences but never wrote a book of his own. He was more affluent before the Second World War than after it, scouting for stories for a film company and (according to his own unreliable account) writing, or perhaps not writing, a script for Robert Donat in Hollywood.

24 August 1938   Laugharne Carmarthenshire S Wales

Dear John,

Thank you for writing. Of course your messages weren't delivered, though Norman and Augustus have both been here to see us, flashing rolls. We hope to be in Hampshire in October, to stay a little bit before our saint or monster,[1] and then we must meet. Unless you have a car and drive one day to Wales: we can put you up somehow any time.

About my books of poems. New Directions is or are, as far as I know, going to publish them both in America; or, rather, one book with nearly all the poems in it. Also, as far as I know again, the stories. This as far as I know nonsense is due to a disagreement between myself and James Laughlin (of New Directions) as to the honesty, or fairness, of the contracts he has sent me to sign. He gave me, when I was broke and hungry, eight pounds, which I regarded foolishly as a present. Later, he sent me a contract to sign that said that the eight pounds was an advance on royalties to be earned by the books which I had, in my gratitude, only promised him. Now I am asking for a proper advance—some lump sum is utterly essential to me right away—or I shall take away the books. If he refuses, hums and ha's, I'll send, with great pleasure, everything to you. Thank you a lot.

The English publication of my stories is in a far worse mess, and I can get nothing clear from Reavey who is certainly not my dream, either, of a literary businessman. I write pathetically to George, but he just won't answer. Publication, he has condescended to tell me on a postcard, of the stories as they stand would lead to imprisonment. What he will not tell me is the particular words, phrases, passages to which objection is taken; these my scruples will allow me to alter without hesitation; but how do I know, without being told, what words etc. the dunder printers and lawyers think

1 The child that Caitlin Thomas was expecting.

objectionable: piss, breast, bottom, Love? I understand, from someone else (Wyn Henderson), that George is going to get the stories done by a Paris smut press first, then allow the lawyers he has apparently consulted to castrate them for English publication. I just sit and hate. Nobody tells me anything. (There will be, Laughlin says, no difficulty about American censorship.)

I am writing, at the moment, a letter of appeal to something called the Royal Literary Fund, asking them for an immediate grant of money to help me live and help me pay for the care of Caitlin and child. This Fund moves slowly, slower than we grind, and I don't hope much from it. But without its help, without some grant—and I am a deserving cause, I have no support at all apart from my earnings as a writer, which won't pay for napkins and doesn't for our food—we are more desperate than you could realise. Do you know of any Society etc. that might give me some little grant, some little immediate living money? And do you know what 'well known writer' would support my bread and butter application? I'm writing to Eliot, but I must, to satisfy these charitable meanies, have some more names.

I'll let you know what happens about New Directions. Thank you again. Regards to you both.

Yours
Dylan T

I didn't know my '25 Poems' were out of print. I could get you a personal copy, though, if you want one, I'm sure.

MS: Texas

ROYAL LITERARY FUND[1]

26.8.38   Sea View   Laugharne   Carmarthenshire   S Wales

Dear Sir,

I am writing on the advice of Mr. Denys Kilham Roberts to ask if I am eligible for a grant from the Royal Literary Fund.

I am 23 years old, and married. I have been trying to live by my writing for five years, and have lived in poverty nearly all that time. So far I have had to be content with poverty, and have always been fortunate to have just enough food and to have a room to work and sleep in. But now my wife is going to have a baby, and our position is desperate. I cannot provide her, by my very small earnings, with the care she needs; and my own health—my lungs are weak—does not let me take, even if it were offered to me, regular employment outside the country. My one hope is that I should be considered deserving enough for a literary grant that would enable me to continue working and to care well for my wife during her pregnancy and

1 A privately supported benevolent society, founded in the eighteenth century, which helps authors whose work is of 'approved literary merit' with grants when they fall on hard times. Thomas was quick to detect a hint of charity for the deserving poor.

afterwards. We have no support at all, apart from what my writing brings us; and my writing is printed mostly in uncommercial magazines.

Mr. Kilham Roberts told me that I should give the names of a few wellknown writers who will support my application. I am sure that, among others, Mr. T. S. Eliot, Mr. Cyril Connolly, Mr. Richard Church, Mr. Richard Hughes, Mr. Charles Williams (of the Oxford University Press), and Mr. W. H. Auden—though I have not written personally to all these gentlemen—would support my claims.

I have published two books of poetry: '18 Poems', in 1934, '25 Poems', in 1936, and a book of my short stories, 'The Burning Baby', is being printed at the moment. I am a contributor to many English and American periodicals, including 'The Criterion', 'The Listener', 'New Verse', '20th Century Verse', 'Contemporary Poetry & Prose', 'New Stories', 'Poetry (Chicago)', 'John O'London's Weekly', 'New English Weekly', 'Life and Letters To-Day'. I have reviewed regularly for the 'Morning Post', and for 'The Adelphi', and contributed reviews to 'The Spectator', and 'Time and Tide'. I am reviewing now, though unfortunately without payment, all novels for the 'New English Weekly'. My work has been represented in most recent anthologies of poetry, including 'The Faber Book of Modern Poetry', 'Poems of Tomorrow', 'The Modern Poet', 'Poems of Today', 'The Year's Poetry' for 1934, 1935, 1936, 1937, and in 'The Faber Book of Modern Stories', and 'The Best Short Stories of the Year'.

My work has been reviewed at length in many periodicals: 'The Sunday Times', (a long review by Miss Edith Sitwell), 'The New Statesman', 'Time and Tide', 'The Spectator', 'The Listener', 'The Criterion', 'Life & Letters', 'The London Mercury'.

A book about my work—'Dylan Thomas: An Introduction' by Henry Treece—is to be published shortly.

My need is urgent. I do most sincerely trust that I am eligible for a grant, and hope to hear from you. Do please tell me if there are any other details you could wish me to supply.

Yours truly,
Dylan Thomas

MS: Royal Literary Fund

JOHN DAVENPORT
31st August 1938   Laugharne   Carmarthenshire   S Wales

Dear John,

Thank you very much. What a list of the boys, the nibs of the P.E.N. Club,[1] pipesucking, carpetslippered, New Statesman in pocket, 'Mr Y has timbre', symposium contributors ('I write in white ink, in a kneeling

1 P.E.N. ('Playwrights, Poets, Essayists and Novelists') is an international organisation for writers.

position'). How can I choose from such richness, rule out a Strauss for a Guinness?[1] No, but I leave it to you if you don't mind choosing, because perhaps you know what sort of writer the Royal Literary Fund will have most faith in. I myself have written to Eliot (who has replied, & has already written 'strongly' to the secretary) and to Connolly, who hasn't yet replied (is he in England, do you know?). I should think the more, and the generally better known, names the better. Huxley?[2] He's famous and respectable, isn't he? but I doubt very much that he knows my name. Does that matter? I heard from the Secretary this morning; he said that his committee doesn't meet again until October, a cold & cheerless way off, so he intends to approach the Government on my behalf for an immediate spot. To do this, he needs, *at once*, a few letters 'authenticating the merits' of my case. So the point is: which of the names you suggest—(it really is terribly kind of you to take this trouble)—would be most likely to write, of their own initiative, an immediate brief letter okaying me? Would it be better to try to choose a few names that have been known to like my poems? or would some of the eminent say, if you asked them, a couple of nice words in a short letter, just for friendlinesses sake and the brotherhood of Art? Of the names you wrote down, I'm known to John Hayward—I mean by 'known' that I know I'm known to them—E. J. O'Brien, Calder Marshall, Collier, Spender, Empson (though I think he's in China, isn't he? and I must have, in my favour, some *at-once* responses), Aaronson, Quennell, Rickword.[3] But I should think more-or-less middleaged people would be safer. It would be grand if you'd write to 3 or 4 of these, telling them about things & asking them to write as soon as possible a short letter to

> H. J. C. Marshall
> Secretary Royal Literary Fund
> Y. Gell
> Trelyllyn
> Nr. Towyn, Wales.

How quickly I get money—and God how much I need it—depends on how quickly any of these people will write an 'authenticating' letter.

That was news about Laughlin who, when he came to England in June, wrote telling me that only the huge price of a railway ticket from London to South Wales prevented him from coming to interview me culturally. Pigiron duke[4] sounds good, and I'll probably try taunting him with it if he still sticks by his disgusting idea of a business advance of £8. He's boosting me now in America, gave a broadcast last month which would have been a joy to hear. In an American paper—I've forgotten which—he wrote an article about me & said that I had the medieval mind. He proved this (a) by

1 Probably the authors Ralph Straus and Bryan Guinness (Lord Moyne).
2 The author Aldous Huxley.
3 John Hayward, critic. Edward J. O'Brien, short story anthologist. Arthur Calder-Marshall and John Collier, authors. Edgell Rickword, poet.
4 See n.2, page 339.

a line of mine, 'May fail to fasten with a virgin o', which he said was 'ballad in origin' and had something to do with raggletaggle gypsies o, and by which I meant a circle, a round complete o, and (b) by my use of the word 'denier' which he said was an ancient coin and which I meant to be a person who denies.

I've just had, from Reavey, at last, a lawyer's list of the objectionable words, phrases, passages & whole chunks in my short stories. The word 'copulation' (used by me in reference to a tree, most innocently), 'pissed', (I said that a man spitefully pissed against the wind in order to wet somebody behind him), 'All Pauls Altar', the actual description of a murder committed by a naked woman (especially the phrase 'her head broke like an egg on the wall'), 'the holy life was a constant erection to these gentlemen', and about 20 long passages, none in the least way tittivating, none using obscene words, none evasively or circumlocutionarily to do with fucking,—all have to go in the English edition. And anyway I'd rather tickle the cock of the English public than lick its arse, which is what even this small and comparatively unimportant piece of unjust censorhip would have me do.

Thank Clement[1] very much for her offer of infant clothes, which Caitlin would love to accept. There won't be any need until about the end of the year, before which perhaps we'll see you. It's very kind of her. Our thing, we hope, won't be too monstrously small or big for the clothes. Write soon & tell me what members of the troupe will perform for me. Thanks again v. much.

Love to both,
Dylan

MS: Texas

ROYAL LITERARY FUND
31 August 1938   Sea View   Laugharne   Carmarthenshire

Dear Mr. Marshall,

Thank you very much for your letter, and for replying so quickly.

Here is the application form. I haven't, in the fifth question, made any reference to the fact that my wife soon will have a child. Question seven I could answer very simply, but, as regards question eight, I haven't kept an exact record of my extremely small earnings.[2] The little money I've received during the last year, and that has somehow kept us alive, has been given to me by a few friends who are, themselves, unfortunately, not well-off and who obviously can't be expected to give me anything more.

In the list of published works I'm not required, am I, to put down all the

---

1 Clement was John Davenport's first wife.
2 Thomas wrote: 'Literary earnings during the past year: under £30.'

poems and stories of mine that have appeared in periodicals and anthologies? I mentioned those in my first letter to you.

About Regulation number II.[1] I have written to several people, asking them for their support for my application, but so far only Mr. T. S. Eliot has replied, saying that he 'will be glad to write strongly in my favour'. He is staying now in Cardiganshire, and I am asking him to send a letter directly to you.

You were kind enough to suggest that, as your Committee does not meet until mid-October, you would approach the Government on my behalf and try to arrange some immediate help: I would be very very grateful if you *would* do that, for October seems, to me in my desperate state, with inevitable debts mounting, a long way off, and I have no idea how, without some such assistance, we can continue living until then. The last thing I want to do—and the first thing I will have to do unless some immediate money can be granted—is to give up the house that we have, with difficulty, half-furnished here and to be forced to move about again hopelessly and helplessly from lodging to lodging. Without some sort of permanent place to live in, without the certainty of regular food & shelter, my own work, necessarily difficult because of its experimental nature, is almost impossible to concentrate upon.

I have written for copies of my two published books of poems; they should arrive here the end of this week and I shall send them on to you at once. Both books are, I believe, difficult to obtain, although they went into two editions. My own copies I was forced to sell some time ago to a man who collected first editions and who offered me a little more than their original cost.

The third book, of stories, will not be ready until the autumn; owing to some difficulty of censorship—the book was actually finished at the beginning of the year—it will appear first in France, then in America (with New Directions Ltd.) & then in England where the Europa Press will publish it. I am afraid that my published work, as you will see it, is very small, for most of my poems and stories, and all that I have done since the publication of my last book—including a long story to appear in the September Life & Letters To-Day, & a poem in the September Criterion—has come out in periodicals.

Thank you again. Mr. Eliot's letter should arrive in a day or two; also, I hope, some supporting letters from other writers.

Yours sincerely,
Dylan Thomas

MS: Royal Literary Fund

1 'No Application for a grant shall be entertained . . . unless accompanied by letters from two or more respectable persons authenticating the merits of the case.'

HENRY TREECE
September 1 1938   Sea View   Laugharne   Carmarthenshire

Dear Henry,

Every apology, true and false, for not having written before. The Old Master[1] stayed on several more days after you left for Harlech; his varnish was cracking visibly; he left us bloated, and dumb from his deafness; then a friend of mine, a Jewish funny drawer with lots to do and say, hitchhiked here from London, on his way to Ireland.[2] He stayed on, occupying all my time in ways you know by now and Caitlin's in the ways a male pig expects, for over a week until my motherinlaw and a neuter friend came for a holiday in the pub. Now they're all disappeared, & I'm forced to work; thank God the sun has gone in and I needn't go out; we've nothing left but our wits and paper. Please forgive me. I really have had no time even for politeness—and anyway I know you too well now to need to be polite—and certainly not for a long letter. The only things I've written have been letters to the Royal Literary Fund, asking them for a grant, and to some respectable persons—Mr. Eliot and minor deacons—asking them to support my application. What I need now urgently is some small regular income; the garret's repugnant; I can't keep a steady head and wag a wild tongue if worry like a bumbailiff sits silently nagging by my side. Poverty makes me lazy and crafty. I'm not a fineweather poet, or a lyrical tramp, or a bright little bowl waiting for the first fine flush, or a man who cuts his face with a grand phrase while shaving; I like regular meals and drink and a table and a ruler—and three pens. Eliot has supported me strongly—he's staying in Wales now, 30 miles from here, and is coming For Tea,—and the Fund secretary is, apparently, going to apply for me to the Fascist Government. Mr. Chamberlain is crazy about modern verse, and I shall send a photograph of myself, in bowler and gasmask, rhyming womb with tomb.[3]

This is only a note to let you know I'm alive, & to apologise, and to say how much we enjoyed your staying here & how much we hope you'll come & stay again & that we'll meet again soon. Little awkwardnesses may have arisen—you took the up path, I took the Brown[4]—but they weren't I hope, anything serious; & one day I'll walk 10 miles with you, & you shall sit 10 hours in a saloon chair with me. Perhaps none of us got really going; in your short stay I had toothache, headache, hangover, rheumatism, & seasickness, & was all the time perfectly healthy; Nelly had a bad Welsh cold. I hope she's better now. Over this weekend I'll write the good letter, with analysis etc. That's a promise.

1 Augustus John. He described his visit in a letter to his wife: 'They live in frightful squalor & hideousness in the house they have taken ... The Dylans are impossible to stand for long.'
2 Mervyn Levy.
3 Neville Chamberlain was Prime Minister of the right-wing 'National' Government. Gas masks were in the news as fears of war continued to grow.
4 Brown's Hotel, the Laugharne pub favoured by Thomas.

I asked John about a drawing; he'll do it when he comes back from France in the autumn. If he does it quickly, in one go, it should be good, & might help the commercial success of your book.

More very soon. Terribly sorry about his rude delay.

Love,
Dylan

Caitlin wishes all the right things for you & Nelly.

MS: Buffalo

VERNON WATKINS

Sunday [?September 1938]   Sea View   Laugharne   Carmarthenshire

Dear Vernon,

Thanks for the letter & the poem which I like immensely now, after many readings; it's one of the very best, & I'll write more about it soon to you (& about 2 others I've got) or read it over with you when we meet.

Here are 2 short ones of mine, just done.[1] Could you type them properly for me? In the ballad-like poem I'm not *quite* sure of several words, mostly of 'great' floods of his hair. I think it's right, though; I didn't want a surprisingly strong word there. Do tell me about it, soon.

What about a weekend here? There's plenty of food, beds, & welcome. Come by bike. What about next weekend? Let me know.

Love,
D.

MS: British Library

ROYAL LITERARY FUND

15th September 1938   Sea View   Laugharne   Carmarthenshire

Dear Mr. Marshall,

I'm naturally very sorry indeed that your efforts to obtain some temporary help for me, prior to the meeting of your committee, have failed. Thank you very much for your kindness, and for the trouble you have taken.

I hope that by this time you've received a letter from Mr. Eliot. I've asked some other writers to send you a letter on my behalf, though, as I asked for their help urgently, I gave them your Welsh address.

---

1 Identified by Watkins as 'The tombstone told when she died' and (probably) 'On no work of words now'.

I have written to the Cymmrodorion Society,[1] not mentioning your name or the name of the Society. Thank you for the address. I'll let you know what happens, though I'm not at all optimistic about this. My position now, as you will hardly need to know, is far more desperate than ever & I cannot continue for long.

Here are my two books of poems. I have been a long time getting hold of them.

I do not think I told you, by the way, that my new book of poems is almost ready to send to a publisher. I hope it will appear next spring. I am working very hard.

Yours sincerely,
Dylan Thomas

MS: Texas

JOHN DAVENPORT

23 ix 38   Laugharne   Carmarthenshire

Dear John,

It's disappointing of course, but I expected it. I know that tolerant sadness, that liberal shrug in the rustling gloom; I've heard 'rather a forlorn enterprise' (resigned but still whimsical), 'there it is what can we do' (palms lifted, ash dropped on the untidy waistcoat drooping on a wrong button), 'we're only the intelligentsia you know' (arch, self-deprecatory and twisted smile), 'yes Spain is terrifying' (serious suddenly, the eyes studiously dilated) echo, like the pad of old slippers in a room carpeted with the competition-pages of the New Statesman, on late summer evenings when nostalgic Hampstead lies half asleep in a briar cloud and the air is full of the soft cries of reviewers and the gentle choosing of books. I react like Beachcomber, and could raise up my club Lewis.[2] The little pessimisms of these Boots-minded[3] thrush-watchers—, calculated to make appear difficult the too-easy occupation of writing,—could drive me to not drinking. When does anyone 'establish his claim to be a professional writer'? When he makes enough money not to want assistance? Are my needs less because I'm young? Must I live celibate on bread and poems until my Novel is Accepted? Anyway, something may come, I suppose, of this lion-prodding; I'd like to print the growls. Eliot and Charles Williams—he's very respectable *and* enthusiastic—have written letters

1 The Honourable Society of Cymmrodorion, founded in the eighteenth century for London Welshmen, promotes cultural Welshness.
2 J. B. Morton's predecessor as 'Beachcomber' at the *Daily Express* was D. B. Wyndham Lewis.
3 Thomas is mocking clients of the lending library run by branches of Boots, the pharmaceutical retailers.

for me. Will *one* of the people you've approached do anything? I hope so. The 'exceptional circumstances' must be stressed. And about what, if anything *does* happen, will the Fund slip over? Any idea? Do write if there's any news, or if there isn't.

Dylan

Haven't managed to get 25 Poems yet. My new book of poems is almost ready. I've no idea who to give it to; I don't like Dent's.

MS: Texas

VERNON WATKINS
Monday [postmarked 14 October 1938]   Sea View   Laugharne

Dear Vernon,

I'm sorry not to have written before, I've been awfully busy with my own work, with reviewing, & muddled up with trying to get money from a sinister philanthropic society. Here's my new big poem and—with no anger at all—the Hardy-like one.[1] I considered all your suggestions most carefully. A 'strange & red' harsh head was, of course, very weak & clumsy, but I couldn't see that the alliteration of 'raving red' was effective. I tried everything, & stuck to the commonplace 'blazing', which makes the line violent enough then, if not exactly good enough, for the last. In the last line you'll see I've been daring, & have tried to make the point of the poem softer & subtler by the use of the dangerous 'dear'. The word 'dear' fits in, I think, with 'though her eyes smiled', which comes earlier. I wanted the girl's *terrible* reaction to orgiastic death to be suddenly altered into a kind of despairing love. As I see it now, it strikes me as very moving, but it may be too much of a shock, a bathetic shock perhaps, & I'd like very much to know what you think. No, I still think the womb 'bellowing' is allright, exactly what I wanted; perhaps it looks too much like a stunt rhyme with heroine, but that was unavoidable. 'Hurried' film I just couldn't see; I wanted it slow & complicated, the winding cinematic works of the womb. I agree with your objection to 'small'; 'innocent' is splendid, but 'fugitive' & 'turbulent' are, for me in that context, too vague, too 'literary' (I'm sorry to use that word again) too ambiguous. I've used 'devilish', which is almost colloquial.

As to the big poem—only provisionally called 'In September', & called that at all only because it was a terrible war month—I'm at the moment very pleased with it, more than with anything I've done this year. Does 'Glory cracked like a flea' shock you? I think you'll see it *must* come there, or some equal[ly] grotesque contrast. The last line of the 2nd verse might

---

1 The 'Hardy-like poem', discussed in the first paragraph, was 'The tombstone told when she died'. The 'big poem', discussed in the second, was later called 'A saint about to fall'.

appear just a long jumble of my old anatomical clichés, but if, in the past, I've used 'burning brains & hair' etc too loosely, this time I used them—as the only words—in dead earnest. Remember this is a poem written to a child about to be born—you know I'm going to be a father in January—& telling it what a world it will see, what horrors & hells. The last four lines of the poem, especially the last but two, may seem ragged, but I've altered the rhythm purposely; 'you so gentle' must be very soft & gentle, & the last line must roar. It's an optimistic, taking-everything, poem. The two most important words are 'Cry Joy'. Tell me about this, please, very soon. I'm surer of the *words* of this poem than of the words in any recent one. I want mostly to know what the general effect of the poem is upon you (though of course you can criticize, as you like, any detail).

Sorry you couldn't come this weekend. Do try to come next. I'm afraid we're much too poor to be able to come up to see you for a long time. So do your best.

All love,
Dylan

[*The following poem was sent on a separate sheet of paper. It was printed that winter, in the magazine* Seven, *but not thereafter in Thomas's lifetime.*]

I, the first named, am the ghost of this sir and Christian friend
Who writes these words I write in a still room in a spellsoaked house:
I am the ghost in this house that is filled with the tongue and eyes
Of a lack-a-head ghost I fear to the anonymous end.

[*On reverse of envelope:*]

Can you send me a typed copy of the long poem?
The word is OGRE, not orge or orgy &, as Prichard would say, I'll listen to no criticisms of it.[1]

MS: British Library

JOHN DAVENPORT
14 October 1938   Laugharne   Carmarthenshire   S Wales

Dear John,
No grant was made me. My literary claims 'were found not strong enough for the purposes of this society'.[2] Who *do* they give their money to? I'm an excellent and most disturbing case. Must you be a Georgian

---

1 In the poem 'On no work of words now'. Watkins had typed it.
2 Among those who wrote to support Thomas as a worthy cause were T. S. Eliot, Edith Sitwell, Charles Williams, Walter de la Mare and John Masefield. Writing to H. J. C. Marshall in 1941 (when a second Thomas application was successful), the author Frank Swinnerton said: 'As I remember it . . . one member of the Committee [probably S. A. Courtauld] read aloud as gibberish one of his poems; and he was turned down because he was only 25 . . .' Courtauld was a businessman. Thomas was 23, not 25.

writer of belle-lettres, suffering in Surrey? Must you be in the evening of your days, with nothing to look forward to but nostalgia, borrowed copies of new books about Wilde, and inclusion in any Gawsworth anthology of the unburied dead? Or is the Royal Fund available only for successful writers having a bad year? Only *recommended* this year by the Medium Book Society! Poor chap, send him a large cheque and a luncheon invitation from a publisher's nark; let Miss DuMaurier[1] knit him a smoking-coat, & don't forget the special, indelible inkstains. But I'm furious. And after Miss Sitwell wrote two pages to the secretary, too. You don't know, do you, any rich person I can try now? I'll dedicate my next poems to him, & write a special sponger's song. Can't I live even on the immoral earnings of my poems? No, but there must be someone, somewhere in England, who'd like to do a poet a good turn, someone who wouldn't miss just enough money to ensure me peace & comfort for a month or two to get on with the work I'm in the middle of now & which I so much want to finish. All my hopes were in that Royal set-up, & now we'll have to abscond from here, as from everywhere else I've ever lived in, leaving, this time, a house full of furniture we had the devil of a lot of cringing trouble to obtain. Thirty bloody pounds would settle everything. If you know any rich chap fond of a jingle, who knows his Peters & Quennells, do let me know at once. Otherwise it'll be traipsing again, no stability at all, no hope, and certainly no work. Try to think of some sap, some saint. There's no reason why I should bother you like this, but here I can't get in touch with anybody with more money than a betty with no cunt or more generosity than a fucked weazel.

> Yours,
> Dylan T.

I'm putting in a poem, someone just typed a few copies of it.

MS: Texas

BBC [R.G. Walford, Copyright Section]
14 October 1938   Sea View   Laugharne   Carmarthenshire   S Wales

Dear Sir,
    In reply to your letter of the 12th, I authorise the broadcast of my poem 'The hand that signed the paper' in the programme on October 18th, and agree to the fee of one guinea which you proposed.

> Yours faithfully

TS: BBC, from original letter in Legal Section

1 Daphne du Maurier, novelist.

BBC
14 October 1938   Sea View   Laugharne   Carmarthenshire

Dear Sir,

I enclose the confirmation sheet, agreeing to broadcast on October 18, etc.

I received a letter today from Broadcasting House, Manchester, inviting me to read a poem at the same date & time; but this letter says that the rehearsal & performance will be from London. My five minutes (stipulated in your agreement) is obviously part of the programme 'The Modern Muse', but the difference of place (London & Manchester) mentioned in the two letters, yours and Mr. Bridson's from the North Region, has confused me a little. I hope you'll clear up these small difficulties by return.[1]

I am now living in Laugharne, outside Carmarthen, and your letter was sent to my old Swansea address. My fare, I am afraid, would have to be paid from Laugharne to Manchester, & not from Swansea. Also, owing to my circumstances, I find it necessary to have to be given the railfare & subsistence allowance *before* I travel.

Sorry if these questions & demands are troublesome, & hope you'll be kind enough to explain etc. by return.

Yours faithfully,
Dylan Thomas

MS: BBC

BBC
15 October 1938   Sea View   Laugharne   Carmarthenshire   S Wales

Dear Sir,

In reference to your last letter, of October 13: I authorise the broadcast of my poem, 'This Bread I break was once the Oat', as proposed, & agree to the fee of one guinea. Is the day for its performance October 22?

I should very much appreciate being paid as soon as possible the copyright fees for both these poems, as I need badly everything I can get.

Yours faithfully,
Dylan Thomas

MS: Texas

---

1 'The Modern Muse. A Recital of Contemporary Poetry' was broadcast from the Manchester studios, 10.30 pm, 18 October. Those who read their own poems included Spender, Auden, MacNeice, Kathleen Raine and Charles Madge. Thomas read 'The hand that signed the paper'. Michael Roberts presented the programme; D. G. Bridson produced it.

HENRY TREECE
[mid-October 1938]   [headed paper:
                              Lyulph's Tower   Ullswater   Penrith][1]
                              Not my address. Still in Sea-View.

Dear Henry,
  If it wasn't that I know bitterly how wild it makes a man or a Caitlin,
how it puts into the head a sense of injury that was perhaps not there
before, I'd say Now don't be huffy. Of course—as you should know; am I a
quivering bundle of temperament, all wind and wet conceit that I can
imagine I could, even if I wanted to, be rude to my equally unconceited, un-
nonsensical friends—I haven't any wish not to fulfil my promises, not to
write you lots of times and lots of pages. It's only that I'm lazy about
writing, and deeply depressed. You mustn't be offended because I'm a lazy
pig—(I know, I bitterly know, 'who's offended, damn your presumption,
jerry-headed conceit that makes you think your lack of writing can offend
me'; & that's true, but I always mean one way less than I say & the other
way more; it is my everpresent conscience, concealed under a Punch
humour, that forces me to make each fact dubious, to attempt to add
suspicion to straight details)—I've wanted to write so often, have thought
about you, what you're doing and why, and several times have written
Dear Henry down, stared at the paper, sunk into coma, picked my nose &
made a small salt meal, though there were many things to tell you and,
even then, many apologies to make. I'm depressed about facts, which no-
money makes dubious; debts are climbing, tradesmen barking, the
Government is too busy, the Royal Literary Fund regards my literary
claims as insufficient (you have, I think, to be a Georgian, a writer of faded
belles-lettres), we will have to abscond from here one day next week,
leaving a furnished (now much better, & more fully, furnished than when
you were here) house behind, a lovely town, some friends. At least, if not
absconsion, a holiday from debts; and that will not pay them. We will go to
Swansea for a week or two, then Hampshire. (On this Tuesday, the 18th,
I'm going to Manchester, to broadcast with Auden, MacNeice, Spender etc.
in a programme, called The Modern Muse, compered by M. Roberts. I
suppose it would be quite impossible for you to meet me in Manchester
that evening? I know only that you're North, I've no idea where. If you
could, come to the B.B.C. offices.)
  Now about your last, full letter: It was odd to hear that Donald Duck of
the New English Weekly has decided that I'm too young for your book. He
wrote me last week, saying he had met you, that he would encourage the
book all he could, & also that I was a swell reviewer. He was enthusiastic,
quacked for pages. What did he tell you? He must change his mind very
quickly; & what a mind, too! Having Gawsworth to edit his anthology!
Gawsworth would be a standing joke if he weren't completely supine. I'm

---

1 Lyulph's Tower was a house that Richard Hughes sometimes borrowed.

glad Seven is doing the surrealist chapter; they want one or two new poems of mine to go in the same number with it; I sent some short ones yesterday, but it may be too late. Your offer—which I should have thanked you for a long time ago—of a percentage of anything that comes from your book is terribly generous. It *was* nice of you to think of it, and I accept it very gratefully. I hope we'll both make out of it, and be able to meet to spend. I'll try to be in London at Christmas; you must meet some of my disreputable friends; I have one of the best collections. Caitlin won't be with me; she looks increasingly robust & our little half-formed monster is kicking & smiting.

There haven't been any visitors here for some time now, & wc live vcry quietly. We have a supper a week with the Hugheses, & they have one here. I am writing poems, & will send them to you as soon as they are typed. One, I think, is as good as anything I've done: a longish poem to my unborn child. You shall see it next week. I want to post this off now, because it's late & I'm going to Swansea tomorrow morning & then on to Manchester. This is the first of a regular series of dull letters. And I've nearly finished for you an analysis of two poems.

Yours ever,
Dylan

I'll send, too, the address—when I can find it—of a new American quarterly edited by Ransom. The first number appears in December. They want new critical work.

MS: Buffalo

VERNON WATKINS
[postmarked 19 October 1938][1] Sea View Laugharne Carmarthenshire

Dear Vernon,

I'm going to Manchester on Tuesday to take part in a programme, that will be broadcast on the National, sweetly called the Modern Muse. About 10.30 at night. Don't forget to listen in. I'll probably read one, at the most two, short poems of my own, &, for that alone, the journey wouldn't be worth while; but I may as well go up to meet Auden, Spender, MacNeice, Day-Lewis & some others who'll be there; Minnie Roberts is compering, which is just about his job. I'll tell you all about it in Swansea, for I'll come back there on Wednesday. Looking forward to seeing you.

Thank you for typing the poems, & for the things you said. I agree that

1 This was the day *after* the broadcast.

'carbolic' & 'strike' cd be bettered,[1] but, at the moment, I'll just leave them; I may be able to go back clearly to the poem some time soon, but I'll publish it now as it is in Life & Letters, & then, we'll see. Glad you liked the straight story;[2] I'm doing another now: illuminated reporting.

That hymn must be great in the original, I wish I could read German.[3]

Love,
Dylan

MS: British Library

CHARLES FISHER
21 October [1938] [card] Sea View House Laugharne Carmarthenshire

So sorry if our sudden change of plans put you out at all. I found suddenly that I had to broadcast—I don't know whether you heard it—with Auden & some others from Manchester, on the Tuesday you were going to collect us. This meant a little money, and that money will keep us for some more days in Laugharne. We'll have to spend, in the future, such a long time with parents that we think it wiser, if only for their sakes, to live for as long as possible on & by ourselves. Can we, in spite of this small muddle, ask you again: and ask you soon?

I've got several new poems to show you. My new book of them is almost ready. It's to be called 'In the Direction of The Beginning', for it will include the long story by that name.[4] Looking forward to showing things to you.

Love,
Dylan

MS: the recipient

VERNON WATKINS
[card, postmarked 24 October 1938]
[*note at side:*] This poem's just a statement, perhaps.

This very short poem is for my birthday just arriving.[5] I know you'll hate the use of the 'Forever' line, but there it is. I scrapped the poem beginning

1 'A saint about to fall' has the phrase 'the carbolic city' and the line 'Strike in the time-bomb town'.
2 Probably 'The Peaches', just published.
3 Watkins had sent Thomas his free translation of 'Wenn Alle Untreu Werden' ('If all were unfaithful'), a poem by the eighteenth-century German writer 'Novalis', F. L. Hardenberg.
4 That story was not included, and the book was called *The Map of Love*.
5 Thomas enclosed 'Birthday Poem' (in *CP* as 'Twenty-four years'). His twenty-fourth birthday was 27 October.

with that line long ago,[1] and at last—I think—I've found the inevitable place for it: it was a time finding that place. I'm pleased, terribly, with this—so far. Do tell me, & type please. In the first version I had 'like a stuffed tailor'. I think stuffed is wrong, don't you? Try to read the end of the poem as though you didn't know the lines. I do feel they're right. In the old 'Forever' poem they were completely out of place—& the rest of the poem wouldn't stand without them. So bang went the whole poem, obviously, & here at last is what it should be.

MS: British Library

D. S. SAVAGE
Oct 24 [1938]   Laugharne   Carmarthenshire   S Wales

Dear D. S. Savage,
    Thank you for the letter.
    The bother about the poems for New Directions and The Partisan Review has been settled. New Directions have persuaded Partisan Review to print another poem, & have themselves kept the one I originally sent to you.
    I don't know what poem I could send for the broadsheet series; I'll try to write something specially for it, but if that doesn't come off I'll let you see a selection of recent poems. Good luck with the series. What sort is it going to be? Woodcut nymphs?

                                        Best wishes,
                                        Dylan Thomas

P.S. Will you let me know the closing date? If the first broadsheet, & if the first is to be mine, comes out early December—how much time does that give me?

MS: Texas

DAVID HIGHAM
27 Oct '38   Sea View   Laugharne   Carmarthenshire

Dear Higham,
    I must apologise for my very long delay in writing to you & in answering your letters. Actually, I never had a letter from you about Laughlin: it must have gone astray in one of my previous, too temporary addresses. It was not laziness, really, that kept me from writing: I've had a very hard time lately,

1 The abandoned poem, beginning 'For as long as forever is', was probably written in 1936. Texas has a twelve-line draft, reproduced in Ferris's biography.

& have been trying, in all sorts of ways, with guile & charity, to set up a house & to live in security. This has almost succeeded, though not quite.

First of all, about the Dent's book. I tried to do it as agreed—a travel book—and failed. Now I'm trying to make it a semi-fiction, semi-autobiographical book, each chapter a short story. One of the stories appeared in the October Life & Letters To-Day. This is rather a big undertaking, & is taking time.

I've nearly got ready my new book of poems, to be called 'In The Direction Of The Beginning'. W. H. Auden tells me that the Hogarth Press, of which he is one of the new advisers or directors, would be very glad to see it and almost sure to want to do it. Is that a good idea, do you think? He also told me—how officially, I don't know—that he thought they'd give me an advance of £50 on receiving & accepting the mss. Even if Dent's *did* want to do this book, I'd prefer it to be published *outside* a series.

I'm enclosing 2 of Laughlin's contracts. Richard Hughes has added a few notes & objections to the first contract, and I can't add much to them.

The contract about 'option & right to publish in U.S.A. any book or books which I shall write or have written' doesn't seem any too good to me. Laughlin says 'in consideration of sums received in advance on royalties', & these sums were two cheques for £4 each, and I can't regard that as anything but a very small advance on the one book of Poems. I think it a good idea for New Directions to do the one book of Poems, as, anyway, nobody else seems to want to do them, & as N.D. has a small but good reputation for modern verse.

My book of stories, 'The Burning Baby', which Dent's refused, & which I eventually gave to the Europa Press because I was sick of the book, is apparently having quite a lot of trouble. No printer'll touch it:—obscene. Now they're thinking of doing it in Paris, which sounds a smelly idea but, perhaps, the only one practicable.

I do hope you'll let me know what you think about these things, & that you'll forgive me for all my past carelessnesses.

Yours sincerely,
Dylan Thomas

MS: Texas

T. ROWLAND HUGHES[1]

29 October 1938   Sea View House Laugharne Carmarthenshire

Dear Mr. Hughes,
    Mr. Bridson, of the North Region, told me to get in touch with you. I mentioned to him, just after broadcasting in a programme of his, that I wanted to read some more poems. He said that Cardiff was obviously the

---

1 Hughes produced 'features' (documentary programmes) for the BBC's Welsh Region in Cardiff.

place for me to do it from and that you were the person to whom I should write. I've broadcast a few times before; I had quarter of an hour for poems of my own from London about eighteen months ago, and recently took part in a programme, The Modern Muse, from Manchester.

One idea that I had was to be asked to broadcast a short series of readings from the work of Welsh poets, or poets of Welsh ancestry, who wrote or write in English: from Vaughan to Edward Thomas, Wilfred Owen, W. H. Davies, & the younger men, contributors to the periodical 'Wales' & to most of the verse periodicals published in London & abroad, who are now making what is really a renaissance in Welsh writing. I don't think anything of the sort has been done before on the air, and I know that there are a great number of people in Wales who are extremely interested in the development of Anglo-Welsh poetry & who have far too few opportunities of hearing that poetry read.

I should be very interested to hear what you think about this, and I do hope that one reading, at least—if not a whole series—could sometime be arranged.

If you find the suggestion at all suitable & to your liking, would there then be the question of an audition? I think Mr. Bridson, or Mr. John Pudney of London, would be kind enough to support me about that. I have done some reading for both of them.

Yours sincerely,
Dylan Thomas

MS: BBC

T. ROWLAND HUGHES
November 3 '38   Sea View House   Laugharne   Carmarthenshire

Dear Mr. Hughes,
Thank you for writing, and for passing my letter on to Mr. Watkin Jones.[1] I hope something comes of my suggestion. Yes, I know that W. H. Davies & Huw Menai etc. have given readings of their own work, but I'm sure there hasn't been any comprehensive broadcast of Welsh-English poetry, no—silly word—survey.

I don't think I'd be able to do one of those long dramatic programmes in verse; I take such a long time writing anything, & the result, dramatically, is too often like a man shouting under the sea. But if you'd let me know a little more about these programmes—length, subjects unsuitable, etc—I'd like to have a try. It sounds full of dramatic possibilities, if only I was.

I should like very much to call & see you & talk over these things & others when I am next in Cardiff, which I shouldn't think will be for a long

1 Alun Watkin Jones produced talks programmes at Cardiff.

time—unfortunately. And I hope if you're in this part of Wales, you'll call & see me.

Yours sincerely,
Dylan Thomas

MS: BBC

---

*GWYN JONES[1]
November 3 1938   Sea View House   Laugharne   Carmarthenshire

Dear Mr Gwyn Jones,
    Thank you for your letter and for wanting me to contribute to your new periodical. Of course I think there's need for something like that; the little magazine 'Wales' did wonderfully well, I thought, but it didn't have any backing.[2] Best wishes; and I hope you'll let me know what contributions are needed.

Yours sincerely,
Dylan Thomas

MS: National Library of Wales

JOHN DAVENPORT
4 November 1938   Sea View   Laugharne   Carmarthenshire

Dear John,
    How very very nice and kind of you. That five pounds helped an *awful* lot, and now our debts are almost all paid off. We want to leave, the middle of this month, to stay in Hampshire, and perhaps now we'll be able to leave owing nothing, which will be grand. Thank you so much.
    Last night we went to Hughes to dinner—you know he lives here, don't you; in the ruined castle—and he gave me a great lot of his prize bitter and this morning I don't know what I am. I've heard nothing yet from the Royal Literary Fund. Are they *definitely* reconsidering their decision? How did you work it? When you said they gave away forty five thousand a year, didn't you mean four to five? I'm waiting anxiously, twitching every time the postman walks over the cockles to our door.[3]
    A couple of weeks ago I read some poems on the wireless in a programme called The Modern Muse. All the boys were in it, and what a mincing lot we were. Did you hear it? All the poets were born in the same house, & had the same mother too.

---

1 Professor Gwyn Jones (b. 1907), writer, translator and Norse scholar.
2 Gwyn Jones founded the English-language magazine *Welsh Review* in 1939, though Dylan Thomas never wrote for it. Thomas's past-tense references to *Wales* were premature, but he and others were disenchanted with its disorganised editor, Keidrych Rhys. See page 400.
3 The path to Sea View was strewn with cockle shells.

I'm sending a copy of 25 Poems, but I couldn't get a first edition. Will this do?

The monster clothes came this morning. Can any child be small as that? Thank you, Clement. Caitlin's writing a note.

Is Chippenham full of bedroom suites? And is it far from Fordingbridge, because we'll be there—or very nearly there—in a fortnight & we must meet.[1] Let me know.

Did you like the poem I sent you? I think the Hogarth Press, under John Lehmann, is going to do my new book: it's called 'In The Direction of The Beginning'.

Thanks a lot. This letter's very weak because of bitter but my gratitude isn't.

> Love to both
> Yours
> Dylan T

MS: Texas

JOHN DAVENPORT
[card, postmarked 21 November 1938]   Blashford Ringwood Hants

This is only to let you know that we've moved at last, for a bit, to Hampshire. Augustus drove us up but now we're getting better. We won't be able to come & see you for a while as we're broke. If you could call here, let me know anytime. Thank you for the postcards. Nothing yet from the Royal Literary Fund. More when there's news or when I meet you.

> Dylan T

MS: Texas

DAVID HIGHAM
November 24 1938   Blashford Ringwood Hants

Dear Higham,

I'm sorry not to have answered your last letter before this. It really wasn't just another bit of my carelessness, for I *did* intend to write at once but I didn't have the chance: I've been moving—but I'll be at this address over Christmas—halfstarving, worrying, and escaping from things. [*In the margin*: tradesmen, not things of the spirit.] Also, I was trying to finish my story so that I could let you have the whole manuscript at once. The story is, I'm afraid, taking longer than I thought, and getting to be a much bigger

---

1 Davenport was moving to a house near Chippenham, in southern England. Augustus John lived at Fordingbridge, not far from Blashford and Yvonne Macnamara's home.

work. So I'm sending you all the poems and (roughly, though probably quite a bit over) half the story. The story, as I'm working hard now, I'll finish by Christmas. You'll see that some of the poems fit in with ideas in the story, and the whole thing does, I believe really, make a comprehensive book, not—as perhaps the suggestion of a book of poems *plus* a story might imply—a hotchpotch. I enclose separately a synopsis of the story, making clear in it where this present manuscript breaks off. It may be a little unfortunate—but surely not so that it will affect consideration—that this manuscript *does* break off at a rather violent part of the story. The rest, I can assure those people on Dent's who thought my Burning Baby stories too violent—is fit enough for any obscure-minded baby to read. The portrait of me by Augustus John, which was promised for the Wales book, could be used as a frontispiece for 'In the Direction', couldn't it? John has done a new portrait, which would reproduce excellently, and he is willing to let it be photographed anytime. Do let me know what you think. Is there—and this is very important to me, as my wife is going to have a baby at the beginning of January and that means a lot of expense, and I am entirely without support—the chance of getting that £50, or some of it at least, on the strength of this manuscript? It isn't complete, but what the book will be like as a whole can easily be visualised. I *must* have some sort of an advance before Christmas.

About Reavey and the *Burning Baby*. He may have told you that he had everything in connection with the stories in hand, but that isn't so. He can't get it printed, as it stands, in England, and Laughlin, who wants to do it in America, doesn't intend even to think about publishing until late next year or the year after. That's far too far away. Reavey is now, as far as I can gather, thinking of doing it in Paris first and getting me to cut out the naughty bits afterwards. His contract with me says that unless he's published it, or has got the publishing of it under way, within a year of the signing of the contract—then the book comes back to me. The contract was signed last December. Nothing practical seems to have been done yet. Some time ago, he wrote me asking me to allow him a further year to try to get it published—and asking me to write down my agreement with that so that he could add it to the contract. I refused. Could you get in touch with him and tell him that, when the contracted year is up, I want the stories back. Then I could get down to the job of 'cleaning' them up so that, after all, perhaps they could be done by a reputable publisher.

I hope to hear from you. Especially about that £50. Something really is essential.

Apologies for the delay.

Yours,
Dylan Thomas

P.S. The Hon. Secretary, Miss M. Gulick L.R.A.M. 15 Belgrave Road, S.W.1., has written to me on behalf of the Association of Teachers of

Speech and Drama, saying that their Individualist Choir, who won the first place in Choric speaking at the Oxford Festival this year, when my poem 'And Death Shall Have No Dominion' was one of the poems 'set', have been invited by H.M.V. to make a record, & they want to recite my poem on it. Can't we get a fee out of them, for the Festival performance of my poem & for this recording? These people can't do what they like with poems without paying the author.

MS: Texas

JOHN DAVENPORT
25 Nov [1938] [card]   Blashford   Ringwood   Hants

Augustus can't drive us over, he's in one of his States, & in bed. But I've just been awarded the Oscar Blumenthal prize for poetry,[1] so there, and can pay you a visit when it's most convenient to you. Tell me when & how.

Dylan

MS: Texas

LAWRENCE DURRELL
30th November [1938]   Blashford   Ringwood   Hants

Dear Lawrence Durrell,

It's nice to hear from you and I'm glad you'll be in England and we *must* meet. I've been living in Wales up until this last week, now I'm here. I'm afraid I can't come to London: no money at all. But this place is much nearer London than my old address; it's about $2\frac{1}{2}$ hours in the train, fare 18/- return. I do hope you can manage to come down. I've forgotten the route; the thing to do is to ring up the Southern Railway, Waterloo Station, & find out about Ringwood, Hampshire. I know, though, that 18/- is right. I'm quite near here to your auntie in Bournemouth.

Could you get me a copy of the Black Book?[2] I'll give you all I've written in exchange, odd poems, small books.

Hoping to hear from you.

Dylan T

MS: Carbondale

1 Awarded to Thomas for the four poems published in Poetry (Chicago) in the August 1938 issue: See pages 330 and 360.
2 Durrell's 'daring' novel The Black Book was published in France and the US in 1938, but not until 1973 in Britain.

*GEORGE DILLON
December 3 1938   Blashford   Ringwood   Hants

Dear Mr Dillon,
  I was delighted and extremely grateful to hear that the Oscar Blumenthal Prize for 1938 had been awarded to me.[1] I cannot tell you how much that generous & so unexpected sum of money meant to me in very poor circumstances. I wish to thank you & the editorial staff of 'Poetry' for the honour you have paid me.
  I'm enclosing 4 poems, three short & more-or-less straight ones & one longer one. I hope you will be able to use some of them in 'Poetry'. If you do not find them suitable, I should like very much to send you some other new poems when they are ready.
  Please accept my sincere thanks again.
                                              Yours,
                                              Dylan Thomas

MS: Chicago

DAVID HIGHAM
December 3 1938   Blashford   Ringwood   Hants

Dear Higham,
  Thank you for your note. I hope Dent's agree.
  I can't find anywhere my contract with Reavey: it was given to me last year when I was living nowhere in particular & that's where I seem to have left it. If I do come across it, I'll send it to you immediately. Otherwise, might Reavey, do you think, send me another copy? Sorry for this.
                                              Yours,
                                              Dylan Thomas

I've just won the Blumenthal Prize for Poetry in America. Worth £20. Is that of any value, apart from the lovely money? I mean, will a thing like that help to influence Dent's or anyone else? I don't suppose so.

MS: Texas

1 The prize, instituted in 1936, was worth $100. Previous winners were Marion Strobel and Thomas Hornsby Ferril.

D. S. SAVAGE
December 10 1938   Blashford Ringwood Hants

Dear D. S. Savage,
Will you forgive me for not writing before? I had the chance of going
pleasantly away for a few days, & have only just returned. And, more
importantly, will you—or can you, after this lapse of time—forgive me if I
do not say anything more about your poems except that I like some of
them? I have tried to make honest sentences, but they were all too vague;
& the more detailed praise or criticism of a particular poem isn't any good
for your present publishing purpose. It is useless, & probably boorish-
sounding, to say, with truth, that some of the lines I like immensely & that
the seriousness of your poems seems to me always admirable. But that is
all, apart from remarks about actual poems in detail, that I *can* say. I do
wish you every success with this book—which, if ever I have a chance to
review it, & I certainly might have if only for a small-circulation paper like
the N.E. Weekly, I shall really try to say a lot of things about &, somehow,
to make up for the apparent, but quite unmeant, rudeness of this apology.
I hope you will write to me soon.
Congratulations on the 'Poetry' award. It was a very nice present, wasn't
it?

                                    Yours,
                                    Dylan Thomas

MS: Texas

DAVID HIGHAM
December 10 1938   Blashford Ringwood Hants

Dear Higham,
Sorry not to have answered at once; I had the chance of going away for a
few days, & have only just come back to find your letter.
I'm glad about the Dent acceptance of the poems, & I'm all for it, of
course. Do you know why Church wants to see me? I don't want to see
him. But I suppose there's some reason. Tuesday or Wednesday this
coming week would suit me all right; so would Thursday or Friday, if it
comes to that, but I'd prefer the beginning of the week if that's possible.
You'll see that I get my expenses *beforehand*, won't you? Otherwise, I
couldn't move.
I've sent letters to the addresses in which my Reavey contract might be
found, & am waiting for answers. I'll let you know at once.
Thank you for getting Miss Gulick's reply.[1] Have to be content with
that problematical guinea.

1 See pages 388–9.

Yes, the anthology rights of my poems published by the Parton Press *are* free. The copyright of those poems is, anyway, mine. No contract was drawn up at all. What do the Oxford U.P. want with Poem Two? For an anthology?

By the way, I haven't been paid yet by Penguin Books for their inclusion of 2 poems of mine in the 2 volume Century's Poetry, edited by Kilham Roberts. The anthology seems to have been out for some time.

Yours,
Dylan Thomas

MS: Texas

C. H. FORD[1]
December 14 [1938] Blashford Ringwood Hants

Dear Mr. Ford,

Thank you for your letter. I'm very glad that you recommended me, in the first place, to Laughlin, and that you like my poetry. I have a new book coming out next spring, which I hope you'll be able to get hold of—if you don't, let me know. Rather different sort of poems, many of them. I hope you'll like them as much.

And thank you for the collaborated poem. I like bits of the language, but it didn't seem to make anything. It was very nice of you to ask me to collaborate, but I don't want to. I think a poet today or any other day is most pleasurably employed writing his own poems as well as he can. With all due lack of respect, I believe this chainpoem to be a pretentious, and lazy, game.

With best wishes,
Dylan Thomas

MS: Texas

VERNON WATKINS
December 20 1938 Blashford Ringwood Hants

Dear Vernon,

It's almost too cold to hold a pen this morning. I've lost a toe since breakfast, my nose is on its last nostril. I've four sweaters on (including yours), two pairs of trousers & socks, a leather coat & a dressing-gown. Who was the French poet who had alphabetically lettered underpants, & wore every one up to H on a cold morning?

I've just come back from three dark days in London, city of the restless

---

1 Charles Henri Ford, American writer, artist and film-maker.

dead. It really is an insane city, & filled me with terror. Every pavement drills through your soles to your scalp, and out pops a lamp-post covered with hair. I'm not going to London again for years; its intelligentsia is so hurried in the head that nothing stays there; its glamour smells of goat; there's no difference between good & bad.

I went to see Dent's—Church, really—about a new book. I'm making it an odd book: 15 poems & 5 stories: all to be called In the Direction Of The Beginning. It may look a mess, but I hope not.

It was a great pity we didn't manage to get down to Bishopston before coming here for Christmas and birth; it's been a long time since seeing you, and I want your new poems. Please write quickly, *for* Christmas, with them & news. I'm enclosing a little new poem; been doing several little ones lately; send you them all soon.

Thank you for 'Poem In the Ninth Month'.[1] It's fine. I'll use it, of course. And sorry about that bracketed line in the birthday poem, but, until I can think of something else or feel, it will have to stay. I thought your alternative line clumsier & more bass-drum (rather muffled, too) than mine. I do realise your objections to my line; I feel myself the too selfconscious flourish, recognize the Shakespeare echo (though echo's not the word). If ever I do alter it, I'll *remember* your line.[2]

Was the American anthology you mentioned one edited by Norman McCaig? I've sent him something. Will you let me see the revised 'Room of Pity'. And the Yeats poem, please.

This morning the secretary of the London Verse-Speaking Choir—I think it was called—rang me up & asked me whether I could attend the final rehearsal, before making an H.M.V. record, of their speaking of my 'And Death Shall Have No D'. I said I couldn't, so there & then the Choir recited it to me down the telephone. Oh dear. Picked voices picking the rhythms to bits, chosen elocutionists choosing their own meanings, ten virgins weeping slowly over a quick line, matrons mooing the refrain, a conductor with all his vowels planed to the last e.

Caitlin's very strong & well & full. She sends love. So do I, as you know. My silence is never sulks. Remember me to your father & mother. Regards to Dot & Marjorie. Have the best Christmas.

Last year at this time Caitlin & I were doing an act in a garret. This time we're just as poor, or poorer, but the ravens—soft, white, silly ravens—will feed us.[3]

Yes, I wish I was in Swansea sometimes too.

Ever,
Dylan

1 Watkins's suggested title for 'A saint about to fall'. Thomas used it for magazine publication but not thereafter.
2 The line, the second in 'Twenty-four years', was: '(Bury the dead for fear that they walk to the grave in labour.)' Thomas didn't change it.
3 Thomas liked the Christian image of charitable ravens and used it more than once of his benefactors. Its origin is I Kings 17:4–6, where God commands the ravens to feed Elijah.

We've got a Monopoly set. Apparently the Monopoly manufacturers have made a new game, called—I think—Families. It's all to do with ages, & the point is not to die.

MS: British Library

JOHN GOODLAND[1]
December 22 [?1938]   Blashford   Ringwood   Hants

Dear John Goodland,

I was interested to hear about Apocalypse, and I'll be glad to see the manifesto when you can send it along. I don't know what to say about your kind invitation to me to contribute, except that, anyway, I haven't started writing a word about Crane[2] yet, and I write very slowly. I couldn't possibly get any material at all ready by January 1. By the end of January, perhaps, I shall have finished a long story on which I've been working, off and on, for over a year. But that, apparently, would be too late.

It isn't for me to criticise, not having read the manifesto nor knowing what you mean by apocalyptic writing; but many of your suggested contributors are, I am certain, by any definition, among the least apocalyptic writers alive; and that says something. (Of course, if you announce well beforehand a symposium of apocalyptic writing, you'll have almost every hack poet, hitherto content with imitations of the queenly social verse, with forced echoes of a schoolboy enthusiasm for jokes and bums, with stupidity about sanity, whipping himself into a false delirium, snatching—in case the apocalyptic game flourishes—at the chance of a frenetic reputation, downing Auden on a pylon for Blake on a bough.)[3] Also, you suggest Read to write the preface if Yeats isn't willing. A preface by Read is suicide; as soon as he gives a 'movement' his good wishes, it dies with indignity; his name on the cover of a new book or magazine establishes its good taste and failure; he has supported, with condescension and theoretical nonsense, almost every popular-at-the-time dud from Blunden to Dali, but the worst of it is that he has also lent his support to some honest writers and writing; he can't always miss, and the good have to suffer with the bad.

I hope you'll let me know more about the definite closing date etc.

Yours sincerely,
Dylan Thomas

MS: Texas

1 John Goodland (1919–78) started *Seven* with Nicholas Moore when both were at Cambridge.
2 Hart Crane.
3 The 'New Apocalypse' movement, then getting under way, believed in lush, visceral poetry that was supposed to be a relief after Auden and Eliot. Treece (see page 397) was a leading light. Thomas, unenthusiastic, never managed entirely to dissociate himself from it.

LAWRENCE DURRELL
28 [?December 1938]   Blashford Ringwood Hants
                                        Tel: Ringwood 110

Dear Lawrence Durrell,
   I couldn't reply before because I've been spending Christmas in a neighbouring house & the letters weren't forwarded.
   I'm very glad you & Miller are in London, and I'm looking forward very much to seeing you. Thanks a lot for the pound.
   You're sure, are you, that you couldn't manage to come down here? I've got the willies of London & it makes me ill as hell. But if you can't possibly, then of course I must come—& thank you for your invitation. I mustn't miss this chance of seeing you both, & God knows when, if ever, I'll come to Paris. And how long are you going to be in England? I could get a lift up next Monday to London. Is that too late? Let me know quickly, won't you? If you could come down here, you could be put up somehow of course—& I'll send you the pound back beforehand, & any other money I might have. But, anyway, I'll see you all.
   Best wishes to yourself, your wife, Miller, Perlès.[1] My wife sends hers.
                                                        Dylan T

MS: Carbondale

VERNON WATKINS
29 December 1938   Blashford Ringwood Hants

Dear Vernon,
   What a lovely Compendium. We play all the games in turn. Halma is a demon's game, but one called Winkle's Wedding is too young and sounds like a mass-poem written by adolescents in Roughton's dead paper.[2] Did Families exist? I had a stocking this year, full of sweets and cigars and mouth-organs and cherry brandy. Thank you also for the pretty croquet card. I wish there was something to send you, apart from my love & the small poem I forgot to enclose last time. Before I forget: there's a new periodical, Poetry (London) which promises to be, if nothing else, well produced. A monthly. Edited by man or woman called Tambimuttu.[3] Contributors, God bless them, to the first number will have their names *engraved* on the special souvenir cover. Will you send it something? It may be honest; if so, it shouldn't want to pack its pages with the known stuff of the known boys; a new paper surely should give—(say)—Barker a rest: he

1 Alfred Perlès, writer, friend of Henry Miller.
2 Roger Roughton's *Contemporary Poetry and Prose* ceased publication in 1937 after ten issues.
3 See page 413.

must be very tired. The address of Tambimuttu is 114 Whitfield St, London W.1.

Is Fig still with you, and how was your holiday? Ours was long and weakening, with parties, charades, and too much. Now we reform again; I have a study with the door compulsorily locked and no thrillers allowed inside; there'll be nothing to do but poems.

Congratulations on the magnificent Yeats poem: so few faults in such noble danger; the fine feeling constant. That may be smug to say, but I'm sick of avoiding clichés of appreciation & expressing a large like in small, tough terms. I think it's one of your most truly felt poems; that's not to say that other poems of yours are not true or felt, but only to say that the purity in it is never less than the poetry. What a poem for the old man after that historic interview.[1] In another letter later I'll tell you the few things in the poem that are, to me, uneffectively understated: one or two instances, especially in the reported speech, when understatement is an excess & moderation, economical sobriety, a wallow. But now I want only to tell you how moved I was by the poem, & how much I admire it.

This is quick thanks. My little news must come with my Yeats' grumbles.

Write soon.

Dylan

Caitlin sends her love, too, to all of you.

This Cwmdonkin poem—minus pandemonium[2]—*must*, please, be typed before read. Don't send me a copy. I've got one. There's a fullstop after 'kill' in the 6th line.

MS: British Library

HENRY TREECE
31 December 1938   Blashford Ringwood Hants

Dear Henry,

Your indignation shames me. In the note of December 19th, it's Ever, Henry. Between that time and the 30th a poison has worked, a bird has told you, and Yours Sincerely, Henry Treece stares and floors me. I had your nice last letter in Laugharne, and was proud and glad to have it. You liked me as a man but did not admire me—(the past tense is open to

---

1 Vernon Watkins was a lifelong admirer of Yeats. In 1938 he visited Dublin during his summer holiday from the Swansea bank where he worked, and telephoned to ask if he could call. The result was the 'historic interview', much of which he incorporated verbatim in a poem, 'Yeats in Dublin'.
2 'Of Pandemonium in Cwmdonkin Park'—the park near Thomas's childhood home—is a line in a Watkins poem. The poem Thomas sent was 'Once it was the colour of saying'.

correction)—which is just as it should be; I have the same feelings about myself. My selfish carelessness and unpunctuality I do not try to excuse as poet's properties. They are a bugbear & a humbug. The selfish trouble is that I myself have had to put up with these seriously annoying faults for so long that I've almost come to think other people can bear them. I am the one who wakes up nearest to myself, and the continual horror that comes from the realisation of this individuality has made me almost to believe that the reactions of others to my horrible self—that would not be itself did it not possess the faults etc. that make me now write this simplified confession of complicated egoism so untidily—are small enough, in comparison, to be counted as the others' loss or to be beaten down by one unsulky thought. But of course I apologise, & sincerely. My silence is never the result of promises for noise. My every intention to be in London over Christmas was kicked in the wish by the thought of [becoming] a father. We were taken away from Laugharne with a rush, & never seem to have recovered. I don't know why your letter returned 'unknown', unless it was a post-official hint at the subsidence of my already rickety reputation. Perhaps this letter to you will be returned, marked 'No Such Person'. Nothing is above red ribbon except a heart.

Answering your first letter: I won't sign, with or without argument, the Apocalyptic Manifesto. I wouldn't sign any manifesto unless I had written every word of it, and then I might be too ashamed. I agree with and like much of it, and some of it, I think, is manifestly absurd. That's not giving my own variety of bird to a thing over which you & others have spent considerable time & thought; it's only to say that the language of such documents is strange to me, that organic reality is all my cock. I cannot see how Auden is unaware of Donald Duck, unless Donald Duck is supposed to be a symbol and not a funny bird. Donald Duck is just what Auden is aware of. To him (Auden), *what* this problematical squirrel of ours stumbles over is more important than the squirrel act of stumbling. Auden often writes like Disney. Like Disney, he knows the shape of beasts—(& incidentally he, too, might have a company of artists producing his lines)— unlike Lawrence, he does not know what shapes or motivates these beasts. He's a naturalist who looks for beasts that resemble himself, and, failing that, he tries to shape them in his own curious image. The true naturalist, like Gilpin, offers his toe to the vampire bat; Auden would suck the bat off. I liked very much your reasonable contradiction of the quotation from Marx. But it's all rather like flogging a dead force. Another thing that's admirable is the insistence, without irrational prejudice, on man's dissolution. I like the title: 'Apocalypse: The Dissolute Man': more than yours. But this isn't the time to argue with a statement of belief in which I mostly believe but with which I cannot sympathise wholly (or even dissolutely), owing to my own dogma of Arrogant Acceptance. If I'm given time—you know I write slowly, & not too often to be interfering—I'd be very glad to write for Apocalypse, whole or corner. I'll try to write something about Crane, but it will come slowly. That's not, I know you know, an affectation. Would you like that chunk of prose I was working on—copying out, once, in affectedly microscopic writing—in Laugharne? The first half is finished. And I'll have a poem, not a very long one, completed by the middle of January.

I shan't quarrel now—this is meant, however misguidedly, for a patching-up letter—with your promise of Apocalyptic 'publicity'. Don't you believe me when I say that I don't want to be publicised? Or don't you? I have all the publicity that my small output deserves, and because some other people's small output has more & undeserved publicity, should I worry? Publicity will not get me more money; the little work I produce is paid for as highly as the rags I contribute to can afford. Publicity would not increase my output—indeed, the opposite—nor would it make it saleable to better-paying magazines, nor would it make pay at better rates those magazines that still would print me.

About the manifesto quotation from that letter of mine. Don't you think, looking at it coldly, that its effectiveness (if any) would be increased by cutting out '. . . but I *am* aware of these things as well'. Surely, my conscious catalogue implies that? I think those last few words—whoever wrote them—sound smug. Imagine me suggesting that I *was* not aware of Oxo, Damaroids, & Bunny Austin.[1] Can't you end the quotation at '. . . tick & revolve in'? Please; & that is, too, if you have to use the bit of silliness at all.

I'd written half this letter when I heard from Henry Miller who'd come to London for a few days; & luckily I managed to get driven to see him. Also I met that sap Goodland the blue-&-water-eyed contact-man, yes-man, no man. I just missed the other boys, Cooke,[2] Moore, etc. They're better than Goodland?

I *have* reminded John of the picture. He now has two portraits finished of me. One I'm going to use in my next lot of poems; the other John is entirely willing to let be used in your book. An expert photograph will have to be taken of it; your publishers will, of course, have to see to that. I'm working on an analysis of a few of my poems *now*, but there have been so many interruptions lately. Now they are over.

I'm glad to hear you're getting married so soon. Remember us to Nellie. And are we seeing you this summer? Thank you for your open house. You know about ours too.

Write soon. This has been an awkward letter to write. I'm sure all our next letters will be easy. Regards from Caitlin.

Yours sincerely,
Dylan Thomas
Ever,
Dylan

MS: Buffalo

1 Oxo, the meat extract. Damaroids, a dubious pill (see p. 290). H. W. 'Bunny' Austin, British tennis player. He was a Wimbledon finalist in 1938.
2 Probably Dorian Cooke, a poet of the period.

LAWRENCE DURRELL
[early January 1939]   Blashford Ringwood Hants

Dear Lawrence,

Thank you for the pretty picture. And thank you and Nancy for giving me such a nice time in London. I wanted to write before, but I've been feeling flabby and careless. What happened to you on the Geographical morning? I waited in the stated pub, leaving only for a few minutes to go to the pub opposite. It was all a pity; I lunched with Cameron, & you should have too. How did Miller get on with him? Goodland's blue eyes make me belch.

I liked Miller enormously,[1] as I'd always expected I couldn't do anything but, and you must please keep him to his promise of coming to stay, in the spring, in Wales, in the live quiet. We all, I hope, had too little time together. And there's time to put that right. Will you write, and will Miller write?

To you & Nancy,
Dylan

MS: Carbondale

*GEORGE DILLON
5th January 1939   Blashford Ringwood Hants

Dear Mr Dillon,

Thank you for your letter. I'm very glad you're going to use the new poems I sent you.[2] And thank you for the nice things you said about the prize.

You asked me about reviewing Delmore Schwartz's[3] book. Though I'd like very much to read it some time, I wouldn't like to write about it. I try to get as much reviewing work as possible, but only novels, the lighter the better, for money. But thank you for asking me. I want to send you some general critical prose this year.

Yours sincerely,
Dylan Thomas

MS: Chicago

1 In Durrell's account (Poetry London–New York, No. 1, 1956), he brought Miller to London, and invited Thomas to a dinner party. Thomas failed to appear, then telephoned from a nearby pub, where Durrell found him, 'too frightened to move'. Durrell persuaded him to go and meet Miller.
2 In 1939 Poetry published only one Thomas poem, 'Her tombstone told when she died', in the November issue. The magazine cover gave the title as 'A Winding Film', using a phrase from the poem that Thomas later changed to 'a hurried film'.
3 American poet.

*KEIDRYCH RHYS
7 January 1939   Blashford   Ringwood   Hants

Dear Keidrych,
      Thank you for writing at last.
      If you want me to write to Niall Montgomery—though why he can't
write to me himself, I don't know—will you give me the *right* address. And
when I write, what do I say? I've never read a line of his.
      Augustus John said, only a few days ago, that he wrote you a letter about
that portrait but that you never answered it. This must be due to the
constant muddle of your addresses. I've had letters to you returned
'unknown.' John *told* Sevier that you wanted the portrait to be reproduced,
and Sevier said that he would 'see about it.' I don't suppose for a moment
he's done anything. Also, Nicholson who runs the gallery in which Sevier
had the exhibition has been warned by John that he must allow the portrait
to be reproduced whenever you wish it. But the best thing is to write again
to John, Fryern Court, Fordingbridge, Hants, & tell him your worries.
      You know, half the trouble is not other people's. You're such a bloody
mystery man. You begin something, get some support, then keep those
supporters, suddenly, in the dark for months. Surely you said your object
was to get 'Wales' out for Christmas: getting a good start on the Welsh
Review.[1] And here you're hanging on into February. Incidentally, in your
contents-list of the new 'Wales'—which looks as though it could be very
good—you have an article on *Mary Butts*.[2] Now *why*, for God's sake? What
has an old, dead Paris-Bloomsbury-Cornwall precious female pasticheur to
do with a young, progressive Welsh magazine? She's a legend for middle-
aged pansies (Cedric,[3] Lett, Herring etc) to present with graceful, rather
catty tributes in camp-quarterlies. All her work was a weak, drugged lie.
Why not an article on Firbank, too? Are you Time-&-Tiding us?
      Nobody, to my knowledge, has 'created dissension,' has tried to spoil
your idea of making an influential group of writers in Wales. You yourself
have been so evasive; you have dragged into your magazine all the little
waste names—Potts, Heseltine, Todd, Symons, Agee—that belong to
London rags & not, in thought or action or feeling, to anything connected
with Wales. At a time when all your energies were needed—at the time of
the conception of the Welsh Review—to keep your contributors, to build
up a new interest in 'Wales,' to keep people like John & Hughes
permanently on *our* side, you vanished. The contributors, thinking 'Wales'
dead, agreed to support the Welsh Review; few, I think, ratted. Now your
writers are dispersed, the policy of 'Wales' seems vague enough to include

---

1 February 1939 saw the first issue of Gwyn Jones's *Welsh Review*, 'A monthly journal
   about Wales, its people, and their activities.'
2 Mary Butts (1892–1937), novelist, is best known for *Death of Felicity Taverner* (1932).
   She liked grand themes—among her subjects for novels were Alexander the Great and
   Cleopatra—and studied mysticism and religions.
3 Presumably the painter Cedric Morris, who was homosexual.

any backstairs London literary clique, & nobody outside a small circle knows whether 'Wales' will ever appear again.[1] I know you've had difficulties, & I'm not a good or happy lecturer. But really you have lacked drive & firmness, you've let the possibility of a possibly *great* magazine almost slip away. It mustn't slip away altogether. Whatever I can do, let me know. I'm no organiser, either. But between us we should manage a little solidity of concentration on making the *basis* of 'Wales' permanent & seeing that its integrity does not degenerate into fashionable, periodical literature such as any sap or crook like Symons or Grigson can produce so deftly & uselessly.

I don't quite know what Treece wants. Some sort of critical, though personal, appreciation from a Welsh point of view I should think. His address now is: The Grammar School, Caistor Rd., Barton on Humber, Lincs. Perhaps you could write & ask, or tell, him.

We'll be back in Laugharne at the end of February. Will you still be near? You must come then. There must be lots of work for us. Write soon.

Love,
Dylan

Are you doing a 'bibliography' of me? I can let you have a lot of material.

MS: (Gabriel Pustel)

VERNON WATKINS
Sunday [postmarked 8 January 1939]   Blashford Ringwood Hants

Dear Vernon,

I was told you telephoned. Caitlin and I didn't get back until fairly late, and as you said it wasn't a call of life & death, we took you at your word and didn't worry. I'll ring you one night. It will be nice to hear you again, those soft Cambridge accents sliding from Wales. Thankyou.

Since you've apparently been taking lessons from John Prichard in refusing to accept adverse criticism, I shall make my grumbles about your good Yeats poem illegible to invisibility. Here come the grumbles, hot, strong, and logical, but you can't see them. Incidentally, the effectiveness of a history of conversation is determined by selection. Though the statements are word for word, the words are still wrong in the poem. You can say to me that effectiveness is less than truth; I can only say that the truth must be made effectively true, and though every word of the truth be put down the result may well be a clot of *truths*.

I'm glad you liked my last poem. I shan't alter anything in it except, perhaps but probably, the 'close & cuckoo' lovers. The 'dear close cuckoo' lovers is a good suggestion.[2] I can't say the same for 'halo for the bruised

1 The issue was published in March 1939 as 'Nos. 6/7'. No. 5 had appeared in summer 1938.
2 The poem was 'Once it was the colour of saying'. 'Close and cuckoo lovers' became 'cold and cuckoo lovers'.

knee & broken heel' which is esoterically *off* every mark in the poem. I see your argument about the error of shape, but the form was consistently emotional and I can't change it without a change of heart.

Last week I went up to London to meet Henry Miller who is a dear, mad, mild man, bald and fifty, with great enthusiasms for commonplaces. Also Lawrence Durrell. We spent 2 days together, and I returned a convinced wreck. We talked our way through the shabby saloons of nightmare London. I saw, too, Cameron who has written a good poem, John Goodland who has no merit, & a man dressed in brown paper.

We still play with the Compendium, & are now the very disappointed owners of brand-new Milestones which is a kiddies' mixture of Ludo & Happy Families & quite without the subversive, serious charm of Monopoly. A woman bought the set for us, so it really was lucky you didn't.

I'll tell you when the great birthday comes. We're waiting now. Caitlin had very few angles before, but now she has none. The word is mellow.

We'll be back in Wales, I hope, at the end of February. Certainly in March. Laugharne will be beautiful in the Spring. You must come often. We'll learn, perhaps, to sail together. Love to your family, &, of course, to yourself.

Dylan

I'll write a better letter soon, with a poem.
But you must write too.
Do you know which stories of mine Francis[1] has translated? A chap called Constantine FitzGibbon[2]—you saw his translation of a little poem in 'La Nouvelle Saison'—wants to do my 'Lemon' story. Is Francis doing that?

MS: British Library

CHARLES FISHER

[January 1939]   Blashford   Ringwood   Hants

We hope to be back in Laugharne
at the end of February. Don't forget
us then: Liberty and Calamity hall,
where a naked man may bury his
towels in peace.

Dear Charles,
I was glad to hear from you; living is even more miserable for all your absences; I should have written a long time ago to find out how all that

---

1 Francis Dufau-Labeyrie.
2 FitzGibbon (1919–83), author, was an American who became an Irish citizen. Eventually a friend of Dylan Thomas, he wrote the official biography in 1965.

curious collection is carrying on in the last days of the fall of the British Empire, but I am fat and slothful, sentimental and unscrupulous, a bag of a boy in the flush of his pulled youth. This flat English country levels the intelligence, planes down the imagination, narrows the a's, my ears belch up old wax and misremembered passages of misunderstood music, I sit and hate my mother-in-law, glowering at her from corners and grumbling about her in the sad, sticky quiet of the lavatory, I take little walks over the Bad Earth. Our baby should be born at the end of next week, we wait and it kicks. Lack of money still pours in.

And I'm glad you're all working, on levitation, rainbow's promises, the drama, & Sketty organs. I heard last week from Bob Rees, who said that he wrote to Fred to find out my address and that, to his great surprise, he got a real letter back from the old umbrella himself. Bob says that he's going to write a book one day, to be called 'The Life and Letter of F. Janes'.

Will you give me, some time, Dan's new address? I still feel Warmley.

Love to you all,
Dylan

Only source: SL[1]

LAWRENCE DURRELL
[?mid January, 1939]   Blashford   Ringwood   Hants

Dear Lawrence,
I forgot to thank you for the pound, crisper than celery and sweeter than sugar oh the lovely sound, not through ingratitude, it's as welcome as a woman is cleft, but through work (half a poem about energy), sloth (in a chair looking at my feet or the mirror or unread novels or counting the patterns on the wc floor to see if I can work out a system for my football pools or watching my wife knit or dance), depression (because, mostly, there weren't more pounds from more people), small habits (from bar-billiards to broadcast talks, slick-bonneted Hampshire roadhouses and socialist teas), love, unqualified, the nearness of Bournemouth, colds and pains in the head and your Black Book about which more in another and longer letter. I liked too very much your eggy poems in Seven. Thank you for the Emily Brontë poem: I thought at first sight it was a rejected manuscript of mine: a great likeness, and yes I can read nearly every word of it.[2] Why are you still in London, has somebody moved Corfu? And do you want another poem from me, for seven shillings and sixpence? Regards to your wife and muse, to Heppenstall if you see him and not to Goodland.

Dylan

MS: Carbondale

1 Charles Fisher later lost the MS that he supplied for *SL*.
2 Durrell, visiting the British Museum, had seen an autograph letter by Emily Brontë and been struck by the similarity between her writing and Thomas's. He sent Thomas a facsimile postcard.

HENRY TREECE
January 26 1939   Blashford   Ringwood   Hants

Dear Henry,
    Thanks for the good letters.
    And straightaway I must say that I haven't got anything for 'Seven'. Half
a poem's on my table, and that's all. I'm sorry my name has to remain on
the cover, but, after all, I had not promised to contribute to this number.
'Apocalypse' is a different affair, isn't it? I mean, surely 'Seven' hasn't
taken that as a new name? Actually, I still have that large chunk of prose I
told you about, and from which I read you bits, but that's got to be bought.
I've spent so much time on that that I don't part with it except for real
money; and I'll stick to that even if it prevents the thing ever being printed.
It applies to my promised contributions to 'Apocalypse', too. From now on,
I'm going to be paid, & paid fairly, for every line of mine that's printed.
Cash-minded Dylan, that's me—if you know the reference.[1] I'll sell
'Seven' seven pages of glamorous prose. Any offers?
    Glad you're feeling better now. I'm not feeling better. I'm worried and
lazy and morose, I've got a hundred headaches and a barbed mouth, I hate
every living person with the exception of a Mrs. Macarthy who lives in
Chelsea. I can't write this letter.
    Keidrych is hysterical. Why should I be interested in the blurb for Glyn
Jones's book in America? And why, anyway, should he send it via
Lincolnshire? He's always doing things like that; once he sent me a lot of
used stamps and the bibliography of Arthur Machen.[2]
    Thanks for the warning about our literary friends' correspondence circle.
I don't want to hurt anybody—much. But Goodland is a sap, 19 or 90. His
blue eyes are pools of piss—aristocratic piss. He's got fallen arches in his
mouth. You say that he might have been frightened of me? Of me? I'm like
a baby in the dark.
    More when I feel good. Caitlin is still waiting, the baby's overdue by 3
days. No worry, though. She sends her regards to you & Nelly.
    This letter's really to tell you about 'Seven' & me. More, about me, when
I don't feel so sick & angry.

                                                    Love,
                                                    Dylan

& more soon, too.

MS: Buffalo

---

1 'Big-hearted Arthur, that's me,' was a catch-phrase of the comedian Arthur Askey, who
  could be heard on radio every week in the BBC's first 'situation comedy', *Band
  Waggon*.
2 Arthur Machen (real name Arthur Jones, 1863–1947), Welsh journalist, actor, author.
  His short story of 1914 about ghosts of the bowmen of Agincourt, coming to the aid of
  British troops in France, was transformed overnight into the myth of 'the angels of
  Mons', widely believed in.

JOHN DAVENPORT
30 Jan 1939   Blashford Ringwood Hants

Dear John,
  Sorry, but I didn't send off those stories as I said I would & as I
wanted to, very much, for advice. Caitlin had to go to Poole Hospital
yesterday evening, is now in The Labour Room, & I'm waiting. I'll ring
you up tomorrow, Monday, & tell you what there is to tell. And I'll
send the stories too. I'm worried & in a bit of a muddle about
everything.

                          Love to Clement & yourself
                                    Dylan

MS: Texas

VERNON WATKINS
1 February 1939   Blashford Ringwood Hants

Dear Vernon,
  This is just to tell you that Caitlin & I have a son aged 48 hours. Its name
is Llewelyn Thomas. It is red-faced, very angry, & blue-eyed. Bit blue, bit
green. It does not like the world. Caitlin is well, & beautiful. I'm sorry
Yeats is dead.[1] What a loss of the great poems he would write. Aged 73, he
died in his prime. Caitlin's address—if you would like to send her a word—
is Maternity Ward, Cornelia Hospital, Poole, Dorset.
                                    Our love to you,
                                         Dylan

MS: British Library

VERNON WATKINS
Saturday [4 February 1939]   Blashford Ringwood Hants

Dear Vernon,
  A very short letter to thank you for your letters to Caitlin and me
about our mumbling boy. He's in the room with me now, making noises
to his fingers, his eyes unfocusing, with his red skull half-covered
in golden cotton. He & Caitlin came back from hospital today. She's
well.

1 Yeats died 28 January.

Here's a new poem.[1] Tell me: is it too short? do I end before the point? does it need more room to work to a meaning, any expansion? I intended it as a longer & more ambitious thing, but stopped it suddenly thinking it was complete. How do you feel about it? And what about a poem from you? Write very soon.

Ever yours,
Dylan

Have you ever seen such insulting rot as that written about Yeats in the respectable Sunday newspapers.

MS: British Library

LAWRENCE DURRELL
Sunday [5 February 1939]   Blashford   Ringwood   Hants

Dear Lawrence,
    Thank you for your letters, and your writing. All at sea on the BB.[2] I'm sickened & excited. If you want—& you say you want—& I believe you—a poem for the new Delta, why not the one you like in the paper of Tambimuttu's, that distinguished Celanese?[3] If not—and perhaps, I hope, as well—here's a new short poem.[4] And I'd rather have the 7/6 than a book-token. My bowels need more than consonants & vowels. When you like, and sooner. Oh, a boy, by the way & the womb. Llewelyn. The homage of his father. You say I'm obscurely worried, but it's too obscure to worry about. I kick against my prick. Everything's OK except why. But is the spring promise of coming to see us in Wales still good? You & yours & Miller. Write soon.

Dylan

MS: Carbondale

1 'Because the pleasure-bird whistles.'
2 Durrell's novel *The Black Book*.
3 Tambimuttu (see pages 395 and 413) edited *Poetry London*, which printed Thomas's 'A saint about to fall' in its first, February 1939, issue.
4 *Delta* dated Easter 1939 printed Thomas's 'January 1939' (= 'Because the pleasure-bird whistles').

JULIAN SYMONS
Feb 5 1939   Blashford   Ringwood   Hants

Dear Julian Symons,
    Sorry for the delay & for the single poem; meant to send you a couple. I
haven't been able to work during the last week because of my new, red son.
Hope this will do.

                                        Dylan Thomas

MS: Texas

*JOHN PRICHARD
14 Feb 1939   [headed paper: Blashford   Ringwood   Hants]

Dear John,
    A late note. Thank you very much for writing. You say that you hardly
know whether to offer your congratulations. Do. I can only deal directly
with implied nonsense. You've heard, by this time, what little—what six
pounds & red—there is to hear. And you can hear him too. I've no other
news. At Christmas I went to London to meet Miller, whom I liked a lot.
Goodland snurged along: a little belch of a boy with no apparent taste or
smell. I don't see many people, either. Locals, usuals, unnecessaries. I had a
funny letter from Bob Rees, who remains honestly nice. Is it true about
Fisher's monocle, or is that another joke? Deepest of all jokes is Fred's
perhaps marriage.[1] I imply nothing absurd in the idea of his marrying.
    My own marriage probably caused him one extra scratch-mark on a
small piece of paint. But to whom? Give his near-wife my regards: up and
down. I hope to see you all quite soon. I see your name in lots of magazines.
I see my own in some of the same magazines. Oh, John, would that they
paid us. My complete lack of money has now been trebled. Yours, at least,
remains singly bloody. Best wishes, & write when you feel like it. I'll be
here for another 3 weeks.

                                        Dylan

MS: National Library of Wales

DAVID HIGHAM
20 February 1939   Blashford   Ringwood   Hants

Dear Higham,
    I'm sorry to be so long returning these stories and suggesting, for Dent's,
the ones which I should like to be included in my book of verse and prose.
But I've been trying hard to raise enough money to keep my wife and son

1 Alfred Janes.

going for the next month or two, and unsuccessfully. Now I'm relying entirely on Dent's. They've got the mss of the poems, and here are the stories. Of the stories I suggest The Orchards, The Enemies, The Map Of Love, A Prospect Of The Sea, and The Visitor. Those are all stories to which no objection, other than literary, could be taken, and anyway they're the best—especially in a book also to contain poems. Church has, among the mss of the poems, part of a prose-piece called 'In The Direction Of The Beginning'—a title I originally intended as the title of the whole book. I have, however, been considering this piece, and have now decided to make it part of a much longer work which I want to spread over many months to come. But that decision doesn't alter the book: there are still sixteen poems and five stories; and two poems, now finished but not polished up enough yet, to be added. So that Dent's *have* the whole mss of the whole book, only not yet finally arranged in order—surely a small consideration considering that the book will not be published until after the spring. (Church can, of course, choose other stories from the enclosed collection if he wants to, but I'm sure my choice is right for the purposes of this book.) And, having the mss in their hands, can't they be persuaded to give me the £30 promised on 'completion of Mss'? If they *can't* be persuaded, then I'm sunk. And this is no begging or joke. I can't return with my family to Wales until some important debts there, principally for rent, have been settled; and there's no money, other than Dent's promised money, coming to me in the world. Do please do your very best for me. After all, here is the book they wanted. The John portrait they can photograph any time they want to—I have all his permission. (By the way, have you heard if they'll do it in colour or not?) And the only thing left to do is to arrange the order of contents. I have, I know, altered the original idea of the book by wishing to cut out the prose-piece already in Church's possession, but I must do that, and five stories and eighteen poems—the two extra ones will be ready and typed by the end of the week—is quite as big a book as Church said he wanted. Please, Higham, do try to get that advance *immediately*. We've got to move, and we can't until our Welsh village has been pacified financially. I can rely on you, I know, to do your best for me as quickly as you can.

Yours,
Dylan Thomas

MS: Texas

RICHARD CHURCH
22 February 1939   Blashford   Ringwood   Hants

Dear Richard Church,
    Sorry not to have got in touch with you for so long.
    Higham now has the complete mss. of my short stories and I've told him which stories I confidently suggest for inclusion in the prose and verse

book. Perhaps you have already seen Higham, and he has explained to you that I wish to cut out the incomplete prose-piece called 'In The Direction Of The Beginning'. I know this will alter the plan of the book, but, I think, alter it for the best. That prose-piece would, I believe, when complete, overbalance the poems and the rest of the stories—by hysterical weight, not by value. I intend now making it quite a long thing, say about the length of Petron, and then I'm sure it would be better to publish it by itself.

If you look at the stories I've suggested, you'll see I had some trouble over the names of the characters. It's fairly unimportant, I suppose, but it should be settled. The name originally used in 'The Orchards' story was Peter, the same as in 'The Visitor', but, on rereading, I took a dislike to the name. It applied more to a character in a slick, fashionable story, and seemed out of place in short imaginative stories or fables. What do you think? I've changed the name in 'The Orchards' but not in 'The Visitor': so that you can see how they compare. Do tell me. Perhaps even 'Marlais' seems an affected choice of name; it was the only one I could immediately think of, being my own.[1]

I hope very much, that's putting it weakly, that Dent's may be persuaded to give me my advance for this book now. It is complete, and only needs arrangement. I've a family to support, and nothing to support it with—just nothing. I do need that advance at once, if I am to keep my wife and son well if only for a short time, and hope you'll help me to get it.

Yours,
Dylan Thomas

MS: (J. M. Dent)

DAVID HIGHAM
25 February 1939   Blashford   Ringwood   Hants

Dear Higham,
Very glad to have your letter & the contract. I knew you'd manage things for me. Thank you.

Here's the contract, initialled.

What a hole there's going to be in my £50.[2]

Have Dent's come to any conclusion yet about the John portrait? Do they want written permission for reproduction from John? It isn't necessary, but I can get it if needs be. What about colour?

Thanks again.

Yours,
Dylan Thomas

MS: Texas

---

1 The names remained Peter ('The Visitor') and Marlais ('The Orchards').
2 £20 of the first £50 for *The Map of Love* had to go to George Reavey, to repay the *Burning Baby* advance.

KEIDRYCH RHYS
Tuesday [?February 1939]   Blashford Ringwood Hants

Dear Keidrych,
    Thanks for the reviews etc. (And I'm looking forward to the editorial
note you spoke about.) I'll see what I can do with these, & show them to
some people. But my influence, as you know, is very small indeed. About
editorship: please, I'd rather *not* go down, printed, as co-editor—though I'd
like very much to have a look at the stuff beforehand, if you feel like
sending it. This number 6/7 is *your* making, and it would be too late now
for me to argue against any of the chosen, and advertised, contributions.
But in future numbers—if there are any, & by God there must be—I should
be very pleased to do something more constructive than merely to grumble
at you while you do all the work. But, really, there's no point at all in me
having anything official to do with this new, already prepared, number.
Though if you want, in spite of that, a hand with comments & reviews *for*
the number, do let me know; I'll do anything you like. What splendid
notices 'Wales' has had, by the way. Surely those, handed to the right
person, should mean something.
    Again—and I'm sorry that all my recent letters seem so disagreeable—I
won't write to Barker asking him for a poem. One of the oustanding things
about 'Wales' is that, so far, it has not printed one of Mr. Barker's
masturbative monologues—as every other verse-magazine of our time has
done, with disgusting frequency. And I think 'Wales's' standard should be
upheld.
    More soon; & please write too.

                                                    Dylan

MS: Location unknown

VERNON WATKINS
Wednesday [postmarked 3 March 1939]   Blashford Ringwood Hants

Dear Vernon,
    Very short note. I've got to do the proofs of my new book of poems this
week, & I'm thinking of putting in this poem just finished. Please, can I
have a quick criticism.[1] It's deeply felt, but perhaps clumsily said. In
particular—is the last line too bad, too comic, or does it *just* work? Have
you any alternatives for the *adjectives* of that last line?—you see obviously
what I *mean.*

---

1 The poem enclosed was '"If my head hurt a hair's foot"'.

Terrific hurry to get this in time for post.

Hope you're well. Back in a fortnight. Letter much sooner. Caitlin & Llewelyn well. Hope you are.

My love,
Dylan

MS: British Library

JULIAN SYMONS
March 3 1939 Blashford Ringwood Hants

Dear Julian Symons,

Thanks for the magazine, and for the congratulations on the birth of my son. Do I get my guinea? Him and me need it. I'll try & send along another poem soon.

Yours,
Dylan Thomas

MS: Texas

DAVID HIGHAM
March 3 1939 Blashford Ringwood Hants

Dear Higham,

Thank you very much for the speedy cheque. Things are a bit easier now.

Here's the contract signed by me, with the extra initialling.

You forgot, by the way, to enclose the counterpart of this contract signed by Dent.

I'm seeing John today, and I'll get a note from him then authorising reproduction of his portrait.

I've seen a review of 'The Year's Poetry. 1938', edited by Denys Kilham Roberts & published by the Bodley Head. It is supposed to have published several of my poems[1]—Roberts asked for them & accepted them months ago—but so far I've had no copy of the book or cheque, & never received proofs. I wonder whether you could enquire for me some time. Thank you again for all you've done.

Yrs,
Dylan Thomas

MS: Texas

---

1 The book contained one Thomas poem, 'In Memory of Ann Jones' (= 'After the funeral').

KAY BOYLE[1]
[?March 1939]   Blashford   Ringwood   Hants

Dear Kay Boyle,

Nicholas Moore[2] wrote to me today, enclosing your letter to him. I've written back to him, telling him that I haven't got a novel but that a book of stories of mine may be free in a few days. New Directions wanted to do it, but I'm quarrelling with them about terms etc, and it will probably end up in refusal all round. But just as I posted the letter to Moore, I realised that I'd been wanting to write to you for a long time, without knowing your address. Ever since you published Monday Night. I thought that was a very grand book indeed, and I wrote a review of it—a meagre little one, it had to be—which I do hope you saw. This is a fan letter. You haven't got a greater admirer than me.

                                         Dylan Thomas

MS: Carbondale

DAVID HIGHAM
March 4 1939   Blashford   Ringwood   Hants

Dear Higham,

I agree with you, of course. Ten years is an absurdly long time, and during which I may write my Gone with The Wind. And I approve, of course again, of your decision to be firm about five years or f-all. And 60 dollars, as you reasonably said, is not a sufficient consideration for a 50 years option: just over, possibly, a dollar a year.

If Laughlin doesn't agree to your terms, can we try another American publisher right away. The little tyke has no legal right to get his 60 dollars back if we do. I've had several letters from American publishers, wanting to see my work, especially prose—Simon and Schuster were the most enthusiastic; extremely so. Also, I heard from Kay Boyle today that a friend of hers, Caresse Crosby Young, has come to Europe to look for books, as she is going to work with a N.Y. publisher. Kay Boyle has boosted me to her.

Thank you for the Dent-signed contract.

                                         Yours,
                                         Dylan Thomas

MS: Texas

---

1 Kay Boyle, American novelist and poet, then living in Europe. Her novel *Monday Night* appeared in 1937.
2 Nicholas Moore, poet; he edited the magazine *Seven*.

RICHARD CHURCH
March 4 1939   Blashford   Ringwood   Hants

Dear Richard Church,
  I've been asked to write, by next Wednesday, a descriptive note of 200 words for my book of poems and stories. I haven't had a reply yet to my last week's letter to you about the choice of stories—I do hope you'll be able to accept mine—and about my wish to cut out that long prose fragment. I do hope you'll tell me what you think about these things before I write the note.
  I shan't finish that fragment for quite a long time; I've decided to make it far fuller & to put in much more detail etc. Is there any point in publishing, in this new book, the fragment as it is now? Anyway, I still think, don't you, that its title should be kept as the title of the whole book, whether the fragment is omitted or not. It does apply to most of the poems & stories in the book.
  I'm having the 2 extra poems typed, & will send them along Monday or, at the latest, Tuesday.
  I'm looking forward very much to hearing from you.
                                          Best wishes,
                                          Yours,
                                          Dylan Thomas

MS: (J. M. Dent)

M. J. TAMBIMUTTU

A poet and literary entrepreneur from Ceylon, where his family was supposed to be descended from kings, the wily 'Tambi' (1915–83) arrived in London in 1938 and founded *Poetry London* as 'the poetry periodical that youth has been waiting for'. While he and his magazine lived hand-to-mouth, he published many of his contemporaries, and T. S. Eliot let him edit a Faber anthology. In the 1950s he ran the short-lived *Poetry London–New York*, but his heyday was the war years, his habitat Soho and Bloomsbury.

March 5 [1939]   Blashford   Ringwood   Hants

Dear Tambimuttu,
  Thanks for your cheque and for the first number of your beautifully produced magazine. The print's always a pleasure to read, even if some of the poems aren't. That's no sneer, believe me. I congratulate you a lot on the handsomest 'intelligent' poetry magazine I know of, and on the courage of your unfashionable introduction. I do understand that you have an extraordinarily large circulation, and that you can't, for that reason, weigh the paper down with too much difficult verse—and I'm not suggesting that the best is difficult, only that most of the best today is bound to be. I suppose there is, there must be, some reason why John Gawsworth,

F.R.S.L., should appear with, say, MacNeice. I think that to include Gawsworth—I mean nothing personal—that leftover, yellow towelbrain of the nineties soaked in stale periods, in a magazine most of whose contributors are, at least, and if little else unites them, nostalgic for nothing but a better *present*, is overdoing your ostensible wish to make 'Poetry' readable to a great number of people on first sight. (I agree, incidentally and only just, with a possible editorial policy which takes the view that if a number of people will only buy the magazine for the not-so-good verse that attracts them easily and immediately, the good verse may do its work on them in spite of themselves and the magazine may prosper.) I *can* see the point in beginning a new magazine with an easily conventional lyric or two, especially if the (problematical now, no fingerpointing offence) editor's real favourites of poems which appear later in the number contain such words as Marx, copulation, and pylon, words very likely, and rightly likely, to put off bookstall tasters. But whether robins, rills, and Mercury woodcuts work the other way I wouldn't know. Please don't take this as a badtempered letter. I want, as much I think as you do, to see 'Poetry'—it's needed alright, verse magazines in England are very sad—grow into something extremely entertaining and popular. Poetry editors are mostly vicious climbers, with their fingers in many pies, their ears at many keyholes, and their tongues at many bottoms. *You've* shown, in your introduction, how much you believe in the good of poetry and in the mischief of cliques, rackets, scandal schools, menagerie menages, amateur classes of novitiate plagiarists etc. More subscribers and power to you. But one trouble I see is that, in an attempt to include many sorts of poetry, you're liable in the end to sacrifice poetry for variety. I know that you dislike as much as anybody whose dislikes have not been patterned for him, the sort of anthology that begins by saying, 'In this we aim to represent every school of contemporary poetry', and the sort of gushing, inaccurate, Professor Daisy textbook beginning 'It is now apparent that there were at the introduction of the twentieth century five poetical channels of thought.' To try, in paper or book, to represent the whole 'field' of contemporary poetry is to take a turd's eye view. Surely the only thing an editor can say about this particular point is, 'This paper's going to print the best poems that are sent to it, and let the contemporary field disappear up its own pansies'. (This may be irrelevant arguing, and I'm sure is badly put.) I lent 'Poetry' yesterday to the butcher's son here, so haven't got it by me to write you in detail about the poems—as you suggested I should try to do. I'll try in a later letter. Just received yours this morning. I heard one of your broadcasts, hope you'll be talking again soon. Lord, what a difficult business it must be, running a poetry paper: and afterward what heavy enthusiasm or condemnation from small and amateur pontiffs like me. Don't take too much notice, only my sincere congratulations. I'm afraid I don't know when I'll be in London again, I can't afford to take a penny bus most days. But when I'm up, I'll let you know at once. Best wishes,

Dylan Thomas

I'll send my poems by Wednesday. Thanks for the extra time you're allowing me.

MS: Texas

RICHARD CHURCH
8 March 1939   Blashford   Ringwood   Hants

Dear Richard Church,
    Thank you for your letter.
    I enclose three more poems. The sonnet I am not sure about, it seems mechanical. What do you think? We do want as many poems as possible, don't we?
    I'm extremely sorry you do not want to include the story, 'A Prospect Of The Sea', which is one of my own favourites. If I removed, or toned down to complete harmlessness, its 'moments of sensuality', would you then consider again its inclusion? I very much hope so, though of course your decision is final.[1]
    I agree with your suggestion of 'The Map of Love: Verse & Prose' as the title.
    The additional poems I should like to be included somewhere about the middle of the collection, where you think fit, but not at either end.
    And I don't really think that I agree with 'The Dress' coming at the very end of the prose? (I suppose the verse will come first in the book? That certainly seems the best.)
    I think 'The Dress' is too pathetic a note to end the book with. I suggest 'The Orchards'—but again, it is not a very important point, and I leave it to you.

                                        Sincerely,
                                        Dylan Thomas

P.S. Here also is the 200 word blurb. I couldn't do one, & got a friend of mine to help. Is it what you wanted?

MS: (J. M. Dent)

1 Church had written on 6 March to complain that 'A Prospect of the Sea' had 'moments of sensuality without purpose [and it] brings us near the danger zone'.

DESMOND HAWKINS
March 12 1939   Blashford   Ringwood   Hants

Dear Desmond,
    I'm very rude but please forgive me because I didn't mean to be. I've been
away from this address, haven't been doing any work, and letters have got
muddled. I *did* receive your note about a poem, but I hadn't got one: I'd
sent away the only one I had a few days before: I wish you'd been able to
give me a little notice. But no blame on you about anything: it's I'm Uncle
Dirty. And I tried to do something with that left-over lot of books, but it
was so flimsy I couldn't make an entertaining article out of it. I'm wanting
very much to review some more, & punctually: give me the closing date.
Thank you, Desmond, I hope you'll send them along soon. Has the N.E.W.
reviewed 'Bitter Victory' by Louis Guilloux—the best modern novel I've
read, I think anyway at the moment. No, perhaps not that, but very grand.
Has your novel been reviewed in the N.E.W.? Or could I have it? I've seen
some very pretty words about it. Best luck with it.[1]
    Dent's are bringing out my new poems, plus $\frac{1}{2}$ dozen stories, in the
summer, under the name 'The Map of Love'. Do get hold of a review copy.
    My son is almost as big as me, but not quite: you'd hardly recognise me.
I've put on over 2 stone & am a small, square giant now. Let me have the
books soon. Apologies again. Give me the news.
                                                    Dylan

MS: National Library of Wales

A. E. TRICK
[mid March 1939]   Blashford   Ringwood   Hants

Dear Bert,
    This is to tell you, with variations, what I'm sure you must know by
now: that I'm the father of a son named Llewelyn, aged six weeks, a fat,
round, bald, loud child with a spread nose and blue saucer eyes. His full
name is Llewelyn Edouard, the last being a concession to Caitlin's French
grandfather;[2] but in spite of this he sounds militantly Welsh, and, though
this is probably national pride seen through paternal imagination or
viceversa, he looks it too. Before anything else, before apologies, recrimina-
tions, and news, how are your wife, Pamela and Kerith? Please do
remember me to all of them, though Kerith I suppose, remembers me as
nothing but a shifting blur with a mop on top.
    For well over a year now, we've failed to keep in touch with each other:

1 Hawkins's first novel, *Hawk Among the Sparrows*.
2 Caitlin's maternal grandfather was a Quaker, Edouard Majolier, a corn merchant from
Provence who married an Irishwoman.

was it my fault or yours? Mine, perhaps—I'm careless, I know, and appear rude but never feel or mean it—though you've not written either. I hear nothing from the boys—is Fred still pineappleing and knifing,[1] consummating in the cinema, expressing down Walters-road with his head full of fruit and stars, has Tom erased himself completely yet?—so nothing about you. Though I'm set in a life now, two stone heavier but not a feather steadier, though never again will I fit into Swansea quite so happily and comfortably as I did—for I'll be a hundred jokes and personal progressions behind all my friends, I'll be almost a dead face, or worse still a new face, in which nothing will interest them but the old shades and expressions—I'm strong and sentimental for the town and people, for long virulent Sundays with you and scrapbooks and strawberry jelly at the end, for readings and roarings with all the grand boys. I'm not meaning to talk like an ancient village outcast; no more than two years separate me; I'll be all the summer, and every summer I hope, in Carmarthenshire. But one small, close society is closed to me, and the social grief is natural. We're all moving away; and every single decisive action happens in a blaze of disappointment.

What's been happening to you? How are the Townhill and Council schemes?[2] Here in this flat, narrow chested and vowelled county, full of fading squires, traditional English romantic outlaws, sour gentlewomen and professional ostriches, I long for my old, but never properly mounted, soapbox of bright colours, and my grand, destructive arguments learned so industriously and vehemently from you on winter evenings after Cwmdonkin sonnets and Lux to sweet ladies—you gave my rebelliousness a direction, and on the black, back-to-the-wall umbrella-man's Day[3] I'll have you to blame, which will be a small recompense.

We come back to Wales in the first week in April, to Laugharne where we rent—though the landlord would disagree—a crumbling house, and to Swansea for a day or two to let my mother see Llewelyn in all his shit, sweetness, and glory. I must see you then. You'll recognise me by belly, black hat, and a nostalgic flavour of the Uplands.

And I want you to see my new poems, which will make a book in the summer. Not quite a book, for the whole thing is called. 'The Map of Love' and has fifteen poems and seven stories. Old stories mostly, but cut and pruned to buggery or sense.

I've got so many questions to ask you that I'll keep them all until we meet. Do write a little soon and let me know how things are and what you are doing.

Love,
Dylan

MS: Ohio State University

1 Fred Janes and his still-life paintings.
2 Swansea's Town Hill was developed in a municipal house-building project between the wars.
3 The 'umbrella man' might be Neville Chamberlain (he always seemed to carry one), and the 'Day' either the 'socialist revolution' or the coming war.

HENRY TREECE
[mid March 1939]   Blashford   Ringwood   Hants

Dear Henry,

Sorry not to reply sooner. I'd decided, until your postcard this morning, not to write a word for some weeks, not a word of anything. It wasn't a moral decision: I wanted to go and play billiards at the conservative club, etc.; all day long. But I'll have to do that little analysis now before you shame me to incoherence, and certainly before your marriage upon which I congratulate you with all the sincerity of a smug, happy, penniless husband and father. I'll finish over this weekend the strongly promised stuff.

I don't know why you have to work yourself up into such an indignant rage when you say that you won't pay me for the analysis. Nobody asked you sir. It never occurred to me.

Of course I don't associate you with Goodland. You're my friend.

I hadn't heard about the anthology.[1] Naturally I'd like to contribute to most things you're likely to do or intend doing, but I won't have anything much *to* contribute for some time. All my new poems belong to the book which Dent's are bringing out in the summer definitely. Your anthology couldn't appear before then, and obviously the same poems couldn't appear in both things. I'll have a few poems I suppose, but I'll have to get them published in magazines—if the anthology isn't under way by that time—as soon as they are completed because I need every halfpenny. I have nothing with which to bring Llewelyn up—he's six or seven weeks old. Nothing is O, not an inadequate income. Is the anthology Apocalyptic?—whatever that means. Barker's paralytic. He should be indecently buried. He grows worse every fake fit and crud of midnight spunk.

I saw your *Seven* article, and I'm looking forward to seeing another one in Poetry. Glad the first one was disliked by Grigson & Symons. What a fancy magazine Poetry is with its wig-and-scroll cover, treesnaps, and woodcuts, Barkers, whistlers, pukers, masturbative monologues, Tambimuttu—although I admire the courage of the queer introduction—wetting his Celyonese[2] Spender with life still Nestling[3] on his lips. The postwar man, as Tambimuttu might have said in his first Indian letter, struggling for watered spirits. The English poets now are such a pinlegged, nibcocked, paperhearted crowd you could blow them down with one bellow out of a done lung. I'm not taking, conscientiously, the inverted attitude, even if it isn't inverted, that insists on the worthlessness of the intelligentsia and the great qualities of those outside it, especially as I am living now—but not for long, Laugharne in April—in the country where the English romantic outlaw is at his loudest in praise of characters and soil—'I wouldn't share a

1 See page 430.
2 Celanese, a proprietary brand of artificial silk, newly fashionable in the 1930s, was often used to make underwear.
3 Perhaps from Nestlé, whose products included tinned milk.

piston with Stephen or Wystan but I'd roll in a sewer with Jan and Bill Brewer'[1]—and I suppose that in finding my sympathetic friends where I mostly do I'm at last on my own level. Don't get me wrong, I'd always prefer to see a street full of lords to a street full of other unemployed. Not that this matters.

Don't worry that anyone else will get hold of your letters: I have no clique, no correspondence club. You know how I live—I'm not, I hope, sentimentalising over this point, over other points I am happy to any time—and that life doesn't contain letter or culture snooping. What you say to me is safe from any but my own misinterpretation.

I'll write more when I send what you want. Sorry about the flimsy delays.

Dylan

MS: Buffalo

DESMOND HAWKINS
16 March [1939]   Blashford   Ringwood   Hants

Dear Desmond,
Waiting for the two promised novels. I'll include a Caldwell review, though it's a weak book. 'Bitter Victory' by Louis Guilloux is published by Heinemann. If you can get me a copy—mine's a library one—I can promise you & the publishers to do a full, praising review.

I'm sorry your book's been reviewed already in the N.E.W. If you'll send me it, I can certainly do a notice of it in *Seven*, if nowhere else. But *Seven*, I'm afraid, is a quarterly, & the Spring number's just come out.

When you see my new book, 16 poems & 7 stories, you'll be disappointed, perhaps,—or perhaps really my violence wasn't much good either—by the choice of stories. Blame that on dirty Church, not on me. I gave him a heap of stories to select from, & he wdn't include one that had 'its moments of sensuality'. A few of the stories were written when I was five or six years younger, & are sure to look tame. That man's a pale beast.

What's your son's name?

Dylan

MS: National Library of Wales

---

1 The names of those who want to go to *Widdicombe Fair* in the rural ballad include 'Bill Brewer, Jan Stewer ... Old Uncle Tom Cobbleigh and all'.

VERNON WATKINS
[postmarked 20 March 1939]   Blashford   Ringwood   Hants

Dear Vernon,

I didn't write sooner because I thought I'd be returning. Now I know it'll be April 6 or 7 when we drive back to the best places. We'll be in Bishopston one day at Easter, the boy with us.

I agree with every word you wrote abt my poem.[1] The 2nd person speaks better than the first, & the last line is false. I haven't been able to alter the first part, & will have to leave it unsuccessful. The last line is now: 'And the endless beginning of prodigies suffers open'. I worked on from your suggestion.

I'd like to go over the final proofs of all the poems with you, but that won't be for a few weeks. Some weeks. Did I tell you the book, which will be priced at 7/6 and have a John frontispiece portrait, includes 7 s. stories as well? All unviolent ones. Church refused to pass the best, 'P. of the Sea' because of its 'unwarrantable moments of sensuality'—the fish. Perhaps I'll make a little money from this book: I think a lot of 'readers' prefer to pay 7/6 for a book to 3/6.

Does Dot know Lawrence's 'Kangaroo' poem? Send her my love. The favourite meal in Australia—'The Ritz couldn't do you better my boy' an Australian told a man I know when he was out there—is a very underdone steak with an over-poached egg on top, followed by a cup of tea.

News when we meet. Quite a lot too.

Love from us,
Dylan

MS: British Library

DAVID HIGHAM
21 March 1939   Blashford   Ringwood   Hants

Dear Higham,

Here is, at last, the authorising note from John. This is what was wanted, isn't it? The portrait's in the Nicholson Gallery—Bond St?—& the people there know all about the fact that Dent's want a reproduction of it.

Yes, do please keep the remaining stories of mine for the time being. Anything about The Year's Poetry?

Yours,
Dylan Thomas

MS: Texas

1 '"If my head hurt a hair's foot"'.

DESMOND HAWKINS
March 25 1939   Blashford   Ringwood   Hants

Dear Desmond,
   This is only to tell you how much I liked the novel. Will it be too late to
say things about it in the next *Seven*? I mean, will it do any good to the
sales etc then? Anyway, I want the Opportunity of stating publicly my
Appreciation and excitement. There were a few things I disagreed with—
towards the middle, when you dealt with Ellen & Milly and their boys, you
changed the style of writing too drastically I thought, even though I liked
what was going on very much—but mostly nothing but congratulations on
one of the best first novels etc. How good to see & hear and feel, too, the
real romance of the out-of-town middleclass; the half-finished buildings,
the last bus home. Oh, I thought the vicar was not a success—the only one
who wasn't completely useful to the book. But Mrs S.[1] You know such a
lot about women, Mr. Hawkins, you *must* be a pansy.
                                        Claps & best wishes,
                                                Dylan

How abt my review books? Nothing's come yet.

MS: National Library of Wales

FRANCES HUGHES (Mrs Richard Hughes)
March 29 '39   Blashford   Ringwood   Hants

Dear Frances,
   We're coming back next Wednesday, the fifth, I think, of April, and we're
looking forward to it a lot. No more muggy south, narrow vowels, flat
voices, flat chests, English Riviera, and housefulls of women. We want to
see again the dilapidated Roman emperors, the giant liars and big women
of Laugharne, Mrs Peounds and Peounds, the petrol-drinkers and bee-
swallowers. It's very damp here. We're being driven down, but not by
Augustus. He's coming later in the month, as soon as, or before, we can
arrange Llewelyn's christening. He's out and more or less about now,
though Mavis's wedding put him back a few beds. We saw the newsfilm of
the departure from the registry office, and Augustus, blowing clouds of
smoke, hopped in the first car before bride or groom could get in.[2] Caitlin
says that she's written to Mrs Williams—we had, apparently, no difference
with her, it was laziness that put her off writing—to ask her to prepare and
air a bit before we return; and she asks you, please, will you see that Mrs

1 Mrs Sparge, a character in Hawkins's novel.
2 Mrs Mavis de Vere Cole, widow of a famous practical joker, Horace de Vere Cole,
  married the archaeologist, Dr Mortimer Wheeler, on 16 March. Between marriages she
  had had a child by Augustus John.

Williams does it & have a look yourself too. (The house must be full of mice by this time, but of course you can't do anything about that.) Love to you and Diccon from Caitlin and me.

Dylan

MS: Indiana

ALLEN TATE[1]
March 30 1939   Sea View   Laugharne   Carmarthenshire

Dear Mr Tate,
  Thank you for writing. Here are two poems. Both have just been printed in English periodicals, but you said that didn't matter. If neither of these is suitable, I'd like to send you some more.

Yours sincerely,
Dylan Thomas

MS: Kenyon College

DESMOND HAWKINS
[4 April 1939][2]   Laugharne

Dear Desmond,
  Forgive all sorts of things. I wish this was a livelier review, I don't feel so hot yet but will be in a few days. If the Caldwell review, & a meagre one it is, is too late now or not good enough, do cut it out. Writing soon.

Dylan

MS: National Library of Wales

KEIDRYCH RHYS
[?April 1939]   Sea-View   Laugharne   Carmarthenshire

Dear Keidrych,
  We came back a fortnight ago. We're expecting you. Any time, the sooner the better. What about this week? Plenty of room here. We'll talk about everything then. No, my letter in 'Poetry'[3] wasn't meant for

1 Allen Tate (1899–1979), poet and editor. He was probably seeking poems for the *Kenyon Review*, with which he was associated, and which published '"If my head hurt a hair's foot"', Summer 1939.
2 Dated by Desmond Hawkins at the time.
3 Tambimuttu printed some of Thomas's 5 March letter in the April issue of *Poetry London*.

publication & *certainly* didn't refer to you; Symons and Grigson were two in particular.

Love,
Dylan

MS: Texas

J. M. TAMBIMUTTU
[?April 1939]   Sea View   Laugharne   Carmarthenshire   S Wales

Dear Tambimuttu,

I liked the second number of Poetry very much. I hope you weren't offended by my first letter, to which you never replied; I thought, at the time, that it may have sounded rather offensively dogmatic. I'm afraid I haven't anything for the May number, but I'll send you my new poem as soon as it's ready.

Am I to be paid a guinea for my poem in the second number?[1] I do very earnestly need it, not having a single penny now. *Please* send it as soon as you can.

Sincerely,
Dylan Thomas

MS: Carbondale

VERNON WATKINS
[April 1939]   Laugharne

        I was too late for the shops in Swansea
        & couldn't get a Life & Letters. I shall in Carmarthen
        tomorrow. Is there any other good news?
                Laugharne is, I've found out,
                        D.C.

Dear Vernon,

Godfather by proxy you shall be, and I'm very glad you can be. As to a gift: honestly don't worry about that, we've just had a big gift from you. Is the wireless set, please, *A.C.* or *D.C.*? The expert here can't tell & daren't test it until he knows for certain; he might blow it up. It was grand to see you, and you must come down soon, a very soon weekend. Until today it's been wonderful here, & we've driven all about Carmarthenshire in the large car you saw. We're still, of course, without a penny. I'll bring the last batch of

1 "'If my head hurt a hair's foot.'" Issue dated April 1939.

proofs to you as soon as they come; or you spend a critical day with them here. We were sorry to miss your mother. Don't forget about the wireless.

Love,

Dylan

& from Caitlin & Llewelyn

MS: *British Library*

VERONICA SIBTHORP[1]

[April 1939]   Laugharne   Carmarthenshire   S Wales

Darling Veronica,

This is the first letter between us for nearly a year, and we should all have our nails pulled out for it, and how are you and where are you? I've been once in London since we saw you last, and then for two days at Christmas: I ran into sinful Wyn,[2] nearly knocked her down, and she told me you spent your life doing crosswords, which seemed very odd and our Inventions is a better game. Will this reach you? If it doesn't, you won't know so I'll write again to Upper Berkeley Street or chase you through Archie[3] through the Etonian Register or Conjugal jails. Please answer, it's terribly foolish us not writing and trying to meet. Caitlin had a baby in January, a son called Llewelyn now weighing one stone, with my Greek nose and chiselled chin. I wired you then, to Berkeley Street, but perhaps I got the number wrong or perhaps you weren't there, because the post office people returned it. And, as soon as they returned it, I should have written to Lamorna, but I got singing drunk for a fortnight and have been lazy and careless almost ever since. Last week we christened the baby, Augustus was here, you should have been too. Augustus could not follow the service, although he had the text, and broke in with the refrain 'I desire it' at intervals. I wish you could come down here for a holiday or longer. Can you? We've got two spare rooms in this crumbling house by the sea, and mice alone occupy them. Be a bigger and better mouse for us. You'd love it here; the beer and the people, the house and the sea, are all very posh in a good sense. I do hope you can afford to come, it's not really very far by train—because that was the reason, wasn't it, that stopped you coming last year. Regular lack of money flows in for us still, we are always with nothing but arrogance, guile, and hope. I'm just about to pawn, for debts and the demon alcohol, a silver christening present to Llewelyn. Little, as they say, the poor boy wots. We still, of course, have the itch and have grown quite attached to it, but, if you have lost it, you needn't worry about getting it again when, & if as I hope, you come down here, for all except our bedclothes conceal nothing worse than moths and mice's breath. How are Archie and Jake?[4] I'm a huge thing now, $12\frac{1}{2}$ stone, and my eyes are

1 See note, page 252.
2 Wyn Henderson.
3 Archie McColl, Veronica Sibthorp's first husband.
4 Jake or John Sibthorp, her second husband.

finally Sprotted. We *do* want to see you; try to see us, & write very soon. Love from Caitlin, & from me, Dylan.

This was bound to be a little letter, because there's so much news & so much nice nonsense that we have to meet to tell it.

MS: National Library of Wales

DESMOND HAWKINS
Mayday [1939]   Laugharne   Carmarthenshire   S Wales

Dear Desmond,
Thank you for the letter. The Date came and went, but still I was not well enough even to blow down a Todd. Now I've nearly finished the review, which I will post tomorrow morning from my bed of asthma. And I want to do a nice lot of work for you. Do you want an article on Miller? Forgive this ill shit.
My regards to your enviable wife and delicious children.
                                        Dylan

MS: National Library of Wales

VERNON WATKINS
[11 May 1939]   Laugharne

I'm sending this to your office
because I've got the idea,
wrong perhaps, that you leave
before the first post arrives.[1]

Dear Vernon,
Glad you're back from Paris. Waiting to hear everything. Herring wrote me & told me you'd been to see him. Impression? Proofs of my poems just come. One poem I want to rewrite, *with* your assistance; but I must do it quickly.[2] Can you come down Saturday—for, if possible, the weekend? Please try, I need your help a lot. It really is important to me.
This Saturday, 13th, of course.
                                        Love from us all,
                                        Dylan
P.T.O.
Bring your masque. Herring wants me to write about it for the July number.
We haven't had the wireless set up in our house yet. It's still in Billy

---

1 Envelope addressed to Watkins at Lloyds Bank, St Helens Road Branch, Swansea.
2 'When all my five and country senses see'.

Williams's—he's the local electrician. He wanted me to get hold of the set's book of instructions for him, or, at any rate, a little 3 plug lead which is supposed to go in at the back of the machine but which wasn't among the parts you gave me. Billy says the set, *without* this little plug thing, will go beautifully in the day-time but makes a bad noise as soon as the Laugharne electric power is started. The plug thing will cut out the bad noise. I meant to ask you about this before, but you were away.

MS: British Library

DAVID HIGHAM

May 11 1939   Sea View   Laugharne   Carmarthenshire   S Wales

Dear Higham,

The Marked Proof of my Dent's book came today. I'll be returning it this week. My contract says, '£20 will be paid the Author on his passing the proofs for press'. Is returning the Marked Proof passing the proofs for press? If it is not, would it be possible—unorthodoxly I suppose, but my need is very urgent—for you to get Dent's to give me £5 advance on that £20 which should soon be forthcoming anyway. My need is urgent because on this coming Saturday, the 13th, I'm to pay a bloody tradesman's bill or County Court proceedings will be taken. Do you think—you've been frightfully good before—you *could* make Dent's let me have a £5 by Saturday. This is a rush, I know, & I'm not too optimistic, but I do need the stuff. If not by Saturday, could you, do you think, manage it quickly?

Dent's will be pleased to hear that my Welsh book, a sort of provincial autobiography, is coming on well. Instalments of it have been printed in the New English Weekly & in Life & Letters To-Day: a new bit will be in the July Life & Letters.[1]

Any news about the other things I asked you?

Sorry for this money bother.

Yours sincerely,
Dylan Thomas

MS: Texas

VERNON WATKINS

[postmarked 12 May]   Laugharne

Dear Vernon,

I don't know if you leave Pennard before the first post comes or not. In case you do, there's a note from me waiting you in your Bank. This is an extra note—because if, & I hope terribly that you can, you do come, you

1 'Old Garbo'.

might want to let your people know *not* by telephone alone, & get a few things, pyjamas perhaps. By 'come' I mean come to Laugharne—as the other note will tell you. I need you urgently to rewrite a poem with me that belongs to the final proofs of my book which have to be sent off almost at once.

Love,
Dylan

MS: British Library

JOHN DAVENPORT
May 11 1939   Laugharne   Carmarthenshire   S Wales

Dear John,
   It's good to hear from you, I'm very sorry too we never met again in the Fitzroys of Salisbury—(I looked about, after you'd told me of Salisbury's literary reputation, & saw crowds of New Forest writers, some tweed and briar, some lankly titled, many going sandalled after Russian tea)—or that we couldn't afford to move across to each other. Yes, of course, Caitlin and I will be looking forward a lot to your all coming here, & make it soon. How is Roger, I haven't seen him for two years or less, he was magnificently prosperous when I did see him, and dressed, I was glad to see, like a capitalist.[1] I say come soon because I'm going to be summoned for a few small debts and unless something happens I shall spend Whitsun picking opium. I haven't dared answer the door all this week; who knows what wired fortunes I've missed that way, invitations to sherry and princesses with Tredegar,[2] fan-mail from Dowlais. When we stayed with you in Marshfield[3] I was richer than I had ever been, I may have spoken scoffingly of small sums, my vistas were misproportioned, even my mind rustled and clinked. Now, at my lowest, I'd sell my soul to Tambimuttu—have you seen his 'Poetry' magazine, Barker's masturbative lack of elegy, Gawsworth's Foreskin Saga, Celanese love-songs? I'm so penniless—the stamp on this letter's stolen—that I'm thinking of trying to work out a small income for myself on these lines: to get as many people as possible, people, that is, of assured incomes and some little interest in whether I do or not avoid the debtors' jug, to promise to send me five shillings (5/-) a week each; if I could get ten people, we'd flourish. I've thought of a possible few, including yourself and Norman, and what do you think of the idea? I've done nothing, except this letter, about it yet. It's not as crazy as it may

1 Roger Roughton.
2 The second Viscount Tredegar, Evan Frederic Morgan (1893–1949) was a writer, and had money. He is said to appear in Ronald Firbank's novel, *The Flower Beneath the Foot*, as an eccentric Englishman from Wales, the Hon. 'Eddie' Monteith, who joins an archaeological expedition to Sodom.
3 Davenport's house was in the village of Marshfield.

sound; I do very much want to go on working here, but I find it very hard when I can't go out in the street for fear of a woman with a shilling owing to her chasing me into the mother sea. As I can't make money by what I write, I think I should concentrate—Miller, incidentally, believes in this too, as you may have found out—on getting my living-money from *people* and not from poems. Do tell me what you think. But it's all a plan for the future, it would take some time to get started; now, now I'm trembling for Saturday which is the final day.

Yes, I believe, too, that Durrell, a very pleasant chap, is over-rated, but I can sympathise with the people who did boost up the Black Book so vehemently when it appeared because the first reading of it does, I think, shock you into emotional praise; it is, on the surface, so much *cleverer* than Miller, and anyway many reviewers of the Black Book hadn't, remember, read a line of Miller before. Durrell's verse is a bad show-up or down; but I think Miller's city nightlife is new and tremendous. We can agree when we meet. My book 'The Map of Love' is due in August; definitely, a notice appears in the Dent's summer catalogue. There wasn't any need after all for us to have gone through the stories, for fish-like Richard Church did the simplest thing by cutting all the best stories out. The ones left are, mostly, very tame, & there will only be the poems—the book is 17 poems & 8 stories—to save it. One story had 'its moments of sensuality', so out it went.

Caitlin and Llewelyn are strong and well. I hope you all are too. Write soon, & come here soon. My love,

Dylan

A few of the people I've thought of approaching about my five bob fund are: Edith S., Norman, John Davenport, Richard Hughes here, Lynette Roberts,[1] Peggy Guggenheim,[2] Augustus, Robert Herring. But of course they won't all agree. I want more possibilities for this Trifling Subscription.

MS: Texas

JOHN DAVENPORT
[?May 1939]   Laugharne

Dear John,

This is a small note to thank you a great lot for the cheque & the names. The cheque saved us; it was marvellously kind of you; Caitlin & I are grateful. No dank debtors' walls obscure us, the fawning tradesmen doff their horns. I'll draft a letter for the fivebob fund & let you have it, it's grand to have your assistance. A witty letter, do you think? I'll write very

1 Lynette Roberts (1909–95), poet, who married Keidrych Rhys later in 1939. See page 16, Vol II
2 Peggy Guggenheim, the American art collector and patron.

soon. Or a straight-from-the-shldr? Love to you all, Caitlin sends hers too. Thanks again, John. And try to come here soon.

Dylan

MS: Texas

J. M. DENT

May 15 1939   Sea View   Laughharne   Carmarthenshire   S Wales

Dear Sir,
    Returning your information sheet. Long delay because I couldn't find a photograph or get one taken. Sorry my answers are so unhelpful. I just live in this small town on the coast & write as much as I can.
    I enclose two photographs; you can use either, they're privately taken.

Yours truly,
Dylan Thomas

MS: (J. M. Dent)

DAVID HIGHAM

May 16 1939   Sea View   Laugharne   Carmarthenshire

Dear Higham,
    Thank you a lot. The cheque was tremendously helpful and has the tradesmen smiling.
    I'll be sending the proofs back this week, & will let you know exactly when.

Yours,
Dylan Thomas

MS: Texas

DAVID HIGHAM

16 May 1939   Sea View   Laugharne   Carmarthenshire

Dear Higham,
    Since posting my letter to you this morning, I've finished my proofs and sent them to Dent's. I'm letting you know this immediately, as you wanted me to.

Yours,
Dylan Thomas

MS: Texas

HENRY TREECE
[mid May 1939]   Laugharne   Carmarthenshire

Dear Henry,
   Congratulations on your marriage. Late, of course, but true. Our son is
screaming outside the window; because this is scrappy and dim blame him.
Thank you both for the cake; Caitlin ate it immediately. I'd heard about
Hendry's anthology before you wrote, from Keidrych who was here some
weeks ago being consciously queer and talking little magazines until the
air was reeking full of names and nonsense and the rooms packed to the
corners with invisible snobs. But I didn't know that you were handling it
with Hendry, I'm glad you are.[1] (What, by the way, is Hendry's criticism
like? His poetry seems to lack it.) I can't keep up with the quarrels that
surround Seven, Delta, & the rest, and only hope that you can work them
out to our advantage: to provide one magazine that publishes without
venom but with some point. About my own contributions to the
anthology: I haven't got anything new—all I've been working on are
straightforward stories, sold now for large (to me) sums to Life & Letters
and Story—but you can, naturally, reprint what you like. When is the
anthology appearing? My own book, under the title of The Map of Love,
comes out on the 1st of August. By that time I should have a new poem, &
may have, though it's unlikely, finished an article on Miller that I've been
preparing since he first hit me in the belly. Sorry to be so unhelpful. I've
done nothing yet on Crane; there's not, in an isolated article, much to say,
(I think) and it's better to read him. Print, of course, your article in 'Poetry'.
How could the publicity offend me? Only one thing: do, for friendship's
sake, cut out that remark of mine about 'I have a beast & an angel in me' or
whatever it was: it makes me sick, drives me away from drink, recalls too
much the worst of the fat and curly boy I know too well, he whose
promises are water & whose water's Felinfoel, that nut-brown prince. (But
no beer-talk, that makes one sicker: Bellocy Bill & Squire John,[2] Bless the
bed that I piss on; Novelists neuter, Catholics chancred, Fill the fucking
flowing tankard; O Georgian blotters and cricketing sops, You'll never
catch me on the hops etc.) At this moment your letter, with blank
postcard, dropped through the door. I found sinister the absence of any
comment on my cowardly delays, but thank you very much for being so
good with me, so consistently good in spite of what must seem my
arrogance and selfish irresponsibility. If your & Hendry's anthology is
appearing in July—that is, before my own book appears—then it's no good
you printing much of mine that will be in my book. The contents of my
book should come as new to people who buy it—most of the stuff's been in

1 J. F. Hendry edited The New Apocalypse (1940). It included a Thomas story, 'The
  Burning Baby', and poem, 'How shall my animal'. Other contributors were Nicholas
  Moore and Treece.
2 Hilaire Belloc, 1870–1953 (who was a Roman Catholic), and John Squire, both of them
  'hearty' poets as seen by Thomas.

little magazines, but not many people read them—& for them to be printed (I mean, for many of them to be printed) in an anthology brought out almost simultaneously with my own book is obviously absurd. (That's very loose writing, the baby's louder, I hope the meaning is clear.) I suggest therefore that you reprint no more than one of my newer poems—either 'A Saint About To Fall', which came out in the first number of Poetry, or 'How Shall My Animal', a copy of which I'll enclose—and one story, 'A Prospect Of The Sea' which is *not* appearing in my book but which Life & Letters printed some time ago. I think it's about my best story to date; Church refused to let me include it in 'The Map of Love'—16 poems & 7 stories—because it has 'moments of undeniable sensuality'. You'll have to ask Herring, I suppose, for permission, which of course he'll give; sorry I've no copy at all of the story: could you get one direct from Herring, do you think, & charge it, if necessary, to Apocalypse—is that the finally decided title?—accounts? I wish I had something fresh to send you; if I do, shortly, you shall have it.

Tell me the new gossip soon. Caitlin and I are well and strong now, happy here as always among friendly people, and in debt to many of them. Is Nelly well? Our regards. I doubt very much that we'll be able to move out of Laugharne this year, in spite of your nice invitation to us. I'd love to move North, though, for a week or two. Are you coming here? There's room and welcome always, you know that. We work, play darts, don't read enough, spend a couple of evenings a week with the hospitable but whimsy Hugheses. I get stouter, burlier, squarer every day: 12 & a ½ stone now. We have a few visitors, Keidrych, Vernon Watkins; Roughton is coming down soon, probably for Whitsun; there's a possibility of Miller in the summer, though what a city-hound like that will do here God knows. No, no truculence now, hardly ever disgruntled. Tell me the names of the new rackets and the number of balls. It'll be nice to hear from you. I've kept to the last the shocking admission that I can't—at the moment anyway—write those analyses you want me to, & which I want to do too. By can't I mean just that: the words won't come: I've tried a hundred times, & have never got further than the lines of a new poem or a series of completely sidetracking ideas. But I'll go on trying. Tell me about your book.

Dylan

MS: Buffalo

J. M. DENT
May 25 [1939]   Sea View Laugharne Carmarthenshire

In Reference to 'The Map of Love'
Dear Sir,

In answer to your wire just received: the reading of the last words of line 14 and the first words of line 15 on page 112 is: 'be swallowed down on to a hill's v balancing on the grave' etc.[1] The isolated letter, in case my handwriting's bad, is v, vee, the letter between u and w. *Not* a capital letter. In its context, its sense is: a triangular hill is turned upside down & looks like the shape of the letter v. (If you call that sense)

Yours truly,
Dylan Thomas

MS: Maggs Bros

VERNON WATKINS
[late May 1939]   Sea View   Laugharne

Dear Vernon,

I don't think I ever wrote to you after you sent the magazine with your Yeats poem in it. Sorry. I liked the poem, of course, and it seemed more closely worked than what I remember the first version to have been. Hughes & I read it together. Did you, by the way, like Hughes? He did you, very much.

Here's my new poem.[2] I hope you'll think it's good; I'm extremely pleased with it at the moment—it was written in a very enjoyable mood, (or any other better word) of surly but optimistic passion—though it is, as you'll see, in places a little awkward. I am not sure of the word 'animal' in the last line but one of the first stanza; it says more or less what I mean, that the rails, the frame if you like, of the bed of the grave is living, sensual, serpentine, but it's a word I've used perhaps too often.

'Crotch'—last line, third stanza—I've also used, once fairly startlingly, but I'm afraid the word is quite essential here. Or so, at the moment, I think. The last two lines I can see you disliking, especially the crude last lump. But that sudden crudeness is (again) essential to the argument, to, if you don't mind, the philosophy. Perhaps I should, or could, have found a stronger & nobler adjective for the light, to be in greater opposition to the very real crudity of the lump of the earth. And is the internal rhyme in the last line but one effective? I think so. Do let me know what you think of the poem, & soon, if you can.

Love,
Dylan

1 In the story 'The Orchards'.
2 An early version of 'Poem (to Caitlin)' (= 'Unluckily for a death').

Don't bother too much about other details in it; apart from what I've mentioned, it's the spirit of this poem that matters.

MS: British Library

*JOHN PRICHARD
[?June 1939]   Sea View   Laugharne   Carmarthen

Dear John,
I was glad to hear from you, but sorry things are no better. Is it the family that's given you autumn notice? Have you any plans? I'm distressingly broke myself, in the shadow of the debtors' jug, but am hoping every moment for improvements. No, I'm sorry I can't find a copy of Mr Sanbow's Rose—I think I gave it back to you a long time ago.

Hughes has been pretty ill, was suspected to have, among other things, consumption and West-Indian fever (it's wonderful what you can pick up in a weekend), but has, after all, only a flabby heart. I told him what you'd said in your letter—about having written him a month ago—and he apologises & will write. He's been in and out of a sick bed—the feather one, not the bunk—for weeks & has, he said, written nothing, answered nobody. You should try to come down here for a week, to spend your time between our crumbling slum and the High palace.[1] The weather's good: we boat: what a pity YellowJacket didn't pay you; I managed to wheedle something from it; demand from Fitzgibbon[2] in future. My two little sketches were, as you must have noticed, very paltry.[3] They were old things I dug up for a guinea each: not, I admit, a good procedure, but I needed money as Hughes needs flattery: bloody badly. It's a well produced paper, isn't it? The editor is very Queer.[4] Write when you can, and I hope you aren't too bowed down. Try, perhaps, to come down with Fisher some Tuesday afternoon.

                                                            Dylan

MS: National Library of Wales

1 Richard Hughes's house.
2 The literary magazine *Yellowjacket* was edited by Constantine FitzGibbon.
3 'The True Story' and 'The Vest' appeared in the second issue of *Yellowjacket*, May 1939.
4 FitzGibbon seems to have been conspicuously heterosexual.

VERNON WATKINS
[early June 1939]   Sea View   Laugharne

Dear Vernon,
   I don't find your way of criticizing at all irritating; you know that. It's the
most helpful there is for me, and I want it to go on. About many
suggestions of yours we'll always, of course, disagree, especially when they
seem completely to misunderstand my meaning; but, as nobody else has
done,—though this is a late and wrong place for a recommendation of your
complete intellectual honesty, a thing we needn't talk about—, without
rancour, affectation, or the felt need to surprise. I think you are liable, in
your criticisms of me, to underrate the value—or, rather, the integrity, the
wholeness—of what I am saying or trying to make clear that I am saying,
and often to suggest alterations or amendments for purely musical
motives. For instance, 'Caught in a somersault of tumbled mantime' may
(and I doubt it) sound more agreeable—we'll leave out any suggestion of it
sounding inevitable because it is, however good the implied criticism, a
group of words *outside* the poem—to the 'prophesying ear' than 'In an
imagining of tumbled mantime', a line I worked out *for* its sounds & not in
spite of them.[1] My criticism of your critical suggestion in this instance is
that your 'ear' is deaf to the logic of my poem;

             'Caught in a somersault etc etc
             Suddenly cold as fish'

is an ambiguous tangle, very like nonsense. (I know your suggestion was
not meant to be the last substitutive word for my first words, but was
meant mainly to suggest further things, allway pointers, to me myself; but
the suggestion still does, I believe, show the way your criticism often
works: towards the aural betterment (ugh) of details, without regard for
their significance in a worked-out, if not a premeditated-*in-detail*, whole).
This is certainly one critical way, but when it suggests 'withered' for
'sheeted', in the last line but one of the first stanza, *I* suggest it cuts across
the poem and does not come out of it. It is a poet saying 'This is what I
would have done'; not a critic saying, 'This, I think, is what the poet should
have done'. I suppose, argumentatively, not randomly speaking, that all
criticism which is not an analysis of reasons for praise must primarily be
suspicion; and that's stimulating. Nothing but the inevitable can be taken
for granted, and it always excites me to find you dealing suspiciously with
a word, a line, that I had, in a naturally blind or artificially blinkered
moment, taken, myself, with too much trust, trusting too much the
fallible creative rush of verse—small or large rushes of verse—that comes,
in many cases, between the mechanical preparations for that (in a way)

---

1 The poem is 'Unluckily for a death'. The *CP* version is much altered from the version
   Watkins first saw; the line 'In an imagining of tumbled mantime' was one that
   disappeared.

accidental rush. (Woolly writing, I'm afraid; hope the meaning comes clearly.) With your annoyance at the word 'chuck' I agree; and my use of it is sentimental. I have tried 'cast', but that is too static a word; I'll find what I really want. And, yes the poem did appear to tire of itself at the end—: (by the way, I resent that 'tire of itself' idea, which arrogantly supposes the self-contained *identity* of the poem even in its forming phases; the poem is not, of course, itself until the poet has left it). The jingle of 'abide with our pride' I'm retaining; I wanted the idea of an almost jolly jingle there, a certain carelessness to lead up to the flat, hard, ugly last line of truth, a suggestion of 'Well, that's over, O atta boy we live with our joy'; a purposeful intolerance—no, I meant an intolerance on purpose—of the arguments I had been setting against my own instinctive delight in the muddled world. Whether that intolerance, carelessness, etc. is *poetically* effective is another kettle of wishes.

It is very fine news of the masque, and Caitlin and I will be there.[1] We will try to bring Hughes too. Why don't you write to him? You want a big audience, of word-boys as well as theatre boys. Who have you asked? I shall do a review for Life & Letters, but after the show you must let me read the masque. We'll be there for the First Night, I hope.

We want a little poem for Llewelyn.

Love till we see you; and before and after. Can you come & see Norman Cameron? He'll be down for a weekend soon, I'll let you know when.

Write soon. Here is a new short poem, nothing very much.[2]

Dylan

The word I used too much—'sucked'—is here bound, I think, to be. 'Desireless familiar' is a phrase in my 'Orchards' & what caused me to write the poem. The best thing is, as you'll perhaps agree, the simple last line of the middle bit.

MS: British Library

CHARLES FISHER
Wednesday June 14 1939   Seaview   Laugharne

(pigeon fucking begins)

Dear Charles,

Yes, of course, Tuesday. I've been hoping you could come down soon; and it's nice very nice, to hear that Fred and fat Tom will be with you. It's a woe or so ago, if I may quote from a wellknown sheepchaser, since I last saw Tom.

1 *The Influences*, to be performed by Swansea Little Theatre. The Thomases weren't there.
2 'To others than you', an uncharacteristic poem in which Thomas writes cryptically of his betrayal by a friend with 'a winning air/ Who palmed the lie on me'.

I won't have a story but I've got one new poem:[1] The G.O.M., Grand Ovary Manica, at his most secretive.

Our baby's getting devilish; I wish we had a *huge* pusher for him.

Keidrych and I are giving a broadcast soon. Tell you about it when we meet.

> I remain your
> humble savant
> Dylan

From a typescript. MS location unknown

JOHN DAVENPORT
23rd June 1939   Sea View   Laugharne   Carmarthenshire

Dear John,

Norman says he's coming here the same time as you: June 31st, next weekend. Hope that's definitely fixed. We're looking forward to you very much. Is Roger driving? Norman, I suppose, can stay for the weekend only; it will be lovely if *you* can stay longer—it's too far to come for such a short time. There's plenty to do here, and even if there wasn't there would be. I've been writing quite hard, got a couple of stories and a couple of poems, plans and beginnings. I've done [one] or two drafts of a 5/- letter—I should have written to you before, but surprise tiny money momentarily wiped out the future; now the nasty future *is*—and I want to go over them with you, if you will, and we'll Get Down and Organise. I want to hear about the Miller visit—fuck fuck fuck—too. Grand to stay with you when he was there (or when he wasn't). I'm going to broadcast poems in August, let you know when—breathless boom boom boom. How is Clement? Caitlin's strong and the baby's piercing. Lots to tell you, not important but jolly. Write to confirm the 31st: we'll be terribly disappointed if you don't all come.

> General love,
> Dylan

MS: Texas

J. M. DENT & CO.
29 June 1939   Sea View   Laugharne   Carmarthenshire

Dear Sir,

Thank you for the proof of the wrapper for my book, which I return.

I suggest that you cut out the statement from the Manchester Evening News, on the back flap. This seems a very dim and tame blurb, and very

1 Probably 'To others than you'.

flat after the praise of the other notices quoted. If you would care to, you could use instead these remarks from a notice in New Directions, America, 1938:—'It is no exaggeration to say that his name is on the tongue of every young poetry reader in England. His poetry is verbal sculpture—almost fiercely strong'. If you don't want to use that, I think the Manchester Evening News remark shd still *not be allowed to stand*; the Evening News is not a paper famous for the value of its literary opinions; & anyway it's a feeble blurb.

Yours faithfully,
Dylan Thomas

P.S. There was a most complimentary review in the Spectator just after the book was published, though I'm afraid I haven't got a copy. Perhaps you can find it; I know Dent's sent me a copy of it through their Press Cutting Agency.

MS: (J. M. Dent)

·

VERNON WATKINS
[early July 1939]   Sea View   Laugharne

Dear Vernon,

This is to tell you, with great regret, that we *may* not be able to come to your play. If Hughes can come—he's not sure yet, he may have to go to London—then we'll be able to; if not, not. I thought I'd have some money this week, but bills took it at once & now we couldn't afford to go to Carmarthen even. But *if* Hughes can go, he'll take us & then everything will be all right. I'd hate to have to miss the play, more than I can tell you. Cameron was supposed to have come here last weekend, but cdn't manage it. Instead, Roger Roughton drove John Davenport down in an impossibly luxurious car; they returned yesterday. I hope very very much to be able to see you on Thursday night; and we *will* try. But if we can't, you must get the Theatre to give us a private performance later on.

Love from us both,
Dylan

MS: British Library

W. T. DAVIES[1]
July 5 1939   Laugharne   Carmarthenshire

Dear W. T. Davies,
Keidrych may have told you that Taig,[2] of the Swansea Little Theatre, intends taking a theatre in London for a night or two at the end of September, and presenting there poems by Welshmen writing in English. Watkins' Masque will probably be included. The poems aren't necessarily to be dramatic, but the audience will be given something to occupy their eyes without sacrificing their ears. All kinds and numbers of speakers will be used. Taig hopes to have some London Welsh actors to read some of the poems. I'm collecting lots of poems together for Taig and myself to go over in more detail—though all the dramatic ideas that come out of the poems, the dramatic possibilities rather, will be Taig's. Would you care to send along a selection of your own poems? I want to include as many *Wales* contributors & supporters as possible. I'd be glad of your help.
                                              Yours sincerely,
                                              Dylan Thomas

MS: National Library of Wales

JOHN DAVENPORT
[July 1939]   Sea View   Laugharne   Carmarthenshire

Dear John,
About Thomas Flotation Ltd:—I wrote to Norman, asking him if he'd give 5/- a week, and he said yes. But his business mind got working, and he suggested: 'the best arrangement for you might be to open a bank-account into which all your sponsors could put a series, say, of monthly post-dated cheques; and John (as he lives in your direction) might act as a funnel'— that, I think, was the word—'if he would be so obliging'. Do you understand that, apart from 'funnel'? Norman says, and vaguely I agree with him, that 'it's too much of a bother for people to send you 5/- every Friday'. What arrangement could be made? Does Norman suggest that these post-dated cheques—why post-dated?—be put into your account? If so, why need I have an account? If they're all put into mine, how are you a funnel? I'm writing to Norman again, but I'd like your views. Surely there must—if people can't be bothered with sending 5/- a week—[be] some very simple method of them sending it to me monthly? The trouble shouldn't begin with that, but with getting these sponsors Thomas-minded. So far

1 W. T. ('Pennar') Davies (1911–96), Welsh writer (chiefly in the Welsh language) and clergyman.
2 See page 452.

only 3 have definitely said yes: you and Roger and Norman. Will *you* ask Peggy G., Guinness, & Redgrave,[1] none of whom (apart from a few envious minutes with Guggenheim) do I know at all. And will Roger ask Penrose? I'll write to Penrose myself, but I think it would be a good idea for Roger to begin. I'm feeling rather miserable at the moment, my head is bloody & bowed,[2] because I can't get this scheme working at once. I do so much need it to work, we're awfully in debt. Sorry, John, to have to ask you so much; I wouldn't if I didn't know that you really wanted to help, & that you had helped such a lot before & so kindly & nicely. Try to send off to those people soon; & then perhaps you can tell me when I should write to them myself. Are there any other names? Like a fool, I lost your first list— though I remember that I didn't know personally many of the people you suggested, & that it would have been too odd perhaps for me to have written to them directly. I've got to get 12 chaps. I'm writing today to Augustus, & asking him to ask Evan Tredegar.[3] Though I don't expect much from that. This scheme has got to get going now; & I'm relying on you a hell of a lot.

We were very very sorry you couldn't manage to come back to Laugharne. I didn't tell too many funny stories, did I? Caitlin thought you might have been bored that last cockle evening. We'd love anyway to come & stay with you soon & have lots of music and things. I've nearly finished a nice new poem I'll send you. Love to you and Clement. Is Roger back with you yet? Caitlin sends love to you both.

Dylan

I want to know something definite about 5/- arrangements—bank accounts, postdated cheques, funnels, how people are to send to me— before writing to Sitwell & a few others. And, I want to write to them soon. Try to puzzle something out.

MS: Texas

JOHN DAVENPORT
[July 1939]   Sea View   Laugharne   Carmarthenshire

Dear John,

Norman asks me to send this letter of his on to you: an explanation of the funnel-&-cheque letter. The arrangement he suggests means a lot of bother to you; I hope you think it's a good suggestion—though it depends on the various sponsors (so far, *definitely* four only)—and that the trouble won't be too awful. If the trouble is, & you don't feel up to it, then I must

1 Probably Bryan Guinness, and the actor Michael Redgrave.
2 An echo of the poet W. E. Henley (1849–1903), who wrote the lines, 'Under the bludgeonings of chance / My head is bloody but unbowed'.
3 Lord Tredegar.

think, or ask someone else to think, of another arrangement. What do *you* think?

Love to Clement & you from us both.

                                                    Dylan

MS: Texas

W. T. DAVIES
July 1939   Sea View Laugharne Carmarthen

Dear W. T. Davies,

Thank you for your letter. Yes, Keidrych Rhys told me about the plan to form a literary society in Wales, but he was vague as to its ideas. And so am I, still. Can I ask some questions first? How is it intended that the young Welsh writers should get together? Is there any suggestion of trying to have an actual Group premises in Swansea or in some other convenient centre? Or of arranging regular conferences? I can certainly see, if not the need for this, the enjoyment to be got from gratifying the wish for that need. That may sound disagreeable; if it does, it's only because group, conference, manifesto, are words for things to be suspected—suspected of giving too many opportunities for official rigmarolling, high-sounding 'party' pronouncements, etc—unless one knows something quite definite about the reasons behind the desire to arrange them. In what manner could the proposed society 'substitute energy and responsibility for the dilettantism and provincialism of life and literature in Wales'? And what does it mean? Does it suggest that a literary society, by being honest and energetic and having as some of its members responsible artists—by 'responsible' I mean here artists who know what they are doing and who go on doing it faithfully to the best of their ability—could strengthen and further the work of its writing members? Or are you suggesting that it could 'give weight' to the work of Welsh writers, that is: that it could influence, by its solidity and (if you like) responsibility, readers in Wales to give a wider and more careful attention to the work of those writers? I doubt if any literary society could, in our time, do this second thing: (that's very arguably open); but I do believe that, through regular discussions, readings of papers and creative work, young Welsh writers could possibly be encouraged to experiment further & not get tired or disillusioned, and that perhaps a new passion and tolerance could be brought to their thinking about and creating of a living literature in this mismanaged, discouraged, middlebrow-beaten, but still vigorously imaginative country. (I'm talking as one of the young writers and can therefore, perhaps, be excused these pompous, old man's phrases.)

Would the society include writers in Welsh and English? Is Welsh Nationalism a part of the proposed Manifesto? And when do you think that a few people could meet and talk about 'policies'? I'm very interested; what

I've said is a sign of my interest, not a quarrel, of course, with you or with the tentative ideas advanced in your letter. I hope you'll write again.

Yours sincerely,
Dylan Thomas

MS: National Library of Wales

W. T. DAVIES
[July 1939]   Sea View   Laugharne   Carmarthenshire

Dear W. T. Davies,
Thank you for writing such an interesting and persuading letter. I still don't like the idea of societies, groups, manifestos. I don't think it does any harm to the artist to be lonely *as* an artist. (Let's all 'get together', if we must, and go to the pictures.) If he feels personally unimportant, it may be that he is. Will an artistic milieu make his writing any better? I doubt it, I'm afraid. God, inspiration, concentration (cool, hot, or camp), John O'London's, opium, living, thinking and loving, hard work, anything you like, may or may not do that. It—the milieu, the organisation for responsibility, though that's an unfair phrase I admit, may make him realise—perhaps, in an extremely lonely case, for the first time—that there are others like himself, other perplexed people who are trying to write as well as possible and to attach an importance to writing. But the result of a consciously-*made* intelligentsia may be to narrow, not to widen, the, if you'll excuse me, individual outlook; and instead of a lonely man—and writing, again, is the result, as somebody said, of certain favourable bad conditions—working in face of an invisible opposition, (the crude opposition, of family, finance, etc. that says 'writing is a waste of time' & 'why don't you do something worth-while' has always, surely, had to be disregarded) there may be just a group of condoling, sympathy-patting, 'I was always bullied at school', 'So was I', 'Down with the philistines', 'They don't understand a poet', mutually acknowledging, ism and isting, uniformed grumblers making a communal opposition to a society in which, individually, they feel alone and unimportant. I'm selfish enough not to feel worried very much about the writer in his miserable artistic loneliness, whether it's in Wales or Paris or London; I don't see why it should be miserable anyway. I think that to fight, for instance, the fascism of bad ideas by uniforming & regimenting good ones will be found, eventually, to be bad tactics. I'm not suggesting for a second that that is what you are suggesting; this rather silly letter is less an argument against your arguments than the expression of my own possibly old-fashioned romantic feelings. Don't take any of it too seriously—not, I suppose, that you would—and let me say that I'd be very pleased indeed to become a member of the proposed society, though a quarrelsome & reactionary one, if that does not mean I have to sign any manifesto. I do appreciate that you

aren't wasting time, and lots of good may come out of the plans. I hope it will. Perhaps we will be able to meet some time. Is Mountain Ash far from Swansea?[1] I'm staying in Swansea—Marston, Bishopston—until next Wednesday. Anyway, best wishes & excuse much of these tantrums.

Dylan Thomas

MS: National Library of Wales

HENRY TREECE

[July 1939]   Sea View   Laugharne   Carmarthenshire

Dear Henry,

I was glad you wrote to me, I like hearing, and I'd feel, I know, very angry if you wrote to me as badly and as irregularly as I do to you. I mean always to send you regular letters full of news and opinions, but what happen are occasional flat bits of grumbling and promises, fully felt and meant, of small worth for your book. And, though I want to be bright and full of opinionated news, this letter won't be any better either, for I'm deep in money troubles, small for some, big as banks for me, my debts are rising, it's raining, my new troubles and poems won't move, and what have I got to sparkle about I'd like to know? We've been staying for a fortnight with my father and mother, who are nice, warm-hearted people forced, by silliness and an almost hysterical greed for safety, to be so penny-cautious, so impatient for my success, (which means for me to have money, a position, and property), that I could run right out and exchange all my happiness for something entirely useless like an old bird-bath or a book of MacNeice's poems. Money and property I should like, but my life's set now towards not getting them. My father's house is stuck on a crowded piece of beautiful landscape—This Way to the Cliff Scenery—and surrounded by 4000 Territorial soldiers. Girls hot and stupid for soldiers flock knickerless on the cliff. We're returning to Laugharne tomorrow. There are only 50 soldiers there. What are you doing for your country? I'm letting mine rot. A girl I knew, sweet and reckless, is Captain Mabel now. Liberals are talking of Hitler's unscrupulous sincerity. MacNeice on the radio asked F. R. Higgins[2] on the radio, and both, if you ask me, were pissed, 'Would it be honest of me, in the present state of the world, to go and live in a little cottage in Ireland and let war and its rumours roar?' (I distrust people who question their own honesty; such people walk critically behind their actions, observe the action of writing a poem before the poem itself; wherever you go and whatever you do, your honesty, or lack of it, goes, and acts, with you.) A schoolmaster in Wales wrote asking me if I would join a Society of Welsh writers and help to attack and crush provincial dilettan-

1 Mountain Ash, about thirty miles from Swansea, was a coal-mining town, and Pennar Davies's birthplace.
2 Frederick Robert Higgins (1896–1941), Irish poet.

tism and the feeling of unimportance and loneliness which young provincial writers are, he says with knowledge, possessed by. (If they feel so unimportant *as* writers it is perhaps because they are; and loneliness, from anything except friendship, hasn't hurt anybody.) A speaker on the wireless said that English dogs don't like foreigners. My liver's rebelled against me, and I have sudden attacks of overwhelming temper, blood rises to my head, and I stamp my little feet. Are you happy in your new state and house? We'd like to visit you—Caitlin and the baby are well—but won't be able to until we can find travelling and during-Lincolnshire money, which may never be. The little I get goes, after a few pleasures, to tradesmen and two landlords. We must, I suppose, live. And I do get little; I'm hoping to sell some new straight autobiographical stories in America for a whole pile of England-trotting money; I'm hoping for retaining money from Dent's. My book[1] comes out on the 24th of August, but I've had all that matters from that and now there are only reviews to come. Have you found a paper to review it for? What about, if nothing with a larger circulation is willing to let its poetry go to anybody who likes poetry,—the dramatic critic of the Times for 30 years has just confessed in a book of memoirs that he always loathed the theatre—the New English Weekly? I should like very much to see your article in MacDiarmid's paper.[2] Could you send me a copy: if you have only one, I'll return it quickly. I'm sure, by the way, that the Oxford University Press, however kind, will not do your book; Charles Williams, who works for it, is a friend but he could not, only 2 years ago, persuade, by any means, the Press to publish my poems; they mightn't be inclined to bring out a book of criticism about work they did not 'see fit to' print themselves. Why won't Symons publish it? He's produced some books, hasn't he: Confusions about Symons by X etc.? Will you send me your long poem? Our handshakes to Nelly.

Love,
Dylan

I've got quite a lot to tell you. Next letter, soon. The baby Llewelyn is singing & eating paper, I can't think now of anything but that. Let me have your news.

MS: Buffalo

DAVID HIGHAM
[July 1939]   Sea View   Laugharne   Carmarthenshire

Dear Higham,
    Any news of Laughlin?
    This is an urgent, and despairing, too, plea for money. Do you think you could persuade Dent's to give me some immediately? Is there, do you

1 *The Map of Love*.
2 The poet Hugh MacDiarmid (Christopher Murray Grieve) (1892–1978) edited the quarterly *Voice of Scotland*.

think, a possibility of getting Dent's to make out a contract for future books of mine—on the lines of Laughlin's proposed contract, covering the next five or more years, but obviously not so mean and ridiculous a one? I would willingly, of course, if you thought it wise and worth-while, let Dent's have first option, or anything else, on all my future work if only they would advance me some money now before it is too late—that is, before I am made to leave, as I certainly *will* be made to leave, this house and town. I am very much in debt here, to landlord and tradesmen, for about £30 altogether, and unless I can begin, at least, to pay off the debts at once, I'll have to move, and move God knows where because, without a certain amount of credit, I can't possibly be expected to carry on week by week or even day by day. I am working a lot now—have more than ten poems towards a new miscellaneous book such as the one Dent's are bringing out next month, and several stories towards the Welsh autobio-graphical book for which Dent's have given me half the advance. But unless I have some money at once I'll have to shift house, which means shift from a house to no house, and get in such a mess of living again that it will be impossible to work on anything. Can you get from Dent's either some more of the advance money still coming to me for the Welsh book not yet completed, or some money as well as a retainer for the promise of my future books? Next year I shd have two new books (including the Welsh one) ready, the second being another selection of prose and verse similar to 'The Map of Love'.[1] And I think that, given some security, and being allowed to go on living here, I'll be able to produce a lot of stuff and work far faster than I have in the past. I find it *extremely* difficult to keep a wife and a child, but the difficulty has now reached a point when only an immediate sum of money, £30, to cover my pressing debts can save me from being chucked out, my books and bits of furniture and beds being taken away, and my work, present and future, being hopelessly spoiled and interrupted. I wouldn't write this unless there was nothing and nobody else for me to ask. I have tried to live without requesting anything further from Dent's, and without troubling you any further—for you have already done a lot for me, though not as yet, I'm afraid, greatly to your advantage—but now I just must get money, and at once. Will you see Dent's, will you tell them what I have told you in this letter? Publishers do, sometimes, give retainers to their authors, don't they? I don't mind what it is—retainer, or contracted promise for all future work—but I must have money for my debts or have everything taken away from me and be quite homeless. I hope you will do your best for me, I know you will, and see how really serious this is for me.

Yours sincerely,
Dylan Thomas

Would it be advisable for me to come up—(though, on my own account, I couldn't)—to see you & Dent's about all this?

MS: Texas

1 No such book appeared; instead, the war came.

JOHN DAVENPORT
August 1 [1939]   Sea View   Laugharne   Carmarthenshire

Dear John,
What about a line on my flotation fund and old Pawk's suggestions?[1] I'm lost without your support. Was Laugharne too much or too little? Augustus wrote to say he wouldn't be here until the autumn. Charles Morgan[2] is staying with Hughes and we're going along tonight to be dazzled. Some man[3] is going to take a London theatre for a night or two in September and give, among other things, dramatic performances of my poems. I'll be there full of cracks etc. Shall we see each other in London? Can I peep inside your club, just a peep? Do let me know something. Recently I may as well have been writing to a malting-house.[4]

                              Love to you & Clement
                              from us both. Dylan

MS: Texas

KEIDRYCH RHYS
[August 1939]

Dear Keidrych,
I'm returning the BBC script. We'd better pacify Mr. Watkin Jones and agree to his alterations.[5] Will *you* make them, in accordance with what he said? I leave it to you, you'll know best: just make it clear that you're talking about English poetry by Welshmen when you refer to the uncultivated tradition, & not talking about their precious Welsh poets. After all, it's the *English* poetry we're bothering ourselves about in this programme; poetry *in* Welsh can be left alone, as far as our talk goes that evening. You should be able to alter the questioned paragraphs very easily. And 'world at large' is a more understandable phrase, I think, than 'the outside world'. But do what you think best. We (or you, rather) *must* alter these 'objectionable' phrases; it's worth agreeing with their piddling suggestions in order to get across what we really want to. I may myself, later & with, probably, the disgust of Mr. Jones, change one of my selected poems; but that can be left until the rehearsal.

1 Norman Cameron.
2 Charles Morgan (1894–1958), novelist and playwright.
3 Thomas Taig. See page 452.
4 Davenport's address was The Malting House.
5 The programme was to be called 'Modern Welsh Poets'; Thomas would read, Keidrych Rhys would discuss. Someone with a long memory at the BBC wrote on the correspondence in thick blue pencil: 'We *must* have this man's script before he appears in the studios.'

Does Harry Roskolenko *pay* for contributions to his anthology?[1] Must they be unpublished poems, or just poems unpublished in America? I don't know Laura Riding, & I think that if she has refused to contribute nothing will make her change her mind.

[*in margin*: Don't forget to answer this, will you?]

I'd like to meet Saroyan.[2] Is he in London?

MS: Texas

BBC
[2 August 1939]   Sea View   Laugharne   Carmarthenshire

Dear Sir,

I'm enclosing the reply sheet you sent me on July 31, and I should like to say that I'm afraid I will need my actual travelling expenses to be paid me, out of the 5½ guineas, *before* the day of the broadcast, as otherwise I may not be able to afford, that day, to travel at all. I hope this isn't inconvenient; I wouldn't insist on it unless it was really necessary.[3]

Yours faithfully,
Dylan Thomas

MS: BBC

DAVID HIGHAM
August 3 1939   Sea View   Laugharne   Carmarthenshire

Dear Higham,

Thank you very much indeed for acting so promptly and so well for me. I agree that Dent's have been really generous; and, of course, as I said in my wire this morning, I accept all the proposals most readily. I'm especially glad—apart from the promise of an immediate £30, which is terribly welcome & urgently needed, even before the contract is completed—that the proposals for the two prose books didn't specify that either had to be a *novel*: for if they had, I'm afraid I'd have had to swear it all off. Both books will probably be stories of some kind or another. The periodical payments will help me greatly. *Thank you* again for all you've done.[4]

Yours sincerely,
Dylan Thomas

1 Harry Roskolenko (1907–80), American writer and editor.
2 William Saroyan (1908–81), American writer.
3 The 5½ guineas (about £5.75) in the contract was to include travel expenses to the Swansea studio on 6 September.
4 Thomas apparently received £30 in August and a further £40 before the end of the year, as well as regular payments of £8 a month that began in September and continued through most of 1940. Neither book was written in the form (or during the period of time) anticipated.

Any Laughlin news? Or are you waiting until my 'Map of Love' comes out? Surely we can get an American publisher to tackle that. I've had a number of v. good American reviews & criticisms lately & a couple of articles on my poems have been published.

MS: Texas

J. M. DENT
August 11 1939   Sea View   Laugharne   Carmarthenshire

Dear Sir,
   I'm glad to hear that my book, The Map of Love, is coming out on the 24th, and that my own copies are on the way.
   You ask me to suggest the names of any periodicals that might not be on your review list. I think that *Seven* might be very useful, it has an important circulation in Oxford and Cambridge and other university towns etc. It is edited by Nicholas Moore whose address is: 68 Chesterton Road, Cambridge. Also, though this is quite possibly on your list, *Wales*, which has a wide following here. Edited by Nigel Heseltine[1] from Cefn-Bryntalch, Abermule, Montgomeryshire. I was one of the founders of this paper & will have an interesting, if nothing else, notice. Also Hugh MacDiarmid's quarterly, *The Voice of Scotland*, which is read by the whole of the Scottish National Party & also by nationalists in Wales & Ireland.
   I don't know if you send review copies to the U.S.A., but 'Poetry, Chicago' has given me quite a lot of attention, including one of their yearly prizes, lately. Anyway, I hope you will be able to send to *Seven*, *Wales*, & *Voice of Scotland*: they're all worth it, I'm sure.

Yours faithfully,
Dylan Thomas

MS: (J. M. Dent)

DESMOND HAWKINS
14th August 1939   Sea View   Laugharne   Carmarthenshire

Dear Desmond,
   Nice to hear. I've been back in Wales a good, in many ways, time now, since April. Too long not to know anything about you. Honestly, Tambimuttu had that buttu of a poem at the time I promised you one; and now of course I've nothing. I've got a short story, but it's longish, about the length of the straightforward stories I've been printing recently (if you saw

1 Heseltine had taken over some of the editing from Keidrych Rhys.

them) in Life & Letters: perhaps 4000, or a bit under. No good? I'm trying to make my living out of straight stories now; I've got a contract too, & must finish a book of stories by Christmas. Autobiographical stories, Provincial Autobiography, Portrait of the Artist as a Young Dog, or something like that. Have you, as we boys are always asking each other, got far with your novel?

I'm very glad you're doing my book for the Spectator, and that you like it. There could have been a better selection of stories, I think, but Church was timid. I know that many of the poems are difficult, and will be called, though not by you, surrealist. (Aren't they, by the way, using 'surrealist' a bit more sparingly now?) I am trying hard to make them less Hide-and-Seek-Jekyll: (cf. your notes on mixed personality in the Spectator once). Few are stunt poems (cf: 'Fog has a bone' in my last lot).[1] And the best are deeply emotional. That said, I agree that much of the poetry is impossibly difficult; I've asked, or rather told, words to do too much; it isn't theories that choke some of the wilder and worser lines, but sheer greed. I'll try to answer, in a discursive way, your questions and natural bewilderments. There isn't anyone living I wd rather write a review of me than you. (For that, which is very true, please substitute *magnificent* for every *interesting*.)

I. Or Nuts to You. Poem 13.[2] 'Nut', yes, has many meanings, but here, in the same line as 'woods', I can't really see that it can have any but a woody meaning. The actual line is a very extravagant one, an overgrand declamatory cry after, in my opinion, the reasoned and quite quiet argument of the preceding lines. The *sense* of the last two lines is: Well, to hell and to death with me, may my old blood go back to the bloody sea it came from if I accept this world only to bugger it up or return it. The oaktree came out of the acorn; the woods of my blood came out of the nut of the seas, the tide-concealing, blood-red kernel. A silly, far-fetched, if not, apparently, far-fetching shout—maybe—but, I think, balanced in the poem.

II. Here I can't get which poem you mean, so I'll take both. First of all, the 3rd & 4th line of poem one (January 1939).[3] Perhaps these lines should have been put in a pair of brackets, but I think that brackets often confuse things even more. The poem begins with a queer question about a bird and a horse: because one thing is made sweeter [*in the margin*: qualify this word] through suffering what it doesn't understand, does that mean everything is sweeter through incomprehensible, or blind, suffering? (Later, the poem has a figure in it standing suffering on the tip of the new year and refusing, blindly, to look back at, if you like, the *lessons* of the past year to help him; and the case, which is really a case for a prayer, begins to make itself clear.) Then I, the putter of the question, turn momentarily aside from the question and, in a sort of burst of technical confidence, say that

1 'How soon the servant sun.'
2 'On no work of words.'
3 'Because the pleasure-bird whistles.'

the bird and beast are merely convenient symbols that just *have* to suffer what my mood dictates, just *have* to be the objects my mood (wit or temper? but here 'mood' alone) has decided to make a meal upon & also the symbolic implements with which I cut the meal and objects up. Loose and obscure explanation; but writing freely like this is the best way, I believe, to get the stuff across, by writing around the difficulties & making notes on them.

III. The next things you wanted to discuss were stanzas three and four of the poem beginning 'I make this In A W.A.', page 4,[1] (Work of Art, Workshop of Agony, Witbite of Agenwar).[2] The stanzas are a catalogue of the contraries, the warring loyalties, the psychological discrepancies, all expressed in physical and/or extra-narrative terms, that go towards making up the 'character' of the woman, or 'beloved' would be wider & better, in whose absence, and in the fear of whose future unfaithful absences, I jealously made the poem. I didn't just say in one line that she was cold as ice and in the next line that she was hot as hell; in each line I made as many contraries as possible fight* together, in an attempt to bring out a *positive* quality; I wanted a peace, admittedly only the armistice of a moment, to come out of the images on *her* warpath. Excuse me, but this note I wrote for a my-eye essay by H. Treece may as well come in now: 'I make one image, though "make" is not the word; I let, perhaps, an image be made emotionally in me & then apply to it what intellectual and critical forces I possess; let it breed another; let that image contradict the first, make, of the third image bred out of the other two together, a fourth contradictory image, and let them all, within my imposed formal limits, conflict'. A bit smug, and old stuff too, but it applies here. And the conflict is, of course, only to make peace. I want the lasting life of the poem to come out of the destroyers in each image. Old stuff again. Here, in this poem, the emotional question is: Can I see clearly, by cataloguing and instancing all I know of her, good and bad, black and white, kind & cruel, (in coloured images condensed to make, not a natural colour, but a militant peace and harmony of all colours), the emotional war caused by her absence, and thus decide for myself whether I fight, lie down and hope, forgive or kill? The question is naturally answered by the questions in the images and the images in the questions—if the vice-versa makes any different sense. Yes, the syntax of stanza 3 is difficult, perhaps 'wrong'. SHE makes for me a nettle's innocence and a soft pigeon's guilt; she makes, in the fucked, hard rocks a frail virgin shell; she makes a frank (i.e.

---

* negate each other, if they could; keep their individualities *and* lose them in each other.

---

1 'I make this in a warring absence', which can be read as an allusion to Thomas's own marriage, was explained more lucidly to Peschmann (page 313). Its new title replaced the earlier 'Poem (for Caitlin)' when it appeared in *The Map of Love*.

2 *Agenbite of Inwit* ('The remorse of conscience') was an influential moral treatise of the fourteenth century.

imprisoned, and candid and open) and closed (contradiction again here, meaning virgin-shut to diving man**) pearl; she makes shapes of sea-girls glint in the staved (diver-prised) & siren (certainly non-virgin) caverns; *SHE IS* a maiden in the shameful oak—: (here the shameful oak *is* obscure, a mixture of references, halfknown, halfforgotten, nostalgic romantic undigested and emotionally packed, to a naughty oracle, a serpent's tree, an unconventional maypole for conventional satyrate figures). The syntax *can* be allowed by a stretch or rack-stretches; the difficulty is the word Glint. Cut out 'Glint' and it's obvious; I'm not, as you know too well, afraid of a little startling difficulty. Sorry to be so conflicting and confusing; I hope this is the only method, though: this rambling and snatchy expansion.

IV. Poem 5. This is a very decorative poem, a poem, if you'll pardon me, on stained glass.[1] There are many ornamental designs, but all, I hope, utilitarian. And I really can't get down to explaining it; you just have to, or just don't have to, let the poem come to you bit by bit through the rather obvious poetry of it. It's not a really satisfactory poem, but I like it. The blue wall of spirits is the sky full of ghosts: the curving crowded world above the new child. It sounds as though it meant the side of a chemist's bowl of methylated spirits, & I *saw* that too and a child climbing up it. (There's a pretty fancy the stout young gentleman has. I'm 12 and a $\frac{1}{2}$ stone now, by the way, a bull of a boy.)

V. *On the angelic etna of the last whirring featherlands.*[2] I wanted to get the look of this stanza right: a saint about to fall, *to be born,* heaven shifting visionarily under him as he stands poised: [*interpolation, linked to the word* visionarily, *which is circled:* changingly, the landscape moving to no laws but heaven's, that is: hills moving, streets flowing etc] the stained flats, the lowlying lands, that is, *and* the apartment houses all discoloured by the grief of his going, ruined for ever by his departure (for heaven must fall with every falling saint): on the last wave of a flowing street before the cities flow to the edge of heaven where he stands about to fall, praising his making and unmaking & the dissolution of his father's house etc—(this, as the poem goes on to talk about, is his father-on-the-earth's veins, his mother's womb, *and* the peaceful place before birth): Standing on an angelic (belonging to heaven's angels & heavenly itself) volcanic hill (everything is in disruption, eruption) on the last feathers of his fatherlands (and whirring is a noise of wings). All the heavenly business I use because it makes a famous noble landscape from which to plunge this figure on to the bloody, war-barbed etc earth. It's a poem written on the birth of my son. He was a saint for a poem's sake (hear the beast howl).

** this is adding to the image, of course, digging out what is accidentally there on purpose.

1 'It is the sinners' dust-tongued bell.'
2 'A saint about to fall.'

All very unsatisfactory. I wrote it down hurriedly for you: not so much as to try to elucidate things but to move them about, turn them different ways, stir them up. The rest is up to you.

Oh yes, *hyleg*.[1] It's a freak word, I suppose, but one or two every now & then don't hurt; I think they help. It was what I wanted & I happened to know the word well. I dessay I could explain this selfishness at intolerable length, but I want you to have this scribble right away.

If you want the story—you *can* pay a bit?—let me know. If you give me a little time, I'll try to do a poem specially.

Dylan

If I can I'm going to be in London at the end of the month.

MS: National Library of Wales

J. M. DENT

August 22 1939　　　　Sea View　Laugharne　Carmarthenshire

Dear Sir,

I wish to have 3 more copies—3 copies, that is, over my author's allowance of 6, which I've received—of my book 'The Map of Love', due out on the 24th of the month. And could the price of these—at 25% less than the published price, as my contract says—be deducted from future royalties on the book? I hope you will let me know if this system of buying extra books is permissible?

Yours truly,
Dylan Thomas

MS: (J. M. Dent)

NANCY PEARN[2]

22 August 1939　　　　Sea View　Laugharne　Carmarthenshire

Dear Miss Pearn,

Thank you for your letter. I'm very glad that you and David Higham are glad about the Dent arrangement. I'm extremely fortunate, and am very grateful to you both.

---

1 O.E.D.: '*astrol*.: ruling planet of a nativity.'
2 Of Pearn, Pollinger and Higham.

Is Higham back yet?

And do you know when my first payment—for the month of August—of £8 is likely to come to me? There's not much of the month left; and I'd relied on having that payment to cover certain commitments—that's a grand way of putting it—that I wouldn't have undertaken hadn't I thought I'd be, for me, very rich before September. Do you think you could find out if it *is* possible for me to be paid *this* month's payment *this* month?

Yes, I see a good deal of Richard Hughes. He's just left for a holiday in North Wales.

Thank you again.

Yours sincerely,
Dylan Thomas

MS: Texas

THOMAS TAIG[1]

23 August 1939　　　　　　　Sea View　Laugharne　Carmarthenshire

Dear Mr Taig,

Here is a selection—out of a great wad of material—of poems that might be suitable for some kind of dramatic presentation.[2] There's lots too much, of course, but you need a lot, don't you, to read over? I suggest—unless you think that alternative scheme, of putting on a certain number of different poems every night or every few nights, is better—that as few *poets* as possible should be chosen. Some of Glyn Jones would be excellent material, I should think; and Alan Pryce-Jones's poem 'Voyage' seems, to me, grand for your purpose. I've included a few more-or-less-journalistic poems about distressed Wales: you could probably make a fine thing of 'Rhondda Poem' & 'Landore'. I've included, too, several of my own; I do hope you'll be able to give me the opportunity of reading: I enjoy reading poems aloud so much, & have got to understand most of the poems turned out nowadays by Our Young Welsh Poets. But we must meet soon; I hope we can as soon as you return. If you'd like a larger selection of poems, or more poems by chaps I've meagrely represented here, do write & tell me please.

I hope everything goes well. I've written to a few people & will let you know at once what does, or doesn't, happen.

Yours,
Dylan

1 A lecturer at Swansea University College, and active in the Little Theatre. The poetry-reading event planned by Taig is described in Thomas's letter dated 5 July 1939.
2 With the letter are four poems copied out by Thomas: his 'Ears in the turret hear' and 'Find meat on bones'; 'Voyage' by Alan Pryce-Jones, and 'Landore' by George Woodcock.

I haven't included anything of Vernon's: mostly because the big number of the show is his Masque, & otherwise because I haven't much suitable of his at hand. We can get hold of one of his excellent ballads, though, if you like, later.

The 2 numbers of Wales I enclose for Idris Davies's two prose poems: Shadows & Cakes, & Land of My Mothers. Bits of these, anyway, might be very effective.

MS: Theodore Brinckman

VERNON WATKINS
[postmarked 25 August 1939]   Sea View   Laugharne

Dear Vernon,
    Sorry not to have written before. I've been busy—over stories, pot-boiling stories for a book, semi-autobiographical, to be finished by Christmas—lazy—messing about in the sun and pub—and worried, by the nearness of this monstrous and still incredible war. No, my book couldn't have come out in a viler month; almost as bad as some woman I was told of who published her first (&, since, her only) novel on the day of the opening of the General Strike & did not have one single review or advertisement (no papers were printed for a week); & not one single copy of the book was sold. I haven't seen Hawkins's Spectator review yet; hope to get it sent on in a day or two. I saw the imbecile Western Mail with striking, if podgy, photograph.
    Your Masque I left with my father in Bishopston. Can you call there for it, or shall I write to him asking him to send it on to you?
    Glyn Jones has been staying in Llanstephan, very near. We saw him a few times; he has, with all due lack of respect, a sly, mean, stupid, shapeless wife with whom we couldn't get on very well. Glyn is all right, but weak; insipid, perhaps; his gentleness has grown in like a soft, jelly-like nail. 'Of course, there's much to be said,' 'You should see both points,' 'No offence meant but.'
    This war, trembling even on the edge of Laugharne, fills me with such horror & terror & lassitude that I can't easily think about the London programme.[1] I've selected a good number of poems—including some by Alan Pryce-Jones which, in their very worldly & wellbred way, are really beautiful. None by you. You can either send a ballad or two direct to Taig, or wait until we all three meet. Perhaps the last would be the best. I didn't want to select anything of yours without your approval, and anyway I haven't much of yours at hand. Taig suggests only 20 minutes for the short poems; I say at least ½ hour. But everything—including all our happiness—depends on Hitler, Poland, & insanity.

1 On 25 August Parliament passed the Emergency Powers (Defence) Act. A week earlier there had been mock air-raids on London to test the defences.

I'm afraid I shan't be able to come Swansea way for a while. If there's no war I'll be broadcasting, with Keidrych, from Swansea on the 6th of September, 6.40 to 7. Could we meet you in Swansea afterwards for a drink? I think I'll try to return to Laugharne that same evening.

Laugharne is a little Danzig.[1]

Wish I could see you soon. When can you come down?

Caitlin & Llewelyn are well. Love to you from us,

Dylan

Regards to your family.

MS: British Library

NANCY PEARN

[late August 1939]   Sea View Laugharne Carmarthenshire S Wales

I'm writing a short note
to Richard Church

Dear Miss Pearn,

Sorry to pester you like this about the Dent's 8 quid due to me *this month*, but I need it most urgently. I know it's difficult to do things in this vile crisis, but it's just because of that vileness that I do need, so badly, the promised money. I haven't anything to buy anything with (not even envelopes), &, even here, all sorts of preparations are necessary—being made officially necessary too. As I don't intend fighting anyone, my position is being made most uncomfortable: and a little money would, at least, ease it. Please do try to buck Dent's up *immediately*.

Yours,
Dylan Thomas

It must be hell in London.

MS: Texas

D. J. THOMAS

August 29 1939   Sea View

Dear Dad,

Grand, *magnificent* dictionary. A lovely surprise. Thank you very very much for it. I will take good care of it and use it often. It is a most valuable thing for me to have; & it appears to be an extremely good dictionary too.

1 The Baltic port of Danzig (now Gdansk) was taken from Germany and made a 'Free City' after the First World War. It had symbolic importance in Hitler's crusade to expand in the east at Poland's expense. Newspapers were full of Danzig that summer.

Immediately, I looked up all sorts of obscure words: & the result couldn't have been better. Exciting to open the important-looking parcel this morning, & find just what I have been wanting. Thank you for the dedication too; I'm glad you enjoyed the *Map of Love*. Do please tell me what you liked best in it, & what seemed most difficult & unattractive. I haven't yet seen the Spectator review, though Vernon wrote to tell me it had appeared & was 'good & sensible'. I saw Fisher's article, which was really about how well he knew me. I haven't seen any other reviews. Was there one in the Observer? I couldn't get hold of it last Sunday.

Yesterday I had the first work done on my teeth: 4 fillings. There is one extraction to come—an unnoticeable stump at the back—& about 6 more fillings. Then, with care, my teeth should last me for good. I wasn't hurt, although, because the teeth needing repair were scattered all about my mouth & not in a cluster, no injection could be made.

These are awful days & we are very worried. It is terrible to have built, out of nothing, a complete happiness—from no money, no possessions, no material hopes—& a way of living, & then to see the immediate possibility of its being exploded & ruined through no fault of one's own. I expect you both are very anxious too. If I could pray, I'd pray for peace. I'm not a man of action; & the brutal activities of war appal me—as they do every decent-thinking person. Even here the war atmosphere is thick and smelling: the kids dance in the streets, the mobilised soldiers sing Tipperary in the pubs, & wives & mothers weep around the stunted memorial in the Grist.[1] Our own position is, *so far*, quite comfortable.

I hope you enjoyed your queer, lackadaisical day here—in spite of bookshelves & Polly's snailing—as much as we did. If there's no disturbance before September 6, I hope to see you in Swansea on that day. We must make arrangements later.

Thank you for everything you brought us on your visit. We were really grateful, although, perhaps, we found it difficult to say much.

And thank you greatly for the very fine dictionary. I am proud to possess it.

I hope mother's well, or better than she has been.

Love to both of you
from us both,
Dylan

This shd have been posted yesterday, but just before the post went I found I hadn't any envelopes—& wasn't in time. Sorry.

MS: (Thomas Trustees)

---

[1] The memorial is a market cross; the Grist is the part of Laugharne at the foot of the hill, by the shore.

DESMOND HAWKINS
29 August [1939]   Sea View   Laugharne   Carmarthenshire

Dear Desmond,
   Are you going to use that story? When—war permitting—does Purpose
come out? I may have a small poem for it. If you don't want the story, do
send it back quickly as I can get some money for it immediately: & Christ,
do I need it.
   Haven't seen your review yet.

                                        Love,
                                        Dylan

MS: National Library of Wales

W. T. DAVIES
30 August 1939   Sea View   Laugharne   Carmarthenshire

Dear W. T. Davies,
   Thank you for your letter, and for the poems you sent. I should have
acknowledged them sooner, but I've been in rather a muddle and this
bloody war buggers the orderly mind.
   It's very doubtful if Taig's programme will come off—or on—this next
month. If it does, your 'Siege' will be included. I would have included
more—or suggested for inclusion—but all the short poems must be packed
into half an hour & that doesn't really allow a chap to be represented by
more than one poem.
   I was interested to know further things about the Society; and of course
I'll still be a member even if I am too snooty to sign the manifesto.
   You said you might be in Carmarthenshire the end of this month. Do
call on us, please.

                                        Yours,
                                        Dylan Thomas

MS: National Library of Wales

VERNON WATKINS
[1 September 1939]   Sea View   Laugharne

Dear Vernon,
   War seems to have begun. But do come on Sunday, if you can. With Taig
too. Any time? Will you make it lunch? If so, arrive by one, please. Perhaps
you can let us know—phone—in the Saturday evening.[1]

1 Germany invaded Poland on Friday 1 September. Britain declared war on Sunday 3
  September.

What are you going to do in the war? I can't kill & so, I suppose, will have to join the dangerous RAMC.

Looking forward to you.

Keidrych & Heseltine—nasty Heseltine—came down yesterday. Went back this morning.

Love to you & family from us.

Dylan

MS: British Library

DAVID HIGHAM
September 1 1939   Sea View   Laugharne   Carmarthenshire

Dear Higham,

Here's the Laughlin contract, signed.[1] I must say that 60 dollars as an advance seems meagre & unsatisfactory to me—£12 or £13, isn't it?—but I am sure you have done the very best possible.

Yes, of course I approve of your permitting Chatto's to have my poem for their anthology.[2] No, the Parton Press have no interest in anthology rights.

This bloody war won't stop Dent's monthly allowance, will it?

Yours sincerely,
Dylan Thomas

MS: Texas

1 Probably for *The World I Breathe*, poems and stories.
2 *A Book of Modern Verse*, 1939, which included 'The force that through the green fuse'.

Index of Recipients

Index